W9-AWN-756

The Iran–Iraq War

The Iran–Iraq War is one of the largest, yet least documented conflicts in the history of the Middle East. Drawing from an extensive cache of captured Iraqi government records, this book is the first comprehensive military and strategic account of the war through the lens of the Iraqi regime and its senior military commanders. It explores the rationale and decision-making processes that drove the Iraqis as they grappled with challenges that, at times, threatened their existence. Beginning with the bizarre lack of planning by the Iraqis in their invasion of Iran, the authors reveal Saddam's desperate attempts to improve the competence of an officer corps that he had purged to safeguard its loyalty to his tyranny, and then to weather the storm of suicidal attacks by Iranian religious revolutionaries. This is a unique and important contribution to our understanding of the history of war and the contemporary Middle East.

WILLIAMSON MURRAY is Adjunct Professor at the US Marine Corps University, a Senior Fellow at the Potomac Institute, and Professor Emeritus at The Ohio State University.

KEVIN M. WOODS is a Historian and Defense Researcher at the Institute for Defense Analyses.

The Iran–Iraq War

A Military and Strategic History

Williamson Murray and Kevin M. Woods

CAMBRIDGE
UNIVERSITY PRESS

CAMBRIDGE
UNIVERSITY PRESS

University Printing House, Cambridge CB2 8BS, United Kingdom

Cambridge University Press is part of the University of Cambridge.

It furthers the University's mission by disseminating knowledge in the pursuit of education, learning and research at the highest international levels of excellence.

www.cambridge.org
Information on this title: www.cambridge.org/9781107673922

© Williamson Murray and Kevin M. Woods 2014

This publication is in copyright. Subject to statutory exception and to the provisions of relevant collective licensing agreements, no reproduction of any part may take place without the written permission of Cambridge University Press.

First published 2014

Printed in the United Kingdom by Clays, St Ives plc

A catalogue record for this publication is available from the British Library

Library of Congress Cataloguing in Publication data
Murray, Williamson.
The Iran-Iraq War : a military and strategic history / Williamson Murray and Kevin M. Woods.
    pages   cm
Includes index.
ISBN 978-1-107-06229-0 (Hardback : alk. paper) – ISBN 978-1-107-67392-2 (Paperback : alk. paper)
1. Iran-Iraq War, 1980–1988.   I. Woods, Kevin M.   II. Title.
DS318.85.M8725 2014
955.05′42–dc23   2014012747

ISBN 978-1-107-06229-0 Hardback
ISBN 978-1-107-67392-2 Paperback

Cambridge University Press has no responsibility for the persistence or accuracy of URLs for external or third-party internet websites referred to in this publication, and does not guarantee that any content on such websites is, or will remain, accurate or appropriate.

For Colonel Karl H. Lowe, USA, retired – soldier, strategist, scholar, mentor, and friend.

Contents

Figures

Tables

Preface

The 1980–1988 war between Iraq and Iran was one of the largest and, yet, one of the least documented conventional conflicts in the twentieth century. Western reporters, regional experts, and a few historians managed during the intervening years to develop useful – if primarily secondary – narratives of the events. Many of these works, cited throughout this volume, remain essential to any study of the Iran–Iraq War.

The relative paucity of primary sources on the Iran–Iraq War changed with the collapse of Saddam Hussein's regime in 2003. Upon entering Baghdad, Coalition forces captured official Iraqi government records and recordings, including thousands from the period of the Iran–Iraq War. Using these records, this book looks at the strategic and military context of the war primarily through the lens of the Iraqi regime and its senior military commanders. The inside view of the war from Baghdad does not resolve the problem of primary source material from the Iranian perspective; however, it does provide a new and significant window into the war.

This book – the third in a series of histories exploring the former Iraqi regime's perspective on its major wars – is also the final product of the Iraqi Perspectives Project. As with the prior studies, the authors believe that in addition to contributing to the existing scholarship on Iraq, this study serves three purposes. First, in keeping with the traditional purpose of military histories, we believe it will contribute to the education of the next generation of military leaders. Second, it provides an unvarnished look at senior military decision making inside of a totalitarian regime. It is hoped that the material cited here, and which is available at the Conflict Records Research Center, Institute for National Strategic Studies at the National Defense University, will lead to additional research across many disciplines. Finally, while the events of the Iran–Iraq War may seem distant from recent challenges in the region, the echoes of that war are just under the surface. Many of the organizations, leaders, and narratives that animate much of the recent sectarian divide in Iraq have their modern roots in the Iran–Iraq War. The men who now dominate Iran's senior leadership were young men on the battlefields of the Iran–Iraq War under conditions of both strict international isolation and the large-scale use of chemical weapons.

More than thirty years after the beginning of the war, Iraq and Iran remain unsettled countries. The reasons, both ancient and modern, seem purposely designed to frustrate all attempts to settle issues by peaceful and violent means. Given this history, it might be tempting for policy makers outside of this region to ignore the past or overinterpret more recent events. This book and the related research seeks to, as a historian once defined his craft, "interpret the past for the purposes of the present with a view toward managing the future, but to do so without suspending the capacity to assess the particular circumstances in which one might have to act, or the relevance of the past actions on them." The past is never predictive of future events; however, it can be instructive.

Acknowledgments

This book is the result of the efforts and support of a large number of people to whom the authors are deeply grateful. For helping in both the research and the review phases of this project, special thanks go to George Mauldin, Dr. Jack Cann, Karl Lowe, Jim Kurtz, Dr. Marcus Jones, Joseph Simons, and Elizabeth Nathan. The authors used both US government and contracted translations for many of the captured records cited herein, but relied on both the translations and the counsel of Laila Sabara for the majority of the material.

For supporting the overall research effort and ensuring continued access to captured records, the authors are indebted to Dr. Thomas Mahnken, David Radcliffe, Heather Peterson, and Richard Johnson in the Office of the Secretary of Defense (Policy); MG John R. Landry in the National Intelligence Council (Military Issues); and Al Musgrove in the Joint Center for Operational Analysis and Lessons Learned. A special debt of gratitude is owed to the staff of the Conflict Records Research Center, Institute for National Strategic Studies at the National Defense University. The staff of the CRRC, especially Dr. Lorry Fenner, David Palkki, Michelle Martinez, and Christopher Alkhoury, were enormously helpful in coordinating the use of the captured records. The authors also want to thank a group of senior Iraqi veterans of the Iran–Iraq War who contributed their personal narratives of the war and provided a human context to many of the documents cited: Ra'ad Majid Rashid al-Hamdani, Aladdin Hussein Makki Khamas, 'Alwan Hassoun 'Alwan al-Abousi, Abid Mohammed al-Kabi, and Mizher Rashid al-Tarfa al-Ubaydi.

Finally, this work could not have been complete without the dedicated efforts of Ana M. Venegas and Carolyn Leonard who endured innumerable rounds of fact checking, rewrites, and drafts before the final edits were complete. Despite all of the assistance noted above, all errors remain the sole responsibility of the authors.

Note to reader

This book draws heavily on Iraqi state records captured during Operation Iraqi Freedom. Most of the Iraqi records cited here can be found in the National Defense University's Conflict Records Research Center (CRRC). In footnoted citations, captured records are indicated by the prefix "SH." An asterisk preceding the prefix "SH" indicates that the record was, at the time of this publication, not yet available through the CRRC. The CRRC will eventually migrate all records cited in this volume into its open research collection.

1   Introduction

Love of power, operating through greed and through personal ambition, was the cause of all these evils. To this must be added the violent fanaticism which came into play once the struggle had broken out. Leaders ... had programmes which appeared admirable ... but in professing to serve the public interest they were seeking to win the prize for themselves. In their struggle for ascendancy nothing was barred; terrible indeed were the actions to which they committed themselves.[1]
                                                                    – Thucydides

The Iran–Iraq War was a struggle for dominance between competing regimes with deeply opposed worldviews. During the course of the eight-year-long conflict, the opposing sides inflicted hundreds of thousands of casualties on each other. The leaders of the two states, Saddam Hussein and Ayatollah Ruhollah Khomeini, each had ambitions greater than their national borders. For his part, Saddam and his Ba'athist colleagues calculated that victory over Iran would be the first step to leadership of the Arab world and to creating an Arab superpower.[2] Khomeini, however, believed Iran should export its revolution to the world, beginning with the countries of the Islamic world.[3]

In retrospect, the opposing sides failed the basic tests of strategic competence. Both leaders began the conflict apparently believing that emotion, simplistic rhetoric, and a motivated population would deliver victory. When those failed, their response was to shovel more men and more resources into the struggle, while issuing ever more fanatical and ferocious pronouncements. Neither side proved competent in applying the most rudimentary ends–ways–means test to the war. The result was a bloody, inconclusive struggle that at times appeared to

---

[1] Thucydides, *The History of the Peloponnesian War*, trans. Rex Warner (London, 1954), 243.

[2] See, in particular, Kevin M. Woods, Michael Pease, and Mark E. Stout, Williamson Murray, and James G. Lacey, *The Iraqi Perspectives Report: Saddam's Senior Leadership on Operation Iraqi Freedom* (Annapolis, MD, 2006), 6.

[3] See Ayatollah Khomeini, "We Shall Confront the World with Our Ideology (20 March 1980)," *MERIP Reports*, no. 88 (1980), 22.

have no possible ending except the collapse of one or both of the contesting regimes.

That Iraq made the battlefield even more gruesome by introducing poison gas – not used extensively in a major war since Mussolini's invasion of Ethiopia in 1935[4] – indicates the desperation and hatred that pervaded the conflict.[5] And once the taboo was broken, the Iraqi regime would later employ such weapons against elements of its own population. Similarly heartless, the Iranians deftly merged notions of religious martyrdom to include symbolic "keys to heaven" with patriotic fervor to send 12 to 17-year-old boys to clear minefields.[6] As though no one had learned anything from World War I, a favorite tactic of the *Pasdaran* and *Basij*, Iran's revolutionary militias, was to launch human-wave assaults into the face of prepared Iraqi defenses. Both sides left few laws of humanity intact. Perhaps the best explanation for the war's character was that it was about quarrels ancient and modern, political and religious. By the time the war ended, both sides had fired ballistic missiles – with only slightly better accuracy than the V-2s the Nazis fired during World War II – at cities of the opposing side. One suspects that, had one or both sides possessed nuclear weapons, they would likely have used them.

In military terms, there were no decisive victories. At the beginning, neither side was capable of applying coherent tactics to the battlefield, much less effective operational concepts or strategic thinking. Initially, fanatical political and religious amateurs determined the disposition of forces and conduct of operations. During the war's course, military

---

[4] There are indications that the Egyptian military forces dropped poison gas during several air raids during their intervention in Yemen's civil war in the mid-1960s. See Jonathan Tucker, *War of Nerves: Chemical Warfare from World War I to Al-Qaeda* (New York, NY, 2006), 190–201.

[5] Evidence that Iraq used chemical weapons is undisputed. From August 1983 until the final campaign in July 1988, Iraq employed various combinations of mustard gas and VX nerve agents against Iranian forces. Iran developed a chemical weapons capability (offensive and defensive) in response to Iraq's first use; however, there is no compelling evidence, including Iraqi intelligence reporting at the time, that Iran employed chemical weapons to any significant degree on the battlefield. See Javed Ali, "Chemical Weapons and the Iran–Iraq War: A Case Study in Noncompliance," *The Nonproliferation Review* 8, no. 1 (2001). A March 1987 Iraqi military intelligence report noted only five small-scale Iranian chemical attacks (specifically one phosgene and four mustard gas attacks; excluding CS and white phosphorus attacks) between 1983 and 1987, but noted the likelihood of captured Iraqi weapons being the source. See Memorandum from GMID to Deputy RE: Chemical Weapons (26 March 1988) in SH-GMID-D-000-898, General Military Intelligence Directorate (GMID) Memoranda Discussing Iranian Chemical Weapons Capability, October 1987–September 1988.

[6] Hooman Majd, *The Ayatollah Begs to Differ: The Paradox of Modern Iran* (New York, NY, 2008), 146.

effectiveness at the tactical level improved somewhat, especially on the Iraqi side. While military professionalism slowly crept into the picture in Baghdad, it never entirely replaced Saddam's amateurish decision making, because he alone made the significant military decisions. On the other side of the hill, military professionalism was rarely evident. Until the end of the war in July 1988, Saddam and Khomeini both equated some degree of military effectiveness with the casualty rates their own forces suffered.

Nevertheless, the war's duration, as well its casualties, forced both Iraq and Iran to adapt and learn. How and what they learned suggests much about the difficulties of learning in the midst of a war, especially a war for which neither side was intellectually prepared.[7] Once again, the conflict underlined that cognitive factors, such as initiative and military professionalism, are of greater consequence on the battlefield than mere muscle and technology. Iran's performance during the war also suggests the lengths to which human beings are willing to go to continue a conflict for a cause in which they fanatically believe.

Equally important in evaluating Iraq's performance in the war from Saddam's perspective is the issue of military effectiveness. An important study on that subject focuses largely on evaluating specific areas of military competence, that is, unit cohesion, generalship, tactical sophistication, information management, technical skills, logistics, morale, and training.[8] However, such an approach poses problems because it rests largely on Western concepts. For Western military analysts, military effectiveness seems to be relatively straightforward.[9] In the West – at least since the military revolution of the seventeenth century, which brought civil and military discipline to Europe's armies – states and their political leaders have taken for granted that military institutions would remain loyal to and supportive of the political structure. Thus, in the West, military organizations exist to protect the state, first from its external enemies, and second from internal enemies who would overthrow it from below. Given the rapacious, fractious nature of European international relations from the seventeenth through the first half of the

---

[7] One of the authors (Murray) has recently completed a study of military adaptation in war, focusing largely on the twentieth century. A major lesson emerging from that study is that military organizations have great difficulty adapting to combat conditions when they embark on war. Organizations careless in their intellectual preparations and training during peacetime, however, will only learn by filling body bags. See Williamson Murray, *Military Adaption in War* (Alexandria, VA, 2011).

[8] Kenneth M. Pollack, *Arabs at War: Military Effectiveness, 1948–1991* (Lincoln, NE, 2002), 4–10.

[9] Among others, see Allan R. Millett and Williamson Murray, eds. *Military Effectiveness, Volumes 1–3*, 2nd edn. (Cambridge, 2010).

twentieth centuries, the focus on the external enemy is not surprising. At the same time, the constant competition for mastery in Europe, accompanied in the eighteenth century by the competition for global dominion, honed military institutions on violence and war. Even in times of peace, those institutions have prepared with the same ruthlessness the Romans had brought to the business of war. Moreover, starting in the nineteenth century, they learned to adapt to the technological world born of the Industrial Revolution.

At times, the military has also provided a crucial bulwark to protect its masters, but for the most part, that has been regarded as a subsidiary, if important, role. Admittedly, in some cases, Western armies have focused on the latter mission to the exclusion of the former – the Italian military in the twentieth century being a particularly good case.[10] Nevertheless, rarely in the history of the West have military organizations overthrown the existing political elite. Napoleon Bonaparte's 18 Brumaire coup, which overthrew the Directorate in France and launched the Napoleonic Empire, certainly springs to mind as one such exception.[11] This reliability of military organizations has rested considerably on the fact that the state's leaders, much of the population, and the majority of the officer corps have accepted the regime's legitimacy, however much they might disagree with some of its policies.

As a result, Western military institutions have been able to concentrate largely on dealing with the external enemy, which has pushed the development of new technologies, doctrinal concepts, and more effective means of projecting military power on the battlefield and over great distances. Thus, the criteria for effective military organizations have come almost entirely to rest on the ability of such organizations, proven in war, to destroy the state's external enemies. Such criteria led many in the United States to rate the German military extremely highly for its performance on the battlefield, but at the same time to miss the salient reality that its approach to strategy was so appalling that Germany not only lost two world wars, but also repeated nearly all of the major strategic mistakes it had made in World War I in the second great conflict.

---

[10] In this regard, see MacGregor Knox, *Mussolini Unleashed, Facist Italy's Last War* (Cambridge, 1983).

[11] Indeed, what goes around comes around. Napoleon was also one of the few state leaders to be overthrown by the military. In March 1814, his marshals refused to fight any longer, and Napoleon, confronted by the massive Allied invasion of France, was forced to abdicate. The Directorate's seizure of power in 1795, as well as Napoleon's 1800 coup, did lead many Bolsheviks to fear the potential of a military coup and led Stalin to execute a massive and devastating coup of the Red Army during 1937 to 1940, which had catastrophic results in the opening months of Germany's invasion of the Soviet Union.

Nevertheless, how Westerners have rated military effectiveness is not necessarily how those from other cultures and backgrounds have viewed the purpose of their military institutions. Some have adapted to the Western military revolutions with alacrity. But even the Japanese failed to adapt to the combined arms lessons that World War I brought in its wake, as their wretched performance in the ground war in 1942 and 1943 underlined.[12]

Middle Eastern militaries began their descent in the seventeenth century from their historic and relative heights and continued through the final collapse of the moribund Ottoman Empire at the beginning of the twentieth. If the peoples of the modern Middle East managed to absorb only a smattering of the Western way of war, it was due largely to their contemporary experience with European military institutions, either as "the colonized" or being on the receiving end of Western military power. The result was that Arab military culture devolved into an echo of its former self, resting on a complex mix of myths and notions of bravery, tribal loyalty, raiding parties, and martyrdom that was, in many ways, indifferent to the effectiveness model inherent in the accoutrements and models of Western militaries.[13] Such attributes have made Arabs extraordinarily brave warriors throughout the ages, but relatively poor soldiers in the context of wars since the nineteenth century.

As Iraq's ruler in 1980, Saddam subscribed fully to the myths of his culture.[14] He would have been entirely contemptuous of George Patton's

---

[12] The exception to this rule would appear to have been the Indians and the Vietnamese. The former having absorbed much from the two centuries of British occupation and education, the latter with the thorough and complete education the French provided to its leaders in the first three decades of the twentieth century.

[13] The authors are aware of the danger of addressing a broader regional culture as a factor in military effectiveness. In addition to the definitional and methodological complexity of the task, as others have pointed out, culture's role in military assessments has a poor legacy, having previously been "spun from an ugly brew of ignorance, wishful thinking, and mythology." However, as noted throughout this work, many of the cultural influences, good and bad, were identified to the authors by former senior Iraqi military officers. See also Norvell B. De Atkine, "Why Arabs Lose Wars," *Middle East Quarterly* VI, no. 4 (1999), 16. For more information, see Pollack, *Arabs at War*, 1–13.

[14] Saddam's aggressive efforts to fashion a common "Mesopotamian" culture to bind Iraq's multi-ethnic–multi-sectarian society under the Ba'ath in the late 1970s culminated at the beginning of the Iran–Iraq War. According to the often crude attempts to rewrite history, not only did Saddam portray himself as the "paramount shaykh" of a tribal culture, but also, in defending the collective Arabs against their historic Persian foe, he had become "a leader who was victorious according to God's will." Eric Davis, *Memories of State: Politics, History, and Collective Identity in Modern Iraq* (Berkeley, CA, 2005), 179–189. See also Amatzia Baram, *Culture, History and Ideology in the Formation of Ba'athist Iraq, 1968–89* (London, 1991).

famous remark that the business of war is not to die for your country, but to make the other bastard die for his. In the largest sense, Saddam's problem was embedded in the nature and the legitimacy of Iraq's political institutions. Secular governance in the Middle East has historically rested on power, particularly military power, rather than on political theory, laws, civil institutions, and a generally accepted legitimacy of the state. A story is told that on his deathbed, the first caliph of the Umayyad dynasty warned his son that "in order to keep the people of Iraq quiet, it was essential to give them a new governor every time they wanted one, however frequently."[15] It seems that the purpose of the military (Iraq's most representative institution) was defined long before the state came into being.

For Saddam, the question of his regime's legitimacy created not only a political problem, resulting in his ruthless purge of the Ba'ath Party in 1979, but also a military one. Saddam knew well that the army was the one institution that could overthrow the Ba'ath regime, as it had done in 1963. In fact, since Iraq had emerged from the British mandate in the early 1930s, the legitimacy of its various governments had been anything but secure, while the army had displayed an enthusiastic willingness to overthrow or participate in the overthrow of the government of the day. Thus, as so many dictators have done throughout history, Saddam aimed to fully co-opt and, failing that, defang the only Iraqi institution with the independence and power to overthrow his regime. From his perspective, the ideal senior commanders were those whom he could point in the general direction of the enemy, and who then, by their toughness and bravery, could destroy the internal as well as the external enemies of his regime. In terms of maintaining his control in Iraq, such an approach was certainly successful.

Like Stalin, Saddam had no qualms with bludgeoning his internal enemies via a minimum effort and maximum of ruthlessness, while ensuring that the army did not develop the kinds of leaders who could launch a coup. Thus, in September 1980 on the eve of a war that would require a very different type of military, Saddam had every reason to believe that he and the Ba'ath Party had created effective military institutions.[16] He would soon discover, however, that a military built on cultural myths and political oratory would not work so well against an opponent three times its size, with an even deeper faith in bravery and

[15] Mohammad A. Tarbush, *The Role of the Military in Politics: A Case Study of Iraq to 1941* (London, 1982), 183.

[16] On the Ba'athification of the military during this period see Ibrahim al-Marashi and Sammy Salama, *Iraq's Armed Forces: An Analytic History* (New York, NY, 2008), 107–129.

martyrdom. Iraq's military, in the 1980s, was as effective as Saddam wanted it to be, but not as effective as he needed it to be.

Politically, the war solidified the religious revolution that Khomeini had set in motion by overthrowing the Shah in 1979. Nevertheless, from the moment the conflict began to its end eight years later, the Iraqis and Iranians consistently overestimated their own possibilities as well as underestimated those of their opponents. The war also underlined the extraordinary capacity of human beings, particularly political leaders, to delude themselves that "war is a good thing or a safe thing."[17]

The Iran–Iraq War also emphasizes societies' capacity to mobilize and commit resources to battle. The West, for all its relative advantages in military effectiveness, routinely underestimates that capacity in less developed nations. Saddam's regime sought to maintain the burden of a great war of attrition through appeals to Arab nationalism as well as via the multiple methods of coercion available to a totalitarian state. With appeals to Persian nationalism and religious fanaticism, Iran proved similarly able to motivate its people to "pay any price, bear any burden."[18]

Stripped of its larger context, the conflict may have little to offer in the way of strategic lessons or battlefield accomplishments. Nevertheless, the study of political and military failure, as much as success, develops a deeper understanding of the past, which in turn sheds light on the future and on the nature and character, as well as cultural dispositions, of potential opponents. As the great Greek historian Thucydides suggested, his history, indeed all history, should be "useful [for] those who want to understand clearly the events which happened in the past and which (human nature being what it is) will at some time or other and in much the same ways, be repeated in the future."[19] The availability of Iraqi documents and media captured during Operation Iraqi Freedom presents a unique opportunity to explore this conflict from within Iraq's decision-making processes.[20] It is on the strength of a unique set of

---

[17] Archidamus, the Spartan king, warning his assembly of warriors that they should not lightly consider going to war with the Athenians at the end of the seventh decade of the fifth century BC. Thucydides, *The History of the Peloponnesian War*, 84.

[18] John F. Kennedy's words to describe the American people on the occasion of his inauguration in January 1961.

[19] Thucydides, *The History of the Peloponnesian War*, 48.

[20] Historians have had no access to the papers and decision-making processes of the regimes of Nasser, al-Sadat, al-Assad, or the other major Arab regimes that have ruled the Middle East since the collapse of the colonial regimes after World War II. The capture of the Ba'athist state records and their availability for scholarship at the Conflict Records Research Center at the National Defense University in Washington, DC, has the potential to change how historians, and ultimately, the people of the region, understand these events.

primary sources that this book examines Iraq's decision-making processes. It does not attempt to provide a comprehensive or detailed historical analysis of the Iran–Iraq War.

Thus, this book, the third emerging from the *Iraqi Perspectives Project*, aims to provide insight into the thinking of Saddam Hussein and his senior leadership in the historical context of the war, offering perspectives on past and future autocrats.[21] It explores the rationale and decision-making processes that drove the Iraqis as they grappled with challenges that, at times, threatened their existence. Where possible, it also aims to present a sense of Iran's actions and perceptions, although without access to the records of the Khomeini regime, this account has less to offer regarding Iran's decision making.

The authors have no illusions that the events in this war will be repeated. Nevertheless, they believe that examining the Iran–Iraq War based on, to a large degree, the high-level perceptions of one of its participants can offer unique understanding and insight into this type of regime, its regional actors, and the worldviews of those in the region who may yet be making decisions. Strategic realities and long-standing national interests all but ensure that America will find its military forces involved again in the Middle East. The thinking and perceptions of America's future allies and opponents in that crucial area of the world will likely reflect the legacy of or share some similarities to the actions and decisions made by Saddam Hussein's Iraq and Ayatollah Khomeini's Iran.

---

[21] The Iraqi Perspectives Project is a trilogy that has worked backwards in time through Saddam's wars. For Operation Iraqi Freedom, see Woods *et al.*, *The Iraqi Perspectives Report*. For Operation Desert Storm, see Kevin M. Woods, *The Mother of All Battles: Saddam Hussein's Strategic Plan for the Persian Gulf War* (Annapolis, MD, 2008).

2   A context of "bitterness and anger"[1]

> *As a rule those who were least remarkable for intelligence showed the greater powers of survival. Such people recognized their own deficiencies and the superior intelligence of their opponents; fearing that they might lose a debate or find themselves out-maneuvered in intrigue by their quick witted enemies, they boldly launched into action; while their opponents, overconfident in the belief that they would see what was happening in advance, and not thinking it necessary to seize by force what they could secure by policy, were more easily destroyed because they were off their guard.[2]* — Thucydides

> *[On] the subject of our relations with Iran – Iran planned animosity for us from the beginning. [It is] as if the change [that] took place in Iran was designed with the intentions to be against the interests of Iraq.[3]* —Saddam Hussein

Not surprisingly, the origins of the Iran–Iraq War lie deep in the past. In fact, until the early twentieth century, when the British stitched together disparate provinces of the Ottoman Empire that they had acquired in the political fallout from that empire's collapse, there was no such political entity as Iraq. Yet, the territory from which modern Iraq emerged has been at the center of world events since the dawn of history. Along with Egypt and China, the Mesopotamian Valley gave birth to the earliest of human civilizations. Beginning in the third millennium BC, small Semitic tribes combined with the Akkadians and Sumerians to build a prosperous city-state culture around Ur and Babylon. Theirs were societies born in the harsh conditions of subsistence agriculture, which forced them to constantly balance their actions in a world caught between disaster and opulence.[4]

---

[1] Keith Mclachlan, "Analysis of the Risk of War: Iran–Iraq Discord, 1979–1980," in *The Iran–Iraq War: The Politics of Aggression*, Farhang Rajaee, ed. (Gainesville, FL, 1993), 26.

[2] Thucydides, *The Landmark Thucydides: A Comprehensive Guide to the Peloponnesian War*, ed. Robert B Strassler (New York, NY, 1996).

[3] SH-SHTP-D-000-559, Saddam and His Inner Circle Discussing Relations with Various Arab States, Russia, China, and the United States, 4–20 November 1979.

[4] For a readable survey of early Mesopotamia, see Georges Roux, *Ancient Iraq*, 3rd edn. (New York, NY, 1992).

Change in Mesopotamia was often swift and violent. The life-giving rivers represented a capricious resource, often failing to flood or flooding too much. This gave rise to a particular fatalism – so-called Babylonian "pessimism" – within a culture where nothing was sure and the future was of little comfort.[5] Nature was not the only source of gloom. During the centuries, Hittites, Assyrians, Persians, Greeks, Romans, Parthians, Byzantines, Arabs, Mongols, Ottomans, Britons, and Americans have all invaded, devastated, and then, in a fashion, ruled, but never fully subdued Mesopotamia.

Past as precedent

For much of its history, the region has straddled a border that has divided, and still divides, great civilizations and religions. It has been the means of transmitting ideas as well as economic production. Not surprisingly, given its position on the frontiers of differing cultures, polities, and religions, Mesopotamia has also seen more than its fair share of human conflict.[6] The geography of Mesopotamia's rivers dominated the political and strategic framework of Iraq to an extent similar to that of the Nile in Egypt or the Yellow River in China. With rainfall limited to relatively short periods during the winter, the rivers represented the lifeblood for sustained agriculture and civilization.

To the south and west, relatively trackless deserts provided considerable protection, except for the occasional explosion of Bedouin tribes into the area. But directly to the east of the Tigris and to the north of the valley rises a range of mountains, from which invasions onto the valley plains have often come. Similarly, invaders from the west like Alexander the Great or the Roman emperor Trajan have moved with considerable facility across the valley and from there into the mountains into the Persian heartland. Nevertheless, in the largest sense, the mountains have been a barrier sufficient to delineate a border between Arab and Persian.[7]

Leading a division of the Indian Army in the invasion of Iran in summer 1941, the future Field Marshal Lord Slim noted:

---

[5] Roux, *Ancient Iraq*, 102.

[6] One study of the history of warfare suggests that the Mesopotamian region boasts the dubious distinction of having had more wars than any other area on the planet. This equates to a war every 2.51 years over a study period of 2,190 years. See Claudio Cioffi-Revilla, "Origins and Evolutions of War Politics," *International Studies Quarterly* 40, no. 1 (1996), 10.

[7] Turkish tribes converted the Persians to the Shi'a version of Islam in the sixteenth century; then in the late eighteenth and nineteenth centuries, Persian missionaries converted substantial numbers of Arabs in the southern portions of the Mesopotamian Valley to their form of Islam.

As it grew lighter, Aizlewood and I pushed on with the advance-guard, and by mid-morning we were almost at the entrance to the Pa-i-Tak Pass. Here we stopped and ... stood on the roof of my station-wagon to study this historic gate through which over the centuries, so many armies had passed or tried to pass.

... The interminable flat plains of the Tigris and Euphrates which stretched behind us for hundreds of miles here came to an abrupt end at the great boundary wall of a mighty escarpment ... The road to Kermanshah which we must follow rose sharply into the mouth of the pass and, climbing in curves and loops, vanished among cliffs and gorges to emerge, three thousand feet higher ... It looked as if a handful of men could hold it against an army many times the size of mine.[8]

In 1941, Slim's division would take only days to reach its goal against indifferent Iranian resistance. It would prove a far harder task for Saddam's divisions at the start of the 1980 Iran–Iraq War.

The creation of the modern Iraqi state resulted from two factors: first, the destruction of the Ottoman Empire by the military forces of Britain and its Commonwealth allies in campaigns from Gallipoli to Egypt and Mesopotamia; and, second, the lack of British political and military leadership's coherent political forethought and planning during the course of those campaigns.[9] Initially, the British planned to rule Mesopotamia as a colony, but a revolt by the tribes in 1920, especially in southern Iraq, and a host of competing priorities for a nation nearly bankrupted by World War I, resulted in London rethinking the area's future.[10]

Gertrude Bell best summed up the slapdash British approach to intervention in the Middle East in 1916, where she was an observer and occasional participant:

Politically, too, we rushed into the business with our usual disregard for a comprehensive political scheme ... The coordinating of Arabian politics and

---

[8] Field Marshal William Joseph Slim, the Viscount Slim, *Unofficial History* (New York, NY, 1962), 182–183.

[9] The Ottoman Empire had been referred to as the "sick man of Europe" since the mid-nineteenth century, and certainly its troubles in the Balkans and North Africa in the decade before World War I might suggest that this was so. Nevertheless, the fact that the empire held on for four long years of World War I against major assaults by the Allied powers suggests it was stronger than experts had supposed before the war. Far and away the best study of Britain's planning for the postwar period during the conflict – or lack thereof – remains David Fromkin, *A Peace to End All Peace: The Fall of the Ottoman Empire and the Creation of the Modern Middle East* (New York, NY, 1989). See also Toby Dodge, *Inventing Iraq: The Failure of Nation Building and a History Denied* (New York, NY, 2003); Peter Sluglett, *Britain in Iraq: Contriving King and Country* (New York, NY, 2007).

[10] On Britain's colonial policies and attempt at a colony-light model of imperial rule, see Daniel Silverfarb and Majid Khadduri, *Britain's Informal Empire in the Middle East: A Case Study of Iraq 1929–1941* (Oxford, 1986).

the creation of an Arabian policy should have been done at home – it could only have been done successfully at home. There was no-one to do it, no-one who had ever thought of it, and it was left to our people in Egypt to thrash out, in the face of tremendous opposition from India and London, some sort of scheme which will, I am persuaded, ultimately form the basis of our relations with the Arabs.

But as she was to admit later in the year, "the real difficulty here is that we don't know exactly what we intend to do in the country."[11]

The eventual result was the establishment of the Hashemite Kingdom of Iraq with three very different constituencies, divided by language, ethnic origins, and religion. In effect, the British stitched together three sections of the Ottoman Empire, the only commonality among them being the Tigris and Euphrates rivers. The southern provinces, largely consisting of Shi'a tribes, received short shrift in the new kingdom, both because of their role in the 1920 revolt and because of Shi'a religious and tribal leaders' refusal to participate in the political negotiations leading up to the kingdom's creation. The Kurds in the north were included in the new state as an afterthought – helped by the discovery of oil near Mosul – thus leaving the Sunnis in the central portions of Iraq in control by default. Not surprisingly, the Sunni elites were delighted to take full advantage of the situation. Thus, Iraq was the fabrication of outsiders who had little understanding of the region, its culture, or its politics.[12] Iraq's first monarch, Faisal, installed by the British and undoubtedly the most effective and humane of Iraq's rulers since its creation, remarked in 1933 that "[t]here is still – and I say this with a heart full of sorrow – no Iraqi people, but unimaginable masses of human beings, devoid of any patriotic idea, imbued with religious traditions and absurdities, connected by no common tie, giving ear to evil, prone to anarchy, and perpetually ready to rise against any government whatever."[13]

The post-mandate Iraqi state faced considerable turmoil. The new Iraqi Army, comprising veterans of the Ottoman army and raw recruits, was trained and organized by officers provided by the British. The British officers struggled with many of the same problems confronting American advisors in Iraq early in the twenty-first century. The most obvious was

---

[11] Sluglett, *Britain in Iraq*, 11–12.

[12] For the period between the world wars, see Silverfarb, *Britain's Informal Empire in the Middle East*; John Gooch, "Building Buffers and Filling Vacuums: Great Britain and the Middle East, 1914–1922," in *The Making of Peace: Rulers, States, and the Aftermath of War*, Williamson Murray and James Lacey, eds. (New York, NY, 2009).

[13] Memorandum written by King Faisal, March 1933, cited in Hanna Batatu, *The Old Social Classes and the Revolutionary Movements of Iraq: A Study of Iraq's Old Landed and Commercial Classes and of Its Communists, Ba'athists, and Free Officers* (Princeton, NJ, 2004), 75.

the problem of how to bring European-style concepts to an officer corps and enlisted troops drawn from an alien social and military culture. A British military report on early operations described the Iraqi Army in the following terms: "Leadership and discipline broke down at a particularly critical stage, and the British officers, whose function was to act only as advisers and who had no legal authority, found themselves compelled to take complete charge and to issue direct orders themselves."[14]

In the early 1930s, sectarian and tribal political intrigues gradually destabilized the Iraqi government. A power vacuum followed the sudden death of King Faisal in 1933 and left the country "drifting into something not far off civil war."[15] Into that vacuum stepped the new army, which enhanced its reputation earlier in the year by squashing a rebellion by Iraq's Assyrian minority with marked brutality.[16] Nevertheless, in the turmoil of tribal rebellions that followed Faisal's death, the army was the only instrument capable of holding the state together, but it could do so only by ruthlessly suppressing Iraq's restless minorities and their tribes.[17]

In October 1936, General Bakr Sidqi, declaring himself the "commander of the national forces of reform," announced to the public that "the army, which is composed of your sons, has lost patience with the present government."[18] Some well-placed divisions and a few bombs dropped on the prime minister's and ministry of the interior's compounds were all that was required to replace the government – a lesson not lost on later Ba'ath conspirators. The new government, which simultaneously fought with powerful tribal sheiks and managed to alienate reformist elements within the officer corps, did not last. Assassins killed Sidqi and the chief of the air force in Mosul in August 1937. Thus began a series of military coups and counter coups that culminated with the April 1941 installation of Rashid Ali al-Gaylani as prime minister. He was backed by the so-called "Golden Square" of senior military

---

[14] Monthly summaries of air operations, April 1932: Air 5/1292 cited in Sluglett, *Britain in Iraq*, 184.

[15] Mohammad A. Tarbush, *The Role of the Military in Politics: A Case Study of Iraq to 1941* (London, 1982), 120.

[16] For the political ramifications see Tarbush, *The Role of the Military in Politics*. For a contemporary account see R. S. Stafford, "Iraq and the Problem of the Assyrians," *International Affairs* 13, no. 2 (1934), 159–185.

[17] The cultural framework within which Iraqi politics occurred is suggested by the following incident. The new king's sister ran off and married a Greek waiter of Italian nationality. An Iraqi politician and military figure suggested that "public feeling was running so high that it might be difficult for King Ghazi to hold his own unless his honor was speedily retrieved. It was his Majesty's first and obvious duty to kill his sister with his own hand." Tarbush, *The Role of the Military in Politics*, 119.

[18] *Ibid.*, 122.

commanders. With encouragement from the German ambassador, Rashid Ali attempted to ally Iraq with the Third Reich. For those Iraqi officers trained at the German-run military academies of the Ottoman Empire, there had always been an affinity for things Prussian.[19]

For most Iraqi politicians, however, the decision came down to issues of who was likely to win the new European war and, harkening back to the effects of the last European war on Iraqi internal power, who was willing to increase Iraq's autonomy and support the growing pan-Arab, anti-colonial movement. The British military response was immediate, short, and swift. Within less than a month, makeshift British forces, cobbled together at the last moment from disparate units in Palestine, advanced across the Transjordan and broke into the Mesopotamian Valley. Once there, they quickly smashed the rebel units of the Iraqi Army, thus ending illusions that Iraq was master of its own fate.[20]

For the next fifteen years, the British attempted to manipulate the politicians in Baghdad to maintain the country's political status quo during a period of increasingly fervent nationalist and pan-nationalist agitation. But the days of overt colonialism in the Middle East were rapidly ending. The European powers were no longer willing, or able, to play an imperial role in the region. In 1958, the winds of change arrived in Iraq as a military coup overthrew the monarchy.[21] Despite the conspirator's plans to exile young King Faisal II, Iraqi soldiers "in a state of frenzy" machine-gunned the royal family following their surrender and then mutilated the corpses.[22] A purge of Iraqi politicians identified with the *ancien régime* followed, as the revolution swept senior military officers and parliamentarians aside.[23] On the eve of the revolution, perennial prime minister and one of Iraq's most accomplished politicians, Nuri al-Said, reportedly told an army plotter, "I hear you are engaged in a plot against the regime. Is this true? Look [added Nuri], if your plot ever succeeds, you and the other officers will be engaged in a

---

[19] For a discussion of the German influence in Iraq during this period, see Reeva Spector Simon, *Iraq Between the Two World Wars: The Creation and Implementation of a National Ideology* (New York, NY, 1986), 20–43.

[20] For a concise description of the campaign, see Roberty Lyman, *Iraq 1941: The Battles for Basra, Habbaniya, Fallujah, and Baghdad* (Oxford, 2006). Somerset Struben de Chair, *The Golden Carpet* (New York, NY, 1945); Major General Ian Stanley Playfair, *The Germans Come to the Help of Their Ally, 1941*, vol. 2 (London, 1956).

[21] This was the period that saw the rise of Nasser, the Algerian revolution against their French occupiers, and the Suez Crisis of 1956.

[22] A good description of the conditions and circumstances of the coup see Batatu, *The Old Social Classes and the Revolutionary Movements of Iraq*, 764–807.

[23] Marion Farouk-Sluglett and Peter Sluglett, *Iraq since 1958: From Revolution to Dictatorship* (New York, NY, 2001), 47–52.

struggle among yourselves which will not end until each of you hangs the other."[24] It was a prophetic warning. Nuri al-Said was caught a few days after the revolution trying to escape the fate of his sovereign and was unceremoniously killed by a mob on the streets of Baghdad. The army officer he warned was, as predicted, among the first executed by his co-conspirators in the euphoric aftermath of yet another military over-throw in Baghdad. What was not clear in the enthusiasm was who or what would ultimately replace the Hashemite kingdom.

Modern factors that contributed to the war

The making of Saddam's Iraq

After a decade and a half of relative stability, the overthrow of the monarchy in 1958 ushered in a period of turmoil – which, in retrospect, reflected the considerable difficulties that Iraq, as well as much of the Arab world, faced in adjusting to the political challenges of the post-colonial era and the Cold War. There were three main contenders for political power in Baghdad: the military; the communists, who received overt and covert support from the Soviet Union; and an emerging Ba'ath Party. During the succeeding decade, a number of coups and attempted coups wracked Iraq. The Ba'ath Party launched two of these. The first in 1963 collapsed due to Ba'ath incompetence, political naïveté, and its murderous cruelty.[25] But the second, launched on 17 July 1968 with the help of key army officers, energized in part by Iraq's passivity in the humiliating defeat of the Arab armies in the Six-Day War, succeeded.[26] Applying the lessons of 1958 and 1963, new president General Ahmed Hassan al-Bakr and his regime moved quickly to consolidate its control over the military. As Nuri al-Said warned in 1958, the Ba'athists, with the help of a loyal tank brigade and a small group of al-Bakr family members from Tikrit, swiftly removed potentially troublesome former co-conspirators on 30 November.

---

[24] Nuri al-Said's warning to Midhat al-Haji Sirri cited in Majid Khadduri, *Arab Contemporaries: The Role of Personalities in Politics* (Baltimore, MD, 1973), 38–39. Brackets in original.

[25] Cruelty in attempting to gain political control were to mark Ba'ath rule throughout its control of Iraq. Tariq Aziz remarked of this period that "to understand why so much blood flowed in those days you have to remember Iraq's history is not one in which political dissent has been allowed." Quoted in Sandra Mackey, *The Reckoning, Iraq, and the Legacy of Saddam Hussein* (New York, NY, 2002), 192.

[26] For the impact of the Six-Day War on the Middle East, see Michael B. Oren, *Six Days of War: June 1967 and the Making of the Modern Middle East* (New York, NY, 2002).

One of the Tikritis in the new regime was Saddam Hussein, a party enforcer, who had acted as a hit man for the Ba'ath Party in the late 1950s. Having participated in the attempted assassination of Iraq's president, Saddam was no stranger to coups. Now older and somewhat wiser, with a deserved reputation as a man willing to perform the party's dirty work, Saddam established himself in the highest ranks of the party's hierarchy. He became the key figure in establishing the centralized Ba'ath bureaucracy and secret police, both of which served as pillars for his seizure of power in 1979. Of course, given the nature of Iraqi politics, it did not hurt his prospects that he was connected by tribe and family to many of the party's senior leaders. An associate at the time stated "there is no real mystery about the way we run Iraq. We run it exactly as we used to run Tikrit."[27]

The authors of pan-Arabic Ba'ath ideology were two Syrians, Michel Aflaq and Salah al-Din al-Bitar, the former a Greek Orthodox Christian, the latter a Muslim, although both could be classified as secularists. Both had studied in Paris in the late 1920s, where they had met. There, they absorbed a hodgepodge of political ideas then circulating among French intellectuals. They drew much from Marxism, but even more from the right-wing, Fascist political philosophies then sloshing around the gutters of Europe in the aftermath of World War I. Given the origin of some of their ideas, and the growing tensions in Palestine at the time, it is not surprising that they were strongly anti-Semitic and emphasized the importance of the charismatic leader in developing a great state.

Aflaq and al-Bitar focused on the nation, in this case the Arab nation, a mystic and thoroughly ahistorical notion. Their new movement, termed *Ba'ath* (*resurrection* in Arabic), began under the slogans "unity, freedom, socialism," and "one Arab nation with an immortal mission." Their aim was to put the Arab nation back in its rightful place, as they defined it, as the leading nation of the world.[28] Here the two political theorists saw the influences of Western civilization as particularly dangerous to the Arab mentality:

---

[27] Interview with Kamran Karadaghi, Iraqi journalist, London, 1997, cited in Andrew Cockburn and Patrick Cockburn, *Out of the Ashes: The Resurrection of Saddam Hussein* (New York, NY, 1999). Reliance on family or tribal bonds was a critical part of Saddam's consolidation of power after the 1968 revolution. While there were notable exceptions, the *hizb al-usra* (family party) consisting of personal and political relationships "forged in blood" was a key source of stability and security for the regime. See Eric Davis, *Memories of State: Politics, History, and Collective Identity in Modern Iraq* (Berkeley, CA, 2005), 177–182; Farouk-Sluglett and Sluglett, *Iraq since 1958*, 212.

[28] For a description of the founding political ideology of the Ba'ath Party as well as the course of its rule through 1988, see Kanan Makiya, *Republic of Fear: The Politics of Modern Iraq* (Berkeley, CA, 1989); Batatu, *The Old Social Classes and the Revolutionary Movements of Iraq*, 722–748; John F. Devlin, "The Ba'ath Party: Rise and Metamorphosis," *The American Historical Review* 96, no. 5 (1991). Makiya's *Republic of Fear* was originally published under the pseudonym Samir al-Khalil.

The philosophies and teachings that come from the West invade the Arab mind and steal his loyalty before they rob him of his land and skies. We want a unified nationalist education program that derives its roots from the peculiarities of the Arab nation, the spirit of its past, and the needs of its future. It should preserve loyalty to the Arab homeland and the Arab cause without sharing in this venture any other homeland or cause.[29]

In their view – a largely secular, nationalistic ideology – once the proper education and mobilization of the masses had taken place, the Arab nation would be able to restore itself to its rightful place as the world's dominant power. Aflaq was not insensitive to the role of Islam in the life of the secular Arab Nation he sought to create. In fact, he occasionally used Islam to color his secular message with statements such as "Islam, in its pure essence, arose out of the heart of Arabism." During the course of the Iran–Iraq War, Aflaq had the pragmatic aim of "harnessing the emotions called forth by Islam in the service of the Arab national movement, or to be specific, the Ba'ath Party."[30]

Ba'ath political philosophy was attractive to the young Saddam. With minimal education, he had found himself influenced by an uncle, Khayrallah Talfah, whose support of the May 1941 coup against the British had cut short an army career at the rank of major. His uncle was a devoted nationalist whose hatred for Britain's colonial domination, mixed with the growing pan-Arabic movement and the anti-Zionist backlash of the day, generated strong sympathies for Nazi Germany. In Khayrallah's writings, the perceived Zionist–imperialist connections of the 1940s were merged with a much older Jewish–Persian connection. In an article entitled "Iranian-Zionist relations throughout the Ages," Khayrallah wrote "Iran has been linked to the pro-Zionist Jewish movement by deep and lasting ties of thousands of years" – a view for which his nephew would find new justification for the geopolitics of the Iran–Iraq War.[31] With these early influences, one should not underestimate the pure anti-Persian bias that festered in Saddam's worldview. The Iraqi

---

[29] Quoted in Makiya, *Republic of Fear*, 193.

[30] Batatu, *The Old Social Classes and the Revolutionary Movements of Iraq*, 733. Unlike Kemal Ataturk's efforts to secularize Turkey by splitting religion from politics, Aflaq, and later Saddam, would treat it as just another lever of power. Despite early reluctance to identify his cause with religion, beginning in the mid-1980s, Saddam increasingly cloaked himself in the role of religion. See Amatzia Baram, "From Militant Secularism to Islamism: The Iraqi Ba'ath Regime, 1968–2003," Occasional paper (Washington, DC, 2011), 24.

[31] Ofra Bengio, *Saddam's Word: Political Discourse in Iraq* (New York, NY, 1998), 127–139. See also Simon, *Iraq between the Two World Wars*, 146–165. From Saddam's point of view, the Persian–Jewish conspiracy went back to the sixth century BC, when Cyrus had restored the Jews to Palestine.

Sunnis were all too aware of the long history of conflict between the Sunni Arabs in the west and Shi'a Persians to the east. In 1981, Saddam gave voice to this tension by republishing another of his uncle's works: *Three Whom God Should Not Have Created: Persians, Jews, and Flies.*[32]

During the 1970s, Saddam's Ba'ath ideology and the need to build support for a powerful central state led him to minimize the role of Islam while emphasizing Mesopotamia's role in history as the center of world civilization.[33] As he suggested to an interviewer shortly after he had taken power in 1979, he believed there was a close connection between Iraq's past and its future:

Nebuchadnezzar stirs in me everything relating to pre-Islamic ancient history. I am reminded that any human being with broad horizons, faith and feeling can act wisely, but practically, attain his goals and become a great man who makes his country into a great state. And what is most important to me about Nebuchadnezzar is the link between the Arabs' abilities and the liberation of Palestine. Nebuchadnezzar was, after all, an Arab from Iraq, albeit ancient Iraq. Nebuchadnezzar was the one who brought the bound Jewish slaves from Palestine.[34]

Saddam's hardscrabble background in Tikrit molded a personality deeply suspicious of the motives and inclinations of others. His sense of distrust led him to rely throughout his career on his family, then his tribe, and then those from Tikrit. But it was his family on which Saddam particularly relied. It was there that he was to make his greatest misjudgment. As a window into Saddam's world, consider his relationship with his second cousin, Hussein Kamel. Through his spectacular career, Kamel rose from the rank of lieutenant in 1980 to become Saddam's close advisor by the late 1980s, and director of Iraq's military–industrial efforts. In the early 1990s, he became the second most powerful man in Iraq. Then, in 1995, he fled Iraq, only to return shortly thereafter to be killed by his own family at Saddam's order.

Yet, in the view of a number of those the authors interviewed, Kamel was a third-rate officer with unlimited ambition and a distinctly ruthless

---

[32] Jerrold M. Post, ed. *The Psychological Assessment of Political Leaders: With Profiles of Saddam Hussein and Bill Clinton* (Ann Arbor, MI, 2003), 337.

[33] Saddam tried to rebuild Nebuchadnezzar's hanging gardens of Babylon. For his architectural and historical efforts to recreate the past, see Kanan Makiya, *The Monument: Art, Vulgarity, and Responsibility in Iraq* (Berkeley, CA, 1991). Makiya's *The Monument* was originally published under the pseudonym Samir al-Khalil. See also, Amatzia Baram, *Culture, History and Ideology in the Formation of Ba'athist Iraq, 1968–89* (London, 1991).

[34] Fuad Matar, "The Young President: An Interview with Saddam Hussein in 1980," in *The Saddam Hussein Reader: Selections from Leading Writers on Iraq*, Turi Munthe, ed. (New York, NY, 2002), 10–11. In fact, the date of the interview was 17 July 1979.

streak. A conversation between Saddam and his advisors in 1980 suggests the kind of sycophants that made up his inner circle as well as a rare blind spot in Saddam's ability to judge the character of those closest to him:

CHIEF OF THE DIWAN:	Lieutenant Hussein [Kamel] is the one who gave the order.
SADDAM:	Lieutenant Hussein [Kamel] is smart ... If we had more like him ... he is smart!
INTERIOR MINISTER:	Hussein Kamel's reaction is very quick!
SADDAM:	He understands and his reaction is quick!
INTERIOR MINISTER:	Yes, this is very obvious.
SADDAM:	He is the smartest and most knowledgeable among the escorts.
CHIEF OF THE DIWAN:	He has a good mentality too!
SADDAM:	Yes! He studies and works hard to improve himself!
MILITARY OPERATIONS DIRECTOR:	It seems he is a hard worker.[35]

In the long-running contest among the Ba'athists, the army, and the Communists for control of Iraq, the Ba'athists won, largely because the army needed their political support, while the Communists were unable to offer an Arab answer to Iraq's problems, at least from the perspective of the army's officer corps. In the 1968 Ba'ath revolution, Saddam was a key player. Unlike other party leaders, he was not a pseudo-intellectual, but a street-smart operator with the requisite ruthlessness to purge the army and politics of the party's enemies. A scholar of Iraq wrote of the Tikritis, a few years after the 1968 revolution, that "their role continues to be so critical that it would not be going too far to say that the Tikritis rule through the Ba'ath Party, rather than the Ba'ath Party through the Tikritis."[36] Saddam, as events would bear out, was the most ruthless Tikriti of them all.

Not surprisingly, Saddam greatly admired Stalin as a role model.[37] In a conversation in early 1981, he remarked: "I tell you, the [Soviets] when they say they have weapons ... This is because of [Stalin], he squeezed their bones to focus on weapons and he was right. Don't tell me [the

---

[35] Transcript of a meeting of the General Command of the Armed Forces (10 October 1980) in SH-SHTP-D-000-573, Transcripts of General Command of the Armed Forces Meetings During the First Gulf War and Correspondence with Other Arab Leaders, October 1980.

[36] Batatu, *The Old Social Classes and the Revolutionary Movements of Iraq*, 1088.

[37] See Robert Fisk, *The Great War for Civilization: The Conquest of the Middle East* (New York, NY, 2005), 160; Simon Sebag Montefiore, *Stalin: The Court of the Red Tsar* (New York, NY, 2004), 25. Saddam also expressed admiration for Hitler's Germany. At the start of the Iran–Iraq War, he remarked to his entourage that the Germans "are honorable; they fought the entire world and by themselves" – an example that Saddam was eventually to replicate.

Soviet Union] would be spreading its clout on the world if it weren't armed."[38] Like Stalin, Saddam possessed untiring energy in administrative matters as well as the ruthlessness necessary to survive in Ba'ath politics. But Saddam was more than just an admirer of Stalin. A number of former regime members commented to the authors that throughout his life, Saddam acted and thought like a Bedouin. Thus, the regime Saddam established reflected the influences of his suspicious Bedouin view of the world, Ba'ath ideology, and a Stalinist desire to control everything.[39]

By 1975, Saddam was vice president of Iraq's revolutionary command council (RCC) – in effect, the country's number-two man behind his relative and president, Ahmed Hassan al-Bakr. Saddam was arguably more powerful than the president due to his control of the intelligence services. As such, Saddam received the irksome task of renegotiating the treaty between Iraq and Iran that governed control of the Shatt al-Arab, the waterway separating the two nations. The confluence of the Tigris and the Euphrates (as well as the Karun River in Iran) flowed into the Persian Gulf and was essential to transshipment of petroleum from terminals and refineries upriver.

The British had established the border between Iraq and Iran along the waterway by treaty in 1937; an arrangement they had forced on the Iranians and that favored Iraq.[40] But by the mid-1970s, the British were no longer a significant power in the region. To a considerable extent, the

---

[38] SH-AFGC-D-000-393, Transcript of a General Command of the Armed Forces Meeting During the First Gulf War and Telephone Conversations, 6–7 January 1981.

[39] Typical of the latter are a series of letters between Saddam's secretariat about a contractor who was supposed to deliver rocks to a building site, but who had died before he could deliver them. The question then was whether he should be fined or not, because he had been late in fulfilling the contract. SH-PDWN-D-000-551, General Administrative Information and Presidential Diwan Correspondence, 28 May 1986. For the Stalinist security procedures of the Iraqi bureaucracy, see, among other documents, RE: Intelligence Service Activities Related to Government Departments (20 March 1986) Memorandum from Ahmad Husayn to the Office of the President Republic of Iraq in SH-IISX-D-000-698, Reports on Iraqi Intelligence Service Activities, October 1985–May 1986. After examining these documents during a five-year period, the authors can only conclude that there were few decisions in which Saddam was not to some extent involved. Among others see "Improvement of Domestic Hens," 5 November 1987 in SH-PWDN-D-000-604, Miscellaneous Memos from the Presidential Diwan Various Directorates About General Administrative and Financial Matters, October 1987– September 1988.

[40] There were earlier treaties between the Ottomans and Iranians delineating the Shatt al-Arab. See Richard Schofield, "Position, Function, and Symbol: The Shatt Al-Arab Dispute in Perspective," in *Iran, Iraq, and the Legacies of War*, Lawrence G. Potter and Gary G. Sick, eds. (London, 2004), 29–70; Hussein Sirriyeh, "Development of the Iraqi-Iranian Dispute, 1847–1975," *Journal of Contemporary History* 20, no. 3 (1985), 483–492.

Iranians had replaced them. With military aid from the United States, Iran had emerged as the region's dominant power, one to which the Iraqis now had to bend. In 1969, the Shah abrogated the 1937 treaty, giving Iran de facto control over the Shatt al-Arab. Two years later, he seized three uninhabited islands in the Gulf, which the Gulf Arabs had long claimed.[41]

During this same period, Iraq was waging yet another phase of its decades-long struggle against armed Kurdish factions vying for control of Iraq's northern provinces. Immediately following the 1968 Ba'ath revolution, the Kurds had taken advantage of the perceived chaos in Baghdad to re-launch a vigorous bid for autonomy. After almost two years of bloody combat, Baghdad came to a tentative agreement over limited Kurdish autonomy with the largest Kurdish faction, the Kurdistan Democratic Party, led by Mullah Mustafa Barzani.[42] Like many such agreements between Baghdad and its minorities, the agreement broke down over disagreements about territorial issues – specifically the oil-rich territory around Kirkuk.

Fighting between Baghdad and the Kurds resumed in 1974. This time the Kurds entered the fray with support from the Shah, the Americans, and the Israelis – all of whom were eager to see the Iraqis distracted and internally focused.[43] In particular, Iranian support for the Kurds jeopardized Iraq's control over its northern provinces and the Kirkuk oil fields. Kurdish forces, operating from mountain lairs and using hit-and-run attacks, dealt the Iraqi Army a number of serious blows. Moreover, the mere threat of a collapse of control over the northern third of the country carried with it the danger that the Shi'a in the south might also revolt. Thus, to end Iranian support for the Kurds, the Iraqis had to negotiate with the Shah, who held all the cards. The Shah played them well.

---

[41] Saddam would list the return of the three islands to Arab control as one of the war's objectives. He was undoubtedly attempting to enlist external Arab support, though in this effort, as in many others, he failed.

[42] For more on the background of the Ba'ath–Kurdish relationship, see David McDowall, *A Modern History of the Kurds* (London, 2004), 302–342. Neither side expected the agreement to last. In October 1980, Saddam and his advisors discussed at length how they might assassinate the Barzani clan, something they carried out in 1982, when Iraqi troops rounded up approximately 8,000 of those associated with the tribe and executed them. See SH-MISC-D-000-695, Saddam Hussein Meeting with Various Iraqi Officials About the Iraqi Position Early on in the Iran–Iraq War, 12–13 October 1980.

[43] See Lokman I. Meho and Michel G. Nehme, "The Legacy of U.S. Support to Kurds: Two Major Episodes," in *The Kurdish Question in U.S. Foreign Policy*, Lokman I. Meho, ed. (Westport, 2004); Mackey, *The Reckoning, Iraq, and the Legacy of Saddam Hussein*, 224; Dader Entessar, "The Kurds in Post-Revolutionary Iran and Iraq," *Third World Quarterly* 6, no. 4 (1984), 920–921.

Negotiations between Saddam and Iran's representatives led to the Algiers Agreement, signed in March 1975, which gave the Shah virtually everything he had demanded, especially a new border along the Shatt. The real losers were the Kurds, because, in accordance with the agreement, Iran withdrew its support immediately after reaching agreement with Saddam. The negotiators addressed numerous other border issues, but failed to reach agreement on most. Technical negotiations between the two sides continued throughout 1975, concluding with agreement to prevent "utterances ... which are offensive to the other party" from crossing the frontier.[44] The territorial matter of the three islands near the Straits of Hormuz, seized by the Shah in 1971, remained a *cause célèbre* for Saddam in his rhetoric at the start of the conflict. In September 1980 he accused Khomeini and Iranian leadership of "unjustly maintain[ing] all the Iraqi territories which the Shah had occupied and maintained – the three Arab islands of Greater Tunb, Lesser Tunb, and Abu Musa."[45] At a press conference two months later, Saddam proclaimed, "Our rights are clear. Our territories are clear. Our sovereignty over the usurped Arab territories is clear."[46]

Much worse – from Saddam's point of view – was what else the Iraqis had surrendered in the 1975 Algiers Agreement. Iraq had to acknowledge Iranian sovereignty over half the Shatt al-Arab, a deep humiliation in a region where even small bits of territory can assume an importance far beyond their economic or strategic value. The Shah made no practical concessions except to stop supporting the Kurds.[47] The Shatt al-Arab is and was critical to Iraq and the transportation of its oil from the south, because it dominates the country's limited access to the Gulf.[48] This loss, while small, symbolized subjugation and humiliation by an ancient rival and displayed Iraq's failure as well as its weaknesses – economic,

[44] "Agreement between Iran and Iraq Concerning Frotier Commissioners," in *Treaties and International Agreements Registered or Filed and Recorded with the Secretariat of the United Nations* (New York, NY, 1976), 224.

[45] Saddam Hussein, "Text of President Speech to National Assembly, 17 Sep (FBIS-MEA-80-183)," *Foreign Broadcast Information Services Daily Reports* (1980).

[46] Saddam Hussein, "Text of President Husayn's 10 Nov Press Conference (FBIS-MEA-80-220)," *Foreign Broadcast Information Services Daily Reports* (1980).

[47] Saddam admitted in a conversation in 1980 that the war against the Kurds in the mid-1970s had cost the Iraqi Army between 16,000 and 17,000 casualties. SH-SHTP-A-000-835, Meeting between Saddam Hussein, the National Command, and the Revolutionary Command Council Discussing the Iraq–Iran War, 16 September 1980. This is almost twice the official Iraqi government casualty count of 9,500.

[48] Iran's coastline, on the other hand, is 1,200 miles long with five naval bases along it, several of them beyond Iraqi operational reach. The sole Iraqi naval bases of Basra and Umm Qasr are on the Shatt al-Arab or nearby, and because of their proximity to Iran, are vulnerable.

military, and political – in light of its desire to become the preeminent regional power, if not leader of the Arab world. For Saddam it was a bitter pill. The former Iraqi foreign minister, Saadoun Hammadi, who also helped negotiate the 1975 agreement, stated acidly that Iraq had to agree to such unfavorable terms, because "it was either that or lose the north of the country."[49] Nevertheless, the treaty represented a bitter pill, one Saddam did not forget.

Saddam: the leader

On 16 July 1979, President al-Bakr announced his resignation and quickly, or advisedly, stepped down.[50] Saddam immediately had himself sworn in as Iraq's president, secretary general of the Ba'ath Party's regional command, chairman of the RCC, and commander-in-chief of the armed forces. To insure his position and eliminate potential rivals, the new president announced before an assemblage of the party's leaders the discovery of a plot involving a number of the Ba'ath Party's most senior members. As the charges were read out, the guilty were dragged from the meeting hall in front of the survivors. The charges were never more specific than "striking at the party and revolution" and "linking Iraq with the capitalist design led by US imperialism."[51]

A quick trial followed, with even quicker executions (in which some of the surviving ministers participated). In short order, Saddam eliminated twenty-two senior party members whom he regarded as rivals, too independent for his tastes, or as conspirators with connections to foreign powers.[52] The message was clear. The new regime's explanation for the purge turned on the supposed collusion between those executed and the Syrians, providing Saddam with a pretext to terminate the ongoing, fruitless negotiations with Damascus.[53] He now set the course for

[49] Nita M. Renfrew, "Who Started the War?," *Foreign Policy* (1987), 100.

[50] While Saddam's role and eventual actions makes this event seem foreordained, the proximate causes and logic of timing still remain shrouded in mystery. Reasons ranging from al-Bakr's health (the least credible), concerns over policy toward the revolution in Iran, disagreements over a potential Ba'ath union with Syria, and a ruthless culmination of a long-standing plan to "transfer already existing bonds of complicity away from the party and firmly into the person of Saddam" are among those offered as the cause. See Makiya, *Republic of Fear*, 70–72.

[51] Efraim Karsh and Inari Rautsi, *Saddam Hussein: A Political Biography* (New York, NY, 1991), 113.

[52] The proceedings remind one of the Queen of Hearts' statements in *Alice in Wonderland*: "First the sentence and then the trial!"

[53] See Phebe Marr, *The Modern History of Iraq* (Boulder, CO, 2004), 178–181; Ofra Bengio and Uriel Dann, "Iraq," in *Middle East Contemporary Survey, Volume III: 1978–79*, Colin Legum, ed. (New York, NY, 1980), 559–565.

himself, Iraq, and "his" Arab nation – a course marked by Ba'ath ideology and a belief in his personal, historic mission.[54]

Saddam's vision

Saddam possessed a combination of intelligence, ruthlessness, and toughness that allowed him to dominate Iraq from 1979 until his fall in 2003. An Iraqi general who dealt with Saddam on a number of occasions described him the following way:

> When [Saddam] looked at you, he paid close attention. He looked you straight in the eye, as if to control you. In general, he was an intelligent person and an amazingly thorough listener. Not knowing what was on his mind was scary. Moreover, the strength of his convictions could be scary; if he believed something was true, even if he were proved wrong, he believed it to be true … Saddam had a number of personality traits. Sometimes he was intelligent, other times he could be as naïve as an illiterate farmer. One moment he would be extremely affectionate, the next moment he would be extremely hostile and cruel. Even Satan was better than Saddam at those times. One minute he could be overly generous, the next he could be extremely stingy. He had a great ability to listen, but then he would not allow you to say anything or he would refuse to listen to what you said. He was extremely courageous. He could take ideas from everyone and create a new idea. At a political level, he was an excellent tactical player; however, at the strategic level, 99 percent of his concepts were wrong.[55]

Another general described dealing with Saddam in these terms: "Saddam would listen if you discussed an issue with him in a logical fashion [but] you just had to be careful how you phrased your answer."[56]

How did Saddam view himself and his role as the leader of Iraq? In 1981, he suggested to a group of ministers, "[My] job is to absorb, analyze, collect intelligence and make conclusions, and relay it to others to analyze and predict, then examine the details gathered from everybody and extract a historic cognitive conclusion for the correct direction."[57] Saddam judged his military subordinates by two criteria. The first lay in

---

[54] For more on the nature of the regime Saddam created, see the exchange of letters dealing with orders emanating from "The permanent committee for hostile activity follow-up" among others in *SH-ISGS-D-001-302, The Permanent Committee for Hostile Activity Recommendations to "Eliminate" Opposition Party Leaders, August 1988.

[55] Kevin M. Woods, Williamson Murray, Elizabeth A. Nathan, Laila Sabara and Ana M. Venegas, "Interview with (Former) Lieutenant General Ra'ad Majid Rashid Al-Hamdani, Amman, Jordan, 6–7 November 2009," *Project 1946: Phase II* (Alexandria, VA, 2010), 59–60.

[56] Woods *et al.*, "Interview with Major General (Ret) Aladdin Hussein Makki Khamas, Cairo, Egypt, 11 November 2009," 121.

[57] *SH-SHTP-A-001-303, Recording of a Meeting between Saddam Hussein and Ba'ath Party Members Discussing the Iran–Iraq War, Circa October 1981–Early 1982.

his belief that Bedouin tribal courage and loyalty were the most important attributes of successful military leadership. That certainly characterized the military leaders Saddam put in the most important army commands by summer 1980. The second was his assessment of an officer's loyalty to Iraq – meaning Saddam. Saddam was no fool. But military professionals were never close to Saddam's heart, even when they were most important. During the Iran–Iraq War, Saddam increasingly came to listen to his head and realized that he needed the advice of his military professionals. However, and often at the worst possible time, Saddam would revert to his gut feelings and defer to the simple-minded but courageous officer who cared little for serious planning or casualty figures.

Saddam's vision of himself as self-appointed leader of a pan-Arab movement sharpened after the signing of the Camp David Accords in 1978. It was to be a driving factor in all of his decision making as Iraq's ruler from 1979 onward. In the words of Saddam's press secretary during the Iran–Iraq War, Sabah Salman: "Saddam had an appointment with Iraqi history because a country with a great history always needs a great historical leader. The real history of modern Iraq began with [Hussein]; other leaders might end up in the 'trash bins of history,' but [Hussein] was inscribed in its annals by 'the pen of history itself.'"[58] Saddam's public speeches as well as his comments in private meetings reflected a striking consistency of strategic vision from the Iran–Iraq War until the American invasion of 2003. In his view, he was foreordained to unify the Arab peoples. That, in turn, would allow the Arabs to expel the "colonial" powers or at least their influence from Arab lands. Once unified and unencumbered under his leadership, the Arab world could drive the Jewish interlopers into the sea.[59] The resulting superpower would recreate a largely secular version of past Arab glories.[60] In terms of its power, Saddam believed his new state, resting on Arab nationalism and oil, would easily equal China and perhaps even the United States.[61]

[58] Quoted in Bengio, *Saddam's Word*, 167–168. The original quotation was translated from Arabic in Sabah Salman, *Saddam Hussein Aq'id Wa-Ta'rikh* (Baghdad, 1986).

[59] Since the late nineteenth century, rallying cries for Arab unification have ranged from the European-inspired nationalism during World War I, opposition to Zionism in the 1930s, euphoria over the end of the colonial era, the existence of a Jewish state, and, finally, to the rise of radical Islam.

[60] For Saddam's views on this, see the discussion in Kevin M. Woods, Michael Pease, Mark E. Stout, Williamson Murray and James G. Lacey, *The Iraqi Perspectives Report: Saddam's Senior Leadership on Operation Iraqi Freedom* (Annapolis, MD, 2006), 6.

[61] In this respect, see Saddam's remarks quoted in Norman Cigar, "Iraq's Strategic Mindset and the Gulf War: Blueprint for Defeat," *Journal of Strategic Studies* 15, no. 1 (1992), 19.

Thus, Iraq's options, timing, and occasional compromises to achieve Saddam's goals would be a matter of circumstances, but what he believed necessary to accomplish his purposes remained at the center of his calculations and actions. Above all, he recognized that military and political force would be necessary to overcome the opposition inside and outside Iraq. He never considered or questioned the potential cost of such purposes. Saddam's rhetoric borrowed liberally from the ideas of an earlier Iraqi pan-Arabist, Sami Shawkat, who served as a government minister in the 1930s. Shawkat delivered a speech in 1933 entitled "The Manufacture of Death." In it he argued, much as Saddam would decades later, that "the ability to cause and accept death in pursuit of pan-Arab ideals was the highest calling."[62] Notwithstanding his occasional bouts of pessimism on the potential for Arab cohesion and unity, Saddam repeatedly emphasized that these were the keys to his strategic vision. Arab unity, after all, lay at the heart of Ba'ath political philosophy. He believed that Arab leaders who did not subscribe to his view would eventually find themselves subject to the "instigation of the people in an organized manner to destroy [their] regime[s]."[63]

While often conflating the concept of self and state, Saddam believed Iraq was the only Middle Eastern state capable of achieving the proper place for the Arab nation in history.[64] Other Arab nations like Syria (also Ba'athist) might play a part, but only when

it becomes part of Iraq ... it cannot do it on its own, even if a sincere ruler takes the helm ... it cannot be the central post of the Arab nation ... Iraq can make this nation rise and can be the center post of its big abode. There are always smaller posts, but it must always be that Iraq feels the responsibility and feels it is the

---

[62] Andrew Parasiliti and Sinan Antoon, "Friends in Need, Foes to Heed: The Iraqi Military in Politics," *Middle East Policy* 7, no. 4 (2000), 131. For more on the role of Shawkat in Saddam's conception of civil–military relations, see Bengio, *Saddam's Word*, 146–147; Makiya, *Republic of Fear*, 177–178.

[63] SH-SHTP-A-000-553, Revolutionary Command Council Meeting after the Baghdad Conference in 1979, 27 March 1979.

[64] Saddam, like Nasser before him, struggled with the Gordian Knot of Arab unity. As a national leader, he appealed to state nationalism to build the kind of strength and political clout necessary to press for a political philosophy (in his case Ba'athist ideology) that embodied state nationalism. To what extent Saddam internalized Louis XIV's famous quip *L'etat, c'est moi* is not clear, but as others have noted, he expended enormous energy to build a cult of personality from the first moments he ascended to power. Leon Trotsky's commentary on his murderous boss seems applicable to a latter-day Stalin acolyte in Baghdad, "the totalitarian state goes far beyond Caesars and Popism, for it has encompassed the entire economy of the country as well. Stalin can justly say, unlike the Sun King, '*La Societe, c'est moi.*'" Karsh and Rautsi, *Saddam Hussein*, 89.

central support post of the Arab Nation. If Iraq falls, then the entire Arab nation will fall. When the central post breaks, the whole house will collapse.[65]

Not surprisingly, Syria, like many of Saddam's neighbors, refused to share the dictator's vision. In 1978, the Syrians refused to become Iraq's junior partner after a frenzied round of negotiations, and from that point, the rulers of each nation became enmeshed in a bitter quarrel.[66] The whole enterprise seemed doomed from the beginning: even as the countries were negotiating what form the unification would take, the harsh realities of Ba'ath politics bubbled to the surface. On 15 December 1979, Iraqi intelligence reportedly listened in on several meetings between Syrian, Iranian, and Libyan leaders who were coordinating operations to create sectarian conflict in Iraq aimed at overthrowing Iraq's Ba'ath regime.[67] Then on 30 December, Saddam was cautioned by his negotiators that he might have to accept certain "temporary sacrifices" in order to make sure Syria's al-Assad remained "confident about his fate." Among the concerns cited was the problem of merging certain unnamed "immoral elements" in Damascus into the new leadership of the party, while at the same time figuring out how to "sacrifice" some of the "comrades in the Syrian state who cannot be tolerated."[68] As one of Saddam's associates had suggested to him a year earlier:

As Arabs, we are unique in our positive and negative emotions that are attached to all of the curves of our major struggle. Between black and white there are no other color levels between destroying the cars of the Syrian diplomatic forum in Baghdad as a response to their [activities] in Syria and greeting their groups with

---

[65] SH-SHTP-A-000-626, Saddam Hussein Discusses Neighboring Countries and Their Regimes, January 1981. "Central post" was an allusion to the Arab nation forming a tent over its people; the individual states were the posts. While there would be many supporting posts, Saddam reasoned, there could only be one central post.

[66] On 27 October 1978, Iraq's al-Bakr and Syria's al-Assad issued a joint statement pledging "a determination to work hard and according to an on-going scientific plan in order to achieve the closest form of unitary relations between the two Arab regions, Iraq and Syria." See "Iraqi-Syrian Charter for Joint National Action Agreed on by Syrian President Hafiz al-Assad and Iraqi President Ahmed Hassan al-Bakr following their Meetings in Baghdad, October 24–26, 1978. [Excerpts]," in "Documents and Source Material: Arab Documents on Palestine and the Arab-Israeli Conflict," *Journal of Palestinian Studies* 8, no. 2 (Winter 1979), 200–202.

[67] Memorandum from GMID to the Revolutionary Command Council RE: Information (15 December 1979) in SH-GMID-D-000-595, Information Regarding Syrian Authorities Secretly Visiting Iran and Libya to Foment Sectarian War in Iraq, December 1979. What angered Saddam was that the Syrians supported the Iranians by providing weapons and training facilities in Syria and Syrian-controlled portions of Lebanon.

[68] Memorandum from Dr. Munif al-Razzaz to Saddam Hussein (30 December 1978) in SH-BATH-D-000-206, Suggestion to Integrate Iraqi and Syrian Ba'ath Parties; Ba'ath Party Structure Notes, 30 December 1978.

all warmth and love ... a few days [later] ... [W]hat separates the definition of betrayal and patriotism between the enemy and the ally is a very thin line.[69]

To the south, Saudi Arabia, and by inference the other oil-rich Arab states, whose rulers Saddam often described as "temporary," could not rise to the leadership challenge because, according to him:

There is a great deal of money. Yes billions, [earned] without sweat ... the human is missing. There is no density of population and no quality. The one who is going to raise the Arab nation should be the one who is richer in scientific knowledge than the others ... There is no escape from the responsibility of leadership. It is not our choice to accept it or not. It is, rather, imposed on us ... [W]e must take this direction. It must be Iraq due to the fact that Iraq has everything going for it.[70]

In discussions, Saddam had a tendency to mix his pan-Arab vision with a decidedly tribal outlook. He often described his burden as the leader or sheik of all Arabs. A time would come, he predicted, when "our people will ask that we revolt against the illegitimate [leaders of the Arab world]." First among these was Muhammad Anwar al-Sadat, who, on 17 September 1978, had agreed to the Camp David Accords that had brought peace between Egypt and Israel. With this single act, Saddam believed, al-Sadat had removed Egypt from its historic role as the leader of the Arab world.[71] Sadat's actions had shocked the Arab world. As a result, Iraq emerged as a more influential force in intra-Arab politics. On 2–5 November 1978, a summit in Baghdad of twenty Arab states along with the Palestine Liberation Organization (PLO) convened to consider the Arab response.

The summit agreed to isolate Egypt and bolster the remaining so-called "frontline states" with financial aid. The Arab leaders, with Saddam's support, agreed to expel Egypt from the League of Arab States – whose headquarters would now move from Cairo to Tunis – to break diplomatic relations with the Egyptians, and to halt all military and economic cooperation with al-Sadat's regime. Finally, the group established a $9 billion fund to provide financial assistance to Syria, Jordan, and the PLO. This aid proved crucial in discouraging Jordan from also defecting. To many, Saddam now appeared as the Arab champion, as well as the only leader capable of unifying the Arabs against Israel.

---

[69] SH-SPPC-D-000-583, Letter Dated 28 October 1978 from Nizar Hamdun to Saddam Hussein Regarding Iraqi and Syrian Ba'ath Commitment, 28 October 1978.

[70] SH-SHTP-A-000-626, Saddam Hussein Discusses Neighboring Countries and Their Regimes, January 1981.

[71] Interestingly, initially Saddam appears to have thought that Iraq would have to accept the Camp David Accords. But he swiftly changed his mind when the outrage in the Arab world at Egypt's "betrayal" became clear. See SH-SHTP-A-000-553, Revolutionary Command Council Meeting after the Baghdad Conference in 1979, 27 March 1979.

Saddam believed the Camp David Accords were evidence of a wholesale Egyptian capitulation to the Arab world's enemies, a betrayal most heinous. Representatives of the Arab League met again in Baghdad on 27 March 1979 to implement the measures agreed on in November 1978. Anti-Sadat emotion ran high. Overnight Sadat went from being the hero of the 1973 war to being reviled in the Arab world. Saddam described the Egyptian president in the most vitriolic terms: "That al-Sadat is the scum of humanity, the scum of humanity. What an immoral man. It is clear why our history names him as the number one traitor."[72]

In Saddam's eyes, Iraq was now the only Arab country capable of dealing with the Palestine issue and ensuring that the other Arab states would honor their promises. During a discussion with unidentified visitors (apparently a Palestinian delegation) after the March summit, Saddam placed this leadership mantle squarely on his own shoulders: "When I asked you who would guarantee that the Arab nations or Arab countries would implement those decisions, you said that we wouldn't have to worry about making sure they are implemented, because you said, 'I am ready, we in Iraq are ready to tour all the Arab nations and hold them accountable to these decisions and also force them to commit to these decisions.'"[73] There were similar thoughts from other attendees, as an unidentified participant commented:

We have an interest in creating a chain of conflict that signals our refusal to give in. And that is where I think the issue requires initiative. And the burden of the initiative falls on the shoulders of Iraq before any other Arab nation, especially in light of the decisions made in [the Baghdad Conference]. That is on the one hand. On the other hand, [inaudible] we feel that there is an Arab national responsibility that falls on the shoulders of the Iraqi nation.[74]

Saddam focused on Arab unity out of respect for his chief enemy, Israel. He often noted, although rarely in public, that "the Zionist enemy is a smart and capable enemy, and we must not underestimate him."[75] It is sometimes easy to discount as mere rhetoric the central place of the "Zionist enemy" in Saddam's long-term strategic calculations.[76] But transcripts from hundreds of hours of recorded conversations reveal that

---

[72] *SH-SHTP-A-001-303, Recording of a Meeting between Saddam Hussein and Ba'ath Party Members Discussing the Iran–Iraq War, Circa October 1981–Early 1982.

[73] SH-SHTP-A-000-553, Revolutionary Command Council Meeting after the Baghdad Conference in 1979, 27 March 1979.

[74] *Ibid.*   [75] *Ibid.*

[76] See Otto Friedrich and James Wilde, "The Gulf: He Gives Us a Ray of Hope," *Time Magazine*, 27 August 1990. For a further examination of the issue see Barry Rubin, "The United States and Iraq: From Appeasement to War," in *Iraq's Road to War*, Amatzia Baram and Barry Rubin, eds. (New York, NY, 1993).

Saddam believed the Jews were both an implacable and devious enemy and a target he could use to achieve larger goals. It is also clear that a major driving force in Saddam's political *Weltanschauung* was a deep and abiding hatred for the "Zionist entity."[77]

Much like Nasser, Saddam used his growing populist credentials to pressure other regional leaders by appealing directly to their populations and as a tool to unify the Arab nations.[78] Saddam also believed that Iraq's people were innately superior to the lie-about Egyptians, who, according to him, possessed little drive, ambition, or vision. He once commented, "One of the things that we noticed is that Abdul Nasser was ahead of his people in his nationalist program. He used to go places, but the [Egyptian] people were standing still and going nowhere."[79] Saddam also believed war was the only path to realizing his historic opportunity to unite the Arabs and deal with the conspiracies of his enemies.[80] Much like Hitler's view of the Versailles Treaty, Saddam reiterated his belief that any future war with Israel must aim to destroy the Jewish state, not just reclaim the territory lost to the Israelis in 1967.[81]

Saddam was determined not to repeat the mistakes of 1973. He had his own conception of what a future war with Israel would look like. In fact, it bore no relationship to any conceivable war against the Israeli state, especially given the fractious nature of Arab states and their militaries and the sophisticated nature of the Israeli Defense Forces:

This is what we envision: we envision a war with the enemy, either with the unity nation (Iraq and Syria) or with the Iraqi, Syrian, Jordanian military effort ... and

[77] At almost every turn in discussions about his enemies, Saddam ascribed his difficulties to the Zionists. *Zionist entity* was the term Saddam and his associates almost always used in reference to Israel. See Kevin M. Woods, David D. Palkki and Mark E. Stout, *The Saddam Tapes: The Inner Workings of a Tyrant's Regime, 1978–2001* (New York, NY, 2011), 59–83.

[78] One Middle Eastern specialist notes that "the importance of Arab public opinion to the foreign policies of Arab states derives from the very absence of electoral legitimacy and the prevalence instead of transnational symbols of legitimacy ... any Arab government must present credentials on those issues." Shibley Telhami, "Arab Public Opinion and the Gulf War," *Political Science Quarterly* 108, no. 3 (1993), 439.

[79] SH-SHTP-A-000-626, Saddam Hussein Discusses Neighboring Countries and Their Regimes, January 1981.

[80] The role of conspiracies in policy-making for this regime cannot be overstated. Saad al-Bazzaz, the former head of the Iraqi News Agency, said in an interview (after his defection) that Saddam would "turn to disasters for silly reasons; they [the regime] base their policy on conspiracy theories." See Saad al-Bazzaz, "Saad Al-Bazzaz: An Insider's View of Iraq," *The Middle East Quarterly* II, no. 4 (1995). This is also the view of General Ra'ad Hamdani, one of the more perceptive observers on the nature of Saddam's goals and aims; see Kevin M. Woods, Williamson Murray, and Thomas Holaday, *Saddam's War: An Iraqi Military Perspective of the Iran–Iraq War*, McNair Paper 70 (Washington, DC, 2009), 41–42.

[81] For Hitler's views see chapter 1 in Williamson Murray, *The Change in the European Balance of Power, 1938–39: The Path to Ruin* (Princeton, NJ, 1984).

for it to be a war that goes on for many months, not days and weeks. Whatever the enemy decides, we can get there. Does the enemy want a war where we quickly cross the miles to attack and then fall back and withdraw? Or do we want the slow step-by-step war where every step we take becomes part of the land and we keep moving forward ... and even more importantly what widespread cheering from the masses that will accompany each step we take forward from every corner of the Arab world. This is more important than the meter and kilometer we gain ... So we can guarantee the long war that is destructive to our enemy. And take our leisure each meter of land, that is bleeding with rivers of blood, we have no vision for a war that is any less than this.[82]

Saddam may have been expecting that the deterrent effect of an Arab nuclear capability would enable the "long war," but his description of such a conflict connected with no coherent military concept, and it certainly bore no relationship to recent Iraqi or even Arab military experience. It may have represented a political set of assumptions designed to unite the Arab nation – the elusive first step in the pan-Arab vision – but the lack of clarity or understanding of the issues involved in really fighting a war is striking. In a preview of the Iran–Iraq War, Saddam described what a united Arab nation needed to defeat the "Zionist entity": "What is required is a patient war, one where we fight for twelve continuous months and after twelve months we take stock and figure out how much we have lost and how much has been gained. And plan for losses amounting to thousands, thousands so that we plan to be prepared to lose in those twelve months, 50,000 martyrs and injured."[83]

Realizing the vision

Although Saddam had a vision of where he thought his journey would end, he had no idea how to realize it. He possessed no immediate means of threatening the Israelis, and there was no one in the neighborhood eager to take on the Israeli Defense Forces again. But from his perspective, a nearer and, at least for the immediate future, more enticing target appeared.

Iraq's leadership had held the Persians in deep contempt for a host of reasons that included competition for regional dominance, long-standing disputes over territory and support for dissident populations, and, at least for many among Iraq's Sunni elite, because they had embraced the Shi'a apostasy in the sixteenth century. In the late

---

[82] SH-SHTP-A-000-553, Revolutionary Command Council Meeting after the Baghdad Conference in 1979, 27 March 1979.
[83] *Ibid.*

1970s, as Ayatollah Khomeini's revolution in Iran gathered momentum, much of the world had difficulty understanding what exactly was transpiring in Iran. Saddam was no different. But he could not have cared less about a political explanation for what was occurring there. What he cared about was first the apparent collapse of the Shah's military machine, a collapse exacerbated by chaotic and often ruthless purges of the Iranian officer corps conducted by the new revolutionary regime in Tehran; second, the political chaos spreading across the Iranian landscape; and third, the opportunity to pay back the Iranians for their humiliation of Iraq (and himself) in the 1975 Algiers negotiations. Iraqi intelligence quickly picked up on the difficulties the Iranian military was having under Khomeini's efforts to remove all vestiges of the *ancien régime*.

Undoubtedly, it also crossed Saddam's mind that a quick victory over his Persian enemy would be a way to easily establish his bona fides with the Arab street and to solidify his claim to the mantle as leader of the Arabs. For Saddam, timing was important. On the more utilitarian timescale of politics, a war against this historic foe offered a chance to consolidate Saddam's "revolution" for control of the Arab nation. For Saddam, on the grand timescale of history, war against the Persians soon came to represent one of the great moments in Arab history, one that would reestablish Arab greatness. In October 1980, after the conflict had begun, he commented to Iraq's senior leadership about the war: "It is a difficult thing to fight people in a foreign land. No one knows it, but the greatest war in the third world is prepared by historians, artists, and writers through their writings, novels, stories, and lectures. That is what this war is about because all of these writings, stories, plays, and photographs can be shown to the next generation."[84] Moreover, Saddam did not forget, nor let others forget, that Persia was a threat to the Arab nation. He suggested in a speech he gave at the Third Islamic Summit in January 1981: "The problem between Iraq and Iran goes back to more than 450 years of history, if we wanted to know its history. It is not a border problem or a secondary question about navigation rights. It is much ... bigger. The problem illustrates the expansionist covetousness of Iran in the nearby and bordering Arabian lands."[85]

---

[84] SH-PDWN-D-000-566, Saddam Meeting with the General Command of the Armed Forces About the Iran–Iraq War, October–November 1980.

[85] Lecture 23: The Address of Saddam Hussein at the 3rd Islamic Summit on 28 January 1981 in *SH-Misc-D-001-304, Lecture 23: The Address of Saddam Hussein at the 3rd Islamic Summit on 28 January 1981.

Saddam's worldview

The old saw has it that "even paranoids have enemies."[86] One cannot understand Saddam's approach to politics and international relations without understanding how deeply he believed malign influences had worked against the Arabs in the past and were continuing to work against Iraq and his vision of a great pan-Arab nation. In fact, Saddam's explanation for the sacking of Baghdad in 1258 by the Mongol General Hulagu Khan was that the international Jewish conspiracy, based in Europe, had persuaded the Mongols to turn south instead of continuing to move west.[87] Not surprisingly, the nature of the Iraqi state created a situation where the sycophants in the bureaucracy and military delightedly reinforced the dictator's paranoia. In 2001, in one of the more bizarre manifestations of such paranoia, the General Security Directorate reported to Saddam that *pokemon* meant "I am Jewish" in Hebrew and that the popularity of the Pokemon craze among Iraqi youth represented a dangerous inroad of Zionism into Iraq.[88]

Given the conspiratorial nature of Ba'ath politics in the 1970s, it is not surprising that Saddam saw enemies hiding behind every bush, while the army's historic meddling in politics gave him every reason to watch its senior officers closely. Indeed, one can argue that it was his ability to manipulate the internal environment to block potential threats that kept him in power for nearly a quarter of a century in the face of otherwise humiliating setbacks. But Saddam also attempted to manipulate the international environment in much the same fashion; however, in the external world, there waited more dangerous and powerful enemies, who, if sufficiently annoyed, could and would bring to bear military, economic, and political power that Iraq would have great difficulty meeting. In the end, his misreading and misunderstanding of the international environment – shaped by a particular view of history and inflamed by a tendency toward a deep-seated belief in conspiracies – would precipitate his fall.[89]

---

[86] One writer described Saddam as having "no constraint of conscience," and a tendency toward an "uncontrolled aggression in pursuit of his goals." Post, *The Psychological Assessment of Political Leaders*, 243–244.

[87] "Full Text: Saddam Hussein's Speech (Part 2)," *The Guardian*, 17 January 2003. www.guardian.co.uk/world/2003/jan/17/iraq2.

[88] SH-IDGS-D-001-213, General Security Directorate Memorandum on the Dangers of the Cartoon Character Pokemon, 2001.

[89] For how Saddam's personality and Ba'ath policies affected Iraq's diplomacy, see Phebe Marr, "Iraqi Foreign Policy," in *Diplomacy in the Middle East: The International Relations of Regional and Outside Powers (Library of International Relations Series)*, L. Carl Brown, ed. (London, 2004), 181–206. See also Makiya, *Republic of Fear*, 270–276.

Saddam believed three great powers were working against him: the United States, which he believed was at the root of his greatest difficulties; the international Jewish conspiracy, exemplified by the "Zionist entity" (Israel); and, acutely throughout his first decade in power, the Iranians. Significantly, in Saddam's worldview, all three collaborated actively to destroy the Ba'ath revolution and his hold on power. At times, given his bitterness at the help the Syrians extended to Iran, Saddam added al-Assad's regime to his "enemies list."

Depending on his troubles or the difficulties Iraq was undergoing, Saddam would focus on one or all of these enemies. Nevertheless, the United States appeared most often as the master conspirator.[90] Such strongly held convictions can often bring about conclusions, which, given the general understanding of events, seem bizarre. In November 1979, he commented that American manipulation had caused the Shah's fall in order to get to the Iraqi regime:

They [the Americans] are involved in the events in Iran, including the removal of the shah, which [was] completely an American decision . . . They [the Americans] will raise the Hormuz issue so that the American fleet will come and do, I do know not what, to Iraq. They will come to an agreement with the Iranians in order to scare the Gulf people, and then turn to Iraq and say that the Gulf people fear us and that we [the Iraqis] do not help them [the Gulf people]. That is why [the Gulf people] were forced to bring the Americans in for protection.[91]

Not surprisingly, the 1986 Iran–Contra affair brought out Saddam's deepest suspicions about the nature and aims of American policy toward the Middle East and especially toward the Iran–Iraq War. He associated American actions in that affair with the Western colonial attitudes of the first half of the twentieth century: "Westerners think they are still capable of doing whatever they want as they used to do 50 years ago, but actually they are like the old man who thinks that he is still capable of doing what he used to do when he was still a young man."[92] While much of the affair appears in the light of history – at least to Americans – to have resulted from bungling at the highest levels of the Reagan Administration, that was not how Saddam saw matters. Shortly after Reagan's speech to the

---

[90] In fairness to Saddam, the Iranians and their leader Khomeini held a similar, paranoiac a view of the world, except that in their case it was the United States, Iraq, and the "Zionist entity" plotting against the legitimate interests of the Iranian people and Iran's religious revolution.

[91] SH-SHTP-D-000-559, Saddam and His Inner Circle Discussing Relations with Various Arab States, Russia, China, and the United States, 4–20 November 1979.

[92] SH-SHTP-A-000-638, Saddam and the Revolutionary Command Council Discuss President Ronald Reagan's Speech in Which He Admitted That the United States Had a Relationship with Iran, Unknown, after 15 November 1986.

American people explaining what had happened, Saddam commented to his foreign policy advisors that:

Reagan said, "We get closer to Iran through weapons." Iran needs weapons the most during the war; therefore, how many more years does Reagan need the war to continue so that he can get close to the goals he set, and for the influence he wants to get out of Iran? This is the dangerous point in the conspiracy. This is connected to old suspicion and I agree and discussed with Comrade Tariq how to be careful and pay attention even to the difference in expression between stopping the war and ending the war. So you see, we are sensitive about this issue to that extent. The Americans are being watched. That is why I am telling you I was not surprised. This level of bad and immoral behavior is a new thing. I swear I am not surprised because I have noticed that even in the nations of the region, there is a Zionist desire that if the [Iran–Iraq] war stops outside of its wish, that the war will stop, but will not end ...

They [the Americans] want you to keep asking for their friendship as long as the war continues, and to continue dealing with them with some measure of flexibility. And they want Iraq to keep dealing with a measure of flexibility at the cost of [its] principles, be it with the Western world or with neighboring countries. And they want some of the governments they want to create illegitimately in the area to remain standing and have influence and be effective, as long as Iran fears that Iraq would return to war and Iraq fears that Iran would return to war. And that is what the conspiracy is, to cease fire and negotiate in this conspiracy.[93]

Somewhat later, in an undated conversation, but clearly one that occurred after the United States had agreed to flag tankers coming out of Kuwait, Saddam explained the various conspiracies he saw at work against Iraq in the Middle East.[94] He suggested to his listeners that "they needed to realize that there is a conspiracy in which the Secretary General [of the United Nations] who looks like a lamb while he is Satan, in fact, is taking part." Saddam then continued to say that "America wants peace somehow so that it can settle the battle in Iran in its favor, but after that America wants the conspiracy [that] the Iranians want since they planned for it and America agreed to play this role ... What made Reagan accept this conspiracy against Iraq is the Zionism in America."[95]

[93] SH-SHTP-A-000-555, Saddam and the Revolutionary Command Council Discussing Reagan's Speech to the Nation on Iran-Contra Revelations (Part 2), 15 November 1986. See also Hal Brands, "Inside the Iraqi State Records: Saddam Hussein, 'Irangate', and the United States," *The Journal of Strategic Studies* 34, no. 1 (2011).

[94] The United States began reflagging and escorting Kuwaiti tankers in July 1987 during Operation Earnest Will. A parallel US operation aimed at stopping Iranian attacks on Gulf shipping named Prime Chance began during the same month.

[95] SH-SHTP-A-000-561, Saddam and His Inner Circle Discussing the Iran–Iraq War and UN Security Council Resolutions Related to the War, Circa December 1987.

But it was not just the Americans who disturbed Saddam's sleep by their malicious plots. The Jews and the Zionists, the latter not necessarily Jews according to Saddam's calculations, in combination or separately were at the root of many of the world's ills and particularly those of Iraq. In a speech to the Iraqi nation shortly before the fall of his regime, Saddam declaimed:

The Jews and their supporters have played a remarkably malicious role against Baghdad in the past and this conspiratorial, aggressive, and wicked role is today reverting to them, to the Zionist Jews and to the Zionists who are not of Jewish origin, particularly those who are in the US administration and around whom stood in opposite front [to] our nation and Iraq ... Zionism and prejudicial people had pushed [America] to search for a role through a devastating brutal instinct instead of ascending to a position of responsible ability and to its civic, cultural role which suits this age and suits the role of balanced nations.[96]

The Israeli air attack on Yasser Arafat's PLO headquarters in Tunisia in 1985 had unleashed the dictator's fury at what he saw as the joint American–Zionist efforts to undermine the potential that the Arab world, manifested in Iraq, possessed:

Now the operation that we are discussing is a new technique worldwide. I mean it has never happened before, worldwide, where Israel or a country other than Israel would carry out such an operation and have a superpower nation support it ... and the action is a joint American-Zionist effort and not a mere Zionist act ... This certainly confirms what we have read between the lines a long time ago that Zionism and the Arabs cannot live together. I have discussed this subject years ago. This issue between the Arabs and Israel will never be resolved. It is either Israel or the Arabs. I mean there is no solution.[97]

But the reader should not assume that to Saddam it was only the Americans and the Jews plotting against Iraq. He suggested to his colleagues in a discussion about the array of enemies that Iraq confronted early on in the war with Iran:

This is a fact, I mean you should not belittle [the Iranians], and regard them as turbans.[98] No, they are not turbans, the Iranians are *satanic* turbans, and they know how to conspire and know how to plan sedition, and they know how to communicate with the world, because they are not the ones doing the communicating. Look can we communicate with the world? Can we achieve

---

[96] "Full Text: Saddam Hussein's Speech (Part 2)."

[97] SH-SHTP-D-000-567, Recording of Saddam and Arafat Discussing the Israeli Attack on the Palestinian Liberation Organization's Headquarters, 5 October 1985. On 1 October 1985, Israeli F-15s attacked and destroyed the PLO headquarters outside of Tunis. Covered in a later chapter is a similar logic leap Saddam made relating to the Israeli raid of Iraq's nuclear facilities in 1981.

[98] Saddam was referring to the Shi'a clergy and the turbans they wear.

the same way the Iranians can? It is Zionism, it is Zionism that is guiding [the Iranians]. Zionism is taking the Iranians by the hand and introducing them to each party, one by one, channel by channel. I mean Zionism – come on comrades – do I have to repeat this every time.[99]

Khomeini: the leader

The sudden collapse of the Shah's regime caught much of the world by surprise. It certainly caught the Iraqis by surprise. Since 1963, Ayatollah Khomeini had been one of the more outspoken religious figures in Shi'a Islam. Unlike most of his fellow clerics in Iran, Khomeini had a distinct political philosophy that he had not hesitated to express openly, even under the threat of SAVAK's retaliation.[100] In particular, as he rose in the Shi'a clerical hierarchy, Khomeini criticized the Shah's efforts to modernize Iran and adapt Western practices in a fashion similar to what Kemal Ataturk had accomplished in Turkey. Despite simplistic descriptions in the West to the contrary, Khomeini was not simply a "fundamentalist" determined to resist change, he was, in his own faith tradition, a theological innovator and maverick. His theory of *valayat-e-faqih* (guardian of the jurist) was as much a threat to the more traditionalist Shi'a leadership in the Arab world as it was to the Shah.[101]

In November 1964, Khomeini's criticisms finally reached the point where the Shah had had enough. The Shah expelled him. After a short exile in Turkey, the Western practices of which he found uncongenial, Khomeini moved to Iraq. He found asylum in the holy city of Najaf. There, he might have simply sunk into regional obscurity, except for the fact that modern technology allowed him to record his sermons and messages on cassettes and to send them to Iran by courier, where the faithful reproduced them and passed them throughout a growing underground movement that rejected the "Westoxification" of Islam.[102]

---

[99] SH-SHTP-A-000-561, Saddam and His Inner Circle Discussing the Iran–Iraq War and Un Security Council Resolutions Related to the War, Circa December 1987.

[100] SAVAK (*Sazamane Etelaat Va Amniate Kechvar*), otherwise known as the Shah's secret police.

[101] Vali Nasr, *The Shi'a Revival: How Conflicts within Islam Will Shape the Future* (New York, NY, 2006), 124–126; Hamid Dabashi, *Theology of Discontent: The Ideological Foundation of the Islamic Revolution in Iran* (New Brunswick, CT, 2005), 409–484.

[102] *Westoxification* was the title of an influential book by Jalal al-e Ahmad published in Tehran in 1962. The theme of which is captured in its English translation (1984) *Occidentosis: A Plague from the West*. Khomeini bemoaned the "dazzling effect that the material progress of the imperialist countries has had on some members of our society." It was not an anti-modernist argument, but rather a call to remain grounded in "our religion and its laws" even as one goes "all the way to Mars or beyond the

Significantly, Khomeini was not especially popular among the Arab Shi'a leadership. In addition to his theological "innovations," Khomeini argued that Qum, the center of the Shi'a religion in Iran, should assume the leadership over the Shi'a religious leaders in Karbala and Najaf. In 1978, Khomeini had become enough of a threat for the Shah to request, on the basis of the 1975 Algiers Agreement and its provisions for non-interference, that Iraq expel the incorrigible ayatollah. This Saddam was delighted to do, since Khomeini was not the easiest of guests. Once again Khomeini found himself traveling the road to exile – this time to Paris.

By then, Khomeini's concepts had crystallized even if his plans had not. Much like Saddam projecting Baghdad's rules onto the external world, Khomeini insisted the details of the revolution would take care of themselves "when the Shah is gone and I have returned." Khomeini's fellow revolutionary and first revolutionary prime minister, Mehdi Bazargan, pleaded with the imam that "the world of politics and the international environment are not like the clerical circle of Najaf and Qom, where logic and truth may be sufficient. We face a thousand difficulties and problems, and they will crush [our] schemes and plans. They won't surrender just because we speak the truth."[103]

Khomeini's increasingly pointed attacks on the Shah found a resonant audience in Iran, where the Shah's corrupt tyranny was arousing more and more opposition. Nevertheless, one should not underestimate the role of other movements in the Shah's overthrow – or the fact that the Shah, terminally ill with cancer, failed to act decisively against his opponents. The various anti-Shah groups had little in common, but all – Shi'a clerics, democrats, student protestors, and communists – were united in their desire to bring the regime down. Confronting mass disturbances, the Shah, regime, secret police, and military collapsed with astonishing suddenness in early 1979, with the monarch fleeing, eventually to die in Egypt.

When Khomeini returned triumphantly to Iran on 1 February 1979, he did not confront a political consensus in Tehran, much less the countryside. In hindsight it is easy to forget that the revolution that ousted the Pahlavi Regime was a broadly popular one, but one with deep fissures. Thus, a wide range of political constituencies spent the first three years of the revolution vying, and occasionally fighting, for their vision of Iran. In understanding the difficulties the Iranians confronted in waging the coming war with Iraq, one must recognize that much of

Milky Way." Quoted in Robin Wright, *In the Name of God: The Khomeini Decade* (New York, NY, 1989), 54.

[103] Quoted in Charles Kurzman, *The Unthinkable Revolution in Iran* (Boston, MA, 2004), 3.

Khomeini's energy focused on establishing political control over the country, particularly during the conflict's early years. This involved not only purging the military, but also controlling, purging, and clamping down on a number of political groups, all of which had deeply differing views on what kind of polity Iran should become.[104]

Perhaps most importantly, these political fractures within the Iranian polity threatened Khomeini's long-term goals. Moreover, as in all revolutions, he found foreign conflict an attractive option to help solidify political control as well as energize the religious faithful at home. In a speech on 20 March 1980, Khomeini warned that to stand up to external threats "our intellectuals [must] give up their fascination with Westernization or Easternization and follow the straight path of Islam and nationalism."[105] The war with Iraq eventually allowed Khomeini's supporters to crush their opponents in the name of national security, while at the same time to spread abroad the flame of Shi'a revolution.[106] In fact, the dynamic of revolution inevitably and inexorably led the Iranians to seek confrontation with their neighbors. It also determined the ferocity and tenacity with which Khomeini's regime would conduct the war with Iraq, the context of which owes as much to its aggressive actions as it does to Saddam's response.

The divine spark

Understanding Khomeini's long-term goals is essential in order to grasp why his republic continued to wage its war in the face of horrendous losses. His political philosophy rested on religious doctrine. The bond between religion and politics is especially clear in the case of Khomeini's Iran, if one remembers that the Shi'a sect was born out of political protests over the question of legitimacy in the succession after the death of the prophet Mohammed. Khomeini, in keeping with Shi'a beliefs, subscribed to the belief that an Imam (the Mahdi), chosen by God, and,

---

[104] For the cut-throat nature of Iranian politics throughout this period, see the memoirs of one of the leading participants: Abu al-Hasan Bani-Sadr, *My Turn to Speak: Iran, the Revolution and Secret Deals with the US* (Washington, DC, 1991).

[105] Ayatollah Khomeini, "We Shall Confront the World with Our Ideology (20 March 1980)," *MERIP Reports*, no. 88 (1980).

[106] See Said Amir Arjomand, *The Turban for the Crown: The Islamic Revolution in Iran* (New York, NY, 1988); chapter 6 in Patrick Clawson and Michael Rubin, *Eternal Iran: Continuity and Chaos* (New York, NY, 2005). For a concise description of the transition of power from the Shah's military to the Revolutionary Guard, see Mark Roberts, *Khomeini's Incorporation of the Iranian Military*, McNair Paper 48 (Washington, DC, 1996). For a sense of the contemporary chaos, see R. K. Ramazani, "Iran's Revolution: Patterns, Problems, and Prospects," *International Affairs* 56, no. 3 (1980).

like the prophet, an infallible servant on earth, was the only legitimate leader. In the time between the occultation of the last Imam and his reappearance, some compromise form of government comprising jurists should rule.[107] Whether for reasons of ego, short-term political advantage, or due to a touch of megalomania, Khomeini did not protest when his followers began using the terms "Imam" or "Imam of the Age and the Lord of Time" to refer to him.[108] Heretofore, such a title had been reserved for the millennial return, for which all Shi'a faithful had waited for many centuries. Khomeini's charismatic nature and the use by some of his most ardent followers of the title *Imam* went a long way to spark the revolution, consolidate power, and create Iran as a revolutionary state with boundless, even divine, ambitions.

One commentator recounts the story of a senior cleric visiting Khomeini during the dark days of the war. The cleric complained, "it is not right for Muslims to kill Muslims ... Hundreds of thousands are dying in a way that has no end and no good purpose." Khomeini responded without emotion and in a way seemingly designed to imply a divine retort: "Do you also criticize God when he sends an earthquake?"[109] The implicit comparison to God by a leader bearing a religious and political philosophy of absolute truth underlines the nature of an adversary incapable of being swayed by the realities of war. The earthly ambitions that derived their legitimacy from such millenarianism were in general aimed at the greater Middle East and, like Saddam's pan-Arab vision, threatened the established order. Khomeini made this clear in a 1979 speech that indicated his revolutionary goals:

Colonialism has partitioned our homeland and has turned the Muslims into separate peoples ... The only means that we possess to unite the Muslim nation, to liberate its lands from the grip of the colonialists and to topple the agent governments of colonialism is to seek to establish our Islamic government. The efforts of this government will be crowned with success when we become able to destroy the heads of treason, the idols, the human images and the false gods who disseminate injustice and corruption on earth.[110]

Once Saddam had unleashed the war, Khomeini seized on the conflict to realize his aim of throttling what he regarded as the corrupt and

---

[107] See J. S. Ismael and T. Y. Ismael, "Social Change in Islamic Society: The Political Thought of Ayatollah Khomeini," *Social Problems* 27, no. 5 (1980), 601–619; Marvin Zonis, "The Rule of the Clerics in the Islamic Republic of Iran," *Annals of the American Academy of Political and Social Science* 482 (November 1985), 85–108.

[108] Arjomand, *The Turban for the Crown*, 100–102.

[109] Nasr, *The Shi'a Revival*, 120.   [110] Ismael, "Social Change in Islamic Society," 616.

authoritarian regimes of the Middle East that had chosen secularization over the righteous path of Islam:

You [Iranians] are fighting to protect Islam and he [Saddam] is fighting to destroy Islam ... There is absolutely no question of peace or compromise and we shall never have any discussions with them [the Ba'athist Iraqi regime and its leaders]; because they are corrupt and perpetrators of corruption.

The damage caused by this criminal [Saddam] is irreparable unless he withdraws his forces, leaves Iraq and then abandons his corrupt government; he must leave the Iraqi people to decide their own fate. It is not a question of a fight between one government and another; it is a question of an invasion by an Iraqi non-Muslim Ba'athist against an Islamic country; and this is a rebellion by blasphemy against Islam.[111]

Thus, the stakes each regime posited in its war aims were quite different. For Saddam, the revolution in Iran represented both an opportunity and a threat. An invasion and quick victory would, he believed, allow him to cast himself in the role of historic Arab leadership and would further his long-range aims and goals in the region. The invasion was also framed as a preemptive move against a potentially aggressive neighbor with strong religious connections to a majority of Iraq's citizenry. Given these two policy objectives, the only outcome less acceptable to outright defeat was a long or indecisive war. Only a few months into the war and while Iraq was still militarily dominant, Saddam's willingness to consider a negotiated settlement exposed the fact that there was little connection between Iraq's military capabilities and Saddam's war aims.

For Khomeini, the conflict also had two aims. The first was simply defending a still unfolding revolution. In this area, Iraq's invasion accelerated a process of revolutionary evolution that may otherwise have collapsed or unfolded at a slower pace. More significantly, the conflict represented a holy war against a regime that to Khomeini possessed the worst traits of attempting to Westernize and secularize the Islamic world while ignoring the duties Islam imposed on its true believers.[112] Some commentators have seen his dogged continuation of the war as an indication of his desire for revenge against Saddam for his exile from Iraq in 1978. Such analysis misses the revolutionary, wide-ranging goals that formed the heart of Khomeini's belief system. He sought no less than

---

[111] Shahram Chubin and Charles Tripp, *Iran and Iraq at War* (Boulder, CO, 1988).

[112] From the beginning, Khomeini made it clear that the influence of the West and Islamic modernizers were the enemies of his revolution. As he commented before the outbreak of the war with Iraq in 1980: "We are not afraid of economic sanctions or military intervention. What we are afraid of is Western universities, the training of our youth in the interests of West or East." Quoted in Chubin and Tripp, *Iran and Iraq at War*, 33.

to overthrow the current, existing order and to return the Islamic world to what he considered its rightful place – not just what it had held in the early Middle Ages, but what Allah had intended for it.

In the long run, Khomeini aimed at creating the conditions necessary to overthrow the entire world order, one that had emerged over the past 500 years. In his theoretical writings he commented:

Holy war means the conquest of all non-Moslem territories. War will perhaps be declared after the formation of an Islamic government worthy of the name ... It will then be the duty of all able bodied men to volunteer for this war of conquest whose final goal is to make Koranic law supreme from one end of the earth to the other. But the entire world should know that the universal supremacy of Islam [will] differ considerably from the hegemony of other conquerors ... To insure the unity of the Moslem nation, to liberate the Moslem homeland from the domination or influence of the imperialists, we have no alternative but to form a truly Islamic government and to take all possible steps to overthrow the other tyrannical pseudo-Islamic governments put in place by the foreigner, and having attained that goal, to install the universal Islamic government.[113]

While Khomeini possessed the skills of a first-rate politician as well as religious leader and thinker, he possessed no skills in the military realm. He was to prove profoundly ignorant of everything having to do with war. First and foremost, he was deeply suspicious of what he termed "the Shah's army" – a suspicion he had every reason to hold.[114] Thus, he purged the Iranian military's senior officer corps on his triumphal return to Tehran. On 15 February, Iranian state radio announced a series of executions to "purify the blood of the revolution and to put new blood of the revolution into circulation." For those unclear as to the depth to which purges would go, or the nature of the judicial process, the same radio announcement stated that "other officers of the hated regime would soon face trial by revolutionary tribunal, followed by death sentences."[115] According to official Iranian announcements, during the first eight months of the revolution, approximately 250 senior ranking officers were executed. Scores of others met a less formal end at the hands of various revolutionary groups. Little wonder then that 60 percent of the Iranian military had deserted by summer 1979.[116]

---

[113] Ruhollah Khomeini, *Principes De L'ayatollah Khomeiny: Poltiques, Philosophiques, Sociaux & Reglieux* (Paris, FR, 1979), 22. Quotation and translation provided by MacGregor Knox, Professor Emeritus, London School of Economics.

[114] The army had been the bulwark of the Shah's regime, which Khomeini never forgot.

[115] Roberts, *Khomeini's Incorporation of the Iranian Military*, 31.

[116] Nikola B. Schahgaldian and Gina Barkhordarian, *The Iranian Military under the Islamic Republic* (Santa Monica, CA: Rand Corporation, 1987), 19–20.

Despite the top-level purges early in 1979, disruptions, strikes, rumors of coups, and open rebellion persisted. In March 1980, an exasperated Khomeini announced, "I shall no longer tolerate disorder within the army in any form. Whoever causes disruption in the work of the armed forces will be presented to the nation as a counterrevolutionary so that the dear nation may settle its account with the remnants of the criminal Shah's army."[117] Throughout the upcoming conflict it appears as though he never trusted officers from the Shah's military, however much they professed loyalty to the state and his regime. In place of that army he supported the buildup of religious militia, the leaders of which possessed few initial military skills except their ability to encourage young Iranians to die by the tens of thousands.

The new regime's behavior from its first days in power underlines the revolutionary nature of Khomeini's attitudes toward the external world. Because Iran was the only country that had established a "Government of God," it had the duty to serve as a springboard disseminating the Ayatollah's sacred message worldwide. For Khomeini and his supporters, this represented the most basic of principles, upon which their theocratic revolution rested. Khomeini immediately made good on his promises. In November 1979 and February 1980, his agents fomented riots in the Shi'a towns of Saudi Arabia's oil-rich Hasa province.[118] Similar disturbances occurred in Bahrain and Kuwait. However, Khomeini remained focused on Iraq and Saddam where the Shi'a accounted for nearly 60 percent of the population.

The most active ayatollahs in the revolution saw Iraq as the largest and most powerful Arab state in the Gulf, a competitor for local hegemony, and thus the main obstacle to realizing their vision. While Khomeini's operatives were spreading discord throughout the Gulf and Iraq, impatient elements within the Islamic Republic were also courting an open confrontation with the United States by seizing the American embassy in Tehran and holding its personnel hostage. Iraq became Khomeini's "near enemy." In the early days of the Islamic Republic, the Iraqis sent diplomatic feelers to Tehran. A cable from Saddam's predecessor as president of Iraq, Ahmed Hassan al-Bakr, to Khomeini expressing Iraq's peaceful intent was simply met with the polite aphorism that "peace is

---

[117] Khomeini, "We Shall Confront the World with Our Ideology (20 March 1980)."

[118] On 31 July 1987, with the Iran–Iraq War ongoing, the Iranians fomented a major riot at the holiest of Islam's shrines at Mecca; more than 400 people were killed before the Saudi National Guard restored order. For a discussion of these events, see Martin Kramer, *Arab Awakening and Islamic Revival: The Politics of Ideas in the Middle East* (New Brunswick, CT, 2008), 161–178. See also Henner Furtig, *Iran's Rivalry with Saudi Arabia between the Gulf Wars* (Reading, NY, 2006), 61–92.

with those who follow the righteous path."[119] Later, Saddam sent a personal emissary, the grandson of a respected Shi'a ayatollah, with a conciliatory message. Khomeini bluntly refused the overture, reportedly declaring, "That dictator will last no longer than six months because he is threatened by a revolution like ours. He wants to find a way out by making us an offer. I will not justify that pig."[120]

In June 1979, Iran's revolutionary regime began publicly urging Iraq's population to overthrow the Ba'ath regime. Saddam, whose regime was already conducting a concerted campaign of intimidation, detentions, expulsions, and murder against prominent Iraqi clerics also responded to Iran's agitation by lavishing public money on Shi'a mosques, shrines, and religious festivals.[121] Iran in turn provided substantial aid to underground Shi'a movements, some of which initiated terrorist attacks against prominent Iraqi officials. Shi'a resistance groups, historically a disparate and ineffective lot, became more aggressive.[122] Even if the revolutionaries in Iran had not increased their overt support, the reality was that the Iranian revolution's success encouraged Shi'a movements across the Middle East.

The historic events in Tehran certainly stirred the followers of al-Sadr's Dawa Party ("the Islamic call") but it was the Ba'ath regime's 30 March decision to make membership of Dawa a capital offense that tipped the balance into open conflict. Attacks by Shi'a radicals reached the heart of the regime when, on 1 April 1980, individuals attempted to assassinate Tariq Aziz, the deputy premier and Saddam's trusted supporter. The regime responded by brutally killing the movement's most public figure, al-Sadr, and his sister. Large-scale deportations and an aggressive policy of suppressing any overt Shi'a sympathy, whatever the form, for the regime in Tehran soon followed with secret police raids.

Yet, for all of its outward aggression against its neighbors, Iran was deeply divided. Khomeini may have appeared as the leader of the revolution against the Shah, but his control over the Iranian political situation initially remained limited. At various points the revolution appeared on the brink of civil war among the political factions vying for power.

[119] Al-Bakr cited in Saïd K. Aburish, *Saddam Hussein: The Politics of Revenge* (New York, NY, 2000), 166.

[120] Quoted in Bani-Sadr, *My Turn to Speak*, 66.

[121] See T. M. Aziz, "The Role of Muhammad Baqir Al-Sadr in Shii Activism in Iraq from 1958–1980," *International Journal of Middle East Studies* 25, no. 2 (May 1993); Rodger Shanahan, "Shi'a Political Development in Iraq: The Case of the Islamic Da'wa Party," *Third World Quarterly* 25, no. 5 (2004).

[122] Modern Iraqi Shi'a activism against the government in Baghdad dates back to the founding of the Dawa Party in the late 1950s. The Ba'ath Party swiftly put down a significant uprising in 1977.

An Iraqi intelligence assessment of Iran's internal situation in 1980 cites
Iranian president Bani-Sadr as saying "in reality we have many problems
in our country – economic, administrative, military, [and] social, in
addition to the problems of regions of Baluchistan, Azerbaijan, Khuzestan, Kurdistan, and Mazandaran."

The same report noted that Iran was descending into "a state of chaos,
crimes and law breaking spreading."[123] This Iraqi equivalent of what the
US government calls a National Intelligence Estimate attributed Iran's
problems to multiple centers of power (it noted divergent religious,
nationalist, and leftists groups) and the fact that many of these movements were armed and hostile to Khomeini as well as Persian rule
itself.[124] Major acts of armed opposition, according to the report, were
occurring in Ahvaz, the Kurdish areas, Baluchistan, and among the
Turkomen along the Caspian Sea (Mazandaran). Added to this was a
steady stream of reports of "military opposition elements" preparing
coup attempts in Tehran.[125]

One commentator has noted about the tenuous situation in Tehran in
the immediate months before the war:

Ayatollah Khomeini presided over a bitterly divided and factionally fragmented
nation, his Islamic Government establishment being only precariously kept in
power by secret trials and executions, wholesale imprisonment without trial and
the perverse activities of the Revolutionary Committees and the *Pasdaran* against
hostile militias. It was Khomeini's immense prestige, power, influence, and
political acumen that held the Islamic Republic together during 1979 and until
September 1980, after which war with Iraq engendered the essential cement of
nationalism. Many considered it problematic how long he could have held his
country together otherwise.[126]

The run up to war

By late 1979, there was little left of Saddam's optimism about accommo-
dation with the revolutionary government next door. He moved to

---

[123] SH-GMID-D-000-842, General Military Intelligence Directorate (GMID) Intelligence
Report on Iran, January–June 1980.

[124] *Ibid.*

[125] *Ibid.* The report notes that more than 100 political parties were active in Iran. Several
Iranian generals and deposed politicians were actively working with Saddam during this
period. In one case, Iran's reaction to an Iraqi-supported coup in July 1980 had a major
impact on Iran's air force when it faced the Iraqi onslaught in September. See Mark J.
Gasiorowski, "The Nuzhih Plot and Iranian Politics," *International Journal of Middle
East Studies* 34, no. 4 (2002).

[126] Edgar O'Ballance, *The Gulf War: Nineteen Eighty to Nineteen Eighty-Seven* (London,
1988), 24.

contain the Iranian subversive campaign. In suppressing the underground organizations, he expelled tens of thousands of Iraqi Shi'as,
attempted to organize his potential allies in the Arab world (particularly
among the Gulf states) into a united pan-Arab front against Iran, had
the spiritual leader of the Dawa Party killed, and supported separatist
Kurdish and Arab elements within Iran. In April 1980, the Iraqis escalated the level of violence. On the last day of the month, a group of Iranian
Arabs, recruited and trained by the Iraqis, seized the Iranian embassy in
London. During the standoff, the terrorists murdered an Iranian diplomat. Prime Minister Margret Thatcher responded by sending in the
Special Air Service (SAS). It was over in a matter of seconds with all of
the terrorists dead except one whom the SAS mistakenly believed to be a
hostage.[127]

On 8 March 1980, Iran announced it was withdrawing its diplomats
from Baghdad. Border clashes, which had been sporadic for months,
began to intensify in April. By the end of summer, serious cross-border
penetrations by aircraft and artillery raids by both sides had
developed.[128] Saddam commented on these developments and asserted
his position as leader and self-appointed champion of the Arab struggle
against the Iranian troublemakers. He positioned himself as the
aggrieved party:

We have tried by every means to keep this area free of armed conflict, particularly
the Arab Gulf area ... Unfortunately, we did not succeed in keeping this area free
of conflicts because conflicts are not to be decided by the will of one side alone.
The will of the Iranian side must coincide with ours, but unfortunately this did
not happen. [T]he will of the Arab citizen has been revived, at least in this place,
in Iraq. Iraq is enough to repulse the hideous threat of Iran.[129]

By early summer 1980, Saddam had decided to confront Iran directly
with large-scale military operations. As early as June 1980, the aerial
intelligence directorate of the Iraqi air force was forwarding detailed
plans for aerial reconnaissance of Iranian territory to the army staff.[130]

---

[127] Steven R. Ward, *Immortal: A Military History of Iran and Its Armed Forces* (Washington,
DC, 2009), 243.

[128] Reporting of these events is generally unreliable, but the Iraqis complained publically of
544 incidents while Iran reported 797 cases involving airspace violations, artillery
strikes, and cross-border raids. Will D. Swearingen, "Geopolitical Origins of the
Iran–Iraq War," *Geographical Review* 78 (October 1988), 406. See also Tom Cooper
and Farzad Bishop, *Iran–Iraq War in the Air: 1980–1988* (Atglen, PA, 2000), 63–71.

[129] Hussein, "Text of President Husayn's 10 Nov Press Conference (FBIS-MEA-80-
220)."

[130] *SH-AADF-D-001-316, Various Reports and Memoranda from the Air Force and Air
Defense Command Relating to Iraqi Reconnaissance and Iranian Incursions into Iraqi
Air Space, 1980.

An intelligence memorandum from late July reported the following about the state of the Iranian military: "An increase in fragmentation and breakup of Iranian forces is expected in case the government [Khomeini's] gets an interim sense of security on the border ... No mobilization [has] taken place since the fall of the Shah ... The existing active individuals in the division[s] do not exceed 50–55 percent."[131] Another report indicated:

We expect more deterioration of the general situation of Iran's fighting capability. It is probable it will send other troops to the Kurdish region to confront the armed Kurds. Moreover, the shortage of spare parts and the continuation of the general dislocation and contradiction will lead to the continuous decline in combat capability ... *it is clear that, at present, Iran has no power to launch wide offensive operations against Iraq, or to defend on a large scale.* However, it is necessary to pay attention in taking protective measures because [we] cannot guarantee that the Iranian enemy could not launch a special operation of a dangerous nature ... if their troops or interests encounter effective losses due to our activities, or when the operation of weakening [the] al-Khomeini regime reaches a more intensive stage.[132]

In July, corps and division commanders of the Iraqi Army and a number of other senior officers met in Baghdad. Interestingly, Saddam was not present. The army's chief of staff warned that war with Iran was a possibility. However, most officers got the impression that such a war would not take place for at least two years. Thus, the army would have enough time to increase training and to incorporate new and more sophisticated equipment.[133] Because neither air force nor navy representatives were at the meeting, one can only assume that it was held for informational rather than planning purposes.[134] Nevertheless, the events of the previous year, the heated rhetoric and antagonism of both sides, and the opportunity that an external threat presented to both regimes conspired to make the war all but inevitable. Throughout the summer, the Iraqis deployed divisions and their logistical-support structure to cantonments along the southern border with Iran.[135] By August, air

---

[131] *SH-GMID-D-001-305, GMID Memorandum to Section 1, 52/Q1/40662, Re: Complete Intelligence Report, 29 July 1980.
[132] SH-GMID-D-000-842, General Military Intelligence Directorate (GMID) Intelligence Report on Iran, January–June 1980. Emphasis added.
[133] Woods *et al.*, "Interview with Major General (Ret) Aladdin Hussein Makki Khamas, Cairo, Egypt, 11 November 2009."
[134] Woods *et al.*, "Interview with (Former) Lieutenant General Abid Mohammed Al-Kabi, Cairo, Egypt, 12 November 2009."
[135] Interestingly, the Iranians, despite their jabbing at Saddam with scurrilous propaganda and a terrorist campaign, appear to have discounted the possibility that the Iraqis would actually attack them. Therefore, they made no serious military preparations.

skirmishes along the border and tit-for-tat exchanges of fire were intensifying.

At present, gaps in captured Iraqi records make it impossible to answer the question of when Saddam truly decided on war. But by early September 1980, war was the only major option on the table. Here, an interesting and revealing document from 16 September records a meeting among the highest levels of the Iraqi government. The meeting took place after an operation on 7 September when the Iraqis had seized two villages the 1975 Algiers Agreement had promised them, but that the Iranians had not returned.

Six days after that meeting, Iraq invaded Iran. Few documents among those available underline more clearly the pervasive amateurism of the decision-making processes in Iraq. The discussions indicate that, while Saddam was considering war, neither he nor his advisors had a clear idea of what military operations might entail. Throughout the discussions, Saddam mused about his options. Those participating in the conversation had not yet considered the strategic and political goals of a war.[136] Saddam commented in this regard: "What is important now is that we can gain back our land ... Getting [our] land back will scare [the Iranians], because it takes [us] to another level of ability [creating a] psychological effect on the Arab people and national public opinion." After further discussion, Saddam continued:

After our forces get the land back, we will tell them. We will say that our forces at this date and at that time got back this land from you, now give us the remainder of the land or we will take it by force. If they do not give it to us, then we shall grab it back ... if they do not act as we wish, we will strike them just as we struck them in Zain al-Qaws and Saif Sa'ad [two border posts the Iraqis had captured a few days earlier] ... we have to put them in a political and military position so they will say yes or have to pull back their army and assume that the matter is over, and that we can do as we please.

It was clear to Abu Hassan "that the situation of the Shatt al-Arab is not like Zain al-Qaws or Saif Sa'ad. It is very complicated, and might lead to a full scale war." In response, Saddam commented:

We have to stick their noses in mud so we can impose our political will over them. This cannot take place except militarily ... we want to twist their hands until they accept the legal fact ... Comrade, minister of defense, what is stopping us from taking Qasar [possibly Shirin] any time we want? What is stopping us from moving forward on all axes and surrounding their armies and imprisoning

---

[136] What is probable, though not provable given the documentary sources available, is that no one in a leadership position in Iraq, either military or civilian, accounted for the fact that the Iraqi invasion would commence just before the rainy season.

them? Or doing as we please with some areas? No one is saying that there is no resistance; no one is saying that there are no losses, or dead. The result in our calculations is that we are able to reach the heartland of Iran ... If they accept with some pressure to preserve their dignity ... then there is no problem. But if they try to bombard oil establishments, then the matters will escalate ... We will retaliate immediately.[137]

Clearly, Saddam was aiming at launching military operations in the near future to warn Iran to cease and desist from interfering in Iraq's internal affairs. Should that not work, the dictator was also eager to take advantage of the revolutionary turmoil in Tehran to push further advances into the "heartland of Iran" if those operations succeeded. Certainly Saddam believed that the oil-rich areas of Arabistan (Khuzestan) were within his reach, a goal his intelligence services seemed delighted to further.[138] Another bonus, not mentioned in the meeting recorded in the 16 September document, was the possibility that military operations would cause Khomeini's regime to collapse, its replacement more amenable to Iraqi interests.

Once the Iraqis had decided on war and military operations had begun, Saddam's Ba'ath regime put forward the most extravagant demands – at least as long as things were going well. As the foremost commentator on the nature of the Ba'ath regime has noted:

Such demands [were] a barely concealed foil for plans to topple the Khomeini regime and bring about the breakup of Iran ... The thrust was wholly destructive, directed at the integrity of Iran, with as many of the pieces gathered into Ba'thist [sic] hands as possible. From a Ba'thist [sic] standpoint, such a real intent was by no means cynically "concealed" by the apparent self-righteousness of their territorial claim; it went hand in glove with a fervent and genuine ideological espousal of the latter.[139]

Events now moved swiftly. On 7 September 1980, Iraq accused Iran of shelling Iraqi villages in the territories of Zain al-Qaws and Saif Saad on 4 September 1980. Iraq demanded that the Iranian forces in those territories evacuate and return the villages to Iraq. Tehran gave no reply. Iraqi forces then moved to "liberate" the villages, and on 10 September announced that its forces had done so in a short, sharp military engagement. Interestingly, on 2 September, the army put out a directive "regarding [captured] weapons and equipment" for disposal in "corps

---

[137] SH-SHTP-A-000-835, Meeting between Saddam Hussein, the National Command, and the Revolutionary Command Council Discussing the Iraq–Iran War, 16 September 1980.

[138] SH-GMID-D-000-620, People of Arabstan (Arabs in Southern Iran) in Al-Ahwaz Area Calling for Independence, 1979.

[139] Makiya, *Republic of Fear*, 269–270.

museums and unit museums" – an indication perhaps that the military bureaucracy remained unaware of Saddam's larger ambitions.[140] On 14 September 1980, Iran announced it would no longer abide by the 1975 Algiers Agreement. Given the scene that was set, it was no surprise that on 17 September, five days before the invasion, Iraq declared the accords null and void. Iraq alleged Iran had consistently violated the provisions of the Accords. Saddam's announcement had the unmistakable ring of a declaration of war: "This *shatt* shall again be, as it has been throughout history, Iraqi and Arab in name and reality."[141] On 22 September, Iraqi units crossed the frontier.

Conclusion

The outbreak of the war between Iran and Iraq was strongly determined by historical, religious, and political fissures separating the two regimes. Five millennia before Saddam, the Akkadian Empire had struggled to hold onto the fractious new civilization it had carved out of Mesopotamia. One commentator has noted of this early Iraq, "[it] offers a perfect preview of the rise and fall of all subsequent Mesopotamian empires: rapid expansion followed by ceaseless rebellions, palace revolutions, constant wars on the frontiers, and in the end, the *coup de grace* given by the highlanders: Guti (in the Akkadian example), Elamites, Kassites, Medes, or Persians tomorrow."[142] But two factors would characterize this most recent incarnation of an ancient war. The first was the religious and ideological nature of the conflict. The opposing sides, particularly their political leaders, were willing to pay an extraordinary price in lives and resources in a struggle, which, at least in its fanaticism, resembled combat on the Eastern Front during World War II. The second was that there would initially be nothing that resembled the relative military competency of the Nazi and Soviet armies.

---

[140] Memorandum from GMID Southern Area Intelligence System to GMID Section 2 No SH/Q/12/261 (19 July 1980) in *SH-GMID-D-001-306, Memoranda from GMID Regarding Prisoners of War, Circa Mid to Late 1980.

[141] Hussein, "Text of President Speech to National Assembly, 17 Sep (FBIS-MEA-80-183)."

[142] Roux, *Ancient Iraq*, 159.

3 The opponents

The problem is that [the Iranian] leadership does not understand the simplest principles of military action, does not understand the simplest principles of psychology, does not understand the simplest principles of economics, and does not see ... they do not have an idea of what defeat means.[1]   – Saddam Hussein, 2 November 1980

To understand the difficulties the opposing sides confronted in the Iran–Iraq War, one needs to understand the background of the military institutions of the two states, as well as how the political leaders understood military power and what they expected to gain from the conflict. Not surprisingly, the military institutions and the conduct of the war reflected the significantly different histories, cultures, religious traditions, and political influences of the two nations. Nevertheless, their initial approach to the war was similar: the Iranians emphasized the religious zeal of their soldiers; the Iraqis, the belief that Ba'athist ideology and Arab nationalism would trump other factors.[2]

Ironically, as the war progressed, the challenges confronting the Iraqis forced Saddam to adopt some of the same phrasing and imagery that dominated Khomeini's approach. The Ba'ath Party tenets of unity, freedom, and socialism soon found themselves augmented after 1981 by calls of *Allah akbar* (God is Great), for Jihad against the Persians, appeals to Islamic history, references to heroic Iraqi soldiers as *Mujahid* (holy warrior), and naming the conflict after a chapter in Islamic

---

[1] SH-PDWN-D-000-566, Saddam Meeting with the General Command of the Armed Forces About the Iran–Iraq War, October–November 1980.

[2] In 1999, an Iranian veteran of the Iran–Iraq War noted "efforts have been made to elevate the ideological [religious] quality of the army; and today we are happy to have among us outstanding Koranic reciters and scholars who are the ones who created the best army in the world." "Iran: General Views Unit's Battle Record; Interview with General Karimi, Commander of the 77th Victorious Samen Al-A'emeh Battalion During Sacred Defense Week (FTS-20000201000513)," *Open Source Center* (1999).

history, *al-Qadisiyya*. Even the most iconic of Ba'ath secular organs, the revolutionary command council, took on an additional name as the "leading *Mujahid* institution" to burnish its Islamic credentials.[3]

For many of the same reasons that Saddam felt compelled to garb himself in a religious mantle, Khomeini increasingly found it necessary to deploy the secular appeal of Persian nationalism, overt claims to international justice rather than religion, references to a colonial past, and invocations of Mohammad Mosaddeq's legacy. As the "inevitability of divine victory" became less attractive in the aftermath of failed military offensives, the Iranians increasingly appealed to Persian nationalism.[4] But in both cases, politicizing the military institutions made it difficult for them to adapt to the conditions of combat. The resulting lack of professionalism in the opposing armies significantly contributed to the length and outcome of the war.

The background of the modern Iraqi military

The British influence

The British founded the Iraqi Army in the 1920s to control the mandate they received over the Mesopotamian Valley as a result of the Paris Peace negotiations of 1919.[5] Their initial policy in the area emerged from their aims during World War I and the fact that during operations their military forces occupied both Basra and Baghdad. As one author has noted, "Imperial ideology justified this annexation [of Iraq] in both strategic and civilizational terms," since the "peoples of the East were considered to be incapable of self-determination in the colonial habit of the day."[6] However, the revolt in 1920 of the tribes persuaded the British they needed to establish a local government under their control to

---

[3] Ofra Bengio, *Saddam's Word: Political Discourse in Iraq* (New York, NY, 1998), 88–90.

[4] Among other sources, see Mateo Mohammad Farzaneh, "Shi'i Ideology, Iranian Secular Nationalism, and the Iran–Iraq War (1980–1988)," *Studies in Ethnicity and Nationalism* 7, no. 1 (2008), 86–103. See also Neguin Yavari, "National, Ethnic, and Sectarian Issues in the War," in *The Iran–Iraq War: The Politics of Aggression*, Farhang Rajaee, ed. (Gainesville, FL, 1997), 75–89.

[5] See Tarbush, *The Role of the Military in Politics*, 73–94. For a discussion of the broader negotiations leading to the creation of the modern Middle East and Iraq in World War I's aftermath, see Gooch, "'Building Buffers and Filling Vacuums'", 8–64; Peter Sluglett, *Britain in Iraq: Contriving King and Country* (New York, NY, 2007).

[6] Toby Dodge, "International Obligation, Domestic Pressure, and Colonial Nationalism: The Birth of the Iraqi State under the Mandate System," in *The British and French Mandates in Comparative Perspectives*, Nadine Meouchy and Peter Sluglett, eds. (Leiden, 2004), 146.

maintain security.[7] That government required military forces to serve as its "enforcement agency" that would stamp down any signs of revolt. The army's other purposes were equally internal: the national army would be a "visible symbol of Iraq's future independence" to engender nationalism, and it provided positions for the "large and articulate group of unemployed and discontented ex-officers from the Ottoman army."[8] Thus, from its earliest days, the Iraqi Army's main mission was internal and political security, not fighting wars with external enemies.

As a result of the methodical approach to war the British developed during the interwar period, it is not surprising that they emphasized carefully planned moves in the army's new officer corps.[9] Because Iraqi officers attended the British staff college at Camberley through 1958, such attitudes affected the army's culture until the Iran–Iraq War.[10] Not unexpectedly, considering its background and purpose, the army's first actions in the mid-1930s were against Iraq's own population – the fractious and rebellious Kurdish and Assyrian tribesmen in the north – operations the army would repeat throughout its history.

Beside its role of maintaining internal security, the army quickly developed a penchant for launching coups against the government in Baghdad. Between 1936 and 1941, its leaders attempted to overthrow the government at least four times, several times successfully. The last and most fateful came in April 1941. With the British military confronting a desperate situation in Greece and Crete as a result of the German offensive in the Balkans and in the western deserts of Egypt with Rommel's arrival, a number of the army senior officers launched another coup, this one aiming to install in power a coterie of pro-Nazi politicians under Prime Minister Rashid Ali al-Gaylani. They then planned to join the Axis.[11]

---

[7] In many ways, the Iraqi revolt against the British in 1920 resembled the one US occupying forces confronted after conventional operations halted in 2003. For more on the revolt against the British, see Lieutenant General Sir Aylmer L. Haldane, *The Insurrection in Mesopotamia, 1920* (London, 1922; repr., Nashville, TN, 2005).

[8] Mark Heller, "Politics and the Military in Iraq and Jordan, 1920–1958," *Armed Forces and Society* 4, no. 1 (1977), 81–82. These purposes also established a pattern of tensions within the officer corps until 1958. Those aligned with the Sharifian veterans – the group that dominated Iraq's early political class – were seen by the early Iraqi (primarily Sunni) nationalists as in collusion with both colonialists and anti-Islamics. Former Ottoman officers (including many of Iraq's minorities) viewed both groups with suspicion.

[9] For British military culture during the period after World War I, see Brian Bond, *British Military Policy between the Two World Wars* (Oxford, 1980).

[10] Kevin M. Woods, Williamson Murray, and Thomas Holaday, *Saddam's War: An Iraqi Military Perspective of the Iran–Iraq War*, McNair Paper 70 (Washington, DC, 2009), 3–4. In the 1960s and 1970s, the Iraqi Army's staff college remained firmly in the British tradition.

[11] For the general strategic framework at the time of the coup, see Playfair, *The Germans Come to the Help of Their Ally*, 177–199. For a concise description of the coups and plots

The units of the army besieged the main Royal Air Force (RAF) base at Habaniya, but even with 20,000 troops, the Iraqis found it impossible to overrun a few RAF aircraft, assorted mercenaries recruited from Iraq's minorities, less than a thousand RAF airmen, and a few armored cars the RAF possessed for local security. The British – largely on Prime Minister Winston Churchill's urgings – acted with dispatch. Field Marshal Archibald Wavell, Middle East commander, warned London on 8 May that with reinforcements he might hold the air base at Habaniya, but would not be capable of taking Baghdad. Churchill would have none of this. The prime minister telegraphed back: "Audacious action now against the Iraqis may crush the revolt before the Germans arrive ... We must forestall the moral effect of their arrival by a stunning blow." He added, "You should exploit the situation to the utmost, not hesitating to try to break into Baghdad even with quite small forces, and running the same kind of risks as the Germans are accustomed to run and profit by."[12]

The British moved two under-strength, patched-together brigades from Palestine and Egypt across what was then known as the Trans-Jordan.[13] The Iraqi rebels received minimal help from the Germans, who flew a few Messerschmitt Bf 109 and Heinkel He 111 aircraft into northern Iraq with the aid of the Vichy French in Syria. But with Operation Barbarossa's approach, the Germans provided no substantial aid. The Iraqis ignominiously collapsed without serious fighting. The army's disintegration would not have surprised the British advisors who observed its performance in the 1920s and 1930s. A British intelligence officer, writing in 1930 noted the following about the army's culture and military effectiveness in this period:

[M]ost ... senior appointments are held not so much through soldierly qualifications as through political graft and knowing the people in high places. Intrigue is ... everywhere and is not confined to army matters; officers mix freely with the local politicians and are prepared to follow anyone whom they think will benefit them. The men as a whole, however, are stupid and dull ... At present there is no reason to suppose that they would refuse to do what they were ordered providing it was not too dangerous.[14]

---

of this period, see Eliezer Be'eri, *Army Officers in Arab Politics and Society* (New York, NY, 1970), 15–40.

[12] Winston S. Churchill, *The Second World War: The Grand Alliance*, vol. 3 (Boston, MA, 1950), 229–231.

[13] The minimal losses the British suffered during the course of the campaign, as well as the patched-together nature of their force, underlines the Iraqi Army's failure to put up effective resistance. For the campaign, see Somerset, *The Golden Carpet*.

[14] Tarbush, *The Role of the Military in Politics*, 119.

In fact, so complete was the army's collapse that the Iraqi generals were unwilling to attempt another coup until a new generation of officers, inspired by events in Egypt, managed to overthrow the pro-Western Hashemite monarchy in 1958.[15] At that point, having once again determined they could control who ruled in Baghdad, the generals indulged themselves in coups and countercoups during the next decade, none of which did anything to improve the military's effectiveness. There were, of course, various conflicts between the Israelis and their Arab neighbors (1947–1948, 1956, 1967), but the Iraqis invariably showed up late and participated only marginally in the fighting.

The memory of the army's political activities would influence Saddam's view of his military organizations once he came to power. It led him to ensure the officer corps' loyalty by having the secret police constantly monitor it and by promoting officers to senior positions based on personal and tribal loyalty. The almost gentlemanly coup of 17 July 1968 was achieved in large measure through the deft manipulation of a small group of colonels in charge of regime security.[16] That coup, in which Saddam was an active participant, reinforced his attitude that Iraq's military required his closest personal attention.

As one of many against Israel

During the first conflict in the late 1940s between Israel and its Arab neighbors, the Iraqis participated in what can only be described as a disgraceful defeat of the numerically and technologically superior Arab armies. One analyst has described Iraq's participation as "unaggressive, unimaginative, and uninspired."[17] Matters improved little in 1956 when Nasser's Egyptian Army, despite massive re-equipment with Soviet arms, lost the whole of Sinai in a few days to the ill-equipped but well-trained Israeli forces before the other Arab nations could intervene. At least the Egyptians could blame their defeat on the interference of Anglo-French forces, which had attacked and occupied a portion of the Suez Canal during the campaign in cooperation with the Israelis.

[15] On this period, see Charles Tripp, *A History of Iraq* (Cambridge, 2000), 108–147. Matthew Elliot, *"Independent Iraq": The Monarchy and British Influence, 1941–58* (London, 1996).
[16] For a detailed description of the coup, see Farouk-Sluglett and Sluglett, *Iraq since 1958*, 107–137.
[17] Kenneth M. Pollack, *Arabs at War: Military Effectiveness, 1948–1991* (Lincoln, NE, 2002), 149–155.

The war of 1967 was another matter.[18] Vast Arab crowds cheered on their leaders and demanded that Arab armies take on the "Zionist entity," this time sure that the militaries of Egypt, Jordan, and Syria – backed up by the Iraqi Army if needed – would crush the Israelis. The result was an even more disastrous defeat in a campaign that lasted barely six days and that left the Israelis occupying the Sinai, West Bank, and Golan Heights. After the Iraqi Air Force's half-hearted, ineffective attempt to strike Israeli cities with obsolete bombers, the Israelis struck Iraq's H3 airfield just east of Jordan. They left the wreckage of twenty-three Iraqi frontline aircraft smoldering on the ground.[19] Again, Iraqi ground forces showed up late. By the time they arrived, the Syrians had already lost the Golan.

Western analysts noted that the major contributing factors for the Iraqi Army's poor performance reflected the fact that, as with the Egyptian and Syrian armies, the enlisted ranks came from the poorest, most unedu-cated segments of society, while the officers played politics and regarded their careers as involving anything other than demanding, serious military professionalism.[20] Where in some armies, such a social gap could be partially compensated for by realistic training or a strict code of discipline, such was not the case in Iraq. Moreover, worried about potential military coups, Iraq's political leaders had had little interest in promoting military professionalism. To do so would merely have served to promote individuals who might offer a serious alternative to the present regime and bring potential replacements forward in the murky world of Arab military and internal politics.[21]

Much of the Arab world concluded that defeat in 1967 resulted from lack of commitment to Arab nationalism. The aftermath of the Six-Day War saw a radicalization of Arab politics, which ultimately threatened the stability of most of the conservative regimes in the Middle East and brought the Ba'ath to power in both Syria and Iraq. In Iraq, despite the

---

[18] For a recent examination of the 1967 war, see Michael B. Oren, *Six Days of War: June 1967 and the Making of the Modern Middle East* (New York, NY, 2002).

[19] Ronald D. Jones, *Israeli Air Superiority in the 1967 Arab-Israeli War: An Analysis of Operational Art* (Newport, RI, 1996), 17.

[20] The culture of Arab armies throughout the twentieth century is best summed up by borrowing from MacGregor Knox's examination of Italian military culture under Mussolini: "The consequence was generally poor performance in war and numerous episodes of collapse under fire. Only the fine record of a few elite units and the good humor and immense capacity for suffering of the troops redeemed the picture." See MacGregor Knox, *Mussolini Unleashed, Facist Italy's Last War* (Cambridge, 1983), 30. See also Pollack, *Arabs at War*, 4–10.

[21] Of all the Arab leaders, only Anwar al-Sadat appears to have encouraged professionalism and effectiveness in senior officers of the Egyptian military.

fact that the army had not reached the fighting before the war ended, the humiliation of 1967 resounded throughout the military and political establishment. In 1968, with substantial support from the military, the Ba'ath Party launched its second coup, this time with the political savvy and ruthlessness to stay in power.[22] In its Proclamation No. 1, the new regime heaped abuse on its predecessors in part for their inaction in 1967 declaring them "a clique of ignoramuses, illiterates, profit-seekers, thieves, spies, Zionists, suspects, and agents."[23] The task of the party's leadership, comprising "cells of valiant revolutionaries ... experts in secret organization ... organizers of demonstrations, strikes, and armed revolutions," was twofold: destroy its political rivals and ensure the loyalty of the officer corps.[24]

Immediately after the Six-Day War, some area political leaders recognized they had to pay attention to military effectiveness more than political loyalty to avoid the defeats that had thus far marked their wars with the Israelis, and military professionalism rapidly increased. While the effect of this is well known in the case of the Egyptian military, it is less well documented in Iraq.[25] Ba'athification of the army took place primarily at the upper echelons where the party sought to demilitarize politics while simultaneously politicizing the army. Preventing another failure like that of 1963 required destroying any trace of a corporate identity in the army independent of the party.[26] This did not, however, dissuade the party from an internally focused effort to professionalize the force. In an interview with the authors, Iraqi Lieutenant General Ra'ad al-Hamdani recalled that as a first lieutenant in the early 1970s, he was required to know the names and study the reputations of all the senior Israeli military commanders. Through this and other anecdotes, Hamdani explained that despite political turbulence at the top, there was a noticeable improvement in training and tactical competency throughout the army.[27]

---

[22] The coup in 1963 brought the Ba'ath to power for a short time, but their inept governance and murderous behavior led to being overthrown by a counter coup.

[23] Hanna Batatu, *The Old Social Classes and the Revolutionary Movements of Iraq: A Study of Iraq's Old Landed and Commerical Classes and of Its Communists, Ba'athists, and Free Officers* (Princeton, NJ, 2004), 1075.

[24] Tariq Aziz from "On Arab–Iranian Relations" quoted in Christine Moss Helms, *Iraq: Eastern Flank of the Arab World* (Washington, DC, 1991), 59. See also, Tariq Aziz, "On Arab–Iranian Relations: To Avoid Confusing the Issues Keeping the Facts Secret and Letting the Conspiracy Pass Unnoticed," Ministry of Culture and Information, 1980, www.al-moharer.net/moh232/aziz80-232.htm (accessed on 29 March 2011).

[25] For insights into the Egyptian reaction to the 1967 defeat, see Pollack, *Arabs at War*, 88–90, 104–106.

[26] Ibrahim al-Marashi and Sammy Salama, *Iraq's Armed Forces: An Analytic History* (New York, NY, 2008), 112–116.

[27] Woods, *et al.*, *Saddam's War*, 3.

When the 1973 war came, the Iraqis deployed substantial forces to the Golan, forces that while an improvement over their predecessors, were not much more successful. On 12 October 1973, during the initial battle with the Israelis, Israeli reserve Sherman tanks destroyed Iraq's more modern Soviet T-55s and T-62s. Nevertheless, the Iraqis, with no advanced warning, had managed to deploy two armored divisions and special force units (500 tanks, 700 armored personnel carriers (APCs) and 30,000 troops) to the battlefront – a significant logistical accomplishment. As one historian noted, the Israeli drive on Damascus was halted in part because the Soviets were making ominous signs toward intervening, but also because the presence of substantial uncommitted Iraqi forces on the Golan convinced Israel that it "did not have sufficient strength on the northern front to force Syria out of the war."[28]

According to Israeli sources, the Syrians and Iraqis had planned a major assault on the Golan front for the day after the Israelis and Egyptians agreed to a ceasefire. Hafez al-Assad, president of Syria, recognizing his forces now confronted the Israelis alone and not willing to anger his Soviet patrons, called off the offensive despite Baghdad's strong objections.[29] This undoubtedly contributed to Saddam's contempt for the Syrians and bolstered his conception of the need for a long war against the Israelis. Regardless of the fighting effectiveness of their army compared to that of the Israelis, the Iraqis had improved.[30] Nevertheless, the Syrian and Egyptian armies had suffered far heavier casualties in the fierce fighting of the Yom Kippur War, since the Iraqis arrived on the Golan after the heaviest fighting was over and had lost far fewer men in the fighting.[31] In the long run, the relatively low number of casualties may have misled Saddam into overestimating his forces when considering his options in September 1980.

Saddam's military

In the aftermath of 1973, the Iraqi Army focused its training at the tactical level.[32] In a number of ways, the lessons of the Yom Kippur

---

[28] Abraham Rabinovich, *The Yom Kippur War: The Epic Encounter That Transformed the Middle East* (New York, NY, 2004), 311–314. Kenneth Pollack indicates Iraq sent 60,000 soldiers and 700 tanks (two armored and three infantry divisions) to the Golan. Pollack, *Arabs at War*, 167.

[29] Rabinovich, *The Yom Kippur War*, 464–465; Patrick Seale, *Asad: The Struggle for the Middle East* (Berkeley, CA, 1988), 219–225.

[30] Nevertheless, there were problems. Because of a lack of tank transporters, most of the Iraqi tanks had to move to the Golan from Iraq under their own power. Nearly half broke down on the way.

[31] Shahram Chubin and Charles Tripp, *Iran and Iraq at War* (Boulder, CO, 1988), 22.

[32] Woods, *et al.*, *Saddam's War*, 3–4. Significantly, the Israelis had not performed well in combined arms at the beginning of the Yom Kippur War (1973 War), but rapidly

War found their way into army preparations. Logistical movement via heavy equipment transporters became a popular subject of study. A regular feature of Iraq's maneuver training and war college education was war games centered on a multi-corps attack into Israel along the same path as that taken in 1973, no doubt anticipating a different result.[33]

Once again, Iraqi officers who had served in the frontlines were impressed by the technological and tactical expertise of the Israeli units they had engaged. As a result, they emphasized realistic tactical training, particularly in the area of combined arms, where the Israelis had again displayed considerable superiority in the last portions of the war.[34] Increasing professionalism in the army included expanding Bakr University for Higher Military Studies in Baghdad. That effort was offset somewhat in the competition for the best-and-brightest talent by the growing size and influence of various intelligence organizations and the party militia – the People's Army – both designed in part to counterbalance the army. Moreover, the hand of Ba'ath politics continued to manipulate the army's higher levels, where political loyalty factored increasingly in promotion.

Throughout the 1970s, the military, particularly the army and air force, shared in the bounty brought by vast increases in oil revenues. During this period, Iraq, driven less by ideological bonds of shared socialist ideology with the Soviet Union than by Third World realities, bought most of its equipment from the Soviet Union and, to a lesser degree, the French.[35] The extent of the technological deficit between top-of-the-line Warsaw Pact equipment and Western weapons was not yet apparent in the 1970s.[36] For the Iraqis, some of the specific

---

recreated the combined arms tactics that had served them well in the Six-Day War. See Williamson Murray, "The 1973 War of Atonement," *Military Adaption in War* (Alexandria, VA, 2009).

[33] See *SH-IZAR-D-001-309, Army Training Course: Research Plan to Study the Effects of Irrigation and Mass Drainage in Southern Iraq, 1997; *SH-RPGD-D-001-307, Plan for the Deployment of the Republican Guard to Fight Israel in Syria, Circa 1992; *SH-AFGC-D-001-310, Joint Staff Course: Chapter 3, Lecture 1, Appendix A: Main Factors that Facilitated the Achievment of Surprise against the Zionist Enemy in the October 1973 War, 1 January 1998; *SH-RPGD-D-001-308, Dispersal Plan for Allah Akbar OC RG, 30 February 2001.

[34] Woods, *et al.*, *Saddam's War*, 4.

[35] SIPRI, "International Arms Transfers Database, 1950–Present," Stockholm International Peace Research Institute, www.sipri.org/research/armaments/transfers/databases/armstransfers (accessed on 20 May 2010).

[36] The first indication of how wide the gap was came in 1982 during an air battle between the Israelis and Syrians, the latter equipped with the latest and best Soviet equipment. The Syrians lost 100 fighters; the Israelis, one. Moreover, the Israeli Defense Forces

weaknesses in Eastern Block technology only emerged in the first days of the war with Iran. As the air force commander in 1980 admitted to Saddam about his reconnaissance capabilities eight days after Iraqi troops invaded Iran, "first, the technicians we have working in the field do not meet the required training level; they said it is because the photography equipment of the Eastern aircraft [was] ... out-dated and non-advanced."[37]

Whatever the qualitative difficulties with Warsaw Pact equipment, the numbers of new weapons the Iraqis acquired were impressive. Between 1973 and 1980, the Iraqis not only re-equipped their ground formations, but also doubled the size of the army – the latter move stirring up considerable turmoil in the officer corps. In total, they bought approximately 1,600 tanks and APCs, most the newest in the Soviet inventory: T-62s, T-72s, and BMPs. The Iraqis also bought more than 200 modern Soviet aircraft, including MiG-23s and Su-22s, which, in the early 1980s, proved distinctly inferior to the American fighters with which the Iranians were equipping their air forces.[38] For Iraq, as with many newly cash-rich nations, new military hardware did not automatically or quickly translate to effective military capabilities. For example, in 1974, Iraq took receipt of four squadrons of MiG-23s. After two years, only two squadrons were operational owing to the lack of trained pilots and maintenance crews.[39]

Unfortunately for Iraq's future, Saddam was fickle. While developing indigenous military technologies and an atomic weapon were prominent features of his regime, he could also be dismissive of technological capabilities. In 1990, after receiving warnings about American stealth aircraft, he commented "[Such aircraft] can be seen by a shepherd in the desert. It will also be seen by Iraqi technology. They [the Americans] will see this Ghost of theirs [their stealth aircraft] will fall just like any other object falls."[40] Saddam was interested in loyalty and numbers, not technology. Like Stalin, Saddam emphasized ideological factors and fear above all else. The ideological factors were for public consumption.

---

destroyed the advanced air defense system the Soviets had established in the Bekka Valley without incurring any losses on their own side.

[37] SH-SHTP-D-000-847, Transcripts of a Meeting between Saddam and His Commanders in Regarding the Iran–Iraq War, 30 September 1980.

[38] In many cases, Soviet export models of frontline weapons were inferior to what the Soviets produced for their frontline divisions in Eastern Europe. Pollack, *Arabs at War*, 182.

[39] Tom Cooper and Farzad Bishop, *Iran–Iraq War in the Air: 1980–1988* (Atglen PA, 2000), 56–59.

[40] Saddam Hussein, "Saddam Hussein Addresses Arab Youth Seminar, 29 Nov (FBIS-NES-90-231)," *Foreign Broadcast Information Service Daily Reports* (1990).

A speech in the mid-1980s underlines Saddam's belief that ideological commitment lay at the heart of battlefield effectiveness:

The soldier who does not carry on his forehead the emblem of victory or martyrdom, the soldier who does not enjoy dying defending [his] honorable life and its ... values, such a soldier cannot achieve victory. However, he will be confronted with the moment he will have the choice between himself and his body, and his ideas and principles ... [M]ilitary power is measured by the period which difficulties become severe, calamities increase, choices multiply, and the world gets dark and nothing remain[s] except the bright light of belief and ideological determination. If the fighter [does] not care about principles and ideals, and his life [becomes] difficult, and [he forgets] his military knowledge in [favor] of his love and fear for himself only. [If] he ignore[s his] values, principles, and ideal[s], all military foundations would collapse. He will be defeated, shamed, and [his] military honor will remain in the same place together with the booty taken by the enemy.[41]

The fear factor was not spoken but demonstrated. Fear, not political philosophy or even nationalism, held much of Iraqi society together. If Iraqi soldiers feared Iran more than their own government, then "they will do what every other rational human being would do in their place: break and run." This explains in part why the Iranians held three times the number of prisoners of war than Iraq by the end of the conflict.[42] While advanced battlefield technology helped to stiffen the Iraqi spine, the traditional interpersonal methods of ruthless military discipline carried the day.

In addition to equipment buys from the Warsaw Pact, Saddam also bought what he thought were large stocks of ammunition and spare parts. He would discover early in the war, however, that sustained modern combat consumes ammunition at an astonishing rate. It was not that he expected a long war with Iran, but rather that he wanted to ensure that shortages of ammunition or spare parts would not force him to accede to a supplier's political demands. He often referred to two examples where Arab states were forced to do the Soviet Union's bidding because they

---

[41] Lecture 22: Raising Enthusiasm and Concentrating on the Positive Aspects of the Honorable and Aware Iraqi Citizens in *SH-MISC-D-001-304, Lecture 23: The Address of Saddam Hussein at the 3rd Islamic Summit on 28 January 1981. On one occasion early in the war, Saddam noted that the Germans deserve greater honor than the Americans because they had fought "the entire world alone." SH-MISC-D-000-695, Saddam Hussein Meeting with Various Iraqi Officials About the Iraqi Position Early on in the Iran–Iraq War, 12–13 October 1980.

[42] Makiya, *Republic of Fear*, 278. "[F]or the Ba'ath, violence is no longer merely the ultimate sanction used periodically ... violence not the threat of it – is institutionalized, forever reproducing and intensifying that all-pervasive climate of suspicion, fear, and complicity ... the fear that creates the complicity that constitutes the power." *Ibid.*, 129.

failed to diversify their suppliers. The first was Egypt, which failed to secure arms from a Western supplier after expelling the Soviets in July 1972 only to return "hat in hand" a few months later in the run-up to the 1973 war with Israel.[43]

The second example was closer to home. In the mid-1970s, Iraq depended heavily on the Soviets for arms. However, various diplomatic tensions with Baghdad over its dealings with Iraqi communists, the Iraq war with the Kurds, and Gulf security policy caused a slow-down in Soviet arms shipments in early 1975. As Saddam described the situation five years later, "we [had] almost used all of the artillery ammunition. Our situation was such that we had only three heavy bombs for the air force ... we only had 1,200 artillery rounds ... [enough] for a day's fighting." Iraq, without assured access to ammunition and spare parts, risked having to pull its troops back from the Kurdish north unless it bent to the demands of an external power. According to Saddam, "if our political and military circumstance would have allowed us a different position, we wouldn't have been pushed into something [referring to the 1975 Algiers Agreement] we did not want."[44] After this, Iraq began to aggressively diversify its arms suppliers, something that began to pay dividends at the start of the war with Iran.

The problems with planning and executing the invasion of Iran underlined the damage Saddam's rule was already doing to the Iraq military. At the tactical level, Iraq's ground forces remained relatively competent because these officers had survived the first round of Ba'athification and even "Takritization" of the military.[45] However, at higher levels, Saddam again extensively purged the senior officer corps immediately after becoming president in July 1979. He focused particularly among those who held combat commands (divisions and corps) and who had been regarded as the most competent among the senior officers. Unlike his political purge of that year, where the unfortunate Ba'athists were shot,

---

[43] See Dina Rome Spechler, "The USSR and Third World Conflicts: Domestic Debate and Soviet Policy in the Middle East, 1967–1973," *World Politics* 38, no. 3 (1986); Karen Dawisha, "Soviet Decision-Making in the Middle East: The 1973 October War and the 1980 Gulf War," *International Affairs* 57, no. 1 (1980/81). To some degree, and despite his desires to remain independent of the superpowers, Saddam's relationship with the USSR during 1980–1982 mirrored that of Egypt's in 1972–1973.

[44] SH-SHTP-A-000-835, Meeting between Saddam Hussein, the National Command, and the Revolutionary Command Council Discussing the Iraq–Iran War, 16 September 1980. On Iraqi Soviet relations during this period, see Francis Fukuyama, "The Soviet Union and Iraq since 1968," *A RAND Note* (Santa Monica, CA, 1980); Oles M. Smolansky, *The USSR and Iraq: The Soviet Quest for Influence* (Durham, NC, 1991), 143–229.

[45] For a description of the first wave of officer purges during 1968–1973, see al-Marashi, *Iraq's Armed Forces*, 112–120.

the officers were simply retired. Saddam then promoted relatively junior officers into those crucial command slots. Some of the officers promoted to divisional and corps commands had not even attended the staff college. None had held brigade-level commands and were, thus, almost totally unprepared for the demands of the coming war, particularly at the operational level. But all were Ba'athists and known for their loyalty to Saddam.[46]

Until then, according to an Iraqi general, the slogan had been *better a good soldier than a good Ba'athist.*[47] That changed:

The turning point came when Saddam Hussein arrived in total control in mid-1979 ... So for the first time in the history of the Iraqi Army, there were a large number of promotions for political reasons ... I watched as Saddam promoted Lieutenant Colonel Hisham to brigadier general, as well as to command one of the first-line divisions. Another officer, Lieutenant Colonel Khaled ... was also promoted to brigadier general, and became the commander of the 3rd Division, our best. Another was a staff major, Tala al-Duri, who was made a full colonel and [later] commander of the 9th Armored Division.[48] Another was Mahmoud Shukr Shahin, promoted from colonel to brigadier general and who then became commander of the 6th Division. So these first four promotions I mentioned were a major shock for the Iraqi Army. All were very dramatic promotions. Then the war with Iran began.[49]

Not surprisingly, family and tribal relations played key roles in these promotions: Saddam's brother-in-law found himself vaulted from the rank of colonel to general and assigned the position of minister of defense.[50] That was not the worst. Having never spent a day in uniform, Saddam promoted himself to the rank of field marshal and in the uniform of that rank took to appearing throughout Iraq. The dictator also decreed that as long as one was a Ba'athist, one could be a military leader, since each Ba'athist was "a truly natural leader. Therefore, there was no

---

[46] A 1971 law made non-Ba'ath political activity within the armed forces punishable by death. Uriel Dann and Ofra Bengio, "Iraq," in *Middle East Contemporary Survey, Volume I: 1976–77*, Colin Legum, ed. (New York, NY, 1978), 518.

[47] Lieutenant General Ra'ad al-Hamdani in Woods, *et al., Saddam's War*, 24.

[48] Al-Duri was one of the more incompetent Iraqi generals, but that never hurt his relations with Saddam. Even after recognizing that al-Duri's 9th Division was so poorly trained and ineffective in combat that Saddam disbanded it in 1982, al-Duri remained in Saddam's good graces. For Saddam's comments on the division as the "mother of all disasters," see SH-SHTP-A-000-710, Saddam Meeting with the Cabinet During Iran–Iraq War About Iranian Advances and Security Council Negotiations, 21 July 1982.

[49] Lieutenant General Ra'ad al-Hamdani in Woods, *et al., Saddam's War*, 24–25.

[50] In April 1978, Colonel Adnan Khairallah Talfah, Saddam's foster brother, brother-in-law, and cousin, was promoted from colonel to full general to his peers' consternation. Interestingly, he came to be highly respected among senior Iraqi officers because of his honesty when representing their views to Saddam. Bengio and Dann, "Iraq," 518.

problem in a Ba'athist switching from being a politician to a military leader."[51]

The result was that virtually none of Iraq's senior generals, particularly commanders of divisions and corps, had the experience and understanding to command large forces. Unsure of their military knowledge, many of them promoted above their competence, Iraq's generals were unprepared, and in most cases unwilling, to provide sensible military advice to Saddam.[52] Many were less than impressive on the battlefield, as Saddam discovered after launching the invasion. By late October 1980, commenting on a brigade commander who had been unsuccessful, Saddam was already railing that:

With all due respect, if you go easy on someone, you do it at the expense of the truth; the results are more important than intentions ... As a result you will kill 20 brave people because of this coward or inefficient person ... It [can] come to the point where the non-commissioned officer recognizes that his brigade commander is a coward, how can you expect him to fight with good morale?[53]

In Saddam's Iraq, autonomous advice was certainly not something the ruler either encouraged or tolerated. At the top, he sat secure in the apparent belief he could master any situation. The army marched into Iran with no clear plan of campaign and with little capacity to adapt to ambiguous or uncertain situations.[54] One of the great military theorist Carl von Clausewitz's simplest and wisest aphorisms is that "No one starts a war – or rather, no one in his senses ought to do so – without being clear in his mind what he intends to achieve by that war and how he intends to conduct it."[55] In every respect the Iraqis violated this precept, because, while Saddam had some idea of what he wanted to achieve, he and his advisors had no idea about how to achieve it.

Saddam's political perception that Khomeini's regime was teetering on the brink of crumbling only exacerbated failures to plan coherently. As the religious revolution gained steam and as civil troubles exploded with various groups contending for power, intelligence reports of events on the other side

---

[51] Woods, et al., Saddam's War, 25.

[52] Even officers with years of experience like General Shanshal, the chief of staff of the Iraqi Army, were widely resented by more junior officers for their unwillingness to make decisions. Saddam kept him in office for much of the war for that very reason. Kevin M. Woods, Williamson Murray, Elizabeth A. Nathan, Laila Sabara, and Ana M. Venegas, "Interview with Major General (Ret) Aladdin Hussein Makki Khamas, Cairo, Egypt, 11 November 2009," Project 1946: Phase II (Alexandria, VA, 2010).

[53] SH-PDWN-D-000-566, Saddam Meeting with the General Command of the Armed Forces About the Iran–Iraq War, October–November 1980.

[54] Woods, et al., Saddam's War, 6.

[55] Carl von Clausewitz, On War, trans. Michael Howard and Peter Paret, indexed edn. (Princeton, NJ, 1976), 579.

of the frontier encouraged the belief there were substantial opportunities in the east. In July 1980, the General Military Intelligence Directorate (GMID) reported that the Iranian Army was in a state of virtual collapse:

Ten thousand officers have been discharged or gone into retirement ... Since June 28, 1980 until now, 100 individuals have been discharged or retired daily. These measures conform to Khomeini's threats of the necessity to purge the national apparatus of those he described as corrupt. An increase in the disintegration and dismantlement of Iranian forces is expected.[56]

Apparently convinced that a few swift victories would lead to an Iranian regime which, if not friendly, would be cowed by Iraq's success, Saddam failed to give his military sensible strategic guidance for the war. This fundamental strategic error was of course made worse by senior commanders who lacked the knowledge, planning skills, and independence of mind required by high command.

The state of the Iraqi military in 1980

Army

In September 1980, the Iraqi military had impressive numbers on active duty. The army comprised approximately 190,000 soldiers with a further 250,000 in reserve organizations. Heavily influenced by its experiences against the Israelis as well as by its Soviet advisors, the army's best units consisted of four armored divisions and two mechanized divisions; a further four infantry and two mountain divisions rounded out the number available. The Iraqis had also trained a special forces brigade, which was relatively effective. In terms of weaponry, the army possessed approximately 2,350 tanks, the bulk of them Warsaw Pact T-54/-55/-62s along with 100 French AMX-30s and 150 top-of-the-line Soviet T-72s, 800 artillery pieces, and 150 pieces of self-propelled artillery.[57]

Despite the presence of modern equipment and Soviet advisors, training levels were not up to even Warsaw Pact standards. Some units hardly trained at all. In late 1980, a staff officer admitted to Saddam that in the case of one particular brigade's training with the RPG-7, "it has

---

[56] SH-GMID-D-001-427, *GMID Intelligence Report on Iranian Military Capability*, 29 July 1980.

[57] IISS, "The Middle East and North Africa," in *The Military Balance: 1981* (London, 1981). The precise order of battle in 1980 is unclear. Iraq had 1,700 tanks available according to Edgar O'Balance, *The Gulf War: Nineteen Eighty to Nineteen Eighty-Seven* (London, 1988), 28. However, according to other sources, it fielded 2,500 tanks. See Chubin and Tripp, *Iran and Iraq at War*, 294.

been more than a year now since the brigade [has] received any training. There is no training going on."[58] There was also a Ba'athist militia, the so-called Popular Army, that had received no significant training, but that represented, along with the secret police, the forces upon which Saddam relied to control his military and suppress dissidents. During the conflict, Ba'ath militia units would guard supply dumps and transportation routes, but were unreliable in combat.

While a cursory look at the religious makeup of the Iraqi military would suggest the potential for insubordination or treason, it was not widespread. The potential was most likely between the officer corps – consisting largely of Sunni Muslims – and the enlisted ranks – drawn principally from Iraq's Shi'a population. Certainly the Iranians believed they would be able to influence Iraq's Shi'a into supporting their efforts against the Ba'athist regime.[59] Despite the often heavy hand of Saddam's security services, the war's sectarian potential remained a relatively minor consideration.

The most widely cited reason was the historic mistrust of Persians by Arabs. While the revolution in Iran appealed to many of Iraq's Shi'a because it seemed to validate the tenets of their faith, many more were repelled by the Persian nationalist trappings of Khomeini's regime. Even within the Shi'a religious community, there was a split between Khomeini's revolutionary brand of religion and the "quietist traditions" of Iraq's senior Shi'a cleric, Abu al-Qasim al-Khoei, who argued against Khomeini's activist version of the Shi'a tradition on the basis that it was an innovation possessing neither theological nor legal basis.[60]

Air Force

The Iraqi Air Force possessed significant numbers of aircraft, but it was less impressive in terms of training and capabilities. Like the army, it possessed a mixture of Eastern equipment and Western training. Of its 340 combat aircraft, most were fighters, but there were a few decrepit

---

[58] *SH-SHTP-A-001-311, Recording of a Meeting between Saddam Hussein and Military Officers, Circa Late 1980.

[59] According to one Middle Eastern scholar, "the historical relationship between Iran and the [Shi'a] communities in the Arab world, and especially that of Iraq, has bedeviled the politics of nationalist identification and has made it extremely difficult for members of the [Shi'a] community to articulate their interest without laying themselves open to the charge of betrayal and disloyalty." Abbas Kelidar, "The Shii Imami Community and Politics in the Arab East," *Middle Eastern Studies* 19, no. 1 (1983), 14.

[60] Kanan Makiya, *Cruelty and Silence: War, Tyranny, Uprising, and the Arab World* (New York, NY, 1994), 73–76; Graham E. Fuller and Rend Rahim Francke, *The Arab Shi'a: The Forgotten Muslims* (New York, NY, 2001), 93–112.

bombers and 230 helicopters. The Iraqis had also recently ordered sixty Mirage F-1 French fighters, a significant upgrade because they were less stressful to fly and had more technologically sophisticated weapons and navigation systems.[61] But as Saddam considered invading Iran, they had yet to arrive.

The Iraqi Air Force's Air Defense Command comprised large numbers of Soviet surface-to-air missiles; SA-2s, SA-3s, and SA-6s.[62] As with their air force counterparts, the relatively modern equipment was not matched by either training or concepts of employment that optimized its potential. What emerged was a highly centralized system that avoided fratricide by rigidly adhering to fixed procedures.[63]

In the two decades before the Iran–Iraq War, Iraqi pilots were trained by a variety of nations. First was the USSR, but as concerns over Communist influence soured relations, training on Soviet aircraft continued under Indian, and to a lesser extent Pakistani, pilots.[64] Despite limited operations in the Yom Kippur War, some Iraqi pilots earned high marks from their allies. The Egyptian chief of staff singled out those flying the British-made Hawker Hunter for the "daring and skill of their anti-tank strikes in the Sinai. They swiftly gained such a reputation that our field commanders, calling for close air support, would frequently ask for the Iraqi squadron." Almost all of them, however, died in the war.[65]

Overall, Iraq's air force was less prepared for war than its army. The technological inferiority of its Soviet platforms does not entirely explain the difficulties its pilots encountered in air-to-air combat. US Navy intelligence assessed Iraqi capabilities far less favorably than the Egyptians had. Even after eight years of combat, a naval intelligence report from 1990 characterized Iraqi pilots as earning "their qualifications and status with a minimum expenditure of personal effort and risk." Pilots and instructors executed their maneuvers "solely by reference to instruments with little attention paid to outside, visual references."[66] Similarly, nearly 80 percent of Iraqi pilots sent to France early in the war failed to

[61] Woods, "Interview with (Former) Major General 'Alwan Hassoun 'Alwan Al-Abousi, Cairo, Egypt, 13 November 2009."
[62] O'Ballance, *The Gulf War*, 28.
[63] Cooper and Bishop, *Iran–Iraq War in the Air: 1980–1988*, 57–59. These procedures included fixed ingress and egress corridors for strike missions. A weakness that Iran would exploit in the early phases of the war.
[64] Major Ronald E. Bergquist, *The Role of Airpower in the Iran–Iraq War* (Montgomery, AL, 1988); David Nicolle and Tom Cooper, *Arab Mig-19 and Mig-21 Units in Combat*, vol. 44, Osprey Combat Aircraft (Oxford, 2004).
[65] Bergquist, *The Role of Airpower in the Iran–Iraq War*, 21.
[66] Williamson Murray, "Part 1: Operations Report," in *Operations and Effects and Effectiveness, Gulf War Air Power Survey* (Washington, DC, 1993), 76.

qualify for the Mirage and washed out of the training squadrons. This, however, appeared to have had little impact on Iraq's system for upgrading pilots. Upon returning to Iraq, nearly all who had failed the French training syllabus found themselves judged as qualified to fly the Mirage in combat.[67]

The Soviets estimated Iraqi pilots' skill slightly higher.[68] Soviet statistics indicated that 50 percent of Iraqi pilots would not have qualified to be assigned to frontline Soviet fighter units.[69] Given that the position of fighter pilot held great prestige in Iraq and was handed out to those with family, tribal, or political connections, the weaknesses that showed up in the early stages of the war are not surprising. In contrast, the Shah's air force had sought out and acquired competent pilots, and the authorities in Tehran were willing to use the expertise of many of those pilots once the war began.[70] This gave the Iranians a distinct advantage, at least as long as they could maintain their complex US equipment without the help of American technicians.

A US intelligence estimate of Iranian and Iraqi capabilities during the Iran–Iraq War provided the following breakdown:

> Air-to-air engagements [on both sides] were correspondingly unimpressive. Both sides appeared to overestimate the capability of their adversary and had an exaggerated fear of radar guided missiles. Iraqi avoidance of air-to-air engagements was continuous ... Lock-on by Iranian fighters would generally cause Iraqi fighters conducting offensive counter-air/strike missions to abort the mission and return to base. Even when the odds were overwhelmingly in favor of the Iraqi Air Force, survival still dominated their tactics. Any engagements that did occur were noteworthy for their lack of aggressive maneuvering. High speed, maximum range missile launches were followed by egress and return.[71]

On the eve of war and despite an increased emphasis on acquiring advanced equipment, the Iraqi Air Force remained "a parade force, designed to fulfill a deterrence role against potential invaders, good-looking on official flypasts, but hardly capable of defending their country."[72]

---

[67] *Ibid.*, 76.

[68] A fact that undoubtedly reflected the lower standards the Soviets set for their pilots.

[69] *Ibid.*, 76–77; Benjamin S. Lambeth, *Desert Storm and Its Meaning: The View from Moscow* (Santa Monica, CA, 1992), 52.

[70] Because the pilots were relatively junior, the ayatollahs feared their reliability far less than that of the senior officers. Despite the dismissal of a number of pilots early in the revolution, many were reinstated when the war broke out.

[71] Quoted in Murray, "Part 1," 75.

[72] Cooper and Bishop, *Iran–Iraq War in the Air*, 59.

Navy

While the navy was the stepchild of the Iraqi military, its relatively low status gave it some important advantages. In particular, Saddam's disinterest in naval matters, as well as its lack of prestige, protected its leadership from too much interference from Ba'athist sycophants. Thus, of all the Iraqi services, it was the most professional and least influenced by the political and patronage concerns that plagued the other services.[73] Despite the navy's lack of standing, Iraq's oil riches led Saddam to supply it with a modicum of up-to-date Soviet equipment that would stand it in good stead.[74]

The initial move to something greater than a coast guard had begun in the early 1960s when the Iraqis purchased a number of torpedo boats from the Soviets. In the 1970s the Iraqis bought a further twelve Osa missile boats, each equipped with four Styx missiles with considerable warship-killing potential, but which were not as lethal against the massive targets that tankers presented. In January 1980, Iraq contracted for four frigates, six missile corvettes, and a replenishment tanker. None of these assets, however, would be available when the war started.[75] The navy also possessed a squadron of eleven French Super Frelon helicopters, armed with Exocet missiles, two medium minesweepers, six coastal and river minesweepers, and four large landing craft, two of which were equipped with banks of Katyusha rocket launchers.[76] It also possessed several patrol boats, a coast artillery battalion (which would eventually be equipped with Chinese Silkworm missiles in 1983), and long-range radar sites at the tip of the Fao Peninsula so the latter could reach out a considerable distance into the northern Gulf.[77]

Because political and military authorities in Baghdad left the navy largely alone, it could attain higher training and preparedness standards than either of its sister services. Nevertheless, the Iraqi high command had little interest at first in using its naval forces aggressively. In fact, the navy was not even informed that war was in the offing until two days

---

[73] Beginning in the early 1970s, Iraqi naval officers were trained at the Indian Defense Services Staff College at Wellington and various schools in the Warsaw Pact.

[74] Woods, "Interview with (Former) Lieutenant General Abid Mohammed Al-Kabi, Cairo, Egypt, 12 November 2009." The Iraqi Navy did not use traditional naval ranks; rather, it used army ranks for its officers. General Kabi was commander in chief of the navy from 1982 through the end of the Iran–Iraq War.

[75] John Moore, ed. *Jane's Fighting Ships: 1980–81* (London, 1980), 241.

[76] The landing craft equipped with Katyusha rockets would play a considerable part in the bombardment of Abadan at the beginning of the conflict.

[77] Woods, "Interview with (Former) Lieutenant General Abid Mohammed Al-Kabi, Cairo, Egypt, 12 November 2009." There are slight differences between Kabi's order of battle for this period and that of authoritative sources like *Jane's Fighting Ships*.

before its outbreak. Thus, two of its landing craft were being repaired in a facility on the Shatt al-Arab north of Basra on 22 September. Not surprisingly, given Saddam's disinterest, the navy's missions during the first two years of the war were limited to protecting Iraq's coast, preventing the Iranians from landing, and monitoring the enemy.[78]

Iraqi intelligence

At the start of the war, the Iraqis had little ability to assess Iranian military capabilities or operations beyond the information their attachés reported from the embassy in Tehran. The GMID had only three officers devoted to gathering military intelligence about Iran.[79] According to one senior veteran of the GMID, there were only three Farsi speakers in the officer corps. In contrast, there were several staff sections in the GMID with a considerable number of officers, many of whom were fluent in Hebrew, assigned to study the strength and capabilities of the Israeli military.[80] Thus, the Iraqis knew almost nothing about Iran's military potential outside of the fact that it had a large population and was equipped with Western weapons. Of the few tactical military maps available to guide advances into Iran, most were incorrect. Human sources, while increasing in number, were largely confined to disgruntled refugees.

The most obvious needs involved preparing up-to-date maps and identifying Farsi speakers who could listen in on Iranian radio transmissions. But the greatest difficulty lay in creating a corps of intelligence analysts who could make sense of the "other side of the hill." By late 1981, six officers were evaluating Iranian intentions and potential operations; by 1986, the intelligence effort on Iran had grown to approximately eighty officers, supported by nearly 2,500 soldiers. The most important advantage the Iraqis enjoyed throughout the conflict was in the realm of signals intelligence.[81] As with the British breaking

---

[78] *Ibid.*

[79] The GMID was separate from the Iraqi Intelligence Service, which did little reporting on military capabilities, most of which was either misleading or wrong. Because the latter was run by Ba'athist Party loyalists, it reflected the prejudices, paranoia, and ideological bent of Iraqi leaders.

[80] Woods, "Interview with (Former) Major General Mizher Rashid Al-Tarfa Al-Ubaydi, Dubai, United Arab Emirates, 9 November 2009."

[81] Pollack notes that "Iraqi signals-intercept capabilities were quite good and often provided a tip-off of an Iranian offensive, according to former Iraqi generals." In fact, the Iraqi intelligence effort was far larger, as the authors discovered in interviews in November 2009; Kevin M. Woods, Williamson Murray, Elizabeth A. Nathan, Laila Sabara and Ana M. Venegas, *Project 1946: Phase II* (Alexandria, VA: Institute for Defense Analyses, 2010). Also see Pollack, *Arabs at War*, 211. For an example of Iraqi signals intelligence, see among others SH-GMID-D-000-726, Reconnaissance Reports on

Germany's enigma codes in World War II, Iraqi success was not so much the result of their brilliance, but a general lack of signals discipline on the Iranians' part. The Iraqis also received considerable help from the Soviets in developing the technological competence to decipher Iranian message traffic.[82]

Such was the technological enfeeblement of the Iranian military in the first months of the conflict that their ground units were transmitting their messages *en clair*. This appears to have contributed significantly to the shattering Iranian defeat in early January 1981, a defeat that played a major role in the fall of Bani-Sadr's government.[83] At some point in 1981, Saddam's propaganda machine inadvertently revealed that the Iraqis were reading enemy transmissions, and the Iranians desperately scrambled to encipher their message traffic. They quickly procured the C52, a mechanical machine for enciphering manufactured by the Swiss company, Crypto.

In fall 1981, an Iranian officer defected with one of these machines and its codes to Kurdistan, and with the help of the KGB, the Iraqis were soon reading Iranian message traffic again.[84] By the mid-1980s, the Iranians had upgraded to the Crypto T450 electronic enciphering machine, but again with Soviet help, the Iraqis were reading Iranian tactical and operational traffic. The deputy of Iraqi signals intelligence operations at the time, General Mizher Tarfa, recalled that he and his fellow officers were drowning in the massive number of messages their organization was deciphering and translating into actionable intelligence. Until the war's end, the Iranians remained consistently careless in their transmissions, sent too many messages, and gave the Iraqis a rich stream of poorly encrypted data.[85] Interestingly, Saddam understood early the value of this intelligence and the need to keep it secret. Thus, in many respects, Iraqi efforts to maintain their signals advantage resembled the British success during World War II, in Winston Churchill's words, in cloaking intelligence "with a body guard of lies."

Iranian Naval Forces and Information About Anti-Iraqi Forces Smuggling Weapons into Iraq, April–October 1982.

[82] Woods, "Interview with (Former) Major General Mizher Rashid Al-Tarfa Al-Ubaydi, Dubai, United Arab Emirates, 9 November 2009."

[83] See Chapter 5 of this book for a discussion of the battle and its significance.

[84] Woods, "Interview with (Former) Major General Mizher Rashid Al-Tarfa Al-Ubaydi." Soviet help was in return for the Iraqis turning over a damaged F-4 that had crash landed in Iraqi-held territory.

[85] *Ibid.* A number of works have attributed the Iraqi successes in 1987 and 1988 almost exclusively to the satellite imagery passed along by US intelligence. See Frank Francona, *Ally to Adversary: An Eyewitness Account of Iraq's Fall from Grace* (Annapolis, MD, 1999). The authors see little evidence of that in the Iraqi record; rather, the Iraqis consistently commented that the imagery was purposely deceptive

The state of Iran's military in 1980

In 1979, Iran appeared to be superior to Iraq in every quantitative index of civil and military power. To begin with, Iran possessed a population three times that of Iraq – thirty-nine million Iranians compared to thirteen million Iraqis. Iran's 2,000-kilometer coastline was fifty times longer than Iraq's, while Iraq was virtually landlocked and surrounded by six neighbors.[86] Moreover, Iraq's foremost strategic and economic resource, oil, lay dangerously close to its two larger and more powerful neighbors, Turkey and Iran. Its only major outlet to the sea, the Shatt al-Arab, was easily controlled by Iran, a fact that the 1975 Algiers Agreement had enshrined. While neither Iraq nor Iran has homogeneous populations, Iraq's ethnic and religious divisions are deeper and more intractable than Iran's.

Iran has a long and mixed military history extending back to the Persian kings, who had contested the eastern Mediterranean with the Greeks and whom Herodotus had described in the following terms: "In courage and in strength, the Persians were not inferior to others." In a passage that might have been written in 1988, he added: "But they were without defensive armor, and moreover, they were unversed in war and unequal to their opponents in skill, and they would dart out one at a time or in groups of about ten together, some more and some less, and fall upon the Spartans and perish."[87]

After the Persians fell to Alexander the Great, the Parthian and Sassanian Empires emerged to contest the Mesopotamian River Valley for more than half a millennium with the Romans. After their wars with the Romans and Byzantines, the Persian Islamic state contested Mesopotamia in interminable wars with their Arab and Ottoman neighbors. But like the Ottomans after 1700, the Iranians found it difficult to keep up with the rapid technological and military advances of the West. What saved the Persians more often than not from invasion was their extraordinarily difficult geography, which, parenthetically, while protecting them from foreign encroachment, also made it difficult for them to project military power from their heartland.

The modern record of Iran's military forces has not been impressive. Despite, or possibly because of, a nearly continuous stream of French, British, Austrian, Italian and Russian training missions and advisors

---

[86] For a description of Iran's military and strategic geography, see Steven R. Ward, *Immortal: A Military History of Iran and Its Armed Forces* (Washington, DC, 2009), 7–9.

[87] Herodotus, *The Histories*, trans. G. C. Macaulay (1890), revised Donald Lateiner (New York, NY, 2004), 483 (Book IX, 462).

during the nineteenth and early twentieth centuries, modernization of the Iranian military generally failed. The American military reformer, Emory Upton acidly caught the state of what he termed the Army of Persia in the late 1870s in his work on the *Armies of Europe and Asia*:

Company officers are wholly ignorant of military affairs, and most of them can neither read nor write ... The price paid by general and field officers for promotion is two years', and for company officers, one year's pay. With such a system only the greatest incompetency can prevail ... [C]orruption pervades every branch of military administration ... With such relations between officers and soldiers it is impossible for discipline to survive. The substitutes only receive the instruction necessary to [im]personate soldiers who are absent, and so ignorant of arms are they and their use that only those that are worthless are placed in their hands.[88]

In the wake of efforts to modernize the military what emerged were two traits that would play a role in the Iran–Iraq War. The first was the concept of "national jihad," which emerged in 1908 as a modern fusion of the religious concept of defensive jihad with a citizen's duty to defend the homeland.[89] The second was the use of paramilitary gendarmeries to suppress dissent under the Shah.[90] As one historian recently noted:

From the Safavid's early refusal to incorporate firearms through the Pahlavi shahs' procurement of sophisticated yet unsustainable systems to the *Pasdaran's* disregard for combined operations in favor of zealous ill-trained volunteers, Iran's soldiers have paid the price of flawed approaches to warfare. Similarly poor leadership by politicized and selfish officers and stingy support and outright mistreatment have regularly undercut the perseverance, resourcefulness, and patriotism of Iranian fighting men.[91]

Iran's introduction to modern war came in a fashion startlingly similar to the collapse of the Iraqi military in May 1941. Two months after the British had destroyed the Iraqi Army, British forces from the west and south and Soviet forces from the north annihilated the Iranian Army and overthrew Reza Shah Pahlavi's pro-German government. They

---

[88] Major General Emory Upton (United States Army), *The Armies of Europe & Asia: Embracing Official Reports on the Armies of Japan, China, India, Persia, Italy, Russia, Austria, Germany, France, and England*. (London, 1878), 90, 93–94.

[89] See Firoozeh Kashani-Sabet, *Frontier Fictions: Shaping the Iranian Nation, 1804–1946* (London, 1999), 144–147.

[90] Stephanie Cronin, "An Experimentation in Military Modernization: Constitutionalism, Political Reform, and the Iranian Gendarmerie, 1910–21," *Middle Eastern Studies* 32, no. 3 (1996); Stephanie Cronin, *The Army and the Creation of the Pahlavi State in Iran, 1910–1926* (London, 1997), 17–53.

[91] Ward, *Immortal*, 4.

placed his son, Mohammad Reza Shah Pahlavi, on the throne.[92] Despite numerous internal challenges to Pahlavi rule by various political, ethnic, and religious movements, the young Shah managed, with significant assistance from the United States and United Kingdom, to retain power.[93] Using the immense wealth conferred on his country by the oil boom of the 1970s, the Shah built the Iranian military into a formidable force, one equipped with the most modern American and Western weapons.

An Iraqi military assessment from July 1979 noted that in addition to reflecting "the American military ideology and tactics related to limited and modern wars, such as [the] Vietnam War, Indian/Pakistani War, and Arab/Israeli Wars," the Iranian military reflected the Shah's "aggressive, expansionist ambitions." This assessment cited the development of new commands (airborne command in Shiraz, naval commands focused on the gulf and sea of Oman, three "field corps" in Tehran, Shiraz, and Khorramshahr), an increase in infantry formations, the addition of twenty-four infantry regiments during the preceding decade, contracting for modern naval and air force weapons, and the steady improvement of military-related infrastructure.[94] Moreover, Iranian air, sea, and ground units consistently trained to higher standards than those of the Iraqis, at least before Khomeini's revolution. Better equipped, better trained, and more numerous, the Iranian military had been a major reason why the Iraqis, to Saddam's considerable shame, had buckled under direct and indirect Iranian pressure in 1975 and signed to the Algiers Agreement.[95]

US policy toward Iran was changing throughout the 1970s, but in the end it was all about security. For the United States, Iran was a client state whose anti-Communist stance and willingness to support US interests in the region – notably Israel and the free flow of oil – represented an emerging pillar, along with Saudi Arabia, of stability in the Persian Gulf. The explosion of oil wealth along with the Nixon Administration's

---

[92] *Ibid.*, 151–169. See also F. Eshraghi, "Anglo-Soviet Occupation of Iran in August 1941," *Middle Eastern Studies* 20, no. 1 (1984); F. Eshraghi, "Aftermath of Anglo-Soviet Occupation of Iran in August 1941," *Middle Eastern Studies* 20, no. 3 (1984).

[93] For a concise overview of the relationship with the United States, see Kenneth M. Pollack, *The Persian Puzzle: The Conflict between Iran and America* (New York, NY, 2005), 72–140; Patrick Clawson and Michael Rubin, *Eternal Iran: Continuity and Chaos* (New York, NY, 2005), 70–85.

[94] *SH-GMID-D-001-312, GMID Report: Iranian Military Ideology and Fighting Methods, 15 July 1979.

[95] Saddam reportedly stated, in late 1979, that he signed because "I had no other choice . . . Due to the battle at the northern front our army was in disarray . . . I had to sign it." Saddam quoted in Richard Schofield, "Position, Function, and Symbol: The Shatt Al-Arab Dispute in Perspective," in *Iran, Iraq, and the Legacies of War*, Lawrence G. Potter and Gary G. Sick, eds. (London, 2004), 54.

policy to sell "Iran those weapons it requested" dominated the large and diverse economic and cultural relationships between Washington and Tehran.[96]

By 1978, the year before Khomeini's revolution, Iran counted 447 aircraft in its air force, fully a third more than those possessed by the Iraqis. Among those aircraft were F-14s, F-4s, and F-5s – all weapons systems superior to the Soviet equipment in the Iraqi arsenal. In addition to the aircraft, American air-to-air missiles and electronic warfare equipment gave the Shah's Eagles a distinct technological advantage over Saddam's Falcons. In the wake of the 1973 Arab–Israeli War, the Shah increasingly emphasized the quality of training and made full use of his relationship with the United States to train Iranian aircrews to a standard far exceeding Iraqi pilots.[97] By 1977, despite the Shah's penchant for "leadership by distrust," whereby officers were played against each other and joint service planning was all but forbidden, Iran's 100,000-man air force was the most powerful in the Gulf.[98]

However, the arrival of the religious revolutionaries in Tehran led to defections and major purges primarily at the top ranks, but occasionally down to the pilot level.[99] Once the war broke out, the regime brought back a number of pilots from prison or civilian life to serve in frontline squadrons against the Iraqis. Nevertheless, the aircraft and pilots proved wasting assets, because soured US–Iranian relations ensured that Khomeini's air force received few American-made spare parts, supplies, and equipment, and no more Iranian pilots would be trained in the United States.[100] Consequently, according to Iraqi intelligence, less than half of Iran's aircraft were flyable, and in some squadrons the maintenance picture was even bleaker.[101] An Iraqi intelligence report from July

---

[96] For a description of Washington's view of this relationship before the Iranian Revolution, see "Briefing Paper from Bureau of near East Affairs, US State Department to the US Secretary of State, Subject: Your Meeting with the Shah of Iran, 13 May 1977 (Declassified)," in *CWIHP Critical Oral History Conference: The Carter Administration and the "Arc of Crisis": 1977–1981: Document Reader*, Malcolm Byrne, ed. (Washington, DC, 2005). See also Gary G. Sick, *All Fall Down: America's Fateful Encounter with Iran* (London, 1985), 25.

[97] On the buildup and training of the Iranian Air Force in the decade before the Iran–Iraq War, see Cooper and Bishop, *Iran–Iraq War in the Air*, 25–47.

[98] Bergquist, *The Role of Airpower in the Iran–Iraq War*, 25.

[99] According to an Iraqi intelligence report, a coup attempt at Isfahan air base on 9 July 1980 had led to the arrest of forty pilots.

[100] War makes strange bedfellows. At its heart, the Iran–Contra Affair was a three-way swap of spare parts and military equipment among the United States, Israel, and Iran. The pressures of the war eventually forced the Iranians to mount a worldwide scavenger hunt for US spare parts.

[101] SH-GMID-D-000-842, General Military Intelligence Directorate (GMID) Intelligence Report on Iran, January–June 1980. These reports indicated that operational readiness

1980 indicated that only five F-14s of Isfahan's two squadrons of Tomcats (approximately forty aircraft) were serviceable. Moreover, there were fewer pilots to fly them, because many had been arrested on suspicion of plotting a coup.[102]

The Iranian Navy fared better than the other services in the purges, and despite logistic problems, maintained its pre-1979 naval superiority over much of the Gulf in the early years of the conflict. The Shah had equipped it lavishly. In 1978, the navy possessed three guided missile destroyers, four frigates, and an assortment of lesser vessels to oppose Iraq's nine fast missile boats.[103] An Iraqi assessment from July 1980 described the navy in the post-Shah period this way: "The Iranian naval force [has] suffered the least from the political events for two reasons. It [has] stayed away from participating in attacking the forces opposing the Shah, and Ahmad Madani, who was appointed as its commander, persisted in protecting its capabilities." Out of a force of more than 28,000 naval personnel, the Iraqis estimated only 3,000–4,000 desertions after the Shah's fall. Overall, the report noted, "fighting qualification can be evaluated average/below average."[104]

The Shah had equipped his ground forces as generously as he had his navy and air force. In 1978, before Khomeini's return, the Iranian Army numbered 285,000 soldiers against the 190,000 soldiers in the Iraqi Army. Relying on American and British suppliers, the Shah had amassed 1,800 tanks by 1978, which served as the backbone for three armored divisions, three infantry divisions, and four independent brigades (one armored, one infantry, one airborne, and one special forces).

Many of Iran's tanks were older model American M-47s and M-60s, but the Iranians also possessed 760 of the newer British Chieftains. The army also deployed 600 of the most modern American and British helicopters.[105] Moreover, at the time of the Shah's fall, the Iranians had a further 1,450 Chieftains on order and were cooperating with funding in the development of the British Challenger tank and its Chobham composite armor.[106] In addition to Western-style training by the British and Americans, the Iranian Army gained some operational and tactical

---

for fighters was 30–40 percent and helicopters 50 percent. The expectation was that the situation would only worsen.

[102] SH-GMID-D-001-427, *GMID Intelligence Report on Iranian Military Capability*, 29 July 1980.

[103] Ward, *Immortal*, 199–200.

[104] SH-GMID-D-000-842, General Military Intelligence Directorate (GMID) Intelligence Report on Iran, January–June 1980. Admiral Ahmad Madani went from the navy to become the first defense minister of the provisional government in 1980 and then fled Iran after a falling out with Khomeini.

[105] Ward, *Immortal*, 196–197.   [106] *Ibid.*, 1.

experience during deployments to Oman in the early 1970s, where it helped suppress Communist rebels. Despite these qualitative advantages, the Shah's army suffered the same fate as most others under totalitarian systems.[107]

The Shah controlled every aspect of military life including promotions above the rank of major. As one study noted, the Shah's ground forces, "although militarily proficient, were lacking any independent decision making capability, sense of identity, or ability to coordinate among themselves."[108] Moreover, the fact that the Iranians in comparison to the Iraqis had a far greater distance to deploy and sustain a fight from their cantonment areas in the central and northern portions of their country considerably made up for the difference in numbers. In terms of divisions and corps and major ground weapons systems, the two countries were nearly equal in the last years of the Shah's rule.

All of that radically changed in the aftermath of Khomeini's return to Tehran. The Islamic Revolution reversed the strategic balance, at least for the short term. The reversal was a result not just of the revolutionary chaos but part of a naïve and ill-timed plan by the revolutionaries to disarm large parts of an armed force which they felt possessed many "excessively and unnecessarily sophisticated weapons."[109] On 6 March 1979, the new government announced that from then forward, Iran would no longer serve as "policeman of the Persian Gulf"; it began converting naval facilities into fishing harbors, canceling military hardware contracts, and expelling Western trainers.[110] An Iraqi military assessment of the Iranian Army shortly after the revolution noted that it was "generally inefficient" and operating at only 50 percent of its prior effectiveness. The report attributed the decline in "discipline and moral" to:

1) Units being "driven by committees" made up of clergy. This "had a bad effect" on the psychological state of commanders . . . 2) Army personnel feel they could be "retired or expelled" from the service at any time. 3) Deployments in the Kurdish region "under undesirable conditions." 4) No training (with the exception of the 16th Armored Division). 5) Lack of maintenance and spare parts.[111]

---

[107] The only exception to this is Hitler's Third Reich, where careers open to talent in the military services were a mark of the Führer's confidence in his position at the top of the Nazi state.

[108] Mark Roberts, *Khomeini's Incorporation of the Iranian Military*, McNair Paper 48 (Washington, DC, 1996), 8.

[109] Cooper and Bishop, *Iran–Iraq War in the Air*, 49.

[110] Nikola B. Schahgaldian and Gina Barkhordarian, *The Iranian Military under the Islamic Republic* (Santa Monica, CA, 1987), 17–18.

[111] SH-GMID-D-000-842, General Military Intelligence Directorate (GMID) Intelligence Report on Iran, January–June 1980. The lack of maintenance on Iranian equipment was confirmed by a British expert the Iraqis employed who indicated that the Chieftains they

Reports from Iraq's military attaché in Tehran added to the assessment that the Iranian military was in a state of collapse. On the occasion of the Army Day parade in April 1979, he noted, "The morale [of] the Iranian soldiers is still low. Comparing uniforms, marching, and general structure of the former Iranian soldier and officer with that of the current ones, you will find a huge gap, whereby the paraded soldiers are marching with uniforms that resemble that of prisoners and most of them are antiques." Moreover, "as for the march, it resembled that of a prisoners' march after combat." The attaché also reported that despite the announcement that ten regiments would pass in review, he counted only five. In conclusion, he noted that "we did not observe any high military ranks in the parade, but the rank was limited to major and lower."[112]

The Pasdaran

Because the army had been a mainstay of the Shah's regime, Khomeini remained suspicious of it, believing the officer corps was a dangerous source for counterrevolution.[113] At least through 1981, he was correct. As a result, Iran's new rulers systematically purged the military, particularly the army, while establishing their own militia of Revolutionary Guards (*Pasdaran*), as a counterweight to the regular military.[114] A number of generals quickly went before the new regime's firing squads, and, while many of these were former SAVAK (the Shah's secret police), many were regular officers.[115] Many more fled or were forcibly

had captured had had no maintenance for a year-and-a-half. *SH-AFGC-D-001-313, Transcripts of Meetings between Saddam Hussein and the General Command of the Armed Forces, 8–9 August 1981.

[112] Memorandum from the Military Attache in the Embassy of the Republic of Iraq–Tehran to the Directorate of the Military Forces General Staff (26 April 1979) in SH-GMID-D-000-845, General Military Intelligence Directorate (GMID) Correspondence About Weapons, Ammunition, and Other Military Equipment Sent from the Soviet Union to Iran and Correspondence to the Iraqi Military Attache in Tehran, January 1978–September 1979.

[113] From Khomeini's return to Tehran to the outbreak of war with Iraq, there were a number of coup attempts. One on 9 July 1980 involved the air force. SH-GMID-D-001-427, *GMID Intelligence Report on Iranian Military Capability*, 29 July 1980. See also Mark J. Gasiorowski, "The Nuzhih Plot and Iranian Politics," *International Journal of Middle East Studies* 34, no. 4 (2002).

[114] *Pasdaran* is short for *Sepah-e Pasdaran* (Army of the Guardians of the Islamic Revolution). Sometimes referred to in English as the Revolutionary Guard.

[115] Reports of wide-scale purges, with imagery of mass executions, may have given Iraqi analysts some comfort. Nevertheless, one should not overestimate the extent of the purges. One analysis found that, while more than 80 percent of the Shah's generals were removed, only half a percent of field grade officers and two-tenths of a percent of company grade officers were removed. Gregory F. Rose, "The Post-Revolutionary Purge of Iran's Armed Forces: A Revisionist Assessment," *Iranian Studies* 17, no. 2/3

"retired." As Khomeini's spokesman announced, the new government had "executed the executioners of the previous regime" to "purify the blood of the revolution and to put new blood of the revolution into circulation."[116]

Iran's new leaders worked diligently to ensure there would be no connection between the regular army and *Pasdaran*.[117] The creation of parallel military formations to protect a revolution represented a concept familiar to the Ba'ath. Iraqi intelligence noted that the announcement of the formation of the *Pasdaran* in June 1979 had exacerbated tensions by "spreading chaos in the ranks." The assessment concluded, "This organization is overwhelmed with ... propaganda. It is not expected to perform any effective [or] practical duties."[118]

In addition to the *Pasdaran*, the Iranians developed a part-time, ill-trained militia, the *Basij e-mustazafin* (the mobilization of the deprived), which, in some cases, individual mullahs organized, trained, and ran from local mosques and religious institutions. In every respect the *Basij* were unprepared for war. At best they were trained to die in human-wave assaults, in which few of their clerical mentors participated. It is with this group that the regime deftly manipulated the Shi'a concept of martyrdom and even mysticism to create the cannon fodder for a desperate "national jihad." One former *Basij* recalled that "the war was not about getting Iraq, but about getting closer to God."[119] These Iranian religious militias had no significant command structure and, more often than not in the early years of the war, appeared at the front as the result of the political ambitions of the clerics who had called them up.[120] While the *Pasdaran* and the *Basij* were virtually useless in fighting on open ground against Iraqi firepower, they proved useful in the initial fighting in marshes, towns, and villages. They suffered a disproportionate level of casualties later in the war.

(1984). According to Rose, the majority of the 1979 purges occurred in the army, intelligence, and SAVAK.

[116] Roberts, *Khomeini's Incorporation of the Iranian Military*, 31.

[117] The Iranian decision was opposite to what the French Revolutionaries had done in 1792, when they had combined the regular army with the flood of volunteers called up to defend the revolution. The result was that the armies of the French Revolution assimilated the military knowledge possessed by the regulars.

[118] SH-GMID-D-000-842, General Military Intelligence Directorate (GMID) Intelligence Report on Iran, January–June 1980.

[119] Roxanne Varzi, *Warring Souls: Youth, Media, and Martyrdom in Post-Revolution Iran* (Durham, NC, 2006), 50.

[120] O'Ballance, *The Gulf War*, 58. An Iranian history of the first two years of the war confirms that impression: *SH-MISC-D-001-350, *The Passing of Two Years of War: Iran–Iraq*, Political Office of the Islamic Revolution Pasdaran Corps.

Nevertheless, whatever their lack of military training, the *Basij* did at times press the Iraqis hard by their numbers and fanaticism.[121] However, as one Iraqi officer recalled:

They come on in their hundreds, often walking straight across the minefields, triggering them with their feet ... They chant Allahu Akbar and they keep coming, and we keep shooting, sweeping our fifty mills [*sic*] [machine guns] around like sickles. My men are eighteen, nineteen, just a few years older than these kids. I've seen them crying, and at times, the officers have to kick them back to their guns. Once we had Iranian kids on bikes cycling towards us, and my men started laughing, and then these kids started lobbing their hand grenades, and we stopped laughing and starting firing.[122]

The *Pasdaran* competed with the army for resources and volunteers throughout the war. According to one of the *Pasdaran*'s co-founders, Mohsen Sazegara, the Iranians envisioned the *Pasdaran* as a "people's army" with a command structure independent from the regular army. In addition to "coup proofing" the new regime, the *Pasdaran*, populated by "students, bureaucrats, farmers, and the like," operated in a decentralized system of "civilian guerilla groups" to fight "alongside the regular army."[123] The *Pasdaran* and the *Basij* were never fully integrated, but rather responded to different centers among the religious and political factions swirling round Khomeini in Tehran.

Khomeini established the *Pasdaran* by decree on 5 May 1979 to provide security against the revolution's internal enemies. Initially it numbered only a few thousand, but by the end of the year it had doubled in size. Not surprisingly, its weaknesses in arms and training were glaring. As one of its commanders admitted after the war:

With the climate that governed the beginning of the war, we had many shortages, and the world had shut its doors to us. So we had to provide our own needs ourselves. In the beginning of the war, we had shortages in light weapons; we had shortages in ammunition; the Guard Corps [the *Pasdaran*] had no medium artillery, or we had only few, a number of mortars. We did not have artillery or

---

[121] By 1983, the Iranian human-wave tactics were such a concern that the Iraqis wrote a doctrinal manual on how to counter them. The manual noted that the "best practitioners of the human-wave attack during this century have been the Chinese" in the 1940s against the Japanese, in the 1950s against the Americans, and in the 1960s against the Indians. See *SH-IZAR-D-001-314, *The Human Wave Attack*, Iraqi Combat Development Directorate, 1983.

[122] The Iraqi officer is quoted in Geneive Abdo and Jonathon Lyons, *Answering Only to God: Faith and Freedom in Twenty-First-Century Iran* (New York, NY, 2003), 109. Brackets in original.

[123] Mohsen Sazegara, "What Was Once a Revolutionary Guard Is Now Just a Mafia," www.sazegara.net/english/archives/2007/03/what_was_once_a_revolutionary.html (last modified on 16 March 2007, accessed on 29 July 2007).

missiles at all, and we had few anti-tank missiles. What the brothers in the military had [was] either out of order or the parts had not come, were left in disrepair, or the ammunition for them had been [used up] in the early months of the war.[124]

With the need to mobilize rapidly, Khomeini turned to the *Pasdaran* rather than the regular army to generate ground forces. By 1983, the *Pasdaran* numbered slightly more than 200,000. By 1986, it was more than 350,000.[125] Nevertheless, in September 1980, this centerpiece of Iran's defense had neither coherent structure nor table of organization. As the prime minister at the time, Abu al-Hasan Bani-Sadr, describes it in his memoirs:

> The 20,000 Revolutionary Guards [*Pasdaran*] were not enough for the task ... Unlike the army, which was becoming a vital, unified corps, the Revolutionary Guards remained totally bound to their social and cultural milieu. Each city had its own Guards with different ideologies and different decision making structures. They were more effective locally than they were nationally ... Some of them, such as those in Khorasan, for example, would refuse any mobilization order from Tehran, while others ignored the directives of such and such an official.[126]

For the first four months of the war, the *Pasdaran* operated without any major headquarters outside of Tehran. In early 1981, the Iranians established a southern operational headquarters in Khuzestan to coordinate the actions of a loose collection of tactical units. One of its functions was to provide *three* days of training for young volunteers eager to fight the Iraqis. Moreover, the *Pasdaran* never possessed the command level or staff to control significant military operations. Its commander summed up its approach to combat in a comment in 1986: "We do not need advanced planes and tanks for victory. [The] employment of infantry forces with light weapons, four times more than the number of Iraqi troops will be enough to overcome the enemy."[127] From its birth, the *Pasdaran* was a revolutionary armed force, not an army.

Purging the armed forces associated "with the former diabolical regime" particularly affected the Iranian Army.[128] By September 1980, the authorities in Tehran had removed approximately 12,000 officers – a move that dealt a devastating blow to Iran's military's operational and

---

[124] "Resalat Interview with Former IRGC Commander: MG Mohsen Reza'i (FTS-19971023000598)," *Open Source Centre* (1997).

[125] James Dingeman and Richard Jupa, "Iranian Elite: The Islamic Revolutionary Guards Corps," *Marine Corps Gazette* 72, no. 3 (1988).

[126] Abu al-Hasan Bani-Sadr, *My Turn to Speak: Iran, the Revolution and Secret Deals with the US* (Washington, DC, 1991), 117.

[127] Dingeman, "Iranian Elite."

[128] Rose, "The Post-Revolutionary Purge of Iran's Armed Forces," 154.

tactical capabilities.[129] Most of those purged had come from the more senior ranks, thus, there remained little expertise in how to plan or execute large-scale, complex military operations. This vacuum of experience had subsumed all fourteen division commanders, independent brigade commanders, and military governors.[130] Perhaps more disastrous for the Iranian ground forces was the fact that the ayatollahs persistently mistrusted not only the remaining officers, but also their professional advice as well.[131]

The 1980 election of Bani-Sadr placed the *Pasdaran*, and its cleric-dominated supporters, outside the new government's national security concept. Iran's new civil government attempted to starve the *Pasdaran* into irrelevance during its struggle to create a stable government in Tehran. Just as the purges of the military and Bani-Sadr's policy of keeping the *Pasdaran* ineffective were hitting full stride, Saddam launched his war.[132] By the outbreak of war, the Iranian Army's numbers had dropped from 285,000 to approximately 100,000 soldiers, whereas the Iraqi Army had increased to 200,000. Not surprisingly, the impact of the purges showed. While Iraq could deploy most of its major weapons systems, Iran could hardly deploy half of its tanks, much less half of its APCs, and its approximately 1,000 artillery pieces.[133] Moreover, virtually the entire maintenance and supply structure had collapsed as a result of the purges and the withdrawal of American contractors.

Introducing the militia into the Iranian equation, particularly given its disparate and disputatious origins, exacerbated the problems that the purge of Iran's regular forces had created. The highly decentralized nature of the *Pasdaran* resulted in a situation where no one in Tehran was in charge of the overall conduct of military operations. The view from Baghdad was that even within the militias, there were independent commands, many of whom were beholden to different ayatollahs in Tehran, who were themselves jockeying for position within the religious

---

[129] Efraim Karsh, "The Strategic Backdrop," *The Adelphi Papers* 27, no. 220 (1987), 14. Both the number and impact of the purges has been disputed. One author notes that in many cases the numbers were inflated by "tendency of the popular media to conflate the purge of the regular armed forces with that of the state security apparatus ... as members of both held military rank." Rose, "The Post-Revolutionary Purge of Iran's Armed Forces," 160.

[130] Schahgaldian and Barkhordarian, *The Iranian Military under the Islamic Republic*, 21.

[131] For an examination of the political attacks and their impact on the army by the mullahs, see Bani-Sadr, *My Turn to Speak*, 108–110.

[132] Kenneth Katzman, "The Pasdaran: Institutionalization of Revolutionary Armed Force," *Iranian Studies* 26, no. 3/4 (1993), 398–402.

[133] "The Middle East and North Africa," *IISS The Military Balance* 81, no. 1 (1981).

and political hierarchy surrounding Khomeini.[134] Since the ancient ayatollah had no personal knowledge of military issues, there would be no coherent direction coming from Iran's leaders.

Instead, most of Iran's religious leaders viewed the revolutionary volunteers as a means to gain Khomeini's attention. Given the distrust of the Shah's old army, none of the militia/religious/political leaders had the slightest interest in cooperating with military leaders or, for that matter, with each other. Instead, the resulting chaotic command structure affected the Iranian military's performance during the war's first two years and continued to influence Iran's competence on the battlefield until the war's end. The Iranians put hundreds of thousands of fighters on the battlefield, but rarely could they control those fighters coherently and effectively. The net result was a continuing slaughter of Iranian soldiers and militia.

There is a larger point here in terms of evaluating military effectiveness on a national level. A simple comparison of the order of battle between the two countries masks the intangible military value of a revolutionary regime capable of mobilizing the Iranian masses. The *Pasdaran*'s "heroic" role in the Iran–Iraq War has become more controversial with time. One recent study has noted that "many Iranians blame the [*Pasdaran*] for an excessively long and futile eight-year war against Iraq. Many believe that Iran, with a population two times larger than that of Iraq, could not defeat [Saddam's] forces because of the [*Pasdaran*'s] inexperience, emotionality, and ideological zealotry."[135] A veteran of the war's early days recalled how Iran's youth considered Khomeini's orders to be the "orders of God." For the faithful of any age, Khomeini's admonition that "the commander in chief of the forces is God, the same God who has ordered you to pray, the same God who has ordered you to defend yourself ... Defense is a religious obligation," was hard to ignore.[136]

Khomeini's revolution did appeal to Iranian hearts and minds. A propaganda book on the war's first two years, published by the *Pasdaran*, placed the official Iranian perceptions neatly:

Victory in war does not always ensure that the desired ends are achieved. Based on this philosophy, [many] victories end up in defeat, and losses [equate to] victory. As Imam Khomeini, our flag bearer says, "this is our duty. God has

---

[134] Woods, *et al.*, *Saddam's War*, 32.
[135] Frederic Wehrey *et al.*, *The Rise of the Pasdaran: Assessing the Domestic Roles of Iran's Islamic Revolutionary Guards Corps* (Santa Monica, CA, 2009), 24.
[136] "Iran: IRGC Commander Attributes Iran's Succes in Iran–Iraq War to Young People (IAP-20040922000113)," *Open Source Center* (2004).

ordered us to fight those who are against Islam and who are against our people. We either win or we don't. If we do, blessed be God, we have accomplished the mission and have been successful. If we die, we have done what we have been told. We do not have defeat, defeat is not for us. For us, we are either victorious or we don't win but we have saved our honor [before] God."[137]

Conclusion

In many ways, the armies that confronted each other in September 1980 were similar. As an observant Iraqi general officer (a major in 1980) noted about the opposing sides:

We see that both militaries were a part of Third-World countries, and, on both sides, the regimes filled up their military institutions in higher positions according to political loyalty rather than expertise. Additionally, both political leaderships failed to allow the professional military officers to participate in making military decisions. Rather decisions occurred with political intent down to the lowest level – all the way down to company level. Both militaries lacked senior level officers sufficiently competent to understand the concept of long-term strategy. But even if these capabilities had existed, or if there were a handful of officers who did have the understanding, their influence was disrupted by the political regimes at all levels. The political limits had a paralyzing effect on virtually every decision.[138]

Sprinkled throughout the officer corps of the opposing sides were professional officers, who, given the chance, could have more coherently approached military effectiveness than the prevailing political correctness and top-down mentality of their leaders. But there were too few such officers and, for the most part, they were distrusted and misused by those above them, while the battlefield would soon consume many of them.

---

[137] *SH-MISC-D-001-350, *The Passing of Two Years of War: Iran–Iraq*, Political Office of the Islamic Revolution Pasdaran Corps.
[138] Woods, *et al.*, *Saddam's War*, 30.

4   1980: The Iraqi invasion begins

We have to stick their nose in the mud so we can impose our political will over them. This cannot take place except militarily.[1]   – Saddam Hussein

Oh great people of Iraq ... We thought the Iranian government was going to learn from the previous lessons after our valiant troops liberated our extorted land on the eastern borders [the two towns the Iranians were supposed to return after the signing of the 1975 Accords], and after we reinstated Iraqi sovereignty in Shatt al-Arab. But the grandsons of the magi who have [a] deep grudge against Iraq and the Arab nation, and who are strong in setting suspicious plans continued in their errors and counter military actions ... Oh ... sons of Iran of all nationalities, religions and sects ... we do not want to inflict any damage on you or seek your land, but the tyrant charlatan Khomeini and his aides want to be in an unfaithful war against us, motivated by an unjustified ... grudge against Iraq ... They wanted to deceive Iraq and [the] Ummah, and the backward ... Khomeini gang committed massacres and caused the Iranian people a blood bath.[2]   – Saddam Hussein

Despite the momentous changes occurring in Iran during early 1979, Saddam was still looking west. At the end of March, a meeting and discussions between the Ba'ath Revolutionary Command Council and members of the PLO, chaired by then-vice president Saddam Hussein, focused on Egyptian President Anwar al-Sadat's defection from the Arab hardline states. Saddam was clear on the policies he believed the Arab world should pursue:

We stated that there would be traitors, and we would deal with them on that basis by [encouraging] the people to [do] all they can to topple the regime for treason. We said it publicly ... We repeated it today, the same words. I fear they think that

---

[1] SH-SHTP-A-000-835, Meeting between Saddam Hussein, the National Command, and the Revolutionary Command Council Discussing the Iraq–Iran War, 16 September 1980.
[2] *SH-MODX-D-001-315, Draft of Saddam Hussein's Declaration of the Iran–Iraq War, 22 September 1980.

those are just words for the public, but that it is not for them also. We stand by what we have said ...

They [the Arab regimes] have signed the resolutions and are now expected to adhere to them, that is from us the revolutionary freedom fighters. And revolutionary freedom fighters have their own methods in dealing with traitors ... And if one of you needs weapons and wants to kill Numari [president of Sudan who had joined Sadat] these ... weapons from our embassy in France [are available].[3]

Saddam was then in his eleventh year as Iraq's vice president. The republic's president, Ahmed Hassan al-Bakr, was reportedly ill and the same could be said for much of the regime's program. Despite aggressively trying to derail the Israeli–Egyptian peace accords, the Iraqis had failed in that attempt. In reaction to Sadat's peace initiative, Iraq sought to reincarnate the idea of a United Arab Republic by joining with Syria. The short-term payoff of such a revival – to blunt any momentum Sadat could muster after the Camp David Accords – worked. The Egyptians were expelled from the Arab League and the Islamic Organization, casting Iraq as the presumptive dominant actor in Arab affairs. However, after initial signs of promise, Iraqi–Syrian relations broke down over Iraq's insistence that it be the dominant partner. As Saddam told a group of senior ministers in November 1979, "any relationship between Iraq and the system in Syria must take one of two directions – there is not a third direction – it is either collision or merger. There is no middle ground in this matter."[4] The Syrians, mindful of Iraq's greater size, were only interested in a military alliance and had no intention of subordinating themselves politically.[5] The failure would cause Saddam to look elsewhere to demonstrate his leadership.

Shortly after Khomeini's return to Tehran, Saddam pontificated about the implications of the ongoing revolution in Iran. He noted that the

---

[3] SH-SHTP-A-000-553, Revolutionary Command Council Meeting after the Baghdad Conference in 1979, 27 March 1979.

[4] SH-SHTP-A-000-911, Discussion between Saddam and Iraqi Officials About Iraq's Relationship with Syria, 26 November 1979.

[5] For an excellent discussion of these efforts, see Malik Mufti, *Sovereign Creations: Pan-Arabism and Political Order in Syria and Iraq* (Ithaca, NY, 1996), 209–220; Patrick Seale, *Asad: The Struggle for the Middle East* (Berkeley, CA, 1988). For the Iraqi perspective on how the "project to integrate" would have affected the Syrian and Iraqi Ba'athist parties, see Memorandum from Dr. Munif al-Razzaz to Saddam Hussein (30 December 1978) in SH-BATH-D-000-206, Suggestion to Integrate Iraqi and Syrian Ba'ath Parties; Ba'ath Party Structure Notes, 30 December 1978. Al-Razzaz was a Jordanian Ba'athi intellectual and member of the so-called pan-Arab leadership. He also held a leadership position in the terrorist group the Arab Liberation Front during the 1960s and 1970s. He would eventually be accused of plotting with the Syrians and arrested after Saddam's July 1979 purge. He died under house arrest in Iraq in 1984.

stability and unity of the revolution in an Iran that "is not hostile to the Arab nation" was in Iraq's interest. In the meantime, and while Iran "stews in its own blood," Iraq should be patient and prepare to deal with "the one who achieves success." Nevertheless, he added, if "they start attacking us, we [will] have no option except the military option."[6] Saddam also examined the events in Iran from the perspective of a self-described revolutionary. Noting that there "is no one organized party," Saddam cautioned that that would change. Khomeini has "support from the population" and "we know that the first phase [of a revolution] is different from the other phases." The opportunity that would compel him to action nearly a year later seemed to already be emerging in Saddam's calculations: "Iran is a country of five nations, bordered by the Soviet Union. [It] has oil and has built a lot of big facilities, but big only because there is a difference between something big in size and the quality of its size. I equate this, my comrades, to a hunter who shoots the wing of a rock-dove with one bullet. It is not the bullet that kills the [bird] but it is [its] fall on the ground that kills it; that is its weight that was its affliction in this situation."[7]

Despite some early attempts to reach out to the emerging regime in Tehran, Iraq saw opportunity in a weakened neighbor. In October, Saddam issued a set of proposals to settle outstanding issues that, if satisfied, would pave the way for its friendship with the "Arab Nation." First, Iran would have to withdraw from the disputed Gulf Islands and drop other "chauvinistic claims." Second, Iran should voluntarily amend the 1975 Algiers Agreement and restore Iraq's claims over the Shatt al-Arab. Finally, Iran should grant autonomy to its Arabs, Kurds, and Baluchi minorities.[8] The answer came in the form of increasingly harsh propaganda and border incidents, communicating to Baghdad that, while it may be weakened, no government in Tehran would ever secure its legitimacy by acceding to such an "offer of friendship."

In November 1979, Saddam, now president, began to focus on the challenge Khomeini's regime represented as well as on Khomeini's intransigence. Meeting with his foreign policy advisors sometime during that month, he commented that Khomeini had "planned animosity [against] us from the beginning," as if the changes taking place in Iran

---

[6] SH-SHTP-A-000-851, Saddam Discussing Khomeini, Iranian Kurdistan, and Iranian Forces with Iraqi Diplomats, 20 February 1979.

[7] *Ibid.*

[8] Ofra Bengio, "Iraq," in *Middle East Contemporary Survey, Volume IV: 1979–80*, Colin Legum, ed. (New York, NY, 1980), 517. An Iraqi ambassador in Lebanon relayed the conditions in such a way that they would generate discussion in the Arab press while giving Baghdad some flexibility with Tehran if negotiations were offered.

had occurred solely with the intention of harming Iraq's interests.[9] Yet, Saddam's anger was also aimed at the Gulf Arabs who, according to him, had no coherent policies toward the Iranian threat:

The Arabs in the Gulf, the Gulf Arabs ... they are the Arabs of decay, the Arabs of shame ... Khomeini will not give them a chance to survive, slaughtering them is a sacrificial blessing, a great deed ... we have to get rid of the ruler of Kuwait, but if anyone overthrows the ruler of Kuwait, he must be able at the same time to safeguard the interests of its people and to safeguard the Arab identity of its people [against Persian influences, i.e., the Shi'a].[10]

Nevertheless, Saddam was still not fully focusing on Iran. Consolidating his own "revolution" would require a significant internal effort. Before seizing power Saddam was busy removing obstacles to his success. In March 1979, he renewed efforts to rid Iraq of the Iraqi Communist Party (ICP). Much of the ICP's leadership fled to Moscow, while many of the rank-and-file sought refuge with sympathetic Kurdish factions in the north. The regime was pleased, as Tariq Aziz stated at the time "[t]here is no need for a Communist Party ... [i]f they want to become martyrs, we will oblige them."[11] Cleaning up the Ba'ath Party was also a top priority. "We are now in our Stalinist era," Saddam reportedly declared; "we shall strike with an iron fist against the slightest deviation or backsliding beginning with the Ba'athists themselves."[12]

The fallout from the Syrian "conspiracy" continued. In November, a joint Libyan–Syrian declaration called for "Arab–Iranian fraternity" and reiterated support for all (including Iranian) liberation movements against "colonialism, imperialism, and Zionism." In December, high-level military meetings between Iranian and Syrian officials in Damascus and Tehran opened the way for direct military and intelligence cooperation.[13] Saddam's intelligence services reported in December 1979 that Syria was working with "Iran and Libya to shape a sectarian civil war in Iraq that would lead to a coup."[14] At the very time Saddam was trying to turn the Arab world toward the looming danger to its east, competitors for leadership in the Arab world were openly challenging his narrative. In Saddam's view, there had to be a more coherent explanation for the

---

[9] SH-SHTP-D-000-559, Saddam and His Inner Circle Discussing Relations with Various Arab States, Russia, China, and the United States, 4–20 November 1979.
[10] *Ibid.*   [11] Quoted in Mufti, *Sovereign Creations*, 214.   [12] Bengio, "Iraq," 505.
[13] Jubin M. Goodarzi, *Syria and Iran: Diplomatic Alliance and Power Politics in the Middle East* (London, 2006), 26.
[14] Memorandum from GMID to the Revolutionary Command Council RE: Information (15 December 1979) in SH-GMID-D-000-595, Information Regarding Syrian Authorities Secretly Visiting Iran and Libya to Foment Sectarian War in Iraq, December 1979.

Iranian Revolution than simply that religious clerics had overthrown the Shah's regime and were trying to overthrow their neighbors' regimes. That explanation was that the United States was behind the revolution! Ironically, the Iranians would explain Saddam's 1980 invasion as the fruit of American encouragement to embark on the war to further US interests. The *Pasdaran*'s history of the first two years of the war noted: "Saddam's ... imposed war against our people's revolution was financed by the United States ... The Imam always looked on Saddam as an American mercenary."[15]

As Saddam continued his November 1979 meeting, he explained his understanding of the larger framework within which events in the Gulf were unfolding:

Have you noticed how disturbed the Americans are lately? They have become nervous ... They are involved in the events in Iran, including the removal of the Shah, which was entirely an American decision ... They raise the Hormuz issue ... They come to agreement with the Iranians in order to scare the Gulf people, so they can have presence and arrange the situation in the region, and then [the Gulf] people turn to Iraq: "We fear you, none of your people help us; that is why we were forced to bring the Americans in to protect us." [The Americans] wanted to change the Iranian regime, come and intervene in the Gulf region, arrange their position and reorganize the Gulf region according to their established laid-out plan, which included the Iranian events ... we talk about the American occupation, the Americans come, the Americans go, they want to embarrass the Iraqi position.[16]

The themes on display in this meeting were remarkably consistent with similar discussions during the course of the conflict. Toward the end of the war, Abd al-Jabbar Muhsen, chief of the ministry of defense's political guidance department, explained the conflict's beginning in the following terms:

There is no way now to explain the many reasons that made the imperialists and Zionists let Khomeini out of his magic bottle and power in Iran. Yet, the principle

---

[15] *SH-MISC-D-001-350, *The Passing of Two Years of War: Iran–Iraq*, Political Office of the Islamic Revolution Pasdaran Corps. For a balanced discussion of Saddam and "conspiracism," see Matthew Gray, "Revisiting Saddam Hussein's Political Language: The Sources and Roles of Conspiracy Theories," *Arab Studies Quarterly* 32, no. 1 (2010). For a comparison of the Baghdad and Tehran versions of the US "conspiracy" at the start of the Iran–Iraq War, see chapter 5 in Daniel Pipes, *The Hidden Hand: Middle East Fear of Conspiracy* (New York, NY, 1996). The idea of an American "green light" for Iraq's invasion is explored and convincingly debunked in Bryan R. Gibson, *Covert Relationship: American Foreign Policy, Intelligence, and the Iran–Iraq War, 1980–1988* (Santa Barbara, CA, 2010), 23–36.

[16] SH-SHTP-D-000-559, Saddam and His Inner Circle Discussing Relations with Various Arab States, Russia, China, and the United States, 4–20 November 1979.

reason was to deal with the situation in Iraq. They allowed him power so that Iran will once again be a tool for aggression against this country, to stop its growth, to rip it apart.[17]

Tariq Aziz explained his take on the issue in October 1980, by saying that, despite the issue over the hostages, "Khomeini's hatred for Iraqis is such that he would support negotiations with the Americans rather than agreeing to a cease fire ... with Iraq." In fact, Aziz continued, "from the political point of view, [I] prefer the Iranian–American alliance be exposed, because [it] will transform the battle ... [f]irst it will transform the Arab stance to our side and [second] the Soviet Union will have no excuse not to support us, then we can push through into Arabistan, in a better manner."[18]

By late spring 1980, Saddam had come to believe that Khomeini's regime was a direct threat to Iraq's stability. The Iranians were increasing their overt as well as covert support for Shi'a revolutionary groups. Iraqi intelligence reports also noted increasing Iranian air activity along the border. One report from May 1980 indicated thirty-seven Iranian penetrations during the preceding forty-five days. The Iraqi analysis of these actions included Iranian resupply of Kurdish forces in northern Iraq and reconnaissance missions in the south. For their part, the Iraqis responded with increasingly aggressive aerial reconnaissance over the Iranian side of the frontier.[19]

Given the extensive intelligence reporting on the collapse of Iran's military forces, it must have appeared to Saddam an ideal time to settle matters and extend Iraqi influence to the east. To those with no real knowledge of military effectiveness or strategy – namely Saddam and his court – war with Iran seemed an increasingly attractive choice. Saddam was assured by a "steady stream of Iranian military visitors to Baghdad ... that the revolutionary guards were an ill-trained rabble."[20] The sporadic artillery duels accompanied the increasingly vitriolic

---

[17] SH-BATH-D-000-300, Lecture on the Iran–Iraq War, February 1987. This view found support in revelations of covert US support for the Kurds in the mid-1970s and the Iran–Contra scandal of 1986.

[18] SH-SHTP-D-000-846, General Command of the Armed Forces Meeting Transcripts During the First Gulf War, 17 October 1980. During this same conversation, Aziz and the Iraqi chief of intelligence expressed concern that the US president and secretary of state had recently described the conflict as "an aggression against Iran." Such a shift from neutral descriptions using words like *conflict* or *hostility* implies that "the American position will be supportive of Iran."

[19] *SH-AADF-D-001-316, Various Reports and Memoranda from the Air Force and Air Defense Command Relating to Iraqi Reconnaissance and Iranian Incursions into Iraqi Air Space, 1980. It is difficult to distinguish at this point which side was "responding to" or "provoking" the other with airspace violations.

[20] Claudia Wright, "Religion and Strategy in the Iran–Iraq War," *Third World Quarterly* 7, no. 4 (1985), 844–845. Wright also credits Iraqi memories of the miserable performance

diplomatic and propaganda exchanges increased through spring and summer 1980. However, Iraqi intelligence reporting of these small clashes did not characterize them as the prelude to larger operations. In fact they were reported as evidence of the Iranian military undergoing increasing levels of "fragmentation."[21]

Pre-war skirmishing

By the end of August 1980, relations between the two nations had reached boiling point. Across the lengthy frontier, artillery barrages punctuated the quiet, while small-unit skirmishes occurred almost daily. Iraqi intelligence reported the following incidents immediately before hostilities:

1 September: Iraqi artillery shelled Qasr-e Shirin and four Iranian artillery positions. Iran responded. Twenty-five Iraqi troops wounded. Estimate ten Iranian casualties. No movement of enemy troops noted.

3 September: Iranian and Iraqi artillery units exchanged fire in the Qawrataw region from 2000 on 2 September until 3 September. No casualties. No movement of enemy troops.

4 September: Iran shelled Khanaqin and the border posts at Qawrataw, Khanaqin, Mandali, Badrah, the headquarters of the 4th Border Brigade at Zurbatiyah, and the town of Zarbatayah. Iraq responded by shelling the cities of Qasr-e Shirin, Khosravi, and Mehran. Iraq suffered three dead and nine wounded. Casualties in Iran were undetermined, but helicopters were seen moving dead and wounded. No military movements noted.

5 September: Iran shelled Zarbatayah, the border posts at al-Darraji, al-Shuhada border post, the 4th Border Brigade, and artillery positions. Iraq responded by shelling Mehran City. Reports say city was burning. Sporadic reports of small arms fire near Jalal border post. No casualties reported. No military movements noted.[22]

Such reports continued for the next three weeks with increasing incidents of small arms fire as well.[23] On 8 September, Iranian troops occupied five

and swift surrender of the Iranian military in the 1941 invasion and occupation of Iran by British and Russian forces with buoying Iraqi confidence.

[21] *SH-GMID-D-001-305, GMID Memorandum to Section 1, 52/Q1/40662, Re: Complete Intelligence Report, 29 July 1980.

[22] Intelligence Report from the GMID to the Bureau of Operations (September 1980) in SH-GMID-D-000-332, Summaries and Intelligence Reports for the General Military Intelligence Directorate (GMID), September 1980–May 1985.

[23] A 1985 Iraqi document indicates there were 245 violations of the Iraqi frontier from 15 January to 4 September 1980, and 451 from 5 September to 12 September. "These violations included artillery shelling, and armed attacks across the border including

small Iraqi border stations, but were quickly driven off. Later that day, during a dogfight between two Iraqi MiG-21s and a pair of Iranian F-4s, one of the F-4s was shot down and its pilot captured. By 9 September, the Iraqis were reporting deployment of Iranian units toward border areas. On 12 September, despite increasing, but intermittent, reporting of Iranian forces moving toward the border, Iraqi intelligence noted: "Diminishing combat effectiveness of the enemy ... enemy troops are unable to withstand confrontation." Nevertheless, the GMID's assessment on 14 September was that "the enemy deployment organization does not indicate hostile intentions and appears to be taking on a more defensive mode."[24]

On 19 September, hostilities spread to a new domain when an Iranian P-3 maritime patrol aircraft fired on Iraqi patrol boats at the mouth of the Shatt al-Arab. The next day, the Iraqi Navy observed the sudden deployment of Iranian naval forces. The following morning, the first naval clash occurred when commercial vessels flying the Iraqi flag and transiting the Shatt al-Arab were fired on. Late that afternoon, Iraqi patrol craft engaged and reported sinking five Iranian boats.[25] The Iranians replied by attacking and reportedly sinking an Iraqi Orsa-class missile boat with helicopter-launched anti-ship missiles.[26] The most interesting feature of these reports from 1 to 20 September was the haphazard nature of the engagements. In retrospect, these were tit-for-tat border skirmishes with no clear objective. Equally interesting were assessments by Brigadier General Abd al-Jawad Thanun, GMID director, that the Iranians were reacting defensively. There was no sense in his analysis that an Iranian conventional offensive was in the offing. Nevertheless, the artillery duel near the obscure towns of Zain-al-Qawa and Saif Saad on 4 September 1980 provided the official excuse for Iraq's decision to invade, a decision that Saddam had been mulling over throughout the summer.[27]

Referring to the 1975 Algiers Agreement, Saddam announced to his senior advisors on 16 September that "we gave Iran all the time to return

---

attacks on security posts and patrols and sorties." SH-GMID-D-000-663, Studies About Iranian Military Activities During the Iran–Iraq War, February 1985.

[24] Intelligence Report from the GMID to the Bureau of Operations (September 1980) in SH-GMID-D-000-332, Summaries and Intelligence Reports for the General Military Intelligence Directorate (GMID), September 1980–May 1985.

[25] Ibid.

[26] Tom Cooper and Farzad Bishop, Iran–Iraq War in the Air: 1980–1988 (Atglen, PA, 2000), 68.

[27] According to the former head of Iraqi military intelligence, Wafiq al-Samarra'i (defected in 1994), a high-level military committee was working on contingency plans for war with Iran as early as January 1978. Phebe Marr, The Modern History of Iraq (Boulder, CO, 2004), 183.

the land, but the Iranians did not return it according to the agreement . . . [Now] we have to gain it back with the blood of our soldiers and by force. Where we have the ability to return what is [rightfully ours], we will do it."[28] The next day, Saddam dramatically tore up the agreement: "This shall again be, as it has been throughout history, Iraqi and Arab in name and reality, with all the rights of full sovereignty over it."[29] While the evidence now available suggests the skirmishes were more a convenient excuse for war, questions still remain. However, it is clear that the Iraqi leadership had no doubts about the ultimate outcome of the conflict. They firmly believed Iraq's military forces would quickly smash Iran's military forces and bring about the overthrow of Khomeini's regime.

The decision for war

On 22 September 1980, Iraq's major military operations against Iran began. The start date underlines how quickly the relations between the two powers had collapsed since spring 1979. The fault for setting the conditions for the conflict lay on both sides: each had been dabbling in its neighbor's internal affairs, both out of a sense of opportunity and fear. Saddam had sent agents into Khuzestan and financed covert "resistance" groups under names like "Arabistan Liberation Front" with the hope of taking advantage of the unrest among the Arabs there.[30] The Iranians had been none too happy about Iraq's efforts to stir up trouble in that area, especially because this was where much of their oil wealth lay. But, regardless of who violated what part of the 1975 Algiers Agreement first, Tehran should not have been surprised that, in response to increasing Iranian support for Iraqi Shi'a groups, Iraq would support Iran's restive minorities, in this case, somewhat ironically, Iran's own Shi'a Arabs. As noted, there were compelling reasons for Iraq to avoid a conflict with Iran, but caution was not Saddam's hallmark, especially when it came to protecting his regime or making his place in history. Nor was it a mark of the Shah's successors in protecting their vision of an

---

[28] SH-SHTP-A-000-835, Meeting between Saddam Hussein, the National Command, and the Revolutionary Command Council Discussing the Iraq–Iran War, 16 September 1980.

[29] Sandra Mackey, *The Reckoning, Iraq, and the Legacy of Saddam Hussein* (New York, NY, 2002), 251.

[30] For the Iranian view on these Iraqi activities, see *SH-MISC-D-001-350, *The Passing of Two Years of War: Iran–Iraq*, Political Office of the Islamic Revolution Pasdaran Corps. See also SH-GMID-D-000-620, People of Arabistan (Arabs in Southern Iran) in Al-Ahwaz Area Calling for Independence, 1979; Ibrahim Anvari Tehrani, "Iraqi Attitudes and Interpretation of the 1975 Agreement," in *The Iran–Iraq War: The Politics of Aggression*, Farhang Rajaee, ed. (Gainesville, FL, 1993), 20.

Islamic Republic spreading its influence over the Middle East and eventually the world.[31]

On the eve of the invasion in a conversation with Saddam, Izzat al-Duri, an intimate confidant, placed the decision for war in the context of the regime's historic mission:

> This is our chance. This is an historical chance … It does not mean that we get back the Shatt al-Arab … It means a whole lot more than [that] … Through this Iraq can take big steps … whether they are within Iraq or the [Arab] nation. Benefits include building the armed forces for the Arab nation and the Arabs. This [war] will elevate [the Arab nation's] psychological level and its spiritual level, and its military and technical level to an elite level. We will save a lot of time [in achieving our goals].[32]

On the risks involved, al-Duri added, "My personal belief is that Iran will not [fight] in a vast way. If they react in a big way, how far are they going to go[?]" Saddam then added sarcastically, "in other words do they have the brains to fight us, while they are in this bad military condition?"[33]

In strategic terms, the situation had forced Saddam temporarily to replace the Israelis with the Iranians as his primary enemy. He also seems to have been willing to accept that, until the Arabs were united under his leadership and possessed their own nuclear weapons, there could be no real fight against the Zionists. Military calculations aside, one can argue that Saddam was acting in accord with his family's attitudes toward the Israelis and Persians. As Saddam's maternal uncle and father-in-law, Khairallah Talfah had written a generation earlier, "many people say that Palestine must be dealt with first … That is true – and yet I say: Iran is bigger in the heart of the Arabs, therefore it must be removed so that the Arabs can regain their health … As the old proverb has it: 'He who lives with us is the worst thief.'"[34]

---

[31] As one scholar noted, "[e]xporting revolution was also a tactical maneuver to intimidate the Arab states into not siding with Iraq, to orchestrate a regional Shi'a awakening, to train a new generation of Arab Shi'a activists, and to elevate Khomeini as the ideological hegemon of the region." Mohsen M. Milani, "Iran's Persian Gulf Policy in the Post-Saddam Era," in *Contemporary Iran: Economy, Society, Politics*, Ali Gheissari, ed. (Oxford, 2009), 351.

[32] SH-SHTP-A-000-835, Meeting between Saddam Hussein, the National Command, and the Revolutionary Command Council Discussing the Iraq–Iran War, 16 September 1980.

[33] *Ibid.* This position was supported by Saddam's most recent intelligence reports on the state of Iran's military. See SH-GMID-D-000-842, General Military Intelligence Directorate (GMID) Intelligence Report on Iran, January–June 1980.

[34] Arshin Adib-Moghaddam, "Inventions of the Iran–Iraq War," *Critique: Critical Middle Eastern Studies* 16, no. 1 (2007), 69.

In September 1980, Saddam believed Iraq's military forces were quantitatively and qualitatively superior to Iran's. Nevertheless, the Iraqis were not entirely ignorant of the regional risks. One of Saddam's advisors warned that rallying the Arabs would be difficult because "they are either spectators rejoicing [in] the misfortune [of others], or they are paid conspirators ... I do not expect, as the president [Saddam] mentioned, that the Arab regimes will help us."[35] He then added that much of Iraq's oil infrastructure was, at present, within reach of the Iranian military and its artillery.

Saddam replied that "both of our [oil installations] might burn. This is war. You cannot say during a war that I have a guarantee [that] my oil [installations] will not burn. When our [installations] are on fire, theirs will be on fire too."[36] Turning to military operations with a comment that underlined his general ignorance of war as well as his own army's capabilities, he addressed the minister of war:

[W]hat is stopping us from moving forward on all axes and surrounding Iran's armies and capturing them? ... No one is saying there [will be] no resistance; no one is saying there will be no losses, or dead. The result of our military calculations is that we will be able to reach the heart of Iran ... They might skirmish with us, a plane might come and we will shoot it down ... However, once a plane attacks Baghdad, then that is that. It is over and done with.[37]

Reinforcing Saddam's belief that the upcoming war would be easy was the fact that Iran was exposed and for once historically vulnerable. Such a situation seemed to invite simplistic military concepts. As one Iraqi former general suggested to the authors:

The Iraqi leadership figured that if the Iraqi Army advanced 10–20 kilometers deep into Iran along the borders, Khomeini would have to send [Iranian] forces from the surrounding area of Tehran to the borders. This would leave Tehran exposed and give the opportunity to the Mehdi Bazargan group to revolt against the religious leadership and gain control of Tehran. So the idea was to bring the militia out of Tehran to weaken the revolution for a counter-revolution.[38]

On the military side, the best units of Iran's regular army had deployed to the northwest of the country against a low-level insurgency among the Iranian Kurds. Moreover, in July 1980 a failed coup plot, emerging from

---

[35] SH-SHTP-A-000-835, Meeting between Saddam Hussein, the National Command, and the Revolutionary Command Council Discussing the Iraq–Iran War, 16 September 1980.

[36] *Ibid.*   [37] *Ibid.*

[38] Kevin M. Woods, Williamson Murray, and Thomas Holaday, *Saddam's War: An Iraqi Military Perspective of the Iran–Iraq War*, McNair Paper 70 (Washington, DC, 2009), 31.

the Nozheh Air Base in western Iran, produced yet another round of purges that further crippled Iran's air force. Frontline Iranian units not deployed against the Kurds appeared to be in a general state of disarray. Consequently, military balance favored the Iraqis. An Iraqi intelligence report on the status of the Iranian 92nd Armored Division underlined the unpreparedness of Iran's military forces:

- No tactical troop drilling has been done since the fall of the Shah until the present.
- Seventy-five percent of the tanks in the division are in working order. [However,] maintenance at this time is poor.
- Existing division personnel manning is at 50–55 percent. Because of this it is not possible to move half the force.
- Morale and fighting strength are poor.[39]

Factional struggles, particularly between the ayatollahs and those interested in establishing a secular regime in Tehran, also wracked Iran, which remained isolated internationally. The Iranians continued holding the American Embassy hostages, which deeply angered the United States and provoked broad international reaction. Moreover, throughout summer and fall 1980, relations between Tehran and Moscow steadily deteriorated. For Moscow, the threat of a militant Islamic state on its border combined with Iran's "neither West nor East" foreign policy moved it to reconsider earlier optimism about a "post-American" era in the region. This emerging reality suggested to those in Moscow that Iran possessed a "frustrating disrespect for geopolitical realities and [an] apparent insensitivity toward traditional calculations of its large neighbor's concerns and interests."[40] From Tehran, public denouncements of Soviet policies in Afghanistan, attacks on the Soviets for various injustices imposed on Iran throughout the twentieth century, complaints about Moscow's support for the "fifth column on the soil of our dear country [otherwise known as the Tudeh Party]," and the complaint that while Soviet "utterances are socialistic," its deeds with regard to Iran were "imperialistic" were all grist for Khomeini's propaganda machine.[41] That the ayatollahs marginalized

---

[39] SH-GMID-D-001-427, *GMID Intelligence Report on Iranian Military Capability*, 29 July 1980.

[40] Mohiaddin Mesbahi, "The USSR and the Iran–Iraq War: From Brezhnev to Gorbachev," in *The Iran–Iraq War: The Politics of Aggression*, Farhang Rajee, ed. (Gainesville, FL, 1993), 72.

[41] Foreign Minister Sadeq Qotbzadeh, "Text of Foreign Minister Qotbzadeh's Message to Gromyko, 14 Aug (FBIS-SAS-80-160)," *Foreign Broadcast Information Service Daily Reports* (1980); Alvin Z. Rubinstein, "The Soviet Union and Iran under Khomeini," *International Affairs* 57, no. 4 (1981), 608.

and eventually banned local communists hardly endeared the Islamic Republic to Moscow.[42] Saddam saw opportunity and commented that the Iraqi invasion might actually improve things for the Soviets: "This distraction is good for them in alleviating the American pressure on Afghanistan."[43]

In fact, the Iranian regime discovered just how unpopular in the international arena it had become in the first months of the war. Bani-Sadr complained at the time, "This is the first time in history that a country is being attacked and is supported by no one in the world. It is total isolation and it should make us think. We have to realize that our words and our slogans satisfy no one but us."[44] Meanwhile, with their own agendas, prominent Iranian exiles in Iraq suggested Khomeini's Islamic Republic would quickly collapse with enough of a push.[45] Thus, a combination of apparent Iranian weaknesses, the contemptuous reception Iraq's emissaries had received in Tehran, and Khomeini's active support for terrorists in Iraq led Saddam to seize on what he perceived as a temporary and unique moment. Besides, according to Saddam's calculations, war was all but inevitable: "A peace decision will never be agreed upon [by the ayatollahs]. In other words, the Iranian mentality is more likely to agree on a decision to go to war than to unite over peace."[46] Saddam also calculated that the insecure and enfeebled Iranian regime would have to disengage in order to survive:

We have to put them [the Iranians] in a political and military position so they will say yes ... They [will] have to pull back their army and assume the matter is over and we can [then] do as we please. We cannot stay on the border forever ... The situation is in our favor ... Expect the situation in Iran to change.[47]

---

[42] The uneasy and often deadly struggle between political members of the revolutionary coalition that eventually swept Khomeini to ultimate power continued through early 1983. Eventually, the Tudeh Party was banned by decree in 1983. See Mohsen M. Milani, "Harvest of Shame: Tudeh and the Barzargan Government," *Middle Eastern Studies* 29, no. 2 (1993), 307–320; Maziar Behrooz, *Rebels with a Cause: The Failure of the Left in Iran* (London, 2000), 95–134.

[43] SH-SHTP-D-000-847, Transcripts of a Meeting between Saddam and His Commanders in Regarding the Iran–Iraq War, 30 September 1980.

[44] Marguerite Johnson, Wilton Wynn, and William Stuart, "Persian Gulf: Choosing up Sides," *Time Magazine*, 20 October 1980.

[45] One of the ironies lay in the fact that the Iranian exile community in 1980 was as badly out of touch with the home country as the Iraqi exile community was to prove out of touch with Iraq in 2003.

[46] SH-SHTP-A-000-835, Meeting between Saddam Hussein, the National Command, and the Revolutionary Command Council Discussing the Iraq–Iran War, 16 September 1980.

[47] *Ibid.*

In fact, the Iraqi invasion involved major miscalculations. Not only were the Iraqi armed forces considerably less effective than Saddam anticipated, but also the Iranian regime saw the attack as a test of its own revolution – a test that allowed Khomeini to crush the political opposition to his rule in Iran under the mantra of national defense, and to mobilize the Iranian nation against Iraq. A "divine" defense of the revolution and the nation became the focus of mobilization throughout the Islamic Republic. The regime used slogans to that effect to rally support among the religious and poor throughout the countryside and thus to consolidate its control of Iran's heartland.[48]

In September 1980, Saddam believed Iraq could kill three birds with one stone. First, he thought the war could topple the revolutionary government in Tehran and replace it with a less hostile regime. Second, that change would enhance his standing in the Gulf and Arab world. Third, he would regain control of the Shatt al-Arab, ceded in the 1975 Algiers Agreement.[49]

The battleground

One can divide the war's geography into three distinct areas (see Figure 4.1). In the north, throughout the border between the Iraqi province of Kurdistan and Iran, great mountains rise to heights over 10,000 feet. They run from the Turkish border to Khanaqin. There are few passes, and the mountain valleys are invariably steep. Only light infantry and artillery can operate in the terrain, while supplying even small forces is difficult in summer and almost impossible in winter. The second and central sector is slightly less mountainous with passes through which major forces can move, though with considerable difficulty. Some of the passes lead toward Baghdad, and they have been a major route for invaders throughout history. This central area stretches from Khanaqin to Susangard. Given how close Baghdad was to this frontier, the Iranians were to launch several major attacks here, but the flat plains beyond the mountains provided ideal killing grounds for Iraqi tanks against Iranian light infantry.

The third area lies in the south, running from Susangard to the Gulf. While the ground is more open here than in the north, innumerable irrigation ditches crisscross the landscape, and four major rivers run into

[48] Charles Tripp, *A History of Iraq* (Cambridge, 2000), 233.
[49] Shaul Bakhash, "The Troubled Relationship: Iran and Iraq, 1930–1980," in *Iran, Iraq, and the Legacies of War*, Lawrence G. Potter and Gary G. Sick, eds. (London, 2004), 21–22.

Figure 4.1 Geography of the war

one of the world's great marsh lands. Even beyond the marshes, mobility has historically been a problem. A British veteran of military operations in World War I, South Africa, and China noted in his account of the 1920 insurgency that:

Until one has paid a visit to Mesopotamia and passed a winter and summer there, one is inclined to treat as travelers' tales the difficulty of getting around the country; but in no part of the world where I have been can movement become more quickly difficult or indeed impossible for a time than, after the fall of rain, on the slippery argillaceous soil of that country. I had after my experiences with the Japanese Army in Manchuria in 1904–05, imagined that nothing could exceed the difficulty of transport in summer over its rain-sodden plains, but the ground there was free from the clay which is mixed with sand in Mesopotamia, and the latter country has not the advantage of being frost bound for several months of the year, when nature makes movement, even across broad rivers, easy.[50]

Nevertheless, the area from Basra to the Gulf is relatively open and in the dry season offers good terrain for armored warfare – at least until the rains come.

All in all, most of the border was not ideal for major unit operations. And both sides knew well those areas that were more open, which robbed planners of the possibility for surprise. An important advantage for Iraq was that its bases were close to the frontier, while the geography and road system of the Mesopotamian Valley permitted reinforcements to be moved easily to meet Iranian attacks. The opposite was true on the Iranian side, where there was a lack of good north–south highways. Even worse, the main Iranian bases lay deep in the center of the country, far from the frontier. Iranian deployments to fighting required considerable movement of troops and logistical support.

1980: the air war

Throughout 1980, the Iraqi Air Force conducted increasingly aggressive reconnaissance flights on the Iranian side of the border. Most of the MiG-21R flights focused on key terrain, towns, and transportation centers. Electronic reconnaissance to pinpoint Iranian air defense radar began in June. However, the distances to major Iranian airfields limited the Iraqis to human sources of intelligence to determine the status and strength of squadrons deployed.[51] Beginning in April 1980, the commander of the Iraqi Air Force, Mohammed Jissam al-Jibouri, directed a series of "non-traditional" exercises. These rehearsed a series of non-specific air strikes at the "maximum range of the aircraft." In June 1980, the minister of defense initiated a program to increase the pilot-to-cockpit ratio from 1:1 to 2:1. These and other subtle events made it clear to members of the air force that war was in the offing.[52] Some portion of the hundreds of airspace violations and raids in the Iranian border areas no doubt supported the planning of an air campaign. For the Iraqi military, cancelled leave and classes at military schools signaled what was coming. Nevertheless, despite these preparations, the Iraqi Air Force

[50] Lieutenant General Sir Aylmer L. Haldane, *The Insurrection in Mesopotamia, 1920* (London, 1922; repr., Nashville, TN, 2005), 14–15.

[51] SH-GMID-D-000-516, General Military Intelligence Directorate (GMID) Memos About the Iranian Air Force, January–November 1980.

[52] Translation of Major General Alwan Hassoun Alwan al-Abousi in *Memoir* (Alexandria, Egypt, unpublished 2003).

"was hardly capable of mounting more than 90 sorties per day ... had only a limited combat experience" and the command system lacked experience in such a large-scale operation.[53]

On 22 September 1980, emulating the Israeli opening gambit of the Six-Day War in 1967, the Iraqi Air Force launched a series of preemptive attacks on key Iranian airfields and other targets, heralding Saddam's invasion of Iran.[54] Sloppily planned and executed, the attempt to destroy the Iranian Air Force on the ground failed. Significantly, prewar reconnaissance had focused on border facilities, and the Iraqis had only limited reconnaissance of Iranian air bases before 22 September.[55] Despite a long-running series of exercises, most squadrons were not at a high state of readiness. In fact, on 12 September the commander of what would be the lead squadron in the attack was released to attend Staff College in Baghdad – only to be recalled to his unit a week later. On 20 September, the air force director of movements made the rounds of the main air bases. He departed each after leaving "a large white envelop wrapped with clear nylon paper and tightly sealed" with the base commanders. The aircrews were informed that another large training exercise was planned for the 22nd.

On the evening of 21 September, squadron commanders opened the sealed envelopes and discovered the details of the strike plans with the targets. In addition to discovering they were attacking Iran, squadron commanders also discovered the air force command in Baghdad had miscalculated fuel requirements. Had they adhered to these orders, returning aircraft would have run out of fuel before reaching their home bases, because bomb loads were too heavy.[56] After hasty consultations with Baghdad, local commanders reduced bomb loads to manageable levels. Aircrews were briefed at 1030 on 22 September that they would cross the frontier at 1200 and strike their targets not later than 1230.

---

[53] Cooper and Bishop, *Iran–Iraq War in the Air*, 72.

[54] Iraq's initial target set included eight airbases, five airports, several early warning and command facilities, four army bases, and three oil facilities. Cooper and Bishop, *Iran–Iraq War in the Air*, 72.

[55] SH-GMID-D-000-516, General Military Intelligence Directorate (GMID) Memos About the Iranian Air Force, January–November 1980; *SH-AADF-D-001-316, Various Reports and Memoranda from the Air Force and Air Defense Command Relating to Iraqi Reconnaissance and Iranian Incursions into Iraqi Air Space, 1980.

[56] The plans, drawn up in Baghdad, prescribed a 2-ton bomb load. In most cases, this combat load would have left the aircraft short of fuel for the return trip. Only a last-minute plea by wing and squadron commanders convinced Baghdad to authorize swapping two 500kg bombs for drop fuel tanks. Kevin M. Woods, Williamson Murray, Elizabeth A. Nathan, Laila Sabara, and Ana M. Venegas, "Interview with (Former) Major General 'Alwan Hassoun 'Alwan Al-Abousi, Cairo, Egypt, 13 November 2009," *Project 1946: Phase II* (Alexandria, VA, 2010).

Thus, two hours after being informed that they were going to war, Iraqi aircraft swept into Iran at 800 kilometers per hour at altitudes of 50 meters and then climbed steeply on approach to their targets. The aircrews were generally surprised at the scale of the Iranian bases. "It was much bigger than the way it appeared in the plans sent to us" was how a Su-22 squadron commander remembered the attack.[57] Some Iranian aircraft were in bunkers and others lined up along taxi-ways, but the attackers were under orders to bomb the runways, where they did little damage.[58] What damage they inflicted was quickly repaired by Iranian airfield repair crews, who had been well trained and equipped by the Americans for just such a contingency.[59]

The fact that the Iraqis failed to launch even 250 sorties during the day – whereas the Israelis had launched 700 sorties on the first day of the 1967 War – partially explains the lack of success.[60] The Iraqis came in two waves: the first with 190 aircraft, the second with 60. The attackers destroyed a few aircraft on the ground and lightly damaged a number of others. Given the Iranians' general unpreparedness to meet the blow (despite the fact that a major crisis was brewing), it is difficult to judge who was the more incompetent. The Iraqi failure is partially explicable when one understands that it was a direct result of Saddam's "coup-proofing" of the air force before the war. He had forbidden air-to-ground training below 5,000 feet lest proficiency in such tactics be used in an assassination plot or coup attempt.[61] By and large, the Iranian Air Force escaped the first blow with little serious damage.

Further difficulties in the air almost immediately beset the Iraqis. On 23 September, the Iranians retaliated with a raid comprising 120 F-4Es

---

[57] Woods, et al., "Interview with (Former) Major General 'Alwan Hassoun 'Alwan Al-Abousi, Cairo, Egypt, 13 November 2009."

[58] The Iraqis reportedly had difficulty with bomb fuses and the setting necessary for effective runway-cratering operations. Cooper and Bishop, *Iran–Iraq War in the Air*, 47.

[59] In a conversation later in the month, Saddam noted to his air force commander that, "striking the runways was not a primary goal of the first strike." SH-SHTP-D-000-847, Transcripts of a Meeting between Saddam and His Commanders in Regarding the Iran–Iraq War, 30 September 1980.

[60] On 5 June 1967, the Israeli Air Force destroyed more than 300 Egyptian aircraft, the majority on the ground. The Iraqi failure was due to several reasons according to General Abousi: the Soviet aircraft the Iraqis were using were so cramped that crews could only fly one long-distance mission, nearly all the Iranian aircraft were in shelters, and the Iraqi aircraft did not possess bunker-busting bombs. Woods, et al., "Interview with (Former) Major General 'Alwan Hassoun 'Alwan Al-Abousi, Cairo, Egypt, 13 November 2009."

[61] Anthony H. Cordesman, *The Iran–Iraq War and Western Security, 1984–1987* (London, 1987), 83.

and twenty F-5s, covered by F-14 Tomcats.[62] The attacks cost the Iranians three F-4Es, but the Iranian attackers inflicted substantially greater damage on the Iraqis, striking fifteens targets, destroying twenty aircraft on the ground, and damaging eight airfields.[63] On 24 September, they shot down six Iraqi fighter aircraft, MiG-21s, MiG-23s, and Su-20/22s, with no aircraft lost. The next morning, the Iranians shot down another three Iraqi fighters with no losses. In addition to the strikes launched on Iranian airfields, on 24 September the Iraqis launched a small raid on Kharg Island, Iran's main oil terminal and the location of its most important refineries. However, the distance to the target meant that the attacking aircraft could only carry small bomb loads, and the oil facilities suffered minimal damage. Furthermore, Iran's refineries were not running at full capacity, so the Iranians readily absorbed the damage.[64]

General confusion in the Iraqi air defense system helped Iran's initial attacks. One Iraqi report recounted the failure in somewhat restrained fashion:

In response to the preventive strike by our air force on 22 September 1980 against ... Iranian air fields, the enemy launched an air attack in large numbers against most of our cities, especially vitally important areas of the country. Our air defense experienced some confusion during the enemy's initial actions, especially inside unit and subunit command points. Enemy targets were not detected by air defense systems, and enemy flights approaching vital targets were not reported. A general weakness was the failure of [the] main command posts to inform officers and enlisted men how to distinguish between our aircraft and those of the enemy ... This happened because our subunit commanders rigidly adhered to fire control principles when weapons' firing was restricted rather than free and because enemy approach routes were unknown.[65]

Within a week of starting the war, it was clear to Saddam that his air force had failed to meet his lofty expectations. Despite public pronouncements to the contrary, he told his air force commander, "I tend to believe that our air strikes were not effective."[66] The situation did not improve. In fact during October, Iranian fighters had shot down twenty-five more

---

[62] Barzad Bishop and Jim Laurier, *Combat Aircraft: Iranian F-4 Phantom II Units in Combat* (Oxford, 2003), 20–21.

[63] Cooper and Bishop, *Iran–Iraq War in the Air*, 80.

[64] Martin S. Navias and E. R. Hooton, *Tanker Wars: The Assault on Merchant Shipping During the Iran–Iraq Conflict, 1980–1988* (London, 1996), 27.

[65] *SH-AADF-D-001-317, Activities of the Iraqi 3rd Air Defense Sector, 4 September 1980–2 September 1987.

[66] SH-SHTP-D-000-847, Transcripts of a Meeting between Saddam and His Commanders in Regarding the Iran–Iraq War, 30 September 1980.

Iraqi aircraft.[67] By the end of the month, Iranian F-14s had come close to establishing air superiority over the border with their Iraqi opponents intimidated and unwilling to engage in air-to-air combat.

Perhaps more disturbing to Saddam than the failure of the initial strikes were reports of cowardice, when Iraqi pilots failed to execute missions and in some cases even refused to take off. On 30 September 1980, in conversation with his minister of defense, Saddam issued an order that underlined his anger. Not surprisingly, given the Ba'ath regime's operating principles, it involved draconian punishments:

According to my authority those pilots who refuse to fulfill their duty should be executed. You need to leave now; take an officer with you and a presidential decree to execute them will be issued tomorrow. So far we have not downed even one aircraft; the pilot takes off and lands, while the pilots of the enemy are like rockets raiding us. Six of their aircraft raid and only one goes back and [yet] they keep raiding us.[68]

On 30 September, the Iranians launched a large air strike against a power generation complex southeast of Baghdad. Two aircraft broke off from the main attack and struck the nearby Osirak reactor project, the center of Iraq's nuclear program.[69] The operation appeared to be well planned and complex. Iraqi air defense failed to react, perhaps overcompensating for earlier fratricide incidents. While the attack failed to destroy the construction on the reactor or any key components, it did damage the site. In conversation with Saddam soon after, his staff was unsure whether the covering aircraft for the raid were F-14s or F-16s.[70] During the discussion, the deputy chief of the general staff for operations plaintively asked whether any Iraqi fighters had intercepted the Iranians and whether a dogfight had occurred. He was told no. Saddam and his advisors then moved on to the need to increase drastically the production of sandbags, so that the reactor could be protected against future attacks.

---

[67] Tom Cooper and Chris Davey, *Combat Aircraft: Iranian F-14 Tomcat Units in Combat* (Oxford, 2004), 24–28.

[68] SH-SHTP-D-000-847, Transcripts of a Meeting between Saddam and His Commanders in Regarding the Iran–Iraq War, 30 September 1980. In this same transcript, the minister of defense assured Saddam that they had already begun executing pilots who failed in their duty.

[69] It is unclear if the strike on 30 September was deliberate or a target of opportunity the crews at the time decided upon. See Cooper and Bishop, *Iran–Iraq War in the Air*, 91–93. The main reactors under construction (Tammuz I and II) were being built under French contracts dating to 1976. Mysterious calamities, such as destruction of crucial components before delivery and the murder of a key scientist, delayed the project until the Israeli strike in 1981 wrecked the entire effort. For more on the Israeli attack, see Chapter 5 of this book.

[70] The implication of this point is that if F-16s were involved, then the Israelis were in collaboration with Iran.

A senior military advisor commented, perhaps in defense of the air force, that intelligence was reporting that "according to their information, Iranian aircraft [are displaying Iraqi insignia] ... to mislead our troops." The minister of defense finally introduced a modicum of sanity by remarking, "Tell them ... a MiG does not look like a Phantom."[71]

Air defense was an early and persistent problem for the Iraqis. Not only were there insufficient resources to cover a large number of fixed sites, but also the combination of poor training and command and control made fratricide a serious threat to Iraqi pilots. Early in the war, radio transmissions of "national songs" were used to alert Popular Army units on rooftop air defense duty. Even then, the air defense units were directed to open fire only after they saw missiles being fired on aircraft or when aircraft bombed a nearby target. But for Saddam, the reporting of air defense success was an early lesson in the difference between raw reporting and intelligence analysis. In mid-October, after being briefed that the Iranians had 350 serviceable planes of an estimated 500 at the start of the war, Saddam reminded everyone that his air defense staff had already told him that Iraq had shot down more than 200 planes! "Do [the Iranians] have a plane hatchery?" he sarcastically asked. The problem, explained the staff officer, was that some air defense units count an aircraft destroyed even when one of the Iraqi air defense "rockets exploded." The rest of the discrepancy came from the reports of several air defense batteries firing on the same target: "everyone claims that they shot down the plane when it was only one plane."[72]

One additional aspect of air defense troubled Saddam in these opening months of the war. Beginning in late 1979, the United States and Saudi Arabia began discussing the possibility of stationing American-manned Airborne Warning and Control System (AWACS) aircraft in the kingdom. The backdrop of the discussion, at least on the American side, had much to do with Cold War fears of Soviet expansionism and the loss of a stable Western-oriented security guarantee over the Gulf given the revolution in Iran. Discussions were still ongoing when Iraq invaded. On 30 September, the United States deployed four AWACS, two tanker aircraft, and 300 personnel to Dhahran Air Force Base in Eastern Saudi Arabia.[73] Their mission was to monitor the air approaches to the

---

[71] SH-MISC-D-000-827, Saddam and Senior Iraqi Officials Discussing the Conflict with Iran, Iraqi Targets and Plans, a Recent Attack on the Osiraq Reactor, and Various Foreign Countries, 1 October 1980.

[72] SH-SHTP-D-000-846, General Command of the Armed Forces Meeting Transcripts During the First Gulf War, 17 October 1980.

[73] Anthony H. Cordesman and Abraham R. Wagner, *The Lessons of Modern War, Volume II: The Iran–Iraq War* (Boulder, CO, 1990), 103.

kingdom and provide early warning of possible Iranian attacks. According to the plan, potential threats could then be handled by Saudi Arabia's new fleet of American F-15 aircraft. Saddam did not see things in quite the same way. On 17 October, his air force commander notified him that "we monitored their (AWACS) plane flying about 70 kilometers south of the neutral zone ... our electronic surveillance equipment detected the plane at about four to ten kilometers," adding that the Americans were "specifically monitoring the war zone."[74] Saddam's response indicates a legitimate concern, but one grounded in his belief that the United States was not to be trusted. He added,

call the Saudi ambassador and tell him, "You said that your planes come to defend us and warn us if the Iranian planes are on a mission to attack us, but according to our radar records your planes are American (AWACS). They are monitoring the operations zone and we do not feel safe from such a procedure ... We are afraid that the collected information will go to the Iranians in one way or another. This implies that these planes are operating against us. We hope you have full control over the operation of these planes ... the situation now relates to our security."[75]

Even as Iraq's air force was struggling to achieve its *sine qua non* mission of protecting Iraqi air space, Saddam was pushing for strikes against a larger number of strategic targets in Iran. This desire may have been in response to Iran's attack on Osirak. In early October, he pressed for attacks against dams north of Tehran in hopes of flooding the Iranian capital. The lack of specific data for the mission was clearly of secondary concern to the dictator:

SADDAM:	Would [bombing] the dams flood Tehran?
PLANNING DIRECTOR:	... it would not be the magnitude that your Excellency is pointing to.
SADDAM:	Would it flood it?
PLANNING DIRECTOR:	No Sir.
SADDAM:	Are there any power plants on [the dam]?
PLANNING DIRECTOR:	Yes, there is one power plant on it sir.

[74] SH-SHTP-D-000-846, General Command of the Armed Forces Meeting Transcripts During the First Gulf War, 17 October 1980. The AN/APY-2 radar on the AWACS could monitor airborne targets to ranges exceeding 250 miles – well into the southern front of the war zone.

[75] *Ibid.* Saddam went on to say that the Saudi's needed to direct their AWACS operations to the Gulf States and southern Saudi Arabia and away from Iraq. In keeping with the confusion over the US position on the war at this point, the Central Intelligence Agency released a warning on 14 November 1980, saying "There is also a danger that US forces in the area could be attacked – either deliberately or in error – by the Iranians. Tehran has already accused the United States of supplying intelligence collected by the AWACS aircraft to Iraq." "The Director of Central Intelligence, Alert Memorandum: Iran–Iraq: Danger of a Wider War, 14 November 1980 (Declassified)," in *CWIHP Critical Oral History Conference: The Carter Administration and the "Arc of Crisis": 1977–1981: Document Reader*, Malcolm Byrne, ed. (Washington, DC, 2005).

SADDAM:	Then let us strike it, we are not losing anything if Tehran flooded or not, the damage would be in the power plant.
PLANNING DIRECTOR:	Okay sir, [but] until we have the complete information about it . . .
SADDAM:	. . . to be confirmed as a target tomorrow . . . tomorrow it should be a target for our air force . . .
PLANNING DIRECTOR:	Yes sir.[76]

During the same meeting, the minister of defense, General Adnan Khair-allah, blasted the air force commander upon learning that some of his aircraft were returning to Iraq with their bomb loads after not finding their targets:

[T]his is a war brother and as you know they [the Iranians] did not spare the children, the electricity, or any civilian target . . . hospital . . . and military targets. I want you to let all of [your pilots] know, if they cannot find their assigned target and still have their load to strike any target . . . okay . . . inform all of them . . . We must strike the enemy hard.[77]

Yet, the realities of sustaining offensive and defensive air operations forced a modicum of realism into Iraqi calculations. In reaction to Iran's success attacking Iraq's airfields, Saddam ordered some of his aircraft to disperse to bases in other Arab countries in the Gulf. Some of what appeared to be just a defensive dispersal plan was part of an aborted plan to extend the operational striking range of Iraqi aircraft by using Arab bases on the southern shores of the Gulf.[78] Nevertheless, losses had reached such a level by early 1981 that Saddam effectively ordered a halt to risky air operations for nearly two months. By then, the dictator was

---

[76] SH-PDWN-D-001-021, Transcripts of Meetings between Saddam and Top Iraqi Officials and Officers Regarding Iran–Iraq War Tactics Such as the Use of Napalm and Cluster Bombs, 6 October 1980. Targeting Iranian dams was an early and long-standing requirement for the Iraqi Air Force. For an example, see *SH-GMID-D-001-318, Iraqi Air Reconnaissance Reports of Iranian Dams, 22 September 1981.

[77] SH-PDWN-D-001-021, Transcripts of Meetings between Saddam and Top Iraqi Officials and Officers Regarding Iran–Iraq War Tactics Such as the Use of Napalm and Cluster Bombs, 6 October 1980.

[78] *Ibid.* Within the first week of the war, Iraq deployed aircraft to airfields in Saudi Arabia, Yemen, and Oman. On dispersion, see also Dilip Hiro, *The Longest War: The Iran–Iraq Military Conflict* (London, 1989), 41. In a transcript of a meeting the week before, Saddam and his senior commanders discuss Iraqi Air Force plans for operations against Iran originating from or recovering to airfields in Yemen, Oman, and Saudi Arabia. SH-SHTP-D-000-847, Transcripts of a Meeting between Saddam and His Commanders in Regarding the Iran–Iraq War, 30 September 1980. It appears that US diplomatic pressure and the prospect of access to AWACS data played some role in convincing Iraq's neighbors to not allow Iraqi air operations from their territories. Such actions, the United States feared, could expand the war and, ultimately, Iraqi dominance in the Gulf. See Zbigniew Brzezinski, "NSC Weekly Report #157, 10 October 1980 (Declassified)," in *CWIHP Critical Oral History Conference: The Origins, Conduct, and Impact of the Iran–Iraq War, 1980–1988: Document Reader*, Malcolm Byrne and Christian Ostermann, eds. (Washington, DC, 2004).

excusing the performance of his "eagles" with the comment that "We will not use our air force. We will keep it. Two years hence our air force will be in a position to pound [the Iranians]."[79]

1980: the ground war

On 22 September, and despite the failure of the initial air strikes, Iraqi ground forces also crossed the border in strength and advanced along three general axes.[80] Altogether, the Iraqis launched six largely uncoordinated drives into Iran, none of which were mutually supporting. The primary thrusts generally moved into the southern Iranian province of Khuzestan and seemingly aimed at separating the Shatt al-Arab from Iran proper to establish a territorial buffer on the southern frontier (see Figure 4.2). Intense shelling and aerial bombardment made short work of Iranian oil installations, petro-chemical plants, and port facilities.

The corps and division commanders had received few details about how operations in a war with Iran might unfold or what the goals might be. In retrospect, the invasion appears to have rested on no overall military plan or conception, nor is there evidence of clear objectives.[81] Instead, the army wandered into Khuzestan in the apparent belief that the invasion would be sufficient, and that matters would sort themselves out on the battlefield. Saddam had high hopes for major military victories in the first days. Two days after the invasion began, he suggested to a meeting of senior commanders, "What we want, we don't want them to escape. If there are people surrounded, we want to capture them and slaughter them." He then urged them to inflate the numbers of prisoners the Iraqis had captured in the first two days of fighting, "We didn't have to say 129 prisoners of war; we should say hundreds. Any number [that] exceeds [a] hundred is [to be] called hundreds. We should say hundreds that will trigger a light in the soldier's psychology."[82]

[79] Major General Edward B. Atkeson (USA retired), "Iraq's Arsenal: Tool of Ambition," *Army* (March 1991), 24.

[80] Major General Aladdin Hussein Makki Khamas, one of the more sophisticated professional officers in the army, indicated to the authors he believed each of the eleven divisions in the invasion moved out on separate axes with no coherent operational goals in mind and with little coordination among the attacking units. Woods, *et al.*, "Interview with Major General (Ret) Aladdin Hussein Makki Khamas, Cairo, Egypt, 11 November 2009."

[81] *Ibid.*

[82] Transcript of a Meeting Held in the Directorate of Military Movement (24 September 1980) in *SH-MISC-D-001-319, Transcript of a Meeting Held in the Directorate of Military Movement, 24 September 1980.

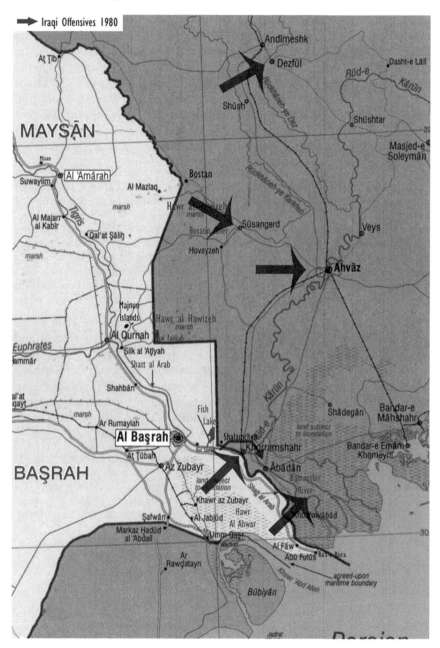

Figure 4.2 Southern battlefield, Iraqi offensives, 1980

Despite the long-running increase in tensions and the cross-border operations, the Iraqis' initial ground assault caught the Iranians by surprise. The latter had only police and militia units in the immediate border areas. Early prisoner of war (POW) reports from interrogations of captured Iranians reinforced prewar intelligence estimates of chaos throughout Khomeini's military forces. A captured Iranian colonel told Iraqi interrogators that 90 percent of the army did not support the new regime.[83] But it was not so much surprise that damaged the Iranians as it was the general lack of training and preparation of Khomeini's *Pasdaran*. A history of that organization records:

At the time of the Iraqi invasion, the only military academy . . . [we] had attended was the war front in the mountains of Kurdistan. Some of our brothers were moved from there to the south with very little military experience. After the war started, the rest attended their academy [in battle] in the deserts of Khuzestan . . . One of the [*Pasdaran*] corps commanders said . . . "in Khuzestan's desert we were able to confront the Iraqi forces with no special [military training], we had not heard the sound of artillery, we did not have combat seasoned commanders, we did not have combat support or the required material for a front this large . . . When this war was imposed on us, we moved from stage to stage with lots of hardships."[84]

The initial results were not surprising: a general advance of Iraqi forces unhindered (see Figures 4.3 and 4.4 for the advance in the central and northern battlefields). Saddam's inner-circle celebrated early successes as a validation of the larger Ba'ath agenda and their assessments of Iranian impuissance. They understood that Iraq was now at war with a country three times its size, but the implications that events would not unfold according to Iraqi logic was only beginning to come into view. A discussion in mid-October between members of Saddam's war cabinet makes that clear:

COMMANDER OF THE AIR FORCE:	Yesterday . . . it occurred to me that those devils [Iran's revolutionary leaders] want to completely destroy their armed forces [which they will do] if they continue with their determination. [After] this they will have no one to challenge them and the Mullahs will be the only decision makers . . .
TARIQ AZIZ:	Today, we had a [propaganda] broadcast with this same meaning.
COMMANDER OF THE AIR FORCE:	. . . their determination is unrealistic!

---

[83] Memorandum from GMID Southern Area Intelligence System to GMID Section 2 No SH/Q/12/261 (19 July 1980) in *SH-GMID-D-001-306, Memoranda from GMID Regarding Prisoners of War, Circa Mid to Late 1980.

[84] *SH-MISC-D-001-350, *The Passing of Two Years of War: Iran–Iraq*, Political Office of the Islamic Revolution Pasdaran Corps.

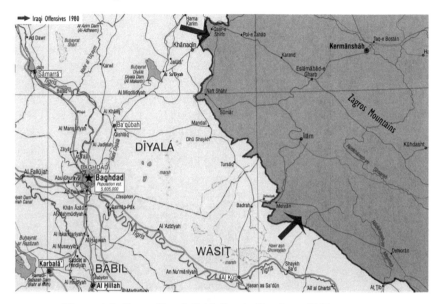

Figure 4.3 Central battlefield, Iraqi offensives, 1980

TARIQ AZIZ:	Any leadership that cared for their army would have stopped the combat two weeks ago, but [Iran's] leadership does not care for their army.
COMMANDER OF THE AIR FORCE:	Not only their army, but also their people …
TARIQ AZIZ:	We transmitted a [propaganda] broadcast and I wrote it myself. I told them [the Iranians] that "Khomeini deceived you when he promised that he would win in a war with Iraq. When he loses, he will not acknowledge that until the last officer and soldier are gone … no tanks are left for use in an uprising and only Khomeini guards will be in control of the situation in Iran."[85]

Despite the generally good news from the front, Saddam was often less than enthralled with the combat performance of Iraqi troops. On 30 September, he was informed that the 30th Armored Brigade had suffered heavy losses. In a situation often repeated across the front, Iraqi armored forces had deployed without infantry in forward, fixed locations. In addition, losses in night fighting were already a serious concern. When

[85] SH-SHTP-D-000-846, General Command of the Armed Forces Meeting Transcripts During the First Gulf War, 17 October 1980.

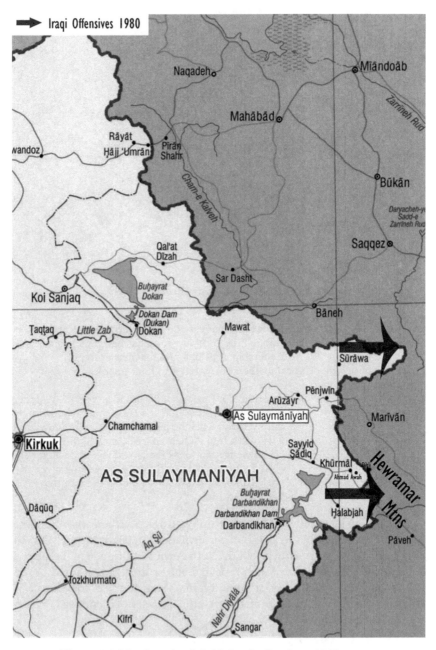

Figure 4.4 Northern battlefield, Iraqi offensives, 1980

challenged by Saddam to explain these losses, the army's chief of staff noted "it appears [the Iranians] know the area."[86]

Within a few weeks, as the reality of the war settled in, Saddam encountered another challenge to his conception of war. It seems that Iraqi troops had a tendency to break when pressured. Saddam referred to it as "the Iraqi spirit I always feared." Tariq Hamed al-Abdullah, head of the presidential secretariat, agreed and added "that is why our mobile defense fails ... We always [abandon] land." Saddam then continued:

I wish we [had been] successful in reaching our goals quickly in [those] first few days. But there was a gap. When units that had not been in combat before fought in the front lines, they were surprised when the enemy fought back and stopped ... and that is why we must arrange to bring the enemy in gradually ... We will deceive them in order to force them to attack ... so that we can drain them and demoralize them.[87]

Khorramshahr

It was not just the tactical issues that gave Saddam pause during those first weeks. In a conversation in October with senior military leaders, the deputy chief of the general staff for operations reported that "the information is that our troops reached [the] Karun River and control the naval base ... They are trying to cross to the other bank, [but] it seems they couldn't make it." Saddam intervened: "We gave instructions to the army chief of staff; we told him that we wanted to seize [ground]. We don't want to [take] a city, therefore destroy the city on their heads." The minister of defense admitted that the top-down leadership from Baghdad was not working all that well. "I would like to understand [why] since for 12 days we [have been] stressing [the importance] of bridging and crossing the Karun River, but no one listens." The conversation then turned to the use of Katyusha rockets (a World War II Soviet tactical rocket) to blast Khorramshahr.[88] Delighted to display his expertise as a connoisseur of World War II documentaries, Saddam waxed eloquent about the impact of Katyushas, "I just want to focus the fire on

---

[86] SH-SHTP-D-000-847, Transcripts of a Meeting between Saddam and His Commanders in Regarding the Iran–Iraq War, 30 September 1980.
[87] SH-PDWN-D-000-566, Saddam Meeting with the General Command of the Armed Forces About the Iran–Iraq War, October–November 1980.
[88] The navy, which had placed Katyusha rockets on two of its landing craft, participated in the bombardment. Woods et al., "Interview with (Former) Lieutenant General Abid Mohammed Al-Kabi, Cairo, Egypt, 12 November 2009."

Abadan ... We want to destroy them, we want their casualties to be as high as when air bursts fall on those who are in the streets."[89]

The Iraqis appear to have believed that a line drawn on a map connecting the towns of Musian, Susangard, Ahvaz, and Khorramshahr would bind the territory they seized in the opening weeks of the offensive and allow them to construct an effective line of defense. They failed, however, to consider the strategic importance of the main highway that lay behind those towns. Controlling it would be essential for the Iranians in preparing their counter-attacks during the coming two years.[90] Even more serious was the failure of Iraqi units to drive on as quickly as possible to the northeast to seal the mountain passes from which Iranian forces moving southwest from Tehran would have to debouch and through which their logistics would flow. Again, there were neither operational nor strategic objectives for the offensive.

Furthermore, senior commanders seemed incapable of providing clear directions to the conduct of operations. They had no clear idea of the campaign's objectives, and for which, given the nature of the regime they served, they were not about to ask. The dichotomy at the strategic level between means and ways was mirrored at the tactical level. Memoirs of an Iraqi officer capture the general level of chaos and lack of military pre-paredness in one of the newer invading divisions: "My initial perception was that the morale and effectiveness of these men were high, but that they formed a disorganized lot lacking the kind of expertise that I [had seen] the night before in the [headquarters] of the 3rd Armored Division."[91]

Nothing demonstrates the disconnect between the thinking in Baghdad and battlefront reality more than Saddam's hope that Iraq might gain a substantial portion of Khuzestan and its oil fields. On one hand, in a meeting with his senior officers in late November 1980, the dictator sug-gested the Iraqis needed to use the velvet glove in dealing with the local Arab tribes in the region. For the benefit of his staff, he noted that Khuzestan should be an autonomous region "closely linked with Iraq." He warned the head of military intelligence that, based on Iraq's experience with the Kurds, Iraq needed to take a "human[e] approach" with the local Arabs in that area: "if a garden is smashed by [our] tanks, they [should] receive a monetary compensation for such losses of up to four times the original worth."[92]

[89] SH-PDWN-D-000-566, Saddam Meeting with the General Command of the Armed Forces About the Iran–Iraq War, October–November 1980.
[90] Woods, *et al.*, "Interview with (former) Lieutenant General Ra'ad Hamdani," Amman, Jordan, 6–7 November 2009.
[91] Translation of Lieutenant General Ra'ad Majid al-Hamdani, *Memoir: From the Golan to the Collapse of Baghdad: Six Wars in Thirty Years* (Baghdad, unpublished 2003).
[92] SH-SHTP-D-000-856, Transcript of a Meeting between Saddam Hussein and His Commanding Officers at the Armed Forces General Command, November 1980.

On the other hand, by then Saddam's own orders had gone a long way toward disabusing the locals of the notion that the Iraqis were their liberators. A few days into the invasion, in a meeting with his advisors, Saddam was told that the 10th Division had captured three Arabs from the area among the POWs it held. He had immediately exclaimed, "Good job, they will be executed today because they are traitors."[93] The 9th Division commander in Khuzestan, Major General Tala al-Duri, a notorious incompetent but brilliant survivor and one of Saddam's favorites, proved particularly enthusiastic in executing the dictator's wishes, shooting large numbers of local Arabs, because they were found with weapons in their possession.[94] The reports of these actions circulated widely among the local tribes and quickly turned them against their Iraqi "liberators."

Initially, the operations on the central and northern fronts were secondary and supportive, designed to secure Iraq against Iranian counterattacks. In the center, Iraqi units occupied Mehran and advanced to the foothills of the Zagros Mountains, supposedly to secure the vital north–south road system. Their lack of drive, however, failed to achieve that goal. In the north, invading forces seized and blocked the traditional Tehran–Baghdad invasion route. Overall, the invading forces encountered no coordinated Iranian resistance, and although not taken by surprise, the Iranian army was unable to deploy for war or react to the invasion with an effective defense.[95]

Despite some difficulties, the Iraqis had made impressive gains, at least in terms of open desert terrain overrun. An Iranian history records:

The Iraqi army very quickly reached its objectives and our [defensive] positions kept falling. Iraqi morale was very high. Their fire power and armor capability was very high, and they felt increasingly stronger to the point that the commander of the Iraqi 10th Armored Division who was fighting in the Shush and Dezful front very proudly and confidently asked Saddam "to give us permission to capture Tehran." On our side poor organization, poor leadership, internal struggles, and other weak points had taken over ... At the onset of the full-scale invasion, the enemy was able to quickly traverse through the Chesaveh Pass, the cities of Bostan and Susangard and advance to [within] one kilometer of Hamidiye.

---

[93] Transcript of a Meeting Held in the Directorate of Military Movement (24 September 1980) in *SH-MISC-D-001-319, Transcript of a Meeting Held in the Directorate of Military Movement, 24 September 1980. It appears that in Saddam's view, because he was the "leader" of the Arab world, any Arabs bearing arms against Iraq were by definition traitors.

[94] Woods, et al., "Interview with (former) Lieutenant General Ra'ad Hamdani."

[95] Edgar O'Ballance, The Gulf War: Nineteen Eighty to Nineteen Eighty-Seven (London, 1988), 36.

There was great danger that the enemy would reach and sever the three main roads Ahvaz-Khorramshahr, Ahvaz-Bostan, and Ahvaz-Andimeshk, which would have put Ahvaz in great peril.[96]

In fact, the Iraqis failed to cut those crucial arteries, which would substantially aid Iranian counterattacks in the future. To the Iraqis it appeared that the tactical setbacks for Khomeini's forces resulted from the fact that everyone and no one was in charge in Tehran. Nor was it clear that there was any Iranian leadership at the front among the units in the border areas. However, the attacking Iraqis were neither able nor willing to exploit Iranian weaknesses. One of the major factors in the sluggishness of the Iraqi advance undoubtedly resulted from Saddam's insistence on monitoring virtually everything occurring on the battlefields.[97]

Success in overrunning Iranian units created the problem of what to do with captured war materiel. At one point, when briefed on the fact that the Iraqi 4th Division had destroyed numerous abandoned Iranian armored vehicles, Saddam responded "what a waste. The price of each tank is 800,000 dinars." The dictator then ordered that the Iraqi military was not to destroy abandoned enemy armor and that the governors of Diyala and Wasit provinces should establish a "civilian service" for the purpose of helping the army "clear out the war spoils" and distribute them throughout Iraq's provinces.[98]

With the Iraqi war machine halted at the outskirts of Ahvaz and Susangard, Saddam appeared willing, at least publicly, to accept the ceasefire proposed by UN Resolution 479 of 28 September 1980. There are some indications he believed Iran was on the verge of collapse and that he was now about to achieve the quick political victory he had hoped for. Nevertheless, in a meeting with Iraqi officers at the end of the month, he commented, "I do not envisage that the war will end. It could stretch on for another year. It is possible it will stretch for six months."[99] In many ways, Saddam's shift from a *Blitzkrieg* to *Sitzkrieg* strategy was working against one of his major objectives, the consolidation of the

---

[96] *SH-MISC-D-001-350, *The Passing of Two Years of War: Iran–Iraq*, Political Office of the Islamic Revolution Pasdaran Corps.

[97] Recordings of Saddam Hussein's meetings with the armed forces high command normally included updates on the current operational situation. Detailed briefings by corps sectors were followed by personal calls from Saddam to corps and division commanders.

[98] SH-PDWN-D-001-021, Transcripts of Meetings between Saddam and Top Iraqi Officials and Officers Regarding Iran–Iraq War Tactics Such as the Use of Napalm and Cluster Bombs, 6 October 1980.

[99] SH-SHTP-A-001-229, Saddam and Military Officials Discussing the Iran–Iraq War and Iraqi Military Capabilities, 30 October 1980.

"Arab nation" under his leadership. In early October, Libya and Syria declared their support for Iran, while other Arab states were announcing "their neutral positions toward the Iran–Iraq struggle," a slight which Saddam informed Kuwait's Prince Jaber "hurts all Iraqis."[100] Thus, he needed a military success, but that success was becoming more and more elusive. It is likely that at some level Saddam was grateful the Iranians turned down the UN Resolution. Their action justified his continuing offensive in order to make highly visible Iraqi gains at the expense of Iraq's Persian enemies clear to the Arab street. If so, Khomeini had not disappointed. In a radio address, the ayatollah announced that there was "absolutely no question of peace or compromise, and we shall never have any discussion with [Saddam's regime] ... we cannot compromise with a perpetrator of corruption. We shall fight against them right to the end."[101]

Not surprisingly, the Iranians also rejected subsequent feelers. Khomeini, motivated by a religious mission and his deep hatred of the Ba'ath regime, decided to continue the war, whatever the initial setbacks to Iranian forces. The conflict was a God-sent gift, because it allowed his supporters to mobilize their strength against the civil-democratic government, which was attempting to run Iran in the shattering aftermath of the Shah's collapse.[102] On 17 October, Iranian Prime Minister Mohammad-Ali Kajai, in what would be his country's last presentation to the UN Security Council for eight years, declared, "the decision of the council, whatever it may be, will not change anything for us, for our people, with the help of God, will fight Saddam and his oppressive regime with their own hands. Our people will win."[103] Khomeini declared that Iran would not stop fighting until the Iraqis had removed Saddam, acknowledged their war guilt, and agreed to pay reparations.[104]

---

[100] Transcript of a Meeting of the General Command of the Armed Forces (10 October 1980) in SH-SHTP-D-000-573, Transcripts of General Command of the Armed Forces Meetings During the First Gulf War and Correspondence with Other Arab Leaders, October 1980.

[101] Ami Ayalon, "The Iraqi-Iranian War," in *Middle East Contemporary Survey, Volume IV: 1979–80*, Colin Legum, ed. (New York, NY, 1981), 21.

[102] Iran's civilian president, Bani-Sadr, was to bitterly attack the religious extremists around Khomeini for undermining the army and "using the war to amass personal power." Roland Tyrrell, "Iran Again Rejects Iraqi Peace Terms," *United Press International*, 19 November 1980.

[103] UNSCOR 2251st Meeting (17 October 1980) cited in Cameron R. Hume, *The United Nations, Iran, and Iraq: How Peacemaking Changes* (Bloomington, IN, 1994), 41.

[104] Ayalon, "The Iraqi-Iranian War," 21. Khomeini "pledged to fight until 'the government of heathens in Iraq topples.'" William Drozdiak, William Stuart, and Spencer Davidson, "War in the Persian Gulf," *Time Magazine*, 6 October 1980.

Reflecting on these events after the war, Saddam's rationale for his error in judgment in believing Khomeini's Islamic Republic would prove a pushover was, as usual, convoluted:

The hardest situation I went through was when we feared that the Iranians would accept our ceasefire suggestion after Muhamarra [Khorramshahr]. We agreed to the decision of the Security Council on the 28th. Do you remember it? On September 28, 1980, we agreed to the Security Council decision [resolution] after six days of a large-scale battle ... Part of the clauses of the resolution was that both parties would agree to an immediate ceasefire and hold negotiations. We agreed, but the Iranians refused. My fear was that the Iranians would agree to this decision after the Muhamarra battle, because that would put us in an awkward position before our people and the world, since we had previously agreed. If we refused, when we would not have had reasons for refusing that would have convinced our people and the world. Even though I know the Iranian mentality, I know they are very devious and are treacherous and play games. When they get a chance to mess things up, they will. So I was hoping that there would not be a ceasefire. For me, that was not the image with which I thought our army should end this war. The appropriate image for our army is to end the war with the Iranians broken and our army strengthened.[105]

In terms of the tactical-level fighting, the performance of Iraqi units was generally superior to that of their opponents. If this were the result of the tactical training they had received since the 1973 conflict or the state of disarray, confusion, and ill discipline among Iran's Army and *Pasdaran* is unclear.[106] But at the operational level (division and corps), Iraqi commanders, many without experience of even brigade command, proved either inept or incompetent. Meanwhile, the higher command in Baghdad, dominated by Saddam, was incapable of providing sensible directions to Iraqi forces. Faced with a paucity of knowledge on either side of the front, ground commanders were giving exaggerated estimates of the strength of the Iranian formations they were confronting. Nevertheless, a stalemate was settling over the front as Iranian reinforcements, *Pasdaran* as well as regular army, were arriving at the front in large numbers by mid-October. Iraq's failure to close the passes leading out of the Zagros Mountains only served to speed the deployment of those reinforcements.

Despite the slowing advance of Iraqi forces, Saddam's enthusiasm for the fight remained unabated. When told of Iran's first public announcements of counterattacks, Saddam commented to Tariq Aziz that Iraq should "insist" that the Iranians attack, as they claim they will, so that "[we can] make them come as an easy meal, then we can vanquish

[105] SH-SHTP-V-000-589, Saddam Hussein and Military Officials Discussing the Iran–Iraq War and the Al-Qadisiyyah Battle, Circa Late 1988.
[106] Interview with Lieutenant General Ra'ad Hamdani, in Woods, *et al.*, *Saddam's War*.

them."[107] A week later, an enthusiastic Aziz remarked to the air force commander that "now is the hunting season for al-Ajam (Persians); if a way can be developed to accelerate the hunt, we do not need prisoners of war."[108]

Despite such enthusiasm, Iraqi aerial reconnaissance struggled to report on Iranian activity. Early in the war, the regime's command post in Baghdad, whence Saddam was running the war, exploded with the dictator's displeasure that aerial reconnaissance had not pinpointed an Iranian division that the 10th Armored Division reported as being deployed to its front. Speaking for Saddam, the air force commander's adjutant, Captain Faruq Ahmed, queried a reconnaissance unit as to why it had not found the Iranian division:

the 10th Armored Division at the sector of Dezful, which there are enemy units in front of it that have become an armored division supported by a battalion of artillery, the artillery battalion of the division is supported by 4–5 additional battalions . . . These units were not seen by you. There were many reconnaissance flights against this division and we received a mission report for each flight . . . It is not acceptable to have this large enemy concentration, which is an armored division plus ten battalions of artillery and when we ask for air reconnaissance, the answer was "Nothing seen in the area." How is that possible? Did the enemies wear invisible hats? Where did they go?[109]

After the first few weeks, *Pasdaran* units bore the brunt of the invasion. Because it was lightly equipped, it could reinforce the battlefront more quickly than the regular army. Late in 1980, Saddam and his senior military advisors discussed reports that the *Pasdaran* was moving tribal levies from the far south of Iran, "individuals unaware of what was going on . . . they did not fear that there was any danger." The reports cited hashish, wine, and beer captured with the Iranian militia as an explanation for the Iranian fanaticism.[110] But events in Khorramshahr seemed

---

[107] Transcript of a Meeting of the General Command of the Armed Forces (10 October 1980) in SH-SHTP-D-000-573, Transcripts of General Command of the Armed Forces Meetings During the First Gulf War and Correspondence with Other Arab Leaders, October 1980.

[108] SH-SHTP-D-000-846, General Command of the Armed Forces Meeting Transcripts During the First Gulf War, 17 October 1980.

[109] SH-PDWN-D-001-021, Transcripts of Meetings between Saddam and Top Iraqi Officials and Officers Regarding Iran–Iraq War Tactics Such as the Use of Napalm and Cluster Bombs, 6 October 1980. The answer might have been either that the Iranian units were figments of the 10th Division commander's imagination, or that due to gross incompetence, Iraqi aerial reconnaissance failed to pick up the location of even portions of an Iranian division.

[110] SH-MISC-D-000-827, Saddam and Senior Iraqi Officials Discussing the Conflict with Iran, Iraqi Targets and Plans, a Recent Attack on the Osiraq Reactor, and Various Foreign Countries, 1 October 1980.

to be forming a logic of their own. A fierce battle had raged over the city's urban terrain, ever since the initial Iraqis attacked in early October. Neither side was prepared to fight in urban terrain, but the Iranians held the advantage by remaining on the defensive, while increasing numbers of *Pasdaran* fighters – willing to fight to the death – arrived from the north. In fact, Saddam had not even wanted his forces to drive into the city, but rather to blast it with artillery fire. In a mid-October discussion with his senior military advisors, Saddam reminded them that "we gave instructions to the army chief of staff. We told him that we wanted to hold the land. We do not want to [take] the city ... Therefore destroy the city on [the Iranians'] heads and don't suffer casualties."[111]

The *Pasdaran's* arrival on the southern front had not been well organized. A *Pasdaran* history of the early war years admits:

At the beginning of the month ... one *Basij* force arrived from Isfahan ... with some of our corps brothers ... in the battle zone by bus. The buses that were carrying the forces without knowing the circumstances, got very close to the Iraqis, and it was not until they came under fire from the enemy that they realized that they had arrived [in the battle zone].[112]

The Iranian history indicates the arriving militia unit then discovered the wreckage of dead and broken equipment from an earlier unit the Iraqis had completely destroyed to the last man. A local Revolutionary Guard commander, Mohammad Jahanara, reportedly offered the following words of comfort to his troops: "Listen guys, everything we have done this far and all our training was for such a day. Of course, 15 days' training course is not enough, but we must demonstrate our power to the enemy."[113] Low-ranking *Pasdaran* soldiers were not the only Iranians ignorant of events at the front. During the first week of November, Iran's oil minister, Muhammad Jawad Baqir, and several of his aides were captured while driving unescorted near the front. During his interrogation, he informed his captors that the Iranian media's "blackout" of military events extended even to the country's ministers.[114]

The Iraqi armored division charged with taking Khorramshahr possessed neither sufficient artillery nor infantry. Nevertheless, its lead units had succeeded in investing the outskirts of the city by mid-September.

---

[111] *Ibid.*
[112] *SH-MISC-D-001-350, *The Passing of Two Years of War: Iran–Iraq*, Political Office of the Islamic Revolution Pasdaran Corps.
[113] Parviz Mosalla Nejad, *The Hub of Resistance Literature and History: Khorramshahr* (Bostan, Iran, 2006), 3. Downloaded from www.sajed.ir/en/content/view/32/201/.
[114] SH-GMID-D-001-025, Interrogation Reports of the Iranian Minister of Oil and His Assistant, 9 September 1980–1 November 1980.

Nevertheless, the initial attacks by tanks of the 3rd Armored Division failed to drive the Iranians out of their defensive positions. At that point, the attacking troops received infantry support from Iraq's special forces brigade. So heavy was the fighting that the Iraqis had to order a three-week pause to retrain the special forces and infantry brought in to reinforce the armor in the house-to-house fighting that was occurring throughout the city.[115] With much of the city in flames and wrecked by seven days of artillery bombardment and with clouds of smoke from the fires in the refineries of Abadan adding to man-made fog hanging over the area, Iraqi tanks fought their way into the city.[116]

The fighting was vicious. Iraqi troops monitoring Iranian radio communications noted appeals from frontline troops "to their commands that they cannot even move ambulance vehicles to evacuate casualties due to heavy artillery [fire]."[117] On the other side of the Shatt al-Arab, Iranian artillery fire destroyed the Iraqi refinery at Fao, causing Saddam to order the evacuation of 70,000 civilians from the city. Khorramshahr fell to the Iraqis on 24 October, by which time both sides had named it *Khunistan* or "city of blood."[118] By the time the battle was over, each side had suffered approximately 7,000 dead and seriously wounded, and the Iraqis had lost more than 100 armored vehicles.[119] Iraqi special forces performed exceptionally well at Khorramshahr, but when the fighting was over few of its soldiers had survived.[120]

Despite its success, Iraq's special forces suffered disproportionate losses that would have a significant impact on their capabilities and utility in the future. After 1980, the army, confronted by its losses as well as the requirements for a massive expansion, would never be in a position to devote high-quality manpower to rebuilding its special forces.[121] Overall, heavy Iraqi losses in taking Khorramshahr reflected the Iraqi military's inability to look beyond the immediate tactical problems at the larger

---

[115] O'Ballance, *The Gulf War*, 38.   [116] *Ibid.*, 37.

[117] SH-GMID-D-001-025, Interrogation Reports of the Iranian Minister of Oil and His Assistant, 9 September 1980–1 November 1980.

[118] Efraim Karsh, *The Iran–Iraq War, 1980–1988* (New York, NY, 2009), 27.

[119] The near equal number of casualties at Khorramshahr suggests a tactical superiority on the part of the Iraqis, because the attacker, particularly in cities, nearly always takes heavier casualties.

[120] Major Kamel Sachet Aziz al-Janabi was one of those feted by the regime for his heroism. He would survive the war, arbitrary imprisonment, redemption, and eventually rise to the rank of general when he commanded the occupation of Kuwait in 1990, only to be executed on Saddam's orders in the 1990s. His story is told in Wendell Steavenson, *The Weight of a Mustard Seed: The Intimate Story of an Iraqi General and His Family During Thirty Years of Tyranny* (New York, NY, 2009).

[121] Interview with Lieutenant General Ra'ad Hamdani, in Woods, *et al.*, *Saddam's War*.

operational picture, such as the fact that it might have been better to have surrounded Khorramshahr and starve the Iranians into defeat, rather than to have their forces fight into and through the city.

While Iraq's soldiers were discovering the difficulty of destroying the fanatical *Pasdaran* in Khorramshahr, Saddam was watching the battle from Baghdad. Less than a month into the war, Tariq Aziz cautioned that "before the international situation changed, Iraq "must gain [its] basic goals." Saddam, the early optimism as Iraqi forces moved into Khorramshahr still prevalent in the headquarters, replied: "Yes ... now the battlefield is from here to here [pointing to a map] ... now we need these two targets [Khorramshahr and Abadan] ... The operation will be excellent ... And if we occupied Dezful – nothing will remain ... Ahvaz will fall spontaneously."[122] The unsettling events around Khorramshahr soon proved a distraction. Saddam noted that the Iraqis had wasted enough time on the city his senior military advisors had called a "secondary priority." The focus needed to be "on Dezful and Ahvaz." Saddam reminded his officers of their error: "After the first attack we were able to occupy [Khorramshahr] without any losses, because our forces entered [the town] and raised the Iraqi flag and [then] left the town. After that the enemy started to assemble in the town. This was a mistake, a real mistake."[123]

Saddam then complained that the lead Iraqi troops were supposed to bypass or surround the city and seize the bridges to Abadan. Popular army units were tapped to take responsibility "for Khorramshahr." His advisors reminded him that in the face of strong resistance, the kind now being offered in Khorramshahr, "the people's army cannot [fight] without the help of the army." The chief of staff informed Saddam that in addition to the commando companies dispatched to "purge" Khorramshahr, the II Corps had sent in several infantry regiments. The director of operations warned that "purging cities is the hardest type of fighting ... The Germans and the Allies were exhausted and suffered much because of this during the Second World War."[124] In the end, the brutal fight for Khorramshahr represented a wakeup call. The dictator's earlier rhetoric about glory suddenly gave way to more somber realism and a candid appeal to the Iraqi people to step up to the challenge of overcoming Iran's "geographical injustice," as well as its superiority in aircraft, artillery, and

---

[122] Transcript of a Meeting of the General Command of the Armed Forces (10 October 1980) in SH-SHTP-D-000-573, Transcripts of General Command of the Armed Forces Meetings During the First Gulf War and Correspondence with Other Arab Leaders, October 1980.
[123] *Ibid.*   [124] *Ibid.*

naval forces. He urged "patience as well as great exertions until the promised triumph was secured."[125]

Almost immediately after taking Khorramshahr, the Iraqis attempted to seize Abadan and its oil refineries. Here they ran into even stronger resistance.[126] Even though the Iraqis had isolated Abadan from land in mid-October, the Iranians moved reinforcements and supplies into the city through the Gulf. Several sharp engagements occurred as the Iranian Navy sought to resupply the desperate defenders. During these skirmishes, the Iraqis lost two Osa missile boats and most of their torpedo boats.[127] The Iraqi Navy did manage to bombard Abadan on several occasions at night from landing craft equipped with Katyusha rocket launchers.[128]

Iraq's offensive against Abadan went nowhere, both because of Iran's ability to reinforce by sea and because the urban fighting in Khorramshahr had exhausted the units involved.[129] Moreover, the Iraqi high command was incapable of shuffling in fresh units to resume the attack on Abadan. Nevertheless, the initial fighting and artillery duels reduced the city to a smoking ruin, while the Iraqi city of Fao across the Shatt al-Arab suffered equally heavily. Despite Saddam's outward confidence, the news from the battlefront was not optimistic. Over a working dinner in early November, the dictator's minister of defense, General Adnan Khairallah, explained the collapse of an Iraqi unit as having been due to "exhaustion" resulting from the recent battles in Khorramshahr. The mechanized unit was operating in swampy terrain and had come under increasing pressure from Iranian infantry. The regimental commander had tried to pull his lead company back, an action "which gave the impression that this [was] the beginning of a withdrawal ... It was impossible to stop it."[130]

---

[125] Ayalon, "The Iraqi-Iranian War," 19.
[126] Interestingly, the assault on Abadan required a river crossing operation. Saddam's military staff had briefed him in detail, and his director of intelligence noted "if the army succeeds, it will be the first [river] crossing operation in the history of the Iraqi Army." Perhaps thinking ahead, Tariq Aziz then asked, "does the Jordan River require all these preparations?" Transcript of a Meeting of the General Command of the Armed Forces (10 October 1980) in SH-SHTP-D-000-573, Transcripts of General Command of the Armed Forces Meetings During the First Gulf War and Correspondence with Other Arab Leaders, October 1980.
[127] Navias and Hooton, *Tanker Wars*, 28.
[128] Woods, *et al.*, "Interview with (Former) Lieutenant General Abid Mohammed Al-Kabi, Cairo, Egypt, 12 November 2009."
[129] O'Ballance, *The Gulf War*, 39–40.
[130] SH-PDWN-D-000-566, Saddam Meeting with the General Command of the Armed Forces About the Iran–Iraq War, October–November 1980.

Three months into the war, Iraq had made few significant gains beyond the initially occupied ground. The farthest advance had been approximately 65 kilometers into Arabistan, while most units had advanced no farther than 20 to 30 kilometers.[131] Perhaps more significant was that they were holding positions and territory that possessed neither operational nor tactical advantage for the defense, but simply because that was where their advance had halted. The failure to exploit the advance to gain suitable defensive positions guaranteed eventual tactical failure. At the very time Iranian frontline troops withdrew to the frontier cities and towns, or beat a disorganized retreat and were thus at their most vulnerable, Saddam's army had settled down and waited. Moreover, the Iraqis appear to have ignored what bad winter weather and rain might do to their vulnerable defensive positions.

Desertion and occasional battlefield panic were not the only disciplinary issues confronting Saddam and his commanders. In late December, the III Corps commander briefed Saddam on the occupation of Khorramshahr. The Iraqi military had planned to confiscate commercial property and loot the homes "occupied by Iranian officers." Of course all of this was for the benefit of the Iraqi treasury. However, local commanders soon found it difficult to keep the soldiers from looting without authority and fighting among themselves over the spoils. Saddam commented that "[looting] is the right of the soldiers ... They fought for it and they should take it." One of Saddam's ministers offered a compromise for future operations: "the army should provide its soldiers a bonus before they enter an urban area ... so there will be no anarchy and so [the soldiers] don't kill the people and plunder the furniture." The issue remained unsettled.[132]

Reality begins to set in

Within several months, the short war Saddam had planned on had become something quite different. Iraqi forces faced significant difficulties. In an early preview of the role that the region's unique terrain would play, the Iranians used the Karun River to stop an Iraqi attack literally in its tracks. In mid-November, the southern-most prong of an Iraqi

---

[131] Pollack, *Arabs at War*, 187.

[132] SH-SHTP-D-000-624, Transcript of Meetings between Saddam Hussein and Iraqi Offiicals Relating to Tactics, 28–29 December 1980. Not surprisingly, the issue of troop discipline and looting became a problem during the 1991 invasion of Kuwait. See *The Mother of All Battles*, 93–123.

armored attack near Susangard ended when 150 Iraqi tanks "sank up to their turrets ... still in battle formation," after the Iranians opened the sluice gates which held back the river water to the north.[133]

In a calculated moment of frankness, Saddam observed: "Despite our victory, if you ask me now if we should have gone to war, I would say: 'It would have been better if we did not go to war. But we had no other choice.' If you ask me now: Would you like the war to last a week or six months, I would say: 'We prefer the war to last a week provided we regain all our rights.'"[134] Nevertheless, he still seems to have believed Iraq was on the road to victory. In conversation with a division commander he commented:

We have touched upon the difficult circumstances [that] some of the divisions have encountered, and this includes your division and the conditions it has gone through ... Victory is within reach, it is evident now. At the beginning we could not talk about difficulties because this could have been misconstrued and misinterpreted as setting the stage for or a front cover for failure ... Victory is defeating the enemy and destroy[ing] its morale, destroy[ing] its weapons, and infiltrate[ing] the depth of its territories.[135]

Later in the conversation, Saddam laughingly dismissed Iranian claims that their forces had destroyed 2,000 Iraqi tanks:

[I]f their claim is true that they have destroyed 2,000 of our tanks and we still have strength to beat them, this is one reason why we should be proud of ourselves. If their claim is true, this means we have a number of super powers providing us with constant air and sea replenishment of tanks ha, ha, ha. [I]t seems that every Iraqi has his tank on his own; perhaps every Iraqi [has] more than one tank.[136]

Despite the difficulties, Saddam was pleased with Iraq's victory in Khorramshahr. However, he was also slowly discovering the reality that strategy represents a delicate balance of ends, ways, and means. He had set Iraq on a course of maximalist ends with minimal means. Early contact with the actuality of war meant that his "demonstration war," as described by two commentators on the conflict, was not going well. The events of November 1980 "made the Iraqi leadership somewhat uneasy about the Iranian leaders' capacity to understand the nature of

---

[133] Ward, *Immortal*, 252.
[134] Saddam Hussein, "Saddam Husayn Address to National Assembly 4 Nov (FBIS-MEA-80-216)," *Foreign Broadcast Information Service Daily Reports* (1980).
[135] *SH-SHTP-A-001-321, Transcript of Telephone Conversation between Saddam Hussein and Unidentified Military Officers Regarding the 1 November 1980 Battle.
[136] *Ibid.*

the demonstration."[137] Saddam's conversations with his senior officers increasingly indicate that he suspected Iraq was engaged in a long war and had reason to be concerned. The commander of the III Corps told Saddam that losses in the 3rd Division had come largely from among its best soldiers. Saddam replied that somewhere between 10 and 20 percent of his soldiers had the necessary "spirit" to lead the rest and that "it is not right to depend completely [on them] till we exhaust them."[138] In a conversation with Major General Hesham Sahah, the 10th Armored Division's commander, the dictator noted, "Yes, you helped your brothers in your area by destroying the enemy. Yes, good, but I do not want your losses to be large." Afterwards he noted to his other listeners, "This commander doesn't care about losses, he doesn't care about losses. We have to [educate] him about that, about losses."[139]

In early January 1981, with no tangible signs that the Iranians would quit, Saddam wistfully commented to his cabinet that "Their [the Iranians'] defeat [has] made them realize that they will not defeat the Iraqi Army."[140] Perhaps Saddam's tone reflected efforts to build support for an external settlement. On 7 December 1980, he announced Iraq would not initiate further attacks.[141] By the end of the month, Iraqi ground operations had become limited to ambushes, patrols, and raids. Saddam set the criteria for success at one Iraqi casualty for every five Iranian. "Ambushes," he instructed his advisors, "have to be well planned and not risk high losses ... This comes with our policy of war that concerns economizing [the lives] of our soldiers." The III Corps commander fulsomely agreed and added that his corps motto was "kill your enemy and keep your own safety."[142] Shortly before the launch of a major Iranian offensive in early January, Saddam stated, "I know that Tariq is going to come up with a result. I mean Tariq will come up with a result at the United Nations. I mean in a few weeks."[143]

---

[137] Shahram Chubin and Charles Tripp, *Iran and Iraq at War* (Boulder, CO, 1988), 54.

[138] SH-SHTP-D-000-624, Transcript of Meetings between Saddam Hussein and Iraqi Offiicals Relating to Tactics, 28–29 December 1980.

[139] SH-AFGC-D-000-393, Transcript of a General Command of the Armed Forces Meeting During the First Gulf War and Telephone Conversations, 6–7 January 1981.

[140] *Ibid.*

[141] Karsh, *The Iran–Iraq War, 1980–1988*, 30.

[142] SH-SHTP-D-000-624, Transcript of Meetings between Saddam Hussein and Iraqi Offiicals Relating to Tactics, 28–29 December 1980.

[143] SH-SHTP-A-000-626, Saddam Hussein Discusses Neighboring Countries and Their Regimes, January 1981. During this period and despite Iran's stern resolutions, Iraq was working with the Islamic Conference, various non-aligned peace missions, Pakistani President Muhammad Zia-ul-Haq, and Olof Palme's UN mission to find an opening that would lock in Saddam's gains.

Saddam's guarded optimism that a settlement of the war might be on the near horizon allowed him to revisit his plans to face his long-term enemy – Israel. In early January 1981, he placed the apparent victory of Iraq's armed forces over the Iranians into his reading of the political and strategic situation in the Middle East. First, he was confident the war with Iran would end favorably. Second, he claimed that regardless of details, the next strategic move could only occur under the protection of an Arab (Iraqi) nuclear deterrent. He noted in late November 1980 that "[h]e who makes a move against Israel before possessing such [atomic] weapons, [the Israelis] will destroy him with the atomic bomb . . . If we do not have one or more of these bombs, they will in the upcoming Arab–Israeli War . . . strike Baghdad." Iraq's air force commander was more realistic: "They will destroy us."[144]

In a pattern that would be repeated in the 1990s, there are indications that Saddam's expectations of technological progress toward nuclear weapons were ahead of reality.[145] A senior Iraqi scientist recalled that, while it was clear the strategic purpose of Iraq's nuclear energy program was a bomb, there was a "mismatch between the idea and reality."[146] In a conversation with his advisors on 1 January 1981, Saddam discussed the implications of nuclear weapons on the balance of power in the Middle East:

SADDAM: If they [the Zionists] are going to hit Iraq, they will hit it before 1985 with an atomic bomb. After that, they will not be able to hit it. That means all of its enemies . . . however, before [1985] it is not so. The building posts have been put in place, but the structure has not taken its final form.

ADVISOR: Sir, after 1985, even the Iranians cannot do anything? You mean the Iranians?

SADDAM: No. I mean all of the enemies of Iraq including Iran.

ADVISOR: I mean even Iran is not able to do anything before 1985.

---

[144] SH-SHTP-D-000-856, Transcript of a Meeting between Saddam Hussein and His Commanding Officers at the Armed Forces General Command, November 1980.

[145] Iraq's nuclear program dated to the mid-1950s and participation in Eisenhower's "Atoms for Peace" program. Small research reactors, supplied by the Soviet Union in the 1960s, helped Iraq develop the nascent knowledge base. Iraq ratified the Non-Proliferation Treaty in 1969, but soon embarked on a clandestine weapons program. In the mid-1970s, the French began to build the Iraqis a large-scale reactor. Saddam even boasted publicly despite the Non-Proliferation Treaty that the French reactor represented "the first Arab attempt at nuclear arming." Lyle Goldstein, *Preventive Attack and Weapons of Mass Destruction: A Comparative Historical Analysis* (Stanford, CA, 2005), 117.

[146] Mahdi Obeidi and Kurt Pitzer, *The Bomb in My Garden: The Secret of Saddam's Nuclear Mastermind* (Hoboken, NJ, 2004), 49. Obeidi is referring to a 1980 conversation with the director of Iraq's Atomic Energy Commission, Dr. al-Hasimi.

SADDAM: No, Iran cannot do anything without the help of the Zionists enemy.
ADVISOR: A Zionist attack, as your Excellency mentioned, is something else.
SADDAM: Only with the atomic bomb and this is a complicated operation and
          not easy.
ADVISOR: That means between now until 1985, God will protect us.
SADDAM: God willing, in 1985 the structure will take its final form ... There are
          matters that need our attention after the war is over. We must put
          up a time schedule. We must take advantage of the experience
          we gained to implement what we did not attend to before ...
          I myself [have] benefited a great deal from this war. We all
          benefited ... You all have had a base and have experience in the
          business of war one way or the other.
          As for me this is the first experience in this form. Even 1974 till
          1975 generally speaking we did not meet and discuss matters
          in such detail ... Also, I used to follow the negotiations of
          the 1973 war as it came and went on the outside ... we were
          not involved in the decision making. This war has added to
          your knowledge, to your situation, [and] your status. On this
          basis, it has added to you say 60 percent, whereas to me it
          added 80 percent. However, the lessons of the war are deep.
          I mean we live all of its details. Not only when we sit here,
          but it lives with us all the time and we are aware of its
          wide ranging details. I mean we take the smallest point
          on the field of operations and apply it to the whole area of
          Iraq and outside of it.[147]

What is instructive about these comments is that Saddam was not only
ignorant about the Israelis and their capabilities, but also obviously
believed he could direct the events in the war against Iran by himself. As
noted in earlier studies, Saddam was a primary driver of lessons-learned
processes within the Iraqi command system.[148] In early January 1981, he
told his staff that unless they personally got involved in that process, some
within the military would use lessons to settle "personal vendettas" against
political enemies. If this happened, he suggested, the real lessons might be
lost. Worse still, faulty lessons "would filter down to even the officers of
the front line of the army," as had happened in 1956 and 1967. However,
this time it would be different. He declared that "we are going to benefit
from this with God's help because we are seeing our soft spots. We are
seeing our own shortcomings and some fundamental shortages."[149]

---

[147] SH-SHTP-A-000-626, Saddam Hussein Discusses Neighboring Countries and Their
Regimes, January 1981. The reference to 1974–1975 relates to the Kurdish revolt. The
reference to 1973 is to the Yom Kippur War.
[148] Woods, et al., The Iraqi Perspectives Report.
[149] SH-SHTP-A-000-626, Saddam Hussein Discusses Neighboring Countries and Their
Regimes, January 1981.

Then, for the benefit of the staff, Saddam described his initial impressions of the past four months of combat:

Alas, we still suffer from a lack of discipline in our army. In this war, the major apparent characteristic was faith and not discipline. Discipline was not the apparent major characteristic. The faith and belief in the march were the major characteristics. However, this may at times fade and weaken; you can compensate for it with discipline. When faith weakens, then you can pick up the slack with discipline that can last for 15 years. These are matters that we should emphasize and consider ... seriously.[150]

Throughout this period, Saddam depicted himself in the guise of the heroic underdog who had succeeded in toppling Iran. His frustrations in dealing with the Iranians after Khomeini had arrived in power occurred on a number of occasions. As he noted the previous fall:

We tried to be extremely patient. But our patience was not a sign of humility, capitulation or inability. We resorted to memoranda and meetings. This continued for about two years. Every time we faced them with more wisdom and patience, they thought that we were becoming increasingly weak. During the first few months after Khomeini came to power – during the first four months to be precise – I used to make all kinds of excuses to my colleagues to give the Persians more time ... [W]e hoped that the Persians had gained some wisdom and realism, but they only became more evil and determined to place Iraq between the hammer and the anvil.[151]

The invasion aimed to push what the Iraqis believed to be a collapsing and chaotic Iranian regime.[152] It represented a preemptive move to exploit a temporary window of opportunity, but one with no clear long-term strategic or operational objectives. Numbers of troops and weapons do not tell the entire story. The quality of military leadership, training, and experience count importantly, and in these areas neither combatant had much to offer. Efraim Karsh aptly termed this post-invasion period as the beginning of a "delicate balance of incompetence."[153] Both armies were stay-at-home forces that had spent neither time nor money to gain a measure of competence. Politicized military leaderships, in which loyalty

---

[150] *Ibid.*
[151] Hussein, "Saddam Husayn Address to National Assembly 4 Nov (FBIS-MEA-80-216)."
[152] According to General al-Hamdani, Saddam believed the invasion of Iran would force Khomeini to send the militia units supporting him away from the capital, which would have enabled the Mehdi Bazargan group to revolt and overthrow the Khomeini's regime. Woods, *et al.*, *Saddam's War*, 103. Bazargan was Iran's first post-revolution prime minster. He resigned after the student take-over of the American embassy in early November 1980, but remained a relatively moderate voice in Iranian politics until his death in 1995.
[153] Karsh, *The Iran–Iraq War, 1980–1988*, 30.

to the regime was a prerequisite for promotion, critical thinking was tantamount to subversion, and religious and social affiliations were more important than professionalism, dominated the high commands in both Baghdad and Tehran.

Saddam was keenly aware that in non-democratic societies force was the primary agent for political change.[154] Consequently, he spared no effort to ensure the military's loyalty. Senior appointments had almost entirely rested on the basis of political, social, tribal, and geographic ties with Tikrit. He had also embedded Ba'ath Party commissars within the armed forces down to battalion level. Those steps resulted in a docile military. Interestingly, Saddam's preferred solution was not that every officer join the Ba'ath Party. In 1983, he warned his senior officers that forcing soldiers into the party would only result in "a long tail of ineffective Ba'athists who will not only be incapable of leading, but [will also] become a burden just as the long negative administrative tail of the army affects its movement [and] fighting ability." Thus, the net result of an overly enthusiastic Ba'ath recruitment effort would result in a loss of control. As he noted,

the security scrutiny will have to be directed more towards the internal affairs of the party rather than the general public. When the general affairs of the party are in good shape, even if you have substantial problems outside [of the party], they [will] be very simple and very easy to resolve because as long as the leader is in good shape, then all other issues can be dealt with; but if corruption reaches the head, then it is all over.[155]

While destroyed facilities at the port of Fao at the mouth of the Shatt al-Arab reduced Iraq's capacity to export oil, Saddam regarded the disruption as a temporary hindrance.[156] During the interim, he believed, Iraq's relatively large foreign exchange reserves could bridge the gap. Despite disappointment with the war's initial results, he believed

---

[154] The Iraqi military had always believed that it was a critical part of the political process. This internal competition resulted in a significant purge of officers who had helped bring the Ba'ath to power in 1968. For further discussion of these issues, see John F. Devlin, "The Ba'ath Party: Rise and Metamorphosis," *The American Historical Review* 96, no. 5 (1991), 1405.

[155] *SH-AFGC-D-001-324, Transcript of a Meeting between Saddam Hussein and the General Command of the Armed Forces, 26 June 1983.

[156] Iraq began the war with a $40 billion foreign exchange reserve. In 1980, Iraq's oil exports dropped from 3.281 million barrels per day to 0.926 million barrels per day. By 1982, Iraq had exhausted its reserves and by 1985 was spending 245 percent of its oil revenues on arms. Solvency was only possible through Saudi Arabian and Kuwaiti grants, foreign credit, and an eventual shift to an austere wartime economy. See Abbas Alnasrawi, *The Economy of Iraq: Oil, Wars, Destruction of Development and Prospects, 1950–2010*, vol. 154 (Santa Barbara, CA, 1994), 79–104.

events would soon force the Iranians to negotiate so that Iraq could devote full attention to its internal problems and the eventual confrontation with the "Zionist entity." Accordingly, Saddam began to formulate a policy of insulating the Iraqi people from the consequences of the conflict.[157]

By January 1981, Saddam's forces had occupied Iranian territory along approximately half of the 735-mile border. The Iraqi advance had seized nearly 10,000 square miles of territory, but it had come to rest in no clear defensible positions on which Iraqi forces could knit effective defensive systems. Saddam's media were full of tales, reports, and pictures of heroic victories and jubilant troops, all forming a new chapter in modern Arab and Islamic history. It referred to Saddam as "the second great conqueror of the Persian enemy," while the dictator regularly appeared in his uniform as a field marshal in martial settings. Intertwined with such propaganda was the carefully cultivated message of an accessible and generous father figure, always ready to shower the populace with gifts.[158] The show was meant not only for Iraqis, but also for the Arab world. To put the seal on his accomplishment, Saddam convened regular sessions of the National Assembly, first elected by the near unanimous vote for Ba'athist candidates in June 1980, to underline popular backing for the war.

The internal war

The war brought to the surface internal security problems that had haunted Iraq from its founding. No central government in Baghdad had ever exercised its full writ over the entire nation. In the north, the Kurds, quiescent after their drubbing by the Iraqis in the mid-1970s, bided their time, but Saddam had little illusion about their long-term reliability. It was the reliability of the Shi'a in the south and their potential ties or sympathies to the Iranians that was of immediate concern.

According to Iraqi military intelligence, Shi'a radicals had established the Dawa Party in 1957 with the purpose of "making [it] the fifth column that has an effective influence for the achievement of the Persian aspirations in the east of the Arab Homeland." Moreover, "Iraqi [citizens] with Iranian origins living in the governorates located in the middle and south of the Iraq state discovered that the Dawa Party was the outlet for

---

[157] In particular, the dictator attempted to follow a policy of guns and butter, continuing the regime's extensive social welfare programs, while supporting the immense costs that the war against Iran involved.

[158] Hiro, *The Longest War*, 68.

their [the Iraqis with 'Iranian origins'] hidden hatreds against the Arab Nation."[159] After the 1977 riots during the so-called Safar Intifada, the movement, which had remained largely underground, had become visible in its opposition to Saddam.[160] In 1979, demonstrations in Najaf included crowds chanting "long live Khomeini, and al-Sadr, and religion. All of us are yours to sacrifice, Khomeini."[161] In June 1979, one of Iraq's leading Shi'a clerics issued a Fatwa forbidding membership in the Ba'ath Party. Saddam's response was to make membership in the Dawa Party a capital offense.[162]

The political and religious tensions had then broken out into an open insurgency with several high-profile assassination attempts, most notably on Tariq Aziz in April 1980. With reports of increased activity among Shi'a groups, Saddam immediately ordered security to be improved to ensure that "none of [these] incidents had gotten out of hand." However, as Saddam reminded everyone, there was a good side to the Dawa Party's focus on the Shi'a population in Basra: "[The Dawa Party] are concentrating on these areas ... however, these individuals will be exposed, then we will get rid of them ... because the battle has become clear now and exposed, therefore, they will have to come out, and then we will deal with them [by] force, whenever they stick their heads out we will cut them off."[163]

Saddam also used the surge of success and patriotic fervor to settle what one can only describe as future scores. He sought to eliminate those he regarded as troublemakers, Shi'a or those deemed to be of excessive "Persian" descent, by deporting them and, in some cases, their families to Iran. This pogrom, like many in history, began with a ritualized creation of new laws meant to "protect" the public, but it descended

---

[159] SH-GMID-D-000-622, General Military Intelligence Directorate (GMID) Studies on the Foundation of the Da'wah Party and the Supreme Council of the Islamic Revolution Party, March–December 1995.

[160] The Safar Intifada began in Najaf Iraq during a Shi'a celebration of a banned religious festival. The pilgrims were attacked by security forces, which led to riots and mass arrests in southern Iraq.

[161] Jerry M. Long, *Saddam's War of Words: Politics, Religion, and the Iraqi Invasion of Kuwait* (Austen, TX, 2004), 62.

[162] Captured documents from 2003 reveal a program run with brutal efficiency. The regime worked hard to ensure that membership in the Dawa Party resulted in a swift execution. The punishment also reverberated throughout the victim's extended family. In one case, a police captain was cashiered because two of his cousins had been executed as members of the party. *SH-IDGS-D-001-325, Memoranda Relating to a Police Captain's Forced Retirement Due to Familial Involvement with the Da'wah Party, June 1981.

[163] SH-PDWN-D-001-021, Transcripts of Meetings between Saddam and Top Iraqi Officials and Officers Regarding Iran–Iraq War Tactics Such as the Use of Napalm and Cluster Bombs, 6 October 1980.

into industrialized slaughter.[164] Deportations began in mid-1980 and continued during the first two years of the war. The number of deportees eventually reached upwards of 100,000.[165] Moreover, Saddam had one of the leading Shi'a clerics in Iraq, Mohammad Baqir al-Sadr, of the famous al-Sadr family, brutally executed with his sister, for anti-regime activities. Reports that Saddam's secret police had raped al-Sadr's sister in al-Sadr's presence, had set his beard alight, and then dispatched him with a nail gun further inflamed the Shi'a faithful, but also served as a useful warning to those considering resistance of any kind.[166]

As the Shi'a pogrom began, the ministry of the interior ordered lower ranking soldiers, whose family members the regime had deported to Iran, dismissed from the armed forces.[167] Documentation of individual events reveals the tragedy and the scope of the events as well as the bitter seeds of future discontent. Example documents include:[168]

- A report on the sale of a business of a recently deported "Iranian as well as stripping them of all their assets." An order from the General Security Directorate banning wives of deported Iranians from joining their husbands.
- An order deporting extended family members to Iran because "they were Turkish descendants from the Ottoman Empire."

---

[164] Since Saddam's fall in 2003, some sixty mass graves have been confirmed of the more than 270 "unopened known" sites being investigated. See United Nations, *Human Rights Report: UN Assistance Mission for Iraq* (2009). Downloaded from www.uniraq. org/documents/UNAMI_Human_Rights_Report15_January_June_2009_EN.pdf. These sites contain an estimated 300,000–400,000 bodies.

[165] *SH-GMID-D-001-326, Intelligence Reports from the Border Regarding Deported Iranians.

[166] Mackey, *The Reckoning, Iraq, and the Legacy of Saddam Hussein*, 249.

[167] *SH-IZAR-D-001-327, Dismissal of Low Ranking Army Personnel, 21 April–29 November 1980.

[168] For example, see *SH-MISC-D-001-392, Correspondence between the General Secretariat for Liquidating Properties of Deported Iranians and the General Aid and Arrangement Directorate, 23 January 1982; *SH-PDWN-D-001-329, Correspondence between Various Security Directorates Regarding Detaining the Wives of Deported Iranians, January 1981; *SH-IDGS-D-001-330, General Security Directorate Memo Regarding the Deportation of Individual Members of a Turkish Family to Iran, 1981; Decrees (30 June 1981) in *SH-RVCC-D-001-328, Decrees and Orders Regarding the Confiscation of Housing from Deported Iranians, 2 May–16 July 1981; *SH-RVCC-D-001-331, Laws Dealing with Various Issues Including the Confiscation of Property from Deported Iranians, Passed between 1981–1982. The Iraqi pogrom was much like that of the Nazis for those Jews lucky enough to escape the Third Reich before the war. It aimed at ensuring that exiles took nothing with them except the clothes on their backs. Among others see *SH-GMID-D-001-332, Correspondence between GMID, the Central Bank of Iraq, and the Central Organization for Standardization & Quality Control Confirming the Receipt of Confiscated Jewelry, Circa January 1981.

- A Revolutionary Command Council Decree, Number 854 authorizing the stripping of Iraqi citizenship and confiscation of the property of "Persians."
- Lists of Iraqi citizens of Iranian origin to be fired from "vital positions" in Iraq and have their property confiscated, and then to be deported to Iran.

Another aspect of Iraq's wartime security developed out of a lessons-learned study from the 1960s. If the Ba'ath revolution were to succeed, then its political arm must have an independent force to counterbalance the army. In Iraq's case in 1970, that meant establishing the Popular Army (al-Jaish al-Sha'bi). That force was charged with preparing citizens for internal and external defense. Its members could keep their weapons at home "in case of need, according to the orders from their superiors."[169] Saddam appointed a regime insider and trusted confidant, Taha Yassin Ramadan, to lead this force. One commentator described the Popular Army as a device "to ensure not only that the regime had a means of mobilizing violence outside military control, but also that [Saddam's] particular group of 'insiders' could successfully dominate any rival faction within the Ba'ath Party itself."[170]

In early 1981, Saddam viewed the Popular Army as a convenient solution to resetting his forces for a defensive campaign. He expressed confidence that Taha Ramadan could provide the numbers required, especially if the latter were to concentrate on training them "on the use of grenades and light weapons." To accelerate the process, Saddam suggested the army command support Taha Ramadan's training mission with special forces officers for "a week or ten days or whatever!" When asked about these Popular Army "commando" units later in the war, Taha Ramadan replied, "We don't need the fighters [of the Popular Army for combat duty], but we want to know who is unreservedly ready to fight. This is ... a sort of plebiscite to dispute claims that the Iraqi people are tired of the war."[171]

It seems that Saddam did not necessarily return the loyalty expected of Popular Army members. In discussion about using the Popular Army to augment regular forces in holding occupied Iranian territory, Saddam commented,

---

[169] Ofra Bengio, *Saddam's Word: Political Discourse in Iraq* (New York, NY, 1998), 150–151.
[170] J. S. Wagner, "Iraq," in *Fighting Armies: Antagonists in the Middle East: A Combat Assessment*, Richard A. Gabriel, ed., *Fighting Armies (Contributions in Military History)* (Santa Barbara, CA, 1983); Chubin and Tripp, *Iran and Iraq at War*, 19.
[171] Bengio, *Saddam's Word*, 151.

the Popular Army needs officers. Every company of the Popular Army needs one officer. Never-mind if the officer is a retired officer as long as he can supervise them! I am sure he will fully execute his duty ... for the protection of the [rear] area, the Popular Army can be depended on and *we should not be too concerned about the losses*. All we need to do is to assign to every company an officer.[172]

When one of his officers suggested that Popular Army troops around the stalled front near Abadan had a tendency to "infiltrate away," Saddam uncharacteristically replied "those who want to take-off let them be ... they should not be made to feel that they either have to fight or die." Whether this response reflected his overall confidence in the frontline situation, or a pragmatic concession as to the limitations of non-professional troops, is unclear. But always true to his nature, Saddam added "He who wants to leave we should let him go ... we can pick them up at a far away distance so that the others will not know the fate of their comrade."[173]

Conclusion

After launching his forces into Iran, Saddam sought to confine the conflict by restricting the army's goals, means, and targets. The Iraqis avoided strikes at Iran's civilian and economic infrastructure (with the exception of the cities and towns in the south that were fought over), and it was only when Iran countered with attacks on soft targets that Iraq responded in kind. Likewise, Saddam's territorial goals were modest at the outset, although they would have stripped Iran of some of its most significant oil fields.[174] He had hoped for a quick and limited campaign that would send a message to the ayatollahs to desist from attempting to overthrow his Ba'ath regime. Saddam did suggest in a press conference in November 1980 that Iraq would demand "additional rights" from the Iranians, although he conceded Iraq was not making any territorial demands, including Khuzestan, on the Iranians.[175]

Nevertheless, in spite of seeming success, there were danger signs. In a dinner with his military advisors, one senior officer admitted that the 16th Brigade had not received any training during the course of a year.

---

[172] SH-SHTP-A-000-626, Saddam Hussein Discusses Neighboring Countries and Their Regimes, January 1981. Emphasis added.
[173] *Ibid.*
[174] However, Saddam made clear on a number of occasions that he would have been delighted to expand his war aims, had Iraqi forces been more successful.
[175] Helena Cobban, "Feisty Saddam Sure Iraq Will Win Gulf War," *Christian Science Monitor*, 13 November 1980.

Saddam's initial comment was, "OK, from next month we'll work on training." That soon led the dictator to a series of bizarre exchanges even by the standards of his court:

SADDAM: The army is on my mind ... but now we need the war to end because there are some trouble areas. Most of the officers in the Iraqi Army are [hardly qualified] ... and they spend their time in eating and drinking. We should preserve our reputation ... we need to increase our good reputation. We should not show such officers on TV because we have youngsters looking at them ...

VOICE 2:   Pardon sir, the war conditions and the stress and anxiety of the war lead officers toward food. It is a natural thing. They consider food as entertainment to pass the time.

SADDAM: Just like prisoners ... If they tend to read and write, they won't feel they have to pass time in eating. I remember I was in prison, some played backgammon, some played dominos, I was always following a reading program ... But they [the officers] don't read. Most of our officers don't read.[176]

In October, Saddam had turned to the issue of training in discussions with his military staff. He

expressed his disapproval of the Iraqi Army's training and irresponsibility, he stressed the importance of training in order to have an army of a specific structure, and he indicated that the annual evaluation report of military officers should be examined carefully. In addition he pointed out the importance of implementing an honest evaluation of each military officer, which has not been implemented thus far.[177]

With the limited invasion Saddam had hoped to reach agreement with the Iranians quickly, hopefully with a replacement government. Tariq Aziz, the Iraqi foreign minister, put it this way: "Our military strategy reflects our political objectives. We want neither to destroy Iran, nor occupy it permanently because that is a country with which we will remain linked by geographical and historical bonds and common interests. Therefore we are determined to avoid any irrevocable steps."[178] However, possession breeds its own logic. As Saddam commented to his army chief of staff in early 1981, "the natural borders [for Iraq] are

---

[176] SH-MISC-D-000-827, Saddam and Senior Iraqi Officials Discussing the Conflict with Iran, Iraqi Targets and Plans, a Recent Attack on the Osiraq Reactor, and Various Foreign Countries, 1 October 1980.

[177] SH-MISC-D-000-695, Saddam Hussein Meeting with Various Iraqi Officials About the Iraqi Position Early on in the Iran–Iraq War, 12–13 October 1980.

[178] Karsh, *The Iran–Iraq War, 1980–1988*, 27.

these borders, because the land that we reached ... enables Iraq to be comfortable to the East."[179]

Establishing a long-term bulwark against the hornet's nest being stirred in Tehran was a task Saddam started planning during the first lull in the fighting. In January 1981, the dictator brainstormed how Iraq could improve the defensive ground to the east of the Tigris between Baghdad and the border. While noting that the work should begin "after we have had a respite from the war," Saddam suggested that the Iraqis cultivate rows of trees separated by open spaces and canals. He told his listeners that such defenses should include in their planting and irrigation plans the need to include anti-tank missile strong points along the tree edges "so that when they [the Iranians] arrive at the open space, they will be killed."[180] Moreover, according to Saddam, by creatively using water obstacles and flooding the ground during nine months of the year, Iraqi troops would only have to be stationed in this inhospitable area during their three-month training cycle. An advisor added that since the eastern portion of the country is flat they should add "artificial hills" that Iraq's military could augment with "watch towers and tanks positions." Everything seemed possible to Saddam then.[181] As he announced in one of his interminable meetings at the start of the New Year: "We can do everything since we have the capabilities of the state and have unusual capabilities at that. In addition, we can use central planning to achieve anything we want."[182]

---

[179] Transcript of a Meeting Held at the General Command of the Armed Forces (10 July 1980) in SH-SHTP-D-000-572, Transcripts from Meetings between Saddam Iraqi Army Officers , January 1981–April 1993.

[180] SH-SHTP-A-000-626, Saddam Hussein Discusses Neighboring Countries and Their Regimes, January 1981.

[181] The similarities between Hitler's table talks during World War II and Saddam's during the Iran–Iraq War are striking for their banality.

[182] SH-SHTP-A-000-626, Saddam Hussein Discusses Neighboring Countries and Their Regimes, January 1981.

5   1981–1982: Stalemate

If they had stood firm for just [a few] minutes, had they opened fire ... and shot just one round off of each tank and then retreated, that would have been bad but they could have hit at least a percentage of the enemy forces coming [at] them. The force that stands firm does not give up losses; I wish to know the reason for this so I can punish them.[1]   – Saddam Hussein

In his decision to invade Iran in September 1980, Saddam Hussein failed to understand his army's limited capabilities and tried to do too many things at once. The Iraqis lost valuable time and surprise with the distractions of attacking Khorramshahr, Abadan, and Susangard. And if Saddam had intended to deprive Iran of Khuzestani oil to protect his gains, then the failure to capture Ahvaz, the crucial pipeline junction east of Dezful, and its associated road and rail infrastructure, all within reach, was a serious mistake. (For the extent of the southern, central, and northern battlefields in 1981 and 1982, see Figures 5.1, 5.2 and 5.3.)

Instead, the invading Iraqi forces focused on the port cities – where the majority of the Arabic-speaking population resided – largely because Saddam's intelligence services had reported those Arabs would rally to the Iraqi cause.[2] But that decision did not pan out when the locals were less than receptive to Saddam's message. To make matters worse, a handful of atrocities by the Iraqis had turned otherwise neutral Arabs in the area into supporters of the regime in Tehran. In fact, the 9th Division commander, Major General Tala al-Duri, admired by Saddam and despised by fellow officers, had ordered the summary execution of locals suspected of supporting Iranians.[3]

---

[1] SH-AFGC-D-000-393, Transcript of a General Command of the Armed Forces Meeting During the First Gulf War and Telephone Conversations, 6–7 January 1981. Saddam and the Director, GMID discussing the collapse of the Iraqi 9th Division during an Iranian surprise attack.

[2] See SH-GMID-D-000-620, People of Arabstan (Arabs in Southern Iran) in Al-Ahwaz Area Calling for Independence, 1979.

[3] Much the same would happen when Iraq invaded Kuwait in 1990. Kevin M. Woods, Williamson Murray, and Thomas Holaday, *Saddam's War: An Iraqi Military Perspective of the Iran–Iraq War*, McNair Paper 70 (Washington, DC, 2009), 121.

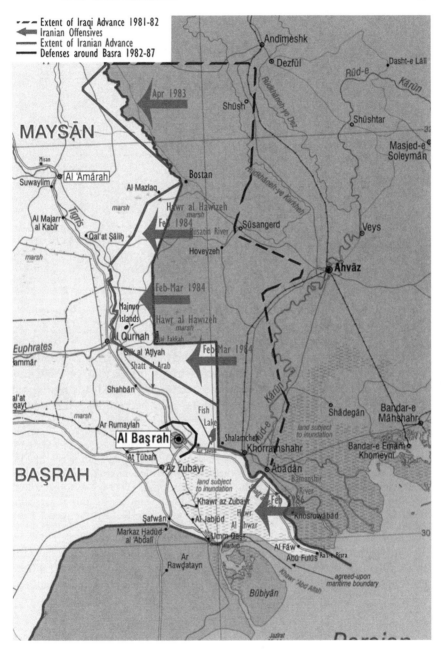

Figure 5.1 Southern battlefield, extent of Iraqi advance, 1981–1982;
Iranian defense of Basra, 1982–1987 Iranian offensives, 1983–1986;
extent of Iranian advance

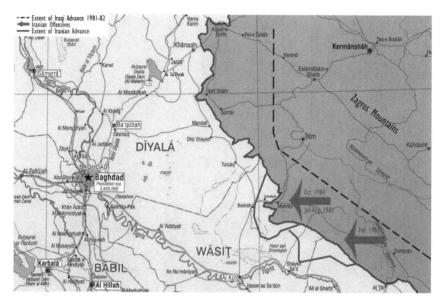

Figure 5.2 Central battlefield, extent of Iraqi offensives, 1981–1982
Iranian offensives, 1983–84; extent of Iranian advance

In a conference with senior officers at the beginning of 1981, Saddam was displeased with the performance of Iraq's military forces. He was especially frustrated with the air force because he could not figure out exactly what the bombers and fighters had been doing during air operations:

As far as the air force command, I have been unable, to this moment, to evaluate or place a single note regarding their performance. As fighters, they are like all fighters in the Iraqi Army, they carry out their work by receiving their orders, fly their airplanes, and go and fight. However … as far as administration, coordination, evaluating, and understanding the events to give directives from these lessons and what is the mentality in the command of the air force, I am unable to make up my mind.[4]

But it was for the gunners Saddam expressed special contempt: "As for the artillery, it is certain that we see some negatives in all phases. There are negatives in the accuracy, coordination, and usage. [Their concentrations are] inaccurate and not hitting the target."[5]

---

[4] SH-SHTP-A-000-626, Saddam Hussein Discusses Neighboring Countries and Their Regimes, January 1981.
[5] *Ibid.*

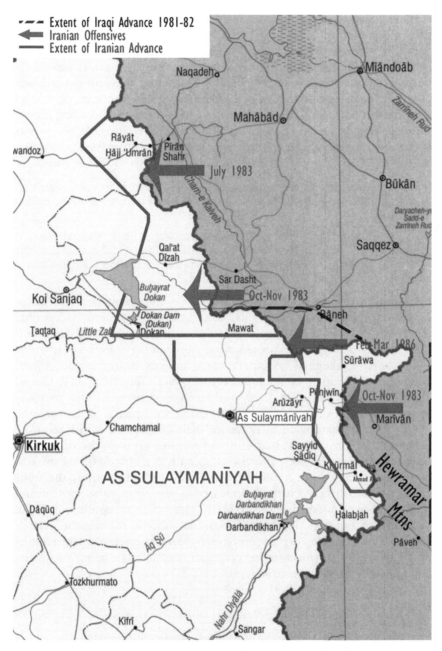

Figure 5.3 Northern battlefield, extent of Iraqi offensives, 1981–1982
Iranian offensives, 1983–1986; extent of Iranian advance

Intelligence reporting early in the war included a considerable volume of tactical information and only occasional operational-level analysis. In the tactical data, Saddam could afford to focus on training and discipline faults because the picture military intelligence was presenting was essentially positive – at least relative to the Iranians. Simultaneously, the general lack of operational analysis allowed Saddam to ignore the campaign-level questions of battlefield geography and sustainment. In effect, the intelligence system was telling Saddam what he wanted to hear. As one report makes clear, both the dictator and his intelligence system were puzzled by the failure of Khomeini's regime either to collapse or sue for peace:

[a] the enemy is determined to continue fighting, and they will not agree to a ceasefire in this current situation out of fear of [an] inevitable increase in civil disturbance ...

[b] The current status of the Iranian economy is not able to support confrontational war for an extended amount of time ... Nevertheless, the nature of the Iranian leadership and the Iranian population's circumstances allows the continuation of the war of attrition.[6]

Confronting the possibility of a longer war, the Iraqis began a major program of mobilizing additional forces, which required widespread purchases of arms abroad, especially ammunition, which the army was using more quickly than expected. Mobilizing and creating new divisions significantly challenged an officer corps already losing junior officers more quickly than it could replace them. Speaking to the III Corps' commander in December 1980, Saddam was concerned that Iraq was losing too many of its "courageous experienced men." Such soldiers, whom Saddam estimated at no more than 20 percent of the total, he believed the army should husband and not use up until the others had been killed or wounded: "The losses should be divided so that the less courageous must have a share [in them]."[7] In this period, the non-commissioned officer corps disappeared as an effective support structure. Increasing losses led the Iraqis to emphasize to commanders the necessity of holding down casualties. An urgent message in March 1981 requested that corps commanders "kindly brief your formations on the necessity of concentrating on organizing defenses in a manner that guarantees the lowest casualties possible."[8]

---

[6] SH-IISX-D-000-841, 1981 Iraqi Evaluation of the Iranian Military Threat, January 1980–January 1981.
[7] SH-SHTP-D-000-624, Transcript of Meetings between Saddam Hussein and Iraqi Offiicals Relating to Tactics, 28–29 December 1980.
[8] Communications between GMID and Various Iraqi Units During the Iran–Iraq War (February–March 1981) in *SH-GMID-D-001-394, Military Orders and Communications

The Iranians also confronted significant internal problems, which may partially explain why Khomeini's regime was willing to release the American hostages in January 1981. Admittedly, Washington played a role with the arrival in office of a tough-talking new president, but part of the deal involved America releasing substantial amounts of the spare parts and weapons systems Iran had purchased during the Shah's regime.[9] The hostage settlement also ended the embargo on arms sales to Iran by some Western European nations.

The Battle of Susangard

The rains had come in November 1980 and fighting along the extended front had died down through to the end of the year. The Iraqis had expected this would last until the weather improved in March, and the ground would be dry enough for military operations to resume. But in early January, the Iranians launched a series of offensives from north to south. The attack in the south, not surprisingly, received the main attention, as the Iranians attempted to drive the Iraqis out of Khuzestan. Unfortunately for the offensive's prospects, the Iranians broadcast much of their tactical radio traffic *en clair* and thus warned the Iraqis as to what was afoot.[10]

The fact that the Iranians chose to launch these offensives at such a bad time indicated the political pressures under which Bani-Sadr was working. He had been one of Khomeini's close advisors when the ayatollah had been in exile in Paris; upon his return, Bani-Sadr had become the

---

between the GMID, the Armed Forces General Command, the RCC, and Various Iraqi Units During the Iran–Iraq War, 1981.

[9] The terms of the deal were in the Algiers Accords (19 January 1981). This agreement, brokered by Algeria, was designed to resolve the "crisis in [US–Iranian] relations arising out of the detention of the 52 United States nationals in Iran," but only contributed to Saddam's suspicions. In addition to releasing certain frozen Iranian financial assets, the Americans agreed to a process whereby they would release "to Iran of all Iranian properties which are located in the United States and abroad." See Charles Nelson Brower and Jason D. Brueschke, *The Iran–United States Claims Tribunals* (The Hague, 1998), 673–725. Iraq already suspected the Iranians were working to obtain US-made spare parts through the Israelis. Ironically, Saddam's suspicions were shared by the revolutionaries in Tehran, who questioned why Iran should accept anything from a country aligned with Iraq to destroy the revolution. See Babak Ganji, *Politics of Confrontation: The Foreign Policy of the USA and Revolutionary Iran* (London, 2006), 206–224; Mark Bowden, *Guests of the Ayatollah: The First Battle in America's War with Militant Islam* (New York, NY, 2006), 248–255.

[10] Kevin M. Woods, Williamson Murray, Elizabeth A. Nathan, Laila Sabara, and Ana M. Venegas, "Interview with (Former) Major General Mizher Rashid Al-Tarfa Al-Ubaydi, Dubai, United Arab Emirates, 9 November 2009," *Project 1946: Phase II* (Alexandria, VA, 2010).

president of Iran.[11] Almost immediately on the onset of hostilities, he was under pressure from the fanatics around Khomeini to attack the Iraqi invaders, because Allah was on Iran's side. When Bani-Sadr did not act as quickly as the ayatollahs thought he should have, they attributed the president's lack of action to outright treason. As one pro-Khomeini account of the war noted, "Bani-Sadr, after becoming the president and commander in chief, sought to build not an Islamic army, but one that was directly under his influence so that he could work [against] the Imam's vision."[12] As a result of such political pressure, Bani-Sadr prematurely committed a disorganized regular army to a series of major offensives against the Iraqis to bolster his political position in Tehran and his influence with Khomeini.

The Iranian regular army conducted the January 1981 offensive with the *Pasdaran* under its control, something that raised suspicions within the clerical establishment. The plan, designed by the new leaders of Iran's regular army, was ambitious. It aimed to smash the Iraqi armored forces surrounding Susangard, drive south behind Iraqi positions to Ahvaz, and then push on to Khorramshahr, having destroyed most of Iraq's ground forces in the area. Had Bani-Sadr allowed the army to wait until the weather was better for major military operations, the Iranians might have succeeded to some degree, which might have had political overtones in Tehran.[13] Members of the revolutionary guard were already accusing Bani-Sadr of suffering from "Bonapartist tendencies" and feared a battlefield victory under the regular army might have encouraged a march on Tehran to seize power.[14] However, the Iranian president rejected the advice to wait.

On 5 January 1981, the Iranian offensive began with much of Iran's armored force attacking Iraqi positions near Dezful and Susangard.[15] Accompanying Iranian armor was the army's parachute brigade, most probably to help clear out the Iraqis from the urban terrain in the two cities it targeted. Iraqi signals intelligence appears to have warned the defenders as to what was coming. The Iraqi Army's chief of staff

---

[11] For Bani-Sadr's political relationship with Khomeini in their Paris exile, see Abu al-Hasan Bani-Sadr, *My Turn to Speak: Iran, the Revolution and Secret Deals with the US* (Washington, DC, 1991); Mohsen M. Milani, *The Making of Iran's Islamic Revolution: From Monarchy to Islamic Republic* (Boulder, CO, 1988), 175–186.

[12] *SH-MISC-D-001-350, *The Passing of Two Years of War: Iran–Iraq*, Political Office of the Islamic Revolution Pasdaran Corps.

[13] Interestingly, Bani-Sadr has nothing to say in his memoirs about his role in pushing for the offensive.

[14] Ahmed S. Hashim, "Civil–Military Relations in the Islamic Republic of Iran," in *Iran, Iraq, and the Arab Gulf States*, Joseph A. Kechichian, ed. (New York, NY, 2001), 38–39.

[15] Susangard is known as al-Khafajiyya in Arabic.

described the scale and intensity of the battles when he informed Saddam that "I cannot imagine a battle like [this] in the area or the entire Middle East ... [it] was walls of fire, one in the direction of the enemy and one in our direction."[16] In heavy fighting, some Iranian tanks achieved significant penetrations and even managed to surround the 9th Division's command post.[17] However, the battle ended up resembling the defeat of Soviet forces in May 1942 at Kharkov.[18] The initial breakthrough soon foundered in heavy rains; the ground surrounding the roads becoming a morass. Armored fighting vehicles of both armies remained confined to the roads.

The advance took the lead Iranian units across the al-Karkh River as far as Hoveyzeh. However, due to the poor conditions, the Iranians failed to widen the salient's neck. There, the Iranian tanks and supporting forces found themselves under fire from Iraqi tanks on both sides of the penetration.[19] Despite the desperate conditions, the Iranians performed well at a tactical level, especially in tank gunnery. They destroyed approximately 100 of the 350 Iraqi tanks involved in the battle.[20] The initial setbacks to Iraqi forces caused significant concern in Baghdad. Early reports described the give-and-take battle as two men pulling on a rope, "sometimes we go and sometime [they go]." In reply, Saddam commented to his staff "I don't get mad about give and take; I get mad when someone leaves their position for no reason."[21] For a time, the Iranian attack produced a chaotic retreat of some of the 9th Division units.[22] That

---

[16] SH-AFGC-D-000-393, Transcript of a General Command of the Armed Forces Meeting During the First Gulf War and Telephone Conversations, 6–7 January 1981. Toward the end of the meeting, after working his way through a confusing flurry of unit designations and equipment descriptions, Saddam commented "from now on let us record all telephone conversations." It is these recordings that will allow historians to reconstruct many of the events and decision-making processes of Saddam's time.

[17] SH-IZAR-D-000-278, Reports on the Al-Khafajiyyah Battle During the Iraq–Iran War, 28 February 1981.

[18] In May 1942, the Soviets launched a major offensive against the Wehrmacht's Army Group South in the area of Kharkov, which was in German hands. The attack broke through and advanced a significant distance behind German lines. But the Germans held the neck of the salient and then, counterattacking, surrounded and destroyed the Soviet forces. For a fuller description, see Earl F. Ziemke and Magna E. Bauer, *Moscow to Stalingrad: Decision in the East* (Washington, DC, 1987), 269–282.

[19] The Iraqi reserves were well positioned to contain a breakthrough.

[20] Steven R. Ward, *Immortal: A Military History of Iran and Its Armed Forces* (Washington, DC, 2009), 254.

[21] SH-AFGC-D-000-393, Transcript of a General Command of the Armed Forces Meeting During the First Gulf War and Telephone Conversations, 6–7 January 1981. Punishment in Saddam's book meant shooting those who had bugged out.

[22] The division's less than impressive performance resulted from its commander's (Major General Tala al-Duri) incompetence. However, while Saddam would later disgrace the

division would soon establish a reputation among the Iraqi high command for gross incompetence.

Nevertheless, an extensive after-action report completed in late February by the commander of the 43rd Brigade of the 9th Infantry Division indicated:

At 0830, on 5 January 1981, the racist Persian enemy began an intense artillery shelling towards the positions of our brigade contingents which were occupying their sectors of defensive responsibility in Khaffaji [Susangard] region ...

The enemy followed his artillery shelling by an approach with three large main convoys, two from al-Kut – al-Hawashem – Umm al-Sukur – al-Jalaliya and the other one from Hawr al-Hawizeh. Each convoy included tanks, BMP combat vehicles, armored troop carriers, part of which were carrying anti-tank missiles, wheeled vehicles carrying 106mm anti-tank weapons ... The fight against the enemy was severe and very fierce and could not be imagined. The enemy's losses were significant with regard to tanks and special forces at the time. The enemy maintained the intensity of his attack with new armored units which advanced very quickly at the expense of the accuracy of [their] firing. Our units were able to destroy a large number of them.[23]

Several months later, Saddam and his senior military staff received a number of reports on Iranian fratricide during these winter battles. Had they resulted from a disagreement among the Persians? Did units arrive on the battlefield in a state of "ignorance" as to situation, terrain, or enemy? Saddam noted the slaughter of Iranian volunteers appeared to be the way that the regular Iranian Army "deals" with volunteers. In the face of Iraqi firepower "it sends them [our] way and whoever gets killed ... is fine." Whatever the cause, the III Corps commander reported to Saddam that "[the Iranians] come to us looking poor and attacked our troops, and that's when God's mercy got active and our youth sweep them away with our machine guns."[24]

In a conversation during the battle in early January, Saddam zeroed in on a more troublesome aspect of the encounter, when some Iraqi units had panicked:

If they [the soldiers bearing the brunt of the initial Iranian attacks] had stood firm for just [a few] minutes, had they opened their tank fire and shot just one round from each tank and then retreated, that would have been bad [but] they could have hit a percentage of the enemy forces coming [against] them. The force that

division by eliminating it from the army's rolls, al-Duri continued to serve in a number of important positions.

[23] SH-IZAR-D-000-278, Reports on the Al-Khafajiyyah Battle During the Iraq–Iran War, 28 Febraury 1981.

[24] *SH-MISC-D-001-334, Transcript of a Meeting between Saddam Hussein and Senior Officers, February–March 1981.

stands firm does not give up losses. I wish I knew the reason for this so I could punish them ... It seems the enemy has brought his armor from everywhere and made us ineffective while they are in a very effective situation. This is attributable to the ignorance of the intelligence; there is no intelligence on the field.[25]

The dictator then indicated the effect of the battle on his psyche:

I slept, yes, I slept. You may be surprised in spite of your knowledge of my sensitivity. I did not expect an Iraqi to retreat even an organized retreat. I mean, I despise it: How could an Iraqi [retreat without fighting?] I was upset with one point; the point is how this force gets ousted by a force smaller or equal to it? But this is what happened.[26]

Perhaps sensing the long-term seriousness of frontline forces not standing their ground, Saddam added: "We have to change this tendency in training ... by education ... I know this from a long time ago. You tell an Iraqi to go forward, two of them run! And they take thousands with them. But if you say to him 'go back,' the first two at the front will go back and also take thousands with them."[27]

In fact, while Saddam was bemoaning the lack of effective resistance to the Iranian offensive, Iraqi forces were already fighting fiercely and inflicting heavy casualties on their attackers. The Iraqi corps commander had reacted with unusual dispatch, reflecting the signals intelligence available. With access to road networks on both sides of the Iranian advance, he concentrated Iraqi armor on the flanks of what turned out to be a murderous killing zone. The brigade commanders were no doubt assisted by the capture of the Iranian 92nd Division's operations order early in the fighting.[28] By the battle's end, upwards of one hundred of Iran's M-60s and Chieftain tanks were destroyed, with an additional 150 armored fighting vehicles captured.[29] More importantly, the Iranians lost tanks they would not be able to replace given the Khomeini regime's pariah status. In particular, the Iranian 16th Armored Division was nearly a complete wreck. On the other side, the Iraqis lost approximately 100 tanks, many reparable.

Almost 300 kilometers to the northwest of Susangard, frontline troops of the II Corps had found themselves after their initial advance 50 kilometers inside Iran without clear objectives. The Iraqi brigades, deployed in defensive positions at the foothills of the Zagros Mountains for four

---

[25] SH-AFGC-D-000-393, Transcript of a General Command of the Armed Forces Meeting During the First Gulf War and Telephone Conversations, 6–7 January 1981.
[26] *Ibid.*   [27] *Ibid.*
[28] *SH-SHTP-A-001-303, Recording of a Meeting between Saddam Hussein and Ba'ath Party Members Discussing the Iran–Iraq War, circa October 1981–early 1982.
[29] Efraim Karsh, *The Iran–Iraq War, 1980–1988* (New York, NY, 2009), 22.

months, had been under constant artillery harassment from the increasingly organized Iranians. Although Iraqi positions blocked the roads leading southwest to the Iran–Iraq border, the Iraqi advance had failed to interdict the network of major roads to the north and east. On 14 January, Saddam's senior military advisors briefed him on the situation of the 6th, 18th, and 50th Brigades. All three were showing signs of psychological "stress" after enduring near constant attacks.

The problem for Iraq's military planners was that they had few infantry units available to secure the foothills near Ilam and the road network that made maneuver by armored vehicles dangerous. The army chief of staff reported losing thirty-five tanks in the attempt, some of which had been lost to American TOW missiles. Saddam's frustration was clear: "Well, what is the solution ... we do not want a common solution; we need a solution to face the current situation ... Our current situation is that our units are losing too much."[30] The normally non-committal army chief of staff General Shanshal suggested that Iraq force Kurdish groups to carry the fight to the Iranians. Iraq should arm "partisans" to augment the armored units. The director of the GMID told Saddam that the Kurdish al-Jaf group could put 1,500 fighters into the hills to conduct ambushes and patrols.[31] Their efforts would cover the flanks of Iraqi armor protecting the road networks. Saddam was not impressed: "We need a big operation to demoralize the Iranians [in the central sector], because they did not have any important losses at the beginning of the war ... The use of the [tactics] they are mastering ... will [result] in crushing our units one after another."[32]

Several days into the offensive, the Iraqi general staff described Iran's tactics to Saddam as a series of "small local battles." The army's senior operations officer remarked that "[t]hey [the Iranians] want local battles. While their air force is working in one direction their army is working in [another]. The [Iranian] air force is planning on hitting targets that may not mean anything to the army."[33] Saddam, expressing some confusion at the direction of the various Iranian attacks, noted "his territory is

---

[30] The Tube-aligned, Optically tracked, Wire-data link (TOW) guided missile was introduced by the United States in the early 1970s and was known as one of the most effective anti-tank weapons of the period. TOWs played a prominent role in the Iran–Contra scandal, after the United States approved the delivery of 2,000 of them to Iran in 1985 and 1986.

[31] This appears to be a reference to elements of the Jaf tribe. The Jaf are the largest Kurdish tribal group with traditional territories straddling the Iraqi and Iranian borders in the area of Halabja.

[32] *SH-MISC-D-001-335, Transcript of Various Meetings between Saddam Hussein and Senior Officers, January 1981.

[33] SH-AFGC-D-000-393, Transcript of a General Command of the Armed Forces Meeting During the First Gulf War and Telephone Conversations, 6–7 January 1981.

occupied and yet he just chops at our territory." Nevertheless, he appeared to miss the significance of the major Iranian defeat that had just occurred.[34]

An assessment of Iranian and Iraqi tactics by Staff Brigadier Abdul Jawad Dhannoun, director GMID, concluded that the Iranians were capable of "limited success" in inflicting losses of soldiers and equipment, capturing Iraqis, and "raising the spirits of the Persians" through localized operations. He went on to note the failings of Iraqi tactics that "may be" enabling this Iranian approach: "The front of [Iraqi] units was [not being] covered by continuous surveillance. [Iraqi soldiers] [were staying] in shelters during the enemy artillery bombardments. There were no minefields and barbed wire within the defensive area of units. There was no alerting (either guard or screening force) in front of the principle defensive sites."[35]

Considering the Iran–Iraq War as a whole, the battles in January 1981 were militarily important for several reasons: the Iranians were unable to rebuild their armored forces because they could not buy enough first-class armored fighting vehicles. Politically, the Iranian defeat placed the secularists, Bani-Sadr in particular, in an increasingly tenuous situation, while it strengthened the hand of radical religious leaders who increased their attacks on the regular army and its reliability. The chroniclers of the *Pasdaran* efforts in the first years of the war argued that Iran's president had launched the offensive with the express political purpose of placing the secularists in control of Iran. Nevertheless, the grand ayatollah had supposedly seen through the president's efforts and understood that "this line of thought would have forced us once again to become dependent on the imperialist powers."[36]

The success in January led Saddam to tell his staff somewhat hopefully that "[the Iranian] defeat [will make] them realize that they will not be able to defeat the Iraqi Army."[37] However, while the Iraqis had repulsed the attack, they failed to build on that success and turn a defensive victory

[34] *Ibid.*
[35] SH-GMID-D-001-020, Information on Iranian Forces Including Their Movements, Casualties and Losses, and the Weapons That They Were Able to Acquire During the Iraqi–Iranian War, 1981. General Dhannoun's assessment of the failings of Iraqi tactical defensive capabilities is supported by interviews the authors conducted with Iraqi generals, particularly Major General Ra'ad Hamdani and Major General Aladdin Makki.
[36] *SH-MISC-D-001-350, *The Passing of Two Years of War: Iran–Iraq*, Political Office of the Islamic Revolution Pasdaran Corps. Khomeini's paranoia about an attempt to overthrow his regime continued to be confirmed. Even as late as May 1982, disaffected air force officers may have been preparing another coup. Sepehr Zabih, *The Iranian Military in Revolution and War* (New York, NY, 1988), 129.
[37] SH-AFGC-D-000-393, Transcript of a General Command of the Armed Forces Meeting During the First Gulf War and Telephone Conversations, 6–7 January 1981.

to operational utility. Despite Saddam's 7 January order to "tell them [the Iraqi division commanders] to continue the momentum and not to [break off] contact with the enemy forces. The enemy will absolutely not be given a chance, [they] must be chased with all [we] have," Iraqi counterattacks had culminated.[38] Perhaps the heavy fighting had drained the Iraqis' willingness to counterattack. Nevertheless, an equally plausible explanation is that their commanders simply lacked the imagination or will to pursue a beaten enemy. Certainly, Susangard was open to an Iraqi repost. But Saddam and his generals were unwilling to push reserves into the area to exploit the defeat of the Iranian armored forces.

Saddam had begun to realize the war would not be short as early as late October 1980. He noted to his senior military leaders:

Yesterday, I was speaking with the Pakistani minister. He said to me, no, they [the Iranians have] started to understand. I told him they do not understand. He said the whole world knows that the Iraqi Army is victorious and that they [the Iranians] are defeated. I told him that they do not understand, because they have no idea of what defeat means ... The situation, the situation is of denial ... he [Khomeini] will not feel anything until blood is at his feet ... and then he will say to his soldiers "advance" and the soldiers will say they will not advance ... because you have made me lose my faith.[39]

Saddam reiterated his belief that the war would last a long time in conversation with his military advisors in early spring 1981. He described the pattern of future events with surprising accuracy:

We start another operation so that we can keep them [the Iranians] occupied ... so we do not give them a chance to pull together and start an [offensive] ... I think they are not going to give up. They will start another offensive and that is it. What will they do afterwards? ... They will begin to think. They will give themselves a year so that they can secure military supplies and American spare parts ... We will then have to think what to counter within that case. The dead will not come to life again in this short period of time.[40]

In March 1981, while discussing a corps commander's request to be allowed to use six Luna missiles in an upcoming operation, Saddam argued that the Iraqis should use these missiles against more lucrative military and psychological targets than enemy troop concentrations.[41]

---

[38] *Ibid.*

[39] SH-PDWN-D-000-566, Saddam Meeting with the General Command of the Armed Forces About the Iran–Iraq War, October–November 1980.

[40] SH-SHTP-A-000-626, Saddam Hussein Discusses Neighboring Countries and Their Regimes, January 1981.

[41] The Luna (or NATO designate FROG-7) was a Soviet-manufactured, unguided tactical rocket with a range of 42 miles. The warheads on the Luna can be modified for high explosive or chemical munitions.

This sparked a conversation between the dictator and his military advisors about how the Iraqis could use such missiles to best effect in the future:

SADDAM:	... the missiles [could] be used tactically ... in [a] chemical war?
HEAD OF THE PRESIDENTIAL COUNCIL:	And bacterial war, also.
SADDAM:	Yes.
CHIEF OF STAFF OF THE ARMY:	The missile?
SADDAM:	Yes, it can be used in bacterial and chemical war.
CHIEF OF STAFF OF THE ARMY:	It can be used for carrying ... warheads.
SADDAM:	And place containers in it.
AIR FORCE AND AIR DEFENSE COMMANDER:	The missile warhead will be replaced by [chemical and biological] containers.
SADDAM:	Let's start the implementation of this program.[42]

A briefing for Saddam in May 1981 suggests how senior officers were describing the military effectiveness of their ground forces to the dictator. The reporting officer described his favorable impressions of one of the two divisions he had recently visited:

The ... officers, sir, are doing a great job ... The major general, sir, of the second division is very organized and excellent in training his soldiers. When I attended their training, he presents his regiment by numbers and in a very organized way. Everyone moves forward very smoothly, as if the major general has measured every inch ... like a robot ... everyone knows his position and his duty, very impressive sir![43]

It is doubtful whether Saddam recognized the weaknesses in such a top-down approach. After all, everything the division commander was doing conformed exactly with the intellectual and cultural nature of Ba'ath ethos.

As the Iranians licked their wounds, contact along the front declined to artillery exchanges. This stalemate led the Organization of the Islamic Conference (OIC) to attempt a brokered peace. In January 1981, a conference of the OIC's foreign ministers and diplomats met in Mecca,

---

[42] *SH-MISC-D-001-334, Transcript of a Meeting between Saddam Hussein and Senior Officers, February–March 1981. The quantity and quality of captured Iraqi documents relating to chemical weapons development and use during the Iran–Iraq War is surprisingly limited given the well-known size of its program. The reason has nothing to do with any lack of effort on the part of the Iraqi bureaucracy to document its work. Rather, it was the legacy of Iraq's efforts after 1991 to hide and then eventually destroy any WMD-related materials to include historical documents relating to WMD in the Iran–Iraq War.

[43] *Ibid.*

Saudi Arabia. It comprised forty-seven Islamic states that were to "reinforce our solidarity and set in motion the process of our renaissance." Iraq forcefully pressed its case. Yet, the best Saddam could muster was a lukewarm restatement of UN Security Council Resolution No. 479 expressing "deep concern at the continuation of hostilities between two Islamic countries" and a call for an immediate ceasefire.[44] The problem of being forced, at least publicly, to choose sides in a conflict portrayed by the combatants as a struggle between pan-Arab and pan-Islamic philosophies proved difficult, if not impossible, for the members.

Equipment and logistical problems

When Saddam's advisors informed him in early October 1980 that the Soviets were refusing to ship Iraq additional arms, he had said, "up to now, we have not requested a screw from anyone. We are not in need."[45] However, he soon changed his tune. Iraq's air force commander confessed to Saddam "we have a shortage of spare parts ... actually it is urgent." The immediate problems were shortages of tires and canopy glass for MiG-21s and MiG-23s. The air force commander assured Saddam that the search was on for suppliers. Saddam, perhaps sensing better than his staff the risk of appearing weak at any level, directed that "requests for weapons from countries, from now on, will be political." He decided he would delegate a "senior comrade to call the designated ambassador and whisper to him our request in complete secrecy."[46] Moreover, Saddam warned,

---

[44] Of the forty-seven members, only Iran and Libya did not attend. Among the measures taken during the conference was one announcing that:

> The Kings, Emirs, and Heads of State of Islamic countries have agreed to declare holy Jihad for salvaging Al Quds Al Sharif [Jerusalem], supporting the Palestinian people and bringing about Israeli withdrawal from occupied Arab territories. In their resolve to launch jihad, the Islamic states have made it clear that jihad has its Islamic concept that permits no misinterpretations or misunderstandings. They have also agreed that the practical measures to put jihad into effect would be taken in accordance with the Islamic concept of jihad and in continuous consultation among themselves.

> See Section F, Paragraph 1 in "The Mecca Declaration of the Third Islamic Summit Conference," Organization of the Islamic Conference, 1981, www.oic-oci.org/english/conf/is/3/3rd-is-sum.htm (accessed 19 February 2014). As noted here, calls from the government in Tehran for a jihad against an OIC member state were problematic.

[45] SH-MISC-D-000-695, Saddam Hussein Meeting with Various Iraqi Officials About the Iraqi Position Early on in the Iran–Iraq War, 12–13 October 1980.

[46] SH-SHTP-D-000-846, General Command of the Armed Forces Meeting Transcripts During the First Gulf War, 17 October 1980.

if such news [of shortages] fell into the hands of our enemy, they [could take advantage] ... we will take precautions. The enemy can imagine and consider our precautions as a critical need for us and assess our fighting stance. Based on this, the enemy will continue to hope for victory. We must give the enemy the impression that our military situation is good and [will be] strong for a long time to come and that we are not in need of help from others, in spite of the imposed – or could be imposed – embargo on us, and this should apply to all types of weapons.[47]

The battles during the first winter underlined that logistics for a sustained war across an almost 800-mile front required more than patriotic rhetoric and purging incompetent officers. As early as January 1981, artillery ammunition shortages had become acute. Divisional artillery units fighting that month were expending upwards of 1,000 rounds per day.[48] In one case in late October 1980, during the siege of Abadan, Iraqi artillery fired 40,000 rounds of a certain type of 122mm howitzer. At the beginning of the conflict, the Iraqi Army stockpiles had only 83,000 rounds of that ammunition.[49] By early 1981 stocks of artillery ammunition in Iraq reached such a crisis level that the resupply of artillery battalions remained limited to the amounts of ammunition produced by Iraq's munitions factories on a daily basis, an insignificant amount compared to what was needed. In fact, both sides were desperately trying to rebuild their ammunition stocks in the face of demands for more ammunition, spare parts, and new equipment.[50] It was a bonanza for those involved on the shady side of international arms dealing.

The new year brought the first new weapons to replace those the Iraqis had lost in the fighting. On 7 January 1981, the chief of staff was able to report to Saddam:

We have contracted for four hundred tanks ... the first shipment arrived ... about two hundred are [already deployed] with the 10th Armored Brigade. If we had another two hundred of them the division would be complete. [The tank's] shell is 125mm which is much heavier than the support guns belonging to the

[47] *Ibid*. Saddam is apparently referring to the possibility of unilateral sanctions emerging from member state interpretations of the recently passed, but distinctly toothless, UN Security Council Resolution 479 (28 September 1980).

[48] Transcript of a Meeting Held at the General Command of the Armed Forces (10 July 1980) in SH-SHTP-D-000-572, Transcripts from Meetings between Saddam Iraqi Army Officers , January 1981–April 1993.

[49] SH-PDWN-D-000-566, Saddam Meeting with the General Command of the Armed Forces About the Iran–Iraq War, October–November 1980.

[50] For other Iraqi efforts to trace what the Iranians were buying, see *SH-GMID-D-001-337, Iraqi Intelligence Estimates on Iranian Weapons Acquisitions, 28 March–1 August 1981; *SH-GMID-D-001-338, Correspondence Relating to Iranian Weapons Acquisition from Brazil and Spain, July 1981; *SH-MODX-D-001-339, Memoranda Relating to the Soviet–Iranian Trade Agreement, 1981.

artillery . . . Heavier! I mean when it hits a target it destroys it . . . It appeared in our first scrimmage with them [the Iranians] which was when we were advancing on them, we destroyed a large number of their tanks, and they lost their balance . . . This time their spirit collapsed. When we moved and engaged them, they were defeated.[51]

In some areas, the Iraqis were already using captured weapons against Iran. After discussing the relative advantage of American TOWs compared to the Soviet anti-tank missiles in Iraq's inventory, Saddam told his staff to go to the Saudis and Jordanians and press them for additional TOW support equipment.[52]

A March 1981 discussion between Saddam, Tariq Aziz, and the minister of defense raised the issue of acquiring American tanks.[53] The minister noted that "according to a contract," America supposedly had the "capability" to supply Iraq with 500 tanks a year. Saddam replied that he had hopes for 2,000 tanks per year: "[I]n fact, we [would be] happy . . . to push it in order to purchase about 6,000 tanks in three years. Yes and we get them ready so that the total [could] reach ten thousand at once and assault in the field all at once." Saddam's numbers were perhaps overstated for effect, and given US policy at the time, the entire discussion seems to have been a wild flight of fancy. Tariq Aziz warned, prophetically, that the unnamed arms merchants they were dealing with "cannot keep a secret" and that "all of their advisors and assistants . . . [are] swindlers." Notwithstanding Aziz's cautions, Saddam wanted to press ahead with the "contract" through Kuwait and Jordan in 1981 and "if the war persists till 1982, we will get back with them."[54] Saddam's

---

[51] SH-AFGC-D-000-393, Transcript of a General Command of the Armed Forces Meeting During the First Gulf War and Telephone Conversations, 6–7 January 1981.

[52] *SH-MISC-D-001-335, Transcript of Various Meetings between Saddam Hussein and Senior Officers, January 1981.

[53] Despite Saddam's oft-stated distrust of the United States, he did on occasion express a pragmatic desire for improved relations. In a meeting early in 1981, for example, he thought Iraq might be able to send officers to the United States for training "in the future . . . when our relations improve." SH-SHTP-A-000-626, Saddam Hussein Discusses Neighboring Countries and Their Regimes, January 1981.

[54] *SH-MISC-D-001-334, Transcript of a Meeting between Saddam Hussein and Senior Officers, February–March 1981. On the question of with whom Saddam was dealing, the transcript is unclear. A June 1981 State Department telegram, referring to a 28 May meeting between William Eagleton and Tariq Aziz, warns that "we recognize that private arms merchants, including possibly Americans, might be attracted by possible sales opportunities growing out of the conflict such as that between Iraq and Iran. We are concerned that private activities not feed rumors of changes in or exceptions to the US position of principles with which the Iraqis are familiar." "Cable from Secretary of State, Washington DC to US Interests Section, Baghdad, Subject: US Policy on Arms Sales and Transfers to Iraq and Iran, 3 June 1981 (Declassified)," in *CWIHP Critical Oral History Conference: The Origins, Conduct, and Impact of the Iran–Iraq War, 1980–1988:*

guidance was clear: "We can ask [an] Arab country that has good relations with the British to make a deal ... on the item that we want to have
and have them [the friendly Arab country] buy it ... After the gun is
delivered, then they can pass it on to us ... We must make use of this
procedure."[55]

Negotiations with potential worldwide suppliers were a constant subject of discussion. Part of the problem was that, like all amateur military
strategists, Saddam had paid relatively little attention to logistics and
supply before the war. In 1981, he suggested to his ministers where his
priority for logistics now lay: "[T]he first thing I take into account is the
psychological aspect, before I examine how much supply we have, how
much ammunition we have, of what type it is and before comparing them
with the enemy's ammunition, supply, and equipment."[56]

The main problem with acquiring ammunition, spare parts, and new
equipment initially lay in the fact that the Soviet Union was sitting on the
fence. It had refused any increase in the supply of Soviet weapons or
ammunition at the beginning of the conflict in September 1980.[57] Why?
First, its leaders were less than happy with Saddam for unleashing the
war with Iran without seeking their blessing. Tariq Aziz travelled to
Moscow in September and November 1980 trying to secure additional
arms shipments in accordance with the 1972 Treaty of Friendship and
Cooperation. Both times, the Soviets rebuffed him because "the war
between [Iraq and Iran] was welcomed by the Imperialist camp." In
the Soviet's view, by fighting each other, Baghdad and Tehran were
destroying their ability to oppose the West.[58] Second and equally important was the fact the Soviets believed as late as early 1981 that the Tudeh
Party (the Communist Party) might win out in the chaos that had

Document Reader, Malcolm Byrne and Christian Ostermann, eds. (Washington,
DC, 2004).

[55] SH-SHTP-A-000-626, Saddam Hussein Discusses Neighboring Countries and Their
Regimes, January 1981. Iraq began receiving military equipment from Egypt through
Jordan as early as March 1981. By 1982, the value of the Arab-supplied weapons had
reached one billion dollars. Bryan R. Gibson, *Covert Relationship: American Foreign
Policy, Intelligence, and the Iran–Iraq War, 1980–1988* (Santa Barbara, CA, 2010), 63.

[56] *SH-SHTP-A-001-228, Saddam Hussein Discussing Ba'ath Party Principles and
History, Military Strategy, and General Administrative Issues.

[57] In December 1980, the CIA reported, "In the arms supply area, the Soviets apparently
told Iraq on 22 September that the USSR would not increase the quantities of military
supplies destined for Iraq or negotiate new sales contracts beyond items already under
discussion before hostilities broke out. The Soviets seem to have been even less
responsive to Iraqi demands than they promised." Director of Central Intelligence
CIA, *Special National Intelligence Estimate: Soviet Interests, Policies, and Prospects with
Respect to the Iran–Iraq War* (Langley, VA, 1980).

[58] Oles M. Smolansky, *The USSR and Iraq: The Soviet Quest for Influence* (Durham, NC,
1991), 231.

followed the overthrow of the Shah.[59] In their view, a Communist or friendly Iran would be of greater value to Soviet prospects in the Middle East than Saddam's Ba'athist regime, which they had little reason to trust.[60] Thus, the Iraqis had to look elsewhere for support.

Despite growing needs, Saddam remained cavalier about the difficulties Iraq was having with its largest arms supplier. He continued to emphasize Iraqi and Ba'ath spirit over material needs. "As for the Soviet Union, or France, or Italy, or Libya, or Syria ... [they] should consider who is with us and who is against us," Saddam opined. Iraqis are dying "in the hundreds and thousands." They were fighting "all of the big powers and all of the middle countries and the rest of the world," but they were succeeding even where the Soviets would have failed: "The Soviet Union cannot comprehend the role that the Iraqi Army has undertaken ... I am confident that the Soviet Union [could not] hold onto the same area that we are holding onto."[61]

On 31 January, the army chief of staff, General Shanshal, informed Saddam that a promised shipment of Chinese artillery ammunition would be delayed for at least four months. He added that, given Iraq's nascent defense industry's inability to predict the output of its munitions factories, artillery batteries would have to "stop shooting." Saddam was incredulous that China, with what he described as a mobilized army approaching 20 million soldiers, could not fulfill its contract on a more aggressive schedule.[62] Moreover, the Soviets were no longer producing ammunition for some of the weapons they had previously provided Iraq, which forced supply officers to scramble after other potential sources.[63]

---

[59] It was only when Khomeini's revolution was relatively secure in spring 1983 that the clerics moved completely against the Tudeh Party. From that point on, the Soviets' strategy of hedging their bets was bankrupt and they became openly pro-Iraqi and stepped up their weapons deliveries. Zabih, *The Iranian Military in Revolution and War*, 129.

[60] The Ba'athists, led by Saddam, had ruthlessly destroyed Iraq's Communist Party after a brief attempt to co-opt them in the early 1970s. See Hanna Batatu, *The Old Social Classes and the Revolutionary Movements of Iraq: A Study of Iraq's Old Landed and Commerical Classes and of Its Communists, Ba'athists, and Free Officers* (Princeton, NJ, 2004), 100–110; Makiya, *Republic of Fear*, 229–257.

[61] Recording of a Meeting Between Saddam Hussein and High Ranking Officials Relating to the Soviet Union (3 October 1981) in SH-SHTP-D-000-711, Saddam Hussein and Iraqi Officials Discussing the King Fahad Initiative, Relations with the USSR, and Perceptions of Other Middle Eastern Countries, October–November 1981. Saddam was obviously not familiar with conditions on the Eastern Front during World War II.

[62] Transcript of a Meeting Held at the General Command of the Armed Forces (10 July 1980) in SH-SHTP-D-000-572, Transcripts from Meetings between Saddam Iraqi Army Officers , January 1981–April 1993.

[63] SH-PDWN-D-000-566, Saddam Meeting with the General Command of the Armed Forces About the Iran–Iraq War, October–November 1980.

The working alternatives indicate how desperate things had become. According to Shanshal, his staff officers were making interim arrangements with smaller nations of even small quantities of ammunition. For example, the Yugoslavs had agreed to ship 3,000 130mm and 5,000 152mm artillery shells immediately. The Czechs for their part agreed to supply 3,000 250mm shells, while the Egyptians had arranged for Somalia to resell to Iraq ammunition Cairo had earlier provided them, albeit the deal taking place at black-market prices.[64] The Iraqis also quietly cut a comparatively large ammunition deal with the Greeks for upwards of 20,000 shells.

During the winter of 1980–1981, the emphasis was "buy, buy, buy,"[65] but for contracting officers, transportation posed an immediate problem. In addition to being inefficient, air transport was politically difficult for some states. In the end, Shanshal told Saddam that by using a combination of suppliers and modes of transportation, he was confident Iraq could "cover the three to four months till the equipment [and ammunition] arrives from China."[66] The Iraqi military sent buyers far and wide to secure not only ammunition, but also all calibers of artillery systems. Purchase orders and bartered oil-for-hardware deals were let for Soviet, French, and American artillery systems from a wide array of countries including Kuwait, Saudi Arabia, Yemen, and, of course, Jordan. Money was no object. Saddam personally told contracting officers that the caliber, make, and price of the weapons were of little importance. The only things that were important were "time" and "keeping the fire upon the head of the enemy, because this makes things better."[67] The challenge was staggering. Table 5.1 presents an extract from the front for late April 1981. At the time, there was relatively little fighting and the three

[64] From the early 1960s through the late 1980s, Egypt and the Soviet Union were the major suppliers of the Somali military. Saddam noted, in early 1981, that Adnan Khairallah was primarily responsible for expanding the program to acquire military hardware from any and all suppliers. SH-SHTP-A-000-626, Saddam Hussein Discusses Neighboring Countries and Their Regimes, January 1981.

[65] According to a 1984 report, before the war, Iraq primarily bought major weapons from three countries. By 1983, it was buying weapons from eighteen countries and was purchasing other military-related support from twenty-two others. Michael Brzoska and Thomas Ohlson, "Arms Trade II: The Iran–Iraq War and the Arms Trade," *Fact Sheets and Policy Briefs* (Stockholm, SE, 1984), 7. Downloaded from books. sipri. org/ files/FS/SIPRIFS8403. pdf.

[66] Transcript of a Meeting Held at the General Command of the Armed Forces (10 July 1980) in SH-SHTP-D-000-572, Transcripts from Meetings between Saddam Iraqi Army Officers, January 1981–April 1993. According to this transcript, in addition to the shipment from China, the Iraqis were hoping for a major shipment from the USSR in the second quarter of 1981.

[67] *Ibid.*

Table 5.1 *Ammunition issue 19–25 April 1981 for I, II, and III Corps Chief of the Army Staff, Field Artillery Directorate*

Type of Weapon	No. Rounds	Type of Weapon	No. Rounds
M46 (130mm) Towed Gun (Soviet)	4,906	M1931/37 or A-19 (122mm) Gun (Soviet)	2,826
D30 (122mm) Towed Gun-Howitzer (Soviet)	9,542	American (75mm) Gun	2
D30 (152mm) Towed Gun-Howitzer (Soviet)	4,517	Russian Mortar (120mm)	2,608
ML-20 (152mm) Howitzer (Soviet)	126	French Mortar (120mm)	0
Yugoslavian Howitzer (155mm)	1,707	American Mortar (120mm)	2,091
S-23 (180mm) Gun (Soviet)	39	Russian Mortar (160mm)	71
8 inch (NFI)	56	Yugoslavian Gun (76mm)	7
M 109 (155mm) Self-propelled Howitzer	153	Spanish (120mm)	1,769
Yugoslavian (105mm)	8,496	American (105mm)	478
Italian (105mm)	1,201	SU (100mm) Self-Propelled Gun (Soviet)	276
D10 (105mm) Anti-tank Gun (Soviet)	1,064	Grad (122mm) Rocket Launcher (Soviet)	1,416
BL (5.5in) Gun (British)	354	Katyusha (132mm) Rocket Launcher (Soviet)	15
QF 25 pounder (British)	806	British Mortar (4.1 inch)	550
M1938 M30 (122mm) Howitzer (Soviet)	3,802	American (155mm) Towed Howitzer	85
MT-12 (100mm) Anti-tank Gun (Soviet)	1	Italian Mortar (150mm)	58
D-44 (85mm) Gun (Soviet)	4,628		
	Total Rounds 53,650		

Iraqi Army Corps expended more than 53,000 rounds from thirty-one different mortar, gun, howitzer, and rocket systems.[68]

These purchases – from sellers who knew how desperate the Iraqis were – bit deeply into Saddam's hoard of foreign exchange.[69] By late spring 1982, the Iraqis had virtually exhausted the war chest they had

[68] SH-GMID-D-001-020, Information on Iranian Forces Including Their Movements, Casualties and Losses, and the Weapons That They Were Able to Acquire During the Iraqi–Iranian War, 1981.

[69] During 1980 to 1988, Iraq imported on average $7 billion-worth of weapons per year. This represented 12 percent of the world's total arms exports. See Rachel Schmidt,

when they had invaded Iran eighteen months earlier. Oil prices were also beginning to fall. Exacerbating Iraq's financial difficulties was Saddam's pursuit of a domestic policy of "guns and butter." Thus, in May 1981, the regime had to seek a $2 billion loan from the Kuwaitis to repair the damage the war had already inflicted on Iraq's infrastructure.[70]

Saddam was also determined to avoid the potentially dangerous problem of a single supplier for Iraq's military needs. He reminded his advisors in early 1981:

From now on we should not remain with one supplier. Before we were dealing with the French, and we stayed with them ... [Then] we would ask if they had something [to sell us], and it would be denied ... It is true, in the beginning, not many countries were willing to supply us, but now the situation is different. There are many who would be willing to sell us weapons.[71]

With friends like these

Intelligence information, often in the form of high-level rumors, raced among senior Iraqi leaders in winter 1981. The tacit objective of using the Iran–Iraq War as a rallying cry for pan-Arab unity (or at the least Ba'ath Party unity) turned out to be a fantasy. In Saddam's world, the security services offered a number of culprits to explain this turn of events. Iraqi intelligence noted that Syrian and Iranian officials were regularly meeting in Damascus, that Syrian-sponsored Palestinian and Shi'a groups in Lebanon were volunteering to join Iranian forces, and that members of the Syrian senior military staff were helping Iran with "preparation and oversight [of] the attack which was launched by the Persian enemy on the 5th of January."[72] Other reports indicated North

"Global Arms Exports to Iraq, 1960–1990, " *A RAND Note* (Santa Monica, CA, 1991), 11–12.

[70] Various Documents Relating to a $2 Billion Kuwaiti Loan to Iraq (21 April 1981) in *SH-RVCC-D-001-393, Resolutions Issued by the RCC Regarding Various Administrative Concerns, 1981; *SH-RVCC-D-001-340, Various Documents Relating to a $2 Billion Kuwait Loan to Iraq, May 1981. During the first year of the war, Saddam's Gulf allies reportedly gave him $16–18 billion in direct financial aid and loans. See Gerd Nonneman, "The Gulf States and the Iran–Iraq War: Pattern Shifts and Continuities," in *Iran, Iraq, and the Legacies of War*, Lawrence G. Potter and Gary G. Sick, eds. (New York, NY, 2004), 175.

[71] SH-SHTP-A-000-626, Saddam Hussein Discusses Neighboring Countries and Their Regimes, January 1981.

[72] GMID to Presidential Diwan of Presidential Directorate (19 March 1981) Memorandum from Director in *SH-GMID-D-001-394, Military Orders and Communications between the GMID, the Armed Forces General Command, the RCC, and Various Iraqi Units During the Iran–Iraq War, 1981. The Palestinian group was identified as the Democratic Front. Members of the Lebanese Amal organization

Korea was suspected of supplying battlefield engineering advice to the Iranians.[73]

Meanwhile, intelligence from early 1981 noted the unsettled nature of the Iranian regime. A GMID study dated 1 March reached the following conclusions:

[The] struggle between [the] Bani-Sadr and Bahashti blocks [is intensifying.] The contradictions are spreading throughout Iran and a wave of anti-government propaganda ... [and] political chaos ... [is] currently sweeping through Iran's cities. Khomeini continues to enjoy general loyalty as a spiritual leader and as a symbol ... [However,] the current [contradictions] in internal affairs ... depends on Khomeini's ability to make [a] decision ... which we see as relatively weak. The enemy is in a state of unrest and the collar of isolation is still imposed on them.[74]

Iran's internal instability and external isolation were important metrics of success for Saddam beginning in early 1981. Changes to either were tracked carefully even if poorly understood. A report from April 1981 detailed Iran's new approach to reach out to the world in order "to break the political isolation which [it] imposed on itself." Khomeini had reportedly approved secret delegations and dispatched them to a large number of First and Second World countries. Nevertheless, according to the GMID analysts, Iran's aggressive attempts to repair relations with a wide variety of nations both inside and outside of the Islamic world had "failed in [their] specific, basic goals."[75]

Iran's revolutionary fervor, a declared non-aligned stance – the so-called "neither East nor West policy" – and a rigid foreign policy that sought to preserve "the principle of non-compromise" did not make for an effective outreach program.[76] Nevertheless, despite initial failures at

were formed into units called the "Khomeinians" and were being "trained and equipped by Syrian forces *en route* to Iran." Some reports indicated that Libyan military supplies were being flown out of Tripoli and Benghazi to Tehran seven to eight times a day. Memorandum from Taha Yasin Ramadan to GMID (19 February 1981) in *SH-GMID-D-001-394, Military Orders and Communications between the GMID, the Armed Forces General Command, the RCC, and Various Iraqi Units During the Iran–Iraq War, 1981.

[73] SH-GMID-D-001-429, Memorandum from GMID to Military Attaches Islamabad, Ankara, and New Deli Relating to Technical Assistance Provided by North Korea, 18 December 1982.

[74] SH-IISX-D-000-841, 1981 Iraqi Evaluation of the Iranian Military Threat, January 1980–January 1981.

[75] SH-GMID-D-000-892, Study by the General Military Intelligence Directorate (GMID) About Iranian Foreign Delegations after the Shah's Fall, 20 March 1981.

[76] Philip G. Philip, "The Islamic Revolution in Iran: Its Impact on Foreign Policy," in *Renegade States: The Evolution of Revolutionary Foreign Policy*, Stephen Chan and Andrew J. Williams, eds. (Manchester, 1994), 123–124.

the diplomatic level, the Iranians were effectively laying the groundwork for an increasingly diverse and complex web of contacts necessary to acquire the military equipment and spare parts its military required to prosecute the war.[77] While not as effective as the Iraqis in securing large weapons contracts, the profit and political influence motives of businessmen and governments alike kept spare parts for the Shah's old military flowing.

Intelligence of a more useful caliber was also making its way into Baghdad. A 17 March 1981 memorandum for the director of the GMID noted that, according to their unspecified US contacts "the Persian enemy will mount a new military attack following the rainy season and to be exact [it] will [occur] in the month of April 1981." A handwritten comment at the bottom of the memorandum by the deputy director of the GMID noted that such information was less than helpful, since it failed to indicate "the nature of the new military attack, the size, the type, the location [and] whether [it was going to be in the] north, south, or the middle."[78] This early exchange hinted at what would become a point of increasing frustration for the Iraqis with respect to the assistance provided by Western intelligence agencies during the coming years – its lack of specificity.[79]

Perhaps part of the explanation for the frustration was not the quality of information American intelligence provided, but the source. In a telling assessment of what appeared on the surface to be the inexplicable Iranian air attack on a Kuwaiti oil facility in October 1981, the GMID argued that the most likely reason was "to push through the AWACS ... to Saudi Arabia deal. America may have instructed the regime in Tehran

---

[77] SH-GMID-D-000-892, Study by the General Military Intelligence Directorate (GMID) About Iranian Foreign Delegations after the Shah's Fall, 20 March 1981.

[78] Memorandum from General Intelligence Service Directorate to GMID (17 March 1981) in *SH-GMID-D-001-394, Military Orders and Communications between the GMID, the Armed Forces General Command, the RCC, and Various Iraqi Units During the Iran–Iraq War, 1981. In fact, that is the difficulty with all intelligence, but as with all amateurs, Saddam assumed the possibility of exact information about his enemy, including intentions. Cooperation and contact between Iraq and the United States was increasing during this period but it is not clear from this or related Iraqi documents if this US contact was an official or unofficial source of information. See declassified US government documents in *CWIHP Critical Oral History Conference: The Origins, Conduct, and Impact of the Iran–Iraq War, 1980–1988*. See also Gibson, *Covert Relationship*, 56–64.

[79] For examples of how such contacts were portrayed in the press, see Tim Weiner, "Iraq Uses Techniques in Spying against Its Former Tutor, the US," *Philadelphia Inquirer*, 5 February 1991; Michael Dobbs, "US Had Key Role in Iraq Buildup Trade in Chemical Arms; Allowed Despite Their Use on Iranians, Kurds," *Washington Post*, 29 December 2003; Patrick E. Tyler, "Officers Say US Aided Iraq in War Despite Use of Gas," *New York Times*, 18 August 2002.

to carry out the mission to demonstrate how important they [the Americans] are to the Kingdom of Saudi Arabia as well as for the security of the Gulf, and to make Congress approve their sale to them [the Saudis]."[80]

This can't-live-with-them-can't-live-without-them dilemma affected both sides of Iraqi–US relations. In 1983, American intelligence summed up the issue:

The current regime [in Iraq] is likely to pursue policies more favorable to the United States than any successor regime. The United States is likely to come in for harsher treatment from new leaders either of a Ba'athist or Islamic fundamentalist variety ... A major upheaval in Iraq, one in which the Iranians were a significant influence, would have severe consequences for US interests in the Middle East.[81]

With regard to arms sales to the Iranians, Iraqi intelligence and diplomats struggled to keep up with the cast of characters in the regional arms *Suq*. In one of the first high-level diplomatic contacts between Iraq and the United States, Tariq Aziz told the head of the US interests section in Baghdad that while "Iraq did not believe that the United States was providing arms to Iran," somehow US arms and spare parts were reaching the Iranians.[82] What was at first a trickle soon became a flood. Within days of the start of the war, Syria became the conduit for sympathetic Arab states and groups to funnel weapons and supplies to Iran.[83] By 1981, a complex network of sometime strange bedfellows had joined the game. A 1981 GMID document noted the activities of a retired Iranian colonel, known to be an arms buyer for the "Iraqi opposition in the north." The GMID reported that he first obtained weapons through a Lebanese arms dealer, who in turn made deliveries through Cypriot businessmen using a shipping company managed by a Palestinian-Jordanian operating out of Kuwait. The weapons were then moved from

---

[80] Memorandum from GMID RE: Results of Iranian Air Raid (2 October 1981) in SH-GMID-D-000-840, Correspondence Discussing Cooperation between Iran and Syria, July 1981–October 1981. The actual reasons for the Iranian raid are unknown. Speculation at the time included a warning about Iran's ability to expand the conflict or specifically a message to the newly formed Gulf Cooperation Council that Iran was the dominant power in the region and a warning to one of Saddam's bankers to stop financing the war. The sale of AWACS to Saudi Arabia was, at the time, embroiled in a major policy fight between the Reagan Administration and Congress. The deal, announced in April, was finally approved in late October 1981.

[81] Director of Central Intelligence, *Special National Intelligence Estimate*, 23–24.

[82] "Cable from US Interests Branch, Baghdad to US State Department, Subject: Meeting with Tariq Aziz, 28 May 1981 (Declassified)," in *CWIHP Critical Oral History Conference: The Origins, Conduct, and Impact of the Iran–Iraq War, 1980–1988*.

[83] Initial shipments, all denied by Syria at the time, were primarily man-portable anti-aircraft and anti-tank missiles. See Jubin M. Goodarzi, *Syria and Iran: Diplomatic Alliance and Power Politics in the Middle East* (London, 2006), 33–42.

Israel to Libya, where they were then flown to Iran aboard Libyan military transports.[84]

Negotiating by fire

Baghdad showed its hand in its eagerness to accept the January 1981 terms of the Organization of the Islamic Conference, which, without addressing the question of who was the aggressor or the facts on the ground, invited "the two conflicting parties to cease fire immediately."[85] Iran perceived Saddam's eagerness for a ceasefire as an indication of Iraqi weakness. Saddam tried to show renewed strength by launching an offensive to capture Susangard on 19 March.[86] The attack failed, largely because of unimaginative Iraqi tactics, as well as the presence of the Iranian army's parachute brigade, which had had two months to prepare defenses and square away the *Pasdaran* in the city. The defeat marked the turning point in the six-month-old conflict. Using the Revolution's second anniversary, Khomeini laid out Iran's position on the "imposed" war: there would be no ceasefire until Iraq is "forced to retreat to [its] own border." He ominously added, "then we will deal with them."[87] Generally, as one commentator has noted, one might characterize Iraqi operations up to this point as the "reinforcement of failure with more failure."[88]

A minor Iranian success in retaking the heights overlooking Susangard in May annoyed the dictator considerably:

The most important issue here is not to allow additional damage and losses. We need to strengthen our armed forces, especially improving morale everywhere ... We are excellent in creating plans; however, we are very slow in responding, and

---

[84] Memoranda (November 1981) in *SH-GMID-D-001-341, Various GMID Documents Relating to Iranian Arms Deals, March 1981. In mid-1981, the clandestine connections between Iran and a small group of Israeli arms dealers that would eventually evolve into the Iran–Contra scandal of 1986 was already in full swing. In July 1981, an Israeli businessman had reportedly already signed a $135 million deal to sell Iran spare parts for its high-tech American weapons. For further discussions of this trade, see Gregory Treverton, "Covert Action: Forward to the Past?," in *Covert Action: Behind the Veils of Secret Foreign Policy*, Loch K. Johnson, ed. (Santa Barbara, CA, 2006), 79.

[85] "Resolution No. 6/3-E(IS): The Iraqi–Iranian Conflict," Organization of the Islamic Conference, 1981, www.oic-oci.org/english/conf/is/3/3rd-is-sum(political).htm#06 (accessed 19 February 2014).

[86] Dilip Hiro, *Iran under the Ayatollahs* (London, 1987), 174.

[87] Statement by Imam Ayatollah Khomeini to the Diplomatic Corps in Tehran (11 February 1981) in *SH-GMID-D-001-342, GMID Memoranda Regarding Iranian Declarations About Iraq, 1981–1984.

[88] Translation of Lieutenant General Ra'ad Majid al-Hamdani, *Memoir: From the Golan to the Collapse of Baghdad: Six Wars in Thirty Years* (Baghdad, unpublished 2003).

that is a fact! . . . I have proof that we have left fully equipped locations in the past where the enemy was able to study them, discover our techniques, and predict our next plan . . . We must take charge of the situation. That is what we need to work on![89]

Saddam was clearly taking stock of the emerging situation and questioning the quality of his military advice. On 27 May 1981, after a briefing on a plan for a broad front summer offensive, he again challenged his military experts:

I do not agree with such a plan! Why should we walk into the fire to fight them in the comfort of their territory? Let them come to us. Why should we meet them in an area where there is no river, no lake, or anything? We have to lure them to a big area, such as [Susangard], in order to spread their forces, exhaust their soldiers and [make them] weak and unfamiliar with their surroundings.[90]

In a shift from the optimism of only a few months before, Saddam altered his strategic guidance in late spring 1981. In doing so he set in motion events that would determine the character of the war for the next six years. When an officer suggested to him that the Iraqi Army "lure [the Iranians] to where our defense is stronger," Saddam enthusiastically replied:

That is right. Our defense will be stronger and our abilities will be stronger as well. However for us to achieve such a goal, we must possess enormous numbers of reserves and equipment for emergency purposes . . . [W]e must study the sectors thoroughly and become capable of shifting soldiers from one corps to another and [then] returning to the next corps.[91]

The Osirak interlude

Summer 1981 was a summer of discontent for Saddam. Not only were Iraqi ground forces running into difficulties, but also the Iraqis ran into an unexpected road block in their efforts to build a nuclear weapon. Within the Iranian and Israeli governments since the mid-1970s, there had been deep concern about Iraqi nuclear ambitions.[92] At the time, with

---

[89] *SH-SHTP-A-001-336, Recording of a Meeting between Saddam Hussein and Ba'ath Party Members, 27 May 1981.
[90] Ibid.   [91] Ibid.
[92] Iran had, in the mid-1970s under the Shah, embarked on a similar program with French and German assistance to develop and build a series of nuclear power plants. There was also suspicion of a clandestine weapons development program at the time. See Yossi Melman and Meir Javedanfar, *The Nuclear Sphinx of Tehran: Mahmoud Ahmadinejad and the State of Iran* (New York, NY, 2007), 76. Israel, by this time, was widely assumed to be an undeclared nuclear power. See Warner D. Farr, "The Third Temple's Holy of Holies: Israel's Nuclear Weapons" in *The Counterproliferation Papers* (Maxwell Air Force Base, 1999).

extensive French aid, Iraq was the only Arab country building a nuclear reactor that could potentially produce the weapons-grade material necessary to construct nuclear weapons.[93] Ostensibly, Saddam was acquiring the reactor for peaceful purposes in general and economic development in particular. Iraq was even a signatory to the Nuclear Non-Proliferation Treaty and had consented to inspections by the International Atomic Energy Agency (IAEA), an organization that would prove ineffective in dealings with the Iraqis.[94]

Nevertheless, a cloud of suspicion hung over the project. If Iraq subverted the nominal intent and built a nuclear weapon, such potentially destructive power would in theory neutralize Israel's nuclear deterrent. Saddam often referred to Iraq as the "central support post of the Arab nation." "If Iraq falls," he reminded his staff, "then the entire Arab nation will fall." Saddam argued that the only way to avoid the loss of the "central support" was to develop a "sound scientific base" for the army. Everyone was going to support the objective, "the young and the old, the soldier, the officer, and the atomic scientist, and the university professor." In early 1981, with a group of senior military officers, Saddam was confident that Iraq's investments were soon going to pay off. "If they [the Israelis] are going to hit Iraq, they will hit it before 1985 with an atomic bomb." "After that," Saddam continued, "they will not be able to hit [us] . . . but before 1985, it is not so. The building posts have been put in place, but the structure has not taken its final form."[95]

Iraqi participation in the 1973 Yom Kippur War had fueled Israeli concerns about Iraq's underlying intentions, intentions Saddam did little to hide. For obvious reasons, the Israelis believed Iraqi nuclear parity represented an unacceptable risk.[96] Israel's declared policy of strict

---

[93] Normally, Saddam had nothing but contempt for Western leaders, but he had a warm spot for Jacques Chirac: "Since my meeting with Chirac [in 1974], [I explained] to him the role of Iraq and its future in the region, and the connection between the unity of the Arab people and their importance and the role of Iraq in leading them and the unity of Europe and their importance and the role of France in leading them." SH-PDWN-D-000-566, Saddam Meeting with the General Command of the Armed Forces About the Iran–Iraq War, October–November 1980.

[94] For commentary on how ineffective the IAEA was in dealing with the Iraqis, see Barry D. Watts, "Part 2: Effectiveness Report," in *Operations and Effects and Effectiveness, Gulf War Air Power Survey* (Washington, DC, 1993).

[95] SH-SHTP-A-000-626, Saddam Hussein Discusses Neighboring Countries and Their Regimes, January 1981.

[96] The day after the Osirak attack, the Israeli government released a statement that stated in part, "we learned this reactor, despite its camouflage, is designed to produce atomic bombs. The target for such bombs would be Israel . . . Saddam Hussein stressed that . . . it was being constructed against Israel alone." Accordingly, the Israeli leadership determined that the facility represented a "mortal danger to the people of Israel."

ambiguity, or opacity with regards to its possible possession of nuclear weapons, dated to the beginnings of its nuclear program in the early 1960s. A serious but unstated corollary to the often repeated official line of "Israel will not be the first to introduce atomic weapons in the Middle East" was the more ominous, "but it cannot afford to be the second state to introduce nuclear weapons into the region."[97]

Saddam certainly had visions of being able to challenge the Israelis successfully, and his aim in the long run was to do this with nuclear weapons. In 1976, Iraq had begun to build a modern nuclear reactor at Osirak to provide the capability to produce weapons-grade uranium. Here the French were of crucial help, providing the expertise to build a reactor not only to manufacture electricity, but also to ultimately produce weapons-grade material. The mastermind behind their support was Prime Minister Jacques Chirac. Saddam, then vice president of Iraq, apparently agreed, when in an interview with an Iraqi journalist in 1976, he noted "the agreement with France is the very first concrete step toward production of the Arab atomic bomb."[98] A quarter of a century later, Chirac "mused publicly that it might not be so dangerous after all if Iran acquired a nuclear bomb."[99]

So long as there were no serious interruptions in ongoing programs, Saddam could clearly foresee the day when Iraq would have nuclear parity with Israel. If achieved, that alone would change the dynamics of the strategic balance not only between the Arabs and Israelis, but also between Iraq and any state that stood between Saddam and his long-range goals. This potential threat could not have been lost on Khomeini. With statements like the following made to military officers studying at Baghdad's Bakr Military University in March 1978, Saddam gave both Israel and Iran reason for concern:

And when the Arabs start the deployment [of conventional military forces], Israel is going to say, "We will hit you with the atomic bomb." So should the Arabs stop or not? If they did not have the atom, they will stop. For that reason [the Arabs] should have the atom. If we were to have the atom, we would make the classical

---

The State of Israel Ministry of Foreign Affairs, "Statements by the Government of Israel on the Bombing of the Iraqi Nuclear Facility near Baghdad: 8 June 1981," www.mfa.gov.il/MFA/Foreign%20Relations/Israels%20Foreign%20Relations%20since%201947/1981-1982/26%20Statement%20by%20the%20Government%20of%20Israel%20on%20the%20Bo (accessed on 15 August 2010).

[97] Haim Shaked, "The Nuclearization of the Middle East: The Israeli Raid of Osirak," in *Middle East Contemporary Survey, Volume V: 1980–81*, Colin Legum, ed. (New York, NY, 1982), 185.

[98] William Shawcross, *Allies: Why the West Had to Remove Saddam* (New York, NY, 2004), 93.

[99] "Let's Keep Squeezing Them Harder," *Economist* 384, no. 8547 (2007), 60.

[conventional] armies fight without using the atom ... [If] they said, "We will hit you with the atom." We will say, "We will hit you with the atom too. The Arabic atom will finish you off, but the Israeli atom [bomb] will not end the Arabs."[100]

On 30 September 1980, two Iranian F-4s had attacked the Osirak facility as part of a raid on a conventional power plant near Baghdad.[101] The Iranians inflicted only superficial damage to the reactor site, which French technicians quickly repaired, and work continued at full speed. Saddam was outraged by the Iranian attack, but in spite of the ongoing war, he publically announced that "the Iraqi nuclear reactor is not intended to be used against Iran, but against the Zionist enemy."[102] It is not clear whether the Iranians got the message, but there were no more Iranian attacks on Osirak.

The Israelis certainly got the message. On 7 June 1981, they sent a robust force of eight F-16s and six F-15s to ensure the reactor's destruction before the French could supply the fuel required for it to go into full operation. The attack succeeded. It caught the Iraqis entirely by surprise: anti-aircraft crews were on dinner break when the bombs fell, while Iraqi combat air patrols had landed to refuel. One Iraqi general suggested to the authors that Israeli intelligence must have had someone on the inside of the facility because their knowledge was exquisite as to weaknesses in Iraqi air defenses and the optimal time to attack.[103]

Saddam regarded the attack on Osirak as a personal affront. He later speculated:

after the failure of their first attempt [by the Iranians], which was spoken of in the Iraqi media and official statements and which took place at the beginning of the war with the Persians, and after the failure of these hits, the hits of the Persian Air Force, against the reactor. And after they reached a conclusion that the air force, the Persian Air Force, was demoralized and had lost a lot of its equipment, they [Israel] made a decision to train their pilots for a long period to carry out this task. And they put in their schedule to train for several months, some said for six months ... I think that they did not intend to reveal the target at the beginning of

---

[100] SH-PDWN-D-000-341, Transcript of a Speech Given by Saddam Hussein at Al-Bakr University "the Role of the Iraqi Armed Forces in the Arabic-Zionist Conflict," 3 June 1978.

[101] It remains a matter of debate as to whether the Iranian aircraft were deliberately targeting the facility or whether it was a target of opportunity. Tom Cooper and Farzad Bishop, *Iran–Iraq War in the Air: 1980–1988* (Atglen, PA, 2000), 91–92.

[102] Quoted in Alan M. Dershowitz, *Preemption: A Knife That Cuts Both Ways* (New York, NY, 2006), 94.

[103] Woods, *et al.*, "Interview with (Former) Major General 'Alwan Hassoun 'Alwan Al-Abousi, Cairo, Egypt, 13 November 2009."

the training, they intended to claim it as part of the war, but there were factors that made them realize that we knew that this hit was from Israel.[104]

Thus, the dictator blamed the Osirak attack on collusion between Iran and Israel as well as other mysterious, unnamed parties who had started the war:

The experience of the first hit [on Iraq's nuclear reactor] was one of the lessons, and that other parties knew of the hit whether before it occurred or during its execution. And that this matter was going to be revealed and so they were forced and also as a reelection factor for Begin, they [Israel] were forced to reveal the hit. If they knew that the war was going to extend at least six more months, to allow them to go in under its cover and carry out this hit, which they trained for several months to carry out, and if they wanted to carry it out under the cover of war, then they must have been fully aware that the war was going to extend for an additional six months. And that is just not possible with just the information and the knowledge of the Mossad. There must have been another international party cooperating with them not only on the hit and on information, but also on giving them information regarding how long the war was going to continue ... and through this and other factors, you can guess why the war took place. Not only to direct a hit on the Iraqi atomic reactor, but also to stop the Iraqi rising/development [ascendancy].[105]

Unable to punish Israel militarily, Iraq attempted to do so diplomatically. However, its efforts to gain sympathy at the United Nations in the aftermath of the attack received limited support there.[106] A subsequent

[104] SH-SHTP-A-000-571, Saddam and His Inner Circle Discussing Israel's Attack on the Tamuz (Osirak) Reactor, Circa Mid-June 1981. This can be understood better when one remembers that Iran refused to accept the first (Iraqi-proposed) UN Ceasefire Resolution of 28 September 1980. This formed the nexus of Saddam's theory that Iran and Israel had unfinished business inside Iraq and that they had continued the war to achieve these objectives. Thus, the war served as a cover for the destruction of Osirak by Israel, a non-belligerent. The assumption of military cooperation between strange bedfellows may also have stemmed from intelligence reporting in late May 1981 that a small number of Iranian fighters (American-made and indistinguishable from those flown by Israel) were operating from a Syrian airbase. See SH-GMID-D-001-020, Information on Iranian Forces Including Their Movements, Casualties and Losses, and the Weapons That They Were Able to Acquire During the Iraqi–Iranian War, 1981.

[105] SH-SHTP-A-000-571, Saddam and His Inner Circle Discussing Israel's Attack on the Tamuz (Osirak) Reactor, Circa Mid-June 1981. A few days before the Iranian raid, the head of Israeli military intelligence voiced surprise that Iran had yet to make an attempt to strike this critical and dangerous target.

[106] UN Security Council Resolution 487 (19 June 1981) "strongly condemned" the attack and called for Israel "to refrain in the future from any such attack." A toothless vote, but one that uncharacteristically the United States joined. An interagency intelligence assessment in the United States was deeply upset at what it regarded as the damage the Israeli attack on the Osirak had done to further the "arms race" in the Middle East. Director of Central Intelligence CIA, *Interagency Intelligence Assessment: Implications of Israeli Attack on Iraq* (Langley, VA, 1981).

comment by Saadoun Hammadi, Iraqi foreign minister, captures Iraq's dissatisfaction. He was instrumental in developing the Iraqi political and diplomatic strategies for protesting the strike and led the delegation in delivering the protest to the Security Council. Although it failed, the Iraqis had crafted their strategy to generate widespread international condemnation of Israel's action and to exact punishment in the form of sanctions. Iraq sought international oversight of Israeli nuclear activity and public visibility of the fact the "Zionist entity" possessed a nuclear reactor and extralegal nuclear weapons:

Iraq [the Iraqi delegation] had prepared the proposed decision from here [Baghdad] and taken it with us. The Iraqi decision proposal contained six points. First: elicit strong condemnation for the Israeli action. Second: insure the right of Iraq and Arab and Third World countries to develop atomic programs that are necessary for the development of their economies. Third: prohibit Israel from undertaking such an operation again in the future. Fourth: establish that the work of Israel is a threat of the international supervision system as presented by the Atomic Disarmament Agreement, which is signed by many nations and which is adopted by the International Atomic Energy Agency based in Vienna. Fifth: Put the Israeli atomic program under international supervision, which would mean that Israel has to join the Atomic Disarmament Treaty. Sixth: most importantly, apply Security Council sanctions in accordance with Chapter VII, Article 41 of the United Nations charter . . .

Usually in the opening session of the Security Council the aggrieved, the accuser and the accused, are asked to be there. So Iraq was asked, and we gave a speech clarifying the Iraqi position. And the Iraqi speech is primarily the Iraqi claim in two parts: The first part is to establish that Israel owns nuclear weapons. And the second was to establish that the Iraqi program with proof, and the proof of the International Atomic Energy Committee, [that the program] is a peaceful program.[107]

Even critics of the raid doubted that Iraq's program was a "peaceful one."[108] Saddam confirmed this in a rambling assertion to his inner circle:

That is why what they pull down today, we can rebuild tomorrow and what they destroy tomorrow we can rebuild the day after, until they become unable to

---

[107] This is Saadoun Hammadi's statement to Saddam about Iraq's actions at the United Nations. SH-SHTP-A-000-571, Saddam and His Inner Circle Discussing Israel's Attack on the Tamuz (Osirak) Reactor, Circa Mid-June 1981.

[108] Anthony Fainberg, a physicist at Brookhaven National Laboratory, argued in 1981 that in its present configuration, "this route to an Iraqi bomb is not believable," but that after the attack, Iraq would most likely emphasize a long-term but clandestine program. Anthony Fainberg, "Osirak and International Security," *Bulletin of the Atomic Scientists* 37, no. 8 (1981). A good survey of initial reactions to the attack is found in Paul F. Power, "The Baghdad Raid: Retrospect and Prospect," *Third World Quarterly* 8, no. 3 (1986).

destroy our new civil buildings, and our new scientific buildings ... That is why I ask that you don't despair that we lost an important link, in spite of the pain of this loss, I can say and I believe that the nation will benefit much. Concerning Iraq, there is no power that can prevent us from dealing with this issue ... Furthermore I say, the lessons that we have learned up to now and which we have utilized into a program, we don't just say it and transform it into a program because the lessons we utilized from this matter and took decisions on ... all of these are richer [more useful] than the results of this hit. We will continue to extract lessons and to utilize these lessons to a working agenda which will add new prosperity which the Iraqis have achieved so far, and which will allow Iraq to be in service to the Arab nation God willing.[109]

For Saddam, the war with Iran was never an end, but a means to both internal goals and progress toward his long-term vision as leader of the "Arab nation." In a 1982 conversation with his senior advisors, Saddam again hinted at the ultimate connection between unfolding events to his East and perceived threats to the West:

Now take a look at Israel ... It cannot tolerate Iraq walking out [of the Iran–Iraq War] victorious because there will not be any Israel ... [T]he Israeli strategic planners are the most knowledgeable on the implication that Iraqi is building and Iraq is winning military-wise. Technically they [the Israelis] are right in all of their attempts to harm Iraq. And I do not put it far from them that they might hit Iraq with an atomic bomb someday if they reach a certain stage. We are prepared, and if God allows it, we will be ready to face it.[110]

---

[109] SH-SHTP-A-000-571, Saddam and His Inner Circle Discussing Israel's Attack on the Tamuz (Osirak) Reactor, Circa Mid-June 1981.

[110] SH-SHTP-A-000-635, Saddam Meeting with His Cabinet to Discuss the 1982 Budget, 1982.

6   Defeat and recovery

Despite all of the improvements in the Iranian situation ... they will weaken and deteriorate ... The zeal of the Khomeini Guards cannot [continue] to grow ... The zeal of the volunteers can only be less than before and so will their number ... These are basic principles.[1]   – Saddam Hussein

During the first half of 1981, Iranian political and military leaders crafted plans to break Iraq's hold on Abadan and retake Khorramshahr. Their efforts occurred, while various counterrevolutionary factions tried to gain support in Iran's cities, as leftist guerrillas and assorted terrorists attempted to overthrow Khomeini's theocratic regime. Over the course of the year, the ayatollahs confronted a ferocious terrorist bombing campaign waged by the People's Mojahedin, a leftist revolutionary group once allied with Khomeini. On 28 June 1981, two bombs destroyed Khomeini's political party headquarters in downtown Tehran, killing the party's leader, Ayatollah Seyyed Mohammad Hosseini Beheshti, fourteen ministers, and twenty-seven deputies.[2] The assassination attempts continued apace in summer 1981. In early July, Iraqi intelligence reported that seventy-one deputies and members of the Shura council "including four ministers" had been assassinated, all of which gave the analysts hope that Khomeini's regime would not last.[3] One authority on Iran has described Beheshti as the potential Lenin of the Islamic Revolution.[4] The loss of this competent, relatively young revolutionary leader likely helped keep Iran's wartime leadership from solidifying around a strong leader below the detached Khomeini.

---

[1] SH-PDWN-D-001-028, Transcript of a Meeting between Saddam Hussein and the General Command of the Armed Forces Talking About Islamic History and the Situation around Al-Huwayzah, 25 August 1981.

[2] Kenneth Katzman, *US Department of State Report: The People's Mojahedin Organization of Iran* (Washington, DC 1992); Fred Halliday, "Year Three of the Iranian Revolution," *MERIP Reports*, no. 104 (1982).

[3] *SH-GMID-D-001-343, Political Reports Relating to the Iranian Domestic Situation and Foreign Relations, 16 February–4 July 1981.

[4] Gary Sick, "Confronting Contradictions: The Revolution in Its Teens," *Iranian Studies* 26, no. 3/4 (1993), 408.

In another attack on 30 August, the People's Mojahedin assassinated both the president of Iran and the prime minister.[5] In June alone, terrorists assassinated nearly 1,000 senior governmental officials and clergy including the chief justice and the prosecutor general. Nevertheless, the regime's operatives were even more deadly. During June, they executed nearly 6,000 activists and those whom they described as terrorists.[6] The People's Mojahedin also made the mistake of directly confronting the army and the *Pasdaran*, which helped the regime's efforts to tame the violence. By the end of the summer, Khomeini was securely in power, while his operatives had largely broken leftist and liberal opposition.

Matters also improved for Khomeini's regime on the battlefield. In July and August 1981, Iran launched several probing attacks northeast of the Shatt al-Arab that pulled Iraqi forces away from Abadan. Iranian counterattacks in this area date to the beginning of the war. An Iranian official history identifies five "limited offensive operations" in this region between November 1980 and August 1981. The attacking formations were brigade-size "irregular battle groups." Their efforts were not intended to push the Iraqis out of the plain of Azadegon, but to "preserve the offensive morale ... and show noncompliance and intolerance towards aggression."[7] In early August, a combined force of *Pasdaran* and elements of the Iranian regular army's 92nd and 16th Divisions moved toward the west of Susangard. The significance of this relatively small gain was lost on the Iraqis. The Iranians, despite the turbulence in Tehran, were learning. They uncovered the nature of Iraqi defensive positions, as Iranian combat engineers spent most of August examining captured earthworks, minefields, and strong points. One Iranian report noted the Iraqis organized "their defenses in a very reliable manner, a deep defensive instrument."[8]

Saddam's assessment of Iranian gains was surprisingly upbeat. In a late August discussion with the director of military intelligence, he noted increasing Iranian casualties. He also laid out a two-part strategy for the remainder of the war: bleed Iran at the front while destroying its economy. Recent losses of Iranian territory were, according to him, of "more psychological than tactical or strategic value." The Iranians had paid a heavy price to occupy land that Iraqi forces could attack with

[5] Katzman, *US Department of State Report*.

[6] Sepehr Zabih, "Aspects of Terrorism in Iran," *Annals of the American Academy of Political and Social Science*, 463 (1982).

[7] *SH-MISC-D-001-344, Supplement to [Iranian] Saf Magazine "The Victory of Victories of the Sacred Defense: Battle of Tariq Al-Quds (29 November–21 December 1981)," November–December 1998.

[8] *Ibid.*

missiles and artillery, inflicting even more casualties. A parallel track, one that Saddam emphasized, would "give decisive results" by hitting four vital targets: "refineries, crude oil, zones of export ... and electricity." Such targets should be "pulverized" to force a "peace solution" and "expand the historic gap in development of the Persians for a period of time." Saddam added that such an outcome would put Iran in a position where "they will not be capable of engaging us in a war ... again."[9]

Testing their knowledge of Iraqi defensive doctrine at the beginning of September, three Iranian divisions crossed the Kharkheh River, with a thrust moving in away from Abadan. Then, on 27 September 1981, the Iranians launched another major offensive. Their 77th Infantry Division and a division-size "corps" of the *Pasdaran* crossed the Karun River and attacked toward Abadan in Operation *Samen al-Ae'mmeh* (Operation Eight Imam). They took the unsuspecting Iraqi defenders, predominantly from the 3rd Division, by surprise. The result was a general collapse. The Iraqi high command ordered a withdrawal operation for which the troops had done no advanced preparations. In a wild stampede to escape over a single pontoon bridge, fleeing Iraqi soldiers abandoned large amounts of military equipment.[10] The Iranians claimed that they had destroyed 90 tanks, 100 BMPs and assorted other vehicles, while capturing 160 tanks and transporters, five 155mm artillery pieces, and 150 assorted vehicles.[11] In a later account, *Pasdaran* historians claimed that Operation *Samen al-Ae'mmeh* "demonstrated the instability and inability of invading forces to preserve their defensive positions in the face of surprise attacks [launched] from several directions."[12]

For Saddam, there was no mystery about what kind of war Iraq was now fighting. Conscious of the cost of panic on the battlefield or loss of confidence in the corridors of power, he framed the setbacks as part of a larger, heroic stand by Iraqi troops to his ministers:

I want to ask about the Iraqi people that die now in the hundreds and thousands. [They] sacrifice daily under the fire of guns and [are] holding tight to the land. With what are they holding onto? It is with the accomplishments ... the achievements of the revolution. They are now fighting all of the big powers ...

---

[9] SH-PDWN-D-001-028, Transcript of a Meeting between Saddam Hussein and the General Command of the Armed Forces Talking About Islamic History and the Situation around Al-Huwayzah, 25 August 1981.

[10] O'Ballance, *The Gulf War*, 62.

[11] *SH-MISC-D-001-350, *The Passing of Two Years of War: Iran–Iraq*, Political Office of the Islamic Revolution Pasdaran Corps.

[12] *SH-MISC-D-001-344, Supplement to [Iranian] Saf Magazine "The Victory of Victories of the Sacred Defense: Battle of Tariq Al-Quds (29 November–21 December 1981)," November–December 1998.

The Soviet Union cannot comprehend the role that the Iraqi Army has undertaken. I am confident that the Soviet Union cannot hold onto the same area of ground that we are now holding onto. They have on their side people from the Afghans, but no one is with us from our neighbors.[13]

Not surprisingly, the victory boosted Iranian morale and motivated them to recover the remainder of the lands lost to the Iraqis. From mid-November 1981 to late May 1982, the Iranians implemented multi-staged offensives to drive the Iraqis from their soil. The first came during the period from 29 November to 7 December 1981 in Operation *Tariq al-Qods* (Jerusalem Way), aimed at recapturing the town of Bostan.[14] The Iranians attempted to regain that town in August, but had run into sophisticated field fortifications, with which they were as yet incapable of dealing. But the offensive in November broke the back of Iraqi defenses and regained that critical junction. For the first time the Iranians used human-wave attacks on a large scale – a move that caught the Iraqis by surprise and overwhelmed the defenders.

The Iranians prepared in detail, including building a road through dunes the Iraqis had assumed impassable. This put a substantial number of Iranian forces on the northern flank of Iraqi defenses. The offensive comprised units drawn from the regular army including one infantry and four armored brigades.[15] The *Pasdaran* did participate, but this was for the most part a regular army affair. On 29 November 1981, Iran attacked Iraq's northern flank once again. The Iraqis collapsed.[16] By midday, the Iranians had recaptured Bostan. Overall, they claimed to have captured equipment for two artillery battalions, ninety tanks and personnel

---

[13] Recording of a Meeting Between Saddam Hussein and High Ranking Officials Relating to the Soviet Union (3 October 1981) in SH-SHTP-D-000-711, Saddam Hussein and Iraqi Officials Discussing the King Fahad Initiative, Relations with the USSR, and Perceptions of Other Middle Eastern Countries, October–November 1981. Saddam complained that neither his European friends nor his Arab neighbors were joining the fight. He noted that Iraq was at the point where it should ask the world "who is with us and who is against us."

[14] This operation was as also named *Karbala 1*. Efraim Karsh, *The Iran–Iraq War, 1980–1988* (New York, NY, 2009), 23.

[15] The armored brigades were drawn from the 92nd and 16th Divisions, the infantry brigade from the 77th Division.

[16] Saddam's propaganda machine had indicated in early 1981 that the Iraqis were picking up the Iranian message traffic that was being sent en clair. Almost immediately the Iranians switched to mechanical enciphering machines. This led to the Iraqis scrambling to break the Iranian codes, an effort that would eventually receive considerable help from the Soviets. Nevertheless, it was not until 1982 that the Iraqis were to succeed. Kevin M. Woods, Williamson Murray, Elizabeth A. Nathan, Laila Sabara, and Ana M. Venegas, "Interview with (Former) Major General Mizher Rashid Al-Tarfa Al-Ubaydi, Dubai, United Arab Emirates, 9 November 2009," *Project 1946: Phase II* (Alexandria, VA, 2010).

carriers, and a vast amount of small arms, as well as to have destroyed three armored and infantry brigades. The victory presaged what was to come in spring 1982. Khomeini called these initial successes "the victory of victories."[17]

The winter of 1981–1982 brought major military operations to a halt. A November GMID assessment of Iranian intent concluded that although "offensive intentions of the enemy still exist," the Iranians seemed satisfied to "control the front with light security troops" while preparing to attack. The assessment recommended that Iraqi forces "carry out limited offensive operations in all sectors in order to increase the impact of [Iraqi air] interdiction and aerial bombardment operations." Such operations would also serve to "prevent the enemy from taking the initiative again and confuse its future planning."[18]

By spring, Iran was ready to launch a series of offensives against the still ill-prepared, badly positioned Iraqi units remaining on Iranian soil. At this point the Iraqis were in serious trouble and they knew it. Saddam even declared a willingness to withdraw from all Iranian territory before the signing of a final peace agreement.[19] Tehran replied with silence while a series of offensives battered the Iraqis back onto their own soil and nearly collapsed the Iraqi Army. At Khomeini's behest, the Iranians now aimed to destroy Iraq's military power and overthrow Saddam's regime.

The first major Iranian offensive, Operation *Fath al-Mobin* (Undeniable Victory), began in March 1982. Again the Iranians prepared carefully and incorporated many lessons from earlier battles. A GMID analysis of Iranian lessons to date concluded that after the destruction of the enemy's armor in January 1981, "no armored victory could possibly be achieved." Instead, Iran would depend on artillery and massed infantry attacks. After Iranian successes in June and September, the report concluded, "the Farsi enemy would continue to apply these methods … despite the losses he [has suffered]."[20]

---

[17] *SH-MISC-D-001-344, Supplement to [Iranian] Saf Magazine "The Victory of Victories of the Sacred Defense: Battle of Tariq Al-Quds (29 November–21 December 1981)," November–December 1998.

[18] *SH-GMID-D-001-345, GMID Report: Iranian Military Activities, 14 November 1981.

[19] Shahram Chubin and Charles Tripp, *Iran and Iraq at War* (Boulder, CO, 1988). In discussions with members of the Popular Army, Saddam characterized the withdrawals not as "defeats," but as a retreat arranged for the purpose of "jumping and killing the enemy or destroying him." *SH-SHTP-A-001-228, Saddam Hussein Discussing Ba'ath Party Principles and History, Military Strategy, and General Administrative Issues.

[20] *SH-GMID-D-001-346, Memoranda from the GMID to the General Command of the Armed Forces and the Ministry of Defense, Re: Al-Khafajiyah Sector.

The GMID report was spot on. The Iranians combined the forces of the regular army, the *Pasdaran*, and the *Basij*. Infantry attacks in waves of massed soldiers suffered heavy casualties at first, but were ruthlessly applied with the exhaustion of ammunition and will eventually breaking Iraqi resistance. Careful reconnaissance by Iranian commandos delineated those sectors of the front held by Saddam's ill-trained and ill-prepared popular army. Once there was a tactical breakthrough, the survivors of the initial wave pushed forward while others widened the neck of a growing tactical salient. Because Saddam was still controlling everything from Baghdad, the Iraqis reacted slowly, and those on the scene refused to take initiative.[21] Moreover, Saddam's orders were to hold all the territory Iraqi units had occupied unless specifically ordered to pull back. The message was clear: the dictator would tolerate no local adjustments. During Operation *Fath al-Mobin*, the Iranians captured 15,000 Iraqi soldiers near Dezful.[22] When it was over, Khomeini's commanders claimed they had destroyed two Iraqi armored divisions and one mechanized division.[23] They also claimed to have destroyed 200 Iraqi tanks and captured enough tanks and armored personnel carriers for the *Pasdaran* to begin organizing an armored unit.[24]

Iraqi intelligence had taken note of Iranian forces building up near Dezful.[25] To counter a potential attack, the Iraqis had positioned a second division (the 3rd Armored) to support the IV Corps' 10th Armored and 1st Infantry Divisions. The Iranians had successfully focused Iraqi attention on the center. In the meantime, to the south of the main Iraqi positions, at 0300 on 22 March, 100,000 Iranians,

---

[21] O'Ballance, *The Gulf War*, 80–81. The extent to which Saddam was controlling everything from Baghdad is suggested by an August 1981 discussion during which Saddam, the army's chief of staff, and the director of military operations spent considerable time discussing how many medals should be awarded to the second regiment of the 29th Brigade. SH-PDWN-D-001-028, Transcript of a Meeting between Saddam Hussein and the General Command of the Armed Forces Talking About Islamic History and the Situation around Al-Huwayzah, 25 August 1981.

[22] Karsh, *The Iran–Iraq War, 1980–1988*, 24.

[23] O'Ballance, *The Gulf War*, 81.

[24] Ward, *Immortal*, 257.

[25] RE: Intercepted message (21 February 1981) Memorandum from 4th Corps/Intelligence to GMID in *SH-IISX-D-001-347, Correspondence between the IIS, GMID, and the Intelligence of the 3rd Corps/Intelligence Regarding Iran; Intelligence report by 4th Corps/Intelligence (21 February 1981) in *SH-IISX-D-001-347, Correspondence between the IIS, GMID, and the Intelligence of the 3rd Corps/Intelligence Regarding Iran; RE: Intercepted message (22 February 1981) Memorandum from GMID Directorate 1 Section 13 to Section Director in *SH-IISX-D-001-347, Correspondence between the IIS, GMID, and the Intelligence of the 3rd Corps/Intelligence Regarding Iran.

including 30,000 *Pasdaran*, infiltrated the gaps in the Iraqi lines and attacked the rear areas of the IV Corps. At the start of the offensive, the corps commander panicked and fled, while poorly conceived Iraqi counterattacks hit the Iranians where they were strongest. The Iranians closed a pincer around several Iraqi brigades, which contributed to the large number of prisoners.[26] An Iranian account, discounting the cost, recorded the "spiritual" and not the instrumental aspects of the battle. The attack, the report continued, "was a moving experience, it was impossible for anyone to enter and not feel the holy atmosphere."[27]

The final stage of the Iranian offensive to regain territories lost in fall 1980 began on 30 April 1982. Some 70,000 troops and 200 tanks attacked badly prepared Iraqi positions north of Khorramshahr. Once again, the GMID had accurately reported the buildup of Iranian forces north of that city. According to Iraqi information, the Iranian preparations included supplies of weapons and spares shipped in from Pakistan; medical supplies from Syria, Libya, and East Germany; and bridging units and equipment "under the supervision" of North Korean combat engineers.[28] The extent and detail of many of these reports indicate the Iraqis were, after a short hiatus, again successfully monitoring Iranian message traffic. Nevertheless, despite the ominous tone of intelligence, it appears that Iraqi military and civilian leaders were slow to grasp the seriousness of the situation.

In late April, the Iraqis still held Khorramshahr with a thin wedge reaching back along the Shatt al-Arab to Iraqi territory. The equivalent of seven divisions defended the area. On the opening night of Operation *Bait al-Moqaddas* (Operation Jerusalem), the Iranians launched a deception to the north, which appeared aimed at cutting the Basra–Baghdad highway. They followed this move with an airmobile–airborne operation in the rear of Iraqi positions. Further disconcerting Iraqi defenses was the Iranian's effective use of helicopter gunships, while attacks on other sectors kept the Iraqis off-balance. Building on earlier successes, Iranian units learned to infiltrate the generally porous defensive lines Iraqi units had established. In an unstructured way, regular

---

[26] Pollack, *Arabs at War*, 196.

[27] *SH-MISC-D-001-350, *The Passing of Two Years of War: Iran–Iraq*, Political Office of the Islamic Revolution Pasdaran Corps.

[28] *SH-IISX-D-001-348, Various Memoranda between IIS and GMID, 1982. For information relating to the Iranian military buildup, look for memoranda dated 26 April 1982 (From II Corps General Staff/Intelligence to 2nd, 7th, 8th, 12th Divisions), 14 May 1982 (From Naval Forces/Intelligence and Naval Reconnaissance to GMID), 22 May 1982 (GMID Eastern Area/Intelligence to II Corps), and 23 May 1982 (From border forces command to the Ministry of the Interior).

infantry and *Pasdaran* units probed Iraqi frontline positions looking for gaps. Large-scale night infiltration followed, forcing the Iraqis to reposition and conduct local counterattacks to hold increasingly tenuous positions. Despite the failure of Iranian attacks to achieve a decisive breakthrough, the Iraqis had no counter and were still reeling from March's devastating defeat.

When the main attack began, the Iranians collapsed the Iraqi defenses. On 2 May, heavy fog settled onto the front between Ahvaz and Khorramshahr. The bridges across the Karun River remained intact despite occasional Iraqi attempts to destroy them by air strikes. As the Iranians had done farther up the line, they infiltrated Iraqi positions in large numbers. The result was that the positions held by one mechanized and two armored brigades began to disintegrate. Four days of fog and spreading chaos on the frontline left the Iraqis isolated and "fighting for their lives."[29] By 8 May, the Iranians had come close to severing connections between the garrison at Khorramshahr and forces farther west. Finally, at the last moment, Saddam recognized the danger and ordered local retreats, pulling Iraqi troops back into the city's urban terrain.

Both sides then regrouped, while the Iraqis announced they were going to make Khorramshahr the "Stalingrad" of the Gulf. By 22–23 May, Iraqi troops were withdrawing from the area around Khorramshahr, while soldiers of Iraq's Popular Army were surrendering en masse. On 24 May, *Pasdaran* units, again using human-wave assaults, broke through Iraqi defenses west of the city, thereby isolating the garrison. According to one account, the 11th Division, charged with the city's defense, "lost command and control over the 15 brigades assigned to its [command]."[30] Two days later, after fierce fighting, 12,000 Iraqis surrendered.

During the month of May, the Iranians claimed they had destroyed 361 tanks and captured 150 armored fighting vehicles, while killing 25,000 Iraqis.[31] However exaggerated Iranian claims might have been, Saddam's forces had suffered a major defeat. Barely half of the Iraqi forces in the area escaped. The former chief of staff of the III Corps and future head of Iraq's combat development directorate attributed the Iranian success to the following Iraqi failures:

---

[29] Hamdani, *Memoir.*

[30] Hamdani, *Memoir.* Given normal military standards for span of control, it is not surprising that the 11th Division with fifteen brigades under its control collapsed.

[31] *SH-MISC-D-001-350, *The Passing of Two Years of War: Iran–Iraq*, Political Office of the Islamic Revolution Pasdaran Corps.

1. The Iraqis failed to control the west bank of the Karun River and left gaps between their positions.
2. There were no plans for reinforcements.
3. The armored forces were assigned to forward positions in infantry terrain.
4. The Iraqis held to the false assumption that the Iranians would only cross the river in daytime.
5. They let the Iranians take and keep the initiative.
6. There were unchecked withdrawals of tactical units.
7. Finally, there was hesitation and interference from the high command in Baghdad in local technical operations.[32]

Not everyone in the regime accepted the military explanation for the defeat. On 23 May, Izzat al-Duri wrote to Saddam that "what happened in this operation and in similar battles that preceded it is clear treason, where the materialistic [factors] and combat will of the enemy had no role at all." Al-Duri claimed that the defending brigades had failed to engage the enemy during the first five hours of the attack. Later that same morning, according to al-Duri, the corps and division requested permission to withdraw due to a lack of ammunition. Saddam had asked, "Where did this ammunition go?" Al-Duri surmised that the answer was "part of the picture of big treason ... I fear the situation [will] continue when we withdraw from inside Iran." Al-Duri then proffered conspiratorial warnings to Saddam of internal threats to the regime and suggested that Saddam establish a "party military plan" to protect the army's security, "because the situation has become much more serious." Al-Duri closed with advice not to abandon Khorramshahr, "so that we can, at least, give the military honor to defend [the city] to the ranks."[33]

For the Iranians, recapturing Khorramshahr was a significant victory that made Khomeini even less willing to consider peace. By the battle's end, each side had between 15,000 and 25,000 dead and tens of thousands more wounded. The *Pasdaran* history describes the collapse of Iraqi forces:

Our invasion started from the Ahvaz-Khorramshahr road toward the border ... The enemy obviously panicked and ... conducted totally uncoordinated and ineffective attacks and strikes. This effort was a laughing matter to our forces, but to the enemy it brought fear for they could see that our force was not concerned, and they realized that they could not stop this force that was

---

[32] Translation of Major General Alwan Hassoun Alwan al-Abousi, *Memoir* (Alexandria, Egypt, unpublished 2003).
[33] SH-MISC-D-000-866, Letter from Izzat Al-Duri to Saddam Hussein Reference the Battle of Al-Hamra in May 1982, 23 May 1982.

moving like a flood because capturing a few kilometers along the border was not the only thing . . . The Iraqis' fear was not without reason, and it was beneficial to us. This fear caused them to launch an immediate retreat even though they had constructed facilities for a long-term occupation . . . The enemy had no choice but to retreat to save its 6th Division and other forces in the area. [The Iraqis] had realized that remaining in place would result in a situation in which they would have to face the invading force from the [North] in addition fight in the rear the forces that were along the border . . . The enemy had tasted encirclement in *Fath al-Mobin* and had [had] enough.[34]

Another Iranian report attributed the victory to a number of factors:

The conquest of Khorramshahr in fact was the result of special methods of conducting war (civilians) and special tactics which the enemy was not prepared to deal with. The enemy, based on their analysis of conventional warfare, felt the Islamic Republic was not capable of conducting such operations. In addition, the special circumstances based on the terrain in the area which dictated the form of defense was the reason the Iraqis were not able to cover and protect their flanks. This exposed vulnerability was the reason for their ultimate defeat. In any event, the conquest of Khorramshahr was the result of both our strengths and the enemy's weakness.[35]

The Ahvaz Battle

Not all of the Iraqi divisions fell apart in the May defeats. While the fight around Khorramshahr was occurring, the Iraqis defending the area near Ahvaz farther north succeeded. Here the soldiers of the 5th Mechanized Division, who defended Iraqi positions, confronted human-wave attacks by *Pasdaran* units in the early hours of 30 April 1982. A particularly detailed and clear analysis of this division's experiences has survived and provides an interesting picture of the nature of the fighting; one that resembles considerably the nature of combat and the defensive approach the Iraqis would utilize in holding their frontline positions during the next five years.

At the beginning of the fight, the division consisted of five brigades buttressed by several additional units. The plan for defending their sectors was based on a simple tactical array: a strong screen of infantry and commando companies, supported by armor and anti-tank weapons and protected by deep minefields and wire entanglements was the first line. The main position – consisting of the 109th, 419th, and 504th

---

[34] *SH-MISC-D-001-350, *The Passing of Two Years of War: Iran–Iraq*.
[35] *SH-MISC-D-001-349, Pasdaran Report: From Khorramshahr to Fao (July 1982–August 1986): A Military and Political Analysis, Circa 1988.

Brigades – lay approximately one kilometer behind the line. Each brigade positioned itself behind extensive earthen embankments, designed and prepared by combat engineers. It was here that the Iraqis stationed their local counterattack forces amongst the main defending units. In reserve were two mechanized brigades, the 15th and the 20th, that were better trained and armed than the other brigades.[36] The Iraqis possessed detailed intelligence on the enemy, which numbered two armored brigades, a commando regiment, and three infantry regiments from the regular army. In addition, the *Pasdaran* provided twelve regiments.[37] The Iraqis clearly had advance knowledge that the Iranians were going to attack in the Ahvaz sector. Extensive precautions included laying 33,864 anti-personnel mines and 4,465 anti-tank mines and accompanied bunkering their artillery positions against Iranian counterbattery fire. Finally, the Iraqis prepared mobile, alternative headquarters for all units from battalion level on up.[38]

The Iranian offensive began at midnight on 30 April 1982 with an intensive artillery bombardment of sectors defended by the 504th and 109th Brigades. Iraqi signals intelligence provided detailed advanced warning of the time and location of the offensive as it would do at every stage of the battle. Iraqi reserves were already moving forward even before the initial Iranian assaults began. The after-action report indicates Iranian human-wave assaults did make several dangerous penetrations of the division's frontline positions.[39] Within two-and-a-half hours, Iraqi commanders had committed portions of the 15th Brigade to restore a portion of the 109th Brigade's front where the enemy had made initial gains. Similarly, the 20th Brigade moved a portion of its forces forward to reinforce the 419th Brigade that had also run into difficulty. Throughout

[36] SH-GMID-D-001-142, 5th Mechanized Division Command Report: Battle of Al-Ahwaz, July 1982.

[37] The Iraqi estimate of the enemy's regular army order of battle was predominately from signals intelligence. The after-action report indicates that the assessment of the *Pasdaran* order of battle was derived from prisoner reports. The report indirectly confirms the authors' interview with Major General al-Tarfa. Woods, *et al.*, "Interview with (Former) Major General Mizher Rashid Al-Tarfa Al-Ubaydi, Dubai, United Arab Emirates, 9 November 2009."

[38] SH-GMID-D-001-142, 5th Mechanized Division Command Report: Battle of Al-Ahwaz, July 1982.

[39] The Iraqi Army made a serious attempt to develop doctrine to counter the Iranian human-wave attacks. In April 1982, the issue was covered in Iraq's military journal, while, by early 1983, the first doctrinal manuals were published with army-specific variations published throughout the conflict. See Methods of Dealing with Mass Infantry Attacks in *SH-MODX-D-001-352, [The Iraqi] Military Journal, vol. 59 issue no. 2, April 1982; *SH-IZAR-D-001-314, *The Human Wave Attack*, Iraqi Combat Development Directorate, 1983; *SH-IZAR-D-001-351, *Armored Corps Platoon Commanders Handbook*, Combat Development Directorate, 1983.

this part of the battle, signals intelligence as well as frontline reports kept Iraqi commanders informed of what the Iranians were doing.[40]

By 0900, Iraqi troops were in full control. Iranian advanced units were calling desperately for reinforcements and artillery support as Iraqi counterattacks chewed them up. By late afternoon, the fighting was over with forward positions restored and the Iranians driven back to their start line. The 109th Brigade reported approximately 6,000 Iranian dead surrounding its positions. These losses deterred the Iranians not at all. On 1 May, they launched another major human-wave attack on the 109th. It achieved a few small penetrations, which armored units from the reserve 15th Brigade quickly smashed. In the early morning hours of 2 May, a further series of human-wave attacks hit the 109th with similar results – more dead Iranians.

On 3 May, another major attack hit forward deployed positions of the 419th and 504th Brigades. The after-action report laconically indicated that "the minefields and artillery had a great impact in inflicting losses on the advancing troops of the enemy and preventing them from reaching the frontlines of the defensive positions, which forced the enemy to withdraw immediately after, fleeing the battlefield and leaving the bodies of its [soldiers]." At the battle's conclusion, the Iraqi estimate (likely inflated) of Iranian losses was 10,000 dead, 151 prisoners, unknown numbers of wounded, three aircraft, five tanks, and other equipment destroyed. In comparison, Iraqi losses were light: thirteen dead, thirty-two wounded, and two missing among the officers; 163 dead, 463 wounded, and 355 missing among the enlisted. Iraqi equipment losses included twelve tanks, eight personnel carriers, and six 105mm howitzers.

The 5th Mechanized Division's report ended with several major lessons. On the importance of counterattacks, it noted:

One of the toughest decisions to make with regards to the using of reserves is the right time to involve them in battle. Based on a study of the enemy's combat methods, characterized by pushing small units deep in order to confuse their opponents and capture a large number of troops, it became necessary to position the reserves close to the units they were supposed to buttress so that they can react quickly to any enemy penetrations.[41]

Not surprisingly, the report also emphasized the role signals intelligence had played in alerting the division to the imminence of enemy attacks and keeping Iraqi commanders up to date as to the success or failure of

---

[40] SH-GMID-D-001-142, 5th Mechanized Division Command Report: Battle of Al-Ahwaz, July 1982.
[41] *Ibid.*

enemy attacks and how well their own units were succeeding in stemming the enemy's efforts.

All in all, the Ahvaz Battle is useful in understanding how the Iraqis would hold their Iranian opponents at bay in future battles. It reflected the work of a skillful division commander, who understood the basics of defensive war. However, it did not yet reflect the general Iraqi approach to defensive warfare, as the disasters that befell those defending Khorramshahr at the same time indicate. But Saddam was not stupid, and he singled out the commander of the 5th Mechanized Division and the division for their successful defense of Ahvaz. Pushed to the wall, the Iraqis were capable of institutional learning. The successful defense of Basra in summer 1982 would reflect many of the lessons the 5th Mechanized Division had learned in those May battles.

The implications of Khorramshahr

In early May, the underwhelming performance of Iraqi troops prompted Saddam to order any soldier fleeing the frontlines to be shot.[42] This was likely counterproductive, since it probably encouraged 12,000 Iraqis, largely Popular Army members, to surrender at Khorramshahr in the following weeks rather than risk being shot for abandoning their positions. This was the second major Iraqi surrender in a matter of months. The surrenders underlined the Popular Army's general unpreparedness to engage in heavy combat, which, given their general lack of training, should have been obvious.

Talking with Popular Army soldiers shortly after this defeat, Saddam the master tactician attempted to undo the damage he had done with his draconian orders. He gave his audience a combination pep talk and fighting advice:

When the commander of a company or even the commander of a battalion dies as a martyr, there is anarchy and chaos among soldiers and even sometimes among officers ... When there is no communication between you and headquarters, you should fight ... You should not consider being cut off a scary condition. When equipment stops working, it does not mean that a person should be weak. On the contrary, this condition should push the person to double his effort to be strong.[43]

Of course, with little training for its leaders, Iraq's Popular Army was hardly more than an armed mob, and in many cases a cumbersome

---

[42] Hiro, *The Longest War*, 62.

[43] *SH-SHTP-A-001-228, Saddam Hussein Discussing Ba'ath Party Principles and History, Military Strategy, and General Administrative Issues.

liability to Iraq's regular forces. And while the Iranian militias were no better trained, they were at least motivated by their fanatical religious beliefs. The questionable inspiration of Ba'athist ideology was a poor substitute for the investment of training, the resuscitation of an officer corps impacted by incompetence and distorted by promotions of those with connections, and the replacement of lost equipment and surrendered troops. The low morale of many regular units, especially in the ground forces, was well documented. But the results on the battlefield now made it obvious to Saddam that something was desperately wrong with morale as well as the army's effectiveness. By late spring 1982, he suspected that he was not receiving complete information on the performance of frontline units and commanders. By 1986, the problem still had not resolved itself and he issued a revealing directive to his senior commanders: "From now on you take the name of the regiment that retreats and you say that this regiment retreated by this distance ... You [will] report precisely their advance and their retreat with the names of the direct commanders and the senior commanders."[44]

It was during 1981–1982 that Saddam began ordering the execution of Iraqi officers from division commanders down to platoon commanders for dereliction of duty. The first of many to go before firing squads was the 2nd Brigade's commander, Lieutenant Colonel Mohammed Jawad Kadhum, for failing to hold his position in the Beit Sa'd area in early 1981. The execution of a company commander and several soldiers followed hard on that of their colonel's. In early 1982, Saddam ordered execution by a firing squad of Brigadier General Juwad Asaad, the 3rd Division's commander.[45] Then, immediately after the defeat at Khorramshahr, Saddam ordered the execution of the commander of the 9th Division, whose unit had collapsed only three days after he had assumed command.[46] In addition to the execution of general officers, the harsh hand of Iraq's military justice fell on the other ranks. One document among many contains a listing of two majors, two first lieutenants, five warrant officers, four master sergeants, and three junior sergeants, all shot by firing squads "due to collaboration with the Farsi enemy," which was a common euphemism for insubordination and failure to do their

---

[44] SH-SPPC-D-000-540, Minutes from a Meeting between Saddam Hussein and Iraqi Army Commanders, February 1986.
[45] Woods, et al., Saddam's War, 38.
[46] Because he favored Major General Tala al-Duri, Saddam transferred him out of command of 3rd Division just before the battle at Khorramshahr. As a result, al-Duri escaped any blame for the division's poor performance despite being responsible for its ill-prepared state.

duty.[47] Such cases were not exceptional as defeats piled up. The spate of executions from 1981 through 1982 may have motivated the officer corps to get its act together and halt the Iranians on the frontier, but it hardly represented a regime that trusted the effectiveness of its officers.

The number of officers Saddam could execute *"pour encourager les autres"* was limited, however.[48] By now the heavy fighting was beginning to exhaust both armies. Between March and June 1982, the Iraqi Army's number had fallen from 210,000 to 150,000. The fighting had reduced two of Iraq's four armored divisions to brigade strength. Combat-ready aircraft had decreased from 335 to approximately 100.[49] Nevertheless, the Iranians were in even worse shape with extremely heavy losses among regular army soldiers and the *Pasdaran* – not surprising given the Iranian penchant for human-wave attacks. The only answer for both sides was a massive expansion of military forces.

For the Iraqis, mass mobilization meant a major expansion of the regular army. The army required officers not only to man combat units, but also to fill out staffs at brigade, division, and corps levels, not to mention the training establishment. Thus, as the expansion began, there was a desperate need for trained officers, whatever their quality. The advantage here for the Iraqis was that the regular army provided a skeleton on which they could construct their new formations, while the Iranians refused to follow such a path. How big was the expansion? In September 1980, the Iraqi Army consisted of thirty-seven brigades and approximately 200,000 soldiers.[50] By 1983, it had more than doubled to 473,000 soldiers. In numbers of divisions, the army increased from twelve to twenty. Perhaps as important as the expansion program in 1982 was the fact that the Iraqis began a major construction program to build fortified zones along the southern front to protect Basra and on the central front to protect Baghdad.

The capture of Khorramshahr was a significant event inside Iran. In many ways, the battle was the most important event in that country since the revolution. The implications of the liberation of Iranian territory reverberated at multiple levels. On a political level, it was what the regime in Tehran needed to energize the population and solidify its control. By summer 1982, Khomeini's regime had crushed political opposition

---

[47] SH-GMID-D-000-423, Correspondence from the General Military Intelligence Directorate (GMID) to Al-Rashid Military Hospital Regarding the Bodies of Executed Personnel for Insubordination in the Iraq–Iran War, July 1982.

[48] The phrase is the one that Voltaire used to describe the execution of Admiral Byng by the Royal Navy for failing to win the naval battle off Minorca at the beginning of the Seven Years' War.

[49] Hiro, *The Longest War*, 60.   [50] Woods, *et al.*, *Saddam's War*, 37.

throughout the country. Soon after recapturing Khorramshahr, the Iranian prime minister placed the battle in a larger framework:

> It is certainly because of this [the victory at Khorramshahr] that we will witness a fundamental upheaval in Muslim countries. The victory of Khorramshahr is in no way a territorial victory. The effects are not limited to one country. This is not the case since this war with Saddam's regime has become very symbolic among the countries of the region and Muslim countries – a war between Islam and blasphemy, and no doubt this victory will heighten Islamic liberation movements.[51]

However the expansion of the opposing forces took place would give the Iraqis an advantage in the long run.[52] For the Iranians, expanding their military forces meant large increases in the size of the *Pasdaran*, while the regular army found itself robbed of the best manpower and the prominent role in defending the nation. Moreover, a second major militia also emerged as a player in the politics of defense. The *Basij*, drawn almost exclusively from the poor of the countryside and mobilized by local mullahs, added to the forces mobilized by Tehran. Given the level of education of these hard-scrabble Iranians, Tehran came increasingly to rely on a low-technological military, which resulted in a military force largely consisting of limited mobility infantry armed with light weapons, rather than on a combined-arms maneuver force. In the end, relying on human-wave attacks was of little use in a stand-up fight against Iraqi forces equipped with superior technology and heavy weapons and with some ability to coordinate combined arms. Thus, the direction Iranian mobilization took ended up in minimizing the potential that the remnants of the Shah's army might have represented to the mobilization of a new, and effective military.[53]

Iraqi efforts to find a ceasefire

A conversation among the Iraqi leaders in summer 1982 indicated how radically their position had changed from fall 1980. Iraq, Saddam now argued, simply wanted peace. Specifically, the dictator told his

---

[51] Christine Moss Helms, *Iraq: Eastern Flank of the Arab World* (Washington, DC, 1991), 188. Brackets in original.

[52] According to a former senior *Pasdaran* member, in 1982, a small clique of *Pasdaran* leaders used the "myth" of their role in the liberation of Khorramshahr to "embark on a mission to convert the Revolutionary Guard into a classic fighting machine." Mohsen Sazegara, "What Was Once a Revolutionary Guard Is Now Just a Mafia," www.sazegara. net/english/archives/2007/03/what_was_once_a_revolutionary.html (accessed 29 July 2007).

[53] Woods, *et al.*, *Saddam's War*, 97.

senior ministers in summer 1982: "We want the peace, which keeps our sovereignty and our dignity intact. We are not going to use military force ... to destroy the Iranian nation and the Iranian army. This is not our tradition. However, we will fight the Iranians when they fight us. We will fight them in an honorable way *as we are supposed to fight them.*"[54]

Regardless of his motives in seeking a ceasefire, Saddam's position was precarious. At home and abroad, the defeats of spring 1982, needless to say, did not project strength. In summer 1982, there was a flurry of activity in the defense ministry's directorate of political guidance to build confidence in the regime's position. In a memorandum to senior officers in June, the secretary general of the armed forces general command, Qaduri Jabir Mahmud, indicated that Iraq's officers needed to focus on a "spirit of revenge ... With regards to recent events, the Iraqi soldier must understand that we are still strong and we should be ready for revenge against the enemy and crush them in the next battle, otherwise we will be exposed to certain danger." Further guidance included Saddam's admonition that commanders should "not suspend leave for the troops regardless of circumstances." In addition, officers responsible for political guidance and commanders were to "visit the units at the front line more often."[55]

Saddam's frustration with the Iranian leadership on this point is instructive. Despite having initiated the war, he complained bitterly that the Iranians were refusing to abide by its self-evident rules: "[d]espite its military defeat [in 1980], the Tehran regime insisted on its aggressive stands and expansionist trends."[56] To him it was obvious the ayatollahs should have agreed to peace by this point, because he wanted it, and from his point of view it was in their interest as well. As Tariq Aziz said in May 1981, the recent battles were important because the results have in effect brought "major hostilities to an end." He went on to express Saddam's conviction that "the Iranian military leadership knows the facts of life, but ... the mullah/politicians are not yet ready to recognize reality ... The

[54] SH-SHTP-A-000-710, Saddam Meeting with the Cabinet During Iran–Iraq War About Iranian Advances and Security Council Negotiations, 21 July 1982. Emphasis added.
[55] RE: Willingness to revenge (11 June 1982) Memorandum from General Command of the Armed Forces to Directorate of Political Guidance in *SH-IISX-D-001-347, Correspondence between the IIS, GMID, and the Intelligence of the 3rd Corps/ Intelligence Regarding Iran; Political Guidance Office to General Command of the Armed Forces Memorandum from Ministry of Defense, RE: Maintaining unit vitality (27 June 1982), in *SH-IISX-D-001-347, Correspondence between the IIS, GMID, and the Intelligence of the 3rd Corps/Intelligence Regarding Iran.
[56] Saddam Hussein, "Saddam Husayn: Troops to Withdraw from Iran (FBIS-MEA-82-120)," *Foreign Broadcast Information Services Daily Reports* (1990).

mullahs will need a cover, a face saver."[57] This realization moved Saddam's concept of the war from "a war of demonstration to the war of survival," a realistic appreciation of what the Iraqis faced.[58] Saddam's war of survival had, however, quickly descended, with the enthusiastic support of the Iranians, into a war of attrition, which neither side could afford, nor apparently end.

Moreover, the defeats of 1982 presaged political troubles at home for the Ba'athist regime. On 8 July, Shi'a terrorists attempted to assassinate Saddam. A terrorist, in Saddam's terms, armed with an AK-47 fired twelve rounds at the convoy carrying the dictator and his security near the village of Dujail sixty miles north of Baghdad. Enraged, Saddam ordered the wholesale round up of villagers in the area for complicity. Iraqi security forces immediately arrested no fewer than 1,400 locals, ranging in age from seventy years to one month.[59] In addition, he ordered the security services to destroy the orchards surrounding the village.[60] Eventually, the Iraqi "justice" system would execute 148 villagers for the attack after all had enjoyed a three-year stay in Abu Gahraib Prison – an act for which the dictator was eventually found guilty by an Iraqi court and hanged in 2006.

Matters had certainly not turned out as the dictator had prophesized. Now he and his country were engaged in a desperate struggle for survival against two enemies: one, an intractable and fanatical opponent, and the other, economic realities created by the war. By this point, the long-term economic costs of continuing the war were becoming clear. Between 1980 and 1982, oil exports had dropped, while Iraq's gross national product had declined from $45.8 billion to $39.1 billion. Furthermore, Saddam had to borrow $1 billion per month from Kuwait and Saudi Arabia to continue financing the war.[61] In a budget discussion with his closest advisors, Saddam began by comparing his decision making in the military sphere to that in the economic sphere:

Before we begin our [economic] review ... whenever I plan something even at the military planning level, I place emphasis on the psychological aspect before I start

[57] "Cable from US Interests Branch, Baghdad to US State Department, Subject: Meeting with Tariq Aziz, 28 May 1981 (Declassified)," in *CWIHP Critical Oral History Conference: The Origins, Conduct, and Impact of the Iran–Iraq War, 1980–1988: Document Reader*, Malcolm Byrne and Christian Ostermann, eds. (Washington, DC, 2004).
[58] Chubin and Tripp, *Iran and Iraq at War*, 56–57.
[59] *SH-MISC-D-001-353, Various Memoranda and Reports Relating to the Al-Dujayl Case, June 1984–April 1985.
[60] See page 3 in Part 1 of "English Translation of the Al-Dujail Judgement (Parts 1–6)," School of Law, Case Western Reserve University, 2006, www.law.case.edu/saddamtrial/dujail/opinion.asp (accessed 20 August 2009).
[61] Kamran Mofid, "Economic Reconstruction of Iraq: Financing the Peace," *Third World Quarterly* 12, no. 1 (1990).

counting how many weapons we have, how much ammunition and supplies, and comparing them with the weapons supplies, preparations available to the enemy ... However, if defeat finds its way within someone before he enters battle, then he is defeated.[62]

Further in the meeting, Saddam tied his approach to military problems to his "guns and butter" analysis. He commented that any reduction in public accounts would be noticed by "merchants, intermediaries, and ultimately the citizens ... [T]hey will realize that it is lower than last year and panic will set in." Such a state of affairs would only serve the interests of Iraq's enemies. Saddam reminded his listeners:

You must guard the citizens [of the] state, do not let [them] panic ... So please pay attention to this point. This is my specialty. I am not educated; I have educated myself ... But I know what turns on the people ... so keep the state stable. If the war is over, and you find yourself with leftovers of a particular item, no problem ... This is required for the psychological balance of the Iraqi citizen.

He chaffed at the suggestion Iraq could maintain its civilian projects in spite of the war by cutting back on the quality of materials used in construction:

We cannot leave for the new generation structures that are not solid. The structure must be flawless and the foundation strong, so that we will not be cussed at, so that we become true and genuine sons for our nation ... At the same time the financial situation, when the war ends, we will be facing an exorbitant burden. Only the war expenditures will end, [the] specific costs. [But] the arming of Iraq will not end, it will not end. Whenever we see a new weapon and we need it, we will buy it, because no one can guarantee that immediately another Khomeini will [not] emerge, or the war cycle will restart in Kirkuk, or another crooked loser [will] show up like Hafez al-Assad.

Despite his intent to maintain a "guns and butter" budget, Saddam was clearly worried about Iraq's financial and economic strength. In this conversation one can see the seeds of the 1990 decision to invade Kuwait:

What are the resources[?] [T]he resources are known and documented ... loans from the Gulf countries and from oil. I have told you from the previous meeting that much of this we cannot rely on ... One day an aircraft from Israel or Iran might attack [the] Tripoli [in Lebanon] pipeline, and the loans really are politics ... What will we do if the father of Qatar told us they cannot loan us anymore? What are we going to do? ... These are our resources; we do not have any other.

---

[62] *SH-SHTP-A-001-354, Recording of a Meeting between Saddam Hussein and Ministers Relating to the Budget, Circa 1982.

After laying out what he described as a veritable "doomsday" situation, Saddam told his ministers he was confident they would "accomplish their objectives." After all, he allegorically noted, "I trust you for my life."[63]

Diplomatic muddle

On 9 July 1982, the Iranians restated their war aims and further announced there would be no end to the conflict until Saddam had fallen and faced trial as a war criminal. Tehran made clear there would be no peace until the Iraqis had installed a proper government (presumably an Islamic one), paid reparations of $100 billion, returned the frontier to that of the 1975 Algiers Agreement, agreed to the repatriation of the 100,000 Shi'a Iraqis whom Saddam had deported, and admitted Iraqi war guilt. There was not a single one of these terms Saddam could possibly have accepted. As he commented to his ministers, "this means they are talking about [creating] a traitor regime that belongs to them."[64] Since no one in Tehran could seriously have believed Iraq would accept these conditions, their diplomatic demands merely presaged an Iranian invasion of Iraq to establish those terms by force of arms.[65]

Meanwhile, Iraqi efforts in the international arena picked up after the new facts on the ground made almost any settlement acceptable, particularly one based on a *status quo ante bellum*. Such a settlement would not require the spectacle of a large-scale Iraqi withdrawal – the defeats of the Iraqi Army having already taken care of that problem. Iraq's efforts focused on three primary international bodies: the United Nations, the Organization of the Islamic Conference, and the ninety-five-member Non-Aligned Movement. Iraqi diplomats continuously tried to influence these forums to build the momentum for an externally "imposed" ceasefire. The Organization of the Islamic Conference was ready to assist, but only after the Iranians and Iraqis had agreed to a solution – hardly much of a help to ending the war.[66]

Similarly, the Non-Aligned Movement, while supportive of statements urging a ceasefire on the two powers, also proved incapable of stepping into a fight between its members. The movement, founded in the early 1960s, ostensibly represented states that did not want to become

---

[63] *Ibid.*   [64] *Ibid.*

[65] The Iraqi minister of health is reported to have suggested to Saddam that he step aside to allow peace to be made before resuming power. He was reportedly executed for his temerity and his body was returned to the family in pieces. Con Coughlin, *Saddam: His Rise and Fall* (New York, NY, 2005), 197.

[66] Cameron R. Hume, *The United Nations, Iran, and Iraq: How Peacemaking Changes* (Bloomington, IN, 1994), 44.

involved in the Cold War. Its rhetoric proclaimed its members were in favor of "national independence, sovereignty, territorial integrity and security of non-aligned countries" in the struggle against "imperialism, colonialism, neo-colonialism, racism, including Zionism, and all forms of foreign aggression, occupation, domination, interference or hegemony as well as against great power and bloc politics." Such an agenda did not lend itself to stepping between warring members. By summer 1982, in addition to the Iran–Iraq War, the Non-Aligned Movement was politically torn between those supporting the 1979 Soviet invasion of Afghanistan such as Cuba, and those bitterly denouncing Soviet actions, like the movement's Muslim members.[67]

Only the United Nations provided the potential of a settlement with which Saddam could live. For Iraq, the period of June–July 1982 appeared to represent a window of opportunity for an external, face-saving settlement between Iran's recapture of Khorramshahr and its transparent buildup for a summer offensive. However, the Security Council agenda in early summer 1982 was full. Among other items, the Falklands crisis dominated UN attention from the Argentinean invasion of the islands on 2 April through the final British victory on 14 June.[68] The council did approve a vapid resolution on 12 July urging both sides to work with the secretary-general to achieve "a just and honorable settlement, acceptable to both sides . . . including respect for sovereignty, independence, territorial integrity, and non-interference in the internal affairs of states."[69] Saddam read the resolution as "a general resolution for both sides." The problem was that "nobody said the Iraqis were right."[70] One can imagine the mirror image of this view in Tehran. Not surprisingly, the Iranians rejected the resolution. Their answer was explicit in a massive assault on Iraqi forces defending Basra the day the UN resolution passed.

To further muddy the waters of the Middle East, the Israelis invaded Lebanon on 6 June in pursuit of the Palestinian Liberation Organization forces that had been rocketing northern Israel from the southern portion of that troubled nation. Operation Peace of the Galilee, as it was known in Israel, appeared to have been timed concurrently with Iranian offensive operations against Khorramshahr, or at least that was how the Iraqis viewed the matter. According to an Iraqi diplomat in a presentation to

---

[67] Chubin and Tripp, *Iran and Iraq at War*, 57.

[68] For the diplomatic aspects of the crisis, see Max Hastings and Simon Jenkins, *The Battle for the Falklands* (New York, NY, 1983).

[69] *Unscr 514*, Public Law Section (12 July 1982). See David M. Malone, *The International Struggle over Iraq: Politics in the UN Security Council, 1980–2005* (Oxford, 2006), 31–33.

[70] *SH-SHTP-A-001-354, Recording of a Meeting between Saddam Hussein and Ministers Relating to the Budget, Circa 1982.

members of the Non-Aligned Movement: "[W]e believe that there is a true connection and a single plan between the Zionists and the Iranian invasion ... we wonder how Iran is supporting the Palestinian cause when they conspire with the Zionist enemy?"[71]

The same set of events in Lebanon was, not surprisingly, interpreted in the exact opposite way in Tehran:

> Naturally, what happened in Lebanon was not without connection to the widespread victories of the Islamic Republic after the conquest of Khorramshahr ... The effect of the Iranian victory scared the Israelis for they had the Palestinians and the Shi'as on their northern border. The [Israeli] invasion ... was designed to prevent an Islamic revolution in Lebanon ... America was forced to show some kind of reaction against the victories of [Iran].[72]

In fact, the Iranians may have delayed preparations for the invasion of Iraq due to uncertainty over what was happening in Lebanon.[73] Nevertheless, given their attitude toward Israel, Iranian propaganda was as shrill about the international "Zionist" movement killing Muslims as was that of the Iraqis. Iraqi intelligence did note that Iranians being trained by the Syrians in Lebanon and along the Lebanese/Syrian border on anti-aircraft and armor missiles were being pulled back to Damascus "for fear of their being hit by Israeli planes."[74]

Operation Ramadan

When Iraq's army relinquished Khorramshahr, it had scrambled to regroup to meet a potential Iranian invasion. The Iraqis correctly divined the Iranians would strike at Basra and the oil fields lying in the southeastern portion of Iraq. Iraqi combat engineers worked feverishly to build elaborate protective fortifications around Basra and Fish Lake, which they soon dubbed the "Iron Ring," while the army concentrated its forces in prepared positions.[75] On 12 July, Iranian radio and television announced that "a grand historic battle is about to take place. The sons

---

[71] SH-SHTP-A-000-710, Saddam Meeting with the Cabinet During Iran–Iraq War About Iranian Advances and Security Council Negotiations, 21 July 1982.

[72] *SH-MISC-D-001-349, Pasdaran Report: From Khorramshahr to Fao (July 1982–August 1986): A Military and Political Analysis, Circa 1988. For background on these events, see Marius Deeb, "Shi'a Movements in Lebanon: Their Formation, Ideology, Social Basis, and Links with Iran and Syria," *Third World Quarterly* 10, no. 2 (1988).

[73] *SH-MISC-D-001-350, *The Passing of Two Years of War: Iran–Iraq*, Political Office of the Islamic Revolution Pasdaran Corps.

[74] *SH-GMID-D-001-355, GMID and IIS Correspondence Regarding Iranian–Syrian Cooperation.

[75] Dr. Stephen C. Pelletiere and Lieutenant Colonel Douglas V. Johnson II (USA), *Lessons Learned: The Iran–Iraq War* (Carlisle Barracks, PA, 1991), 12.

of Khomeini have gone to the front, with the intention of marching to occupy Karbala."[76] The route to the holy city lay through Basra.

Beginning on 13 July 1982, the Iranians launched a series of major attacks, code named Operation Ramadan. The attacking forces numbered approximately 90,000 against 70,000 Iraqis.[77] But the latter had the advantages of knowing the terrain, standing on the defensive, and possessing greater firepower. The Iranians had the disadvantage of far longer lines of supply than had been the case earlier in the year. These now reached back deep into Iran. So badly equipped were *Pasdaran* units that some of their soldiers did not even possess weapons. The Iranians used the unarmed to clear minefields.

The attackers were initially able to penetrate up to ten miles into Iraq, but then became bogged down and were driven back almost to the border. Indeed the Iranian 92nd Armored Division advanced into a cul-de-sac surrounded by three Iraqi armored divisions, the 3rd, 9th, and 10th.[78] The Iraqis then butchered the 92nd and its accompanying *Pasdaran* units. On 22 July, a determined Iranian Army advanced again with similar results. The Iraqis thwarted a third effort on 28 July. For a time, Iranian units penetrated to the command post of the bad-luck 9th Iraqi Division, capturing the commander's Mercedes, "destroy[ing its] staging area, and perform[ing] ablution on the waters of the fish canal and the Katiban stream."[79] As before, these Iranian efforts utilized human-wave attacks to break through, which resulted in heavy casualties. But Khomeini had decided Iran was going to crush Saddam's Iraq whatever the cost. Thus, Iranian commanders ordered one more major effort on 1 August, which again failed dismally. Later, the Iranians were to admit the loss of more than 10,000 men killed in action. Iraqi intelligence calculated the enemy's losses at 9,000 dead, 12,000 injured, and 1,000 captured. In addition, the Iraqis captured 200 armored vehicles from the 92nd and 30th Divisions, along with 300 other vehicles and "large amounts of ordnance and artillery."[80]

The Iranian explanation for the failure was straightforward:

Another important factor was the enemy [the Iraqis] was fighting in their own land and naturally they were familiar with the area . . . [T]he enemy, by retreating

---

[76] O'Ballance, *The Gulf War*, 93.   [77] Ward, *Immortal*, 258.

[78] In these battles, Iraqi intelligence was clearly breaking into Iranian transmissions whether enciphered or *en clair*. As in the May battle of Ahvaz, signals intelligence had a major impact on the battle.

[79] *SH-MISC-D-001-349, Pasdaran Report: From Khorramshahr to Fao (July 1982– August 1986): A Military and Political Analysis, Circa 1988.

[80] Branch 13 Memorandum from GMID Southern Area Intelligence Organization to GMID, RE: Iranian Materiel and Personnel (12 August 1982), in *SH-GMID-D-001-356, Various GMID Correspondence Regarding Iranian Material and Personnel, August 1982.

to its borders, in fact deepened and thickened its defensive line and reached a stronger defensive posture. In addition to this, they prepared themselves to fight against the invasion of infantry forces and to stop and control the invading waves. They also were able to release their main forces from the defensive line and use them as the reserve force ...

The enemy, up until the conquest of Khorramshahr, had looked at this city as the key to Basra and the thought of losing the city [Khorramshahr] never entered their mind. During the time that our forces mentally were involved in Lebanon and the operation [Ramadan] was postponed, the Iraqis made important changes to the area, most of [them] based on their lessons learned from previous operations.[81]

A recent history of Iran's military puts the Iranian difficulties directly on the shoulders of the *Pasdaran*'s fanaticism and lack of training:

The failed offensive against Basra shone a spotlight on Iran's most significant military shortcomings. Iran's basic strategy was equivalent to trying to use a hammer to destroy an anvil. The Guard formations allowed the commanders to commit large numbers of infantry in repeated attacks, but the divisions were slow and plodding and lacked the training and mobility needed to counter Iraq's ... armored reserves. Because command and control capabilities were limited, lead Guard units were nearly autonomous, which, when coupled with the *basijis'* desire for martyrdom made it difficult for commanders to redirect or recall their units.[82]

In spite of Iraq's defensive success against the first Iranian offensive on Iraqi soil, Saddam was less than pleased at the failure of Iraqi forces to follow up on their success. He provided his assessment to a group of generals and ministers at July's end. He began on a positive note: "I would like personally to say in the beginning that I consider this battle with its military and political results, as equal to all our successful battles that the Iraqi army had during the last two years." Nevertheless, "colleagues, all of you know that we do not lack a military success, or the military capabilities to stop the enemy. But we have to present the facts as they are. During the past six months, Iran achieved several successful military operations against our troops."[83]

Saddam then turned to the failure of Iraqi operations during the fighting that saw the recapture of Khorramshahr by the Iranians:

The [Iraqi] counterattack did not happen at all. Cases like these and how to deal with these differ according to the diligence and according to the nature of each

---

[81] *SH-MISC-D-001-349, Pasdaran Report: From Khorramshahr to Fao (July 1982–August 1986): A Military and Political Analysis, circa 1988. The Iraqi changes may well have reflected their breaking the Iranian codes.

[82] Ward, *Immortal*, 260.

[83] SH-SHTP-A-000-710, Saddam Meeting with the Cabinet During Iran–Iraq War About Iranian Advances and Security Council Negotiations, 21 July 1982.

system and the composition of the people who lead the regime. Some of them correlate matters as if these matters are a personal issue to look innocent. And some of them collapse. And some of them manage matters correctly. Our regime is not of the first sort, but of the second sort. When a mistake or carelessness or a gap happens, we do not leave this case or attribute these matters not to their truth. And we are not of those sorts who try to find a scapegoat in any given situation and assume that was enough. We face the difficulty as is, so when we go to bed we do not have to take valium. This means that we do not put an insulator between the bitter [truth] and ourselves.[84]

Finally, Saddam delivered a few words of encouragement:

I have a conviction, that the Iraqi people have accomplished [a turnaround]. And this will continue with Allah's will and the will of the Iraqis. I mean it will continue. One division here. One division there ... I can tell you about any of these battles, and if it happened [to] any regime in the Arabic world, the regime might fall with its army. But look at us! We reach the formation. We attack. We calculate the losses of equipment, the weapons, [and] the individuals. We get together. And after two weeks, we stand on our feet and the reformation takes place and [we] get back to the fighting. This is the right and healthy state of armies. There is no such thing in Third World countries.[85]

By the beginning of August, the fighting was again on the verge of bleeding both of the opposing armies white. An Iraqi summary of the fighting estimated the Iranians had suffered 28,095 soldiers killed with large numbers wounded in the July fighting and had lost 300 tanks and 108 armored personnel carriers. It also claimed the Iraqis had captured sixty-five tanks and twenty-six armored personnel carriers.[86] While the Iraqis had prevailed, though barely, they had done so only at a terrible price. The 9th Armored Division, which had taken the brunt of the Iranian assaults, sustained such heavy losses north of Fish Lake that the army, with Saddam's approval, disbanded it. By his decree, it would not be reformed.[87] An apparently unappreciative and uninformed Saddam inaccurately demeaned the division's fight, perhaps as a rationale for its disbandment for having lost so many battles earlier in the year:

The 9th [Armored] Division was the mother of all disasters. And I have to say that this division, unfortunately, held the key to all of the military gaps or most of them ... Therefore, yesterday we dismantled this division which does not have a

---

[84] *Ibid.*

[85] Obviously, Saddam did not regard Iraq as a Third World nation. SH-SHTP-A-000-710, Saddam Meeting with the Cabinet During Iran–Iraq War About Iranian Advances and Security Council Negotiations, 21 July 1982.

[86] SH-GMID-D-000-663, Studies About Iranian Military Activities During the Iran–Iraq War, February 1985.

[87] Pollack, *Arabs at War*, 205.

single person of the personnel of the 9th Division ... This division did not record a single victory in any battle, and the enemy chased it everywhere it appeared ... Therefore, yesterday we dismantled this division and decided to remove it from the ... army. We established a new division that does not have a single person from the former 9th [Armored] Division ... This division should have been dismantled a long time ago.[88]

The fate of the division's commander was straightforward. Saddam ordered him executed even though he had taken over from the incompetent Tala al-Duri three days before the Iranian attack. Saddam's failure to understand the battle appears again in his criticism of the 9th Armored Division to the chief of staff, General Shanshal:

Notice that [Iranian] victory is attached to a group that is not very good [disorganized] ... The retreat of some groups from their defensive positions, such as what happened with the 9th Armored Division, for example. They change the whole picture. This is not only unacceptable behavior by any one, they are a lost group. It is not fair for all those thousands of men on the frontline fighting there, and the martyrs and others. A small group gets up and leaves their defensive positions; they impact the defensive positions as a whole and leads to their retreat. What happened to you? You [must] at least fight for two hours – stand firm.[89]

The Iranian Air Force now intruded on one of Saddam's pet projects. He had persuaded the Non-Aligned Movement to schedule its seventh summit meeting in Baghdad. As an apparent message to prospective attendees, the Iranians launched a carefully planned attack to destroy Baghdad's conference center. The Iraqis had some warning: naval intelligence reported on 15 August that eight F-4 Phantoms and four F-14 Tomcats had transferred to Tehran "for training and in preparation for carrying out an air strike on Baghdad ... prior to the conference of non-aligned countries."[90] The attack failed to destroy the center, but inflicted sufficient damage on the surrounding area to cause summit planners to move the meeting to Delhi because of the danger of holding the meeting on Iraqi territory. No excuses from the movement could appease a furious Saddam.[91]

---

[88] SH-SHTP-A-000-710, Saddam Meeting with the Cabinet During Iran–Iraq War About Iranian Advances and Security Council Negotiations, 21 July 1982.

[89] SH-AFGC-D-000-393, Transcript of a General Command of the Armed Forces Meeting During the First Gulf War and Telephone Conversations, 6–7 January 1981.

[90] The specificity of the intelligence indicates it rested on decrypts. Intelligence and Reconnaissance Section to GMID Memorandum from Naval Forces and Coastal Defense Command, Branch 13, Subject: Information regarding Iran (15 August 1982) in *SH-GMID-D-001-356, Various GMID Correspondence Regarding Iranian Material and Personnel, August 1982.

[91] Barzad Bishop and Jim Laurier, *Combat Aircraft: Iranian F-4 Phantom II Units in Combat* (Oxford, 2003), 66–69.

Following the costly fighting outside Basra, King Hussein of Jordan visited Saddam and made an offer of Jordanian troops. At the start of the war, Jordan had immediately sided with Iraq. It viewed Iran as a threat not only from its possible military expansion, but also as a supporter and example of Islamist revolutionary militancy against conservative monarchies. A recent biography of King Hussein notes that his support for Iraq was "the central plank" of Jordanian statecraft in the 1980s. The reasons behind this support were a complex mix of "national interest, ideology, domestic politics, budget security, dynastic ambition, and personal affinity."[92] The king was under intense internal pressure from the always restive Palestinians. In April 1981, the Palestinian national council had met in Damascus and had "adopted an anti-Hashemite line ... indirectly distinguishing between the monarch and his people."[93] Thus, to the king, Iran and Syria represented threats to the security of his kingdom as well as to the Arab Gulf monarchies and their oil, on which Jordan relied. Throughout the war, Jordan supported Iraq politically and economically. Indeed, Jordan's port of Aqaba and its overland trucking routes provided the main supply lines to Iraq throughout the conflict.[94] In return, Jordan received oil from Saddam at prices far below market value.

While Saddam was grateful for Hussein's offer of military support, it turned out to be an unfulfilled promise. Saddam's expectations of his "brother Arabs" were invariably cynical, and he was rarely surprised when they disappointed. At the conclusion of the war, he reminisced over the incident:

Another one [story], because it seems that when we don't tell our stories, Iraqis are easily fooled by people and what they do. We don't tell details, but when he [King Hussein] claims big favors to Iraq, Iraqis must know the truth as it is. To be fair to him, he used to come to Iraq often, and whenever he would come, he would say that we were embarrassing him by not giving him a bigger role in the war, and that this was an Arab war and for the whole Arab world and that our sacrifices were for all the Arabs. Everything he said was true, it was a true description. And that we didn't give our brothers a chance to fight in this war. Every time he came he would say that, and I would respond and tell him that I understood that his circumstances were different and that as brothers every Iraqi is like a Jordanian in his army. That there was no difference in the national sense

---

[92] Nigel Ashton, *King Hussein of Jordan: A Political Life* (New Haven, 2008), 210.

[93] Alexander Bligh, *The Political Legacy of King Hussein* (Portland, OR, 2007), 178.

[94] The magnitude of the material shipped from Jordan to Iraq is suggested by the following figures. In 1981, the total was 6,293 tons. One year later it had reached 745,021 tons. By 1988, more than 1.2 million tons of goods made the journey. See David Schenker, *Dancing with Saddam: The Strategic Tango of Jordan–Iraq Relations* (Lanham, MD, 2003), 52.

between the Iraqi Army and the Jordanian one to us ... In 1983 we were sitting together, I believe the whole command council was there ... [s]o we were talking and I told him that we were in need [of soldiers], so he said that he would send a division in addition to a brigade, and that when he went back he would try to make it either two divisions or a division plus a brigade, in any case no less than two divisions. I thanked him. He left, and our military men who were present had procedures they had to follow.

The second or third day, I am not sure, Abu Muthana saw me in the war room and stated that since there was an army coming, they needed to make arrangements for them ... He took a message ... from [King Hussein] to the chief of staff of the Jordanian Army, who of course had been at the meeting. It was Zaid bin Shaker at the time. So we told him that we wanted to make arrangements in anticipation of their arrival, in terms of timing and needs. But he was surprised, so we explained that King Hussein had promised Saddam Hussein. So bin Shaker responded and basically said that it wouldn't work out and that it was too much, and I told him not to tell anyone about it and to kill the story, because it was embarrassing even in front of the council ...

What can I tell you about Arabs [or] Arab rulers? I hope that I forget all their stories and not remember any, not even one. With hopefully keeping my memory in other areas, but I hope God allows me to forget their shortcomings, even though they don't affect us. We always look at the Arab world in one sense and look at the rulers in another. You look at Jordan and expect that they could do more.[95]

Still Saddam was disappointed that while many Arab states were willing to support Iraq with loans and military equipment, none, including Jordan, were willing to provide direct military support. He commented at one point:

[T]he Arabs think that the Iraqis will always be Iraqis. If any of them get in trouble, and he calls for help no Iraqi will come to his aid ... If you (the Arabs) really want honor, this battle is still going on, there are two volunteer armies to join. Now after 18 months it is clear we can fight without you (the Arabs). We are not saying that we need fighters, but we need a principle.[96]

The air and naval wars

The frenzied combat of the early months of the war had a significant impact on Iran's Air Force; however, despite combat losses and internal purges, according to a December 1981 GMID report, the Iranians could

[95] SH-SHTP-V-000-589, Saddam Hussein and Military Officials Discussing the Iran–Iraq War and the Al-Qadisiyyah Battle, Circa Late 1988.
[96] *SH-SHTP-A-001-357, Recording of a Meeting between Saddam Hussein and Advisors Regarding Various Administrative and Financial Issues and Arab Nationalism, circa 1982.

still match qualified crews to operable aircraft. Nevertheless, from a force structure of 386 frontline aircraft (F-4Es, F-4Ds, F-5Es, and F-14s) at the start of the war, the Iranians had lost 168 aircraft. What was seriously affecting their capabilities was an inability to maintain the aircraft they had. While the F-4s and F-5s were operating at a reasonable readiness rate of 60–70 percent, the F-14s could only achieve 20 percent. The Iraqis remained wary of their opponents however: Iran, the report continued, "still [possesses a] relatively effective air defense" and "does not suffer noticeable shortages in fighter pilots." Moreover, the report's author warned that "the Persian enemy's combat capability for current and future [operations] should not be underestimated."[97]

Meanwhile, the air balance was swinging in Iraq's favor. In summer 1981, the Iraqis had taken their first deliveries of Mirages, a significant upgrade over the Warsaw Pact aircraft they already had. While the navigational and weapons systems on the French aircraft were more complex, the aircraft were easier to fly and placed less strain on the aircrew.[98] It would take the Iraqis a long time to master the Mirage, but during the next six years, they would receive a constant flow of new aircraft from the French and the Soviets, while the Iranians would receive next to nothing.[99] The majority of Iraqi Air Force operations through the end of 1981 were tactical, disjointed, and of only passing effect. Even where strikes were made against "strategic targets," they were of a rather limited scale and achieved an equally limited effect. As one history noted, "the strategic exchange took on the aspect of a blood feud with both sides retaliating, expecting the other to be the first to back off."[100]

As the air force began to regain its balance, the naval war in the Gulf continued as a series of intermittent skirmishes between missile and patrol boats with an occasional strike by Iraqi aircraft and Super Frelon helicopters. The targets were primarily oil facilities and tankers loading at Kharg Island or strikes against shipping to or from Bandar-e Khomeini.

---

[97] SH-AADF-D-000-228, Correspondence between the Air Force, the Air Defense Command and the General Military Intelligence Directorate Concerning Reports on Iranian Air Force Capabilities During the Iran–Iraq War, 25 December 1981. For a description of Iranian operations during this period, see Cooper and Bishop, *Iran–Iraq War in the Air*, 111–136.

[98] Woods, *et al.*, "Interview with (Former) Major General 'Alwan Hassoun 'Alwan Al-Abousi, Cairo, Egypt, 13 November 2009."

[99] Iran did purchase and take delivery of approximately twenty-five Chinese F-7A aircraft (copies of Soviet MiG-21) between 1982 and 1986. SIPRI, "International Arms Transfers Database, 1950–Present," Stockholm International Peace Research Institute, www.sipri.org/research/armaments/transfers/databases/armstransfers (accessed 20 May 2010).

[100] Major Ronald E. Bergquist, *The Role of Airpower in the Iran–Iraq War* (Montgomery, AL, 1988), 45.

Despite the critical role that operations were to play in this war, there was virtually no operational cooperation between the Iraqi Air Force and Navy. As the navy's commander noted to the authors, "there was an unbridgeable wall between the two services."[101] The general lack of air cover forced Iraqi missile boats and helicopters to fight almost exclusively at night when there was little threat from Iranian fighters. Operating under such conditions also explains why the Iraqis were unable to identify their targets, but simply fired at the first target that appeared on their radar screen.[102]

Thus far, the Iranians had enjoyed a relatively free ride when loading tankers at Kharg, as well as when transporting cargo and military supplies to Bandar-e Khomeini to support the southern front. But as the war turned against the Iraqis toward the end of 1981, Saddam ordered more aggressive attacks. On 19 October, an Iraqi Exocet missile damaged the Liberian bulk carrier *Al Tajdar* near Bandar-e Khomeini. Within the week, two Exocets had hit another bulk carrier in the same area. Nevertheless, there was as of yet no sustained campaign to shut down Bandar-e Khomeini or the oil terminals at Kharg. By this point, both sides were feeling the economic pinch. In a desperate effort to earn foreign exchange, the Iranians were offering substantial discounts on the price of crude loaded at Kharg. Thus, the waters off the terminal were soon flooded with tankers awaiting the opportunity to take on cut price crude.[103]

In May 1982, the Iraqis warned foreign ship owners to keep their vessels away from Kharg and the waters of the northern Gulf or risk attack. The Iraqis then upped the ante with more attacks. According to Iraqi sources, attacks beginning in May and continuing throughout the summer achieved mixed results. Most post-strike assessments came from media and commercial sources, but reports of suspended loading operations, increased insurance premiums, and occasional damage to terminals encouraged further Iraqi attacks.

During the summer, Saddam replaced the commander of the Iraqi Navy with Lieutenant General Abid Mohammed al-Kabi, a more aggressive leader. Kabi's brief was clear: attack Iranian shipping from Kharg to Bandar-e Khomeini, tankers uploading at Kharg or that the navy could reach, and any tankers moving up to Kharg or leaving the terminal

---

[101] Woods, *et al.*, "Interview with (Former) Lieutenant General Abid Mohammed Al-Kabi, Cairo, Egypt, 12 November 2009."

[102] *Ibid.*

[103] Martin S. Navias and E. R. Hooton, *Tanker Wars: The Assault on Merchant Shipping During the Iran–Iraq Conflict, 1980–1988* (London, 1996), 50–51.

loaded. Kabi immediately released the Super Frelon helicopters and missile boats to pursue a more aggressive posture. Several factors aided his effort. Using long-range radars located at the tip of the Fao Peninsula and on one of the oil terminals off Fao, the Iraqis could pick up ship movement in the northern Gulf. According to Iraqi intelligence, the Iranian Navy, which had avoided the major purges in the early days of the revolution, was in the throes of a major purge in June 1982. According to one report, the regime forced the retirement of more than sixty senior officers, including the navy's commander, because of doubts about their loyalty. As a result, desertions and acts of sabotage had increased.[104]

More significant, however, was the fact that Iraqi signals intelligence was breaking into Iranian message traffic that guided military and civilian ship movements in the northern Gulf. Deciphering these messages gave Iraqi naval forces detailed knowledge of when Iranian convoys would move to and from Bandar-e Khomeini, their intended speed and course, and the nature and number of naval escorts.[105] Iraqi attacks increased in August. On 9 August, Exocets launched from Super Frelons hit two ships, both flying neutral flags, and sank both. Three days later, the Iraqis, following the British practice in the Falklands, declared a maritime exclusion zone in the waters within thirty-five nautical miles from Kharg.[106]

Throughout this period skirmishes increased between Iraqi missile boats and Iranian escorts protecting shipping heading to Bandar-e Khomeini. Overall, the Iraqis got the better of the fighting with the Iranians losing two PF103 class corvettes. In early September, the Iraqis launched a number of attacks and claimed to have sunk two tankers off Kharg and two freighters off Bandar-e Khomeini. In November, Iraqi attacks on Iranian and other flagged shipping increased again; missiles from Super Frelons and missile boats hit five Iranian and other assorted shipping. The Iraqis claimed they had hit five tankers; in fact, they hit only three and the damage was relatively limited. In December, the Iraqis successfully attacked shipping attempting to reach Bandar-e Khomeini, in one case hitting the Greek tanker *Scapmount*, causing an enormous explosion from its kerosene cargo.[107] Nevertheless, while Iraqi attacks increased dramatically, they were too few to affect the willingness of foreign flagged

[104] *SH-GMID-D-001-358, Various Intelligence Reports and Memoranda Regarding Kharg Island, 1982.

[105] Woods, *et al.*, "Interview with (Former) Lieutenant General Abid Mohammed Al-Kabi, Cairo, Egypt, 12 November 2009."

[106] Navias and Hooton, *Tanker Wars*, 52.

[107] *Ibid.*, 53–55. *Tanker Wars* credits virtually all of the damage and sinking of Iranian and other vessels to Exocet missiles. In fact, in a number of cases, the Iraqis were firing Soviet and French surface-to-surface missiles from their missile boats.

carriers to use Kharg or Iran's economic situation. But the turn to war against shipping was an indication of how the war had moved from limited conflict to a war without limits.

Military effectiveness and the long war

Despite a spate of "victories" that blunted Iranian offensives in the last half of 1982, Saddam again questioned the quality and morale of his forces. Late in 1982, he asked an advisor "right now can you evaluate the morale to be better than at the beginning of the war?" Not surprisingly, the officer answered "Yes sir, just like I told you sir, victory is one of the factors that can raise moral[e]." In an almost candid discussion with a few commanders, Saddam, reflecting on the fall of Khorramshahr the previous July, noted "[s]ince the beginning of the war, they [the Iranians] have been using their artillery in a smart and accurate way. They are more skilled in using artillery than us." In addition, Saddam was not happy with the performance of his infantry, specifically the 5th Infantry Division. Saddam said he assumed the soldiers of the 5th Division had been "seasoned" in earlier battles in the north and would therefore "fight more" than they did around Khorramshahr. He added, "What happened is that our infantry in general is not effective. I mean they did not show efficiency that would match with the experience that they had lived through, trained for, and studied from 1961 until 1980. What is the explanation for this?"[108]

The commander of the 3rd Infantry Division offered Saddam an explanation that would become a recurring theme in the dictator's conversations with his officers:

[The] first [problem is] the training sir. I think that all of our training was wrong ... our training no longer generates the psychological features that need to be generated inside the people who are in fact fighting. These features consist of fighting, determination, and the hatred of the enemy. Hatred, sir. If you do not hate the enemy, [Saddam finished his sentence "You will not fight them."] Exactly, you will not fight them sir. Our training was only training to breakdown or to put together weapons.

... Sir, [our] training does not include psychological factors. The psychological factor is very important. Training is not only about knowing how to use the weapons, training is also about knowing how to use the human psyche in order to

---

[108] *SH-SHTP-A-001-359, Recording of a Meeting between Saddam Hussein and Military Officers Regarding the Iran–Iraq War, circa July 1982. According to the transcript, the commander of the division was also, at the time of the battle, the commander of a special forces brigade. He had previously served as commander of Iraq's special forces' school.

improve the consistency and determination to fight. Sir, if we are able to breed such soldiers, we will be able to fight.[109]

This was music to Saddam's ears. In February 1982, talking to a group of commandos soon to be committed to the fighting, he declared "if 12 elements defeat 12 elements, this is not good according to our standards. No [what] we want is that 12 Iraqis equal 14 Iranians or to be more accurate 36 Iranians. Because they are three times our number."[110] In May, he angrily confronted senior officers and berated them about the slovenly approach to war too many soldiers were displaying:

SADDAM:	The most important issue here is not to allow additional damage and losses! We need to strengthen our armed forces especially improving morale everywhere. I was not aware of the whole situation until my last visit, since no one brought it to my attention before ... We are excellent in creating plans, however, we are very slow in responding and that is a fact! ... as far as deceiving maneuver for the enemy, we have not created one yet!
UNIDENTIFIED MALE VOICE:	Yes, of course sir!
SADDAM:	No, it is not of course! I have proof that we have left fully equipped locations in the past where the enemy was able to study them, discover our techniques and predict our next plan ... What you really need in your bureau is [to hire] three competent individuals for follow ups and not weak and stupid individuals [laughs].[111]

Conclusion

From late 1980 through 1982 was a time of disillusion for Saddam. The war he had believed would be short had become a long war against a tenacious opponent. The standoff of 1981 when there was no response except defiance from Khomeini's regime, led to a series of major defeats in 1982 that destroyed much of the Iraqi Army. For a short time, those defeats threatened to overthrow the Ba'ath regime. Moreover, the severity of the fighting had resulted in a casualty bill beyond anything the

---

[109] *Ibid.* During this meeting, Saddam suggested that division commanders might exempt their officers who had distinguished themselves in combat from the promotion examinations.

[110] *SH-SHTP-A-001-228, Saddam Hussein Discussing Ba'ath Party Principles and History, Military Strategy, and General Administrative Issues.

[111] *SH-SHTP-A-001-336, Recording of a Meeting between Saddam Hussein and Ba'ath Party Members, 27 May 1981.

Iraqis had conceived in initiating operations. As Saddam admitted after the war: "Even so, we can notice that our losses on the political side and the party ... [were] not much, except the batch of 1982."[112]

But Saddam was learning. In July 1982, he held a long discussion with senior officers during which he examined the causes of the defeats around Khorramshahr. The dictator enumerated the following factors as important:

Another thing is not executing the counter attack plan correctly; like the hesitation that took place at divisional headquarters at Ibn al-Walid brigade headquarters. [The] lack of intervention [by] the corps was the beginning of [the] emboldening [of] the enemy ...

Some [of our] troops continued fighting to the afternoon ... Some withdrew and some were bypassed by the enemy. Some fought and fought, and they pain me most. They fought and we said the [Iraqi] army will arrive at dawn in a counterattack and decimate the enemy; [as a result] they stood and fought. But as it turned out [the counterattack] divisions did not do their duty ... Once a soldier has been in a trench for a whole year, he invariably finds that he cannot fight except in a trench ... Sixteen brigades [commanded] by one division. Even if one wanted to call out to this division there were not enough headquarters to run 16 brigades. There was no adequate headquarters outside of the city of [Khorramshahr] that was in control.[113]

Admittedly the Iraqis had weathered the initial storm. But it was clear that Khomeini's regime would not settle for anything less than the overthrow of Saddam's regime. And so the Iraqis confronted an uncertain future against an opponent with superior manpower and who was willing to take enormous numbers of casualties. The war had now become one of attrition. Thus, it represented a conflict the Iraqis seemingly had little chance of winning, unless their opponent proved even more incompetent and incapable of weighing the tactical and operational realities than Iraq's leaders had proven in September 1980.

---

[112] SH-SHTP-A-000-631, Saddam Hussein Discussing General Issues and Iraqi Military History, Circa July–August 1988.

[113] Transcript of a Meeting Held in the Directorate of Military Movement (3 July 1982) in *SH-MISC-D-001-319, Transcript of a Meeting Held in the Directorate of Military Movement, 24 September 1980.

7   1983–1984: A war of attrition

My brothers, as long as our army has strong morale and has an ability to wage an attack there is no fear, even if the enemy [is] able to occupy some of our lands, as long as we are strong we can [regain] these lands, now, a year from now, or two years from now. [However,] if we lose our morale and our ability to wage an attack then we could lose the whole of Iraq.[1]   – Saddam Hussein

As early as fall 1981, Saddam had ordered his army commanders to begin preparing defenses in case Iran invaded.[2] During the next several years, the Iraqis constructed extensive field fortifications, especially in the south, to defend their territory. Meanwhile, with Khomeini's blanket refusal to consider peace, the Iraqis massively expanded the army. At the war's outset, the army was approximately 200,000 soldiers in thirteen divisions and three brigades. By early 1983, the expansion was well on the way to reaching what it would reach by late 1984, nearly half a million men in twenty-three divisions with nine additional brigades.

The sources of equipment and weapons for the expanding army and air force were diverse. Once again in 1982, the Soviets refused to contract for increased deliveries of weapons and spare parts; however, Soviet attempts to remain "neutral" were quickly overcome by the pressure to maintain their standing with the Arabs and the cold reception they received from the Iranians. In early 1983, Iraq finally concluded a set of amendments to arms contracts with Moscow worth $230 million

---

[1] SH-SHTP-A-001-022, Recording of a Meeting between Saddam Hussein and High Ranking Military Officers Regarding Military Operations During the Iran–Iraq War, Circa February 1984.

[2] The creation of these fortified positions was somewhat out of step with the dictator's approach to the war, which eschewed the defensive in favor of the offensive. Nevertheless, he was a careful man when it came to his long-term security, and he may well have taken these steps given the surprises that had already occurred in the war. Also, the one area where the Iraqi military displayed consistent competence and military effectiveness throughout the war lay in its engineering efforts.

to build a rocket manufacture facility and aircraft repair depot, and to provide "certain special military equipment."[3]

In contrast to 1980, the Iraqis were either manufacturing simple items themselves or purchasing them from other sources by 1983. In June 1983, an air force supply officer reported to Saddam:

Sir I have to be honest with you that ... the Soviet Union stopped supplying us seven to eight months ago, which forced us to take the step of approaching the Socialist countries that supplied us with the products related to the MiG-21, so that we were not as much surprised as at the beginning of the war. Sir, where the fight was continuous and when we had many patrols and duties, and, therefore, we had no other choice but to approach the Western industrialized countries. [F]or instance, Sir, we approached the United Kingdom to manufacture tires ... We also adopted [ways] to manufacture these materials during this period. Sir, we were able indeed to provide the important spare parts that affect [the combat readiness] of combat aircraft.[4]

A chronic lack of ammunition and spares was a constant topic of discussion for Saddam. The public picture was one of abundance and administrative efficiency. In a May 1983 issue of the Ministry of Defense's journal of administrative affairs, retired Brigadier General Hassan Mustafa argued that the Arab failure to defeat Israel in the 1948–1949 War was due to "the gross failure of the political and military leaders of the Arab countries to prepare their armies for war." Mustafa dutifully added "that there is such a big difference between our commanders today, headed by our unique commander, Field Marshal Saddam Hussein, and Iraq's commanders at the time."[5] Saddam drew important lessons from depending on a single-source supplier:

It will not be embarrassing to say that we forgot this in peacetime; we forgot indeed and it is not a shame. Why do people forget to learn lessons in wartime?

---

[3] Memorandum from the Judical Department to the Office of the Secretary of the RCC (15 September 1983) in SH-PDWN-D-000-552, Arms Agreements Signed between Iraq and the Soviet Union in 1981 and 1983, 1981–1989 On the shifting diplomatic relations between the USSR and Iraq during this period, see Oles M. Smolansky, *The USSR and Iraq: The Soviet Quest for Influence* (Durham, NC, 1991), 237–243.

[4] *SH-AFGC-D-001-324, Transcript of a Meeting between Saddam Hussein and the General Command of the Armed Forces, 26 June 1983. For a description of Britain's economic relations with Iraq during this period, see The Right Honorable Sir Richard Scott, The Vice-Chancellor, *Report of the Inquiry into the Export of Defense Equipment and Dual-Use Goods to Iraq and Related Presecutions (HC 115)* (London, 1996). For a detailed review of Iraqi arms imports during the Iran–Iraq War, see Rachel Schmidt, "Global Arms Exports to Iraq, 1960–1990," *A RAND Note* (Santa Monica, CA, 1991).

[5] "How Arab Armies' Neglect of Administrative Affairs Affected the Outcome of the First Palestine War," in *SH-MODX-D-001-360, Administrative Affairs Journal, no. 3, May 1983.

Isn't [it] because they do not remember things in peacetime? No, we wanted only one supplier and that [was] the Soviet Union in general; we were not even aware of the other Socialist countries [who are] members of the Warsaw [Pact]. I mean we did not search their markets. We did not even search the Western markets … We [had] everything from missiles to aircraft, but [we forgot that] aircraft stop running for simple things during war.[6]

Saddam also hit on a novel appeal to his would-be suppliers to increase their exports of arms to Iraq. In a discussion about purchases of arms from China, Saddam suggested:

If a country like Iraq, an oil producing and warring country, [were to sing] the praises of Chinese weapons to the Arabs, it [would] mean that the Arabs will buy their weapons from the Chinese … We will tell them that Chinese weapons are excellent … [and sales] of Chinese weapons will reach sky high [levels] and bring economic returns [for the Chinese].[7]

The Iranians tried just as strenuously to mobilize their nation's man-power and to equip their soldiers. Their advantage lay in a more numerous population. In addition to the *Pasdaran* and *Basij*, by spring 1983, the Iranians had mobilized or were setting up twenty-one div-isions along with twelve armored brigades and a number of commando units in the regular army. Their sources of military equipment, unlike the Iraqis, however, remained limited: the North Koreans, Syrians, and Libyans provided considerable support, but not much heavy equipment. According to Iraqi intelligence, there were even thrice-weekly flights of Iranian Boeing 747s between Tehran and Pyongyang crossing Pakistan and China on their way to pick up weapons and spare parts.[8] Nevertheless, whatever the purchases abroad, the Iranians continued to depend on infantry units, which, given their lack of armor and artillery, inevitably suffered heavy casualties.[9] In addition to other help, the

---

[6] *SH-AFGC-D-001-324, Transcript of a Meeting between Saddam Hussein and the General Command of the Armed Forces, 26 June 1983.

[7] Transcript of a Meeting between Saddam Hussein and Military Commanders (31 May 1983) in SH-SHTP-D-000-539, Records of Saddam Meeting with the General Armed Forces Command Leadership and Jordanian King Hussein Bin Talal, 1983. Despite concerns over minor technical issues with Chinese tanks and artillery, the Iraqi high command liked the fact that the Chinese were prepared to deal directly with Baghdad and that their prices were one-tenth those of other sellers.

[8] RE: Transport of weapons from North Korea to Iran (18 May 1981) Memorandum from Military Attache–Islamabad to GMID in *SH-GMID-D-001-361, Memoranda between the GMID and Various Iraqi Military Attaches Regarding the Transport of Weapons from North Korea to Iran and Flights from Iran to the Gulf States, 1981. The increasing use of China and North Korea as weapons suppliers during the war undercut Iran's qualitative technology edge over Iraq.

[9] O'Ballance, *The Gulf War*, 121.

United States and Israel provided spare parts for US equipment on the sly, as both involved themselves ever more deeply in the murky politics of the Middle East.[10]

Syria's continued willingness to supply armaments to Iran enraged Saddam, especially because its leaders were supposedly fellow Arabs and Ba'athists. The dictator remarked in September 1982: "The Syrian position is conspiratorial and malicious which has been expressed in their spiteful acts."[11] Saddam's Iraq was not a passive player in the relationship. Some reports indicate that an Iraqi-supported military coup against al-Assad was timed to start with the assault on the Muslim Brotherhood's stronghold at Hama in February 1982.[12] The reported plot was foiled and provoked a large number of arrests and executions.[13] Al-Assad later described the events at Hama as a part of an unfolding conspiracy: "We were not just dealing with killers inside Syria, but with those who masterminded their plans. The plot thickened after Sadat's visit to Jerusalem and many foreign intelligence services became involved. Those who took part in Camp David used the Muslim Brothers against us."[14]

Tariq Aziz, presumably expressing the anger and frustration of Iraq's leaders with Damascus, drew an altogether different conclusion – Syria's support for Iran in the ongoing war was, above all else, proof of Syria's complicity with, if not direct control by, the Zionists:

On the other hand the Syrian people [have] experienced bloody tragedies ... Syria used to form the central beam of the Arab national movement and now it has become the [heart] of the Zionist conspiracy. I have stated this in the past and I am convinced that the government in Syria is a Zionist government and not governed by an individual but by Zionists ... If you want my opinion, I think that even if the Muslim Brotherhood was leading [in Syria], I would not be against it ... I am not against this draft [damning Assad's regime], but I am against [its]

---

[10] In the long-term, the help declined as the Iranian inventory of US military hardware was lost in combat.

[11] SH-SHTP-D-000-864, Transcripts of Meetings between Saddam Hussein and Senior Military Commanders Discussing Nominations to Ba'ath Party Leadership and Iran–Iraq War Battles, 8 April–18 September 1982.

[12] In February 1982, Syrian troops moved into the town of Hama and violently crushed a long-simmering rebellion against the regime led by members of the Muslim Brotherhood. Casualty figures are unreliable but range from 7,000 to more than 30,000. For a detailed description and analysis of the implications of events at Hama, see Thomas L. Friedman, *From Beirut to Jerusalem* (New York, NY, 1989), 76–105.

[13] The plot reportedly involved an odd combination of pro-Iraqi Syrian Ba'athists, members of the Islamic opposition, and Syrian air force officers. See Eberhard Kienle, *Ba'th v. Ba'th: The Conflict between Syria and Iraq, 1968–1989* (London, 1990), 161–162.

[14] Interview with President Asad, Damascus, 12 May 1985. Cited in Patrick Seale, *Asad: The Struggle for the Middle East* (Berkeley, CA, 1988), 335.

religious [emphasis], because I am a Ba'athist. However when the situation in Syria [has] reached the level of Zionism, I agree on any alternative.[15]

The battles of 1983

The main threat the Iranians posed to Iraq lay in their offensives in the south aimed at Basra and toward the Shi'a centers further to the west along the Euphrates (see Figures 5.1, 5.2 and 5.3 in Chapter 5). But the Iraqis could not ignore the threat of an Iranian thrust out of the mountains toward Baghdad which more than almost any other threat might well have precipitated the regime's collapse. The Iraqis possessed one considerable geographic advantage: the Mesopotamian Valley and its road network allowed for transferring mechanized divisions between the two main theaters of operations relatively quickly. However, Iran's mountainous terrain made it difficult for the Iranians to transfer forces from Baghdad to Basra and vice versa. Nevertheless, Khomeini's forces enjoyed the initiative and could decide where and when the next battles would occur.

The question was how the Iraqis would dispose their forces and how quickly they could move to counter Iranian thrusts. The battlefield defeats in 1982 had shaken Iraqi confidence, yet despite that, they had stymied the first enemy offensive into Iraq while inflicting heavy casualties on the Iranians.[16] Many Iraqi officers understood the implications of the shift in Iranian strategy to limited attacks. One participant noted, "the Iranians adopted the tactic of serial battles and prolonged war, with constant gnawing at the battlefields. [The Iranians] hoped that since 60 percent of the Iraqi labor force was deployed on active service and Iran had a larger population ... this could [allow] them to win the war."[17] In 1983, the Iraqis deployed three of its available corps along the frontier to guard the main invasion routes with one corps in reserve. In addition, Iraqi engineers drew extensively from Soviet doctrine to construct field fortifications in depth behind which Iraq troops could shelter. These defenses were critical to defending the approaches to Basra.

The Iraqis deployed the three forward corps as follows: III Corps, consisting of eight divisions, defended Basra; II Corps, consisting of

---

[15] SH-SHTP-D-000-864, Transcripts of Meetings between Saddam Hussein and Senior Military Commanders Discussing Nominations to Ba'ath Party Leadership and Iran–Iraq War Battles, 8 April–18 September 1982.

[16] That they were defending their own territory also helped. Here, Arab sensibilities trumped Shi'a loyalties.

[17] Hamdani, *Memoir*.

ten divisions, defended the approaches to Baghdad; in the north, I Corps comprising two divisions safeguarded access to Kurdish areas and the oil fields in the north and kept a watchful eye on the locals, whom Saddam had good reason to distrust. Finally, IV Corps was the strategic reserve, one that would increasingly consist of the Republican Guard.[18] These preparations served well in fall 1982, when the Iranians could not penetrate Iraqi defenses despite massive human-wave attacks and tenacious fighting that resulted in heavy casualties for both sides.

The Iranians had their own explanations for their failure to drive into Iraq and overthrow Saddam's regime in the previous year. A postwar study by the Iranian military admitted, "[T]he enemy, by retreating to its borders, in fact deepened and thickened its defensive line and reached a stronger defensive posture. In addition to this, [the Iraqis] prepared themselves to fight against the invasion of infantry forces and to stop and control the invading waves."[19] Moreover, the advance of Khomeini's forces into Iraq created lengthening supply lines, while "the feeling of our soldiers and military, while defending their own land and rights, is very different than when they are 80 kilometers into enemy territory."[20] Those lengthening logistical lines were increasingly open to interdiction by Iraqi armored units in local counterattacks, a tactic against which the *Pasdaran* and other militias had precious little protection.

Iran's large-scale counterattack into Iraqi territory also widened the gap between the regular army and the *Pasdaran*. For the remainder of the war, the two would rarely cooperate and when they did, it was unwillingly. Furthermore, this fragmentation strengthened the *Pasdaran* and the *Basij*, the latter consisting largely of schoolboys between the ages of twelve and eighteen, who were widely reported to have received "passports to paradise" and plastic keys to heaven before going into battle.[21] The continuing erosion of Iranian military professionalism increased reliance on human-wave attacks by poorly trained, ill-equipped militia troops without adequate armor, artillery, and air support, an almost complete absence of combined arms.[22] Nevertheless, even the militias displayed some improvement in their tactics.

---

[18] For the disposition of the corps, see O'Ballance, *The Gulf War*. They are confirmed in an interview with Lieutenant General Ra'ad Majid al-Hamdani: Woods, *et al.*, *Saddam's War*, 50.

[19] *SH-MISC-D-001-349, Pasdaran Report: From Khorramshahr to Fao (July 1982–August 1986): A Military and Political Analysis, circa 1988.

[20] *Ibid.*

[21] Karsh, *The Iran–Iraq War*, 62.

[22] Born of revolution and mistrust of the established military institutions, the *Pasdaran* was hobbled by a lack of ordnance and logistics support for most of the war. In some cases

The general failure of Iranian offensives had, by 1983, resulted in serious recriminations among Iran's leaders. On the one hand, the moderates underlined that the invasion had already led to exorbitant human, material, and political costs. On the other hand, hardliners, led by Khomeini's strongest supporters, argued for accelerating military operations before others could rally to Iraq's defense. In the end, Khomeini's support for an aggressive war tipped the scales in favor of continuing the conflict. The initial offensive in 1983, codenamed *Dawn*, began on 6 February. Hojatoleslam Rafsanjani, speaker of the Iranian parliament and a leading hardliner at the time, heralded its opening with a bold statement: "This *Fajr* [Dawn] offensive is the final move toward ending the war, and it should determine the final destiny of the region."[23]

The first Dawn offensive failed dismally.[24] Beginning just before midnight on 6 February, two Iranian divisions launched human-wave attacks on either side of the frontier town of Fakkeh. Iraqi signals intelligence had already alerted the defenders.[25] According to Iraqi intelligence, the Iranians threw twenty-six regiments against the Iraqi obstacle belt to capture al-Amara and cut the main highway from Baghdad to Basra.[26] A postwar Iranian account indicates how quickly the offensive ran into trouble.

[T]he operation began on three fronts. The forces, under complete darkness began their advance to clear the mine fields, break the enemy's defensive line, and penetrate into their territory. The enormity of the obstacles and fortifications, coupled with several canals that the enemy had built in previous months,

---

they relied on captured Iraqi heavy weapons which, despite its temporary utility, only added to their logistic challenges. As late as 1985, the *Pasdaran* leadership complained that Tehran had purchased no heavy weapons for its use. Kenneth Katzman, "The Pasdaran: Institutionalization of Revolutionary Armed Force," *Iranian Studies* 26, no. 3/4 (1993), 391.

[23] O'Ballance, *The Gulf War*, 114. Hojatoleslam Ali Akbar Hashemi Rafsanjani, an Iranian politician and cleric, founded the Islamic Republic Party when Ayatollah Khomeini returned from exile in 1979. He became Iran's president upon Khomeini's death in 1989 and was succeeded by Seyyed Muhammad Khatami in 1997.

[24] The choice of *Fajr* reflected a belief that the offensive would be a new beginning for the Middle East.

[25] Kevin M. Woods, Williamson Murray, Elizabeth A. Nathan, Laila Sabara, and Ana M. Venegas, "Interview with (Former) Major General Mizher Rashid Al-Tarfa Al-Ubaydi, Dubai, United Arab Emirates, 9 November 2009," *Project 1946: Phase II* (Alexandria, VA, 2010).

[26] RE: Standarized Briefing Formal (19 January 1985) Memorandum from the Army Chief of Staff to Corps and Shatt al-Arab Operational Commands in SH-GMID-D-000-649, General Military Intelligence Directorate Reports About Various Activities During the Iran–Iraq War, January–February 1985. The report recapitulates the battles over the previous two years.

prevented our forces from advancing with speed. As a result, even though they broke through the enemy lines, daylight approached prior to the completion of the clearing operations, and it now appeared that we would not be able to stabilize the battlefield ... In fact, the darkness of the night, our inability to clear all mine fields, and the alertness of the enemy as a result of their knowledge of the operation, all were factors which contributed to our inability to accomplish our objectives.[27]

The main attack, launched at midday on 7 February, fared no better. A third human-wave attack on 8 February upped the battle's casualty bill. On 9 February, the Iranians finally achieved a small measure of success with an armored attack that soon became a disaster. Iranian heavy units succeeded in punching a hole in the defenses, but, as with their attack in January 1981, the armor received little support from the *Pasdaran*, while the Iraqi corps commander concentrated his forces, moved up available reserves, and crushed the attacking force. Both sides suffered heavy losses. The Iraqis "were successful in crushing the enemy," according to General Shanshal, who reported enemy losses at 16,722 killed, a "large number" injured, and more than 10,000 prisoners.[28]

These battles significantly boosted Iraqi confidence and demonstrated the defensive system's effectiveness, which, during the next five years, would devastate the youth of Iran. In a briefing to King Hussein on 6 April 1983, Saddam's army chief, Shanshal, described how the "complete system" of fortifications, tank traps, minefields, and wire barriers was in place for the first time. Before the twenty-six brigades of Khomeini Guards could cross no-man's-land, they had to face concentrated fire from up to twelve artillery battalions per Iraqi brigade. Shanshal noted, "if you grab a handful of dirt [from this battlefield], you will see that half of it is gravel and the other half is iron." By leveraging lessons from the defensive operations of 1982, the Iraqis shifted reinforcements quickly to critical points. By amassing twenty-two artillery battalions behind fifty-four brigades, ensconced behind a six-kilometer defensive system of World War I proportions, the defenders decimated the Iranian attacks. In agreement with Shanshal, Saddam emphasized to the king that "not one soldier fled from his position on the front line ... This is an important point." As in so many battles during World War I, the frontline

---

[27] *SH-MISC-D-001-349, Pasdaran Report: From Khorramshahr to Fao (July 1982– August 1986): A Military and Political Analysis, Circa 1988.

[28] Memorandum from the Army Chief of Staff to Corps and Shatt al-Arab Operational Commands in SH-GMID-D-000-649, General Military Intelligence Directorate Reports About Various Activities During the Iran–Iraq War, January–February 1985.

hardly moved, but Iranian losses were staggering.[29] Nevertheless, the defeat made little impression on Iranian leaders. Rafsanjani announced, "Operation 'Dawn' will continue."[30]

The heavy fighting, as well as their losses, led the Iranians to pause and regroup before launching their next offensives. Codenames for the next two offensives were "Dawn 2" and "Dawn 3." Both struck north of Basra to pull Iraqi reserves away from the city. The first struck positions defending the Kurdish areas in the north. To Saddam's outrage, the Kurds, despite earlier agreements, cooperated with the Iranians and attacked Iraqi positions. The Iranians won a small victory, capturing a number of dominant heights along the border. The offensive's goal seems to have been to inflict heavy casualties on the Iraqis rather than achieve a major military success.[31]

At the end of July, the Iranians struck at the central sector to break the Baghdad to Basra highway, an obvious attempt to limit the ability to shuttle reserves to meet Iranian attacks. Three divisions of *Pasdaran*, approximately 35,000 strong, attacked. Again the Iranians made minor gains, but at heavy cost. Three days of human-wave attacks, some supported by armor, failed. On the fourth day, the Iranians broke through Iraqi frontline positions, but the tactical success led nowhere. Both sides made extravagant claims about their opponents' heavy losses.[32] The fourth and last offensive, this one imaginatively codenamed "Dawn 4," came in the north in late December 1983; the Iranians hoping to receive significant help from the Kurds. But Kurdish help failed to strengthen the attack enough for either victory or territorial gains. Instead, the Iranians only seized a few border outposts and squalid mountain villages.

The Iranian attacks in the center and north reflected a change in operational approach, at least in the short term. They were easier to supply logistically, because they were closer to Tehran. In addition, the mountainous terrain played to Iranian strengths, particularly in light

---

[29] Transcript of a Meeting between Saddam Hussein and Military Commanders (31 May 1983) in SH-SHTP-D-000-539, Records of Saddam Meeting with the General Armed Forces Command Leadership and Jordanian King Hussein Bin Talal, 1983. At the height of one of the battles in 1983, the Iraqis were firing 34,000 shells per day.

[30] O'Ballance, *The Gulf War*, 114–116.

[31] *SH-MISC-D-001-349, Pasdaran Report: From Khorramshahr to Fao (July 1982–August 1986): A Military and Political Analysis, Circa 1988. According to Iraqi documents, the Iranians suffered 14,900 dead of 70,000 committed during the Dawn 2 offensive alone. Memorandum from the Army Chief of Staff to Corps and Shatt al-Arab Operational Commands in SH-GMID-D-000-649, General Military Intelligence Directorate Reports About Various Activities During the Iran–Iraq War, January–February 1985. The report recapitulates the battles during the two previous years.

[32] O'Ballance, *The Gulf War*, 119–120.

infantry. Nevertheless, Khomeini's soldiers had little hope of succeeding because the terrain quickly descended to the plains of the Mesopotamian Valley, where Iraqi armor dominated. The Iranians hoped that with Kurdish help they could capture the dams northeast of Baghdad, but even here they were disappointed. Their forces simply were not skilled enough to capitalize on tactical success achieved at heavy cost.[33] According to one report, the Iranians had thrown a large force of regular infantry and *Pasdaran*, backed by nineteen artillery regiments, into the battle. In three major thrusts between 19 October and 19 November, they suffered 46,000 killed. While the number likely reflects Iraqi exaggeration, the Iraqi estimate was higher than reports on battles earlier in the year.[34]

Lessons learned in 1983

During 1983, Saddam had reason to reflect on the war. In a conversation with senior officers in fall 1983, he launched into a monologue:

To be the same in your style is deadly in a long war. Using the same style of warfare will teach your enemy your style of fighting ... [T]he principle weapons in a long war are the tank and the cannon [artillery]. Since we have destroyed their air force; now more than ever the principle weapons are the cannon and the tank ... We bought 123,000 artillery shells. We went to war with an average of 130 shells to each cannon and 23,000 shells of ... artillery; but we have three times as much of that ammunition. The numbers are big; we bought so much ammunition that it is hard for me to forget the number. Memorizing numbers is not my cup of tea; but the extraordinary numbers and the need of this equipment and ammunition changed that. Now you mention any number that has to do with weapons of any kind only one time, and I will remember it.[35]

The dictator turned to his worries that others, particularly the Israelis, might benefit from the military experience the Iraqis had gained during the past three years:

The whole world knows that Iraq will be in war for three or four years and the arms that would be used in this [war] will be evaluated after the war ends. There [will] be a new evaluation of weapons; we will be careful not to give anyone

---

[33] Woods, *et al.*, *Saddam's War*, 13.

[34] Memorandum from the Army Chief of Staff to Corps and Shatt al-Arab Operational Commands in SH-GMID-D-000-649, General Military Intelligence Directorate Reports About Various Activities During the Iran–Iraq War, January–February 1985.

[35] SH-SHTP-A-000-627, Saddam and Senior Military Officials Discussing Arms Imports and Other Issues Related to the Iran–Iraq War, Circa Fall 1983. Because of the failure to mention specific dates or events in the transcript, it is impossible to give an exact date. Our best estimate is that the conversation occurred sometime in the fall.

feedback on how these weapons performed during war. Since those arms we are using can be used against us and the suppliers can raise the price of the better weapons, it would be disadvantageous for us to tell anybody how those arms performed ... Countries learn how to fight through fighting in actual wars ... The Jews ... see the experience we are gaining of the war as it goes on will be intact after the war and that will be a threat to them [the Israelis] later on ... Sure we are aware of the basics of warfare [before the war]; but to attack, gain ground, and have the enemy counterattack us and cause us to react in many ways, that was a learning experience. We did not have the military background of how to balance, defend and counterattack and how to react to specific situations [on] the battlefield.[36]

Saddam then addressed the nature of war and death and the courage of the warrior:

Death and its effect on people usually is overwhelming; but by now the Iraqis have encountered death in the martyrs of this war and are accustomed to handle it properly ... If it ever happens the Iraqi people were in a conflict with their Israeli enemy; then the Iraqis would be able to withstand three years of fighting in a war. However, the Israelis cannot withstand one year of fighting in a war.[37]

He added that "the Israelis they use their brains, they get smarter after six months of fighting. That is why they are masters of warfare."[38] However, he suggested that the Iraqis represented a warrior nation with immense potential:

Throughout history Iraqis have been pioneers in warfare and the world learned from them how to fight wars. Now can you tell me how they could have managed to do that if they were not smart? We are the first nation that knew how to wage war, but look at us now; we are trying to learn from here and there ... We should create our own Iraqi expressions and vocabulary in the military manuals that would fit our needs. I have already started adapting a process. From now on my secretary will send me two training manuals at a time so I can go over them and check them out.[39]

Nevertheless, the human material from which the Iraqi military drew its frontline forces left something to be desired in terms of education levels and quality of schooling – a reality Saddam recognized. In a conversation with air force officers in early summer 1983, he mentioned that the qualification for entrance into the armor branch was a sixth-grade education, but then admitted that those who possessed such a level of education were still functionally illiterate.[40] The influence of Saddam's

---

[36] *Ibid.*   [37] *Ibid.*   [38] *Ibid.*   [39] *Ibid.*
[40] *SH-AFGC-D-001-324, Transcript of a Meeting between Saddam Hussein and the General Command of the Armed Forces, 26 June 1983.

views of military history on the Iraqi Army is suggested by an article in one of the Iraqi military journals appearing at this time:

The military's power and the combatant's heroism are measured in times of growing calamities and mishaps, when the world becomes dark for all except those who possess shining faith and the awesome inspiration of their creed. A fighter who does not attach importance to principles and idealism becomes dejected ... and forgets his art, knowledge, and skills. A soldier who loves himself and fears for his life thereby rejects his principles and ideals ... Arab commanders are the most faithful, most intelligent, and most vigorous. They do not fear death, rather they seek it.[41]

The most useful outcome from these discussions was Saddam's decision that the army needed to focus on retraining combat units after the fall battles. He excoriated the state of training in the army in 1980, a state of affairs for which no one was willing to suggest that the leader bore some responsibility. Saddam ordered frontline army commanders to withdraw two brigades from each division, leaving one in place, for extensive retraining in rear areas during the winter. The emphasis on retraining extended to the regime's propaganda efforts, which underlines why the army needed extensive retraining in the midst of war. The army's psychological warfare committee urged soldiers to shape their tactics around the following principles, an astonishing list, considering that the Iraqis had been engaged in combat for nearly three years:

For the review of all fighters at the fronts: precise execution of the points below at the combat fronts will help us achieve victory over Godlessness [i.e., the Iranians].

- Complete obedience to command.
- No shooting ... at the ranks of the first line.
- Not firing RPGs without a target.
- Do not fear intense fire of the enemy in the area [of combat].
- [You are] obliged legally and traditionally to remain until the end of the operation (desertion [in] war puts a stain on one's name ...)
- The troops advancing in the rear ranks must be aware of the presence of their forces in the lines forward of them. They must pay attention to not firing on our forces ...
- An enemy counterattack is considered an important matter in operations. You must defend against it in place ...
- Firing is prohibited unless [you] see the targets.[42]

---

[41] Concept of the Military Profession in the Heritage of Arab Warfare in *SH-MODX-D-001-360, Administrative Affairs Journal, No. 3, May 1983. Such attitudes explain much about Saddam's contempt for the United States and its military forces in the run up to the 1991 Gulf War.

[42] *SH-GMID-D-001-362, Various Memoranda between the Psychological Warfare Committee, GMID, and the RCC, 21 February–4 July 1983.

1983: blood for peace

While the desultory fighting on the ground dragged on, Saddam searched for alternatives to force the Iranians to the peace table. Both sides considered attacking the opponent's cities and towns with aircraft and missiles. Here, the Iraqis enjoyed a considerable advantage because both the Soviets and the French were willing to sell them frontline aircraft. However, Khomeini's regime had angered virtually every one of the major powers, greatly limiting its ability to import spare parts except through dubious and unreliable means like those that eventually became the Iran–Contra affair and from the Syrians, Libyans, Chinese, and North Koreans.[43] Consequently, control of the air shifted to the Iraqis, although the skill of Iraqi pilots was, for the most part, less than impressive.[44]

One chronic weakness of the Iraqi Air Force system was airspace command and control. Throughout the war it remained inept, which helps explain how the Iranians were consistently able to slip F-4 formations into Iraqi airspace and attack targets throughout Iraq. In a conversation with Saddam, the officer responsible for an air defense sector commented on the technological weaknesses of his controllers and the need to upgrade training:

Sir, as far as the air controller's preparation, as your Excellency knows, we get those who failed at the air force academy. For those the academy will either send them to fighter control or to the fire department, if [airspace] control does not need them. The traditional training curriculum is backward; it consists of blackboard teaching ... We [have suggested that] this method does not help us ... We contracted with a trainer specialized in air controllers, radar training, direction aiming training [navigation] and an optical trainer [for aircraft] within the airport's range.[45]

This made little sense to Saddam, who failed to see why he should spend resources to train air controllers. When an attendee suggested specialty pay might be useful, Saddam exploded, "They are air controllers and when they want half of the pilot's allocation we need to ask them how

---

[43] Iran managed to extend the combat readiness of its American-made aircraft through various clandestine connections. In addition, by 1983 there were increasing public reports of Chinese-built F-6 fighters making their way to Iran through North Korea with training provided by East Germany. Clarence A. Robinson Jr., "Iraq, Iran Acquiring Chinese-Built Fighters," *Aviation Week & Space Technology* (1983).

[44] For an examination of the difficulties the Iranians were having in equipping the vast numbers of troops they were able to raise, see Ward, *Immortal*, 260–261.

[45] *SH-AFGC-D-001-324, Transcript of a Meeting between Saddam Hussein and the General Command of the Armed Forces, 26 June 1983.

many of them [have been] killed in this war. Maybe no one, while how many pilots [have been] killed?"[46]

Meanwhile, the war heated up in the Gulf. The Iraqis attempted to pressure Iranian exports of crude so that Khomeini would agree to peace. Mirage F-1s and Super Etendards made it possible for the Iraqis to gain control of the Gulf's air space and increased the damage their air force could inflict on Iranian shipping. The story of Iraq's acquisition of these aircraft from France is a complex, and, in some cases, long-standing, mix of political, diplomatic, and commercial interests.

Relations between Iran and France began to deteriorate in early 1981 after the delivery of French Mirage F-1s to Baghdad. In August, two refugees from the revolution arrived in Paris, Iran's former prime minister, Bani-Sadr, and the leader of the People's Mojahedin of Iran, Massoud Rajavi. Both used the French media to attack the government of the ayatollahs. An increasingly deadly reply to these events by Iran and its surrogates began almost immediately on French targets with attacks on French government personnel and interests throughout the Middle East and especially in Lebanon between August 1981 and September 1983. This helps to explain why Iran found so little support for its entreaties to the international community during the war.

Iraq made headway while Iran was damaging its own interests, and in October 1983, France was set to deliver five Super Etendards on lease to Baghdad. Some in the French government were against leasing the planes to Iraq; they feared the Iraqis might use the fighter bombers to attack the main Iranian oil terminal on Kharg Island with Exocet missiles, thereby driving up oil prices. Then, after an Iranian-supported suicide-truck bomb killed fifty-eight French troops in the French barracks in Beirut, the French immediately released the Super Etendards for export.[47]

Throughout 1983, before crews were trained on the Super Etendards, Iraqi attacks by missile boat, helicopter, and aircraft increased, but fitfully. The attacks were particularly effective against the Iranian convoys moving to Bandar-e Khomeini, but Kharg was a more difficult target.

---

[46] *Ibid.*
[47] David Styan, *France and Iraq: Oil, Arms, and French Policy-Making in the Middle East* (New York, NY, 2006). See also O'Ballance, *The Gulf War*, 124. This was either a case of Iran's inability to control its proxies or another example of ineptly executed foreign policy on the part of Tehran. Although the United States has generally maintained that Hezbollah was responsible for the attacks on the US Marine and French barracks, the specific organization responsible for the attacks is still a matter of some debate among experts. However, Iran's support for the perpetrators is generally not disputed. The same day, a truck bomb killed 241 US military personnel in Beirut.

During the year, the Iraqis hit thirteen tankers and bulk freighters, nine of which were sunk or written off by their owners. The Exocet missile attacks succeeded less than half of the time, because the missile warheads often were not powerful enough to damage super tankers more than marginally. In addition, the Iranians opened up a new transshipment point on Sirri Island, located 250 miles southeast of Kharg and out of the range of Iraqi air strikes.[48]

As soon as the crews were trained, Saddam launched the Super Etendards in a campaign to shut Kharg down and end Iranian oil exports.[49] An article in an Iraqi military journal in 1984 indicates what the Iraqis had hoped to achieve:

The next stage of the naval blockade imposed on Kharg Island involved decisive warnings issued by President Commander Saddam Hussein in November 1983, when he said, "It is obvious that the Iranian regime's launching of any new attack against Iraqi civilian centers, or any military attack against our armed forces defending our international borders, will be an additional cause for us to undertake deterrent actions."[50]

The article then discussed how effectively the Iraqi operations and blockade had shut down Iranian oil exports.[51] In fact, while the Iraqis had substantially damaged Kharg's facilities and Iranian exports, they had neither the expertise nor the capabilities to prevent the Iranians from repairing the damage. Nevertheless, the campaign in the northern Gulf did have an impact. Ship owners' increasing unwillingness to risk vessels in the waters off Kharg forced Iran to expend its increasingly overtaxed financial resources to buy tankers either to export their own oil or to move it to safer locations down the Gulf, where it could be transferred to other carriers. By the end of the war, the Iranian fleet had expanded from 450,000 tons to 2.1 million tons. Moreover, the Iranians had to mark down crude oil prices by approximately $3 per barrel, a price that attracted a considerable number of foreign tankers to Kharg despite the dangers of missile attacks.[52]

Not surprisingly, given the stalemate on the war's battlefronts, the war against civilian populations increased. Each side apparently fired off

---

[48] Anthony H. Cordesman and Abraham R. Wagner, *The Iran–Iraq War*, vol. II (Boulder, CO, 1990), 71.

[49] The Iraqis planned sophisticated mission profiles, but lacked both the maintenance support and the number of aircraft to make their campaign work.

[50] Strategic Dimensions of the Kharg Island Blockade in SH-MODX-D-000-853, [The Iraqi] Military Journal, July 1984.

[51] *Ibid.*

[52] Navias and Hooton, *Tanker Wars*, 57–60.

Scuds and other assorted missiles as fast as they could get them from the Soviets or various client states that had bought them from the Soviets. The Soviets' willingness to increase the delivery of Scuds sometimes depended on Iraq's ability to supply them with captured American equipment. In particular, in conversations during 1984, the Soviet military attaché in Baghdad made clear the Soviet desire to acquire Phoenix, Sparrow, and Sidewinder air-to-air missiles, all of which the United States had supplied to the Shah.[53]

By this point in the war, Saddam was increasingly interested in how to apply military means to psychologically impact his Iranian enemies. In a June 1983 discussion with his air force advisor and the commander of his air force and air defense, Saddam pressed them on the lack of effect that Iraqi air and missile attacks had on the Iranian air bases near Dezful:

As you know the air base could only be struck by luck and if we wanted to strike it, we would have to fire approximately 15 missiles on it, hoping that one of them would strike it. In addition, one of the missiles might drop on a residential area and kill a large number of residents ... Therefore, we will continue firing only on the big cities, because wherever the missile strikes, it will cause damage.[54]

Saddam then proceeded to provide tactical targeting guidance for attacking Iran's cities:

SADDAM:	We will fire the missiles at the industrial site, and we will specify a missile to strike Dezful city at night, because striking the city at night will have a better effect, since there will be larger numbers in the city at night than there would be during the daytime. Therefore we will strike Andimeshk city during the daytime and strike Dezful at nighttime in the same day.
MILITARY OPERATIONS DIRECTOR:	Sir, that is to say for us to strike Andimeshk during its business hours.
SADDAM:	Yes, during their business hours.[55]

[53] RE: The Soviet Military Attache in Baghdad (28 July 1987) Internal GMID Memorandum in SH-GMID-D-000-550, General Military Intelligence Directorate Memoranda About the Soviet Military Attache to Baghdad and Information on Plans for Iraq to Provide Russia with Missiles, 1982–1987.

[54] SH-PDWN-D-001-029, Meeting between Saddam Hussein and Various Iraqi Military Leaders, 11 May 1983.

[55] *Ibid.* Previously it was assumed that the missile that hit Andimeshk was "meant for Dezful and had failed to strike its target." See Anthony H. Cordesman and Abraham R. Wagner, *The Lessons of Modern War, Volume II: The Iran–Iraq War* (Boulder, CO, 1990), 496.

Saddam also explored other avenues for forcing the Iranians to end the war. As early as 1982, the Iraqis began using chemical weapons, as they rationalized it, to offset their enemy's superior numbers. In a November 1983 memorandum from the GMID titled, "Effects of Chemical Weapons," the director candidly assessed Iraq's use of chemical weapons thus far in the conflict. "Chemical weapons were used during the battles east of Basra" (July 1982), but the "effectiveness [of these weapons] was not established." Furthermore, the 10th Armored Division's use of chemical weapons was disappointing. Interrogations of prisoners of war taken from the target area reported "only light dizziness." Other operations in Khanaqin and Penjwin had similar results. The memorandum, however, noted the psychological potential of such weapons. The Iranians had reacted by launching a "propaganda campaign about our troops' use of chemical agents."

The memorandum then warned that because the Iranians were feeling increasingly threatened by "the use of chemical bombs," they would, in all likelihood, develop their own capabilities in gas warfare. Based on Saddam's analysis, the GMID recommended three things:

1. Avoid the use of chemical agents now . . .
2. Take advantage of current production and stockpile it to obtain an extensive striking power when needed.
3. . . . Achieve production of toxic agents in large quantities as quickly as possible for use as a deterring factor and for sudden attacks directed at enemy concentrations of troops and his main civilian gatherings.[56]

A letter signed by the secretary of the Armed Services General Command, under Saddam's authority, concurred with the GMID director's analysis and directed stockpiling agents. The Iraqi military began accumulating chemical stocks for some ongoing use, but the emphasis was still in general anticipation of an emergency situation, or when it would be to Iraq's best advantage. Saddam ordered commanders not to use such weapons without his permission, a move undoubtedly

[56] SH-AFGC-D-000-094, Iraqi Armed Forces General Command Memos Proving That Iraq Produced and Used Chemical Weapons against Iran and Along the Border During the Iran–Iraq War, June–November 1983. During this period, Iran accused Iraq of using chemical weapons on almost 100 occasions. Iraq denounced as fabrications and "full of lies" public statements by US officials concluding that at least some of Iran's accusations were true. See SIPRI, *Fact Sheet: Chemical Warfare in the Iraq–Iran War* (Stockholm, 1984). Downloaded from www.sipri.org/research/armaments/transfers/databases/armstransfers; Javed Ali, "Chemical Weapons and the Iran–Iraq War: A Case Study in Noncompliance," *The Nonproliferation Review* 8, no. 1 (2001), 47–50.

influenced by the fact that UN inspectors were sniffing around for just such a thing.[57]

Since early in the war, it had been clear to the Iraqi high command that despite the international backlash against using chemical weapons and despite the risk that Iran would respond in kind, the psychological impact of the weapons on Iranian troops might be their most redeeming attribute. One of the main themes of the 27 November memorandum was that "[d]espite [its] limited effect, the continued use of the aforementioned agents has led to the issuing of a number of warnings by Iranian higher headquarters to regular and non-regular units. The majority of the non-regular troops do not possess individual protective gear and the enemy's ability to undertake protective actions and collective decontamination is extremely limited."[58]

The GMID's analysis supported a psychological operations campaign directed at Iranian troops: even while denying they were using chemical weapons on the battlefield, the Iraqi high command took every opportunity to remind the Iranians they had the capability and intent to use chemical weapons. In September 1983, the Iraqi high command issued a less-than-subtle warning that it was

armed with new weapons. These modern weapons will be used for the first time in war … were not used in previous attacks for humanitarian and ethical reasons … If you execute the orders of Khomeini's warmongering regime and go to the fronts, your death will be certain because this time we will use a weapon that will destroy any moving creature on the fronts.[59]

The commander of the III Corps was quoted in early 1984 saying "[i]f you give me some insecticide that I could squirt at this swarm of mosquitoes, I would use it so that they would be exterminated, thus benefiting humanity by saving the world from these pests."[60] Iraq's efforts to play up the threat were no doubt assisted by Iran's complaints to the international community. The reports of chemical attacks against unprepared troops accompanied by photographs of causalities only served to play up the fear that Iraq sought to create in the minds of Iran's soldiers.

---

[57] SH-AFGC-D-000-094, Iraqi Armed Forces General Command Memos Proving That Iraq Produced and Used Chemical Weapons against Iran and Along the Border During the Iran–Iraq War, June–November 1983.

[58] *Ibid.*

[59] Unattributed, "Commentary on New Lethal Weapon, 12 Apr (FBIS-MEA-83-071)," *Foreign Broadcast Information Service Daily Reports* (1983).

[60] Barry Hillenbrand, William E. Smith, and Raji Samghabadi, "The Gulf: Clouds of Desperation," *Time*, 19 March 1984.

1984: no end in sight, planning for the campaign

As 1984 opened, both sides had successfully mobilized much of their manpower and economic resources. The Iranians had suffered heavy losses for no appreciable gains against Iraqi defenses in 1983. One of their histories of this period admits, "On the third and fourth year of the war, based on the lessons they [the Iraqis] had learned in the battlefield, the Iraqis decided to employ new tactics and reorganized their forces to meet the new method of [our] operations. For us, confronting the 'new' enemy required new planning and different tactics, if we were to preclude a stalemate."[61] For the Iraqis, the question was how much longer they could stay the course with increasing losses in manpower and material. Even Iran, with its manpower advantage, was not immune to the losses. Iraqi intelligence noted increasing numbers of Afghan and Pakistani "volunteers" on the other side. One report even claimed that 45,000 Afghans had been "forced or coerced" into service during the 1983 battles.[62]

In an extended conversation with senior officers in February 1984, Saddam examined the possibilities. In particular, he emphasized the need to share combat lessons throughout the army, because there probably would be time between each enemy offensive. Shortly after these conversations, the Iranians launched a series of heavy attacks in both the central sector and the south, the latter aimed at capturing Basra, and thus opening the door to the Shi'a cities along the Euphrates.[63] Saddam began his exposition of the changes to Iraqi military culture with an admonition no officer would have taken seriously: "Even myself when I make mistakes, I need someone from among my colleagues to notify me." He continued saying that senior commanders needed to "exchange analyses with each other in regard[ing] the way we need to treat the enemy ... and then ... apply [the results] from one corps to another in

---

[61] *SH-MISC-D-001-349, Pasdaran Report: From Khorramshahr to Fao (July 1982– August 1986): A Military and Political Analysis, Circa 1988.

[62] RE: Afghan Volunteers (12 March 1984) Memorandum from the Military Attache– Kabul to GMID in SH-GMID-D-000-465, Correspondence from the Iraqi General Military Intelligence Directorate Regarding Iranian–Afghan Relations, December 1983– March 1984. The reporting was likely exaggerated for effect by the Afghanistan government. During this period, the Iranians began training Shi'a or ethnic Persian Afghan refugees and helped to create or support several Afghan resistance groups. Martin Kramer, "The Routine of Muslim Solidarity," in *Middle East Contemporary Survey: Iraq, 1976–1999, Volume IX: 1984–85*, Itmar Rabinovich and Haim Shaked, eds. (Tel Aviv, 1986), 159–160.

[63] Cordesman, *The Iran–Iraq War*, 142–150.

a good manner and at the same time we will be able to fill the gaps and fix any mistakes."[64]

Saddam then turned to the difficulties the Iraqis had planning anything less than a lengthy timeline:

[W]hen we ask the commander of [a] division to ... attack an enemy position, and it takes him almost a month to put the required plan together, I don't understand and how can I understand his psychology ...

[M]oreover, the opportunity is there to take, you as a hunter [must take it] because the enemy will not stay frozen waiting for you. One of the most important things we know is that to put the enemy in a state of confusion [you] use the elements of surprise to put his [understanding of the situation] in doubt, but if it takes us one month to put a plan into effect, the enemy could surprise us and launch an attack, let's say within 15 days ...

How can we prepare ourselves to put plans quickly into action to confront the enemy not within a month ... but dynamically, so we will [not] tell our enemy, "please wait because it will take us two months or one month to put the required plan into action?" So my brothers the usual military methods we are using against the enemy ... was born of our training. [W]e thought we could use these same methods to confront another enemy with different characteristics ... [However,] we are dealing with these irregulars now, but at the same time we have to prepare ourselves to confront a modern regular army with good armament, so we have to prepare for both situations ... not only in theory but [also in] practice.[65]

The dictator commented on the fighting around Basra the previous year and noted the Iranians had been watching how the Iraqis fought and were learning about Iraqi behavior on the battlefield. He particularly believed the emphasis the Iraqis had put on the defensive in 1983 had persuaded the Iranians they had little to fear from Iraqi counterattacks. His implication was clear: the defensive mindset must change. For 1984, he estimated:

The enemy will maneuver with all his strength and possibly will use one fourth of his strength to preoccupy along the front of three corps and concentrate on several axes of one specific corps area ... This is our impression that the enemy will occupy our army along a three corps area as a secondary attack, but will concentrate on one specific corps area and keep attacking it ... attack the first day and get nothing ... attack the second day ... the third day ... the fourth day ... but on the fifth day he will be able to penetrate into our rear areas and on the sixth day he will surround us. Thus, he will choose certain army units and keep pounding them using the human wave technique. How then can we face up to this kind of approach?[66]

---

[64] SH-SHTP-A-001-022, Recording of a Meeting between Saddam Hussein and High Ranking Military Officers Regarding Military Operations During the Iran–Iraq War, circa February 1984.
[65] *Ibid.*   [66] *Ibid.*

The question before Saddam was where the Iranian offensives would come:

And before that the enemy started talking about a final ... battle indicating that a decisive battle will be waged against us and we decided to challenge him to produce this decisive battle ... The enemy is using this rhetoric as an essential part of his propaganda ... but I also think that the enemy as far as planning goes wishes to wage a decisive battle, so if he wants to wage a decisive battle, where will he wage it?[67]

For Saddam it was obvious that, considering the enemy's previous efforts and the nature of the terrain, the enemy's main effort would come against Basra. Iraq's second city was the obvious target, because Baghdad was simply too distant from Iranian lines.

To meet the enemy's offensive, Saddam stressed that the army could not simply stand on the defensive:

So my brothers as field military commanders we have a responsibility to take a risk on seizing the initiative, because if we do not we will cause the demoralization of our fighters and also motivate enemy forces when they see you do not take action on the enemy's territory nor on your own territory. Thus, one of the most distinguishing factors among military personnel is the ability to attack successfully and defeat the enemy instead of waiting for the enemy to wage his attack.[68]

An unidentified officer proceeded at this point to ask the dictator: We are entering this war now for the fourth year, so all the questions we had before the war we are supposed to have answered them for now, because our experience before the start of this war was based on books and publications dealing with wars that lasted two or three weeks and the international community was able to stop them. Sir, I would like [you] to comment on your first point of this discussion that this war is a very rich experience for our armed forces, and its lessons and consequences are much different than the ones we had with the Zionist entity.[69]

Saddam interjected a piece of self-justification that was not only patently false, but also revealing about his psychological makeup and decision making, which would reappear in the days before the 1991 Gulf War. He commented on the Iraqi "withdrawal" from Iran in 1982: "We did not withdraw because of the enemy, but because we wanted to provide a psychological cover for our army. I swear to God, if the whole world wanted us to withdraw, we would never have withdrawn and would have stayed there and [fought] the enemy the same way, but because of some losses our army suffered we decided to withdraw."[70] Of course, based on the disaster at Khorramshahr and related actions,

---

[67] *Ibid.*   [68] *Ibid.*   [69] *Ibid.*   [70] *Ibid.*

these comments were false. But the larger point is that no one had put political pressure on Saddam to withdraw from Iran. Thus, he had ordered his troops to retreat rather than stand fast. What then to do about the gains that the Iranians had made in driving Iraqi forces back over the fighting in summer and fall 1983? Here Saddam was more realistic: "My brothers, as long as our army has strong morale and has the ability to wage an attack there is no fear, even if the enemy were able to occupy some of our land. As long as we are strong, we can get this land back now, a year from now, or two years from now, but if we lose our morale and our ability to wage an attack, then we [will] lose the whole of Iraq."[71]

At the end of these discussions, Saddam reiterated a number of major points he believed were important to conducting military operations. He reemphasized his desire that Iraqi officers display initiative at different levels and that his forces not allow the Iranians to attack unhindered. The Iraqi Army must launch spoiling blows and counterattacks:

On this subject ... I have stressed two essential points: maneuver and the ability to wage attacks to disperse the enemy effort and ... the need to take risks in the process of decision making with an understanding of the psychological and technological aspects of our army, because I follow my army in very precise detail. So my final point is that we have to wage attacks on enemy forces and by this will take the initiative from the enemy and at the same time we can train our soldiers and keep their morale high. As I said before, I would prefer to lose land with a well-trained army rather than to hold the land, but possess a weakened army. With a strong army we will soon regain what we have lost. The solution is [that] field commanders should have the ability to make a decision during the battle without going back to their corps commanders even if there is a 30 percent error rate. Nevertheless in normal circumstances we should discuss our plans through regular channels ...

One of the notorious ills of the long war is the dependence factor. During a long war it could take us two full weeks to put a plan into action, but no, I want our commander to put a plan into action within 48 hours, as in a decisive war.[72]

Leveraging lessons accumulated in 1983, Saddam directed a series of measures to prepare for the coming year. First, he created a field command designed to cover the gap between the III and IV Corps. The new command was to control the 10th Armored Division and a collection of non-corps units in the area of the Shatt al-Arab. A new reserve command to relieve frontline corps of the need to respond to the immediate defense

[71] *Ibid.*   [72] *Ibid.*

of the area was a major change in the Baghdad-centric command processes of 1983. Other changes included:

1. Minor operations must stop; instead a force must be dedicated to keeping the enemy engaged.
2. Reallocation of artillery support.
3. When losses of any brigade exceeded 50 percent, the brigade must be replaced immediately.
4. Special forces must not be used as infantry.
5. The air force must take risks in striking targets.[73]

At the same time, Saddam's overall guidance was being integrated into an increasingly professionalized military. Under its new director, Major General Aladdin Makki, Iraq's combat development directorate began to publish tactical and operational lessons gleaned from the war. One such product, published in July 1984, summarized the shift of Iraq's strategy "in order to upgrade [to] a long term defense effectively":

1. Revalidation of the legitimacy of continued fighting ... Strengthening of a spirit of steadfastness in confronting the enemy and acceptance of extremely costly sacrifices ...
2. Constant reviewing, reformulation, and crystallization of the objectives of the war in a way which harmonizes ... political and military situations.
3. Tighten relations with other fraternal countries be they friendly or neutral, regardless of their own strategies.
4. Exploit victories in the field to keep the public mobilized.
5. A careful balance must be achieved in reconciling war requirements and development requirements.
6. [Pursue] the conflict ... in other than a traditional or expected manner. Surprise must be used to confront the enemy at every turn ... on [the] military field at times and on political and diplomatic ... at other times.
7. Rely on preventative warfare ... by thwarting [the enemy's] preparations ... Sap his resources and fragment his capabilities ...
8. Conduct ... psychological and media warfare ... a word directed to the mind and heart of the adversary and his supporters ... is no less influential than the able sword.
9. Design ... strategic and operational deception plans to place the enemy in constant doubt.[74]

Fighting flared almost immediately in 1984. The Iranians launched a series of major attacks in mid-February on the central and southern

---

[73] Orders of the President and Commander-in-Chief of the Armed Forces (26 February 1984) in SH-AFGC-D-000-686, Orders of the President and Commander-in-Chief of the Armed Forces, February–December 1984.

[74] Upgrading a Defense in Long-Term War in SH-MODX-D-000-853, [The Iraqi] Military Journal, July 1984.

fronts. US satellite imagery and intelligence estimated that along the front, the Iranians had deployed approximately 300,000 *Pasdaran* and *Basij* in thirty divisional-sized groupings.[75] Not surprisingly, the code name for the first offensive was "Dawn 5," but for the second the Iranians came up with a new codename: Operation "Khyber."[76] The first attack was a small affair aimed at dominating, or at least interdicting, the Baghdad–Basra highway farther north. It was meant to divert Iraqi attention from the Basra defenses and draw reserves away from the south, where the main blow came. Nevertheless, the Iranian high command threw nearly 100,000 men into the offensive north of the Hoveyzeh Marshes.[77]

The second and main offensive came on 22 February. Its mission was to cut the Basra–Baghdad highway and thus split Iraqi defenses. Its specific goal was the town of al-Qurnah, where the Tigris and Euphrates meet and the Shatt al-Arab begins. Here, the Iranians caught the Iraqis by surprise by using a flotilla of boats to cross the supposedly impassable Hawr al-Hawizeh, on the far side of which the Iraqis had established few defenses.[78] These marshes lie north of Basra and run northeast to southwest along the border between the two nations for approximately 30 miles. Iranian planning played on the nature of the terrain:

the reasons for selecting the marshes were to take advantage of the following:

- Prevent a frontal attack. In other areas the enemy's defense had generally forced us into a force-on-force frontal attack.
- Attack the enemy's flank. The enemy's deployment east of Basra was such that by linking our forces in Talaiye and then attacking the enemy's rear in Neshve we could prevent any lateral movement to their flank and destabilize their defense . . .
- The enemy's ill-defended positions and their belief that no major operations would be conducted in the marshes . . .
- Difficult if not impossible to maneuver armor.

The purpose of Operation Khyber was the destruction of the [Iraqi] III Corps forces, securing the northern and southern Majnun islands, [and a] continuation of the attacks from the islands [to consolidate several fronts]. In this operation, we also planned to capture the hard surface (dry land) east of the Euphrates

---

[75] O'Ballance, *The Gulf War*, 143.

[76] The codename for the second offensive referred to the prophet Mohamed's attack on the Jewish commercial and agricultural town just to the north of Medina before his triumphal return to Mecca. Significantly, his cousin Ali, the great saint and martyr of the Shi'a faith, played a major role in Mohamed's victory at Khyber.

[77] Ward, *Immortal*, 263–264.

[78] O'Ballance, *The Gulf War*, 143–144.

through the marshes. In this manner, we would deny the enemy the capability to strengthen its III Corps from the north.[79]

The Iraqi III and IV Corps shared responsibility for defending the area, but neither had made extensive defensive preparations, given the terrain. Nevertheless, despite the surprise, the Iraqis reacted quickly and soon had blunted the offensive. Again the Iranians ran into the problem that was to beset them throughout the war: once out in the open, light infantry could not hold together against Iraqi armor and firepower. The Iranians reached the outskirts of al-Qurnah but were halted by Iraqi counterattacks.[80] A series of human-wave attacks by *Pasdaran* and *Basij* units collapsed during the following week in the face of Iraqi firepower and weaponry.[81] Iranian sources reported that the Iraqis used chemical weapons extensively, which may explain the sudden halt of the Iranian advance on the far side of the marshes.[82] Several sources reported the Iraqis had used "a crude sulfur-mustard, similar to that used by Germany in 1917 on the Western Front."[83] Along with firepower, the gas depleted Iranian strength and broke the back of the offensive. As a report noted:

chemical agents are effective in degrading command and control, fire support, and lines of communication. One of the most dramatic examples of this was during Operation "Kyber 1" in February 1984. In this operation, the Iranians attacked through the Hoveyzeh Marshes, attempting to cut the Basra–Baghdad road. In a notable example of battlefield interdiction, the Iraqis isolated the forward elements of the attacking force with Mustard, cutting it off almost entirely from resupply by land. When the Iraqis counterattacked, they encountered Iranians who had no ammunition and who had not eaten for several days.[84]

One estimate places Iranian casualties from mustard gas at 2,500.[85] Nevertheless, Iran's attacks had clearly scared the Iraqis enough that

---

[79] *SH-MISC-D-001-349, Pasdaran Report: From Khorramshahr to Fao (July 1982–August 1986): A Military and Political Analysis, Circa 1988.

[80] Uriel Dann, "The Iraqi–Iranian War," in *Middle East Contemporary Survey: Iraq, 1976–1999, Volume VIII: 1983–84,* Haim Shaked and Daniel Dishon, eds. (Tel Aviv, 1985), 184.

[81] For further discussion of these attacks, see O'Ballance, *The Gulf War,* 142–143.

[82] *SH-MISC-D-001-349, Pasdaran Report: From Khorramshahr to Fao (July 1982–August 1986): A Military and Political Analysis, Circa 1988.

[83] Dann, "The Iraqi–Iranian War," 184.

[84] "Subject: Task Force v Lessons Learned: The Iran–Iraq War, Appendix B–Chemicals," US Office of the Secretary of Defense, 1996, www.gulflink.osd.mil/declassdocs/af/19961205/120596_aaday_01.html (accessed 19 February 2014).

[85] Anthony H. Cordesman, *Iraq and the War of Sanctions: Conventional Threats and Weapons of Mass Destruction* (Westport, CT, 1999), 529.

Saddam was willing to relent on his earlier policy of conserving stocks of chemical agents, but threatening their use.[86]

By the time Operation Kyber ended early in March, the Iraqis had driven the Iranians back from the solid ground on the western side of the swamps. The Iranians did hold on to most of the island of Majnun in the swamp area, which possessed no tactical or operational value, but was inside Iraq's territory and did have substantial deposits of oil.[87] As usual, casualty figures on both sides were horrendous. One estimate calculates that the *Pasdaran* and *Basij* lost between 12,000 and 20,000 killed in action, while the regular army lost a further 6,000.[88] In fact so heavy were their losses that the Iranians were able to launch only small probing attacks for the remainder of 1984.

An Iraqi lessons-learned manual published in summer 1984 discusses how the Iranians were attempting to overcome the Iraqi superiority in tanks and armored fighting vehicles in their attacks as well as the Iraqi response. Saddam provided the introduction: "The enemy may not be bound by traditional factors in selecting routes and axes over which to attack. They may choose to attack our army from directions and over routes they believe to be covered by weak troops."[89] The Iraqis developed the manual to deal with the hastily prepared earthen berms the Iranian combat engineers were throwing up immediately behind attacking *Pasdaran* units and to explain how their forces could best counterattack and drive out the enemy before they could develop

---

[86] There is some controversy around the motivation and timing of Iraq's decision to use chemical weapons so heavily in late February 1984. Joost Hiltermann argues that the generally passive nature of US warnings and a willingness to pursue broader bilateral interests (including a renewal of full relations) despite Iraq's use of these weapons, may have led Iraqi leaders to believe "they were not more but less constrained on the battlefield." However, it does not appear from the Iraqi materials reviewed that the decision was anything more than a cold military calculation based on earlier Iraqi assessments of the cost of failure. See Joost R. Hiltermann, *A Poisonous Affair: America, Iraq, and the Gassing of Halabja* (New York, 2007), 46–56.

[87] An Iraqi report from early 1985 describes the Majnun area and its oil deposits as follows: "The Majnun [oil] fields are two islands in the region of Hawr al-Hawizeh. The southern field is 13 kilometers long and 10 kilometers wide. The width decreases until it becomes 7 kilometers south of the field at a total area of 100 square kilometers. The largest portion of it is currently submerged except for a section of the south on which our troops are located ... The northern field is eight kilometers long from the west and six kilometers from the east. Its width is seven kilometers. Its total area is 53 square kilometers." SH-IZAR-D-000-781, Intelligence Report About the Area within the Fourth Corps Command Sector, January 1985.

[88] Ward, *Immortal*, 265.

[89] *SH-MODX-D-001-363, Dealing with Hastily Prepared Earthen Berms*, Combat Development Directorate, August 1984.

permanent defensive positions: "Swift reaction by armor and mechanized infantry troops, heavy fire, and intense artillery support is required to ensure a shock force that will make it impossible for the enemy to hold out in a hastily-prepared berm, forcing them to withdraw or be wiped out."[90]

The manual's lessons can be succinctly summed up by a selection from the preface:

- Due to the obvious and eminent superiority of our armor and mechanized infantry troops over enemy troops and to limit our superiority and hamper the work of our troops, the enemy resorted to constructing berms – either deliberate berms inside defensive positions or hastily-erected berms built during [offensive] engagements ...
- Having reached a certain depth in the area of penetration, the enemy resorts to hasty construction of berms after a successful attack on our defensive positions (usually at night). They quickly send in engineering equipment behind assaulting troops to construct these berms for protection against armor counterattacks we usually launch at first light. The enemy then makes every effort to complete these berms (four kilometers in length, based on our experience with them in battle) during the hours of darkness ...
- The following information about the enemy, their organization, and their arms has been gathered through battles and combat experience ...
- An Iranian infantry battalion or guard unit will be dispersed along 3–4 kms. During the first night of an attack, the berm is constructed that night for their protection and to center their defense.
- ... we can expect the following weapons (considered the most dangerous) to be present. In the worst case, they are a threat to our armor within 1 to 1.5 kms of the berm; however, our attack will not be along a 4 km front. It will be against 1–1.5 kms to ensure concentration against a particular area of the berm; 54 RPG-7 launchers, 16 Dragon missiles, 6 TOW missile platforms, and 6 106mm AT guns.
- ... Most of the casualties inflicted on our troops have occurred because of halting between the stop line and the enemy berm, failure of the tanks to fire while moving, failure to provide sufficient concentration of fire against the enemy berm, failure to use smoke screens to limit or reduce enemy opportunities to observe our troops and aim at them while they mount their assault and assaulting the enemy at slow speed.[91]

At the end of March, a somewhat shaken Saddam met with his senior commanders. This conversation seems to bring full circle the GMID's warning from 1982 that wide-scale use of chemicals would eventually drive the Iranian's to respond in kind. Iraq's renewed use in its operations in February and apparent intent to continue meant that Iraqi

---

[90] *Ibid.*   [91] *Ibid.*

troops were at increased risk from not only a presumed Iranian response but also a downwind hazard from their own munitions:

SADDAM: ... this is our chance to train our army on the use of protection and tools against chemical war. This is also a chance to eliminate any panic state they might have should chemical strikes take place.

OFFICER: Yes, sir.

SADDAM: They should be ready with all means. I recommend that we lay out a plan for chemical strikes for us to carry out and ask our formations nearby to wear masks and that ... I mean truly the locations in the front ... they should be ready to be somehow affected; No, No, we strike the enemy ... we strike the enemy, [unintelligible] but in areas close to the front lines [unintelligible]. The doctors do their jobs by treating occurring cases in a way we eliminate ... and when this happens it is like nothing. So we want to eliminate any panic state our Iraqi Army might have if the enemy succeeds one day to [use chemical weapons].[92]

Saddam's decision to use chemical weapons reflected the pressures under which his regime was laboring. One file among many from April 1985 indicates that hundreds of soldiers were executed for desertion in 1984. Like all Iraqi security bureaucratic correspondence, the file covers in great detail the implementing messages and acknowledgments for executions between the military discipline command and other military organizations including the al-Rashid military hospital. In this case, the executions occurred on the Bismayah execution field with detailed instructions for the firing detail, the requirement to have doctors and an Imam present. Between 20 and 24 January 1985, at least ten soldiers were executed per day, all judged and delivered for actions that had occurred in 1984. Clearly discipline was becoming a problem.[93]

Equally distressing for Saddam was that there appeared little hope of bringing the war to a close. The Iranians indicated no interest in making peace while continuing to mobilize their larger population. The Arab states were still supporting Iraq financially, but now mostly in the form of

---

[92] *SH-SHTP-A-001-247, Recording of a Meeting between Saddam Hussein and Military Officers, 27 March 1984. See also, SH-AFGC-D-000-094, Iraqi Armed Forces General Command Memos Proving That Iraq Produced and Used Chemical Weapons against Iran and Along the Border During the Iran–Iraq War, June–November 1983.

[93] Presidential order to execute officers and soldiers (9 April 1985) in *SH-MISC-D-001-364, Presidential Order to Execute Officers and Soldiers, 1985. According to some reports, despite a 1982 law making desertion a capital offense, the number of deserters reached 120,000 by 1985. As a deterrent, deserters were shot in their home towns. Ofra Bengio, "Iraq," in *Middle East Contemporary Survey: Iraq, 1976–1999, Volume IX: 1984–85*, Itmar Rabinovich and Haim Shaked, eds. (Tel Aviv, 1986), 465.

loans. Mobilizing Iraq's manpower had reached the point where the regime had to import more than a million Egyptian guest workers to keep the economy functioning to free its male population for duty at the front.[94] Moreover, disaffection among Iraqis with the seemingly endless conflict and its losses was growing.

For the short term, the Iranians stood back and reexamined their options. During the spring, debates took place in Tehran as to whether or not to continue the war. The president, Hojatoleslam Rafsanjani, argued that the losses suffered so far in the conflict were too heavy for the nation to bear. But others led by the commissioner of the Revolutionary Guard, Mohsen Rezaee, pursued a hard line. Summer came, and the Iranians did not launch major attacks, but temporarily demobilized and sent home 300,000 *Pasdaran* and *Basij*. On the political front, Rafsanjani, concerned with the economic and political implications of a long war, stated that "Iran is willing to follow the diplomatic path to achieve its war aims ... A qualified tribunal might depose Saddam Hussein."[95] The radicals reiterated Khomeini's 1980 conditions and argued for a long war of attrition. According to Rafsanjani, Iranians were victorious when the Iraqis were not because Iranians "prefer not to have life, not to have bread or house, but to have their faith."[96] Elections in Iran strengthened the hardline position. In the end, perhaps swayed by the hardliners confidence or the potential implications of backing down from his self-declared divine mission, Khomeini supported the call for a military solution. There was one small offensive in mid-October, Dawn 7, that attempted to dislodge the Iraqis from their positions holding the high ground overlooking Mehran in the central sector. After five days of heavy fighting, which brought small gains, the Iranians called off the offensive.[97]

The Iraqis were considering their situation as well. Despite Saddam's desire for a more aggressive posture, the emphasis remained on the

---

[94] Dann, "The Iraqi–Iranian War," 183.   [95] O'Ballance, *The Gulf War*, 149.

[96] Hojjat ol-Eslam val-Moslemin Hashemi-Rafsanjani, "Hashemi-Rafsanjani 26 November Sermon (FBIS-SAS-82-230)," *Foreign Broadcast Information Service Daily Reports* (1982). For more on the internal debate, see also Ray Takeyh, "The Iran–Iraq War: A Reassessement," *The Middle East Journal* 64, no. 3 (2010).

[97] The Iraqi military leadership appears to have been well informed about Iranian military dispositions during summer and fall 1984. See RE: Evaluation of the Iranian Military (18 August 1984) Memorandum from GMID to the General Command of the Armed Forces in *SH-GMID-D-001-365, Various Memoranda between the Defense Ministry, GMID, the General Command of the Armed Forces, and IIS Regarding Evaluations of the Iranian Military, 1984. This series of intelligence reports indicates that Iraqi intelligence had a pretty good idea of the location of major Iranian units and the major intentions of the Iranian enemy.

defensive. An article in Iraq's leading military journal in July 1984 commented:

There is no doubt that a defense is a relatively stable, if not occasionally static combat situation in warfare. The greater the relative permanence and stability of a defense, the greater the needs are to refresh and reactivate movement in a defense, so that a monotonous defense does not lead to total stagnation of the leakage of signs of weakness in material and psychological aspects of the structure and resistance of the defense.

The problem of upgrading, if this is a good term, a defense becomes more pressing in a protracted war, especially when the opposing forces are approximately equal, or a decision favoring one of them is not possible because of foreign intervention. Therefore the constant modification and development of the defender's position provide a primary basis for a favorable tipping of the balance with time. Such modification and development also reinforces the resistance of the defense regardless of the duration of the war.[98]

In mid-October 1984, Saddam held another meeting with his senior military leaders to review the general situation. Saddam was loquacious, but there was little his commanders could grasp in terms of the dictator's ambiguous orders and directions. Much of the conversation involved pressing ahead with the development of an unspecified secret weapon, most probably a reference to a missile that could reach Tehran. This was an indication perhaps of how seriously Saddam viewed the situation at the front. The discussions also indicate that Iraqi leaders were worried about the level of training and competence of junior officers, who were now leading platoons and companies of a vastly expanded army and most of whom had had little preparation. About all Saddam could offer were platitudes about the importance of rigorous training:

Back to the subject of Iran, they stated that their soldiers receive training and support from European countries, but we do not receive such support. Therefore, we must emphasize the provision of advanced training for our soldiers. In order for a soldier to advance, he must prove his devotion towards his citizens, master advanced training, possess common sense when initiating an attack, especially tank soldiers, those are some of the basic requirements.[99]

The War of the Cities and the War of the Tankers

In 1983, the majority of the military target analysis for firing Scud missiles into Iranian cities focused on the economic nature of

---

[98] "War" in SH-MODX-D-000-853, [The Iraqi] Military Journal, July 1984.
[99] SH-SHTP-A-000-735, Saddam and Officials Discussing Military Operations and Secret Project During the Iran–Iraq War, 18 October 1984.

the targets and, not explicitly, the population (even though the weapon's accuracy would not allow for a distinction in any meaningful way). Guidance from Saddam in 1983 to his senior officers increasingly made population targeting a clear but important sub-set of economic targeting. At times, the president stepped in and provided specific guidance. A note, appended to a September 1983 targeting memorandum from the GMID, stated: "Directions of Mr. President as follows: Attack on Saturday afternoon. Launch two missiles and after one hour launch another two missiles at the same location (an hour before sunset). President's Order: We should attack Masjid-i-Sulaiman as well. The launching will be two missiles toward Dezful and two missiles toward Masjid-i-Sulaiman."[100]

By early 1984, planners in the GMID were making population centers an explicit target for missile attacks. As a memorandum from the GMID to the Army Chief of Staff on 18 February made clear, the campaign required not only economic but also ethnographic intelligence.[101]

Economic targets ("The following are ... located within the range of [our] missile systems."):

- The port and the petro-chemical complex located at Khomeini Port
- Al-Kharji Island (electrical power station and control equipment)
- Bushehr Port, which requires highly accurate measure
- Iron factory located in Ahvaz
- Gas production and isolation factor in Ahvaz
- Tabriz petrol refinery

Iranian cities ("The following are suggested for R-17 missiles."):

- Ahvaz (489,000) 90% Arab, 5% Persian, and 5% Lur (A note adds that there is also a "large number of Revolutionary Guards there.")

---

[100] Section 13 to Section Director Memorandum from GMID, RE: Missile Attacks (20 October 1983), in *SH-GMID-D-001-366, Various GMID Reports and Correspondence with the General Command of the Armed Forces and Air & Air Defense Force Regarding Suitable Iranian Targets, Economic and Military. Masjid Sulayman is city of approximately 175,000 people located in the central Khuzestan province. Historically, it was one of Iran's centers of oil production.

[101] Section 13 to BG Miyassar Memorandum from GMID, RE: Missile Attacks (20 October 1983), in *SH-GMID-D-001-366, Various GMID Reports and Correspondence with the General Command of the Armed Forces and Air & Air Defense Force Regarding Suitable Iranian Targets, Economic and Military; Section 13 to BG Miyassar Memorandum from GMID, RE: Movement Time (20 October 1983), in *SH-GMID-D-001-366, Various GMID Reports and Correspondence with the General Command of the Armed Forces and Air & Air Defense Force Regarding Suitable Iranian Targets, Economic and Military.

- Khurram Abad (515,361) 90% Lur, 5% Kurd, 5% Persian
- Nahawind (119,255) 80% Persian, 10% Kurd, 10% Turk
- Masjid Sulayman (179,000) 85% Persian, 10% Arab, 5% Lur
- Khorramshahr (562,334) 90% Shi'a Kurd, 10% Persian
- Brujard (231,834) 90% Lur, 10% Turk.

While every major Iraqi city was within easy range of Iranian aircraft, the two great centers of Iranian political and religious life, Tehran and Qom, remained at the outer edge of Saddam's reach. Iraq's surface-to-surface missile attacks, beginning in early 1981, but becoming a sustained campaign by 1983, started to chip away at Iran's geographic advantage. The Iranians immediately warned they would reply to any missile attacks with artillery bombardments of Basra and against other cities with missiles and aircraft.[102] On 11 February, Saddam showed how much the Iranian warnings deterred him by ordering a Scud-B missile launched against Dezful, which killed thirty-six and injured 140, according to Iranian reports. Iran's response was immediate: on 12 February, artillery shelled Basra and three days later F-4s struck Baghdad. Meanwhile, the Iraqis continued to fire off the Scuds at Iranian cities. By mid-February, both sides had had enough, and attacks on the cities declined. It picked up again in early June, but UN mediation finally brought a temporary halt to such attacks, which had no military purpose other than to kill civilians. In December, however, the Iraqis recommenced firing Scuds at Iranian cities.[103]

Contributing to the Iranian desire to end the War of the Cities was the fact that, by this point in the war, they had lost or could no longer operate a substantial number of their American aircraft. Replacing trained pilots was even more difficult than obtaining spare parts. According to Iraqi intelligence, of the 196 F-4s Iran had possessed at the beginning of the war, only eighty remained; of the 141 F-5Es, only forty-six remained; and of the seventy-eight F-14s, seventy-two remained.[104] The large number of F-14s still in the Iranian table of organization reflected their domination over Soviet aircraft and the Soviet-trained pilots the Iraqis possessed as well as the fact that they were not used in low-level attacks. But even here, shortages of spare parts and trained technicians meant that much of the F-14 fleet was out of commission.

---

[102] O'Ballance, *The Gulf War*, 153.

[103] *Ibid.*, 154–155. Iran would acquire and retaliate with its first Scuds from North Korea in 1985. See Cordesman, *The Lessons of Modern War, Volume II*, 495–506.

[104] The Iraqi figures appear relatively accurate. *SH-GMID-D-001-367, GMID Assessment of the Iranian Air Force, 15 November 1984.

After the war, Saddam claimed that during this period he had further diminished the usefulness of the F-14s by a skillful piece of deception that played on Khomeini's paranoia:

Thank you Abu Zaid. Let me tell you one of our war stories. It has some interesting points in terms of camouflage and "sound deception" as they put it ... The Iranian F-14s were assigned to defend [Kharg] as an alternative to anti-aircraft weapons ... So we were watching out for [them], because we knew [they] could hurt [our] airplanes in either the trip over or the trip back ... So I asked a certain party to go tell the political [leaders] in a certain Gulf nation that there were some Iranian pilots who wanted to desert with their F-14 planes and if they could please allow them to land, because arrangements have been made for them to seek asylum in Iraq.

According to Saddam, the message went straight to the Iranians as he had hoped, who then proceeded to temporarily ground their F-14s.[105]

Meanwhile, the naval war in the Gulf had accelerated as the Iraqis increased attacks on Iranian and on neutral shipping plying the waters around and to the north of Kharg (for a depiction of the shipping lanes under attack, see Figure 7.1). The arrival of 180 Exocets from their French manufacturers allowed the Iraqis to increase the scope and number of their attacks beginning in May 1983.[106] Yet, the Iraqis overestimated the effect of their attacks. For example, in March, their propaganda claimed their aircraft and missile boats had hit five tankers near the Kharg, when in fact they hit none.[107] Nevertheless, the threat was there, and there was not much that the Iranians could do to stop the attacks.

The year 1984 also saw a continued escalation of Iraqi attacks. The Iranians escalated their threats to blockade the Straits of Hormuz if the great powers refused to force Saddam to desist. In February, Super Frelon helicopters and missile boats hit a slow-moving convoy

---

[105] SH-SHTP-V-000-589, Saddam Hussein and Military Officials Discussing the Iran–Iraq War and the Al-Qadisiyyah Battle, Circa Late 1988. The discussions make it clear that the meeting occurred after the war was over. The actual date of this supposed incident is unclear. The Iranian Air Force reportedly suffered a mini-purge of officers in late 1983 and early 1984. In May 1984, a group of air force officers were executed for plotting to bomb Khomeini's residence. Cooper and Bishop, *Iran–Iraq War in the Air*, 175.

[106] According to the SIPRI Arms Transfer Database, Iraq took delivery of a total of 352 AM-39 Exocet missiles from 1978 to 1988. At the time, sales to the Middle East constituted more than 75 percent of all French arms exports. From 1980 to 1984, Iraq alone purchased $5 billion-worth of French arms. For a summary of French interests in arms sales to Iraq at this time, see Rex Tareq Y. Ismael and Rex Brynen, "Western Europe and the Middle East," in *International Relations of the Contemporary Middle East: A Study in World Politics*, Tareq Y. Ismael, ed. (Syracuse, 1986), 115–120.

[107] Navias and Hooton, *Tanker Wars*, 56–57.

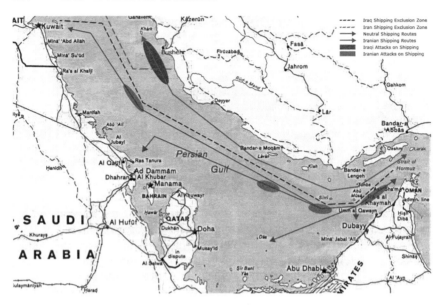

Figure 7.1 Persian Gulf, Tanker War

proceeding to Bandar-e Khomeini; at the end of the month, the Iraqis hit another three ships close to the same port. During the year, they hit no fewer than fifty-eight tankers and freighters with various missiles – most of them Exocets. These attacks now ranged deep into the Gulf, in some cases as far as 50 nautical miles south of Kharg. The extended range reflected the additional capabilities the Super Etendards offered. More-over, Iraqi attacks in the summer managed to significantly damage the Kharg terminal for the first time.[108]

Still, the Iraqis could not pressure the Iranians sufficiently to force Khomeini to the peace table. Iraq did not have the electronic monitoring capabilities or enough missiles to impose a true blockade on Iranian exports. Putting the Iranian war effort where it could no longer gain even limited access to the weapons on which its ground and air forces depended alone would have been sufficient at this point in the war. However, while the Iraqis might have hoped to succeed, their efforts caused barely a ripple in the world's oil markets, where a glut had already driven prices down. The number of ships damaged in 1984 was minuscule compared to the number of ships the Iraqis claimed to have

---

[108] *Ibid.*, 74–85. It appears the Iraqi secret police were suspicious of Iraqi pilots who failed to fire their Exocets. Thus, the pilots had a tendency to fire at any target appearing on their radar screens.

attacked. In the words of Lloyd's underwriters, they "had lost count of the number of claimed attacks."[109] While there was some nervousness among those transshipping oil, the only result of Iraqi efforts was that Iran had to offer discounts of between \$2 and \$4 per barrel to attract tankers to Kharg's terminals.[110]

The Iranians did attempt to reply to Iraq's blockade effort, but with the closure of the Shatt al-Arab in the early days of the war, the Iraqis had turned to shipping their crude through the limited pipelines that ran through Turkey and by tanker truck through Jordan to Aqaba.[111] Thus, there was no avenue for the Iranians to attack Iraqi oil shipments. Nevertheless, Tehran decided to strike Iraq's financiers and indirectly impact Iraq's war-making ability. Iranian aircraft would attack tankers loading Saudi oil in the hopes of changing Riyadh's strategic calculus (where the Saudis went, Tehran no doubt hoped, the small Gulf States would follow) and drive up the price of oil, which, despite the war, had fallen by 40 percent between 1981 and 1985.[112] In April and May 1984, Iranian aircraft attacked several tankers in Saudi waters. But the entire effort ended when two Saudi F-15 aircraft, directed by a US AWACS, shot down two Iranian F-4s on 5 June. The Saudis established the so-called "Fahd Line," a line beyond their territorial waters, within which they declared they would shoot down any aircraft not on a peaceful mission.[113] Despite the failure, the Iranians did try to attack Iraq's supporters in the West indirectly, but with no greater success. In July, they used a Libyan Ro-Ro ship to drop off 190 mines on both sides of the Suez Canal, which damaged a number of ships, including ones flying the flags of China, Poland, East Germany, North Korea, and the Soviet Union – hardly the intended victims.[114]

---

[109] "Gulf War: Iraq's Confidence Trick," *Economist*, 294, no. 7378 (1985).

[110] Dann, "The Iraqi–Iranian War," 185.

[111] Syria closed the Iraqi oil pipeline that ran through its territory to the Mediterranean Sea (300,000 barrels per day capacity) on 10 April 1982 after it made a lucrative deal with Iran for its oil needs. Iraq's other pipeline to the north continued to operate but at less than capacity due in part to sabotage.

[112] Joseph A. Kechichian, "The Gulf Cooperation Council and the Gulf War," in *The Persian Gulf War: Lessons for Strategy, Law, and Diplomacy*, Christopher C. Joyner, ed. (New York, NY, 1990), 91–110.

[113] Dann, "The Iraqi–Iranian War," 186.

[114] Navias and Hooton, *Tanker Wars*, 90–91. Palestinian Islamic Jihad claimed responsibility for the incident, and while Egyptian intelligence identified the culprit as the Libyan cargo vessel, it is generally accepted to have been a proxy attack conducted on behalf of Iran. See Moshe Gershovich, "The Red Sea Mining Affair," in *Middle East Contemporary Survey, Iraq, 1976–1999, Volume VIII: 1983–84*, Haim Shaked and Daniel Dishon, eds. (Tel Aviv, 1984), 188–192.

Conclusion

The military events of 1983 and 1984 underlined that neither side was in a position to overthrow the other. The Iraqis had abandoned the simplistic hopes and assumptions with which they had wandered into Iran in 1980. Saddam would have accepted almost any settlement that left him in power at this point. But the Iranians under Khomeini remained adamant that war would continue; there would be no peace until either Iranian actions or an internal revolt in Iraq had overthrown Saddam's regime.

Militarily, Iran's population advantage forced Iraq to mobilize virtually every male of military age and placed enormous pressure on Iraq's ground forces. That pressure manifested itself on the battlefield in the human-wave attacks that broke again and again on Iraqi positions throughout 1983 and 1984. That pressure also showed up in the three initiatives Saddam took during this period: first, using gas warfare on the battlefield to increase Iranian casualties substantially; second, waging the War of the Cities with missile attacks on Iran's population centers; and third, attempting to cut off Iranian oil exports, particularly from Kharg. None achieved its desired goals.

8   1985–1986: Dog days of a long war

One of the important matters in battle is to stretch your imagination as far as you [can]; perhaps imagination allows us to discover things that we weren't able to reach practically as we were overburdened with details. That is why our meeting today falls within this context. This political group ... is to survey what is on the enemy's mind; let us visit carefully the enemy's mind, and let everyone speak his own mind without limitation and with liberty on the subject matter that he wishes to speak about ... [Let us] recall events that took place and critique them, so we can decide how we [will] deal with the enemy in the next few months.[1]
          – Saddam Hussein

By early 1985, the opposing sides were beginning to resemble punch-drunk fighters. They had now fought for more than four years. Thus far in the war, their casualties had numbered in the hundreds of thousands. They had exhausted their holdings of foreign currency, while a fall in oil prices had exacerbated the economic difficulties both faced. For the Iraqis, the need to import tens of thousands of workers to replace those whom the regime's massive mobilization had dragooned into the army compounded the difficulties (see Table 8.1).[2] The attitudes of the two regimes toward the war, however, remained fundamentally different. For his part, Saddam could not understand Iran's unwillingness to consider peace on anything other than its own terms. As he had commented to a *Time* reporter in 1982:

The chances for peace appear slim because Khomeini is a politician, not a man of principle. As time goes by he reveals his superficiality. The more he talks, the more he makes himself a laughingstock. I wish the whole world would read his

---

[1] SH-SHTP-D-000-607, Transcripts of Meetings between Saddam, Vice President of the RCC Izzat Ibrahim Al-Tikriti, Minister of Defense Adnan Khairallah, and Army Chief of Staff Abd Al-Jawad Zinun During the Iraq–Iran War, 25 February 1985–31 July 1986.

[2] Iran did not have this problem, because of its larger population and a substantial number of unemployed. According to one source, while upwards of three million Iranian males (of a population of 8.5 million males aged 15–35) served during the eight years of war, this was in a total population of fifty million. Rarideh Farhi, "The Antinomies of Iran's War Generation," in *Iran, Iraq, and the Legacies of War*, Lawrence G. Potter and Gary G. Sick, eds. (New York, NY, 2004), 105.

Table 8.1 *Estimate of the cost of the Iran–Iraq War: 1980–1988*

	Iran	Iraq
Human Costs (Number of lives in thousands)	1,050–1,930	550–1,040
Casualties (thousands)	600–1,200	400–700
Wounded (thousands)	450–730	150–340
Killed (thousands)	2,000	400
Refugees (thousands)	45	400
Prisoners of War (thousands)	45	70
Economic Costs (Marginal costs in $B)		
Arms Purchases	7	25
Oil Revenue	10	55
Pipelines	NR	3
Transportation	1	9
War-Risk Insurance	1	NR
Petroleum-Product Imports	5	NR
Compensation to Families	10	4
Military Salaries	10	10
Repairs to War-damaged Facilities	5	3
Non-oil GDP	20	50
Total Economic Costs in $B	$69	$159

Source: Anthony H. Cordesman and Abraham R. Wagner. *The Lessons of Modern War, Volume II: The Iran–Iraq War.* Boulder, CO: Westview Press, 1990, 3.

statements to form an impression of this shallow devil. The actions he has carried out do not indicate that he is a rational person.[3]

An Iranian account of the war highlights the assumptions under which Khomeini was conducting the war: "The slogan 'war-war until victory' was a ray of light based on the Koran's slogan 'war-war until the eradication of the sedition.' In fact, the Imam's expressed opinions killed any prospects for reconciliation."[4] Iraq's extensive use of chemical weapons beginning in 1984 had only served to harden the Iranian's resolve for revenge. In their view, Iraqi behavior had steadily worsened during the war; consequently, they had no desire to seek any sort of compromise. Moreover, the war was settling into a particular Shi'a

---

[3] Dean Brelis and Murray J. Gart, "An Interview with Saddam Hussein," *Time Magazine*, 19 July 1982.

[4] *SH-MISC-D-001-349, Pasdaran Report: From Khorramshahr to Fao (July 1982–August 1986): A Military and Political Analysis, circa 1988.

narrative with roots in the bloody founding of the sect. The call for "victory of the blood over the sword" validated losses as it encouraged increasingly reckless tactics. It would also provide the so-called "victory narrative" that would echo for decades.[5]

Meanwhile, the Iraqi Army continued to expand. Here, Saddam was profligate with Iraq's oil revenues as well as the billions of dollars Iraq was borrowing from its Gulf neighbors. While refusing to supply military forces to help the Iraqis – to Saddam's disgust – the Gulf States, Saudi Arabia, and Jordan, were at least willing to provide the financial resources necessary to meet Iraq's burgeoning expenses.[6] Whatever their doubts about Saddam's trustworthiness, they certainly had no desire to see Iran's Shi'a regime triumph over Iraq. However, underscoring the general lack of unity in the Arab world, the Syrians and Libyans persisted in selling arms and missiles to the Iranians, with the latter immediately firing off their purchases at the Iraqis. By the beginning of 1986, the Iraqi Army had expanded to 700,000 soldiers by drafting much of the nation's military-age male population. Thus, it had placed an increasingly shaky economy in the hands of foreign workers, a bill largely paid by foreign loans. To equip its military forces, the Iraqis continued to scour foreign arms markets. The army now possessed a vast array of equipment: approximately 4,000 tanks and 3,800 assorted other armored fighting vehicles, such as the most modern infantry fighting vehicles (BMPs) and T-72s, 3,500 artillery pieces, and 600 aircraft.[7]

In addition, Saddam expanded the Republican Guard. It had grown from one brigade in 1980 to six brigades by 1985 and received not only the best equipment, but also the pick of those officers who had proven themselves on the battlefield.[8] The dictator also continued to push for extensive training programs, which increased the Guard's military effectiveness.[9] By 1985, that organization formed the heart of Iraq's reserves and the objective standard of performance for the rest of the force. The Iraqis used it primarily as a counterattack force against significant Iranian

---

[5] Steven Ward defines this narrative as "how Iran's armed forces, allied militant groups, and the Iranian people draw on religious feeling and the concept of martyrdom to confront stronger and more technologically sophisticated opponents." Steven Ward, "Iran's Challenging Victory Narrative," *Historically Speaking* 10, no. 3 (2009), 41.

[6] Which, in retrospect, Saddam appears to have had little intention of repaying.

[7] Pollack, *Arabs at War*, 206. Saddam always placed the internal security of the regime as his first priority.

[8] *Ibid.*, 229; Ibrahim al-Marashi and Sammy Salama, *Iraq's Armed Forces: An Analytic History* (New York, NY, 2008), 156–157.

[9] Woods, *et al.*, *Saddam's War*, 77–78.

penetrations. The bulk of this force remained stationed near Baghdad, whence it could move quickly to reinforce threatened sectors in the south or center, but where it was also ideally situated to protect the regime from internal threats. Placing the Guard near Baghdad also reflected Saddam's belief that the regime would survive losing Basra, but could not lose the capital and survive.[10]

In 1985, the pace of operations picked up after the lull in the aftermath of the failed Iranian Operation Khyber in February and early March 1984. The clerics in Tehran refused to accept the results of that defeat and demanded another series of offensives to break Iraq's will. As Iran's Prime Minister Mir-Hossein Mousavi proclaimed in early January: "Iran did not need to change its approach because the 'power of faith' can outmaneuver a complicated war machine."[11] In January 1985, Iraqi intelligence noted the "large number of enemy units" massing across from the III Corps to the east of Majnun Island – indicators that an offensive was in the works. Iranian preparations included supply trains, the accumulation of assault boats, and increased engineering work to control the flow and depth of water barriers separating the combatants.[12] Nevertheless, on 28 January the Iraqis struck first, launching an offensive to regain Majnun Island and its oil wells. The attack caught the Iranians by surprise and made initial gains. But by its end, the Iraqis had only recaptured the island's western end. Despite repeated attempts to drive the Iranians back, the offensive stalled in the face of obdurate enemy resistance.[13]

A high water mark

Slightly more than a month later, on the evening of 11 March, the Iranians struck with their first major offensive since "Khyber 1" in 1984. Here, the Iranian military drew the wrong conclusions from the

---

[10] Among other documents, see Saddam's comments about the relative importance of Basra and Baghdad in a meeting with his senior commanders: SH-SHTP-A-000-634, Saddam and Military Corps Commanders Discuss the Great Day and Great Harvest Battles, Analyze Iranian Intentions, and Discuss Iranian Efforts to Capture Basra, 28 March 1987.

[11] Quoted in Ray Takeyh, "The Iran–Iraq War: A Reassessment," *The Middle East Journal* 64, no. 3 (2010), 369.

[12] RE: Bimonthly Analysis of Enemy Activities (3 March 1985) Memorandum from III Corps Command/Intelligence to Divisional Commands in SH-RPGD-D-000-706, Reports on Iranian Military Activities, November 1984–March 1985.

[13] O'Ballance, *The Gulf War*, 160.

initial success of the first Operation Khyber. In nearly every respect, the Iranian offensive reflected previous tactical concepts. Human-wave attacks followed one after another, all involving lightly armed infantry, none of whom were prepared to handle massive doses of Iraqi firepower. The offensive, largely conducted by the *Pasdaran* rested on the optimistic assumption that human-wave attacks could achieve a decisive success. The Iranians deployed 45,000–65,000 *Pasdaran* and *Basij* troops to conduct the offensive, this one code-named *Badr*.[14] Astonishingly, they attacked across the same al-Hawizeh marshes that had seen their defeat a year earlier. However, *Pasdaran* planning and capabilities had improved somewhat.

The Iranian plan was for infantry to cross the marshes and, after achieving a lodgment on dry land to the west of the swamps, to reach and cross the River Tigris and then to cut the Basra–Baghdad highway. After that move, a second force of two divisions would strike across Majnun and after reaching solid ground, swing south behind the Iraqis. The two drives were then to meet and trap a substantial Iraqi force.[15] All in all, Operation *Badr* was ambitious, but conceived and executed by amateurs incapable of handling its complexities, especially after the normal frictions of war intervened. Besides being better equipped with small arms than in the past, the *Pasdaran* had begun to receive protective gear against Iraqi chemical weapons.[16] Unfortunately for *Badr*'s prospects, the Iraqis had substantial forces in the area and had fortified the surrounding territory, including berms, field fortifications, bunkers, minefields, and engineering work that would allow them to flood much of the terrain.[17] After the battle, Saddam compared the military forces of the two sides: "Our strength is in the awareness of our soldiers and their strength is the lack of awareness by their soldiers."[18] He may have overstated the abilities of

---

[14] Ward, *Immortal*, 265.

[15] O'Ballance, *The Gulf War*, 160.

[16] The protective gear was less successful than its makers – North Korea and East Germany – had promised. They were designed for paint fumes, not chemical warfare. In one case, the filters only lasted for 15 minutes. Besides the question of quality, the fact that most of the *Pasdaran* refused to shave their beards reduced the tightness of the fit between mask and face. The result was an increased number of gas casualties. Jean Pascal Zanders, *Iranian Use of Chemical Weapons: A Critical Analysis of Past Allegations*, Center for Nonproliferation Studies (2001), cns.miis.edu/archive/cns/programs/dc/briefs/030701.htm.

[17] Ward, *Immortal*, 266.

[18] *SH-AFGC-D-001-368, Transcript of a Meeting of the Armed Forces General Command, Saddam Hussein in Attendance, 13–14 February 1985.

his soldiers, but his assessment of Iranian training and tactics was accurate.

Given their experience of the previous year, the Iraqis did not expect the enemy to come through the same area. In fact, for a short period, 3,000 *Pasdaran* reached and cut the Basra–Baghdad highway, but after that the operation fell apart.[19] Initially, some Iraqi units panicked, abandoning their positions after only slight resistance. The commission Saddam established to examine the initial Iranian success submitted its interim report on 21 March. Its members rendered a dismal report card. They ascribed the Iraqi difficulties to the following causes:

- The enemy had specific information about the defensive plan of our forces ...
- A large number of leaders and commanders [of Iraqi frontline units] were either killed or injured ...
- Not enough forces [were] charged with holding the defensive positions ...
- [Defensive position lacked] depth and [there was] the failure to provide suitable reserve forces ...
- Some commanders took leave despite the confirmed information about the enemy plan to attack ...
- Delay in evacuating martyrs and wounded soldiers negatively affected morale ...
- Some of the enlisted from [the 93rd infantry regiment] fled to the enemy side four days before the attack ...
- Putting the artillery support battalions in forward positions made it easy for the enemy to attack early and deprived [our] forces [of] fire support ...
- Most command posts were too close to the front of the battlefield including the command post of east Tigris operations and the other main command posts ...
- A limited breakdown in some units and battalions after the enemy's attack from the rear [occurred] ...
- Based on the above, we have concluded there was a general state of panic and chaos that led to an inability to conduct the defensive battle [which] made it easy for the enemy to succeed.[20]

A subsequent report was equally forthright. None of this could have made happy reading for Saddam, who again confronted failure in the army and among its officers. According to the report, in addition to Iraqi failures, there were a number of things the Iranians had done well in preparing for and conducting the fight:

---

[19] Ward, *Immortal*, 266.

[20] Reports by the Committeee Investigating the Causes of Military Failure (21–22 April 1985) in *SH-GMID-D-001-369, Correspondence between the GMID, the Ministry of Defense, and the Ministry of Interior Regarding Iranian Military Movements and the Distribution of Iranian Troops, 1985.

- The manner in which the enemy penetrated the defensive position ...
- First: [They destroyed] visible firing positions on the western dam of Hur with rockets and machine gun fire mounted on boats before they attacked.
- Second: [The enemy attacked] fast with boats into the front of the defensive position ...
- Third: [they moved] north and south of the western dam to widen the area of penetration by destroying fire position ...
- Fourth: [They attacked] the command posts of units and artillery positions ... toward the Tigris River.[21]

Despite all of that, the Iraqis had reacted quickly, and because most of their army now consisted of either armored or mechanized units, they moved counterattacking units to threatened points quickly. Moreover, they had substantially reformed their organizational approach, relying more heavily on brigades than on divisions. The former represented the Iraqi maneuver force, while the latter controlled an unspecified number of brigades, which allowed for greater flexibility in command and control. Thus, one Republican Guard division controlled no fewer than seven brigades at one point. Once again, Iraqi firepower dominated to the detriment of the attackers.

Within several days, the Iraqis were attacking Iranian units that had reached and crossed the Tigris with massed artillery and armor from three sides. Chemical agents exacerbated the carnage and suffering of Iranian troops. The bridgehead across the Tigris became a trap, worsened by the Iranian's difficulties in reinforcing spearhead units. Iraqi helicopter gunships placed a heavy toll on *Pasdaran* supply boats attempting to funnel reinforcements across the marshes, while Iraqi aircraft flew their attack missions into the battle areas largely unhindered by the Iranian Air Force.[22] Saddam suggested to his staff that "the enemy fights to the death because [after crossing at night] it becomes daylight and there is nothing behind the enemy but water. Where would he go? Therefore the fight will be merciless ... The enemy will endure great losses with Allah's help."[23]

By 18 March, Iraqi forces had driven the Iranians back to their start lines on the eastern shores of the al-Hawizeh Marshes.[24] The Republican Guard Division's outstanding performance helped convince Saddam that expanding that force into a number of additional divisions was in his – and Iraq's – best interest. Nevertheless, despite the drubbing their

---

[21] *Ibid.*   [22] Ward, *Immortal*, 266.
[23] *SH-AFGC-D-001-368, Transcript of a Meeting of the Armed Forces General Command, Saddam Hussein in Attendance, 13–14 February 1985.
[24] O'Ballance, *The Gulf War*, 162–164.

forces had received in the southern portion of the marshes, the Iranians still decided to launch their two-division assault from Majnun. It was too late. Again the attackers suffered a major rebuff, barely advancing beyond their start positions.

At the battle's conclusion, both sides made extravagant claims. One source placed Iraqi casualties at 2,500–5,000 soldiers, with losses on the Iranian side ranging between 8,000 and 12,000.[25] The defeat of Operation *Badr* was a significant blow to Iran's hopes. Such heavy losses appear to have caused some of Iran's leaders to lose confidence. Saddam sensed as much. While the battle raged, Lieutenant General Ala Kazim al-Janabi, army chief of staff, informed the dictator that the Iranians had complained to the United Nations that Iraq was violating the Secretary General's 1984 "truce" to avoid attacks on urban areas. Saddam, who until this point had been eager for a ceasefire, declared: "Beginning now, we will not approve of any agreement." Al-Janabi then stated what the officers in the room likely hoped to be true: "Sir, this proves that our operations [have begun] to affect them and the solution is in our favor." Building on this optimism, Saddam added, "We will not stop the chemical strikes; we will not stop the shelling of the cities."[26]

Nevertheless, political disquiet in Tehran was not enough to change Khomeini's strategic goals. The Grand Ayatollah and his closest advisors remained steadfast in their decision to continue the conflict.[27] Much like Sir Douglas Haig in assessing his German opponents in 1916 and 1917, they believed the Iraqis were on the brink of collapse and the next offensive would break their enemies. It is difficult to reconstruct Saddam's mood, although Iraqi propaganda trumpeted the victory. In fact, the Iraqis went so far as to let Western media reporters tour the battlefield. Those reporters, however, could confirm what the Iraqis had denied – that Iranian troops had crossed the Tigris and reached the

---

[25] Anthony H. Cordesman and Abraham R. Wagner, *The Lessons of Modern War, Volume II: The Iran–Iraq War* (Boulder, CO, 1990), 203.

[26] *SH-AFGC-D-001-368, Transcript of a Meeting of the Armed Forces General Command, Saddam Hussein in Attendance, 13–14 February 1985. The transcript was edited by a committee of active and retired Iraqi generals at a later date. All references to chemical weapons, including the one above, were lined through in what appears to be preparation to excise references to weapons of mass destruction from official Iraqi records.

[27] Steven Ward points out that while the Iranians were confronting the difficult situation on the battlefield against Saddam's Iraqis, they were also spending significant resources dabbling in the politics of Lebanon and other areas of the Middle East to further Khomeini's aim of world revolution for the Shi'a. Ward, *Immortal*, 267.

Basra–Baghdad highway.[28] All the same, the detritus of the battlefield made clear that the Iraqis had won a substantial victory.

In a conversation with senior officers in April, Saddam commented on the current situation and what the Iranians were up to:

The enemy has been maneuvering for over a year and one month since February of 1984 until March of this year. He stayed there in Majnun preparing to repeat his action ... Then he began to maneuver between the III and IV Corps. He then came near the II Corps and attempted that small operation in Saif Saad. He did not gain the results he was hoping to achieve and planned for. Even though he had taken all of Saif Saad, it was a political move rather than an operational move when considered in the light of a long, drawn out war. I mean psychologically speaking, taking a few kilometers does not have a significant effect on the results of a war ...

... [The enemy's] latest move is to the place that we are discussing now is indicative of a lack of strategy on the part of the enemy. He has not decided what tips the balance on the field and allows him to attack from one place or the other. Our reactions, as they were detailed by our intelligence ... were effective in preventing him from reaching his desired goals! We should like to know how effective were our reactions and what specific variables work[ed best]?[29]

The discussion turned to the problem of defending Basra against a direct attack. Here Iraqi intelligence warned that the Iranians were preparing to launch an offensive against that city. One of the officers from the III Corps interjected to assure the dictator that "we have set up our defensive formations over the entire III Corps which we think that they are well prepared for the task [of defending the city against an Iranian attack]."[30]

That same month Saddam spoke before the Second Popular Islamic Conference.[31] As usual, he portrayed Iraq as the aggrieved party in the war that he had started. For those who remembered how the war had begun, Saddam's comments must have sounded strange:

The Security Council did not tell the Iraqis when they were in Iranian territories that they must withdraw to their borders. The Security Council said it when

---

[28] O'Ballance, *The Gulf War*, 164.
[29] *SH-SHTP-A-001-370, Recording of a Meeting between Saddam Hussein and High Ranking Officers Regarding the Iran–Iraq War, circa March 1985.
[30] *Ibid.*
[31] The conference brought together 300 Islamic religious leaders in a transparent Ba'ath propaganda ploy to "show that the Iraqi regime revered Islam, and that the Muslim world was behind Iraq in its struggle against the heretical leaders of Iran." Hiro, *The Longest War*, 149.

Khomeini attacked us on the 4th of September 1980, and whatever came after that, we were patient time and again ...

[A]nd anyway what does Iraq want? What does Khomeini want? You are exposed to what Iraq wants. Iraq does not want anything. Iraq wants to live freely on its territories and within its international boundaries ... But Khomeini insists on, he insists on war. Who can prove that any Iraqi official from these documents, as all uttered words in the media, or stated in the newspapers ... who can prove that any Iraqi official from the beginning of the war till this day has uttered a word that could be understood or clearly imply any ambition inside Iran?[32]

While Saddam was lecturing his officers and addressing the conference, the Iranians appeared to be preparing a major offensive against Basra. At least, that was what the indications of Iranian deployments suggested to Iraqi analysts, who remained wary, given the initial surprise and success of the *Badr* offensive in March. In late April they reported "[a] very large force [had] gathered [in] the Basra area ... They [the Iranians] consider it the final attack."[33] In fact, the Iranians launched no major offensives for the remainder of 1985. In early April, the Iraqis quickly rebuilt their defenses and launched interdiction attacks into the Iranian rear areas that appear to have disrupted or dissuaded an attempt to repeat the March offensive. Some part of Iraq's success in dissuading further large-scale Iranian attacks was likely the result of American-supplied intelligence pinpointing Iranian logistics buildup.[34] In this case, the intelligence appears to have been forwarded, indirectly, through King Hussein of Jordan.[35] And of course, the Iraqis could monitor Iranian operations,

---

[32] *SH-SHTP-A-001-371, Recording of a Speech by Saddam Hussein on the Iran–Iraq War at the Second Islamic Conference, April 1985.

[33] RE: expected Iranian attack in Basra region (26 April 1985) Telegram from General Secretariat Directorate to GMID in *SH-GMID-D-001-369, Correspondence between the GMID, the Ministry of Defense, and the Ministry of Interior Regarding Iranian Military Movements and the Distribution of Iranian Troops, 1985.

[34] US policy toward Iraq at this time was complex and at times in conflict with itself, other polices, and, in the case of Iraq's use of chemical weapons, some of its own principles. Putting aside the specific details and personalities, two factors tended to shape the relationship. First was the logic of Cold War competition with the USSR. Soviet operations in Afghanistan and efforts to recover its position in the region were a constant theme in US policy deliberations. The second factor was articulated by the former secretary of state at the time: "If Iraq collapsed, that could not only intimidate but inundate our friends in the Gulf and be a strategic disaster for the United States." George P. Schultz, *Turmoil and Triumph: My Years as Secretary of State* (New York, NY, 1993), 235.

[35] In early April 1984, the Regan Administration approved approaching "friendly states (e.g., France and Jordan)" that were "capable of providing overt and covert military support to Iraq" as a part of the policy to "avert an Iraqi collapse." *NSDD 139: Measures to Improve US Posture and Readiness to Developments in the Iran–Iraq War (Declassified)*, 1984. Evidence of apparent Jordanian participation in this policy was found in the records of King Hussein of Jordan. Ashton, *King Hussein of Jordan*, 220–221. See also

especially higher-level logistics and movements, through their signals intelligence, as previously noted. The relative effect or relationship between these two sources is, as far as can be determined through Iraqi sources, unknown. Instead, the Iranians kept the pressure on with raids, ambushes, artillery bombardments, and limited attacks on Iraqi positions in the central and the southern sectors.[36]

Regardless of the specific cause, the Iranians adopted a more economical approach aimed at wearing the Iraqis down. The Iranian Army's chief of staff suggested as much:

Our blitzes are planned so as to make it hard for the enemy to redeploy its forces to the areas attacked. In our various operations, while we aim to avoid sustaining heavy casualties, we seek to surprise the enemy and to wear him out psychologically [as well as physically] ... We wish to render it almost impossible for enemy commanders to plan properly; our operations enable our men to fight an enemy [equipped] with heavier hardware.[37]

This was, of course, what the Iraqis feared, because a sustained war of attrition with lower Iranian casualty rates and higher Iraqi casualty rates was the kind of war Saddam could not afford to fight.[38] Discussing that summer's fighting, Saddam spoke philosophically about the distinction between Iranian and Iraqi tactics. Noting that the Iranians learned to be creative in marsh fighting because they had to, he suggested that the Iraqis could benefit from adopting some of the enemy's techniques. However, he also warned that "we cannot rely on this ... since the enemy is going to remain superior in this regard."[39]

Thus, throughout the remainder of the year, there was a steady drain on Iraqi forces. Even with the reduction in fighting, the Iraqis were losing nearly one hundred men per day – "wastage" in World War I terms. Moreover, in the course of a single day's attack on the northern front in

---

Bryan R. Gibson, *Covert Relationship: American Foreign Policy, Intelligence, and the Iran–Iraq War, 1980–1988* (Santa Barbara, CA, 2010), 136–137, 148–149.

[36] Ward, *Immortal*, 265–266; Uriel Dann, "The Iraqi–Iranian War," in *Middle East Contemporary Survey, Volume VIII: 1983–84*, Haim Shaked and Daniel Dishon, eds. (Boulder, CO, 1985), 170.

[37] Cordesman, *The Iran–Iraq War and Western Security*, 74.

[38] Every year of the war, more than 400,000 Iranian males turned eighteen years old, compared to only 150,000 Iraqi males. Iran's high birthrate added twelve million people (almost half the size of Iraq's entire population) between 1978 and 1988. James A. Bill, "Morale vs. Technology: The Power of Iran in the Persian Gulf War," in *The Iran–Iraq War: The Politics of Aggression*, Farhang Rajaee, ed. (Gainesville, FL, 1993), 203.

[39] *SH-SHTP-A-001-372, Recording of a Meeting between Saddam Hussein and the Armed Forces General Command, 7 June 1985.

July, the Iranians inflicted 2,000 casualties on the defending Iraqis.[40] In the month of July, Iraqi intelligence focused on more extreme measures the Iranians might take. In early April, a report that the North Koreans were training the Iranians on the finer points of flying aircraft loaded with explosives into Baghdad buildings put the Iraqi air defenses on their highest warning state.[41] An account of the Iranian efforts lays out the principles under which their military forces operated for the remainder of 1985:

Significant Details of Limited Operations:

1. Operations should not require more than 30–40 battalions.
2. Casualties should be minimized in order to preclude an adverse effect on future operations.
3. They should be short in duration and executed with speed.
4. They should have both economic and military value.
5. They would have to contribute to and be in the path of our war strategy.
6. They have to guarantee victory.
7. The area [chosen for these operations] should support dispersal operations.[42]

An Iranian raid that resulted in a three-hour battle near the town of Sumar suggests the kind of fighting that marked the last half of 1985. At its end, the Iranians claimed they "had captured 19 positions and three ammunition depots, and destroyed four tanks."[43]

Even though Iranian attacks were smaller in the latter half of 1985, the Iraqis continued to prepare to operate in a battlefield environment where chemical weapons might be used. A training report for a live chemical agent exercise the army executed in August 1985 indicated:

First, it was noted that most soldiers wore their gas masks and their commitment to orders was high ... Second, the soldiers had the impression that any chemical attack will have a great impact and may result in the annihilation of the whole intended area. But taking precautionary measures which resulted in no injury made them realize the importance of gas masks ... Third ... the perceptions that chemical weapons are not decisive widened.[44]

---

[40] Cordesman, *The Iran–Iraq War and Western Security, 1984–1987*, 80.
[41] *SH-AFGC-D-001-368, Transcript of a Meeting of the Armed Forces General Command, Saddam Hussein in Attendance, 13–14 February 1985. During the meeting, Saddam decided to issue a no-fire order to all of Iraq's air defense forces, lest Iraqi forces mistake the UN aircraft for an Iranian Kamakazi.
[42] *SH-MISC-D-001-349, Pasdaran Report: From Khorramshahr to Fao (July 1982–August 1986): A Military and Political Analysis, Circa 1988.
[43] O'Ballance, *The Gulf War*, 167.
[44] Memorandum from the Office of Political Orientation Ministry of Defense to the Army Chief of Staff (No. 4451) (2 July 1985) in SH-IZAR-D-001-246, Correspondence from the Iraqi Army Chief Regarding an Experimental Chemical Weapons Attack on 27 June 1985, July–August 1985.

The other wars

Throughout 1985, the Iranians continued to try to undermine Iraq by subversion. Nevertheless, whatever political pressure they placed on Iraq through terrorism and subversion or attempts to assassinate Ba'athist leaders, Saddam had already made clear to Iraqis the penalty for disloyalty.[45] In March, the Iraqi authorities hanged 148 males from the village of Dujail for the assassination attempt on his life in summer 1982. The warning was clear: even if you were not involved in a plot to kill Saddam, if it occurred near your village, you were going to pay. The penalty would be several years under the tutelage of Saddam's none too merciful secret police, followed in most cases by execution.[46]

Although Saddam's attention remained on Iran, there was always time for the Kurds. The regime was successfully forestalling dissention by Shi'as and communists, but "[b]y contrast, the Kurdish opposition, assisted by Iran, Syria, and Libya, did constitute a real menace."[47] A report from the as-Sulaymaniyah Governate at the end of 1985 on its efforts to bring the Kurds to heel via a campaign Saddam had ordered, noted the following about operations in October:

Our office had a distinct and effective role in this campaign, in addition to the role played by our comrade brothers ... The presence of our militant brother, the respectable Mr. Ali Hassan al-Majid, President of the General Security Office, played a distinct and effective role. His recommendations and instructions were a practical guide which made us avoid errors and mistakes and gave us the required flexibility to deal with the events.[48]

The "distinct and effective role" of one of Saddam's most infamous confidants would soon earn him his sobriquet "Chemical Ali." During 1985 (most probably the end of the year), Saddam discussed the

---

[45] Efforts from within the military continued to try to sabotage Iraq's war effort. In late April 1985, Saddam signed the death sentence for a sergeant who had placed a piece of metal in a Sukhoi fighter-bomber's intake and admitted to being a member of the al-Da'wa Party. The incident happened in November 1984. SH-PDWN-D-000-240, Letter Authorizing the Execution of an Air Force Warrant Officer for Sabotaging a Plane Engine, May–April 1986.

[46] *SH-RVCC-D-001-373, an Execution Order Issued by the RCC Related to the Al-Dujayl Case, 23 March 1985. The Iraqi executioners made careful preparations to ensure that nothing would go wrong. For further information on the incident, see the Saddam Hussein trial documents: "English Translation of the Al-Dujail Judgement (Parts 1–6)," School of Law, Case Western Reserve University, 2006, www.law.case.edu/saddamtrial/dujail/opinion.asp (accessed 20 August 2009).

[47] Ofra Bengio, "Iraq," in *Middle East Contemporary Survey, Volume IX: 1984–85*, Itamar Rabinovich and Haim Shaked, ed. (Boulder, CO, 1987), 470–473.

[48] *SH-MISC-D-001-374, Report on the Al-Sulaymaniyah Security Governate from 1985–1988 Including Al-Anfal.

possibility of using chemical weapons against carefully chosen leadership targets in Kurdish areas where Iraq's conventional power could not reach:

SADDAM: Today, we are meeting to discuss a matter that could be
           irrelevant or it could be characterized as important. This
           meeting is about those who [are carrying] out sabotage in
           northern Iraq. We need [to utilize our technological
           advantage since] our army is preoccupied with the major
           battles against the Iranian foe ... It has been five years since
           the war started ... [U]nlike peaceful times, we need to hit
           hard. I mean you can attribute [a rebellion] during peaceful
           times to social reasons. However, during time of war,
           even the international arena views the rebellion as an
           attempt to weaken Iraq and to exploit the war to benefit
           forces whether inside or outside Iraq ...
           We mobilize in a way that we are certain that our attacks,
           including the use of the special arsenal that will be used
           against a specific location that harbors the leadership. We
           need to use the air force that is equipped with the special
           arsenal to attack leadership and command centers. Then
           we execute special forces' air drops from planes to destroy
           those who have managed to survive ...
UNIDENTIFIED   I suggest that we utilize ammunition and gas attacks. That is
SPEAKER: why we need approximately eight hours so that we can enter
               the area, so that we are not affected by the gas effects. This
               is important, gas effects last a long time.[49]

Saddam then turned to what to do about the headquarters of Kurdish leaders.

SADDAM: All their [head]quarters will be forced to scatter and when [head]
           quarters scatter, it is not same as you are located in a central
           command, when you are comfortable, and make your decisions
           accordingly. I mean we will carry out a series of steps that will force
           them to scatter their forces. This way they will not be able to scatter
           their forces against you [his commanders] or give them the chance
           to deploy forces that will surprise you because they will know
           better not to attack you as they will realize the repercussions.[50]

One commander suggested they did not need special weapons. Saddam replied that "I believe that we as commanders, we should be prepared

---

[49] SH-SHTP-A-001-045, Saddam and High Ranking Officers Discussing Plans to Attack Kurdish "Saboteurs" in Northern Iraq and the Possibility of Using Special Ammunition (Weapons), Undated (Circa 1985). While there is no date on the tape, during discussions Saddam mentions that the war has been going on for five years.
[50] *Ibid.*

that if the target is not critical then we do not need the special arsenal of course, brothers ... resort to conventional weapons." General Adnan suggested: "Whatever we can accomplish ... whatever we cannot defeat, we should use special ammunition to secure the areas, we should burn them and come back."[51] Thus, the Iran–Iraq War, for all of its risks and costs, provided a wonderful smokescreen to settle matters with the fractious Kurds.

1985: more blood for peace

Both sides turned to other means to break the deadlock that was costing so many lives and resources. Previously we discussed the air and naval attacks in the Persian Gulf during the first years of the war as each side attempted to interfere with the movement of the world's supply of petroleum. That war continued to escalate throughout 1985. In the first months of that year, the Iraqis claimed they hit ten naval targets south and southeast of Kharg. In fact they hit only five. Part of the problem was that Exocets did not pack sufficient punch to sink the great oil tankers. It was not until February that the Iraqis sank a tanker, the Liberian tanker *Neptunia*, although ship owners had written off a number of other vessels because of damage.[52]

Iran's response to the unwillingness of shippers and insurers to risk their ships in the increasingly dangerous waters around Kharg was to institute a shuttle service whereby small tankers would move the crude down to the islands of Lavan and Sirri, where foreign tankers could take on their loads with relative impunity. In summer 1985, with a swelling air fleet of Mirages, including the F1EQ-5-200s, dedicated to anti-shipping missions, the Iraqis launched a more sustained campaign against Kharg and the Iranian shuttle fleet (for a depiction of the Iraqi air raids on Iranian islands, see Figure 8.1). During the last five months of 1985, they claimed to have struck the land facilities at Kharg fifty-nine times, and, while they failed to shut down Iranian facilities, they inflicted severe damage. By the end of the year, attacks on shipping near Kharg had hit thirty-three ships, two of which were sunk and twelve written off by either their owners or insurers.[53]

[51] *Ibid.*
[52] Navias and Hooton, *Tanker Wars*, 101. See also Uriel Dann, "The Iraqi–Iranian War," in *Middle East Contemporary Survey, Volume IX: 1984–85*, Itamar Rabinovich and Haim Shaked, eds. (Boulder, CO, 1987), 170–171.
[53] Navias and Hooton, *Tanker Wars*, 105–108.

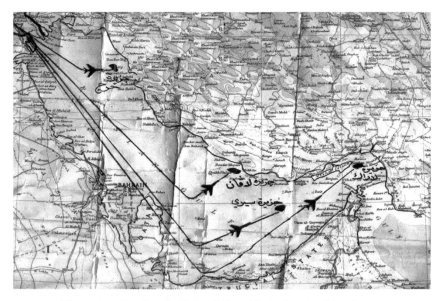

Figure 8.1 Persian Gulf, Iraqi air raids on Iranian islands

Overall, Iraq's attacks in 1985 on Gulf shipping failed to impact the world's oil supplies, though it did spur a general internationalization of the conflict to Iran's detriment.[54] The campaign was now beginning to bite into Iran's position, forcing the Iranians to react by building a new pipeline to their southern coast and building up the air defenses on Kharg, both of which efforts used up significant resources.[55] Generally, Iran's response remained restrained. Its naval forces began to search ships entering the Straits of Hormuz that were not under the flags of the major powers; here the potential for a major confrontation with Western powers lingered. In October, the Iranians attempted to search a French merchant vessel only to be warned off by a French warship, part of a US–British–French force keeping the Straits open.[56]

---

[54] As a result of increasing attacks on shipping, American, British, and French warships became increasingly involved in the Gulf. US-supplied AWACS support to Saudi Arabia became more important as members of the Gulf Cooperation Council began to fly defensive combat air patrols over their shipping. The so-called Fahd Line was first tested in June 1984 when a Saudi Arabian F-15 shot down an Iranian F-4 approaching its oil facilities. Christin Marschall, *Iran's Persian Gulf Policy: From Khomeini to Khatami* (New York, NY, 2003), 62–99.

[55] A good description of the tactical air operations around Kharg in 1985 is found in Cooper and Bishop, *Iran–Iraq War in the Air*, 183–186.

[56] Navias and Hooton, *Tanker Wars*, 111.

The year also saw the "war between the cities" renewed and amplified. Both air forces spent a lot of time attacking civilian targets. The Iraqis renewed attacks on Iran's civilian population on 4 March, when aircraft broke the UN moratorium on such raids on Iranian cities. The bombing caused significant civilian casualties.[57] The Iranians replied in kind, but neither air force possessed enough aircraft or the maintenance and supply infrastructure to sustain an air campaign.[58] Nevertheless, Iraqi aircraft dominated the air-to-air arena. In fact, because of the increasing unreliability of the Phoenix missiles with which F-14s were equipped, the Iranians attempted and failed to adapt Hawk anti-aircraft missiles to the F-14 fire control systems.[59]

In spring 1985, Saddam pressed his staff for new solutions to a variety of problems that ranged from tactics on the battlefield to worries about the possibility that Iran might retaliate with chemical weapons. An intelligence report in early April described Iran's still limited but growing ability to employ or defend against chemical weapons. Training in defense against chemical weapons was improving. Eighty percent of Iran's regular army possessed defensive equipment against chemical weapons, though only 40 percent of the *Pasdaran* did. The report noted Iran's attempts to purchase chemical defense equipment, but was most concerned with recent reports that West German and Swiss firms were supplying chemicals, Pakistan was supplying a chemical fertilizer plant "fit for military purposes," and North Korea was prepared to sell nerve and mustard agents to the Iranians. The report concluded that with the exception of chemical weapons captured from Iraq, intelligence had yet to confirm an immediate threat. However, "Iran is striving with all their access to obtain chemical weapons and to manufacture [them] locally, [in order to] use [them] as soon as possible as a surprise lethal weapon against our troops." The director of military intelligence urged Saddam to upgrade Iraq's defensive capabilities, training, and the psychological ability of Iraqi troops "to accept chemical blows."[60]

---

[57] O'Ballance, *The Gulf War*, 169.

[58] The Iraqi attacks may have been, in part, a reply to Iranian artillery shelling of various targets in the suburban areas surrounding Basra. The reality that Iraq could not sustain an air campaign for anything more than a few days most probably misled Saddam in 1991 into believing that Coalition air forces could not sustain an air campaign for anything longer than a week to ten days.

[59] Ward, *Immortal*, 272.

[60] Memorandum from the Office of the Secretary of the General Command of the Armed Forces to the Army Chief of Staff (10 April 1985) in SH-GMID-D-000-153, Correspondence between the General Military Intelligence Directorate and the Armed Forces General Command About Iranian Chemical Weapons Capabilities, April–October 1985. In June, the army began conducting large-scale live-agent experiments

Besides worrying about chemical weapons, Saddam remained unhappy with the air force. In April, he expressed his displeasure at the failure of Iraqi pilots to hit their targets accurately:

I think we do not have a guided weapon that can be launched and directed to the target, but the pilot throws the bomb on the target and does not know exactly where the bomb will fall especially when the distance is far away ... We want to get information from any sources to know the effect of air strikes and how they deal with them and what the factors [are] that can weaken their effect. According to such information, we will see what we are going to do. Because using these air strikes has a political price. If our work has a political price and results are not [significant], then why [do] we insist on using [it]?[61]

Negotiation by Scud

In 1985, the two opponents returned to launching missiles at each other as a means of ratcheting up the pressure. The move to missiles made sense, because Scuds cost slightly more than $1 million per missile, and attrition rates for far more expensive aircraft were still unsustainably high. Significantly for both sides was the fact that missiles did not risk the loss of pilots, who required a great deal of resources to train and prepare. Moreover, the Iraqi pilots' skill made them no more likely to hit targets accurately than were the Scuds, which says a great deal about their training, given the inaccuracy of the missiles.

Iraqi intelligence indicated that as a result of a secret visit by Rafsanjani to Tripoli in late December 1984, "transport aircraft were seen at Tehran airport carrying large numbers of [surface-to-surface] missiles." By February 1985, an air bridge was moving military equipment between Tripoli and Tehran with the help of Soviet aircraft. The Iraqis estimated the value of those shipments at $3 billion including the surface-to-surface missiles. The Iranians reportedly had bought approximately fifty Scuds from the Libyans.[62]

---

on Iraqi units. The first experiment, conducted with an infantry brigade of the I Corps, was considered successful because Iraqi troops recognized that "chemical weapons [were] no longer a decisive weapon in battle." Memorandum from GMID to the Army Chief of Staff (No. M1/SH12/Q1) (11 July 1985) in SH-IZAR-D-001-246, Correspondence from the Iraqi Army Chief Regarding an Experimental Chemical Weapons Attack on 27 June 1985, July–August 1985.

[61] 11 April 1985 Transcript in *SH-MISC-D-001-375, Transcripts of Meetings between Saddam Hussein and Military Commanders, April 1985.

[62] Memorandum from the Military Attache–Juddah to GMID (26 February 1985) in SH-GMID-D-000-524, General Military Intelligence Directorate (GMID) Memos Regarding Iranian–Libyan Military Cooperation, November 1981–November 1985; Memorandum from GMID to RCC/Intelligence Service (3 August 1985) in SH-

During the second week of March, in reply to the Iraqi air attacks of 4 March, the Iranians fired several Scuds at Kirkuk and Baghdad, strikes that outraged Saddam.[63] The Iraqis initially reported that the first Iranian Scuds to hit Baghdad were car bombings by Iranian terrorists. However, the Iraqi military attaché in Paris warned that such claims, especially after a fifth Scud hit Baghdad, might be counterproductive. Such a line, he warned, might suggest to the Europeans that Iraq was facing internal difficulties.[64] Moreover, suggesting to the Iraqi populace that an effective underground opposition existed in Iraq would not help keep the majority of Kurdish and Shi'a populations passive. By the end of 1985, both sides were nearly out of missiles. Having been denied the newer long-range Scuds from the USSR, the Iraqis would develop a domestic industry to extend the range of their Scuds with an eye on Tehran.[65]

Throughout this second War of the Cities, Saddam's mood varied between a desire for ruthless revenge and calculating deterrence in the belief that such efforts might persuade Khomeini to act rationally. In one meeting, he furiously interjected, "We will strike you [the Iranians] with such strikes that [will] make your turbans roll in the streets." Later in the meeting, he commented:

Do not expect the Iranians to be like Iraqis and understand that, when they strike, the Iraqis may not strike back. They may not understand that, so when we want to strike back we will let them know we have already warned and threatened them. Since the essential goal for us is not to kill more Iranians, but to isolate the Iranian regime from its people, to isolate it from its source of power, silence may not always benefit us.[66]

GMID-D-000-524, General Military Intelligence Directorate (GMID) Memos Regarding Iranian–Libyan Military Cooperation, November 1981–November 1985. The GMID's files were filled in early 1985 with reports of Iranian efforts to obtain Scud missiles. Among others see *SH-GMID-D-001-376, Various Memoranda between GMID, IIS, the Armed Forces General Command, and Military Attaches Regarding Iran's Acquisition of Surface-to-Surface Missiles.

[63] Steven Zaloga, "Ballistic Missiles in the Third World: Scud and Beyond," *Jane's International Defense Review* 21, no. 11 (1988).

[64] *SH-GMID-D-001-376, Various Memoranda between GMID, IIS, the Armed Forces General Command, and Military Attaches Regarding Iran's Acquisition of Surface-to-Surface Missiles.

[65] By the end of the decade, Iraq had the "largest technical and scientific base in the Middle East." Close to 40 percent of Iraq's industrial labor force (100,000 workers) were working in military industries. Timothy D. Hoyt, *Military Industry and Regional Defense Policy – India, Iraq, and Israel* (New York, NY, 2007), 123.

[66] SH-SHTP-A-000-556, Saddam Meeting with Cabinet Ministers to Discuss the Iran–Contra Revelations, circa late 1986.

In the end, the missiles fired did not inflict enough damage to significantly affect morale, but they did kill and maim thousands of innocent civilians.[67] Iranian Scud attacks, however, moved the Iraqis to mount a full court press to persuade the Soviets and Eastern Europeans to stop supplying weapons to the Persians. At the end of March, Tariq Aziz traveled through Europe ending up in the United States to persuade the Americans to stop supplying spare parts for the US weapons systems the Iranians possessed. At the same time, the Iraqis put a number of fighter bombers on alert to search for the Iranian launchers firing Scuds. Their sorties proved no more successful than those launched by Coalition forces to find Iraqi missile launchers during Operation Desert Storm.[68]

One might have thought that the war would have been sufficient to keep Saddam focused on his local enemies, the Iranians and Kurds. But in fact, Saddam always reserved his deepest hatred for the Israelis. In early October 1985, Israeli aircraft, flying across the eastern Mediterranean, bombed Yasser Arafat's PLO headquarters in Tunisia and almost killed the Palestinian leader. That act brought forth all of the dictator's fury combined with his paranoia. He immediately announced to his entourage that someone must have informed the Israelis as to where Arafat was ensconced. Saddam declared that the Iraqis needed to make ever more rigorous security arrangements, given the Israeli threat:

How do we find a balance here? I mean between this situation and the security matter? Because the use of phones is necessary; besides the country's secretariat and the council resort to correspondence sometimes. If they use correspondence, more often than not, it will go though their secretaries, companions, bodyguards, and other employees at the office. Thus the entire office of that comrade is going to know that comrade Na'im has a meeting at such and such a time of day.

Saddam worried that Ba'ath leaders did not possess enough bodyguards, but soon turned back to the complex conspiracy he believed was aimed at Iraq:

---

[67] The Iraqi strikes into Tehran temporarily affected morale. As reported at the time, Tehran was a "curious mix of despondency and panic," with citizens evacuating the city and even participating in occasional protests. Thomas L. McNaugher, "Ballistic Missiles and Chemical Weapons: The Legacy of the Iran–Iraq War," *International Security* 15, no. 2 (1990), 9. Casualty estimates as a result of these attacks are difficult to verify. Official Iranian figures for its own citizens place the number of civilian missile casualties at 12,931 (2,226 deaths). See S. Taheri Shemirani, "The War of the Cities," in *The Iran–Iraq War: The Politics of Aggression*, Farhang Rajaee, ed. (Gainesville, FL, 1993), 37.

[68] *SH-GMID-D-001-376, Various Memoranda between GMID, IIS, the Armed Forces General Command, and Military Attaches Regarding Iran's Acquisition of Surface-to-Surface Missiles.

Either the Arabs are slaves to Israel and Israel controls their destiny, or the Arabs can be their own masters and Israel is like Formosa's location to China at best ...

By God, do we remain silent? I mean at least from the national standpoint and a political standpoint, we should do something. Something that would make humans feel, make the world feel, make the universe feel that we tell them, "Hey people, this is rejected by the Arabs"' I swear by Allah if we weren't tied up, we would have attacked Tel Aviv by God ... The Americans are still conspiring bastards and this thing is their doing ... What I am calling for is not to forget our special condition and that does not mean that we hesitate, remain silent, or do not do anything but to take into our special condition which we are going through because we are at war with Israel, at war with Iran, at war with Hafez al-Assad, and at war with al-Gaddafi. All of them are at one side and coordinate, whether with information, with bases, or with all the available methods.[69]

1986: persistence and delusion

The interminable conflict gave both sides a sense that their military forces were reaching new levels of competence and that combat experience on its own was enough to produce military effectiveness. Saddam was now devoting substantial effort to building up the Republican Guard. Still, he could not entirely break his habit of appointing officers on the basis of Ba'ath loyalty and familial ties to himself to the most important commands, such as divisions, no matter how incompetent they were. One former Republican Guard officer commented on his experiences with such a commander in 1986:

[T]here were difficulties with the division commander, whose name was Brigadier General Ahmed Hammash al-Tikriti. He was courageous but plainly stupid. I had many clashes with him over division plans, and so it was hard for me to build the division, because he always had objections to my recommendations and the decisions I made ... It [was] hard for anyone to work under the command of a stupid leader of limited education, not knowing how [not] to cross him and needing to comply with [his orders and directions], but at the same time wanting to do the right thing.[70]

In the case of Iraq's military organizations, there was also the need to ascribe much of the learning from the battlefield to Saddam's wisdom, because he was quick to remind his military advisors that he had discerned fundamental truths in the experiences of war. An article in

[69] SH-SHTP-D-000-567, Recording of Saddam and Arafat Discussing the Israeli Attack on the Palestinian Liberation Organization's Headquarters, 5 October 1985.
[70] Woods, *et al.*, *Saddam's War*, 79.

an Iraqi military journal in January 1986 suggests the extent to which such efforts went:

It is worth noting that this aspect – i.e., the aspect of military doctrine – continues to be a weak point among Third World countries in particular. These countries purchase their weapons from foreign suppliers and borrow those suppliers' tactical doctrine. The tendency of Third World armies to borrow or become saturated with foreign military doctrine and concepts is inevitable, because the developing countries lack combat experience in current, mechanized warfare comparable to the experience of [the advanced] countries. The aforementioned of course does not apply to our warrior country, which has gained combat experience during the war years which is superior to that of any foreign country, because it is baptized in blood . . .

Foreign military doctrines must not be borrowed along with all their defects. Rather they should be treated as broad working guidelines . . . In this regard, President Commander Saddam Hussein . . . states, "The army is a big family which has its own doctrine. This doctrine is born of and linked to, society's doctrine. However, it has its own special nature. While the army shares society's doctrine, it develops its own doctrine for combat purposes based on the society's doctrine."[71]

On the other side of the hill, the Iranians were continuing to re-equip their military forces. By late 1984, they had reestablished their access to global arms markets. In 1985, arms from the United States had begun arriving in what would become known as the Iran–Contra scandal. Despite the political and strategic implications of the indirect and direct arming of Iran by the United States, the material impact on the course of the war was marginal.[72] During 1986, the United States and Israel delivered 2,000 anti-tank missiles, 300 Sidewinder air-to-air missiles, and 25 Hawk ground-to-air missiles. This compares to the 10,500 anti-tank missiles from China and North Korea, or the hundreds of artillery systems funneled through Austria, Argentina, China; combat aircraft from China, Ethiopia, North Korea, and Switzerland. Armored fighting vehicles, ships, Scuds, helicopters, and a wide variety of spare parts from those nations rounded out the collection.[73] From the North Koreans and

---

[71] A Suitable Doctrine for the Next Mechanized War in *SH-MODX-D-001-377, [The Iraqi] Military Journal, Issue No. 1, January 1986.

[72] The TOW missile was effectively used against Iraqi tanks in the 1986 Fao and Mehran battles but not in numbers that could have changed events. One estimate found that due to "training and operating problems," Iranian anti-tank gunners "rarely achieved more than a 0.1 hit probability. Cordesman and Wagner, *The Lessons of Modern War, Volume II*, 442.

[73] For a complete breakdown of international arms transfers by country and date, see SIPRI, "International Arms Transfers Database, 1950–Present," Stockholm International Peace Research Institute, www.sipri.org/research/armaments/transfers/databases/armstransfers (accessed 20 May 2010).

the Chinese, the Iranians received approximately $4.5 billion-worth of weapons, including Scuds, SA-2s, Silkworm anti-ship missiles, and a large number of armored fighting vehicles.

Nevertheless, the Iranians remained substantially inferior to the Iraqis in virtually every category of weapons system. At the beginning of 1986, the Iraqis possessed 4,000 tanks, the Iranians barely 1,000. The Iraqis had approximately 3,800 other armored fighting vehicles; the Iranians only 1,400. Of the Shah's once formidable air force, the Iranians could keep somewhere between sixty and eighty aircraft in flyable condition; the Iraqi Air Force numbered 600 aircraft and could keep approximately two-thirds in commission with the help of foreign technicians.[74] (For a complete Order of Battle during the war, see Appendix E.) Nevertheless, the ayatollahs in control of war policy in Tehran persisted in believing they could defeat Iraq. That belief rested almost entirely on the willingness of the *Pasdaran* and *Basij* to, at some level, still believe the motivational billboards erected near the battlefield with slogans such as "The sword does not bring victory, it is blood that brings it" and "The blood of martyrs decides the fate of the Islamic Revolution."[75]

Fao: Iran's hollow victory

Major ground combat erupted almost immediately at the beginning of 1986 and followed a pattern similar to that of the previous year. The Iraqis began major operations with a well-planned attack to finish the job of driving the Iranians off Majnun Island, which they had failed to recapture in 1985. After two days of heavy fighting and massive use of firepower and chemical agents, Iraqi artillery and armor drove the Iranians off most of the island. With their advantages in firepower, even though they were the attackers, the Iraqis inflicted heavier casualties on the Iranians. Nevertheless, the Iranians still held a small portion of the island from which they continued to harass the Iraqis.[76] The offensive itself was probably the result of the pressure Saddam was exerting on his commanders for more aggressive operations. Its success once again underlined that when and where the Iraqis could bring sufficient firepower to bear, they could defeat their opponents.

---

[74] Ward, *Immortal*, 273.
[75] Saskia Gieling, *Religion and War in Revolutionary Iran* (London, 1999), 118. These phrases are typical of the language and allusions Khomeini deployed to mobilize the Iranian population. It is difficult, if not impossible, to separate the Iranian war rhetoric, cited above, from the religious and overtly sacrificial rhetoric of such Shi'a ceremonies as *Ashura*.
[76] O'Ballance, *The Gulf War*, 173.

But the main fighting in the winter of 1985–1986 came as the Iranians launched a major offensive to take the swamp-inundated Fao Peninsula. The peninsula was strategically important because it was the site of important Iraqi oil installations and controls access to the Shatt al-Arab and then to Basra 75 miles to the north. Northwest of Fao lies the port of Umm Qasr, formerly a fishing port, but which in the 1980s served as the main Iraqi naval base. Capturing the port would have put the Iranians west of Basra and opened up access to the Shi'a cities lying along the Euphrates. The peninsula itself was lightly inhabited: most of its terrain was a mix of mud flats, canals, and swamp land covered with marsh grass.

From the Iraqi point of view, the peninsula was terrible ground on which to wage a major battle. For the Iranians it maximized their capabilities at infiltration and small unit infantry tactics. One Iraqi general described the peninsula's terrain as

so dusty in dry periods and muddy when raining, that it was always difficult to maneuver. We could only stay on the roads, and with all the traffic funneled along the only two roads; it was terrible – the infantry, the BMPs, the armor. Because of the fact there were only two roads, the Iranian forces were able continually to shell both. They knew about the terrain conditions and that the roads were the only way in or out for transportation. The enemy was just on the other side [of the Shatt al-Arab], and so they were able to see us.[77]

Between early December 1985 and January 1986, the Iranians built an assault force totaling nearly 250,000 soldiers, with approximately 150,000 deployed for the Fao operation and 100,000 northeast of Basra.[78] Most of those in the south were *Pasdaran*, the leaders of which appear to have planned the operations with some help from the regular army. During the previous summer and fall, the *Pasdaran* had trained its assault forces extensively deep in Iran, far from Iraqi intelligence.[79] Training included exercises and extensive training for the attacking amphibious units on the lakes and rivers of central and northern Iran. Finally, the Iranians appear to have received considerable help from North Korean engineering experts on how to build and maintain the tactical and logistical infrastructure once they had captured Fao. In retrospect, Iranian military commanders hoped the offensive against

---

[77] Woods, *et al.*, *Saddam's War*, 75.
[78] Major Michael E. Hoffpauir (USA), *Tactical Evolution in the Iraqi Army: The Abadan Island and Fish Lake Campaigns of the Iran–Iraq War* (Army Command and General Staff College, 1991).
[79] *SH-MISC-D-001-349, Pasdaran Report: From Khorramshahr to Fao (July 1982–August 1986): A Military and Political Analysis, circa 1988.

the peninsula would not only be a major tactical victory, but also outflank Iraq's southern line and lead to the capture of Basra.

An Iranian account relates the offensive's planning and objectives:

[I]t is apparent that our objectives [could not have been] satisfied through prolonged limited objectives.[80] In spite of their effectiveness, they [would] not be a decisive factor in determining the final outcome of the war. Based on our objectives, and taking into consideration the enemy pressure across the front ... the enemy's situation in the area [Fao] and the geopolitical sensitivity of the area (control over the northern part of the Persian Gulf and its proximity to neighboring Kuwait ...). The wide-spread operations of al-Fajr 8 ["Dawn 8"] were planned ...

[T]he experience from the previous three years, had taught us that we had to reach a sufficient military capability suitable for the accomplishment of our political–military strategy ... The area of [Fao], based on geography and the natural situation, solved some of [our] security problems as well as those associated with confronting the pressure from the enemy. By this we mean that as a result of the lack of trafficability in the swamp areas and artificial obstacles such as salt factories, for the enemy the area was practically unusable. The area was covered by water on three sides, so naturally confronting the enemy from only one direction was much easier and [during] a counterattack, the enemy would be vulnerable from two sides.[81]

Iraqi intelligence picked up the buildup, but misread its significance. Nobody in Baghdad believed the Iranians could put together both a major deception and the capabilities to attack the peninsula all at once. Some of those on the spot warned that the main Iranian effort would come south of Basra. According to General Hamdani, who visited the area before the battle:

I saw personally that the enemy was going to attack the VII Corps when I went on reconnaissance missions. We could see that they were dropping boats they were going to use, building observation posts, and making gaps between the orchards to stockpile their war supplies. They were building logistics roads with their corps of engineers. So we could see the Iranians were going to attack in this direction, but back [in Baghdad] they dismissed this as just a trick and believed that the main attack was going to come against the VI Corps.[82]

---

[80] This is a reference to a rejection of the attrition strategy of small attacks that had marked the Iranian approach during much of 1985.

[81] *SH-MISC-D-001-349, Pasdaran Report: From Khorramshahr to Fao (July 1982–August 1986): A Military and Political Analysis, circa 1988. The last sentence references the fact that Iranian artillery could fire from the left bank of the Shatt al-Arab onto the peninsula.

[82] Woods, et al., Saddam's War, 70–71. An interview with a senior Iraqi intelligence officer assigned to the Iran Branch during the Iran–Iraq War confirmed Hamdani's story. See Kevin M. Woods, Williamson Murray, Elizabeth A. Nathan, Laila Sabara, and Ana M.

However, the intelligence center in Baghdad, Saddam, and the corps commanders defending Basra discounted such reports from the peninsula and believed the Iranians would renew their assault on Basra from the northeast, as they had during the previous three years.[83] Adding to Baghdad's miscalculations was the fact that there was only one decrypt that indicated that a major Iranian attack on Fao was in the offing. The lack of signals intelligence resulted from the offensive being run by the *Pasdaran*, which possessed limited signals capability. Their message traffic in the planning stages of the campaign went either by telephone lines or via messengers. At the time, the chief of Iraqi intelligence, General Mahmoud Shahin, an armor officer with no intelligence background, was trying to please his bosses in Baghdad, who believed the Iranians were going to attack north of the Iraqi capital. Thus, he refused to pass along any intelligence suggesting the possibility of an Iranian attack on Fao.[84]

Astoundingly, Saddam and his advisors in Baghdad persisted in their assumptions that no attack would occur against Fao even during the first several days of the Iranian offensive. The source of this confidence is unclear. However, information reportedly provided to Iraq through King Hussein of Jordan appears to have played a significant role in misleading Saddam and his senior officers. Just as the attack began on 9 February, the king, who was allegedly passing on US intelligence information, warned Saddam that the attack on the Fao was only "a limited diversionary assault ... the main Iranian offensive would come later in the central sector."[85] Between the Iranian deceptions, inept analyses on the part of Iraqi intelligence, and the apparent confirmatory intelligence from the United States, the Iranian attack was a complete surprise.[86] According to Hamdani,

---

Venegas, "Interview with (Former) Major General Mizher Rashid Al-Tarfa Al-Ubaydi, Dubai, United Arab Emirates, 9 November 2009," *Project 1946: Phase II* (Alexandria, VA, 2010); "Iraq Ascribes A Key Defeat in '86 to Misinformation from the US," *New York Times*, 19 January 1987. www.nytimes.com/1987/01/19/world/iraq-ascribes-a-key-defeat-in-86-to-misinformation-from-the-us.html.

[83] Woods, *et al.*, *Saddam's War*, 71.

[84] Woods, *et al.*, "Interview with (Former) Major General Mizher Rashid Al-Tarfa Al-Ubaydi."

[85] Ashton, *King Hussein of Jordan*, 221; Gibson, *Covert Relationship*, 168. Such information would presumably be passed in accordance with the US Administration's National Security Decision Directive (NSDD) 139 (5 April 1984). News reporting on 13 February indicated that US officials believed, based on "confidential discussions with Iraqi officials and on intercepted radio communications," that the attacks on the Fao were a feint and a possibly prelude to attacks farther North. See Charles Mohr, "New Iranian Drive Seen as Diversion," *New York Times*, 13 February 1986.

[86] Later Iraqi claims that the Americans had fed Iraq faulty intelligence on the eve of Fao to purposely damage its position owes more to scapegoating than logic. Despite the confused and often conflicting nature of US policy toward Iraq and Iran in 1986,

[the Iranians] demonstrated a high-quality performance of integrated operations. There were thousands of boats that fit 400 [soldiers], rushing in before dawn. These were rubber boats, wooden boats, and big boats all transporting thousands of soldiers in a few moments under the cover of intense artillery and air bombardment of the area ... But even with report[s] and headquarters acknowledging that this was part of the main attack, Baghdad still had worries about a secondary attack in the [central] VI Corps sector.[87]

On 11 February, the Iranians began their main attack and achieved their second substantial victory of the war. That the defending division, the 26th Infantry Division, was a second-class unit with only a few field fortifications behind which to shelter, exacerbated the difficulty of defending the peninsula against waves of attacking Iranians.[88] At the start of the offensive, the first wave of Iranian troops moved out with the shout of "Oh God increase the calamity."[89] They got their wish. In the midst of a storm, Iranian frogmen swam the Shatt al-Arab to remove Iraqi obstacles. Almost immediately, a full division of *Pasdaran* made an amphibious landing on the peninsula.[90] The 26th Infantry Division immediately fell apart. However, the Iraqi Navy, which had picked up what was afoot in the days preceding the attack, succeeded in removing its Silkworm batteries and radar units from the peninsula and back to Basra without significant losses. Even as the 26th Infantry Division was collapsing, Saddam refused to recognize that the tip of the Fao was where the Iranians were placing their major effort.[91] For the first three days of

---

actively setting conditions for a major Iranian battlefield victory would clearly run counter to the classified US policy at the time. The Iraqi line of reasoning also presumes US intelligence was not also deceived, or at least not clear, as to the Iranian main effort of the spring 1986 campaign. On the Iraqi accusations of deceit, see "Iraq Ascribes a Key Defeat in '86 to Misinformation from the US." It was also during this time that some intelligence information was provided to Iran as part of the Iran–Contra operation in order to, as National Security Advisor Admiral John M. Poindexter later testified, "establish bona fides that the U.S. really was intent on moving in this direction, then give [the Iranians] 1,000 TOW missiles and then see what the [they] did, like release a hostage." The information passed reportedly covered "only a segment of the Iraqi front ... without giving the Iranians a fighting edge." Even if the data included the southern front, the fact that it was not passed until 5 February would likely have merely confirmed to the Iranians that their Fao deception was working. See John Tower, Edmund Muskie, and Brent Scowcroft, *The Tower Commission Report: Full Text of the President's Special Review Board* (New York, NY, 1987), 238–245.

[87] Woods, *et al.*, *Saddam's War*, 74.   [88] *Ibid.*, 73.   [89] Ward, *Immortal*, 274.
[90] *Ibid.*, 274–275.
[91] One of the Iraqi explanations for the fact that the Iranian offensive had caught them by surprise was that they had "erected sites for their artillery about a year ago and they left the sites and went away." SH-SHTP-D-000-607, Transcripts of Meetings between Saddam, Vice President of the RCC Izzat Ibrahim Al-Tikriti, Minister of Defense Adnan Khairallah, and Army Chief of Staff Abd Al-Jawad Zinun During the Iraq–Iran War, 25 February 1985–31 July 1986.

the offensive, the Iraqis reinforced their collapsing positions on the peninsula with only a few units from the 5th Infantry Division. Meanwhile, the well-executed Iranian deception operations north of Basra persuaded Saddam, his advisors, and the corps commanders on the scene, that a major attack was about to occur in that area.[92]

On that first day, the Iranians captured the town of Fao while other of their forces advanced to capture the remainder of the peninsula.[93] They then moved quickly to northwest to try to outflank Basra before the Iraqis could react. Here the Iraqi Navy saved a deteriorating situation: it moved its marine units to block the main highway out of the peninsula. Those troops held on long enough for army reinforcements to arrive and hold the peninsula's neck.[94] An Iranian account describes the operation's opening and initial successes:

Understanding that there was a possibility of a high state of alert among enemy units and preparing for it, allowed us to break through the front lines, clear the area of enemy forces and establish a suitable beachhead ... The enemy, during the first moments of the operation as they came face to face with the waves of our forces ... was completely surprised. One of the enemy's commanders was giving the following preliminary report to his headquarter: "The enemy like a flood by boats is discharging forces into our land. If you don't do something they will probably capture Om-al-Qasr [Umm Qasr], and our situation is very bad."[95]

By landing in six locations, all successfully, the Iranians created further panic and uncertainty among the defenders. The hesitancy, with which the Iraqi high command responded, allowed the Iranians to consolidate their position and establish defensive positions. Because there were only two paved roads running the length of the peninsula, the Iranians knew from whence Iraqi counterattacks would come, while the road that ran along the Shatt al-Arab was open to heavy bombardment by Iranian batteries on the other shore of the waterway. Amplifying the Iranian advantages, the Iraqi counterattack began just as a major storm hit, further constraining Iraqi mobility. The rains turned the peninsula into a sea of mud, which substantially diminished the effectiveness of Iraqi artillery and air attacks, including those using gas.

While Saddam and his advisors in Baghdad had refused to shift reserves from Basra to the peninsula until too late, they did rush special

---

[92] *SH-MISC-D-001-349, Pasdaran Report: From Khorramshahr to Fao (July 1982–August 1986): A Military and Political Analysis, Circa 1988.

[93] *Ibid.*

[94] Woods, *et al.*, "Interview with (Former) Lieutenant General Abid Mohammed Al-Kabi, Cairo, Egypt, 12 November 2009."

[95] *SH-MISC-D-001-349, Pasdaran Report: From Khorramshahr to Fao (July 1982–August 1986): A Military and Political Analysis, circa 1988.

weapons to the area. They immediately decided to use gas as notes from their discussions indicate:

Date 11 February 1986: The mission: To study the needed requirements for establishing a strong chemical strike by aircraft or artillery against al-Bishah has first priority and against the Eastern side of Shatt al-Arab as a second priority . . .

Characteristics of target:

The enemy is located in (Ra's-e Bisra–Fao) area between the two northern lines and two eastern lines according to information received at 2000 [hours] on 11 February. It could be engaged with special ammunition considering the safety of the sectors . . . the area occupied by the enemy is estimated at least 40 KM (which equals 4,000 Hectares). The enemy is considered a fixed target and their chemical protection equipment [is] 100 percent.

56 aircraft to be used, one battalion of 155mm artillery: 360 bombs with chemical weapons for each of two strikes; one at 1100 [hours] the second at 1700 [hours].

155mm artillery shells, 5,000 shells for a shelling of 45–60 minutes with three battalions.

Reserve ammunition 700 chemical bombs, with 100 more each day: up to a total of 2,000 bombs of mustard and nerve gas.

1,500 extra artillery chemical shells available – 200–250 daily with a grand total of 10,000 more available if needed.

Recommendations:

Strikes by air force and artillery 12 February as fast as possible beginning at 1100 [hours].[96]

In an after-action report, the Iranians described the conundrum Saddam confronted:

It should be mentioned that it was necessary to predict how the enemy would confront this situation. The two problems, the land and the forces, were critically important considerations to the enemy. In spite of the Iraqis' past performance, the Iraqi Army's ability to choose between the two was going to be problematic. On the one hand, the military–political value of the land would force the Iraqis to recapture the area at all costs. On the other hand, the geography of the area practically took away a considerable portion of the enemy's capability and was certain to result in significant damage to the Iraqi battle structure. As a result, the enemy would not be able to satisfactorily achieve both the recapture of the land and at a low cost and therefore would have to sacrifice one at the expense of the other. In any event, whatever the choice, it would eventually lead to the loss of the other.

---

[96] SH-PDWN-D-001-024, Saddam Hussein and High Ranking Military Officers Discussing the Possible Use of Chemical Weapons against Iranian Troops, 22 December 1988.

If the enemy decided to save the land, it would result in the heavy loss of forces and in the long term [he] would not be capable of defending other operational areas. If they selected to save [their forces], [he] would have to face the psychological damage to the force as well as place [himself] in a tenuous social and political loss of a very important and sensitive area.[97]

Once it was clear the Iranians had captured the peninsula, Saddam jumped into the trap. On 14 February, three days later, the Iraqis began rushing reinforcements south, including some of the prized Republican Guard. The aim was to retake the peninsula and drive the Iranians into the Shatt al-Arab. There was not enough time to plan. General Hamdani pointed out to the authors:

[A] weakness in Iraqi strategic thinking [is that] it was Bedouin and not professional. I was very resentful of the Iraqi strategic approach at the time, thinking it was wrong. However, [Fao] was Iraqi territory taken by Iranians, so I was determined to retake it. We considered this attack as a stab at the dignity of the Iraqi leadership. This ... is Bedouin and not strategic thinking ... Part of [the problem] was a mentality among the high-ranking general officers, but it also stemmed from Saddam Hussein's insistence on recapturing Fao. It was in part Saddam's ignorance about how to use armor, but it was also a flaw that we [Iraqi professional soldiers] had in our understanding about how to use armor.[98]

The counterattacks were a dismal failure. Appalling weather did not help, but the larger geographic problem was that there were only two roads down which Iraqi armored columns could advance against a well dug-in opponent. The hurried response from Baghdad piled reinforcements on top of reinforcements without a coherent plan, thus exacerbating the confusion and increasing losses.[99] But Saddam felt the political consequences of losing the peninsula might be disastrous to his regime's political stability. Throughout the battle, Iraqi superiority in artillery and short-range missiles counted for little in the swampy, water-logged soil, without their being able to inflict significant damage on the defending Iranian infantry in their dug-in positions. The result was heavy casualties in soldiers and equipment with little ground retaken.

A furious and embarrassed Saddam urged his commanders to press their counterattacks, regardless of losses and in spite of the weather:

---

[97] *SH-MISC-D-001-349, Pasdaran Report: From Khorramshahr to Fao (July 1982–August 1986): A Military and Political Analysis, Circa 1988. One might take the Iranian claim with a grain of salt, because the evidence suggests they had larger aims than forcing the Iraqis into a battle of attrition.

[98] Woods, et al., Saddam's War, 75–76.

[99] Hamdani, Memoir.

This will be decisive in terms of the fate of the battle; this will decide a battle, it will decide the war. I mean from now on, he who wins the battle here, he will win the war. Especially if we win this battle, we will win the war, because all of Iran will burn in that location, but do your level best Abu-'Ali to reduce our casualties our sacrifices ... I mean from my point of view, I have no objection to the slowness; it seems that this will be our pace and I do not envisage that we will be faster than that or that our pace would increase. We will remain advancing [a] few meters at [a] time, we will achieve progress and crush them in that bottom area. The only thing that we must do is to reduce our sacrifices throughout daily efforts, and I emphasize the word daily, daily, daily, we have to improvise new techniques, because this is [a] battle [which] will settle this war, no doubt about that.[100]

Whatever hopes the Iranians had had of pushing on to Umm Qasr or even Basra died in the mud and blood of the Fao Peninsula. On the other side, the Iraqis suffered exceedingly heavy casualties in men and equipment without being able to push the Iranians any significant distance down the peninsula. With their well-placed artillery, the Iranians could interdict the Republican Guard moving south from Basra to Fao.[101] Targets were not only in plain sight, but also on the hardened surfaces of the highway were more vulnerable to artillery fire than Iranian soldiers in the swamps. An Iranian report indicated:

the [Iraqi] enemy, from the last point in their rear which would go the Umm al-Rasas front to the connecting line in Fao was under our observation and in the line of fire of our artillery forces. The volume of our artillery fire on the enemy was so heavy that they had no defense for it. The Iraqi forces had very rarely confronted this volume of fire in the five years of war.[102]

In early March, Saddam abandoned the counterattacks and left the Iranians with their gains. One source estimates Iranian casualties as high as 30,000 and Iraqi losses at 7,000 after barely three weeks of fighting.[103] Despite the fact that the Iranians finally possessed adequate chemical defensive gear, most members of the *Basij* still refused to shave, which rendered their gas masks of little use.[104] The Iraqis also lost a substantial number of tanks and BMPs in the mud, victims of Iranian anti-tank missiles and mines. Nevertheless, such tribulations never

[100] SH-SHTP-A-000-628, Saddam Being Briefed About the Iraq–Iran War and Discusses Iraqi–Syria Relations and Hafiz Al-Asad, Circa February 1982.
[101] One of the Iranian accounts of the battle claims that Iranian artillery inflicted 30 percent casualties on the Republican Guard formations. *SH-MISC-D-001-349, Pasdaran Report: From Khorramshahr to Fao (July 1982–August 1986): A Military and Political Analysis, Circa 1988.
[102] *SH-MISC-D-001-349, Pasdaran Report: From Khorramshahr to Fao (July 1982–August 1986): A Military and Political Analysis, Circa 1988.
[103] O'Ballance, *The Gulf War*, 179. Later estimates place the Iraqi casualty figures much higher.
[104] Ward, *Immortal*, 276.

prevented Saddam from spinning the results. In a meeting with Ba'ath Party officials in March, he commented:

The true meaning for us as commanders [is] that the people observed the resistance and the strength of Iraqis [willing] to fight for their country. Although we lost Fao, we retained our strong will and our resistance. The enemy's strategy was [to] destroy our will power; the world will never forget how the Iraqis handled the situation and converted it from a defeating situation, to a prevailing situation. We [have] shocked the world, especially the Western [world], although the Iranians [have] achieved their partial victory on land, they were surprised [by] the Iraqi strength in fighting to the end, and they admit it.[105]

A more sober appraisal came from the minister of defense, General Adnan Khairallah Talfah, who commented that "the Iranians have turned their weaknesses and backwardness into points of strength in [confronting] our superior capabilities in battle."[106] His opposite number among the Iranians, Mohsen Rezaee of the Revolutionary Guard, agreed and used the improbable victory at Fao to press for a continuation of a war policy of passion over reason.[107]

For the next half a year there would be no major Iranian offensives. A series of smaller battles contributed to burgeoning casualty figures. The Iranians returned to the attrition strategy they had employed in 1985. In fact, in July 1986, senior military leaders were considerably worried that the Iranians were shifting to an attrition strategy. The minister of defense noted: "In my estimate, the enemy's plan for the next three or four months ... will open with distant battles that will wear us out and wear our reserves and plan for grand operations."[108]

Iraqi leaders obviously also realized the effectiveness of Iranian deception operations. The director of planning in the ministry of defense, Major General Mohammed Abd al-Qadir, remarked to Saddam in a July meeting of senior military leaders, "The important point [is] the danger of differentiating between deception and reality. The [Iranians] included in their calculation that we might have responded to [both] operations

[105] SH-SHTP-A-001-023, Saddam Hussein and Ba'ath Party Members Discussing the Iran–Iraq War, 6 March 1987.
[106] SH-SHTP-D-000-607, Transcripts of Meetings between Saddam, Vice President of the RCC Izzat Ibrahim Al-Tikriti, Minister of Defense Adnan Khairallah, and Army Chief of Staff Abd Al-Jawad Zinun During the Iraq-Iran War, 25 February 1985–31 July 1986.
[107] Shahram Chubin and Charles Tripp, *Iran and Iraq at War* (Boulder, CO, 1988), 77; Farhi, "The Antinomies of Iran's War Generation," 106–107.
[108] SH-SHTP-D-000-607, Transcripts of Meetings between Saddam, Vice President of the RCC Izzat Ibrahim Al-Tikriti, Minister of Defense Adnan Khairallah, and Army Chief of Staff Abd Al-Jawad Zinun During the Iraq-Iran War, 25 February 1985–31 July 1986.

[meaning the Fao and North Basra buildups] and augmented both sectors." If Iraq did not respond to the deception and move forces to meet the threat at Basra "then, it is possible to turn the deception into reality, a real operation."[109]

The Iraqis struck first in these smaller battles. Saddam ordered his troops to recapture the Iranian border town of Mehran on the central front. He hoped to close one of the passes so the Iranians could not use it to attack Baghdad, and because it provided him a chance to hold Iranian territory. According to the Iranians, Iraqi forces numbered three armored and five infantry brigades, an indication of how much smaller an operation this was compared to the fighting around Basra.[110] Beginning on 14 May, the three-day Iraqi offensive regained Mehran, approximately one hundred square miles of Iraqi territory lost earlier in the war, and the two key peaks, overlooking the town.[111] Interestingly, having taken Mehran and with an opportunity to pursue the defeated Iranian forces, Saddam forbade any advance into Iran. That alone was enough to provoke the Iranians. Having suffered a tactical defeat, they almost immediately replied with a counteroffensive on 20 June, codename Karbala 1. Again they surprised and inflicted heavy casualties on the Iraqi defenders. By the time Iraqi reinforcements arrived, the Iranians had regained Mehran and its heights.[112] This defeat, like the Fao Peninsula, was a significant military and political setback for Saddam.

Whatever moderating voices in Tehran had left to say about the direction of the war were finally silenced when, in his annual New Year's speech, Khomeini announced that Iran would win by the start of the next Persian New Year (March 1987). The moderate camp (those who would support a political outcome of the war that did not include installing an Islamic government in Baghdad) led by Rafsanjani, tried to moderate expectations by qualifying the ayatollah's pronouncement with "we hope to gain more considerable victories," rather than the final victory. However, they had little effect after the triumph at Fao.[113] As one observer notes "paradoxically, Fao was to be the culminating point of Iran's

---

[109] *Ibid.*
[110] *SH-MISC-D-001-349, Pasdaran Report: From Khorramshahr to Fao (July 1982–August 1986): A Military and Political Analysis, Circa 1988. Cordesman estimated the Iraqi's attacked with two divisions – approximately 25,000 men. Cordesman and Wagner, *The Lessons of Modern War, Volume II*, 227.
[111] O'Ballance, *The Gulf War*, 179–180.
[112] *SH-MISC-D-001-349, Pasdaran Report: From Khorramshahr to Fao (July 1982–August 1986): A Military and Political Analysis, Circa 1988.
[113] Hiro, *The Longest War*, 177.

success, the point at which it both over-reached itself and misled itself as to the implications."[114]

In August and September, the Iranians launched two smaller offensives – Karbala 2 and Karbala 3 – that involved no more than three brigades each.[115] Both achieved little. In a lessons-learned conference in late September after Karbala 3, Iraqi senior officers from the army and air force discussed the lack of cooperation between ground and air. General Mohammed Fathi Muni noted in a comment, "I have a comment on the point General Nazzar regarding the lack of joint understanding. We have six years of war; until now there is no joint understanding between army air [close air support] and ground forces."[116]

Nevertheless, late in the year, closing universities to support, mobilize, and conscript large numbers of Iranians indicated that something was afoot. In early October, alarmed by their agents in Iran, Iraqi intelligence reported:

The high state of readiness indicates that it is possible that Iran will launch its attack before or shortly after the beginning of winter … It is very likely that the main goal of the attack will be to seal off the city of Basra or capture it. The rulers in Tehran believe that the fall of Basra will be a huge military and moral blow to Iraqi forces and the Iraqi people. It would be the first step in establishing a Shi'a republic in Iraqi territory. Iran is aware that Iraqi defenses on this front are very strong, although they believe that achieving a limited success, like cutting off the Baghdad–Basra roads, would result in the collapse of these defenses.[117]

Undoubtedly buttressed by decrypts of Iranian message traffic and possibly external intelligence sources, Iraqi intelligence had matters right. Khomeini ordered his forces to attack with the aim of capturing Basra and crushing the Iraqis in the south. On the evening of 23 December 1986, the Iranians launched Operation Karbala 4. Spearheaded by frogmen and commandos, backed by amphibious forces, the Iranians attempted to break out from the Fao Peninsula and capture Umm Qasr. The Iranians believed they could isolate Iraqi forces blocking the exits from Fao, cut Basra off from reinforcements, and eventually drive up the Euphrates to the Shi'a cities lying on the river. Alerted by signals intelligence about Iranian plans, the Iraqis had reserves well positioned. Thus,

---

[114] Shahram Chubin, "The Last Phase of the Iran–Iraq War: From Stalemate to Ceasefire," *Third World Quarterly* 11, no. 2 (1989), 5.

[115] O'Ballance, *The Gulf War*, 189.

[116] Transcript of a Meeting between Saddam Hussein and Military Advisers (24 September 1986) in SH-SHTP-D-000-411, Transcripts of Iraqi Leadership Meetings Discussing Responses to Iranian Missile Strikes, 12–24 September 1986.

[117] *SH-GMID-D-001-378, GMID Intelligence Report on the Current Military Situation in Iran.

the size and extent of the blow failed to surprise Baghdad. At the opening of the Iranian landings on the upper Shatt al-Arab, a deluge of Iraqi artillery fire blasted the attackers and in a three-day battle, the Iraqis defeated the Iranians. Iraq later claimed a 100:1 ratio of dead Iranians to Iraqis. Total casualties of up to 90,000, with 10,000 dead were later estimated to be the butcher's bill.[118]

One commentator on the war has noted, "Iraqi television showed piles of Iranian dead on the sandbars, beaches and in the date palm groves; and Iraqi combat commanders spoke, with some truth, of the waters of the Shatt al-Arab turning red with Iranian blood in what was described by [one general] as the 'three-day assault on a 25-mile front.'"[119] Tehran attempted to put the best face possible on the defeat. President Ali Khamenei described the operation as only "*a small operation with limited aims.*"[120]

Distractions from the ground war

Both sides continued to attack military and population targets as well as targets in the Gulf with the Iraqis leading the way. The defeat on the Fao Peninsula led to focusing on the air war and the War of the Cities. In one case, Iraqi fighters successfully shot down an Iranian C-130 transport carrying eight *Majlis* deputies, several senior military officers, and Khomeini's representative to the *Pasdaran*. By this point in the war, the balance in air-to-air capabilities had swung decisively in favor of the Iraqis. In 1980 and 1981, the Iranians had dominated the skies with their F-14s and F-4s. The Iraqis, with their MiG-21s and MiG-23s, had been at a distinct disadvantage. By 1986, even with the help of spare parts provided by Iran–Contra, the Iranians could keep only a small percentage of their fighters in operational condition.[121] Moreover, the Iranians had lost most of the pilots trained under the Shah, either through combat or due to purges and desertions. Now, in 1986, the Iraqis possessed upgraded MiG-23s, new MiG-25s, and French Mirage F-1s, all in substantial numbers.[122]

---

[118] Cordesman and Wagner, *The Lessons of Modern War, Volume II*, 247.

[119] O'Ballance, *The Gulf War*, 191.   [120] *Ibid.*, 191. Emphasis in original.

[121] An Iranian colonel who had deserted to Iraq claimed that in late 1986 the Iranian Air Force had fewer than fifty fighters operational, none of the Orions could be flown, and barely 10 percent of the C-130s were in commission. Navias and Wagner, *Tanker Wars*, 121.

[122] Iraq would take delivery of twenty-four MiG-29 Fulcrums from the USSR in April 1987.

Despite the forbearance marking the air and missile war for much of the year, fall 1986 saw a return of the War of the Cities that surpassed the carnage of previous years and lasted into 1987. In this case, Iraqi aircraft and missiles attacked explicitly civilian targets. A February 1987 Iraqi intelligence memorandum to Saddam describes in detail the forty-one-day bombing blitz between 9 January and 19 February. According to this memorandum, 860 aircraft sorties attacked fifty Iranian cities and inflicted somewhere between 5,000 and 14,000 fatalities on their populations.[123] The Iranians replied by firing Scud-Bs at Baghdad.[124] The resumption of attacks on population centers led to a meeting among Iraqi leaders in September on the subject of deterrence and the use of chemical weapons against civilian targets:

SADDAM:	This escalation is a result of the modern order where people fight and say: The Iranians or the Iraqis are escalating the situation ... there are Geneva agreements; they include sections prohibiting the use of chemical weapons.
VICE PRESIDENT:	The civilian areas.
SADDAM:	The civilian areas or the residential areas?
VICE PRESIDENT:	Residential.
TARIQ AZIZ:	Sir, Geneva protocol (24) prohibits using chemical weapons in any situation. Geneva agreement (48) prohibits shelling areas such as cities and places; I mean residents.
SADDAM:	I think what they meant by that is cities.
TARIQ AZIZ:	Yes cities. But there are specifics to military installations that are close to residential areas. This is a gray area. It is prohibited to attack cities and residential areas and districts.
SADDAM:	We hit their concentrations with force, we inflict [it] upon them ... Sometimes a person has a certain weapon and the war is about to end. He will say: use all of it, why keep it? The war is going to end anyway, hit them over the head while they are enemies, and we are still at war. When for example the 24th gets here don't hit them. But from now to the (24th), bomb them over their heads with all the bombs available. This is the personality of the person

---

[123] Memorandum from GMID to the President of the Republic RE: 9 January–19 February 1987 Bombing of Iranian Cities (25 February 1987) in *SH-GMID-D-001-379, Memoranda from GMID to the President of the Republic Regarding the Bombing of Iranian Cities, February 1987.

[124] Iran's ability to obtain Scuds on the "black market" or through its limited pool of allies severely restricted its options. Some Scud-B missiles were obtained through Syria, Libya, and North Korea. The inability to respond in kind helped drive Iran toward a program of self-reliance in the area of ballistic missiles. Kamran Taremi, "Beyond the Axis of Evil: Ballistic Missiles in Iran's Military Thinking," *Security Dialogue* 36, no. 1 (2005).

at war ... If it is just a continuous escalation process, it may lead to negative results in the psychological mobilization of public buildup. So how far are we going to escalate and what is the final result we will meet ... So in front of these two main choices, we decided not to retaliate. A third consideration ... is that [the Iranians] want us to broaden the [focus] of our air force instead of concentrating it. We don't have 5,000 aircraft to assign 1,000 ... to bomb cities and 4,000 to hit economic targets. It may be, one of their methods is to say the Iraqis have destroyed us and our economy, let's keep them busy with something.

TARIQ AZIZ: One thing you pointed to, your Excellency is that our blow to them was very effective and afflictive. This is a fact that can't be denied. Hitting the sensitive infrastructure.

SADDAM: To Iran the continuation of this operation is a disaster. And we, as a government, can realize the meaning of hitting a refinery, a power plant, or a bridge and to repeat hitting another refinery, a power plant or a bridge. After a year of these kinds of operations, the economic base will crumble especially when it is a country that is in ruins to start with, weak and unable to do quick repairs and suffering economic hardship which is clear to us. So the effectiveness of the blows is just as you stated. Any side of a conflict, when it is hit and hit, it has to react in some form or fashion or hit the cities or hit our economic infrastructure and this reaction is eminent ... I think it is beneficial [for] us to deal with the issue from the angle of the conflict that is reaching its final phase.

TARIQ AZIZ: ... Yes sir, the Iranians have proclaimed the decisive year and are rebuilding. It became clear to us and with no doubt that they want to engage in a battle or a series of battles to accomplish their military objective and then the political objective ... If we wish to retaliate for their bombing of cities, this time, we have to prove with documents that it is true they hit Basra; we should take the Red Cross to the residential area where they hit, and also, take the diplomatic delegation today where the missile hit in Baghdad, if there are military objections.

SADDAM: No to the contrary, we should proceed as such ...

DR. SA'ADUN: ... I totally agree with you sir that every wisdom and every attempt [at] self control by us is seen by the Iranians as a weak point. I think that is their perception of our total halt to hitting cities in the past, even though the reason we halted hitting cities is based on analysis and decisions and by a wise motive ... When they hit Baghdad the first time, they thought they succeeded by hitting Baghdad with missiles and killing a few of our citizens and our fear of the internal factors, we halted the bombing the cities as it looks now Mr. President. Our blows to the economic infrastructure are an effective action, and they are aware, if this action continues, it will be the demise of the Iranian regime ...

ALI HASSAN AL-MAJID: If we keep quiet and do not react, maybe the Iranians will interpret it as a sign of weakness. I agree with not hitting cities. But we have to announce when we hit any economic target that this is retaliation for hitting Baghdad or Basra. We gain in two [ways] with this. First the mobilization process will continue. And second, we could say, instead of noticing the Iranian side hit our cities, [that] we are retaliating by hitting economic and military targets ... Escalation is a must. If there is no retaliation, we will not benefit from escalation. I agree with the comrades in their analysis which is that hitting their cities at this time is not necessary. If the enemy continues and after a few missiles, we should announce that and start hitting Tehran because if they hit our capital, we hit their capital.

PILOT LT. GEN. HAMID SHA´BAN: ... Last week ... we accomplished great destruction on the Tabeer refinery, we inflicted on [the Iranians] losses totaling 400 dead as we saw the destruction from aerial photos. As you know sir, it was one of the most successful attacks. We also hit [Kharg] Island and we are sure it was a successful attack in spite of the distance to it. Iran exports a quarter of its oil production from the island. We also totally destroyed a huge storage facility as well as inflicted physical damage to the boats ... All of these attacks are a result of Iran escalating the attacks whether hitting Baghdad or Basrah, it doesn't make any difference, and the objective is the same, to affect the morale. As for hitting Tehran with our planes, we have plenty of information about the air defense systems around the city. We don't have to hit [Tehran] with our planes, we have plenty of other options. We could hit the city of Qom, for example, it is the head of the country and the head of the snake.

SADDAM: We could hit a big village ... The issue is now clear, our reaction is not going to be as they expect. We have to hold ourselves and continue our course, we are amongst our people. Our position has not changed.[125]

---

[125] Transcript of a Meeting between Saddam Hussein and Military Advisers (24 September 1986) in SH-SHTP-D-000-411, Transcripts of Iraqi Leadership Meetings Discussing Responses to Iranian Missile Strikes, 12–24 September 1986.

At this point, Iraq began receiving a shipment of Scuds from the Soviets – estimated at 300 – virtually the entire year's production. Aiming for Khomeini's regime, Saddam had created a program with North Korea's help to extend the range of these missiles, so they could reach Tehran and other targets deep inside Iran, which so far had been out of range. The first improved Scud, ironically dubbed *al-Hussein* after the martyr of Shi'a Islam, was successfully fired in early 1987.[126]

Meanwhile, a war against shipping in the Gulf intensified as Saddam made every effort to wreck Iran's ability to export its crude. The pattern of Iraqi attacks during the first half of the year suggests the limits of their capabilities. In January, Exocets struck five ships (one written off); in February, six (one written off); March, four (three written off); April, four (one written off); May, five (one sunk, one written off); in June, four (two written off); and in July, three (one written off). Iraqi strikes aimed at Kharg and its oil terminals significantly damaged the facility. In late January, the Iraqis even shut off transshipment of crude out of Kharg for a short time.[127] Yet, the Iranians escaped serious economic damage. By either buying or leasing tankers they were able to store substantial amounts (nearly 2.2. million tons) of crude off Sirri for those instances when they could not move oil from Kharg.

The Iraqis responded by launching a strike against the Sirri transshipment base. In August 1986, using Mirages as tankers for the strike aircraft, they slipped four Mirages down the Gulf to the area off Sirri.[128] There, they hit three tankers with four Exocets. Two of the missiles hit the *Azarpad*, which was loading, and forced the Iranians to beach her to prevent her from sinking.[129] In November, Iraqi attacks increased, hitting a new high of nine tankers. During the whole of 1986, the Iraqis struck sixty-two ships in Iranian waters with four of those sunk with a further eighteen written off.[130]

The Iranians could not attack the tankers or freighters the Iraqis were using, because they were shipping their oil through the Mediterranean and using Aqaba for supplies.[131] So the Iranian response was to continue to strike neutral shipping in the Gulf, much of it moving through the

---

[126] Zaloga, "Ballistic Missiles in the Third World: Scud and Beyond."; Frank Francona, *Ally to Adversary: An Eyewitness Account of Iraq's Fall from Grace* (Annapolis, MD, 1999), 13–14.

[127] Navias and Hooton, *Tanker Wars*, 115–116.

[128] Woods, *et al.*, "Interview with (Former) Major General 'Alwan Hassoun 'Alwan Al-Abousi, Cairo, Egypt, 13 November 2009."

[129] Navias and Hooton, *Tanker Wars*, 119.   [130] *Ibid.*, 116–117.

[131] Tankers picking up Iraqi oil were loading in either the Mediterranean or Aqaba, while military supplies were moving to Iraq mostly through the Red Sea and the Mediterranean.

territorial waters of the Gulf States. Nevertheless, the operational ready rates for their aircraft were so low they did far less damage than the Iraqis despite their more advantageous geographic position. From the perspective of World War II shipping, the tanker war had already reached impressive levels: one authority estimated that the two combatants had damaged beyond repair an amount of tonnage equal to 20 percent of the merchant ship tonnage the Allies had lost during World War II. Yet, less than one percent of the ships that entered the Gulf each month were attacked.[132] That figure, more than any other, underlines why the tanker war was regarded by the shipping industry and its insurers as not much more than a nuisance.

Conspiracies and Saddam's mind

Both the Iraqis and the Iranians believed the West and the Israelis were supporting the other side with extensive shipments of arms and supplies. Throughout the Iraqi documents dealing with the conflict are sprinklings of conspiracy theories involving the United States, Israel, the Iranians, and even the Soviets. In summer 1986, the director of general military intelligence, Major General Sabar Abd al-Aziz al-Duri, commented to Saddam:

The Americans want to stretch the war as this contributes to the national security of Israel. When Iraq is consumed with war and its problems, the American/Soviet agreement, if the war is stretched to the nineties, the Soviet Union will occupy Iran in agreement with the Americans. That is why they want to stretch the war for the purpose of destroying the Iranian economy through Afghanistan; Iran will not be able to confront this. Therefore, the Soviets are betraying us, likewise the Americans, all of them Sir.[133]

However, the Iranians expected the Americans would do everything in their power to help Saddam. By the summer of 1985, the United States, with the encouragement of Israel, became convinced that TOW and Hawk missiles could be sold to Iran in return for improved relations and the release of hostages held by Iranian proxies in Lebanon. The covert operation eventually expanded to include spare parts for other weapons and military intelligence on Iraq.[134] The scandal – known as Iran–Contra, in reference to the illegal diversion of funds to the anti-

---

[132] Navias and Hooton, *Tanker Wars*, 130–131.

[133] SH-SHTP-D-000-607, Transcripts of Meetings between Saddam, Vice President of the RCC Izzat Ibrahim Al-Tikriti, Minister of Defense Adnan Khairallah, and Army Chief of Staff Abd Al-Jawad Zinun During the Iraq–Iran War, 25 February 1985–31 July 1986.

[134] As Hezbollah and the other Iranian proxies in Lebanon released hostages, they simply kidnapped others, so in effect the whole Iran–Contra effort simply encouraged further bad behavior.

communist forces in Nicaragua, the Contras – in the end did little to improve relations or resolve the hostage crisis.[135]

Given their situation, the Iraqis tried to improve relations with the United States to open up the possibility of arms purchases. But in fall 1986, the Iran–Contra affair broke in Lebanon with a devastating impact in Washington to the astonishment of most in the West, but not to Saddam. In November, Saddam had an extended conversation with his cabinet ministers about what had transpired in Washington between the Reagan Administration and the Iranians:

TARIQ AZIZ: [The Iran–Contra affair] has impeded the Israeli and American preparation operations. At least definitely the American, as long as this scandal is going on and the inquiries, the examination and paralysis of the organizations that controlled this operation in this field, in this case the National Security Agency and the CIA, who are now under scrutiny and therefore cannot carry out any operations in current situation …

SADDAM: Our policies have gone well – have served their purpose and are still good. But the real American conspiracy – the real American–Israeli–Iranian conspiracy, and which they stated in their speeches, which it seems they know, and the Iranian administration is in agreement with … And one of the most important things that would produce such an agreement amongst them would be a conspiracy against us. Meaning that it has a positive influence on the war, otherwise they wouldn't agree … I do not imagine that the [United States] will stop conspiring against Iraq. I do not imagine it, even if the Democrats come to power … Common sense tells us we should be loved, because we are good people and we don't have – we don't harm anyone, we only harm those who harm us. For a long time now, we have been pruning all those who work on their own and sometimes surprise us with bad behavior and statements … In terms of Arab unity, we have come to understand it as a large tent with all our little tents inside it, and what we see is one tent. Meaning the large tent with the small one inside it, indicating the privacy of each small tent, while sharing in public opinion in the topics that strengthen all of us, and make us serious, national, country loving, handsome with clean hands … So then whenever there are conspiracies, they don't destabilize our policies and line, because we have become used to the circumstances of life …

[135] US Congress, House Select Committee to Investigate Covert Arms Transactions with Iran; US Congress, Senate Select Committee on Secret Military Assistance to Iran and the Nicaraguan Opposition, *Report of the Congressional Committee Investigating the Iran–Contra Affair: With Supplemental, Minority, and Additional Views* (Washington, DC, 1987); Tower, *et al.*, *The Tower Commission Report.*

they have taught us to be more patient and bear more kicks, but sometimes we worry that we will get tired of the game and react in an improper manner ... Because even if we fight on ten fronts once we focus on a person, we keep after him until we break his head, out of frustration ... So what if we are at war with Iran, if we discover that someone has been conspiring against us, we will slice his neck ... we will have him ... Of course the whole situation with Iran is not an understandable one. That is something else ... Well we must – in all truth we sometimes need to become like Christ. This whole Arab situation is so corrupted – and as much as one wants to get mad, the others must calm him down[136] ... and bear it ... But our national duty and the weakness and the state the Arabs are in, we are required as Arabs, even if three-quarters of their dirt falls on our heads, we must shake it off and move. It really is an unhealthy situation. In a situation that has this much money, humans should be cherished instead of dehumanized. Instead of cleaning them up, it is making them dirty, and instead of empowering them, it is making them weaker. So it is our duty, our duty to bear and bear, not for the sake of our situation, not for our sake. Thank God, there is nothing wrong with our situation, they are ones who are fearful, and want to stay out of our way, otherwise we can daily hit them one of Abu Zaid's hits ... let's say with the sandal[137] ... Ha, ha, ha![138]

In another meeting, Saddam examined the nature of the conspiracies the Americans were spinning. "What would a conspiracy look like? The continuation of the war and the high death toll, that is, a conspiracy and stopping the war, while maintaining a state of war is also a conspiracy." He then turned to the subject of why the Americans would not sell certain modern arms to the Kuwaitis:

The war either continues without ending which is the only state that Reagan can get (according to his speech) close to the desired influence in Iran. And in this, in all cases, it must not be at a cost to Iraq, and it can only be as a conspiracy against Iraq. What would a conspiracy look like? The continuation of the war and the high death toll, that is, a conspiracy and stopping the war, while maintaining a state of war is also a conspiracy ... [D]id that mean that they intended for Kuwait to be weak before the Iraqi threats and the Iranian danger? Did they want to corner Kuwait and put [it] in danger of Iran so that it would cooperate more with

---

[136] Saddam was referring to his anger at the Syrians and Libyans for supplying Khomeini with Scuds.

[137] Hitting someone with a shoe or a sandal is, of course, one of the great insults in the Arab world.

[138] SH-SHTP-D-000-609, Saddam and His Inner Circle Discussing the Iran–Contra Affair, Circa November 1986.

the [United States]? So you see, I am not just sitting there, [but] my mind is mulling over even the little things and taking them into account.[139]

Later in December, Saddam instructed his senior advisors, "What is needed at this stage is to focus on the existing relationship between the Iranian enemy, Israel, and [the] USA which exposes how the war happened, the role of Israel, and the interests of America in the war."[140]

But Saddam also found time to examine the plots and dangerous cultural tendencies among the Iraqi people. The connection between the Iraqi Shi'a and their coreligionists in Iran was of great concern. It also helped to explain why the Iranians seemed to be much better informed about what was going on in Iraq than the Iraqis were about events in Iran:

[There are] two important things in this conflict. The first is the intelligence operation. The enemy knows more about us than we know about him. The enemy knows in great detail about our theater of operations for some known reasons and some unknown reasons. As for me I do not know the enemy's capability and whether there is a foreign body that feeds him with intelligence.[141] Another aspect is the presence of this a popular link between our people and the enemy. I mean the presence of this strong sectarian, cultural tendencies and intellectual [links] between our people and the enemy, [which] has been used to the enemy's favor up to this point.[142]

From Saddam's point of view, such treacherous connections had clearly led to the military defeat that Iraq had suffered thus far in the war. The Iran–Contra scandal (or Iran-Gate, as many of the Iraq documents refer to the issue) plays an important role in the Iran–Iraq War not because the weapons or intelligence supplied to Iran as a result of an ill-conceived and poorly executed covert operation tipped the military balance. But because it provided tangible proof, in the mind of Saddam Hussein, of a long-running American conspiracy to undermine his regime. The reality, something only tangentially important to a good conspiracy theory and

---

[139] SH-SHTP-A-000-555, Saddam and the Revolutionary Command Council Discussing Reagan's Speech to the Nation on Iran–Contra Revelations (Part 2), 15 November 1986. For further discussions between Saddam and Tariq Aziz concerning the Iran–Contra affair, see SH-SHTP-A-000-715, Saddam and the Iraqi Command Discussing the Suicide of an Iraqi Minister, 20 December 1986.

[140] SH-SHTP-D-000-608, Minutes of Meeting between Saddam Hussein and the General Command of the Armed Forces on Turkey Using Guerilla Warfare and Blocking Iranian Terrorists, Raid Damages, Attack Plans, and America and Israel Supplying Weapons to Iran, November 1986.

[141] Saddam is probably referring to the United States.

[142] SH-SHTP-D-000-607, Transcripts of Meetings between Saddam, Vice President of the RCC Izzat Ibrahim al-Tikriti, Minister of Defense Adnan Khairallah, and Army Chief of Staff Abd al-Jawad Zinun During the Iraq–Iran War, 25 February 1985–31 July 1986.

rarely knowable at the time of the event, was that the US policy-makers never seriously considered Iraq or, for that matter, wider US policy objectives in the region.[143] These events had a significant impact on Saddam's views of the United States for the remainder of the war and beyond.

In a meeting with US Ambassador April Glaspie on the eve of Saddam's disastrous invasion of Kuwait, Saddam described recent American criticism of his policies as a continuation of the hostile policy revealed by Iran–Contra. "New events remind us that old mistakes were not just a matter of coincidence," he said.[144] A few months later, as Iraq found itself confronted by a broad, US-led military coalition, Saddam told advisors that his war against Washington had not begun in August 1990 or even in the months prior, but rather that "the war launched on us long before all this. It officially started in the 1986 meeting, and was exposed under the title 'Iran-gate.'"[145]

Conclusion

The year 1986 of the war strained each opponent extraordinarily. Both countries were in serious trouble economically and in terms of morale. A discussion among Saddam and his advisors underlines this:

SPEAKER 3:   We added a large number of soldiers to our troops as if we were about to face a major battle, therefore they started to attack us seven months ago . . .

SPEAKER 4:   They were very surprised by the size of our [forces], therefore, they started to face a major crisis inside, including their [air force] and that is the main reason for them to [cease operations].

SADDAM: I believe they were trying to buy time! They were using the political and morale crises that occurred in their country as an excuse to buy more time . . .

---

[143] US Secretary of State, George P. Schultz noted as the scandal broke that the whole Iran–Contra scheme "assaulted our own Middle East policy." Schultz, *Turmoil and Triumph*. For a view of how the scandal played in the Arab world, see Jerrold D. Green, "Arab Politics and the Iran–Contra Affair," in *The Middle East from the Iran–Contra Affair to the Intifada*, Robert O. Freedman, ed. (Syracuse, NY, 1991). For repercussions in Tehran, see Shireen T. Hunter, "After the Ayatollah," *Foreign Policy*, no. 66 (1987).

[144] "The Glaspie Transcript: Saddam Meets the US Ambassador," in *The Iraq War Reader: History, Documents, Opinions*, Micah L. Sifry and Christopher Cerf, eds. (New York, NY, 2003), 62.

[145] SH-SHTP-D-000-557, Saddam and His Senior Advisors Discussing Iraq's Historical Rights to Kuwait and the United States' Position, 15 December 1990. For a detailed analysis of how these events shaped Saddam's views, see Hal Brands, "Inside the Iraqi State Records: Saddam Hussein, 'Irangate', and the United States," *The Journal of Strategic Studies* 34, no. 1 (2011).

SPEAKER 4:   No we should not allow this to happen. Our economy is worsening; if they do not strike us again this month, when will they? Every day economically and politically we are worsening …

SADDAM: I must order you to slaughter them; after the spring season, we must prepare our fifth and first divisions to start moving forward, as we previously mentioned in the previous meetings. God willing we will slaughter them and you will do whatever you please with them.[146]

Shortly before that conversation, Saddam issued explicit orders to his commanders. A number of them are useful in understanding the Iraqi situation and state over the last two years of war:

- Avoid the excessive use of chemical weapons, except for striking vital targets at the strategic level … not to mention that the non-use of chemical weapons by the enemy against us is going to have [a] psychological impact on our troops when used by the enemy. The army staff headquarters must enforce the chemical [training] on our troops without any delay …
- Protect oil installations by all means since their destruction is going to give the enemy superiority at the economic level as well as other levels because the enemy does not need the technical [expertise] with which we can overcome the large number [of people he possesses] and at the same time, the need of their fighters to survive is less than ours …
- The Zionist enemy will always consider Iran in order to win it in a joint hostility to Iraq …
- Change the general type of Iraqi characteristics (general education, special education, the comprehensive conception of universe and life in addition to the high usage skills) in addition to aiming the majority of muzzles towards the enemy and reduc[ing] the administrative size of the armed forces is what we should always do and remember in order to balance the natural superiority factors [that our enemy possesses] (population and land capacity).[147]

What *was* clear was that Iran had not stopped trying to break Saddam's military forces by drowning them in a sea of blood. The defeat of Operation Karbala 4 in late December only presaged further Iranian attempts to capture Basra and deal the Iraqis a major political and military defeat. Khomeini was still firmly in control in Tehran, and he had no intention of ending the war on any other terms than the complete defeat of Iraq.

---

[146] *SH-SHTP-A-001-380, Recording of a Meeting between Saddam Hussein and High Ranking Iraqi Officials Regarding the Iran–Iraq War, 26 December 1986.
[147] *SH-PDWN-D-001-381, Various Memoranda and Reports between the Presidential Diwan, the Ministry of Defense, and Various Military Units.

9   1987–1988: An end in sight?

> So we have to continue to create hoopla that we support this resolution so and
> so 598. But we should not hurry [in] forging peace, because this [Resolution
> 598] will not produce peace. [P]eace will be achieved when Iran is
> incapable ... and this Iranian incapacity, God willing, is on its way to
> being achieved.[1]
>   – Saddam Hussein

The year 1987 began, as had the previous six years in the war, with no
end in sight. Yet within the next year-and-a-half, the outcome on the
battlefield – as well as Iran's almost complete isolation in the world –
finally forced Khomeini to agree to a humiliating peace. The international community's virtual silence after the USS *Vincennes* shot down
an Iranian airliner in July 1988 underlined for the Iranians that they had
no worthwhile friends, something even Khomeini could no longer
ignore.[2] Battlefield results during 1987–1988 should have been equally
clear to the true believers in Tehran. Their great winter offensive of 1987,
which had aimed at destroying the Iraqi Army and overthrowing the
Ba'athist regime, failed in a welter of blood and chemicals that devastated
the attacking troops. In the spring of 1988, Iraq went on the offensive
with refurbished forces and inflicted a series of devastating defeats. By
July 1988, the Iranian Army was in tatters, approaching collapse that, had
the war continued, might have threatened the stability of an Islamic
Republic already confronting serious internal difficulties.

A number of factors shaped the character of the war's final acts. First
was the increased sophistication of Iraqi tactical operations. By this point
in the war, Saddam was supporting military professionalism over political, tribal, and regional loyalties when choosing his senior commanders.
The resulting changes in the high command coupled with hard-earned

---

[1] SH-SHTP-A-001-217, Saddam and His Inner Circle Discussing the Performance of
Iraq's Army in Northern Iraq, Relations with the United States and Russia, and UN
Security Council Resolution 598, 21 January 1988.

[2] Khomeini's chief advisors still had to exert considerable pressure to persuade the
Ayatollah to agree to peace. Robin Wright, *In the Name of God: The Khomeini Decade*
(New York, NY, 1989), 179–202.

experience finally began to influence Iraq's fielded capabilities. The problems the army had run into during the winter 1987 Iranian offensive encouraged Saddam to bestow his trust and responsibility on competent, proven officers. This move was, at least for the short term, a significant break from Saddam's and the Ba'ath Party's traditional approach to the army. As a General Hamdani noted in his memoirs:

Saddam had a conspiratorial personality; he always conspired against the closest people to him because of his personal ambitions to dominate ... [Thus] he tried to undermine the army. One of my uncles, killed in an aircraft accident in 1971, told me that Saddam had once commented to him, "The Iraqi Army was the only force capable of conspiring against me. The only power we fear is this army will take over the party's leadership. The army is like a pet tiger." Therefore [Saddam] pulled out its eyes, teeth, and claws.[3]

Nevertheless, whatever improvements occurred in the Iraqi's battlefield performance, a pervasive distrust of his military commanders continued to mark Saddam's attitudes. Not for a moment did he forget that only the military could replace him. Immediately after the conflict's end, a dispute between senior commanders as to what had occurred in a major battle arose during a meeting presided over by the dictator. Saddam stepped in and informed the disputants:

the intelligence [branch][4] will settle this matter, because [it] was eavesdropping on you, [it] was assigned to eavesdrop on you. [It] was assigned to eavesdrop [on the corps]; this way we [could] find out whether the corps [was going] to comply with operational security.[5] I mean the corps responsible for execution, so every time we have a battle going, the intelligence officer instructs the technical departments to ensure the corps is adhering with guidelines, and we hear what they are [saying], whether such talk will reveal the plans.[6]

On the other side of the hill, the continuing split between Iran's professional military and the *Pasdaran* ensured that next to no learning was happening, and then mostly haphazardly. The Iranian successes in 1986 on the Fao Peninsula, a success resulting from operational surprise as much as from tactical virtuosity, led the revolutionary stalwarts in Tehran to believe they need not change the basic tactical and operational framework within which they were waging the conflict. Yet, already the

---

[3] Woods, *et al.*, *Saddam's War*, 90.

[4] In this case, the GMID.

[5] The intelligence branch was undoubtedly eavesdropping to ensure that the corps commander and his staff were also not planning to launch a coup.

[6] SH-SHTP-V-000-612, Saddam and Senior Military Officials Discussing Efforts to Retake the Majnun Area, circa late 1988.

Iranians had suffered huge numbers of casualties in their efforts to overthrow Saddam's regime, numbers increased by incompetence as well as Iraq's use of poison gas. In internal memoranda, Iraqi intelligence estimated Iranian losses from the beginning of the war through August 1986 as: killed or missing, 228,000–258,000; wounded, 405,000–415,000; prisoners of war, 18,000–20,000.[7]

According to Iraqi intelligence, contentious debates within the Iranian leadership on the operational way ahead began in late 1986. Baghdad believed that Iranian leaders remained split between the "more of the same" group, led by Rafsanjani, and a growing number of pragmatists, supported by the regular army.[8] In fact, this assessment incorrectly described Rafsanjani's position. According to numerous sources he was, at this point, quietly pushing for a series of pragmatic changes in both operations and strategy. It was the *Pasdaran*'s leadership, notably Mohsen Rezai, who argued that Fao validated the current approach.[9] Iraqi intelligence assessed that the Iranian public was "apprehensive," as a result of their government's inability to end the war, of the growing casualties and of Iraq's successful attacks on Iran's economy. One assessment went on that while "morale is still high" owing to recent, but ultimately limited, battlefield successes, it "will begin to deteriorate with the beginning of the winter season."[10] In terms of the patterns of history, what occurred during this period was analogous to events in 1918. Then, the great attacks of spring 1918 brought the German Army perilously close to victory by early June, but the extent of losses suffered in those battles contributed to the army's swift collapse in that fall.[11] Similarly, Iran's desperate efforts to achieve a decisive victory beginning

---

[7] *SH-GMID-D-001-382, Various Memoranda between GMID, IIS, and Military Attaches Regarding the Iranian Army and Navy, 1985–1986.

[8] SH-MISC-D-000-449, Report Detailing the Iranian Military Presence Along the Iraq–Iran Border, Iranian Current Affairs, Reports on Weapons Sales, and Analysis, 29 October 1986.

[9] Interestingly, during the heated political campaign in 2006, Rafsanjani released a previously secret 1988 correspondence between Rezai and Khomeini where Rezai argued that despite his earlier confidence, the war could not be won without a massive increase in conventional weapons and even atomic weapons. This contradicted Rezai's public position at the time and the postwar myth-making on the part of the Islamic Revolutionary Guard Corps. Frederic Wehrey, *et al.*, *The Rise of the Pasdaran: Assessing the Domestic Roles of Iran's Islamic Revolutionary Guards Corps* (Santa Monica, CA, 2009), 4. See also "RFE/RL Iran Report," *Radio Free Europe*, 9, No. 38 (2006).

[10] SH-MISC-D-000-449, Report Detailing the Iranian Military Presence Along the Iraq–Iran Border, Iranian Current Affairs, Reports on Weapons Sales, and Analysis, 29 October 1986.

[11] For a discussion of the flawed nature of the German offensives in spring 1918, see David T. Zabecki, *The German 1918 Offensives: A Case Study in the Operational Level of War* (New York, NY, 2006).

with the Fao offensive were to prompt a significant decline in Iranian morale by 1988.

The terminal decline of Iran's internal position was still not apparent at the start of 1987. The unwillingness of other Arab states to physically join in the war continued to disturb Saddam. Bitterness over the Syrian and Libyan betrayal only hardened as the war continued. A comment Saddam made in early 1987 underlined his contempt for his enemies in the Arab world:

As far as the war, we do not need Hafez al-Assad ... to fight with us. He cannot fight and he does not want to fight, and even if he is willing to fight, he is incapable of fighting, because this war only Iraqis will handle it. We do not need him for the war ... I hope this day will never come, wherein I have to shake al-Assad's dirty hand, with the blood of Iraqis on it.[12]

A year later, he was equally furious with the leaders of the major Arab states: "What can I tell you about Arabs? What can I tell you about Arab rulers? I hope I forget all their stories and [do] not remember any, not even one. With hopefully keeping my memory in other areas, but I hope God allows me to forget their shortcomings, even though they don't affect us." The dictator then acidly commented on Syrian claims they were only waiting for the Iraqis to show up before destroying Israel:

So we told Abd al-Salam, that these Syrians and I meant their government [consists of] liars, crooks and cowards and worriers. And to prove it we would, as the old Iraqi proverb says, "show up so fast that our heads would arrive before our feet" at whatever place they needed us to go to liberate Palestine and that we would go in front of [the Syrians] and not even wait and walk with them.[13]

---

[12] SH-SHTP-A-001-023, Saddam Hussein and Ba'ath Party Members Discussing the Iran–Iraq War, 6 March 1987. In many ways, Assad was trapped by his unpopular decision to support Iran in 1980. The initial logic was to avoid being caught between a post-Camp David "victorious" Israel and a victorious Iraq. As the war dragged on, Assad needed an ending that did not leave a vengeful Saddam in place – regardless of the outcome. Patrick Seale, *Asad: The Struggle for the Middle East* (Berkeley, CA, 1988), 357–359. King Hussein of Jordan worked furiously behind the scenes in 1986 to reconcile his Ba'ath neighbors. With the help and encouragement of Soviet diplomats, Saddam and Assad met in the Western Iraqi desert in late April 1987, but came to no major agreement. The biggest result was a frantic effort on Iran's part to offer additional economic incentives (mainly oil) to Syria to remain its most important regional ally. See Eberhard Kienle, *Ba'th v. Ba'th: The Conflict between Syria and Iraq, 1968–1989* (New York, NY, 1990), 166–169. For Iraq's view on the behind-the-scenes deals at the time, see *SH-GMID-D-001-383, GMID Intelligence Report on Syria, 16 December 1985–20 March 1986.

[13] SH-SHTP-V-000-589, Saddam Hussein and Military Officials Discussing the Iran–Iraq War and the Al-Qadisiyyah Battle, circa late 1988.

Another cloud appearing on the horizon in the waning years of the war was what, in just over a decade, would eclipse the influence of the Ba'ath as the animating force in regional politics. In a conversation about the rise of Islamist movements (specifically the Muslim Brotherhood) in Sudan, Egypt, and Syria, Saddam cautioned his staff that because Iraq was already in a struggle against an enemy that clothed itself in religion, "I don't believe it would be wise to engage in a clash with the religious current in the Arab world when it is possible to avoid it." He then added,

[i[f they want to clash with us we will clash with them, if they get close to power we will expose them, and if they are in power and open fire on us we will open fire on them. But if there is a chance of avoiding [placing] ourselves in a direct clash position with them during [this] striving period, this would be beneficial.

Perhaps anticipating the risks ahead, Saddam uttered a variation of the old saying "keep your friends close and your enemies closer." When the inevitable happens, he told Tariq Aziz, and Khomeini's religious government falls, Iraq should "not let the [Islamists] feel that the collapse of Khomeini means their collapse." An unidentified advisor picked up on Saddam's logic and added "the [Islamists] agree with us regarding many things" and because "the religious current is not only directed against the Ba'ath ... it is directed towards the prevalent circumstances in the Arab world, which no one is satisfied with" it may prove useful.[14]

The second half of 1986 was a transitional period in the war for Saddam. Despite setbacks at Fao and later Mehran, his confidence in the quality of his force was increasing. However, at the same time the chronic impact of the long war exposed major cracks in his ability to control Iraq's disparate populations. Heavy casualties and setbacks at the front forced Saddam to deal directly with the decline of morale in the army and throughout the Iraqi populace. Despite domestic concerns and in a move that set the military context for the final two years of war in July 1986, Saddam recommitted to a rational military approach to recent setbacks during a speech at a congress of the Ba'ath. In a move that exposed him to domestic pressures over casualties, Saddam authorized expanded infantry-based forces to balance Iraq's heretofore armor-heavy counterattacks.[15]

That the Iraqi ground and air forces had been expanding since the conflict's onset suggests the extent of the strain of the war on Iraq. In

---

[14] SH-SHTP-A-001-167, Saddam and Ba'ath Party Members Discussing the Status of the Party in the Arab World and Exploitating of the Muslim Brotherhood as an Ally, 24 July 1986.

[15] Ibrahim al-Marashi and Sammy Salama, *Iraq's Armed Forces: An Analytic History* (New York, NY, 2008), 165–167.

1980, the army had numbered 190,000 soldiers; at the beginning of 1988 it counted nearly 1,000,000 men under arms. In 1980, it had possessed 1,900 tanks; in 1988 6,310. In 1980, the air force and army had possessed 339 combat aircraft and 231 helicopters; by 1988 those numbers had grown to more than 500 combat aircraft and 422 helicopters.[16]

The failure of Khomeini's victory pledge: the battles of 1987

By 1987, the Republican Guard had grown steadily, from six brigades in early 1985 to eighteen brigades.[17] During late summer and fall 1986, the Iraqis had also pulled a number of the regular army's better divisions out of the frontlines to retrain and re-equip them to higher standards of tactical performance than the remainder of the army. Included in this refurbishment were the 3rd, 6th, and 10th Armored Divisions and the 1st and 5th Mechanized Infantry Divisions. To keep staffing this force with higher quality candidates, Saddam called up large numbers of university students. That move affected Iraq's privileged classes, but also provided better raw material from which to build combat units than had been the case earlier.

The Iraqis had developed relatively sophisticated defense systems at the operational level. They relied on regular army divisions to hold the frontline in heavily fortified positions, particularly around Basra and along the valleys issuing out of the Zagros Mountains with avenues of approach that threatened Baghdad. Backing up the regular army was an increasingly well-trained and well-equipped Republican Guard, which by early 1987, had grown to a corps. For the most part, the guard deployed its units near Baghdad, but the layout of Iraq's highways and railroads allowed it to rapidly redeploy to areas threatened by the Iranians.

The Iraqis' defeat of the Iranians at the end of 1986, however, was only the beginning of a sustained battle around Basra, in which the Iranians threw in formation after formation desperately trying to break the Iraqi hold on the city and open up the way for an exploration up the River Euphrates. The Iranians appear to have believed that if they captured Basra and the Iraqi forces on the lower Euphrates collapsed, this would

---

[16] Farouk-Sluglett and Sluglett, *Iraq since 1958*, 272. The Iranian forces had expanded to a similar extent, but its emphasis was on the *Pasdaran*.
[17] Woods, *et al.*, *Saddam's War*, 77–78; Pollack, *Arabs at War*, 219.

lead, domino style, to the fall of Saddam's regime thereby fulfilling Khomeini's New Year's victory pledge.

Khomeini's declaration, however, notwithstanding the success of the Fao operation, was not supportable by the facts on the ground. Perhaps it was indicative of how disconnected the ayatollah was from the realities of the war. His chief subordinate, Rafsanjani, had the onerous task of "reinterpreting" what his boss had really meant. Khomeini's declaration, Rafsanjani noted, "did not mean that the war will come to an end … we hope to gain more considerable victories this [coming year] … And we believe that when all the supporters of Saddam Hussein have become disappointed … then victory will be ours."[18] Despite his reasonable caveats, Rafsanjani's later statements make clear that Tehran was incapable of rationalizing the relationship between ends and means. In October 1986, Rafsanjani commented that one of the lessons of the Fao victory was that Iran should stop ad hoc operations and instead carry out "an extensive and destiny-making offensive." The aim "is to reach our objectives through a huge movement, *without shedding too much blood.*"[19]

The next stage in the Iranian offensive and the first battle of 1987 began on 6 January with Operation Karbala 5.[20] The Iranians concentrated a force that numbered between 150,000 and 200,000 soldiers, a combination of some of the better *Pasdaran* units, and the usual militia forces. The attacking units possessed better equipment than those in previous offensives, and the Iranians made some effort to ensure that experienced officers and non-commissioned officers (NCOs) spearheaded the offensive.[21] Large arms purchases from abroad aided the mobilization efforts considerably. The Iranians had bought well over $1 billion in arms from the Chinese alone, as well as substantial imports from Eastern Europe.[22] However, the ability to exploit breakthroughs remained problematic. The major factor in the initial Iranian success was that Karbala 5 followed so closely on the heels of Karbala 4. Moreover, early January brought bad weather, which the Iraqis may have assumed would prevent the Iranians from attacking. As was the case for many of their offensives, the Iranians

---

[18] Hiro, *The Longest War*, 177. The last comment underlines the extent to which Iran believed Iraq could only withstand Iran's efforts through the support of external powers.

[19] Gary G. Sick, "Iran's Quest for Superpower Status," *Foreign Affairs* 65, no. 4 (1987), 706. Emphasis added.

[20] Gideon Gera, "The Iraqi–Iranian War," in *Middle East Contemporary Survey: Iraq, 1976–1999, Volume XI: 1987*, Itamar Rabinovich and Haim Shaked, eds. (Tel Aviv, 1988), 181.

[21] Ward, *Immortal*, 278.

[22] Gera, "The Iraqi–Iranian War," 180.

achieved a substantial initial success. The offensive came on both sides of Basra, and attacking forces punched through frontline Iraqi defenses in a number of places. Immediately to the south of Fish Lake, the attackers achieved major gains as Iraqi defenses crumbled and a path behind Basra appeared to be opening. Farther south, the Iranians made gains that brought them close to the city's suburbs.

As with many cases previously, the incompetence of Iraqi higher-level command contributed to the surprise. Apparently the corps commanders defending Basra, both of whom were Ba'athists and Saddam's cronies, had competed to make themselves look good in the dictator's eyes in the reports they submitted about the "success" of their troops during Karbala 4:

In order for the III Corps commander [General Tala al-Duri] to prove that he had defeated the Iranian attack, he gave some figures for Iranian losses – a large number that was completely unrealistic. General Maher Abd al-Rashid [VII Corps commander] ... [wanted] to be Saddam Hussein's favorite, and so he gave an even larger number ... The III Corps Commander [then] came back and said, "We made sure we doubled the losses of the enemy." What happened is that Saddam Hussein felt satisfied because of the large losses for the Iranian Army following Fao. To make matters worse the Iranians then came back with propaganda that ["Karbala 4"] was, "The attack of a million." So, to the strategic leaders back in Baghdad, the corps commanders repeated that they had caused all this damage in the sectors of the 6th and 3rd Divisions. Such losses would obviously affect the capability of the Iranian forces all along the border, so everyone relaxed ... [T]he peace of mind that the enemy had suffered such big losses led people to think that Iran would need at least six months to plan for a major attack. In the meantime, after just two weeks, the enemy staged an extremely sudden attack.[23]

The main attack, south of Fish Lake, broke through into the suburbs of Basra; it was only after fierce fighting that the Iraqis were able to contain the attackers and throw them back.[24] The Iranians penetrated five of the city's six defensive rings. Both sides suffered heavy casualties.[25] But well after the prospects for success had disappeared, the Iranians continued to throw fresh forces into the killing zones the Iraqis had established. Khomeini's demand that his forces achieve victory by March undoubtedly contributed to reinforcing failure. Only after the situation north of Basra threatened the city, did Saddam wake to the danger. Republican Guard units immediately trundled down the Baghdad–Basra highway to meet the offensive. Two of the Iraqi divisions in the area, the 3rd Armored and the 5th Mechanized Divisions, were effective units, but

---

[23] Woods, *et al.*, *Saddam's War*, 80.   [24] Gera, "The Iraqi–Iranian War," 181.
[25] Pollack, *Arabs at War*, 223.

the other three divisions defending the area were second class. Still, the Iraqis fought well with the support of heavy doses of mustard and other types of gas. Nevertheless, the Iranian superiority in numbers drove the defenders steadily back, while adding to the confusion and uncertainty in rear areas.

Reinforcing Republican Guard units arrived to chaos. General Hamdani, serving on the staff of a Republican Guard division, recorded his impressions of the situation:

When we arrived, Diej had just fallen to the enemy as well as Khasm, Buhaira, Kut Sawadi, and the eastern shore of the Fish Lake. Baghdad [Republican Guard Forces Command] and the 2nd Republican Guard Armored Division were determinedly pushing toward the east of the battleground, while the 11th Division responsible for this front was fighting bravely . . .

The time of [our] attack was decided as 1500 hours of that day, while the units were moving slowly and with great difficulty because of the blockage created by the frontal combat and administrative units. Entering the battleground at Jasim before nightfall we needed a miracle, let alone trying to be there at 1500 hours to start the battle. The whole situation was based on imprecise information, since the deputy chief commander was under the impression that the roads were open (they were on maps, but not in reality). Poor judgment on behalf of the general command, embarrassment and optimism were all additional factors in keeping the top command unclear about the situation . . . Our forces succeeded in halting the enemy's thrust and the fighting shrunk to ten kilometers from Shalamja [Shalamcheh] and seven from the Fish Lake, having various depths at various points. We were surprised by the enemy's conduct and could not understand what they wanted from this tiny sliver of breached sector . . . There were more than 5,000 artillery pieces on both sides and the battle raged to one of costly attrition.[26]

In some areas, the horror of the battlefield was extraordinary. In a conversation with the authors, General Hamdani described his experiences:

The situation worsened to the point where my commander, [Brigadier General] Ahmed Hammash, could not use the phone to talk to higher headquarters and get support. No one was able to reach a phone or even a communication station, because of the extensive [shelling] and the Iranian presence . . . At one point an armored personnel carrier arrived at our headquarters. I went to the driver, who was a captain in one of the companies. They were desperate [terrified and disoriented]. I told them to keep moving to the front. He just looked at me without answering me. So I joined him and again told them to move and they did until we reached al-Da'ich, the first line. Nothing but massacred tanks and dead people surrounded the area – tens of people every 100 meters [and] tens of

[26] Hamdani, *Memoir*.

tanks burning. The situation ... was the same as I had only seen in the movies ... I got out and started looking for division headquarters ... There were tens of soldiers on the area above ground [of the headquarters], most injured and bleeding. You could see their blood dripping through the stairs in the structure.[27]

The Iraqis eventually halted the Iranian offensive by using chemical weapons extensively. Even as using them had become routine, Saddam was in a strange position, at least for him, in having to restrain his more enthusiastic colleagues.[28] In a series of March 1987 conversations with senior ministers, one advisor recommended ramping up Iraq's attacks on Iranian cities: "Even if there are international interventions ... we should not cease such severe blows." Specifically, he suggested that,

[t]he situation is ripe for us to choose an important city ... of Iran and attack it with a chemical blow, in a very violent and severe manner. I mean ... [we] should wipe it from existence, and whatever happens, happens ... we have the capability ... We should mount a heavy chemical blow that will be the equivalent of an atomic weapon ... to annihilate the city totally, that no living soul will survive.

However, Saddam was not so sure: "This matter crossed our mind that these are one type of weapon that we might need to use in our attacks." He went on to explain that a review of Iraq's chemical weapons policy "resulted in our belief that this weapon is strategic and we should not rule out its use. However, we should be very careful in our timing for its usage ... The current situation does not call for the use of this weapon now." To distinguish between "strategic" targets and operational or purely military ones, Saddam later assured his advisors that "we have not stopped using the chemical weapon. With regard to military formations ... this is continuous ... we are using it."[29]

Yet in another conversation, which appears to be from the same day, Saddam played the role of chemical enthusiast:

UNIDENTIFIED   I have a military question, Sir. Is the chemical weapon as
  MALE: effective as we think ... ?

---

[27] Woods, et al., Saddam's War, 81–82.

[28] According to Anthony Cordesman, the Iraqis used chemicals extensively during this period: December 1986, mustard gas (air delivered) near Umm arRas (heavy casualties); January–February 1987, mustard gas (air delivered), near Khorramshahr (disrupted buildup); February–April 1987, nerve and mustard (air and artillery delivered), near Basra (heavy casualties; and April 1987, mustard (air delivered) near Basra (disrupted buildup). Anthony H. Cordesman, *Iraq and the War of Sanctions: Conventional Threats and Weapons of Mass Destruction* (Westport, CT, 1999), 529 (Table 517.521).

[29] SH-SHTP-A-000-896, Saddam and Other Government Officials Discussing the State of the Country During the Iran–Iraq War and the Use of Chemical Weapons, 6 March 1987.

SADDAM: Yes, effective on he who does not use the mask at that
                   moment . . .
UNIDENTIFIED   You mean it exterminates by the thousands?
MALE:
SADDAM: Yes, it exterminates by the thousands . . . it exterminates by the
                   thousands and restrains them from drinking and eating . . .
                   and leaving the city for a period of time until it is fully
                   decontaminated . . . he cannot sleep . . . eat or drink . . . they
                   [must] leave . . . naked.

In this second conversation, an unidentified advisor offered a note of practical, not strategic or moral, caution:

I agree in everything we discussed, but as far as chemical weapons . . . we should be economic as much as possible when using it at the front because it is possible that some strikes at the front may not have the effectiveness of the weapon we envision . . . due to the soldiers' position in the front [and] the Iranians almost [all] started to use the mask.[30]

The decisive factors for Iraqi success around Basra lay in superior firepower, discipline, and training. As early as 19 January, the Iranians probably realized they were not going to capture the city. On that date, Rafsanjani declared that Basra was not the aim of Karbala 5, but the "demoralization of the Iraqi regime and the partial destruction of its war machine" was.[31] Nevertheless, the Iranians persisted. But once they lost surprise, they had little chance against Iraqi firepower and the Republican Guard. The Iranian casualty figures for the January offensive were appalling, ranging from 70,000 to 80,000, or slightly less than 50 percent of the attacking force.[32] Iraqi casualties were high, but nowhere near the same level.

Sporadic fighting continued throughout February into April.[33] The Iranian aim was, as Rafsanjani declared, to inflict the maximum casualties possible on the Iraqis. In fact, it was their side that was suffering the heavier losses, which even with superior numbers, they could ill afford.[34]

---

[30] SH-SHTP-A-001-023, Saddam Hussein and Ba'ath Party Members Discussing the Iran–Iraq War, 6 March 1987.

[31] Gera, "The Iraqi–Iranian War," 181.   [32] Pollack, *Arabs at War*, 223.

[33] In April, the Iraqis reported that the Iranians used phosgene gas in an attack, but such use never reached the extent of Iraqi use of such weapons. SH-GMID-D-001-125, General Military Intelligence Directorate Correspondence About Iranian Use of Chemical Weapons on Iraqi Troops in the Battlefield, 14 April 1987.

[34] A 13 April memorandum detailing Iranian losses during the first two weeks of April noted that the Iranians sent 13,500 troops into the Battle of East Basra (Operation Karbala 5) and suffered 60 percent casualties "in addition to losses resulting from strikes deep into enemy [territory] as well as special strikes [euphemism for chemical attacks]. Despite the huge effects these strikes had on influencing the course of the

There were no breakthroughs; advances occurred on the order of hundreds of meters. It was Iraqi firepower that made the difference, because Iraqi counterattacks did not seem to have improved in their effectiveness.[35] The Iraqis were still struggling with implementing combined-arms warfare.

But there was an equally important issue beyond the battlefront that alarmed Saddam. After the Iranian offensive petered out, he held a discussion with senior Ba'ath leaders at the beginning of March 1987. Portions of the discussions centered on the difficulties the Iraqis were having maintaining morale as well as with drafting young Iraqis,[36] but more worrisome was that the number of deserters from frontline units was reaching epidemic proportions. Three weeks after that discussion, an Iraqi general would report that between 1 December 1986 and 20 March 1987, 24,952 Iraqi soldiers had deserted.[37] Because Iraqi losses on the battlefield continued to mount, Saddam was confronting significant problems on the home front in the regime's ability to recruit while the holding down of the numbers of deserters and discouraging Iraqis from sheltering those deserters was becoming more difficult.

Trying to energize, buck up, and perhaps intimidate the party faithful, the dictator noted:

To be more specific [in discussing Iraqi mobilization methods], the most effective method is the passion method, which works on the public's mentality, soul, and heart, not through analyzing that is what we require. We need to influence parents and families to reach a level wherein they force their sons to

battles, little information is known about their actual results." Memorandum from GMID to the General Command of the Armed Forces RE: Enemy Losses (13 April 1987) in SH-GMID-D-000-266, General Military Intelligence Directorate (GMID) Correspondence About Iranian Military Sites and Plans During the Iraq–Iran War, 1–14 April 1987.

[35] For a discussion of factors lying behind the Iranian failure, see Pollack, *Arabs at War*, 224.

[36] Morale in Iran was no better. As an Iraqi observer commented later, "Most importantly, though, is that the charm of the revolution and the charisma of their leader, Ayatollah Khomeini, languished. The losses and the amount of destruction inflicted on the Iranian economy by the war of the tankers were a factor, and in addition, Iraq had destroyed much of their economy ... Moreover, the willingness of Iranian soldiers to sacrifice themselves weakened considerably." Woods, *et al.*, *Saddam's War*, 85. For more on Iraqi morale, see SH-SHTP-A-001-023, Saddam Hussein and Ba'ath Party Members Discussing the Iran–Iraq War, 6 March 1987.

[37] SH-SHTP-A-000-634, Saddam and Military Corps Commanders Discuss the Great Day and Great Harvest Battles, Analyze Iranian Intentions, and Discuss Iranian Efforts to Capture Basra, 28 March 1987. In the late March meeting, the number of deserters did not alarm Saddam, perhaps because, as the discussion below makes clear, there were other issues vexing him about the army's performance.

go and fight. The mother needs to say to her son: "Pick up your weapon and go and fight, otherwise you are not welcome in my home and I will not feed you." ...

If you would ask me, "How would you measure the difference?" I would say, "It is like the difference between an individual, when we tell him that we killed his son because he [deserted]," [this individual] then spits on his [dead] son's face ... Moreover, [the family] will say, "[we] refuse to bury him." [However], there is another type of individual who would actually hide their son, support him, and say to him, "I am glad what you are doing. Wait until everything settles down and then join the army." We must [eliminate this] contradiction and retain progression, mental and humane progression ... I mean we must execute the number of those individuals between the ages of 18 and 25 ... However [some] parents are in denial ... now even after seven years, the family denies their son betrayed [his country] ... they must be ill. Our responsibility is to change those ill-people mentally and emotionally.

At this point, a certain Commander Mezban Khider Hadi chimed in to comment that:

As far as ... 1982, we did not lose our war, or our national land, although it is Arab land; it is not Iraqi land. We succeeded in achieving our goal, however, in Fao, we lost and we were able, thanks to your leadership to convert [defeat] into victory. The whole world talked about the Iraqi victory, and the role of the Iraqi president towards his nation and his effectiveness in mobilizing the right quality which led to our victory.

Never one to miss the chance to rewrite history, Saddam replied, "People explain the meaning of [victory and defeat differently]. The true meaning for us as commanders [is] that the people observed the resistance and strength of the Iraqis [in fighting] for their country; although we lost Fao, we retained our strong will and our resistance."[38]

These worries about Iraqi morale, particularly among the troops, help to explain the propaganda campaign the regime launched to remind the population of Arab greatness as well as the role Iraq had played and would play in the future. In a stridently Islamic speech to Ba'ath Party branches in mid-April, Saddam emphasized that role:

Since [God] assigned the Arab *Ummah* with all heavenly missions, this means He decided that there is no *Ummah* more capable of this mission [than] the Arab *Ummah* ... There is no movement, revival, religion, or cause that can reach its level without [a] cadre that is psychologically, intellectually, and practically prepared for this role ... [God] is going to express the essence of this mission through human beings ... He did not send any more prophets or assign anyone

---

[38] SH-SHTP-A-001-023, Saddam Hussein and Ba'ath Party Members Discussing the Iran–Iraq War, 6 March 1987.

with this mission. I believe in my full conscience that God assigned the Iraqis, this generation, with carrying the Prophet's mission in an era with no prophets in order to awaken the *Ummah*'s conscience.[39]

In late March, Saddam held an extensive lessons-learned discussion to examine the army's tactical mistakes over the past several months, what needed to be done to repair those weaknesses, and the implications for coming operations. Throughout, he was caustic about how some Iraqi commanders and units had performed:

SADDAM:	[Referring to the VII Corps Sector] . . . [the Iranians] failed to provide momentum in all directions as they should have done. So what happened? . . .
GENERAL NIZAR AL-KHAZRAJI, ARMY CHIEF OF STAFF:	Sir, if we wanted to go back to old battles, I believe that the Iranian enemy was targeting the VII Corps during the battles of the Great Day. Basically, the first priority was to finish the VII Corps. The effort toward the III Corps in order to detain the biggest possible number of troops was serious. If the VII Corps was gone, we would not have been able to fight in Basra sir . . . Right now sir what are the expected things? In my opinion the central direction and the central concern for the enemy would still be the direction of Basra, the III Corps with all its divisions, the northern wing of the corps, the southern wing of the VI Corps, and the northern direction of the VII Corps. This means Basra, north of it to the borders, part of the VI Corps, the southern part until the borders, and the northern part of the VII Corps would be the center of concern. If the enemy were to carry out limited operations or missions, it would be aiming towards weakening our presence in this direction. After that the enemy would carry out a direct action or a semi-direct action, and this would be carried out from the northern part of the III Corps, inside the III Corps sector, or from the southern part of the VI Corps. If the enemy were to do such a thing, they would do that so that they can pull some of our deployments and troops from in front of the

[39] SH-SHTP-A-000-618, Saddam Hussein Speech to the Ba'ath Party Branch in Mosul, 12 April 1987.

> III Corps, so that they can carry out an action
> later on in the III Corps Sector or in these
> directions that we indicated. The direction
> stays the same. In my opinion, this is the
> central and the important direction to end the
> war.[40]

As the discussions continued, the army's chief of staff then made an astonishing admission:

Sir, our soldiers are not used to digging. We made a habit for them to come and sit [on prepared positions]. I have seen brigades and I have said to soldiers: "Why do you fight like that?" They would say to me, "They did not prepare [positions] for me. The bulldozers did not come and build us [defensive berms] so that we could sit down and fight." This [situation] does not exist in any other army in the world. Once the battalions, companies, cavalries, and brigades show up, they should start digging and within two to three hours, everyone should be done with their defensive site.[41]

After this admission of the army's inability to get its soldiers to follow a basic principle at the heart of military discipline, namely to dig defensive positions when in combat, Saddam rounded on his generals:

I want specific analysis. This means measured analysis. It means it should be established on an [argument]. The [argument] could be logical, scientific or both. For example, why does the enemy surprise us? Do you have fewer weapons than the enemy? ... No excuses shall be accepted by me from any leader, nor will you accept any excuses from a commander [u]nless the enemy secures a superiority against him with the ratio of three to one.[42] It has to be clear to the commanders and superiors that unless the enemy outnumbers you with a three to one ratio, we will not accept anything from him but a confession that he is a coward or that he failed to [conduct] his battle properly ... From now on I will not accept any illogical statement from a comrade. One of the comrades said to me, "They achieved superiority." I said to him, "Silence," or something with the same meaning during my comment. I said to him, "The intelligence had informed you with the number of people who were going to show up in that place." I will not accept any incorrect statements ...

Is the enemy's training better than our training? Are they better armed than us? Is their psychological situation in comparison [pauses]. Everything should be wrapped together when it comes to the commanders. Your responsibility is to prepare the [soldiers] for the fight. My responsibility is to provide you with the

---

[40] SH-SHTP-A-000-634, Saddam and Military Corps Commanders Discuss the Great Day and Great Harvest Battles, Analyze Iranian Intentions, and Discuss Iranian Efforts to Capture Basra, 28 March 1987.

[41] *Ibid.*

[42] The traditional ratio required for the offense to overcome the defense in battle has usually been calculated at three to one.

people and my job is to make sure that you will not be shorted in regards to weapons . . .

My responsibility requires me to be on the right side when it comes to analysis and strategic leadership. Your job and the responsibility of the rest of the division [commanders] and the brigade commanders is how to use all of these pieces in order to create a team spirit that could achieve the [desired] results . . . Whatever had happened in [location unclear], it will not be allowed again! [The commander] knew that he was going to be under attack and the enemy did not [possess] superiority against him. We are not going to sit here and babysit people! Not all people do things in this manner. They do not care about a brother, a friend, or a mustache . . .

I want every leader to cancel the excuses and become a soldier. Ba'ath and human issues, leave them alone! You should tell him, "You are a commander, [and] this is how many weapons that you have, these are your preparations, this is your food, and this is your drink. The enemy is in his worst situation. Fight him."

The dictator then turned to what he regarded as an unspoken conspiracy among his generals to cover for and excuse the mistakes of their comrades in the fight against the Iranians:

I notice that the military spirit is vanishing among you and this is because of the human relationships that were built up during the circumstances of war. So instead of it working in a positive direction, sometimes it is becoming more active towards the negative direction. This means that the commander . . . feels safe from judgment. "Oh I have this guy to cover for me." This is not good in the military life! This is not proper! . . . Instead of sitting around until they come to you on the hill and achieve superiority with a ratio of five-to-one on an isolated hill, go after him, according to intelligence information. Right now we have connected everything with one person. This person is Ali Hassan al-Majid. All of the state's authorities and their private agencies are connected to him . . . Go to the enemy and strike him. Wherever they tell you he is at, they tell you that the enemy is in a village, go to the enemy and hit him in that village . . . Any army, [which] will not keep confronting until the last moment of the war, will also not be considered a true fighting leadership. Our army is capable of being this way . . . No one has the features of the Iraqi fighter. Let's just prepare them in a real way.[43]

The discussions turned to current matters in terms of the defense of Baghdad, but then quickly led to an explosion from Saddam as to what was really important in defending Iraq and what was not. An Iraqi general commented:

Similar to what was indicated by [the] commander of the III Corps, some activities that would catch the attention had appeared. They consist of constant

---

[43] SH-SHTP-A-000-634, Saddam and Military Corps Commanders Discuss the Great Day and Great Harvest Battles, Analyze Iranian Intentions, and Discuss Iranian Efforts to Capture Basra, 28 March 1987.

movement of motorized convoys in critical timings, right before the sunset and at night ... We believe these activities are part of a trick, but we have to be cautious that they might use a trick to deceive us and carry out a real [attack] ... Exactly like we had indicated in our reports, the enemy does not possess the capability of resuming their large scale attacks with the same momentum of the large scale attacks that were carried out previously, right after the battles of the Great Day and the Great Harvest.

Another general then chimed in: "Right now we agree that the dangerous strategic goal for the enemy is the city of Basra. Basra directly and Basra indirectly ... There is no serious target that would tip the strategic scale other than this important city." The comment immediately caught Saddam's attention. "Basra is more important than Baghdad?" The general replied: "Not important, it is just closer to the heart [of the Iraqi people]." That was simply too much for Saddam, who furiously rounded on the unfortunate officer:

No it is not closer! As the leader of the Iraqi state, I am telling you that Basra is not closer to my heart ... I am telling you that if Basra were to fall, we will fight, and if they were to reach the gate of the Republican palace in Baghdad, we will fight them and push them back to the border ... But the theory if they were to take over Basra, it would be the end of the world; it would not be the end of the world. Even if they were to take it, it would not be the end of the world.[44]

Despite increasingly optimistic intelligence reporting on Iran's weakening condition, Saddam still felt the need to improve the talent in Iraq's high command.[45] As the above discussions in late March indicate, Saddam was groping toward imposing higher performance levels on senior commanders. At the end of July, he ordered a major shakeup in the high command.[46] He replaced the commander of the Republican Guard with General Ayad Fayid al-Rawi, an officer with a reputation for competence and battle-tested leadership. And in a particularly significant break with the past, al-Rawi had no connections with either Saddam's tribe or Tikrit. As a result, General Hamdani recalled, "there would not be any flattery from the rest of the command; it would

---

[44] *Ibid.*
[45] Iraqi intelligence assessments from fall of 1986 noted reductions (compared to 1985) in Iranian oil revenues of 40 percent, industrial production down by 65 percent, and unemployment had reached four million (one-third of Iran's non-mobilized work force). The report concluded that based on information out of Tehran, "the government will not be able to finance the current level of military efforts for more than one [more] year." SH-MISC-D-000-449, Report Detailing the Iranian Military Presence Along the Iraq–Iran Border, Iranian Current Affairs, Reports on Weapons Sales, and Analysis, 29 October 1986.
[46] Hamdani, *Memoir.*

all be on a professional level. He was the kind of commander who, if you [were told] to execute a plan, you'd [better] do it right away, because he would not cut [you] any slack."[47]

Because there was a substantial decrease in the intensity of military operations, al-Rawi was able to focus the regular army and Republican Guard on improving staff work, tactical performance, and unit proficiency. However, the new commander and his staff set the bar lower for the performance of commanders at the division level and below in terms of combined-arms tactics and operations. Al-Rawi and his staff no longer expected the army to employ the complex combined arms operations that the army had attempted with a distinct lack of success thus far in the war. Instead, he emphasized doing a few things well, but keeping the tactical framework simple and rigid while at the same time reaching only for achievable goals.

Thus, there was little expectation of initiative and improvisation in the army's tactical philosophy. In effect, the new high command was dealing with the kind of officers, NCOs, and soldiers they *had*, as opposed to building up the army on a theoretical construct based on Western experiences. The retraining aimed at producing units capable of following simple, scripted tactics to the letter, but as effectively as possible. The emphasis would be on officers performing assigned tasks, something that had rarely, if ever, occurred before al-Rawi assumed command. If officers could not follow simple orders, they soon found themselves on the outside looking in. The tactical system now expected officers to obey orders ruthlessly and completely.[48]

Finally, when not in the frontlines, units trained day-in and day-out. Al-Rawi's efforts were strongly supported by the corps commander, General Maher Abd al-Rashid, one of the more competent Tikritis, whom Saddam singled out by having the general's daughter marry his son Qusay.[49] As one commentator noted after the war about the reforms

---

[47] Lieutenant General Ra'ad Majid Rashid al-Hamdani quoted in Woods, *et al.*, *Saddam's War*, 83. Hamdani was serving on the Republican Guard general staff at this time.

[48] This approach to tactics was similar to what the Soviets had done in 1942 to simplify the Red Army's tactics, and in many ways, what General al-Rawi did with the Iraqi Army was similar to what Sadat's generals had done with the Egyptian Army in preparing for the 1973 War with Israel.

[49] Farouk-Sluglett and Slugett, *Iraq since 1958*. Immediately after the war, Saddam ordered Qusay to divorce the general's daughter, while General Rashid's brother, also a competent commander, died in a helicopter crash. Generals who could execute complex military operations competently could also execute *coup d'etats*. That was certainly the basis of Saddam's approach to his senior commanders. He preferred those he could trust no matter how stupid or incompetent over the competent and independent.

that occurred in the army, "they tried to overcome all of the failings of Iraqi junior officers by writing operations orders so detailed that, simply by following this guidance, Iraqi field commanders would do everything they needed to win."[50]

Luckily for the Iraqis, nothing similar occurred among the Iranians. While the Iranians were licking their wounds, the paradigm of a religious war continued to dominate their thinking. For the rest of 1987, while they held on to their gains, including territory close to Basra, they launched only small-scale attacks. They apparently concluded that surprise was an enabler, but it was not an intelligent approach to launch major operations without a significant chance of victory. One Iranian document noted that "when we want to bring several thousand combatants to the war zone and use a vast amount of military resources, we must be relatively sure ... of victory."[51] Thus, for the remainder of 1987 there were only small-scale battles. The Iranians focused on a war of attrition and stirring up troubles in both northern and southern Iraq. In the north they provided substantial military and armaments aid to Kurdish insurgents, while in the south they aided the Marsh Arabs.

The continued war on cities and the naval war

The fighting around Basra that had broken out in late December 1986 and continued into January 1987 led the opposing sides to look for avenues other than the ground battles to take the pressure off their states. Early January saw the "Battle of the Cities" recommence. The Iraqis acted first with a series of missile attacks on Tehran, Shiraz, Tabriz, and Isfahan, and escalated the violence with missile hits on the holy city of Qom. The Iranians, within artillery range of much of Basra, bombarded that city intensively.[52] And now that they had Scud-Bs, they fired ten of those at the Iraqi capital during January and February of 1987. The Iraqis continued to fire missiles at the Iranians throughout the year, letting up only when their supply of missiles ran out. The Iranians replied in kind. Throughout October they fired a number of missiles at Baghdad, one of which hit a primary school, killing thirty-two children and injuring 182 others.

On the naval front, the war against tankers escalated as well. In fact, 1987 would be the high point of attacks on shipping in the Gulf during the conflict. The Mirages, with sophisticated electronics and the ability to perform air-to-air refueling, enabled the Iraqis to reach deep into the Gulf, in one case targeting a tanker 115 nautical miles south of Kharg.

---

[50] Pollack, *Arabs at War*, 221.   [51] Gera, "The Iraqi–Iranian War," 181.
[52] *Ibid.*, 183.

Iraq aircraft focused almost entirely on interdicting the shuttle of tankers Iran was running from Kharg to Sirri, where they transferred the crude to tankers of other nations. In January, Mirages, bearing the bulk of the effort in the Gulf, hit seven tankers, no fewer than three of which were total write-offs. Despite hitting thirty ships during the next seven months, it was only on 1 September that they managed to wreck another tanker.[53]

The Iraqis ratcheted up their attacks in the last quarter of 1987; they hit thirty-six tankers and other vessels, five of which were either written off or sunk. Moreover, at the end of the year, they launched ultra-long raids that reached all the way down to the Straits of Hormuz. These attacks required no fewer than fourteen Mirages: two as ECM (electronic counter measure) aircraft for the first stage of the flight to get by the Iranian air defenses. Then, six of the Mirages refueled the other six and returned home. The six remaining flew until three tanked up the three mission aircraft.[54] On 5 October, one of these strike packages managed four hits on four different tankers.[55] Later, the Iraqis successfully used a Chinese "Badger" bomber modified to carry a Silkworm missile to the Hormuz area and fire the missile at a tanker.[56] The Iraqis also continued to attack Kharg, but it was becoming a more dangerous target: the Iranians were steadily increasing their anti-aircraft defenses that protected the terminal. Nevertheless, at one point Saddam's minister of information trumpeted, "We are capable of demolishing Iran brick by brick ... We do this daily ... We have decided to return Iran to [a condition of] ... relying on rugs rather than oil."[57] Yet the Iraqi efforts, while they turned up the pressure, were still not enough to bring the Iranians to the peace table.

Having largely remained on the defensive in the Gulf in the past, the Iranians aggressively tried to disrupt tanker and other traffic moving crude and goods from the neutral Gulf powers lying to their south. They particularly targeted the tankers moving Kuwaiti oil. Initially, they used the frigates the Shah had acquired during his reign, but moved on to sowing mines throughout the Gulf and launching attacks with *Pasdaran*

[53] Navias and Hooton, *Tanker Wars*, 132–133, 157.
[54] Kevin M. Woods, Williamson Murray, Elizabeth A. Nathan, Laila Sabara and Ana M. Venegas, "Interview with (Former) Major General 'Alwan Hassoun 'Alwan Al-Abousi, Cairo, Egypt, 13 November 2009," *Project 1946: Phase II* (Alexandria, VA, 2010).
[55] Navias and Hooton, *Tanker Wars*, 149.
[56] Nabila Megalli, "Who's Shooting What? Gulf Tanker Targets Laden with Confusion," *The Associated Press* 1988. The first indication that Iraq was modifying these aircraft came after two Iraqi Silkworms passed near the USS *Chandler* on 12 February 1988.
[57] Gera, "The Iraqi–Iranian War," 184; Jack Reed, "Iranian Missile Attack on Baghdad School Kills 32," *United Press International*, 1987.

units equipped with speedboats. During 1987, the Iranians actually attacked fifty-eight more ships than did the Iraqis, but with less success. If the Exocets the Iraqi Mirages fired had difficulty sinking or damaging tankers beyond repair, the rocket propelled grenades and mines the Iranians were using had even greater difficulty. The advantage in using mines and *Pasdaran* speedboats was that there was a certain plausible deniability. For a while, the Iranians attributed the mines to the "hand of God"; however, this explanation no longer held, when, on 21 September, US helicopters caught the *Iran Ajr* laying mines. After blasting the Iranian ship with rockets, US Navy SEALs stormed her, captured a trove of documents on her mine-laying activities, and photographed her cargo of mines before sinking her.[58]

Iran's efforts to internationalize the cost of the war served to accelerate, not forestall, military defeat. First, it brought the navies of the major powers into the Gulf that Iran's ramshackle navy had no chance of matching. Admittedly, the initial commitment of naval forces to convoy reflagged tankers out of Kuwait through the Gulf was less than impressive. When the tanker *Bridgeton* ran into a mine that inflicted minimal damage, the escorting naval vessels had to follow in her wake, because mines were a mortal danger to their smaller ships. The commander of the task force had to admit that in spite of intelligence warnings, no one had thought it necessary to check the convoy's route for mines.[59] Eventually, the navies of the world sorted out the mine danger, and in the end, the Iranians only managed to damage a number of ships. In return, they brought over-whelming naval forces to the Gulf and saw sanctions tightened, which affected their ability to fight the ground war.

The *Stark* incident

One of the unintended effects of the Iraqi war on tanker traffic near Kharg was an attack by an Iraqi aircraft on the USS *Stark*. The American side has documented its side of the story well through a declassified investigative report.[60] According to the investigation, the *Stark* was

---

[58] Navias and Hooton, *Tanker Wars*, 146; Cordesman and Wagner, *The Lessons of Modern War, Volume II*, 318.

[59] Navias and Hooton, *Tanker Wars*, 144.

[60] "Memorandum from Radm Grant Shart (USN) to Commander in Chief CENTCOM, RE: Formal Investigation into the Circumstances Surrounding the Attack on the USS Stark (FFG 31) on 17 May 1987," (1987). Downloaded from www.dod.gov/pubs/foi/reading_room/65rev.pdf. See also Harold Lee Wise, *Inside the Danger Zone: The US Military in the Persian Gulf, 1987–1988* (Annapolis, MD, 2007); Jeffrey L. Levinson and Randy L. Edwards, *Missiles Inbound: The Attack on the Stark in the Persian Gulf* (Annapolis, MD, 1997).

operating near but outside of the declared Iraqi exclusion zone when two Exocet missiles struck it. The report records the ship's leadership's confusion and failure to defend against the attack as well as the heroism of its crew in reacting to control the extensive damage and fires the missiles caused.

However, several aspects to the attack remained puzzling, including the fact that, while the Iraqis were cooperative with the US Navy's investigative team, they inexplicably refused to allow the Americans to interview the pilot who conducted the attack. The report of the AWACS that monitored the flight path of the Iraqi aircraft from take-off through its attack also contained a number of inexplicable anomalies. The attacking aircraft flew much slower and lower than normal for Iraqi Mirages flying into the Gulf to attack tanker traffic. Moreover, its course was erratic for the Mirages that had thus far flown that mission, and it approached the *Stark* more closely than the normal Mirage profiles before firing its Exocets. Normally, the Mirages fired at maximum range to limit their exposure to Iranian anti-aircraft missiles. The aircraft attacking the *Stark* had fired its missiles at a range of only 13 nautical miles, while Mirages normally fired at a range of 40 nautical miles.

It turns out that the aircraft that fired at the *Stark* was not a Mirage, but a French-made Falcon 50 transport aircraft that the Iraqis had purchased from the French as a part of its larger arms deal.[61] In 1983, the Iraqis, desperate for aircraft that could reach out into the Gulf more deeply than their Super Frelon helicopters, had ordered the Mirage F-1EQ-5 strike aircraft with a much upgraded fire control system that could fire Exocet missiles. The French manufacturer Dassault was about to produce these aircraft but deliveries would not begin for more than two years.[62] As a stop-gap measure, the Iraqis had then modified two Falcon 50s with the F-1's firing radar and firing control systems.

One of the Falcon's was fully equipped to carry Exocets, while the second was pre-wired for rapid reconfiguration to an anti-shipping role, but most of the time served as Saddam's private aircraft. Apparently, the transport crews that flew the Falcon missions over the Gulf were not as

[61] Woods, *et al.*, "Interview with (Former) Major General 'Alwan Hassoun 'Alwan Al-Abousi, Cairo, Egypt, 13 November 2009."; Lon O. Nordeen, *Air Warfare in the Missile Age*, 2nd edn. (Washington, DC, 2002), 197.

[62] The first F-1 Mirages had arrived in the Iraqi inventory in 1981, but these aircraft lacked the fire control system and radars necessary to fire Exocets. For a discussion of the politics and controversy of this deal, see David Styan, *France and Iraq: Oil, Arms, and French Policy-Making in the Middle East* (New York, NY, 2006), 143–146.

well trained as the Mirage fighter pilots; this partially explains why the mission profile looked strange enough to the AWACS crew that they reported its divergence from the usual practices of Iraqi Mirages on Exocet missions.[63] Significantly, neither the Falcon nor the Mirage crews ever attempted to get close enough to identify the targets at which they were firing. It was simply a case of their picking up a target, locking on to the target, and firing. Not surprisingly, the Iraqis did not want American investigators to talk to the pilots of the Falcon, since to do so would reveal to the Iranians how the Iraqis were reaching so deeply into the Gulf in an aircraft significantly more vulnerable to countermeasures than the Mirages.[64]

Initially, the regime expected a sharp and most likely military response to the attack. However, as Tariq Aziz explained the events to a small group of advisors a short time later, the rapid reaction on the part of Saddam and his Foreign Ministry kept the "American reaction ... balanced and normal." The exchange of letters with President Reagan, Aziz continued, prevented "Iraq's enemies' or the anti-Arabs in the United States from taking advantage of this incident to cause problems between Iraq and the US." In the end, Aziz explained, questions from the United States, referring to the visiting American investigation team, "were in regards to avoiding such incidents from recurring in the future [and were] not based on suspicions, threats ... and they did not insist on meeting our pilot."[65]

The internal wars

While the War of the Cities and naval confrontations in the Gulf played out, the fighting around Basra ended and Saddam turned to clearing out the Marsh Arabs, or the *Madan*, as they were known locally, and securing the area once and for all. This was a seemingly intractable problem for Saddam. Four years earlier, he had sought to subdue the predominantly Shi'a Arab population who for thousands of years had made their living in and on the marshes that once covered 6,000 square miles of south-eastern Iraq.[66] This distinct population survived through the age-old behavior of the weak caught between two warring sides: they temporized, attempting to cooperate with both sides. That was not good enough for Saddam. Beginning in 1983, the cleansing of the Marsh Arabs began.

---

[63] Wise, *Inside the Danger Zone*, 18.   [64] This was the last of these Falcon missions.
[65] SH-SHTP-A-000-958, Saddam and High Ranking Iraqi Officials Discussing the American Frigate "Stark," 27 May 1987.
[66] On the Marsh Arabs, see Wilfred Thesiger, *The Marsh Arabs* (New York, 2007).

Saddam commented in November of that year to senior officers about the operations:

Do you know how the marshes operation was carried out? It was organized in a wonderful way and it had an element of surprise . . . I gave the orders to the People's Army force that were mobilized there, whereas, it was carried out by 11,000 fighters of the corps' commandos that were on standby for the operation, also army aircraft were involved. [T]hey killed 180 individuals at that location, and they arrested 800 individuals. They brought them tied up . . . The marsh was cleaned up in three days. It was considered an offensive operation, and I told them whoever resists among the 800 individuals, kill him. They carried out 600 death sentences on these individuals. We gathered large numbers from all the marsh villages and from the draft evaders . . . to watch [the execution] of the 600 individuals . . . So, the next time when a person from the marshes evades the draft, he [will] run to the desert, because he [will] say to himself, I would rather be judged there and sentenced to five–ten years; however, in the marshes he would be sentenced to death.[67]

As was the case with Saddam's other restive minorities, such "demonstrations" would not be enough. On 17 May 1987, the General Security Directorate sent a letter to Saddam suggesting how they might execute his desires to take care of this problem:

Implementing security operations against the saboteurs in the marsh areas such as poisoning, bombing, and burning their homes through friends and entrusted persons to make them feel the marsh areas are not safe . . .

Choosing a number of good and capable sources among the deserters and draft evaders [who] are found in the marshes area so that they can be assigned assassination missions against the hostile elements. In return they would be spared from their desertion and evasion crimes in case they do accept . . .

Taking punitive and deterrent actions from time to time against the persons who cooperated with the saboteurs in the marshes area such as burning and destroying their homes in order to restrain the others.[68]

A follow-on letter from Saddam's national security council informed its recipients how the campaign had progressed. Other letters in the same file detailed other "successes" by the regime's security detachments against a primitive, but centuries-old culture and people.

They favor poisoning, bombing, and burning homes of the saboteurs in the marshes areas and such suggestions were still being implemented by the security directorates in the region as such:

---

[67] SH-PDWN-D-001-029, Meeting between Saddam Hussein and Various Iraqi Military Leaders, 11 May 1983.

[68] Memorandum from the Ministry of the Interior to President of the Republic (17 May 1987) in SH-RVCC-D-000-218, Plan for the Marshes Which Includes Killing, Poisoning, Burning Homes, and Economic Punishments, May–September 1987.

- In the Dhi Qar Governorate: kidnapping five hostile elements inside the marshes, assassinating fifteen hostile elements and criminals and sending fifteen strikes by means of different sources on the places where hostile [groups] can be found.
- In the Misan Governorate: assassinating four hostile elements and wounding one, kidnapping seven persons, and burning thirty homes of the fugitives inside the marshes.
- In the Basra Governorate: assassinating three fugitives.
- A plan was put into action to chase the draft evaders and deserters in the southern governorates and strike their hideouts. The result was as such up to 28 August 1987: 4,943 arrested, 29,544 remorseful, 402 dead, 104 executed, and 35 wounded . . .
- A proposition was already presented to the President Saddam Hussein to gather all the village residents in one single dry area but was rejected. On the other hand, [the president] formed a committee to open roads inside the marshes and to drain some of the areas according to [their] importance in order to reach the depth of the marshes.[69]

It was not just the Marsh Arabs who suffered the regime's murderous attention. While the fronts near Basra and east of Baghdad drew most of the focus of military operations, Saddam refused to allow the Kurds to remain untouched. Because there were insufficient troops to launch an offensive against the mountain tribesmen, the regime used air and chemical attacks on the rebellious tribesmen. Iraqi documents indicate that a number of such attacks took place in late 1986 and early 1987, though the goal seems to have been to intimidate the Kurds, rather than breaking their resistance as was the case with the Marsh Arabs.[70]

The program to suppress the Kurds, soon known as the al-Anfal Campaign, began with the appointment of Saddam's cousin Ali Hassan al-Majid, aka Chemical Ali, to the position of secretary general of the northern command. Saddam sent his cousin north to allow the regime to focus on the conventional battles building around Basra. As one former associate described the appointment: "In tough cases, in which [Saddam] needs people without a heart, he calls upon Ali Hassan al-Mahid."[71] A 30

---

[69] Memorandum from the RCC to the Secretariat of the North Organziation Office (6 September 1987) in SH-RVCC-D-000-218, Plan for the Marshes Which Includes Killing, Poisoning, Burning Homes, and Economic Punishments, May–September 1987. There are other documents in this file chronicling atrocities Saddam's security directorate carried out against the Marsh Arabs.

[70] *SH-GMID-D-001-384, Correspondence between the GMID, the Iraqi Military Attaché in Jordan, the Air & Air Defense Force, and the President of the Republic Regarding Attacks on Iran and Using Chemical Weapons on the Kurds. Other correspondence confirms these reports.

[71] Appendix A, Section 4: Northern Bureau Meeting to Review the Campaigns of 1987 and 1988; [Circa] 21–22 January 1989, in "Genocide in Iraq – the Anfal Campaign against the Kurds," *Middle East Watch Report* (New York, NY, 1993). This report, bolstered by extensive fieldwork and thousands of pages of Ba'ath records captured during the chaos

June 1987 memorandum that summed up the campaign thus far suggests the lengths to which the Iraqi forces, under the enthusiastic guidance of Chemical Ali, were willing to go. To pacify critical terrain of potential threats, Saddam directed that Chemical Ali and his police force clear huge swaths of northern Iraq of "saboteurs." In early June, hundreds of villages were declared "prohibited" and, according to the memorandum, after 21 June any persons found in these areas would be guilty of either "harboring saboteurs, agents of Iran, members of the KDP [Kurdish Democratic Party], and ... traitors of Iraq." Since the "presence of any human or animal [in these villages] is completely forbidden, they are subject to attack." Moreover, it ordered corps commanders to "use special strikes from time to time, using artillery, helicopters, and airplanes ... to kill large numbers of the individuals ... found in the prohibited areas." Finally, the memorandum ordered that individuals between 15 and 70 years of age were to be executed "after benefitting from their information."[72] The efficiency with which the Iraqi forces carried out this specific order is unknown.

1988: dénouement

In a conversation with his ministers at the end of 1987, Saddam noted that "this is not the time for peace yet and there will be another political and military round."[73] In this case, one of the few times during the war, events proved him right. Nevertheless, the "year of decision" did not begin auspiciously (for the 1988 Iraqi offensives in the southern and central battlefields, see Figures 9.1 and 9.2). The opening battle erupted in Khurmal, north of Halabjah.[74] The Iranians caught the Iraqis by surprise and in the initial attack captured the 34th Infantry Division's commander and almost entirely destroyed the division.[75] In terms of

---

of 1991, provides a chilling and detailed analysis of the campaign against the Kurds during 1987–1988.

[72] *SH-IDGS-D-001-385, Correspondence within the Directorate of General Security Regarding Directions from Ali Hassan Al-Majid Related to the Northern Areas of Iraq, 4 December 1987. The general nature of these operations was well publicized in Iraq. In a documentary produced by the military, Iraqi troops are shown enthusiastically destroying the town of Barzan including all dwellings, the water supply, food storage and even a mosque. *SH-MODX-V-001-386, *The Knockout Operation* by Iraqi Military Photography and Cinema Command, 10–11 August 1987.

[73] SH-SHTP-A-000-561, Saddam and His Inner Circle Discussing the Iran–Iraq War and UN Security Council Resolutions Related to the War, Circa December 1987.

[74] Hamdani, *Memoir*.

[75] Hamdani characterized the 34th Division in the following terms: "we refer[red] to this division as the 'unlucky division,' especially as the division commander [another one] was killed in 1992 by the Kurds." Hamdani, *Memoir*.

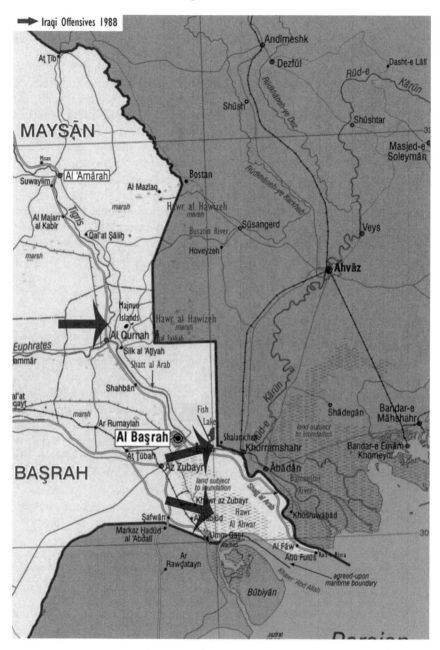

Figure 9.1 Southern battlefield, Iraqi offensives, 1988

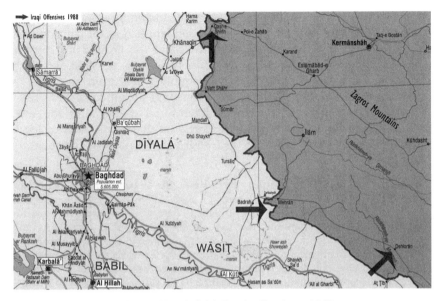

Figure 9.2 Central battlefield, Iraqi offensives, 1988

overall military effectiveness, it represented a terrible performance. An after-action report, written by a group of Iraqi senior officers immediately after the opening days of the battle, reported:

Below listed are our remarks about the reasons that led to what happened in Halabjah sector:

- The complete loss of command and control.
- The military units that were specified to hold the defense location were weak ...
- The boats required to transport the withdrawing forces through [Khazzan] Darband Khan Lake were not provided. Thus we had enormous losses of the withdrawing force that was notified that the boats were ready to transport them to the west side of the lake ...

This is what led to the [psychological breakdown] of all the combatants ...

- The notable weakness in the corps operations staff ...
- The weakness of the 43rd Forces [Division] Command and specifically Major General Ali Hussein Uwayyid ...
- Despite the availability of sufficient information regarding the axes, the direction, and the timing of the [Iranian] attack, the corps command mishandled this information and dealt with it superficially.[76]

---

[76] Memorandum from Intelligence System of the Eastern Zone Section 1 Department 1 to GMID (HQ) RE: Battles at Halabja (18 March 1988) in SH-GMID-D-001-026, Reports Related to the General Military Intelligence Directorate Concerning the

Substantial Iraqi counterattacks in April, including one by the 10th Armored Division, one of the divisions Saddam had spent considerable effort refitting and retraining, failed to regain the ground lost by the collapse of the 34th Division. Nevertheless, it is possible the 10th Armored Division's counterattack was simply a deception operation to cover the larger operations the Iraqis were about to launch farther south. That was certainly how the Iraqis interpreted events after the war. Nevertheless, documentary evidence suggests that at the tactical level, they made every effort to regain the lost ground. A postwar commentary did note:

During the first and second battles east of Basra, the "Battles Crown" battle, the great liberation battles that lasted from 17 April 1988 to July 1988, both our troops and the enemy used deceptive plans. There were troop movements for deception to attract attention, the use of additional wireless networks and cancelling other networks besides engineering activities in sectors that were not part of the plan to attract attention away from the selected sectors. The harmony between the al-Anfal battles and the liberation battles was one of the most successful deception strategic and tactical plans [in history].[77]

Even the extensive use of chemical weapons, including large lay downs of nerve agents, failed to dislodge the Iranians from the positions they had seized:

As a result of the chemical attack the enemy sustained the following losses: 500 people were killed in addition to a significant number of injured in Dizli; 500–600 people killed and a large number injured in Tarkhan Ayad; [and] 25,000 people killed, including a significant number of injured, including those among the Iranian Revolutionary Guard, the saboteurs, and the local residents, in Halabjah.[78]

The target of these chemical attacks was not just Iranian and Kurdish forces, but civilian Kurds as well, in the hope their morale and

---

Status of the Iraqi Corps and Regiments During the Iraqi–Iran War in Different Sectors of the Battlefield and Discussions About Halabja, March 1988. For additional information on the 43rd Division's operations at Halabjah, see "Genocide in Iraq," 117–118. The "availability of sufficient information "probably, decrypts of Iranian signals had warned the Iraqis that an attack was coming – a warning the corps commander mishandled. Woods *et al.*, "Interview with (Former) Major General Mizher Rashid Al-Tarfa Al-Ubaydi, Dubai, United Arab Emirates, 9 November 2009."

[77] SH-IZAR-D-000-347, Research Paper: *Tactical Deception on the Battlefield*, 13 July 1988. According to an officer in signals intelligence, the Iraqis used decrypts to gain a picture of how the Iranians were reacting to Iraqi deception measures and then emphasized those that were making an impact. Woods, *et al.*, "Interview with (Former) Major General Mizher Rashid Al-Tarfa Al-Ubaydi, Dubai, United Arab Emirates, 9 November 2009."

[78] SH-IZAR-D-000-646, Telegram from the Intelligence System of the Eastern Zone Revealing the Use of Chemical Weapons against Halabja, 20 March 1988.

willingness to support the Iranians would collapse.[79] By mid-March 1988, Saddam's frustration with the Kurdish "saboteurs," Iranian penetrations into northern Iraq, and the difficult terrain led him to overcome his occasional reservations about using chemical weapons. On 22 March, the general secretary of the ministry of defense issued broad authority on the release of chemical weapons: "Permission is obtained to strike the enemy with the special ammunition in the air force, [army] aviation, and the artillery along the front, giving the priority for the I Corps front."[80] An intelligence report from that same date coldly states:

Due to the bombing of Halabjah city by the airplanes and our artillery, the casualties of the enemy were large and reached around 3,000 slain guards and Iranian volunteers, whose bodies were transported to Alvar City. Moreover, there were lots of injured people who were all from Halabjah City and the residential complexes in addition to the surrounding villages. Most of the casualties were the result of the chemical attack.[81]

An April letter from the GMID makes clear the results of such authority: "It is suggested that Ahmad Awah area and the village of Bustan' Inab al-Qadima would be handled by the special weapons, and in the late hours of the night, when most of the enemy are sleeping."[82] One Iraqi source suggests the gas attacks on Halabjah and surrounding towns killed 5,000, most of them innocent civilians, and caused more than 100,000 Kurds to flee to Turkey and Iran.[83] Yet, the chemical attacks failed to drive the Iranians from their positions, an indication of

---

[79] Not surprisingly, when he was interviewed by American interrogators after the war, Chemical Ali "denied personal knowledge or responsibility regarding the Iraqi government's use of chemical weapons during the Iran–Iraq War, against the Kurds, or at any other time. He added, 'I have never had any involvement with chemical weapons in my life.'" *FD-302 of Ali Hasan Al-Majid Al-Tikriti on 31 January 2004 in Baghdad, IQ* (Washington, DC, 2004).

[80] *SH-MODX-D-001-387, Orders by the Ministry of Defense to Strike the Enemy with "Special Munitions," 22 March 1988.

[81] Memorandum from Intelligence System of the Eastern Zone Section 1 Department 1 to GMID (5th HQ) (22 March 1989) in SH-GMID-D-001-026, Reports Related to the General Military Intelligence Directorate Concerning the Status of the Iraqi Corps and Regiments During the Iraqi–Iran War in Different Sectors of the Battlefield and Discussions About Halabja, March 1988. The source of the information was a Kurdish informant, "whose reliability is good." Another Iraqi report placed the casualty figures "as a result of the chemical attack" as 900–1,000 "killed and a large number wounded" near Halabjah and some 2,500 in the city itself. These numbers included "Khomeini guard, saboteurs, and the rest were civilians." SH-IZAR-D-000-646, Telegram from the Intelligence System of the Eastern Zone Revealing the Use of Chemical Weapons against Halabja, 20 March 1988.

[82] SH-GMID-D-000-299, General Military Intelligence Directorate Correspondence About Iranian Military Activities and Other Issues, March 1988.

[83] Farouk-Sluglett and Sluglett, *Iraq since 1958: From Revolution to Dictatorship*, 273.

the ever-increasing Iranian defensive capability and the extraordinary motivation some Iranian units still possessed.

Still, a survey of Iranian prisoners of war in June 1988 supports the Iraqi doctrinal belief that chemical weapons were primarily a psychological weapon at the operational and strategic levels.[84] It noted that, first, cyanide and nerve agent weapons "have the greatest impact on the Iranians and are the most feared by them"; second, the impact of chemical weapons is "intense especially after the first strike"; third, rumors in Iran say that "Iraq will use chemical weapons in every future attack," which generates "fear and panic"; and fourth, another rumor says the Iraqis will use "chemical agents in the warheads of long-range missiles to strike at [Iranian] cities."[85] Despite rumors of Iranian chemical threats and occasional battlefield use (mostly CS gas and captured Iraqi chemical rounds), by 1988, the Iraqis were satisfied that there was no near-term threat. An intelligence report discussing North Korea's help to the Iranians to develop an indigenous mustard gas capability, however, pointed toward a future where Iraqi troops might need to worry about chemical attacks.[86]

The outcome of the battle around Halabjah and the failures of Iraqi counterattacks had a considerable impact on Iraqi morale. General Hamdani noted in his memoirs:

After a long series of unsuccessful counter-attacks by our forces, we tragically lost the mountainous barricade of Shimeran, [the position of] which was essential for our reclaiming of Halabjah ... On April 2, the 10th Armored Div[ision] and a number of other formations staged an unsuccessful attack on the enemy in an attempt to change the deteriorating situation around Halabjah. Things kept deteriorating further as if a long night descended on the battlefields. There was little hope for success.[87]

---

[84] Timothy V. McCarthy and Jonathon B. Tucker, "Saddam's Toxic Arsenal: Chemical and Biological Weapons in the Gulf Wars," in *Planning the Unthinkable: How New Powers Will Use Nuclear, Biological, and Chemical Weapons*, Peter R. Lavoy, Scott D. Sagan, and James J. Wirtz, eds. (Ithaca, NY, 2000), 62–63.

[85] SH-GMID-D-000-079, Memorandum from the General Military Intelligence Directorate to the Director of the Military Industrialization Commission About Information on Chemical Weapons Obtained from Iraqi Prisoners in Iran, 6 June 1988.

[86] Memorandum from GMID to the Assistant RE: Chemical Weapons (27 June 1988) in SH-GMID-D-000-898, General Military Intelligence Directorate (GMID) Memoranda Discussing Iranian Chemical Weapons Capability, October 1987–September 1988. For a broad outline of Iranian programs of the period, see Gregory F. Giles, "The Islamic Republic of Iran and Nuclear, Biological, and Chemical Weapons," in *Planning the Unthinkable: How New Powers Will Use Nuclear, Biological, and Chemical Weapons*, Peter R. Lavoy, Scott D. Sagan, and James J. Wirtz, eds. (Ithaca, NY, 2000).

[87] Hamdani, *Memoir*.

Nevertheless, in spite of the failures in the north, the balance of power had shifted substantially in favor of the Iraqis. Heavy losses of life since the war's beginning had substantially eroded Iranian morale with many Iranians expressing their unhappiness. There were now considerably fewer volunteers for the *Pasdaran* and *Basij* than in previous years. As a result, the leaders in Tehran had to call back to the colors survivors who had fulfilled their service obligations. In one Iraqi intelligence report from early 1988, the Iranian Joint Staff was reportedly desperate for fresh troops and was pressing Khomeini to issue an order stating: "In order to favorably put an end to the war, all Iran must actively participate and send fighters and monetary assistance to the front. Each Iranian must be ready to actively participate and that all Iranians must execute his religious creed willingly or forcibly."[88] Despite its enormous population advantage, by the end of the war, Iran's ground force numbers only totaled 600,000, while the Iraqi Army contained approximately 1,000,000 soldiers.[89] In every category, weapons, numbers of soldiers, and tactical preparations, the Iranians were at a distinct disadvantage.

The situation in the north around Halabjah led Saddam to resume "the Battle of the Cities." In late February 1988, the Iranians hit Baghdad with two Scud missiles. Once again, the clerics in Tehran misjudged how the Iraqis would respond: Saddam replied with a barrage of their new "al-Hussein" missile, which could hit Tehran with ease.[90] For every missile the Iranians fired, the Iraqis fired four back. By the time Saddam unilaterally ended the "battle," the Iraqis had fired 140 Hussein missiles, most at Tehran, and another forty Scuds at cities closer to Iraqi territory. The bombardment of Tehran led nearly a million of the capital's citizens to flee into the countryside.[91] After the war, the Iranians would admit that they had suffered approximately 10,000–11,000 deaths as a result of air and missile attacks on their cities, most in 1988.[92]

In a conversation with Adnan Khairallah, minister of defense, Hussein Kamel, then head of the military industrialization commission and charged with Iraq's missile and WMD programs, argued strongly for a more aggressive war against Iran's cities:

---

[88] Directorate 5 to Section Director Memorandum from GMID, RE: the source (21 January 1988), in *SH-GMID-D-001-388, Various Correspondence between the GMID and the Presidential Diwan Regarding the Iranian Army and Air Force.

[89] Ward, *Immortal*, 292.

[90] In fact, it was little more than a modified Scud with greater range, less payload, and no greater accuracy, the Scud having the general accuracy of a World War II V-2 missile.

[91] Ward, *Immortal*, 297; Cordesman, *The Lessons of Modern War, Volume II*, 500.

[92] Shahram Chubin, "The Last Phase of the Iran–Iraq War: From Stalemate to Ceasefire," *Third World Quarterly* 11, no. 2 (1989), 11.

Sir to be honest, my personal point of view is that the war will stop when Iraq becomes capable of deeply harming the Iranians at the front lines – and not only at the front lines, [but] harming the enemy in locations deep inside Iran as in its cities. [This] is the way to reach the Mullahs in Tehran, who do not see, who do not hear, who are holed away in rooms, and do not care about the thousands who die there. As for us ... we are concerned for a single person who dies without justification. We execute people when they go astray, but our people are very precious to us and we try to protect them and we strive to help them live happily. The ability to harry Iran deep inside, in their main cities, as well as on the battlefield, is what is required of us.[93]

During the remainder of the war, the two sides exchanged missiles and aircraft attacks on population centers. The military effectiveness of these missile attacks was near zero. However, the strategic effects in terms of increasing pressure on Iran to agree to a UN-brokered ceasefire were significant. As one analyst points out, the 1988 War of the Cities "ranks as one of the smallest strategic bombing campaigns in history." During a seven-week period, Iraq's modified Scud missiles rained 40 tons of high explosives on Tehran. The effects on the city were "wildly disproportionate" when compared to the 20,000 tons dropped on Hanoi-Haiphong in 1972 during an eleven-day period; the 153,000 tons dropped on Japanese cities in August 1945; the 1,200,000 tons dropped on German cities in 1944; or the more than 1,000 tons that fell on London in the nose-cones of German V-2s.[94] Despite the historically small scale of the missile campaign, it did achieve its intended effect. In spite of the constant appeals to religious and nationalist obligations from hardline Islamic revolutionaries, the chronic effect of a long and costly war clearly lowered the resistance of Iran's population, especially its urban populations, to new shocks.[95]

The cumulative effects of battlefield setbacks beginning in late 1987 and the demonstration that the chemical weapons could be delivered to Tehran in the increasing barrage of Iraqi missiles tipped the psychological balance of the war. Ironically, Tehran's own propaganda machine, which sought to trumpet the Iraqi chemical attack on Halabjah for world condemnation, may have only added to the demoralization and dread of its own urban populations.[96] In the end, these events

---

[93] SH-AFGC-D-000-731, Meeting of the General Command of the Armed Forces, March 1988.

[94] Thomas L. McNaugher, "Ballistic Missiles and Chemical Weapons: The Legacy of the Iran–Iraq War," *International Security* 15, no. 2 (1990), 10–11.

[95] As late as June 1988, the Revolutionary Guard spokesman was still arguing in public that "the war will be decided on the battlefield and not at the conference table." Ray Takeyh, "The Iran–Iraq War: A Reassessment," *The Middle East Journal* 64, no. 3 (2010), 381.

[96] Dilip Hiro, *The Iranian Labyrinth: Journeys through Theocratic Iran and Its Furies* (New York, NY, 2005), 232.

were finally achieving what Saddam naïvely thought could be accomplished at minimal cost in 1980, namely that "the continuation of the war would threaten the very existence of the Islamic Republic" and "Khomeini's legacy."[97]

While the Iraqis were dealing with difficulties in the north, Saddam began planning a major operation in the south to regain the Fao Peninsula and another to drive the Iranians back from the positions they held close to Basra. These offensive operations changed the war's framework and finally persuaded the Iranians to make peace. The reason for the victories lay in the changes Saddam made to the Iraqi military. Planning and preparation for the offensives remained close-hold to prevent leaks that might have alerted the Iranians. Only a select few initially advised Saddam when preparing the offensive: the commander of the Republican Guard, his chief of staff, and an intelligence officer from the Republican Guard. Detailed planning was restricted to a small team in the Republican Guard. At first, even the army chief of staff and the head of the general staff were not informed about the upcoming offensive.[98] Eventually, the planning group expanded to include the regular army's deputy chief of staff for operations, General Hussein Rashid, who had been al-Rawi's predecessor as the commander of the Republican Guard. The army's chief of staff was informed of the general concept, but not about the timing or details, nor were the participating regular army units apprised of their part in the offensive until the last moment.[99]

There are several possible factors behind Saddam's desire to launch a major offensive. The most important was perhaps the psychological need to sustain the initiative. After retaking the Fao Peninsula, one Iraqi officer suggested that:

When [the Iranians] started to shout ... that 1987 will be the decisive year, the president stood up and said, "I defy you, and if there is a settlement, then it will be towards the other party." The factor that ... broke the [Iranians'] spirits ... was the confrontation, losses, and lack of confidence in the promises of their leaders ... the Iranians ... entered the conflict of missiles ... the war of the cities, [which brought] the Iranian family, Iranian society, and the people outside the battle frame fall under the influence of this battle ... That's when the president, may God protect him, started to plan the Fao battle that he

[97] Chubin, "The Last Phase of the Iran–Iraq War," 10.
[98] The lengths to which Saddam went to keep the attack on the Fao Peninsula secret is suggested in a conversation between Saddam and his senior military advisors that took place after the first Gulf War. SH-SHTP-A-000-813, Saddam and Senior Military Officials Discussing Various Military Operations Including Re-Capturing the Al-Fao Peninsula, Unknown, after 1991.
[99] Woods, et al., Saddam's War, 85.

thought ... [would] be the decisive one that [would] change the war formula until the settlement of this conflict.[100]

A more prosaic explanation is that Saddam, in serious trouble both in the north in Kurdistan and south around Basra, needed a major battle-field success to turn around a growing suspicion in the army and among the population that Iraq was losing: "This was his last chance to rectify these losses that had happened along the borders of Iraq."[101] According to General Hamdani, who coordinated the planning group, which was spread between Baghdad and Basra:

Once I got these recommendations and other ideas [from a senior officer in Iraqi intelligence], I would take them and go back to Baghdad Palace, the command headquarters for Saddam. I would go there to talk to General Rashid, the assistant of the chief of staff. I would hand the plan over to him and he would explain the points to Saddam. If Saddam had any questions, or anything requiring clarification, he would call me in. If he would make any recommendations or additions to the plan, I would take it back to the director of intelligence, meet with the deputy director of Iraqi intelligence, and then fly from there back to Basra. So there was a circle.[102]

Several factors helped the Iraqis plan and execute their effort to regain Fao. The center of gravity for the Iranians had shifted to the north. As a result, they deployed their best units in that theater, which, of course, explains why the Iraqis failed so completely in their attempts to regain Halabjah in March and April. The focus on the north had also led to a progressive weakening of Iranian forces on the peninsula and near Basra. But the greatest weakness in the Iranian position lay in the general decline in their military power and the fact that the leaders in Tehran were consistently overestimating the capabilities of their troops. More-over, their strength in the north made it difficult to transfer forces to the south given the primitive north–south roads on their side of the fron-tier.[103] In effect, they would have to transfer troops in the northeast to Tehran before directing them back to the southwest to reach the south-ern front. This had not mattered so much when they possessed the initiative, but it did now as the Iraqis again seized the initiative.

Aiding the operational framework was a deception campaign the Iraqis conducted in the weeks preceding their offensive. It is likely that the deployment of the 10th Armored Division and a Republican Guard

---

[100] *SH-SHTP-A-001-389, Recording of a Military Lecture Given in the Presence of Saddam Hussein, Circa Early 1989.

[101] Woods, et al., Saddam's War, 85.   [102] Ibid., 86.

[103] See Chapter 2 for a more detailed discussion of the impact of geography on the strategic and operational framework within which the war was waged.

headquarters to the north aimed at persuading the Iranians that Saddam was determined to regain Halabjah. In addition, signals intelligence and decrypts gave the Iraqis a clear picture of Iranian dispositions, a picture made clearer by American and Soviet satellite imagery.[104]

The information obtained about the occupied areas [of Fao] was excellent. The last satellite images of the area were taken on March 30th 1988 and contained very specific details of the distribution of their forces, equipment, defense nodes, and supporting arms. Based on this information we recreated a similar battleground in the al-Amara marshes and trained most of our forces on similar terrain and with similar targets to those that they were going to face in battle.[105]

One can gauge how important Saddam considered the offensive to be by the fact that he arrived at the controlling headquarters the day before the assault began and took direct, personal command of the operation. His two sons served as observers at Republican Guard Corps head-quarters and VII Corps headquarters.[106] The movement of two corps, tanks, infantry, and artillery to their jump off positions occurred without Iranian intelligence picking up that a major Iraqi offensive was in the offing. As General Hamdani noted to the authors, "This was the highest point of experience and expertise that the Iraqi Army reached."[107]

The offensive began at 0430 hours on 17 April with an opening bombardment of high explosive and chemical shells fired by 1,400 artillery pieces. The Iraqis had planned to deluge the Iranian defenders with poisonous gas, but in the end they limited the use of chemical weapons because of winds that approached 40 knots.[108] They concentrated

---

[104] According to members of the US Defense Intelligence Agency liaison team in Baghdad in 1988, the United States "had prepared the plans for an air war against Iran comprising more than 20 targets behind Iranian lines that were critical to sustaining the Iranian war effort." The Iraqis received accurate "drawings made from [satellite] images." Patrick E. Tyler, *A World of Trouble: The White House and the Middle East – From the Cold War to the War on Terror* (New York, NY, 2009), 336; Frank Francona, *Ally to Adversary: An Eyewitness Account of Iraq's Fall from Grace* (Annapolis, MD, 1999), 18–28. For examples of Soviet intelligence-sharing with Iraq, see Directorate 5 Memorandum from GMID, Section 20 to the President of the Republic, No. 11717, RE: Analysis of Information (29 May 1987), in *SH-MODX-D-001-390, Iraqi Military Documents Discussing Iranian Military Movements and Activities, Including the Iranian Use of Chemical Weapons, 1987. This memorandum refers to and comments on letters from the Soviets on Iranian military plans and dispositions. See also Internal GMID Memorandum RE: The Soviet Military Attache in Baghdad (28 July 1987) in SH-GMID-D-000-550, General Military Intelligence Directorate Memoranda About the Soviet Military Attache to Baghdad and Information on Plans for Iraq to Provide Russia with Missiles, 1982–1987.
[105] Hamdani, *Memoir*.   [106] *Ibid.*   [107] Woods, *et al.*, *Saddam's War*, 89.
[108] SH-SHTP-A-000-568, Saddam Hussein and High Ranking Officers Discussing the Liberation of Al-Fao, circa summer 1988.

100,000 soldiers and a large number of tanks. Against this force, the Iranians had somewhere between 8,000 and 15,000 troops defending the peninsula.[109] Because the start date coincided with the start of Ramadan, Saddam code-named the operation "Blessed Ramadan."[110]

Across the front the Iraqis achieved surprise. Almost immediately the Iranian defenses crumbled:

> We didn't have to wait long before we started to hear on the radio [the] first news of the victory, followed soon after with reports on the situation, each announcing the achieved victory. We were taken aback by the speed of these events ... Six hours into the fray, all our frontal formations were at their targets except the 16th Republican Guard Special Forces Brigade which was faced with a large and deep area of water with a large enemy force concentrated on the other side. A second column of infantry was thrust through the positions reclaimed by the 6th Brigade and they were able to surprise the enemy from behind and destroy their resistance ... On the night of April 17 all our frontal units had occupied their targets, and the same applied to the VII Corps units.[111]

By the following day, the Iranian's resistance had collapsed. The defenders fled, abandoning their equipment. On 18 April, the victorious Iraqis occupied Fao and the rest of the peninsula fell into their hands. Saddam ordered the air force not to attack the bridges across the Shatt al-Arab, so that fleeing Iranians could spread disorder and fear among those not directly affected by the offensive.[112] The Iraqis had won at a cost of only 1,000 soldiers killed in action. Two years earlier, they had lost many times that in their failed efforts to halt the Iranian offensive and regain the peninsula.[113]

During a conversation sometime in late April, Saddam and his senior Ba'ath colleagues discussed the victory's implications in regaining the peninsula. Tariq Aziz noted that Iraq should use the victory to mount a "jolting and decisive" campaign in terms of regional politics. The Fao victory was bigger than its battlefield impact, he argued: it "manifests [itself] in Arab dreams" and is on the scale of the victories won by Mohammed and Umar bin al-Khattab. Aziz was confident that Fao's fall would ultimately lead to the war's termination, but warned Saddam, after placing him on a historical pedestal, that "there is an international trend toward settlements ... This direction is ... one of the most

---

[109] Ward, *Immortal*, 292.   [110] Hamdani, *Memoir*.   [111] *Ibid.*
[112] Woods *et al.*, *Saddam's War* 87.
[113] Hamdani, *Memoir*. In the aftermath of the offensive, the Iraqis estimated their casualties as 3,000 from the Republican Guard and the VII Corps killed and wounded. SH-SHTP-A-000-568, Saddam Hussein and High Ranking Officers Discussing the Liberation of Al-Fao, circa summer 1988.

dangerous phases in the history of nations." And then he specifically asked Saddam whether it was "possible that we achieve peace, but the question here, is under what circumstances." The Jews and Persians might "steal away this opportunity."[114]

The opportunity, according to Aziz, was to use Iraq's military achievements, "our gain in weaponry ... capability and the great successes that we achieved in military and missile industries," to bring "equality between us and Israel, and between the Arabs and the oppressed, these jihadist people in Palestine, who are mounting *Jihad* against Israeli arrogance." The Fao campaign, continued Aziz, will eradicate from "the Jews' mind" that land can "remain occupied." The larger meaning of Fao was that "the Arabs are capable of going through bold and assaulting battles and [capable] of uprooting the sneaky enemy from the land that it occupied ... no matter how long it takes." Saddam could not have agreed more enthusiastically. He noted, "the whole world has started to talk about the new standards of the Iraqi Army ... Countries are watching how the Iraqis are fighting." He directed that Iraq bring representatives of various countries to Fao "so that they can see themselves ... There is no military secret here, bring them in ... There is no message more important that Fao."[115]

In a post-operation conversation between Saddam and senior Iraqi generals, a number of points emerged. One of the generals noted:

We were successfully able to liberate the first supreme division after seven years of defending [the] al-Fakah region. We conducted extensive training in the battle and resistance schools and we merged them with [the] IV Corps in the beginning of 1988 ... Of course, the purpose of the ... VII Corps was to liberate [Fao] through extensive training program[s], which liberated cities, villages, fords, or any rivers ...

It took us three or four days to infiltrate the entire division [in]to the region, to ground zero ... [At the start of operations], we forgot that Basra [Fao] old road was [to be] utilized by the 16th Brigade and part of the 25th, which caused congestion ... Therefore, we had side and front fire artillery besides the nature of the land and the blockages, which limited the roads and caused major congestion.

Saddam then interjected and indicated that he set up a competition in the planning between the 7th Armored Division and Republican Guard to see who could liberate Fao first. The conversation turned to the subject of an unfortunate officer who had failed in his assigned task. There is not

---

[114] SH-SHTP-A-000-857, Saddam and Iraqi Officials Discussing the Liberation of Al-Faw and Its Broader Implications, circa 18 April 1988.
[115] *Ibid.*

much doubt about the officer's fate. One of the generals got the ball rolling with the comment to Saddam:

GENERAL: That officer [a staff officer], sir, caused depression and
                      confusion among everyone . . .
                      I said to him, "What do you mean we are done? You better
                      attack." The [Republican Guard] was achieving a
                      tremendous success at the time and the tanks of the 6th
                      Division were moving normally . . . He was already exposed
                      with the soldiers, what was he thinking? He was ignorant
                      by stating we were done!
ANOTHER   He was at the doorsteps of Fao and wanted to quit . . . He used
GENERAL: to be a respectable officer and now [was] a loser joining
                      the insurgents.
SADDAM: Is that right, I guess he is a betrayer . . .
                      I guess he did not want to put [out] extra effort, what did he
                      mean by "we are done," and as soon as we liberated Fao,
                      he acted as if he were a superman. At that time
                      I considered him a betrayer . . . Whoever imitates
                      Americans, Zionists and Europeans are low class
                      individuals; they shave their beards and mustaches . . . and
                      what about the betrayer's family? They have been
                      destroyed as well, now you see.[116]

The conversation turned back to the battle:

GENERAL: We visited the 6th Division and discovered that their situation was
           good, of course not on the same level as the Republican
           Guard . . . I am certain sir that you are aware of the difficulties in
           operating tanks in such limited space, regardless of the
           competence level of a division . . . The second point sir is to
           clarify the role of the 1st and 6th Divisions. [T]he 7th Division's
           location was complicated due to palm trees, blockages, and
           Iranian attacks from the Shatt al-Arab. The main reason we
           prevailed in the Fao Battle is the delay of the 7th Division, since
           it possessed a strategic location besides enduring major
           attacks . . . Their position was complicated, the 6th Division was
           attacked from the side as well and the 1st Division was crossing
           from the same road along with the 7th Division, which
           complicated issues even further. The 7th Division crossed with
           the 6th Division . . . and they were fired at from both sides that is
           what caused delay to the division sir more than others did . . .
SADDAM: We did not only want to liberate Fao, we wanted to end the war and
           we were very certain, based on our plans, that we would prevail.
           We trusted in God, the greatest, it was not based on adventure, it

---

[116] SH-SHTP-A-001-231, Iraqi Officials Discussing the Iran–Iraq War and the Battles to
Recapture Al-Fao, Undated (circa late 1988–1989).

> was based on faith, overall expanded and defined plans in every aspect and remembering the habits of the enemy during previous battles and how to handle them. We also remembered that the enemy underestimated our abilities in winning such a major battle and would never expect us to prevail. We engaged in a major battle with the enemy, we attacked them in two areas on a high level of attacks, a level that liberated Fao. There were two major battles, a battle that the enemy initiated, which at times affected us, and another we initiated ... and after that, they attempted hard to defeat us, however, we were determined to achieve our goal.[117]

Iraqi morale skyrocketed after Fao. And it was clearly time to exploit the disarray of Iranian forces. The latter had stepped up the fighting in the north, but Saddam refused to be diverted from cleaning up the situation in the south. A conversation between him and his military advisors in May underlines his focus. Talking about upcoming operations against Kurdistan, the army's assistant chief of staff, Lieutenant General Hussein Rashid, noted: "The third point is ... working with small covert units; this is a weak point for us and an advantage to them. The enemy can work with small covert units because the northern area is ideal for this type of operation." Saddam replied:

Anything after Fao including Shalmaja [Shalamcheh], we are not in a hurry for. Do you know why we [are] hurried in regaining Shalmaja [Shalamcheh] ... ? To tell the enemy to wash his hands of Basra completely ... There is nothing that requires us to be in a hurry after Fao ... we don't want to exhaust our forces but I want effective plans that assure us not having to surprise them in a way we are not comfortable with.

The dictator moved on to the more mundane matter of rewarding the troops who had displayed exceptional valor:

From now on, I will not ask the commanders to tell me, even the Republican Guard forces ... I will deal with them separately. I will say, your share is this number of bravery medals ... tell me, what are your suggestions on how to distribute them ... because it appears that the commanders reached a not so good situation ... they only want to assess, to the point that they spoil even the honor process ... So, this regiment has thirty bravery medals.[118]

At the end of April, Saddam ordered the team that had planned the Fao offensive to prepare the way for a major offensive immediately north of Basra to remove the Iranian threat to that city. By 10 May, planning

---

[117] *Ibid.*
[118] SH-PDWN-D-000-730, Transcript of an Armed Forces General Command Meeting Discussing the Iran–Iraq War and Al-Fao, 26 May 1988.

had advanced sufficiently so that he could issue a directive for the offensive to begin on 1 June. One of the chief planners noted, "The III Corps [was] to participate in the attack by performing secondary duties in the direction of Kut Sawadi. [But] the main thrust [toward] the Shatt al-Arab fell to the [Republican Guard] forces ... We began the final documentation and accompanying slides."[119]

One week later, the Iraqis moved the jump off date, probably at Saddam's instigation, to 26 May to coincide with the end of Ramadan. Again, Saddam paid close attention to the planning. In this case, he ordered the offensive to include a detailed deception plan aimed at deceiving not only the Iranians as to what was coming, but also the Americans. As he later commented to his senior advisors:

And this [is] what makes us careful, also in previous battles the Americans did not concern themselves with the technical outcome of the battle ... [A]fter the recent victories of the Blessed Ramadan Battle [the liberation of Fao] it became evident to the Americans that the outcome of the battles will have a noticeable effect on logistics. That is why they started to get interested in the technical aspects with regard to the battles that take place between us and Iran. This has added an additional factor with regard to the importance of secrecy and extra precautionary measures in all aspects be it technical, tactical, and operationally in liberation battles.[120]

On 25 May at 0345, the controlling headquarters was informed the offensive would not begin on the 26th after all, but on the 25th within five hours.[121] A flurry of activity allowed the Iraqis to launch the effort, and again they caught the Iranians by surprise. The result was a general collapse of the enemy's defensive positions around Basra.[122]

At 0930 hours sharp on 25 May, hundreds of mortars provided timed protection to our crossing units. The front line pushed through the crossings prepared the previous night by the engineering corps. The missiles formed a blanket of smoke and dust that completely enveloped our fighters and made them invisible. Only the shouts of "Allah Akbar" could be heard over the din of the shelling. Fierce fighting began. No sooner had the front units crossed the minefield than the engineering corps began their task to widen the crossings to allow our tanks to follow.

---

[119] Hamdani, *Memoir*.

[120] SH-SHTP-V-000-612, Saddam and Senior Military Officials Discussing Efforts to Retake the Majnun Area, Circa Late 1988.

[121] There appears to have been no explanation for the change, except that Saddam may have believed the plans for the offensive had been divulged to the Iranians. By moving the attack up by twenty-two hours he would still catch them by surprise. As an amateur, he failed to understand such an alteration so late might cause the offensive to break down.

[122] Since the Iranians had been on the offensive for the previous six years, their defensive positions may well have been less sophisticated than those of their opponents.

At 0142 hours of that same morning we received the first good news: the enemy's first line at Jasim had been taken. Sounds of praise and rejoicing filled the air. By 1107 the whole combat [force] of the 17th [Republican Guard] Armored Brigade had crossed the Shatt al-Arab via a breach 500 [meters] wide ...

At 1200 the 16th [Republican Guard] Special Forces Brigade moved in to complete the liberation of Tawilat Island ... At 1250 hours Baghdad and Medina Munawwarah [Division of the] RGFC pushed with full force into Deij to complete the second part of the plan. At 1325 hours they reached their targets, as did the Hammurabi [Division of the] RGFC. At 1445 hours our forces occupied the barricade through which the international border passed.[123]

This second offensive resulted in an even more devastating defeat for the Iranians than Fao. In ten hours, the Iraqis regained the ground they had lost in 1987. In many areas Iranian troops simply ran away in commandeered vehicles. The amount of materiel the Iraqis captured suggests the extent of the defeat: one hundred tanks from Iran's ever-shrinking inventory of armored fighting vehicles and more than one hundred artillery pieces. The tide of the war had turned against Khomeini, and the Iranians had little hope of overthrowing Saddam's Ba'athist Republic. Despite the defeat at Fao, the Iranians appear to have done little to prepare themselves for this second offensive, while the ayatollahs in Tehran still refused to recognize the extent of the defeats.

Almost immediately after the second victory had freed Basra from the Iranian threat, Saddam ordered planning and preparations for a third major offensive, this one to liberate the area around the Majnun islands and its valuable oil fields. On 12 June, the Iraqis began planning. The III Corps and Republican Guard were responsible for executing the plan. Against them were arrayed the 85th *Pasdaran* Brigade and the 3rd Armored Brigade of the 23rd *Pasdaran* Division in the north, with two *Pasdaran* regiments to the south. The defenders possessed only sixty tanks against the deployment of more than 2,000 Iraqi armored fighting vehicles.[124] The fact that Khomeini had dismissed the army's commander in chief and ordered Rafsanjani to take over command of the fighting at the front suggests the extent of Iranian desperation.[125]

By now, Iraqi planners were well trained in preparing set-piece offensives that took advantage of their considerable superiority in firepower:

The [Republican Guard] plan was based on the deployment of two divisions to repossess the southern oil fields (south Majnun) as [the] first part of the plan, followed by [a] push into the northern fields in the second part. Each of the plans had a huge artillery support in the form of the preliminary shelling and then protective

---

[123] Hamdani, *Memoir.*   [124] Ward, *Immortal*, 293.   [125] *Ibid.*, 107.

firing. The [Republican Guard] commander had previously personally trained the [Republican Guard] artillery in the use of protective firing techniques ... A force equivalent to a regiment was to be airdropped behind the enemy's lines to cut their withdrawal and capture as many [of the fleeing Iranians] as possible and to keep in communications with the units of the VI Corps.[126]

On 25 June at 0345, the Iraqis began their preparatory shelling of Iranian defensive positions. Again, the Iranians were caught flat-footed. By the evening of the same day, the Iraqis had captured their objectives while collecting large numbers of prisoners of war. By the end of the fighting, the Iraqis had mauled or destroyed elements of between six and eight Iranian divisions. On 27 June, Saddam held a conference to discuss the extent of the Iraqi victory and the rewards the dictator was going to pass out to the victorious troops and their commanders: "If we honored everyone equally without considering what he [achieved], no fighter will distinguish himself. That is human nature. Has the money assigned to reward III Corps that captured enemy fighter[s] been transferred? Two million is not enough for them. Are 1,000 prisoners of war enough for you [the generals attending Saddam]."

The attendees replied: "Two thousand, sir."[127] The conversation turned to the subject of captured Iranians and weapons, as well as how to force some of the recalcitrant Iranians to surrender. There was a clear air of jocularity throughout the discussions.

SADDAM:	Then that is enough for III Corps. I called the commander of the Republican Guard yesterday and asked him about enemy weapons they gained during the battle. He said he didn't know. I asked him to count them accurately and get the price list specific to enemy weapons and prisoners of war from [Ali Abdullah] Saleh, III Corps commander. The Guard Corps started collecting weapons and prisoners of war. III Corps counted no less that 3,000 enemy fighters. But, his hastiness and not searching the field of operations cost him a number of prisoners of war.
ARMY ASSISTANT CHIEF OF STAFF FOR OPERATIONS:	Sir let's hit the Qasab al-Bardi area with aerial explosives, there is a large number of enemy hiding there.

---

[126] *Ibid.*

[127] SH-SHTP-D-000-538, Transcript of a Meeting between Saddam and His Commanding Officers at the Armed Forces General Command Regarding the Iraq–Iran War, 27 June 1988.

MINISTER OF DEFENSE:	Where are they going to go? The area is not conducive to walking. Anyone who doesn't know how to swim very [well] will drown, or he will stay there until hunger will compel him to come our way.
SADDAM:	They will come out to the dry land. There is no one bigger than man but God, and when he makes a decision, it will be it. Two steps between Majnun and land, the dam will open and when he comes to this broken place, he will get out to dry land and return. As for food, he will live on the grass available.
MINISTER OF DEFENSE:	Because of the artillery bombardment, the lagoon is full of dead fish.[128]

The final discussions examined the remaining weaknesses of Iraqi forces to conduct complex operations:

SADDAM:	The last operation conducted by III Corps and the Republican Guard was satisfactory and there are some corps that are still using old theories, capturing territories in a slow fashion. I consider advancing just a few feet after hitting the enemy with intense fire very harmful ...
REPUBLICAN GUARD DIRECTOR:	Sir, in spite of the successes achieved in Fao ... and other battles, we still have a deficiency in understanding the use of artillery even when we are victorious. If we look closely, we will find deficiency and weaknesses even in the Republican Guard['s] use of firepower in spite of the superiority showed in the latest battles ...
SADDAM:	In general, the forces we now have number-wise are able to crush the Iranians even if Iran developed its resources. The only thing is how are we to act? When we regain our lands, we should chase the enemy anywhere he gathers and destroy him, this will be our program. We have to hold our defensive positions with as [few] fighters as possible with the presence of reserve[s] in all our corps in addition to the general command reserve will always be [prepared to] attack not defend ...
	From now on, if the enemy attacks Ashalamja, we hold him at the front and attack him from there as deep as we can and hit him from behind. We shouldn't

[128] *Ibid.*

> engage the enemy head on and give up martyrs and wounded for no reason. The plan we will apply if the enemy attacks and outs us from this location is to hold him at the front and attack him from the left and right completely cutting him off. That way we don't subject our forces to danger, nor does the enemy gain any land, and we do not exhaust our armed forces.[129]

The defeat of the Iranians in the south was almost complete. Despite the clear military opportunity to pursue and defeat a broken force in detail, Saddam had the sense to hold. Not only would pursuing Iranian forces into the depths of their own country once again expose Iraq's military weaknesses, but it would also undercut Saddam's diplomatic track designed to end the war on terms favorable to Iraq.

The war in the Gulf

The Tanker War continued unabated into 1988 with the Iraqis once again taking the lead in terms of both attacks and damage inflicted. The initial set of attacks in January and February hit fourteen tankers. Nevertheless, only one had to be written off because of extensive damage. By now, the Iraqis were skilled at launching strikes deep into the Gulf. These raids ranged from Farsi and Lavan Islands; however, most Iraqi attacks centered on Kharg. The expanding Iraqi inventory now included the C-601 Kraken air-to-surface missile. The attacks continued into mid-March with another Iranian tanker written off. But a hit on the *Sandandaj*, while only damaging the tanker, killed twenty-six of her crew.[130]

There was then a puzzling six-week lull in Iraqi air operations over the Gulf, explicable perhaps only in terms of the Iraqi use of the air force to fly interdiction missions in support of the ground forces. Not until mid-May did the Iraqis return to the Gulf to launch a sustained number of sorties against Iranian tanker traffic. In less than a week, they hit thirteen tankers and salvage tugs. On 14 May, the Iraqis launched their fourth attack on shipping near Larak Island in the Straits of Hormuz. This raid was perhaps the most successful of the war. The Cypriot tanker *Seawise Giant* was a write-off. The Liberian tanker *Argosy* was damaged, but repairable. The crew of the Spanish tanker *Barcelona*, burning after being hit by several bombs, had to beach her to prevent her from sinking. Four

---

[129] *Ibid.*   [130] Navias and Hooton, *Tanker Wars*, 166–167.

days later, just as salvage tugs were pulling the tanker off, an unexploded bomb went off sinking one tug and damaging three others.[131]

Iraqi attacks tailed off in June with the last attack of 8 July rendering the tanker *Star Ray*, sailing from Kharg to Larak as part of the Iranian shuttle fleet, a total write-off.[132] Meanwhile the Iranians vented their anger at these raids by attacking as much neutral shipping as they could get away with. As a result, once again, they involved themselves in a direct confrontation with the United States. The mining of the frigate USS *Samuel B. Roberts*, sister ship of the *Stark*, on 14 April was a final straw for the Americans. They responded four days later. Operation Praying Mantis occurred at the same time that the Iraqis were blasting their way through Iranian defenses on Fao. Led by the cruiser USS *Wainwright*, four destroyers and three frigates attacked the Sassan and Sirri oil platforms, which were being used by *Pasdaran* naval units. After the platforms had been destroyed, the Iranians attacked shipping in the United Arab Emirate's territorial waters; A-6 Intruders replied by sinking two of the *Pasdaran* craft involved and so terrorized the crew of one of the Iranian boats that they ran their craft aground. The *Wainwright* and one of its accompanying destroyers sank the fast-attack craft *Joshan* after it had fired a missile at them. The final blow came when the Americans sank the Iranian frigate *Sabalan* with a combination of smart and dumb bombs and two Harpoon missiles.

Heightened tension between the Americans and their European allies on one side and the Iranians on the other had unfortunate consequences. The cruiser *Vincennes* engaged in combat with *Pasdaran* craft when her radar picked up what her crew interpreted as an F-14 taking off from Bandar-e Abbas. It was not, but rather was an Iranian civilian Airbus en route to Dubai. The cruiser fired its anti-aircraft missiles and nearly 300 civilians died.[133] Khomeini's initial reaction was to order the preparation and implementation of an Iranian response to the disaster. According to a senior cleric, such a response would have included "cells at home and abroad ... [making] the material, political, economic, and military interests of the US targets of their struggle." However, Khomeini demurred from his usual "victory of spirit over blood" path and directed that Iran seek its justice through the UN Security Council. This was, no doubt, a result of Rafsanjani's ongoing lobbying for a diplomatic end to the war, in place of, as many in the *Pasdaran* continued to advocate, the expansion of a losing cause. The tragedy of the Iranian Airbus shoot-down would, as Dilip Hiro described it, "prove to be the curtain raiser to

[131] *Ibid.*, 167–168.   [132] *Ibid.*, 168.   [133] *Ibid.*, 175.

something more profound: Iran's acceptance of Security Council Resolution 598."[134]

What had the naval war in the Persian Gulf achieved? The most thorough study has this to say about the Iraqi perspective:

[A]lthough Saddam Hussein made many mistakes, his decision to attack merchant shipping proved extremely perceptive. The Iraqi strategy of striking merchant vessels to bring indirect pressure upon the Iranian war effort, as well as emphasizing the international aspect of the war, was fully vindicated, for Baghdad was able to manipulate such attacks for [its] political ends.[135]

The al-Anfal Campaign

Having disposed of the Iranians in the south by liberating Fao, the territory occupied by the Iranians around Basra, and the Majnun islands, Saddam turned his eyes to the north. He aimed to re-conquer the territory held by Kurdish "saboteurs" and Iranians. He also hoped to extort a full measure of vengeance for what he regarded as the traitorous activities of Kurdish rebel groups. By early 1988, even pro-Baghdad Kurdish forces, known as the national defense battalions, were suspect. Saddam directed that the Kurdish forces be separated from Iraqi units, for whom they served in an auxiliary function. Iraqi forces would concentrate on a firepower-heavy solution to its tactical problems. Saddam directed a different approach for his Kurdish allies:

Each of them is given a target and you say ... "This is your target, if you capture it, you will have to keep it and after that we will use you no more to advance even one step." You should abide by this direction and practice it [because] if you don't achieve your target, we will push you to your target until you all get killed.[136]

An early summer 1988 discussion among Iraqi leaders suggests the extent of Saddam's desire for revenge. After a lengthy discussion about the legality of using chemical weapons, Saddam turned directly to the

---

[134] Hiro, *The Longest War*, 211–212. Despite Rafsanjani's belief that Iran needed to seek a diplomatic solution to the war, he believed that the Airbus accident was part of a larger (presumably American) conspiracy to "prevent our victory" or as one Iranian newspaper article stated, "this was in no way an accident, and in our view was a notification." Quoted in Takeyh, "The Iran–Iraq War," 381.

[135] Navias and Hooton, *Tanker Wars*, 187–188.

[136] Transcript of a Meeting between Saddam Hussein and the Military Advisers (Tape 4; 21 January 1988) in *SH-MISC-D-001-391, Transcripts of Meetings between Saddam Hussein and the Armed Forces General Command, January–February 1988.

subject of the Kurds. At the height of discussions, the dictator made his intentions clear:

To all the Kurds [who] are contending that we are afraid to discuss or tackle this issue; our message is that we are willing to discuss the subject of capitalism, communism, Kurds, and so forth or any other subject that they want to discuss. That will teach them a painful lesson; so next time before they think to raise the issue against us they will think twice as they remember the pain that they have suffered in this lesson. We will ask all parties or countries that are for Kurdish self-rule or for improving the current self-rule status to attend these discussions ... Ha Ha Ha ... Our Kurdish elements that are involved in sabotage will be killed this time and if they return a second time they will be killed again until we are rid of them forever.[137]

As the overall pacification czar for the campaign, Saddam had chosen his hatchet man, Chemical Ali, who lived up to his name. On 15 April 1988, he met with local authorities, members of the northern bureau of the Ba'athist Party, and the governors of the supposedly Autonomous Kurdish Region of northern Iraq. He was ruthlessly honest with his listeners about what the pacification plan for the region was going to entail:

What went wrong? What happened? Thirty, twenty-five, twenty years of saboteur activity. Imagine how many martyrs we have! ... Now you can't go from Kirkuk to Erbil any more without an armored vehicle. All of this basin, from Koysinjaq to here [Kirkuk] ... I am going to evacuate it. I will evacuate it as far as Gweir and Mosul. No human being except on the main roads. For five years I won't allow any human existence there. I don't want their agriculture. I don't want their okra and cucumbers. If we don't act in this way the saboteurs' activities will never end, not for a million years. These are all just notes, but with the help of God we will apply them very soon, not more than a month from now. In the summer nothing will be left.[138]

In January 1989, Chemical Ali summed up his campaign's success and his reaction to Saddam's order to ease up the pressure on the Kurds. This time the audience consisted almost exclusively of members of the northern Bureau of the Ba'ath Party, which had provided political and security direction to the units in the al-Anfal campaign:

So we started to show these senior commanders [army commanders who were objecting to some aspects of the murderous campaign] on TV that [the saboteurs] had surrendered. Am I supposed to keep them in good shape? What am I supposed to do with them, these goats? Then a message reaches me from

---

[137] SH-SHTP-A-000-788, Saddam Discussing the Iraqi Stance toward Respecting International Law, Circa June–July 1988.
[138] Section 1 "Meeting With Members of the Northern Bureau and Governors of the Autonomous Region of Iraqi Kurdistan, 15 April 1988" of Appendix A *The Ali Hassan al-Majid Tapes* in "Genocide in Iraq."

that great man, the father [Saddam], saying take good care of the families of the saboteurs and this and that. The general command brings it to me. I put his message to my head.[139]

But take good care of them? No, I will bury them with bulldozers. Then, they ask me for the names of all the prisoners in order to publish them. I said, "Weren't you satisfied by what you saw on television and read in the newspaper? Where am I supposed to put all this enormous number of people? I started to distribute them among the governates. I had to send bulldozers hither and thither."[140]

The combination of Chemical Ali's campaign of extermination and the fighting that destroyed the last vestiges of Kurdish resistance left somewhere between 150,000 and 200,000 Kurds dead.[141]

With the collapse of the Iranian position in the south, Saddam and his generals could concentrate nearly all their military power against the Kurds. With the devastating defeats in the south, the morale of Iranian forces supporting the Kurds hit new lows. Undoubtedly the heavy fighting in March and April around Halabjah had drained off much of the combat effectiveness of Khomeini's forces in the area. Thus, the Kurds and their Persian allies had little chance against the combination of Iraqi armored forces, their huge superiority in firepower, and the consistent use of chemical weapons against military and civilian targets.[142] The military results were a foregone conclusion while the losses due to chemical attacks devastated Kurdish villagers. One Iraqi report indicates 500 Kurds "killed in addition to a significant number injured in Dizli ... 500–600 ... killed and a large number injured in Tarkhanb Ayad ... near Mariwan, [and] 2,500 killed and a significant number injured, including those among the Iranian Revolutionary Guards, the saboteurs, and the local residents in Halabjah."[143]

---

[139] Note in the translation: "The sense conveyed in the Arabic phrase is that Saddam Hussein's wish is always al-Majid's command – but not, he goes on to say defensively, in this instance."

[140] Appendix A, Section 4: Northern Bureau Meeting to Review the Campaigns of 1987 and 1988; [Circa] 21–22 January 1989, in "Genocide in Iraq."

[141] Farouk-Sluglett and Sluglett, *Iraq since 1958*, 270.

[142] For further evidence of the Iraqi use of chemical weapons against the Kurds, see SH-PDWN-D-000-678, Various Memoranda Relating to the Iraqi Use of Chemical Weapons against Halabja and Other Kurdish Villages, 1988. Specifically, memorandum dated 21 April 1988.

[143] SH-IZAR-D-000-646, Telegram from the Intelligence System of the Eastern Zone Revealing the Use of Chemical Weapons against Halabja, 20 March 1988. One Iraqi document suggests "dealing with the area of Ahmad Awa and the old Bistana 'Anab village using special ammunition during the late hours at night when most of the enemy are sleeping." SH-GMID-D-000-299, General Military Intelligence Directorate Correspondence About Iranian Military Activities and Other Issues, March 1988.

So too were the political consequences. Those Kurds who could escape fled to Iran and Turkey. Most could not. The unlucky ones, who had not been executed or died in the fighting, were deported to miserable enclaves scattered throughout southern Iraq, where many died as a result of the appalling conditions the Iraqis imposed on them. The majority, but a bare majority, eked out a living until Saddam's power collapsed in much of Kurdistan as a result of fallout from the 1991 Gulf War.

10   Conclusion

The hardest point I went through was when we feared the Iranians would accept our cease fire suggestion [Referring to June 1982] ... that was not the image that I thought our army should end this war with. The appropriate image ... is to end the war with the Iranian broken and our army strengthened by God ... [w]hat was accomplished was the highest of my hopes for this bloody route that has taken eight long years.[1]   – Saddam Hussein, late 1988

Even after the disastrous defeats of Iran's military forces as well as indications that morale in the army and on the home front was collapsing, Khomeini made every effort to keep up appearances. Despite a growing pragmatism among many senior clerics, the Majlis election resulted in a victory for "candidates who called for the most extreme policies."[2] Propaganda broadcast to the Iranian people described the defeats as "planned withdrawals."[3] There is some indication the regime increased the naval confrontation with the United States in the Gulf – a set of incidents that contributed to the shoot-down of the Iranian Airbus A300 – to distract the Iranians from the bad news on the battlefield.[4] Finally, confronted with the possibility of greater defeats at the hands of the Iraqis and growing opposition at home, Khomeini yielded to the

---

[1] SH-SHTP-V-000-589, Saddam Hussein and Military Officials Discussing the Iran–Iraq War and the Al-Qadisiyyah Battle, Circa Late 1988.

[2] This result owed much to the regime having promoted the election as "religious duty" and as a patriotic way to show support for the war while the shower of Iraqi Scuds, which in part drove a substantial portion of Tehran's reform-minded population (the middle class) into the countryside and away from the polls. Bahman Baktiari, *Parliamentary Politics in Revolutionary Iran: The Institutionalization of Factional Politics* (Gainesville, FL, 1996), 148; David Menashri, "Iran (Jumhuriyye Islamiyye Iran)," in *Middle East Contemporary Survey, Volume XI: 1987*, Ami Ayalon and Haim Shaked, eds. (Boulder, CO, 1988), 489–490.

[3] Ward, *Immortal*, 294.

[4] The United States admitted the "tragic and regrettable accident" and agreed to compensate the families. Harold Lee Wise, *Inside the Danger Zone: The US Military in the Persian Gulf, 1987–1988* (Annapolis, MD, 2007), 219–232; US Department of Defense, "Investigative Report: Formal Investigation into the Circumstances Surrounding the Downing of Iran Air Flight 655 on 3 July 1988" (1988).

advice of Iran's senior religious and political leaders and agreed to a ceasefire.

On 20 July, the Grand Ayatollah announced to the Iranian people, "Taking this decision was more deadly than poison. I submitted myself to God's will and drank this drink for his satisfaction."[5] Khomeini's humiliation was hardly sufficient for Saddam. Shortly after the conclusion of the armistice, Saddam rubbed salt in his enemy's wounds by commenting publicly on the ceasefire:

Who deeply understands history knows that history plays an essential role in [what] people believe [and national policies] and this present day will become history in the future . . . For the above mentioned reasons, in addition to reasons related to our faith and the great history of our nation and people, we offer the hand of friendship, forgiveness and peace to the Iranian people regardless of the bitterness we feel and regardless of [their] assault and violation that [we were] exposed to.[6]

Why then had the Iranians lost? One perceptive commentator on the Iran–Iraq War noted the following in the conflict's aftermath:

If Iran's military successes between 1982 and 1986 were ephemeral and costly, with long gaps between major offensives from 1984–86, the problem stemmed as much from deficiencies in strategy as from logistics. Alternating between frontal offensives and attrition along the length of the frontier ("defensive jihad"), between enthusiasm for the daring of the revolutionary guard and the more sober appraisals of the professional military, Iran's leaders were unable to frame a strategy that tied their war aims – the overthrow of the enemy – to their military capabilities, which in terms of equipment dwindled with each offensive.[7]

Throughout the war, Khomeini had rejected every possibility of peace to pursue regime change in Baghdad. Iranian actions in Lebanon, attacking tankers carrying crude from the Gulf States, and confronting the United States meant that its ability to deploy well-equipped forces on the various battlefronts decreased steadily during the war.[8] Rafsanjani admitted in July 1988 that "in the revolutionary atmosphere, we made enemies of

---

[5] Ward, *Immortal*, 296.

[6] SH-SHTP-A-000-913, Saddam and Advisors Discussing a Forthcoming Speech, circa July 1988.

[7] Shahram Chubin, "The Last Phase of the Iran–Iraq War: From Stalemate to Ceasefire," *Third World Quarterly* 11, no. 2 (1989), 4.

[8] According to one source, Iranian forces, beginning in May 1988, were ordered to avoid direct confrontation with the United States, but should continue to fly "harassing missions" to keep US Navy ship crews at general quarters and their skippers "nervous." Cooper and Bishop, *Iran–Iraq War in the Air*, 276.

[some Western countries] ... we pushed those who could have been neutral into hostility."[9]

Throughout the conflict, Khomeini and his hardline advisors believed that religious enthusiasm, engendered by their revolution, could replace military expertise, weapons systems, and technology. While this "way of war" may have affected a few tactical engagements, it was a recipe for disaster as a strategy. Given the disparity in population size between the two countries, the Iranians had the raw material to prevail in a long war of attrition; but through their religious fanaticism, disdain for their enemy, and ignorance of things military, they squandered every advantage. They set impossible strategic goals for their military forces. When the balance tipped against them, they tried to expand the conflict by attacking the world's energy supplies flowing through the Gulf.

Despite all evidence to the contrary, they maintained a fanatical belief that God would give them victory. As Khomeini had commented in 1984, "Those that think that the Koran does not say 'war until victory' are mistaken."[10] Iran did not create a single overarching military command until 2 June 1988. On taking his position as acting commander of the armed forces, Rafsanjani issued a sweeping decree that established an organization for national defense that all but admitted the ineptitude of the previous seven years. Khomeini's heir apparent, Ayatollah Hussein-Ali Montazeri, agreed, admitting on Tehran radio in early June, "Do you know why the war has lasted so long? ... We had no planning, [no] coordination, [nor] a unified campaign."[11]

Had Iraq won? Saddam had survived, but Iraq had hardly triumphed. The nation was bankrupt. It had lost huge quantities of manpower and equipment. It owed vast sums to the Gulf States, which had supported its war effort. Its oil infrastructure had suffered considerably. However, the corrupt and murderous Ba'ath regime remained in power, while its leaders had learned little or, perhaps worse, the wrong lessons from their careless and ill-thought-through decision to invade Iran in 1980. Saddam would soon embark on new adventures, this time putting Iraq's military forces in a position to counter a power against which they had no chance.

Iraq's survival also resulted from the ruthlessness with which it waged the war against the Iranians. The War of the Cities was one example of its struggle to survive; the decision to use chemical weapons was not only a

---

[9] Interview with Hashemi-Rafsanjani 6 July 1988 cited in Robin Wright, *In the Name of God: The Khomeini Decade* (New York, NY, 1989), 192.

[10] Chubin, "The Last Phase of the Iran–Iraq War," 4.

[11] Gideon Gera, "The Iraqi–Iranian War," in *Volume XII: 1988*, Ofra Bengio, ed., *Middle East Contemporary Survey: Iraq, 1976–1999* (Tel Aviv, 1989), 212–213.

desperate measure to halt the human waves of *Pasdaran* militia but also a statement of will. Tariq Aziz best caught the regime's rationale for using chemical weapons in a conversation with the Swedish diplomat Rolf Ekéus that he recounted to Saddam in the 1990s:

I mean that [when] the Israelis reached the Suez Canal [the superpowers] told them to "stop." They arrived to the Golan [and the superpowers] told them after the Golan this is it ... As to our conflict with Iran, no one came to tell us [or tell the Iranians] Basra or Baghdad or I mean any spot in Iraq [represents] a red line you cannot cross ...

Second, the people we wanted to fight [the Iranians], they do not live on the same planet on which we live ... Hundreds of thousands of fanatics blind in their mind and in their hearts used to come to us who wanted to die ... A threat of this kind requires ... special confrontation ... So you [Ekéus] come and search for European contexts or classical contexts in the behavior and you want to apply it on a case that is not a classical case. That is the first thing. Second, when we were confronted we faced this kind of aggression and this danger that threatened the existence of our people and our land, we ... took a decision as a political leadership ... that whatever we can [do] to face this aggression, we [did]. ... I told him so we authorized the workers [involved in] military production that any weapon they can produce, let them produce it. They asked, can we improve the missile? We told them to improve it. They said, can we produce chemical weapons? We told them to produce chemical weapons?[12]

Iraq's "victory" involved a number of factors. The military's increasing professionalism as well as Saddam's own learning curve played their parts. Iranian incompetence also played a major role. Finally, there was the ruthlessness with which the Iraqis pursued the conflict. Chemical weapons had cast a long shadow beyond their use on the battlefield. The bombardment of Tehran in 1988 carried with it the message that the Iraqis, given how they had prosecuted the war thus far, were capable of adding chemical warheads to their bombardment of Iranian cities. The massive exodus from Tehran carried with it a message that even Khomeini's regime could not ignore.

With the war over, Saddam proceeded to trumpet Iraq's victories as indicating the arrival of a new great power in the Middle East. Many believed him, not only in the Arab world, but also in the West. Many accepted his claims of a battle-hardened and highly effective Iraqi Army. Thus, when the confrontation over Saddam's occupation of Kuwait occurred in late summer 1990, the conventional wisdom among too many pundits and so-called experts outside and even within the military

---

[12] SH-SHTP-D-000-760, Saddam and Political Advisors Discussing the Production of Biological Materials in Iraq, the Iran–Iraq War, UN Inspections, and the Arab–Israeli Conflict, circa 1990–1999.

in the United States pictured an Iraqi army as if its soldiers were the reincarnation of the *Waffen* SS. They were not. Those who had survived eight years of futile blood-letting were simply the survivors of a horrible event that had consumed much of Iraq's youth in support of Saddam and his ideology.[13]

As for military effectiveness, during the war, the Iraqi military had gained the ability to utilize firepower and control, and in a relative sense, large bodies of soldiers. But even on the battlefields of 1988, it had displayed little initiative and less flexibility. As one commentator on Arab military organizations noted about the Iraqi Army:

At a tactical level, the Iraqis exhibited the same problems that had plagued them throughout the war. While the [Republican Guard] and the best regular-army units performed better than the rest of the armed forces, their improvement can only be said to have been relative. In particular, the same old problems could be seen when, for one reason or another, the situation did not develop as anticipated by Baghdad's plan. Whereas combined-arms integration generally was stilted but adequate in most of the assaults, on numerous occasions when Iraqi units were caught off guard by an Iranian ambush or an unexpected defensive position, this cooperation disintegrated, leading to losses in infantry and tanks. Unfortunately Iranian counterattacks continued to take a disproportionate toll on Iraqi forces; the Iraqis were slow to react, and in every case their only response was to try to beat the Iranians back with overwhelming firepower.[14]

Iraq's triumph had come largely as a result of the fact that Iraq could spend more lavishly on equipping its military forces at the end of the war than the Iranians. The spending levels of the two opponents during the last three years of the conflict suggest how and why the military balance tipped so drastically against the Iranians in 1987 and 1988. From 1984 through 1987, the Iraqis spent approximately $12–14 billion each year on arms purchases abroad. In 1985, the Iranians spent $14 billion, but the next year their purchases dropped to $5.89 billion with $6–8 billion in 1987. To a considerable extent, the drop in Iranian purchases reflected the drop in oil prices. The Iraqis suffered the same drop, but were able to make up the difference with loans from their Arab neighbors. Given Iran's consistently bizarre international policies that seemed aimed at making enemies of the entire world, no one was going to lend the Iranians a penny.

The numbers of weapons systems available as a result of the differences in financial resources available to the opposing sides explain much

---

[13] And on the other side, there had been the fanaticism of Khomeini's brand of Shi'a radicalism, which had refused all the opportunities to end the slaughter.
[14] Pollack, *Arabs at War*, 230–231.

about the crushing defeats Iran suffered in 1988. By spring of that year, the Iraqis enjoyed a four-to-one superiority in tanks, a three-to-one superiority in artillery, and a ten-to-one superiority in aircraft, with most of the Iranian aircraft grounded for lack of spare parts. As the commander of the *Pasdaran* admitted after the war, "They had armor and we did not ... We were unarmed infantrymen against the enemy's cavalry."[15] A decided advantage for the Iraqis was also that their military and signals intelligence organizations had broken Iran's codes through most of the war and hence could determine where and when the major Iranian offensives were going to occur during the desperate years of the conflict. That advantage was equally important in providing Iraqi air and naval forces with intelligence on Iranian tanker traffic and convoys in the Gulf.

The disadvantages under which his opponents had worked throughout the conflict, much of it do to their own unwillingness and inability to adapt, were not obvious to Saddam, who almost immediately began to bask in the glow the sycophants of his court shone on him, endlessly declaiming Iraq's great triumph. Saddam was sowing the seeds for the invasion of Kuwait and further catastrophe for this country.[16] In a meeting with senior ministers after the war, Saddam attempted to place the conflict in what he believed to be its historical setting:

I am sure that in a thousand years, [if] the Iraqis [were] in dire need, they would appeal to this al-Qadisiyyah the same way that we appealed ourselves to the other al-Qadisiyyah fourteen hundred years ago.[17] All of this could not have happened had it not been for the insistence and the togetherness of [our] leadership. It so happened that the togetherness was not a case of belief, but rather it was a case of intellect and humanity ... It is based on the belief in confrontational strategy ... This tremendous capital and this great experiment is the first event in the history of the Arab nation ... the world has not fought [such a long war] for a long time ... [In] a thousand years and for a thousand years to come, no country from the Arab nation has faced such a great challenge and such dangerous intermingling between the fighting arenas, the ditches, and, let us call it, the sacred land ... You remember the Arab experiment during the period of Gamel Abdel Nasser ... the Abdul Nasser experiment collapsed and was finished within six hours ...[18] In 1973 a

---

[15] Chubin, "The Last Phase of the Iran–Iraq War," 7.

[16] For the Iraqi perspective on that conflict, see Woods, *The Mother of All Battles*.

[17] The Battle of Qadisiyyah occurred in 636 AD not far from the Euphrates in Iraq and saw the Arab army destroy the Persian army, which led to the collapse of the Sassanid Empire and its eventual replacement by an Arab-Islamic regime.

[18] Here Saddam was referring to the Six-Day War when, in the first hours, Egyptian air power was destroyed by the Israeli strike.

war that was initiated by the Arabs took place against Israel. The whole war officially lasted for no more than fourteen days.[19]

Saddam had learned little from his experiences during the war.[20] After its conclusion, he dismissed a number of his more competent commanders, while other competent military leaders had a penchant for dying in helicopter crashes. The old cronies swiftly crept back to reassure Saddam of his military genius. A conference of senior officers immediately before the war ended in July 1988 suggests how little had changed from the days of the invasion in September 1980. One of the officers suggested to Saddam:

We have a third issue sir, which is updating and informing us during the battle, although we still receive communications to be prepared, either through our intelligence, through security or other forces, we must take in[to] consideration that it will be impossible to continue training at that time, which could jeopardize the safety of our nation. The other issue sir [is] that long periods of training could cause boredom and carelessness ... Our forces are supposed to be always prepared and they are sir, especially air defense. They are prepared night and day; however if we receive orders instructing us to be prepared and ready to attack, the forces fear if they do not have their equipment and radar running continuously, they will appear they are not following orders. If they have their equipment running 24 hours, they will need to rest it for hours afterwards.

Saddam replied:

Like we have seen before where we watched soldiers tied up to vehicles and dragged throughout the city and we watched through those cameras people running and screaming ... We should capture whoever we can, hammer them to the vehicles and drag them all around until they are totally dismembered, we must perform such act[s] ... Listen! I do not ever want to hear [about] weather again. The weather does not relate to what I am talking about here! ... I was trying to provide you with a solution and you were complicating the issue.[21]

The authors leave this account of Saddam's "triumph" with a suggestion the dictator made in the celebratory atmosphere that characterized his discussions with the Iraqi high command after the Iranians had asked

---

[19] SH-SHTP-A-000-631, Saddam Hussein Discussing General Issues and Iraqi Military History, Circa July–August 1988.

[20] Nor for that matter had his senior advisors. One of them commented in the meeting quoted directly above: "The war is going to end and if nothing happens, God forbid, then we will start another war that singles the present one out." SH-SHTP-A-000-631, Saddam Hussein Discussing General Issues and Iraqi Military History, circa July–August 1988.

[21] SH-SHTP-A-000-637, Saddam Meeting with Military Advisors Regarding the Iraq–Iran War, circa 1988.

for a halt in the fighting. Saddam proposed the following as a monument to the success of Iraq:

The weapons and military equipment that are the spoils of the three months from the Ramadan al-Mubarak Battle, the Battle of Tawakalna 'Ala Allah and the Battle of Mohammed Rasul Allah, in other words the battles of the three months ... I have assigned the chief of the presidential *Diwan* to coordinate with the ministry of defense to measure the weight of all the weapons and equipment, and its equivalent weight of soil. Then we [will] make a mountain, a mountain of soil, and in 5,000 years, we will say do you see these ancients, it is equivalent to the amount of weapons that we have gained within the three months.[22]

---

[22] SH-SHTP-A-000-816, Saddam and Ba'ath Party Members Discussing the Iraqi Victory in the Iran–Iraq War, 9 August 1988.

Appendix A Timeline

1979	11 February	An Islamic revolutionary regime, headed by Ayatollah Khomeini, assumes power in Iran.
	16 July	Saddam Hussein named president of Iraq, chairman of the Revolutionary Command Council, and general secretary of the Regional Command of the Ba'ath Party.
	30 October	Iraq demands a revision of the 1975 Algiers Agreement.
	14 December	Tehran announces that it repulsed an attempted Iraqi incursion into Iran.
1980	26 January	Abol Hassan Bani-Sadr elected president of the Islamic Republic of Iran.
	February	Periodic border clashes between Iran and Iraq begin and continue until the outbreak of war.
	17 April	Khomeini urges the Iraqi people and military to overthrow the Ba'athist regime.
	4 September	Iranian shells Iraqi towns of Khanaqin and Mandali (retrospectively noted by Iraq as the first act of war).
	17 September	Iraq declares the 1975 Algiers Agreement null and void due to Iranian violation and claims full sovereignty over the Shatt al-Arab.
	22 September	Initial Iraqi air strikes target ten airfields in a failed attempt to destroy the Iranian Air Force on the ground.
	23 September	Iraqi ground forces invade Iran, advancing as far as Ahvaz and Susangard and offers Iran a ceasefire.
	28 September	UN Security Council Resolution 479 calls for the cessation of hostilities.
	5 October	Iran rejects the offer of a ceasefire.

	22–24 October	Iraq gains control of area around Abadan and Khorramshahr.
	10 November	Iraq captures Khorramshahr
	7 December	Saddam announces that Iraq will employ a defensive strategy in Iraqi-held Iranian territories.
	24 December	Iraq begins air raids on Iranian oil terminals at Kharg Island.
1981	5–10 January	Iran's counteroffensive in Dezful–Susangard area is unsuccessful.
	7 June	Israeli air strike destroys Iraq's Osirak nuclear reactor.
	28 June	Iran rejects Ramadan ceasefire offered by Iraq.
	27–29 September	Iran regains Abadan.
	5 November	Iran rejects Muharram ceasefire offered by Iraq.
	November–December	Iran retakes territory around Abadan and north of Susangard in a series of small attacks.
1982	12 April	Saddam offers to withdraw Iraqi troops from Iran in exchange for a guarantee that the conflict will end, which he does not receive.
	22 May	Iran liberates Khorramshahr.
	10 June	Iraq offers another ceasefire, which is rejected by Iran.
	20 June	Iraq declares its withdrawal from Iran by 30 June.
	13 July	Iran rejects UN Security Council Resolution 514, which calls for a ceasefire and the withdrawal of warring forces to the international border.
	13 July–2 August	First Battle at Basra (Operation Ramadan): failed Iranian offensives intended to capture Basra.
	12 August	Iraq declares a maritime exclusion zone around Iran's Kharg Island.
1983	10–17 April	Operation Dawn: Iranian offensive near al-Amara.
	7 June	Iraq offers a ceasefire, which Iran rejects.

	2 November	Iraq warns merchant vessels to avoid the "war zone" in the northern Persian Gulf.
1984	February	Tanker War: with the intention of shifting the war away from the battlefield stalemate, Saddam orders increased aerial bombing of Iranian commercial tankers in the Persian Gulf. His intention is to force Iran to close the Strait of Hormuz, resulting in foreign intervention on behalf of Iraq.
	7–22 February	First "War of the Cities": Iraq targets eleven Iranian cities with ballistic missiles. Iran targets Iraqi cities in retaliation. Iraq fails to achieve its main objective of preventing an Iranian offensive.
	24 February–19 March	Second Battle at Basra (Operation Khaibar): Iranian offensives intended to capture Basra. Iran fails to capture Basra but does capture Majnun Island.
1985	28 January–early February	First Iraqi offensive since the opening of the war. Occurs along the central front, in the region of Qasr-e-Shirin.
	11–23 March	Third Battle at Basra (Operation Badr): failed Iranian offensives intended to capture Basra.
	22 March–8 April	Second "War of the Cities."
	August–December	Iraq launches approximately sixty air raids on Kharg Island.
1986	9–25 February	Operation Dawn 8: Iran captures Fao Peninsula.
	12 August	Iraqi long-range air raid on Sirri Island.
	25 November	Iraqi long-range air raid on Larak Island.
	24–26 December	Fourth Battle at Basra[1] (Operation Karbala 4): failed Iranian offensive intended to capture Basra.
1987	9 January–25 February	Fifth Battle at Basra (Operation Karbala 5): failed Iranian offensive intended to capture Basra.

---

[1] Named the "Battle of the Great Day" by Saddam after hearing about the massive number of Iranian losses.

	17–25 January	Third "War of the Cities."
	February–April	Fourth "War of the Cities."
	6–9 April	Sixth Battle at Basra (Operation Karbala 8): failed Iranian offensive intended to capture Basra.
	17 May	USS *Stark* is struck by two Exocet missiles fired from an Iraqi aircraft.
	20 July	UN Security Council passes Resolution 598 calls for a ceasefire between Iran and Iraq and the withdrawal of troops from foreign soil. Accepted by Iraq but rejected by Iran.
1988	29 February–30 April	Fifth "War of the Cities."
	15–16 March	Iraqi forces launch a chemical attack on the Kurdish stronghold of Halabja, killing thousands of civilians.
	18 April	Iraq recaptures the Fao Peninsula.
	25 May	Iraq recaptures Majnun Island.
	13–17 July	Iraqi forces cross into Iran for the first time since 1982, then withdraw and offer a peace settlement to Iran.
	17 July	Iran accepts UN Resolution 598.
	20 August	Ceasefire goes into effect.

Appendix B People

Abousi, Maj Gen Alwan
  See *al-Abousi*
Aflaq, Michel
  (Syrian) Author of pan-Arabic Ba'athist ideology
Ahmed, Cpt Faruq
  Air Force Commander's Adjutant
Al-Abdullah, Tariq Hamed
  Head of the Presidential Secretariat
Al-Abousi, Maj Gen Alwan Hassoun Alwan
  Air Force Deputy Commander of Training
  Commander of Air Force Administration
Al-Assad, Hafez
  President of Syria, 1971–2000
Al-Bakr, Ahmed Hassan
  Prime Minister of Iraq, 1963, 1968–1979
  President of Iraq, 1968–1979
  Chairman of RCC, 1969–1979
Al-Duri, Izzat Ibrahim
  Vice-Chairman of RCC, 1982–2001
  Asst Secretary-General of RC
  Member of NC
Al-Duri, Maj Gen Sabar Abd al-Aziz [Hussein]
  Director of GMID
Al-Duri, Maj Gen Tala [Khalil Ibrahim]
  Commander of the Presidential Guard
  Commander of 9th Armored Division
Al-Gaddafi, Muammar Abu Minyar
  Leader of Libya
Al-Gaylani, Rashid Ali
  Prime Minister of Iraq, 1933, 1940–1941, 1941
Al-Hamdani, Lt Gen Ra'ad Majid Rashid
  Senior Training Officer, Republican Guard

Al-Sabah, Prince Jaber al-Ahmed al-Jaber
Sheikh of Kuwait, 1977–2006
Al-Janabi, Lt Gen Ala Kazim
Chief of Staff of the Army
Al-Janabi, Gen Kamel Sachet Aziz
Special Forces Commander
Al-Jibouri, Gen Mohammed Jissam
Commander of Iraqi Air Force
Al-Kabi, Lt Gen Abid Mohammed
Director of Naval Operations
Commander-in-Chief of the Navy
Al-Majid, Ali Hassan
Director of General Security
aka Chemical Ali
Member of RCC, 1991–2001
Secretary of the Ba'ath Party Northern Bureau
Al-Qadir, Maj Gen Mohammed Abd
Commander of IV Corps
Director of Planning, Defense Ministry
Al-Rashid, Gen Abdullah Maher Abd
Commander of III Corps
Commander of VII Corps
Al-Sadat, Muhammad Anwar
President of Egypt, 1970–81
Al-Sadr, Grand Ayatollah Mohammad Baqir
Iraqi Shi'a cleric
Founder of Islamic Dawa Party
Al-Samarra'i, Maj Wafiq
Head of the Iran Branch, GMID
Al-Saud, King Faisal ibn Abdul Aziz
King of Saudi Arabia, 1904–1975
Al-Tarfa al-Ubaydi, Maj Gen Mizher Rashid
Intelligence Officer in the Iran Branch, GMID
Al-Tikriti, Brig Gen Ahmed Hammash
Republican Guard Commander
Arafat, Yasser
Chairman of the Palestine Liberation Organization, 1969–2004
Asaad, Brig Gen Juwad
Commander of 3rd Division
Ataturk, Mustafa Kemal
President of Turkey, 1923–1938

Aziz, Tariq
Deputy Prime Minister
Foreign Minister
Member of RCC, 1977–2001
Member of NC
Bani-Sadr, Abu al-Hasan
President of Iran, 1980–1981
Barzani, Mullah Mustafa
Leader of the Kurdish Democratic Party
Bazargan, Mehdi
Prime Minister of Iran, 1979
Beheshti, Ayatollah Seyyed Mohammad Hosseini
Chief Justice of Iran, 1979–1981
Secretary-General of the Islamic Republic Party (Iran), 1979–1981
Bin al-Khattab, Umar
Companion to the Prophet Mohammed
Second Caliph after Mohammed's death
Bin Laden, Osama
Founder of al-Qaeda
Dhannoun, Gen Abdul Jawad
Chief of Staff of the Army
Faisal, King
See *al-Saud*
Hamdani, Lt Gen Ra'ad
See *al-Hamdani*
Hammadi, Saadoun
Minister of State for Foreign Affairs
Member of the RCC and RC
Speaker of the National Assembly
Hammash al-Tikriti, Brig Gen Ahmed
Republican Guard Division Commander
Hanash, Mohammed Jassam
Commander of the Air Force and Air Defenses
Hussein, Saddam
Vice President of Iraq, 1968–1979
Prime Minister of Iraq, 1979–1991, 1994–2003
President of Iraq, 1979–2003
Commander-in-Chief of the Armed Services
Chairman of RCC, 1979–2001
Deputy Chairman of RCC, 1969–1979

Secretary-General of RC
Deputy Secretary-General of NC
Ibn Shaker, Prince Zaid
Commander-in-Chief of Armed Forces (Jordan), 1976–1988
Prime Minister of Jordan, 1989, 1991–1993, 1995–1996
Jaber, Prince
See *al-Sabah*
Jahanara, Mohammad
Revolutionary Guard Commander
Kabi, Lt Gen Abid
See *al-Kabi*
Kadhum, Lt Col Mohammed Jawad
Commander of 2nd Brigade
Kajai, Mohammad-Ali
Prime Minister of Iran, 1980–1981
President of Iran, 1981
Kamel al-Majid, Hussein
Supervisor of Military Industries
Minister of Industry and Military Industrialization
Khairrallah Talfah, Gen Adnan
Deputy Commander-in-Chief of the Armed Forces
Deputy Prime Minister
Minister of Defense
Member of RCC, 1977–1989
Khaled, Brig Gen
Commander of 3rd Division
Khamenei, Ayatollah Syed Ali Hoseyni
President of Iran, 1981–1989
Supreme Leader of Iran, 1989–Present
Khomeini, Ayatollah Sayyed Ruhollah Moosavi
Supreme Leader of Iran, 1979–1989
Madani, Ahmad
Commander of the Navy (Iran)
Makki Khamas, Maj Gen Aladdin Hussein
Chief of Staff of III Corps
Director of Combat Development Directorate, Ministry of Defense
Montazeri, Ayatollah Hussein-Ali
Deputy Supreme Leader of Iran, 1985–1987
Mosaddeq, Mohammad
Prime Minister of Iran, 1951–1952, 1952–1953

Mousavi, Mir-Hossein
Prime Minister of Iran, 1981–1989
Muhsen, Abd al-Jabbar
Chief of Department of Political Guidance, Ministry of Defense
Mussolini, Benito Amilcare Andrea
Prime Minister of Italy, 1922–1925
Head of Government of Italy, 1925–1943
Head of State of Italy, 1943–1945
Nasser, Gamel Abdel
President of Egypt, 1956–1970
Pahlavi, Reza Shah
Shah of Iran, 1923–1925
Pahlavi, Mohammad Reza Shah
Shah of Iran, 1941–1979
Rafsanjani, Hojatoleslam Ali Akbar Hashemi
Chairman of Parliament of Iran, 1980–1989
President of Iran, 1989–1997
Rajavi, Massoud
Leader of the People's Mojahedin of Iran
Ramadan, Taha Yassin
Commander-in-Chief of the Popular Army
Member of RCC, 1969–2001
Member of RC and NC
First Deputy Prime Minister
Rashid, Lt Gen Hussein
Commander of I Corps
Rezai, Mohsen
Commissioner of the Revolutionary Guard
Sachet [Aziz al-Janabi], Maj Kamel
See *al-Janabi*
Sahah, Maj Gen Hesham
Commander of 19th Armored Division
Saleh, Ali Abdullah
Commander of III Corps
Salman, Sabah
Press Secretary for the President of Iraq
Sazegara, Mohsen
Co-founder of Pasdaran
Sha'ban al-Tikriti, Lt Gen Hamid
Commander of the Air Force and Air Defenses
Air Force Advisor to Saddam Hussein

Shahin, Gen Mahmoud Shukr
  Commander of 6th Division
  Chief of Iraqi Intelligence
Shanshal, Gen Abd al-Jabbar
  Chief of Staff of the Army
  Minister of State for Military Affairs
Sidqi, Gen Bakr
  Acting Commander of Iraq Army who staged coup d'etat in
  1936
Talfah, Gen Adnan Khairrallah
  See *Khairrallah Talfah*
Tarfa, Maj Gen Mizher Rashid
  See *al-Tarfa al-Ubaydi*
Thanun, Brig Gen Abd al-Jawad
  Director of GMID
Uwayyid, Maj Gen Ali Hussein
  Commander of 43rd Special Forces

Appendix C Place names

Location, **description**, *Country*: map number

Abadan, *Iran*: 4.2, 5.1, 9.1
Ahmad Awah, *Iraq*: 4.4, 5.3
Ahvaz, *Iran*: 4.2, 5.1, 9.1
Al-Amara, *Iraq*: 4.2, 5.1, 9.1
Al-Fakkah, **oil well**, *Iraq*: 4.2, 5.1, 9.1
Al-Karkh, **river**, *Iraq*: east of Tigris
Al-Kut, *Iraq*: 4.3, 5.2, 9.2
Al-Qadisiyyah, **province**, *Iraq*: 4.1
Al-Qurnah, *Iraq*: 4.2, 5.1, 9.1
Andimeshk, *Iran*: 4.1, 4.2, 5.1, 9.1
Arabistan (Khuzestan), **province**, *Afghanistan, Iran, Turkmenistan, Uzbekistan*: includes Ahvaz, Dezful, and Bandar-e Khomeini
As-Sulaymaniyah, **province**, *Iraq*: 4.1, 4.4, 5.3
Baghdad, *Iraq*: 4.1, 4.3, 5.2, 9.2
Bandar-e Abbas, **port**, *Iran*: 7.1, 8.1
Bandar-e Khomeini, **port**, *Iran*: 4.2, 5.1, 9.1
Basra, *Iraq*: 4.1, 4.2, 5.1, 9.1
Bostan, *Iran*: 4.2, 5.1, 9.1
Bushehr, *Iran*: 7.1, 8.1
Dezful, *Iran*: 4.2, 5.1, 9.1
Dhi Qar, **province**, *Iraq*: 4.1
Diyala, **province**, *Iraq*: 4.1, 4.3, 5.2, 9.2
Dizli, *Iran*: 4.4, 5.3
Dujail, *Iraq*: 4.3, 5.2, 9.2
Fao, **peninsula**, *Iraq*: 4.2, 5.1, 9.1
Fish, **lake**, *Iraq*: 4.2, 5.1, 9.1
Habaniya, **lake**: 4.1
Halabjah, *Iraq*: 4.4, 5.3
Hawr al-Hawizeh, **marsh**, *Iran and Iraq*: 4.2, 5.1, 9.1

Appendix D Order of battle

	1980		1984		1988	
GROUND FORCES	Iran	Iraq	Iran	Iraq	Iran	Iraq
TOTAL REGULAR ARMED FORCES	240,000	242,250	555,000	642,500	604,500	1,000,000
Manpower						
Regular Army/Active	150,000	200,000	250,000	600,000	305,000	475,000
Regular Army/Active Reserves	400,000	250,000	350,000	75,000	350,000	480,000
Para-Military[1]	75,000	79,800	2,755,000	654,800	2,945–3,045,000	654,800
Divisions/BDEs						
Armored/Mechanized	3dv + 1bde	4dv/4dv	3dv	6dv/5dv	4dv	7dv
Infantry	3dv + 1bde	4dv	7dv	5dv	6dv	39dv
People's Army, Volunteer (Inf)				15 bde		
Presidential Guard (Armd, Inf)						5bde
Republican Guard (Armd)		1bde		2bde		
Reserve				9bde		
Revolutionary Guard					30dv	
Special Forces	1bde	2bde	3dv	3bde	1dv	20bde
Major Equipment						
Tanks[2]	1,985	2,850	1,050	4,920	1,810	6,310
Armored Fighting Vehicles[3]	825	2,500	1,190	3,200	540	1,000
Artillery[4]	2,900	2,240	5,660	7,750	1,908	3,400
Fixed-Wing Aircraft[5]	65	NR	65	NR	48	NR
Rotor-Wing Aircraft[6]	660	NR	320	NR	320	412[7]

(*cont.*)

	1980		1984		1988	
NAVY	Iran	Iraq	Iran	Iraq	Iran	Iraq
TOTAL REGULAR ARMED FORCES	240,000	242,250	555,000	642,500	604,500	1,000,000
Manpower						
Naval Forces	20,000	4,250	20,000	4,500	14,500	5,000
Marines	3bns	NR	3bns	NR	3bns	NR
Major Equipment						
Amphibious	NR	4	NR	4	10	6
Mine Warfare	3	5	5	5	3	8
Patrol and Coastal Combatants[8]	34	27	29	15	34	38
Principal Surface Combatants[9]	7	NR	10	1	8	5
Support and Miscellaneous	6	NR	5	1	8	3
Fixed-Wing Aircraft[10]	17	NR	11	NR	14	NR
Rotor-Wing Aircraft[11]	56	NR	19	NR	12	NR

	1980		1984		1988	
AIR FORCE	Iran	Iraq	Iran	Iraq	Iran	Iraq
TOTAL REGULAR ARMED FORCES	240,000	242,250	555,000	642,500	604,500	1,000,000
Manpower	70,000	38,000	35,000	38,000	35,000	40,000
Major Equipment						
Fixed-Wing Aircraft[12]	546	388	161	631	142	511
Rotor-Wing Aircraft[13]	84	276	76	391	76	NR

Source: "The Middle East and North Africa," *IISS: The Military Balance* 80, no. 1 (1980, 1984, 1988)

[1] Para-military in Iran include Basij, border tribal militia, Gendarmerie (border guard), Hezbollahi (home guard), Mostazafin (guards), Pesh Merga (Kurds), and Revolutionary Guard (Pasdaran). Para-military in Iraq include frontier guard, People's Army, and security troops.

[2] Iranian tanks include Chieftain Mk 3/5, CH T-59, M-47, M-48, M-60A1, Scorpion, T-54, T-55, T-62, and T-72 tanks. Iraqi tanks include AMX-30, CH T-69, PT-76, Romanian M-77, T-34, T-54, T-55, T-59 II, T-62, T-69 II, and T-72 tanks.

[3] Iranian armored fighting vehicles (AFV) include BMP-1, BTR-40, BTR-50, BTR-60, BTR-152, EE-9 Cascavel, and M-113 AFVs. Iraqi armored fighting vehicles (AFV) include BRDM, BMP, BTR-50, BTR-60, BTR-152, EE-3 Jararaca, EE-9 Cascavel, E-11 Urutu, ERC-90, FUG-70, M-113A1, MOWAG Roland, Panhard M-3, OT-62, OT-64, and VCR(TH) AFVs.

[4] Iranian artillery included M-101 105mm, 130mm; M-107 155mm, 175mm; M-109 155mm; M-110 203mm SP; M-114 155mm; and M-115 203mm towed guns. Iraqi artillery included 23mm, 37mm, 57mm, 85mm 100mm towed guns; 75mm, 85mm, 122mm, 130mm, 152mm howitzer guns; SU-100, ISU-122 SP guns; ZSU-23-4 and ZSU-57-2 SP guns.

5 Iranian fixed-wing aircraft included Cessna 185, Cessna 310, F-27, O-2A, Shrike Commander, and Falcon planes.

6 Iranian rotor-wing aircraft included AB-205A Iroquois, AB-206 JetRanger, AH-1J SeaCobra, Bell 214A Isfahan, and CH-47C Chinook helicopters.

7 Data equals the sum of itemized (attack and transport) helicopters rather than the given total.

8 Patrol and Coastal Combatant ships include corvettes, missile craft, torpedo craft, and inshore patrol craft.

9 Principal Surface Combatant ships include destroyers and frigates.

10 Iranian fixed-wing aircraft include F-27, Mystere 20, P-3F Orion, and Shrike Commander planes.

11 Iranian rotor-wing aircraft include AB-205A Iroquois, AB-206 JetRanger, AB-212 Twin Huey, RH-53D Sea Stallion, S-65A Sea Stallion, and SH-3D Sea King helicopters.

12 Iranian fixed-wing aircraft included Aero Commander, Boeing 707, Boeing 747, C-130E/H, F-4D/E, F-5E/F, F-14A, F-27, Falcon 20, RF-4E. Iraqi fixed-wing aircraft included An-12, An-24, An-26, Tu-22, Tu-124, Il-14, Il-28, Il-76, MiG-21, MiG-23B, Su-7B, Su-20, Heron, Hunter FB-59/FR-10.

13 Iranian rotor-wing aircraft included AB-206A Twin Huey, AB-212 Twin Huey, Bell 214C Huey Plus, CH-47C Chinook, HH-34F Huskie, S-61A4, [SA 321] Super Frelon. Iraqi rotor-wing aircraft included [SA 316/319] Alouette III, [SA341/342] Gazelle, Mi-4, Mi-6, Mi-8, Mi-24, [SA 321] Super Frelon, [SA 330] Puma, Wessex Mk 52.

Bibliography

CAPTURED DOCUMENTS IN THE CONFLICT RECORDS RESEARCH CENTER

Most of the Iraqi records cited in this book can be found in the National Defense University's CRRC. Captured records are indicated by the prefix "SH." An asterisk preceding the prefix "SH" indicates that the record was, at the time of this publication, not yet available through the CRRC.

*SH-AADF-D-001-316, Various Reports and Memoranda from the Air Force and Air Defense Command Relating to Iraqi Reconnaissance and Iranian Incursions into Iraqi Air Space, 1980.

*SH-AADF-D-001-317, Activities of the Iraqi 3rd Air Defense Sector, 4 September 1980–2 September 1987.

*SH-AFGC-D-001-310, Joint Staff Course: Chapter 3, Lecture 1, Appendix A: Main Factors That Facilitated the Achievment of Surprise against the Zionist Enemy in the October 1973 War, 1 January 1998.

*SH-AFGC-D-001-313, Transcripts of Meetings between Saddam Hussein and the General Command of the Armed Forces, 8–9 August 1981.

*SH-AFGC-D-001-324, Transcript of a Meeting between Saddam Hussein and the General Command of the Armed Forces, 26 June 1983.

*SH-AFGC-D-001-368, Transcript of a Meeting of the Armed Forces General Command, Saddam Hussein in Attendance, 13–14 February 1985.

*SH-GMID-D-001-305, GMID Memorandum to Section 1, 52/Q1/40662, Re: Complete Intelligence Report, 29 July 1980.

*SH-GMID-D-001-306, Memoranda from GMID Regarding Prisoners of War, Circa Mid to Late 1980.

*SH-GMID-D-001-312, GMID Report: Iranian Military Ideology and Fighting Methods, 15 July 1979.

*SH-GMID-D-001-318, Iraqi Air Reconnaissance Reports of Iranian Dams, 22 September 1981.

*SH-GMID-D-001-326, Intelligence Reports from the Border Regarding Deported Iranians.

*SH-GMID-D-001-332, Correspondence between GMID, the Central Bank of Iraq, and the Central Organization for Standardization & Quality Control Confirming the Receipt of Confiscated Jewelry, Circa January 1981.

*SH-GMID-D-001-337, Iraqi Intelligence Estimates on Iranian Weapons Acquisitions, 28 March–1 August 1981.

*SH-GMID-D-001-338, Correspondence Relating to Iranian Weapons Acquisition from Brazil and Spain, July 1981.

*SH-GMID-D-001-341, Various GMID Documents Relating to Iranian Arms Deals, March 1981.

*SH-GMID-D-001-342, GMID Memoranda Regarding Iranian Declarations About Iraq, 1981–1984.

*SH-GMID-D-001-343, Political Reports Relating to the Iranian Domestic Situation and Foreign Relations, 16 February–4 July 1981.

*SH-GMID-D-001-345, GMID Report: Iranian Military Activities, 14 November 1981.

*SH-GMID-D-001-346, Memoranda from the GMID to the General Command of the Armed Forces and the Ministry of Defense, RE: Al-Khafajiyah Sector.

*SH-GMID-D-001-355, GMID and IIS Correspondence Regarding Iranian–Syrian Cooperation.

*SH-GMID-D-001-356, Various GMID Correspondence Regarding Iranian Material and Personnel, August 1982.

*SH-GMID-D-001-358, Various Intelligence Reports and Memoranda Regarding Kharg Island, 1982.

*SH-GMID-D-001-361, Memoranda between the GMID and Various Iraqi Military Attaches Regarding the Transport of Weapons from North Korea to Iran and Flights from Iran to the Gulf States, 1981.

*SH-GMID-D-001-362, Various Memoranda between the Psychological Warfare Committee, GMID, and the RCC, 21 February–4 July 1983.

*SH-GMID-D-001-365, Various Memoranda between the Defense Ministry, GMID, the General Command of the Armed Forces, and IIS Regarding Evaluations of the Iranian Military, 1984.

*SH-GMID-D-001-366, Various GMID Reports and Correspondence with the General Command of the Armed Forces and Air & Air Defense Force Regarding Suitable Iranian Targets, Economic and Military.

*SH-GMID-D-001-367, GMID Assessment of the Iranian Air Force, 15 November 1984.

*SH-GMID-D-001-369, Correspondence between the GMID, the Ministry of Defense, and the Ministry of Interior Regarding Iranian Military Movements and the Distribution of Iranian Troops, 1985.

*SH-GMID-D-001-376, Various Memoranda between GMID, IIS, the Armed Forces General Command, and Military Attaches Regarding Iran's Acquisition of Surface-to-Surface Missiles.

*SH-GMID-D-001-378, GMID Intelligence Report on the Current Military Situation in Iran.

*SH-GMID-D-001-379, Memoranda from GMID to the President of the Republic Regarding the Bombing of Iranian Cities, February 1987.

*SH-GMID-D-001-382, Various Memoranda between GMID, IIS, and Military Attaches Regarding the Iranian Army and Navy, 1985–1986.

*SH-GMID-D-001-383, GMID Intelligence Report on Syria, 16 December 1985–20 March 1986.

*SH-GMID-D-001-384, Correspondence between the GMID, the Iraqi Military Attaché in Jordan, the Air & Air Defense Force, and the President of the

Republic Regarding Attacks on Iran and Using Chemical Weapons on the Kurds.

*SH-GMID-D-001-388, Various Correspondence between the GMID and the Presidential Diwan Regarding the Iranian Army and Air Force.

*SH-GMID-D-001-394, Military Orders and Communications between the GMID, the Armed Forces General Command, the RCC, and Various Iraqi Units During the Iran–Iraq War, 1981.

*SH-IDGS-D-001-302, The Permanent Committee for Hostile Activity Recommendation to "Eliminate" Opposition Party Leaders, August 1988.

*SH-IDGS-D-001-325, Memoranda Relating to a Police Captain's Forced Retirement Due to Familial Involvement with the Da'wah Party, June 1981.

*SH-IDGS-D-001-330, General Security Directorate Memo Regarding the Deportation of Individual Members of a Turkish Family to Iran, 1981.

*SH-IDGS-D-001-385, Correspondence within the Directorate of General Security Regarding Directions from Ali Hassan al-Majid Related to the Northern Areas of Iraq, 4 December 1987.

*SH-IISX-D-001-347, Correspondence between the IIS, GMID, and the Intelligence of the 3rd Corps/Intelligence Regarding Iran.

*SH-IISX-D-001-348, Various Memoranda between IIS and GMID, 1982.

*SH-IZAR-D-001-309, Army Training Course: Research Plan to Study the Effects of Irrigation and Mass Drainage in Southern Iraq, 1997.

*SH-IZAR-D-001-314, The Human Wave Attack, Iraqi Combat Development Directorate, 1983.

*SH-IZAR-D-001-327, Dismissal of Low Ranking Army Personnel, 21 April–29 November 1980.

*SH-IZAR-D-001-351, Armored Corps Platoon Commanders Handbook, Combat Development Directorate, 1983.

*SH-MISC-D-001-304, Lecture 23: The Address of Saddam Hussein at the 3rd Islamic Summit on 28 January 1981.

*SH-MISC-D-001-319, Transcript of a Meeting Held in the Directorate of Military Movement, 24 September 1980.

*SH-MISC-D-001-334, Transcript of a Meeting between Saddam Hussein and Senior Officers, February–March 1981.

*SH-MISC-D-001-335, Transcript of Various Meetings between Saddam Hussein and Senior Officers, January 1981.

*SH-MISC-D-001-344, Supplement to [Iranian] Saf Magazine "The Victory of Victories of the Sacred Defense: Battle of Tariq Al-Quds (29 November–21 December 1981)," November–December 1998.

*SH-MISC-D-001-349, Pasdaran Report: From Khorramshahr to Fao (July 1982–August 1986): A Military and Political Analysis, Circa 1988.

*SH-MISC-D-001-350, The Passing of Two Years of War: Iran–Iraq, Political Office of the Islamic Revolution Pasdaran Corps.

*SH-MISC-D-001-353, Various Memoranda and Reports Relating to the Al-Dujayl Case, June 1984–April 1985.

*SH-MISC-D-001-364, Presidential Order to Execute Officers and Soldiers, 1985.

*SH-MISC-D-001-374, Report on the al-Sulaymaniyah Security Governate from 1985–1988 Including al-Anfal.

*SH-MISC-D-001-375, Transcripts of Meetings between Saddam Hussein and Military Commanders, April 1985.

*SH-MISC-D-001-391, Transcripts of Meetings between Saddam Hussein and the Armed Forces General Command, January–February 1988.

*SH-MISC-D-001-392, Correspondence between the General Secretariat for Liquidating Properties of Deported Iranians and the General Aid and Arrangement Directorate, 23 January 1982.

*SH-MODX-D-001-315, Draft of Saddam Hussein's Declaration of the Iran–Iraq War, 22 September 1980.

*SH-MODX-D-001-339, Memoranda Relating to the Soviet–Iranian Trade Agreement, 1981.

*SH-MODX-D-001-352, [The Iraqi] Military Journal, Vol. 59 Issue No. 2, April 1982.

*SH-MODX-D-001-360, *Administrative Affairs Journal*, No. 3, May 1983.

*SH-MODX-D-001-363, *Dealing with Hastily Prepared Earthen Berms*, Combat Development Directorate, August 1984.

*SH-MODX-D-001-377, [The Iraqi] Military Journal, Issue No. 1, January 1986.

*SH-MODX-D-001-387, Orders by the Ministry of Defense to Strike the Enemy With "Special Munitions," 22 March 1988.

*SH-MODX-D-001-390, Iraqi Military Documents Discussing Iranian Military Movements and Activities, Including the Iranian Use of Chemical Weapons, 1987.

*SH-MODX-V-001-386, *The Knockout Operation* by Iraqi Military Photography and Cinema Command, 10–11 August 1987.

*SH-PDWN-D-001-329, Correspondence between Various Security Directorates Regarding Detaining the Wives of Deported Iranians, January 1981.

*SH-PDWN-D-001-381, Various Memoranda and Reports between the Presidential Diwan, the Ministry of Defense, and Various Military Units.

*SH-RPGD-D-001-307, Plan for the Deployment of the Republican Guard to Fight Israel in Syria, Circa 1992.

*SH-RPGD-D-001-308, Dispersal Plan for Allah Akbar OC RG, 30 February 2001.

*SH-RVCC-D-001-328, Decrees and Orders Regarding the Confiscation of Housing from Deported Iranians, 2 May–16 July 1981.

*SH-RVCC-D-001-331, Laws Dealing with Various Issues Including the Confiscation of Property from Deported Iranians, Passed between 1981–1982.

*SH-RVCC-D-001-340, Various Documents Relating to a $2 Billion Kuwait Loan to Iraq, May 1981.

*SH-RVCC-D-001-373, an Execution Order Issued by the RCC Related to the Al-Dujayl Case, 23 March 1985.

*SH-RVCC-D-001-393, Resolutions Issued by the RCC Regarding Various Administrative Concerns, 1981.

*SH-SHTP-A-001-228, Saddam Hussein Discussing Ba'ath Party Principles and History, Military Strategy, and General Administrative Issues.

*SH-SHTP-A-001-247, Recording of a Meeting between Saddam Hussein and Military Officers, 27 March 1984.

*SH-SHTP-A-001-303, Recording of a Meeting between Saddam Hussein and Ba'ath Party Members Discussing the Iran–Iraq War, Circa October 1981– Early 1982.

*SH-SHTP-A-001-311, Recording of a Meeting between Saddam Hussein and Military Officers, Circa Late 1980.

*SH-SHTP-A-001-321, Transcript of Telephone Conversation between Saddam Hussein and Unidentified Military Officers Regarding the 1 November 1980 Battle.

*SH-SHTP-A-001-336, Recording of a Meeting between Saddam Hussein and Ba'ath Party Members, 27 May 1981.

*SH-SHTP-A-001-354, Recording of a Meeting between Saddam Hussein and Ministers Relating to the Budget, Circa 1982.

*SH-SHTP-A-001-357, Recording of a Meeting between Saddam Hussein and Advisors Regarding Various Administrative and Financial Issues and Arab Nationalism, Circa 1982.

*SH-SHTP-A-001-359, Recording of a Meeting between Saddam Hussein and Military Officers Regarding the Iran–Iraq War, Circa July 1982.

*SH-SHTP-A-001-370, Recording of a Meeting between Saddam Hussein and High Ranking Officers Regarding the Iran–Iraq War, Circa March 1985.

*SH-SHTP-A-001-371, Recording of a Speech by Saddam Hussein on the Iran–Iraq War at the Second Islamic Conference, April 1985.

*SH-SHTP-A-001-372, Recording of a Meeting between Saddam Hussein and the Armed Forces General Command, 7 June 1985.

*SH-SHTP-A-001-380, Recording of a Meeting between Saddam Hussein and High Ranking Iraqi Officials Regarding the Iran–Iraq War, 26 December 1986.

*SH-SHTP-A-001-389, Recording of a Military Lecture Given in the Presence of Saddam Hussein, Circa Early 1989.

SH-AADF-D-000-228, Correspondence between the Air Force, the Air Defense Command and the General Military Intelligence Directorate Concerning Reports on Iranian Air Force Capabilities During the Iran–Iraq War, 25 December 1981.

SH-AFGC-D-000-094, Iraqi Armed Forces General Command Memos Proving That Iraq Produced and Used Chemical Weapons against Iran and Along the Border During the Iran–Iraq War, June–November 1983.

SH-AFGC-D-000-393, Transcript of a General Command of the Armed Forces Meeting During the First Gulf War and Telephone Conversations, 6–7 January 1981.

SH-AFGC-D-000-686, Orders of the President and Commander-in-Chief of the Armed Forces, February–December 1984.

SH-AFGC-D-000-731, Meeting of the General Command of the Armed Forces, March 1988.

SH-BATH-D-000-206, Suggestion to Integrate Iraqi and Syrian Ba'ath Parties; Ba'ath Party Structure Notes, 30 December 1978.

SH-BATH-D-000-300, Lecture on the Iran–Iraq War, February 1987.

SH-GMID-D-000-079, Memorandum from the General Military Intelligence Directorate to the Director of the Military Industrialization Commission About Information on Chemical Weapons Obtained from Iraqi Prisoners in Iran, 6 June 1988.

SH-GMID-D-000-153, Correspondence between the General Military
    Intelligence Directorate and the Armed Forces General Command About
    Iranian Chemical Weapons Capabilities, April–October 1985.
SH-GMID-D-000-266, General Military Intelligence Directorate (GMID)
    Correspondence About Iranian Military Sites and Plans During the
    Iraq–Iran War, 1–14 April 1987.
SH-GMID-D-000-299, General Military Intelligence Directorate
    Correspondence About Iranian Military Activities and Other Issues, March
    1988.
SH-GMID-D-000-332, Summaries and Intelligence Reports for the General
    Military Intelligence Directorate (GMID), September 1980–May 1985.
SH-GMID-D-000-423, Correspondence from the General Military
    Intelligence Directorate (GMID) to Al-Rashid Military Hospital Regarding
    the Bodies of Executed Personnel for Insubordination in the Iraq–Iran War,
    July 1982.
SH-GMID-D-000-465, Correspondence from the Iraqi General Military
    Intelligence Directorate Regarding Iranian–Afghan Relations, December
    1983–March 1984.
SH-GMID-D-000-516, General Military Intelligence Directorate (GMID)
    Memos About the Iranian Air Force, January–November 1980.
SH-GMID-D-000-524, General Military Intelligence Directorate (GMID)
    Memos Regarding Iranian–Libyan Military Cooperation, November
    1981–November 1985.
SH-GMID-D-000-550, General Military Intelligence Directorate Memoranda
    About the Soviet Military Attache to Baghdad and Information on Plans for
    Iraq to Provide Russia with Missiles, 1982–1987.
SH-GMID-D-000-595, Information Regarding Syrian Authorities Secretly
    Visiting Iran and Libya to Foment Sectarian War in Iraq, December 1979.
SH-GMID-D-000-620, People of Arabstan (Arabs in Southern Iran) in
    Al-Ahwaz Area Calling for Independence, 1979.
SH-GMID-D-000-622, General Military Intelligence Directorate (GMID)
    Studies on the Foundation of the Da'wah Party and the Supreme Council of
    the Islamic Revolution Party, March–December 1995.
SH-GMID-D-000-649, General Military Intelligence Directorate Reports About
    Various Activities During the Iran–Iraq War, January–February 1985.
SH-GMID-D-000-663, Studies About Iranian Military Activities During the
    Iran–Iraq War, February 1985.
SH-GMID-D-000-726, Reconnaissance Reports on Iranian Naval Forces and
    Information About Anti-Iraqi Forces Smuggling Weapons into Iraq,
    April–October 1982.
SH-GMID-D-000-840, Correspondence Discussing Cooperation between Iran
    and Syria, July 1981–October 1981.
SH-GMID-D-000-842, General Military Intelligence Directorate (GMID)
    Intelligence Report on Iran, January–June 1980.
SH-GMID-D-000-845, General Military Intelligence Directorate (GMID)
    Correspondence About Weapons, Ammunition, and Other Military
    Equipment Sent from the Soviet Union to Iran and Correspondence to the
    Iraqi Military Attache in Tehran, January 1978–September 1979.

SH-GMID-D-000-892, Study by the General Military Intelligence Directorate (GMID) About Iranian Foreign Delegations after the Shah's Fall, 20 March 1981.

SH-GMID-D-000-898, General Military Intelligence Directorate (GMID) Memoranda Discussing Iranian Chemical Weapons Capability, October 1987–September 1988.

SH-GMID-D-001-020, Information on Iranian Forces Including Their Movements, Casualties and Losses, and the Weapons That They Were Able to Acquire During the Iraqi–Iranian War, 1981.

SH-GMID-D-001-025, Interrogation Reports of the Iranian Minister of Oil and His Assistant, 9 September 1980–1 November 1980.

SH-GMID-D-001-026, Reports Related to the General Military Intelligence Directorate Concerning the Status of the Iraqi Corps and Regiments During the Iraqi–Iran War in Different Sectors of the Battlefield and Discussions About Halabja, March 1988.

SH-GMID-D-001-125, General Military Intelligence Directorate Correspondence About Iranian Use of Chemical Weapons on Iraqi Troops in the Battlefield, 14 April 1987.

SH-GMID-D-001-142, 5th Mechanized Division Command Report: Battle of Al-Ahwaz, July 1982.

SH-GMID-D-001-427, *GMID Intelligence Report on Iranian Military Capability*, 29 July 1980.

SH-GMID-D-001-429, *Memorandum from GMID to Military Attaches Islamabad, Ankara, and New Delhi Relating to Technical Assistance Provided by North Korea*, 18 December 1982.

SH-IDGS-D-001-213, General Security Directorate Memorandum on the Dangers of the Cartoon Character Pokemon, 2001.

SH-IISX-D-000-698, Reports on Iraqi Intelligence Service Activities, October 1985–May 1986.

SH-IISX-D-000-841, 1981 Iraqi Evaluation of the Iranian Military Threat, January 1980–January 1981.

SH-IZAR-D-000-278, Reports on the Al-Khafajiyyah Battle During the Iraq–Iran War, 28 Febraury 1981.

SH-IZAR-D-000-347, Research Paper: *Tactical Deception on the Battlefield*, 13 July 1988.

SH-IZAR-D-000-646, Telegram from the Intelligence System of the Eastern Zone Revealing the Use of Chemical Weapons against Halabja, 20 March 1988.

SH-IZAR-D-000-781, Intelligence Report About the Area within the Fourth Corps Command Sector, January 1985.

SH-IZAR-D-001-246, Correspondence from the Iraqi Army Chief Regarding an Experimental Chemical Weapons Attack on 27 June 1985, July–August 1985.

SH-MISC-D-000-449, Report Detailing the Iranian Military Presence Along the Iraq–Iran Border, Iranian Current Affairs, Reports on Weapons Sales, and Analysis, 29 October 1986.

SH-MISC-D-000-695, Saddam Hussein Meeting with Various Iraqi Officials About the Iraqi Position Early on in the Iran–Iraq War, 12–13 October 1980.

SH-MISC-D-000-827, Saddam and Senior Iraqi Officials Discussing the Conflict with Iran, Iraqi Targets and Plans, a Recent Attack on the Osiraq Reactor, and Various Foreign Countries, 1 October 1980.

SH-MISC-D-000-866, Letter from Izzat al-Duri to Saddam Hussein Reference the Battle of al-Hamra in May 1982, 23 May 1982.

SH-MODX-D-000-853, [The Iraqi] Military Journal, July 1984.

SH-PDWN-D-000-240, Letter Authorizing the Execution of an Air Force Warrant Officer for Sabotaging a Plane Engine, May–April 1986.

SH-PDWN-D-000-341, Transcript of a Speech Given by Saddam Hussein at Al-Bakr University "The Role of the Iraqi Armed Forces in the Arabic–Zionist Conflict," 3 June 1978.

SH-PDWN-D-000-551, General Administrative Information and Presidential Diwan Correspondence, 28 May 1986.

SH-PDWN-D-000-552, Arms Agreements Signed between Iraq and the Soviet Union in 1981 and 1983, 1981–1989.

SH-PDWN-D-000-566, Saddam Meeting with the General Command of the Armed Forces About the Iran–Iraq War, October–November 1980.

SH-PDWN-D-000-604, Miscellaneous Memos from the Presidential Diwan Various Directorates About General Administrative and Financial Matters, October 1987–September 1988.

SH-PDWN-D-000-678, Various Memoranda Relating to the Iraqi Use of Chemical Weapons against Halabja and Other Kurdish Villages, 1988.

SH-PDWN-D-000-730, Transcript of an Armed Forces General Command Meeting Discussing the Iran–Iraq War and al-Fao, 26 May 1988.

SH-PDWN-D-001-021, Transcripts of Meetings between Saddam and Top Iraqi Officials and Officers Regarding Iran–Iraq War Tactics Such as the Use of Napalm and Cluster Bombs, 6 October 1980.

SH-PDWN-D-001-024, Saddam Hussein and High Ranking Military Officers Discussing the Possible Use of Chemical Weapons against Iranian Troops, 22 December 1988.

SH-PDWN-D-001-028, Transcript of a Meeting between Saddam Hussein and the General Command of the Armed Forces Talking About Islamic History and the Situation around al-Huwayzah, 25 August 1981.

SH-PDWN-D-001-029, Meeting between Saddam Hussein and Various Iraqi Military Leaders, 11 May 1983.

SH-RPGD-D-000-706, Reports on Iranian Military Activities, November 1984–March 1985.

SH-RVCC-D-000-218, Plan for the Marshes Which Includes Killing, Poisoning, Burning Homes, and Economic Punishments, May–September 1987.

SH-SHTP-A-000-553, Revolutionary Command Council Meeting after the Baghdad Conference in 1979, 27 March 1979.

SH-SHTP-A-000-555, Saddam and the Revolutionary Command Council Discussing Reagan's Speech to the Nation on Iran–Contra Revelations (Part 2), 15 November 1986.

SH-SHTP-A-000-556, Saddam Meeting with Cabinet Ministers to Discuss the Iran–Contra Revelations, Circa Late 1986.

SH-SHTP-A-000-561, Saddam and His Inner Circle Discussing the Iran–Iraq War and UN Security Council Resolutions Related to the War, Circa December 1987.

SH-SHTP-A-000-568, Saddam Hussein and High Ranking Officers Discussing the Liberation of Al-Fao, Circa Summer 1988.

SH-SHTP-A-000-571, Saddam and His Inner Circle Discussing Israel's Attack on the Tamuz (Osirak) Reactor, Circa Mid-June 1981.

SH-SHTP-A-000-618, Saddam Hussein Speech to the Ba'ath Party Branch in Mosul, 12 April 1987.

SH-SHTP-A-000-626, Saddam Hussein Discusses Neighboring Countries and Their Regimes, January 1981.

SH-SHTP-A-000-627, Saddam and Senior Military Officials Discussing Arms Imports and Other Issues Related to the Iran–Iraq War, Circa Fall 1983.

SH-SHTP-A-000-628, Saddam Being Briefed About the Iraq–Iran War and Discusses Iraqi–Syria Relations and Hafiz Al-Asad, Circa February 1982.

SH-SHTP-A-000-631, Saddam Hussein Discussing General Issues and Iraqi Military History, Circa July–August 1988.

SH-SHTP-A-000-634, Saddam and Military Corps Commanders Discuss the Great Day and Great Harvest Battles, Analyze Iranian Intentions, and Discuss Iranian Efforts to Capture Basra, 28 March 1987.

SH-SHTP-A-000-635, Saddam Meeting with His Cabinet to Discuss the 1982 Budget, 1982.

SH-SHTP-A-000-637, Saddam Meeting with Military Advisors Regarding the Iraq–Iran War, Circa 1988.

SH-SHTP-A-000-638, Saddam and the Revolutionary Command Council Discuss President Ronald Reagan's Speech in Which He Admitted That the United States Had a Relationship with Iran, Unknown, after 15 November 1986.

SH-SHTP-A-000-710, Saddam Meeting with the Cabinet During Iran–Iraq War About Iranian Advances and Security Council Negotiations, 21 July 1982.

SH-SHTP-A-000-715, Saddam and the Iraqi Command Discussing the Suicide of an Iraqi Minister, 20 December 1986.

SH-SHTP-A-000-735, Saddam and Officials Discussing Military Operations and Secret Project During the Iran–Iraq War, 18 October 1984.

SH-SHTP-A-000-788, Saddam Discussing the Iraqi Stance toward Respecting International Law, Circa June–July 1988.

SH-SHTP-A-000-813, Saddam and Senior Military Officials Discussing Various Military Operations Including Re-Capturing the al-Fao Peninsula, Unknown, after 1991.

SH-SHTP-A-000-816, Saddam and Ba'ath Party Members Discussing the Iraqi Victory in the Iran–Iraq War, 9 August 1988.

SH-SHTP-A-000-835, Meeting between Saddam Hussein, the National Command, and the Revolutionary Command Council Discussing the Iraq–Iran War, 16 September 1980.

SH-SHTP-A-000-851, Saddam Discussing Khomeini, Iranian Kurdistan, and Iranian Forces with Iraqi Diplomats, 20 February 1979.

SH-SHTP-A-000-857, Saddam and Iraqi Officials Discussing the Liberation of Al-Faw and Its Broader Implications, Circa 18 April 1988.

SH-SHTP-A-000-896, Saddam and Other Government Officials Discussing the State of the Country During the Iran–Iraq War and the Use of Chemical Weapons, 6 March 1987.

SH-SHTP-A-000-911, Discussion between Saddam and Iraqi Officials About Iraq's Relationship with Syria, 26 November 1979.

SH-SHTP-A-000-913, Saddam and Advisors Discussing a Forthcoming Speech, Circa July 1988.

SH-SHTP-A-000-958, Saddam and High Ranking Iraqi Officials Discussing the American Frigate "Stark," 27 May 1987.

SH-SHTP-A-001-022, Recording of a Meeting between Saddam Hussein and High Ranking Military Officers Regarding Military Operations During the Iran–Iraq War, Circa February 1984.

SH-SHTP-A-001-023, Saddam Hussein and Ba'ath Party Members Discussing the Iran–Iraq War, 6 March 1987.

SH-SHTP-A-001-045, Saddam and High Ranking Officers Discussing Plans to Attack Kurdish "Saboteurs" in Northern Iraq and the Possibility of Using Special Ammunition (Weapons), Undated (Circa 1985).

SH-SHTP-A-001-167, Saddam and Ba'ath Party Members Discussing the Status of the Party in the Arab World and Exploitation of the Muslim Brotherhood as an Ally, 24 July 1986.

SH-SHTP-A-001-217, Saddam and His Inner Circle Discussing the Performance of Iraq's Army in Northern Iraq, Relations with the United States and Russia, and UN Security Council Resolution 598, 21 January 1988.

SH-SHTP-A-001-229, Saddam and Military Officials Discussing the Iran–Iraq War and Iraqi Military Capabilities, 30 October 1980.

SH-SHTP-A-001-231, Iraqi Officials Discussing the Iran–Iraq War and the Battles to Recapture al-Fao, Undated (Circa Late 1988–1989).

SH-SHTP-D-000-411, Transcripts of Iraqi Leadership Meetings Discussing Responses to Iranian Missile Strikes, 12–24 September 1986.

SH-SHTP-D-000-538, Transcript of a Meeting between Saddam and His Commanding Officers at the Armed Forces General Command Regarding the Iraq–Iran War, 27 June 1988.

SH-SHTP-D-000-539, Records of Saddam Meeting with the General Armed Forces Command Leadership and Jordanian King Hussein Bin Talal, 1983.

SH-SHTP-D-000-557, Saddam and His Senior Advisors Discussing Iraq's Historical Rights to Kuwait and the United States' Position, 15 December 1990.

SH-SHTP-D-000-559, Saddam and His Inner Circle Discussing Relations with Various Arab States, Russia, China, and the United States, 4–20 November 1979.

SH-SHTP-D-000-567, Recording of Saddam and Arafat Discussing the Israeli Attack on the Palestinian Liberation Organization's Headquarters, 5 October 1985.

SH-SHTP-D-000-572, Transcripts from Meetings between Saddam Iraqi Army Officers , January 1981–April 1993.

SH-SHTP-D-000-573, Transcripts of General Command of the Armed Forces Meetings During the First Gulf War and Correspondence with Other Arab Leaders, October 1980.

SH-SHTP-D-000-607, Transcripts of Meetings between Saddam, Vice President of the RCC Izzat Ibrahim al-Tikriti, Minister of Defense Adnan

Khairallah, and Army Chief of Staff Abd al-Jawad Zinun During the Iraq–Iran War, 25 February 1985–31 July 1986.

SH-SHTP-D-000-608, Minutes of Meeting between Saddam Hussein and the General Command of the Armed Forces on Turkey Using Guerilla Warfare and Blocking Iranian Terrorists, Raid Damages, Attack Plans, and America and Israel Supplying Weapons to Iran, November 1986.

SH-SHTP-D-000-609, Saddam and His Inner Circle Discussing the Iran–Contra Affair, Circa November 1986.

SH-SHTP-D-000-624, Transcript of Meetings between Saddam Hussein and Iraqi Offiicals Relating to Tactics, 28–29 December 1980.

SH-SHTP-D-000-711, Saddam Hussein and Iraqi Officials Discussing the King Fahad Initiative, Relations with the USSR, and Perceptions of Other Middle Eastern Countries, October–November 1981.

SH-SHTP-D-000-760, Saddam and Political Advisors Discussing the Production of Biological Materials in Iraq, the Iran–Iraq War, UN Inspections, and the Arab–Israeli Conflict, Circa 1990–1999.

SH-SHTP-D-000-846, General Command of the Armed Forces Meeting Transcripts During the First Gulf War, 17 October 1980.

SH-SHTP-D-000-847, Transcripts of a Meeting between Saddam and His Commanders in Regarding the Iran–Iraq War, 30 September 1980.

SH-SHTP-D-000-856, Transcript of a Meeting between Saddam Hussein and His Commanding Officers at the Armed Forces General Command, November 1980.

SH-SHTP-D-000-864, Transcripts of Meetings between Saddam Hussein and Senior Military Commanders Discussing Nominations to Ba'ath Party Leadership and Iran–Iraq War Battles, 8 April–18 September 1982.

SH-SHTP-V-000-589, Saddam Hussein and Military Officials Discussing the Iran–Iraq War and the Al-Qadisiyyah Battle, Circa Late 1988.

SH-SHTP-V-000-612, Saddam and Senior Military Officials Discussing Efforts to Retake the Majnun Area, Circa Late 1988.

SH-SPPC-D-000-540, Minutes from a Meeting between Saddam Hussein and Iraqi Army Commanders, February 1986.

SH-SPPC-D-000-583, Letter Dated 28 October 1978 from Nizar Hamdun to Saddam Hussein Regarding Iraqi and Syrian Ba'ath Commitment, 28 October 1978.

BOOKS

Abdo, Geneive and Jonathon Lyons. *Answering Only to God: Faith and Freedom in Twenty-First-Century Iran*. New York, NY: Henry Holt and Company, LLC, 2003.

Abousi, Major General Alwan Hassoun Alwan. *Memoir*. Alexandria, Egypt: Unpublished, 2003.

Aburish, Said K. *Saddam Hussein: The Politics of Revenge*. New York, NY: Bloomsbury, 2000.

Alnasrawi, Abbas. *The Economy of Iraq: Oil, Wars, Destruction of Development and Prospects, 1950–2010*. Santa Barbara, CA: Greenwood Press, 1994.

Arjomand, Said Amir. *The Turban for the Crown: The Islamic Revolution in Iran.* New York, NY: Oxford University Press, 1988.

Ashton, Nigel. *King Hussein of Jordan: A Political Life.* New Haven, CT: Yale University Press, 2008.

Ayalon, Ami. "The Iraqi–Iranian War." In *Middle East Contemporary Survey, Iraq, 1976–1999, Volume IV: 1979–80*, edited by Colin Legum. New York, NY: Holmes & Meier Publishers, 1981.

Bakhash, Shaul. "The Troubled Relationship: Iran and Iraq, 1930–1980." In *Iran, Iraq, and the Legacies of War*, edited by Lawrence G. Potter and Gary G. Sick. London: Palgrave MacMillan, 2004.

Baktiari, Bahman. *Parliamentary Politics in Revolutionary Iran: The Institutionalization of Factional Politics.* Gainesville, FL: University Press of Florida, 1996.

Bani-Sadr, Abu al-Hasan. *My Turn to Speak: Iran, the Revolution and Secret Deals with the US.* Washington, DC: Brassey's Inc, 1991.

Baram, Amatzia. *Culture, History and Ideology in the Formation of Ba'athist Iraq, 1968–89.* London: Palgrave MacMillan, 1991.

Batatu, Hanna. *The Old Social Classes and the Revolutionary Movements of Iraq: A Study of Iraq's Old Landed and Commercial Classes and of Its Communists, Ba'athists, and Free Officers.* Princeton University Press, 2004.

Be'eri, Eliezer. *Army Officers in Arab Politics and Society.* New York, NY: Praeger, 1970.

Behrooz, Maziar. *Rebels with a Cause: The Failure of the Left in Iran.* London: I. B. Tauris, 2000.

Bengio, Ofra. "Iraq." In *Middle East Contemporary Survey, Iraq, 1976–1999, Volume IV: 1979–80*, edited by Colin Legum. New York, NY: Holmes & Meier Publishers, 1980.

"Iraq." In *Middle East Contemporary Survey, Iraq, 1976–1999, Volume IX: 1984–85*, edited by Itamar Rabinovich and Haim Shaked. Boulder, CO: Westview Press, 1987.

Saddam's Word: Political Discourse in Iraq. New York, NY: Oxford University Press, 1998.

Bengio, Ofra and Uriel Dann. "Iraq." In *Middle East Contemporary Survey, Iraq, 1976–1999, Volume II: 1977–78*, edited by Colin Legum. New York, NY: Holmes & Meier Publishers, 1979.

"Iraq." In *Middle East Contemporary Survey, Iraq, 1976–1999, Volume III: 1978–79*, edited by Colin Legum. New York, NY: Holmes & Meier Publishers, 1980.

Bergquist, Major Ronald E. *The Role of Airpower in the Iran–Iraq War.* Montgomery, AL: Air University Press, 1988.

Bill, James A. "Morale vs. Technology: The Power of Iran in the Persian Gulf War." In *The Iran–Iraq War: The Politics of Aggression*, edited by Farhang Rajaee. Gainesville, FL: University Press of Florida, 1993.

Bishop, Barzad and Jim Laurier. *Combat Aircraft: Iranian F-4 Phantom II Units in Combat.* Oxford: Osprey Publishing, 2003.

Bligh, Alexander. *The Political Legacy of King Hussein.* Portland, OR: Sussex Academic Press, 2007.

Bond, Brian. *British Military Policy between the Two World Wars.* Oxford University Press, 1980.

Bowden, Mark. *Guests of the Ayatollah: The First Battle in America's War with Militant Islam*. New York, NY: Atlantic Monthly Press, 2006.

Brower, Charles Nelson and Jason D. Brueschke. *The Iran–United States Claims Tribunals*. The Hague: Kluwer Law International, 1998.

Chubin, Shahram and Charles Tripp. *Iran and Iraq at War*. Boulder, CO: Westview Press, 1988.

Churchill, Winston S. *The Second World War: The Grand Alliance*. Boston, MA: Houghton Mifflin Company, 1950.

Clawson, Patrick and Michael Rubin. *Eternal Iran: Continuity and Chaos*. New York, NY: Palgrave MacMillan, 2005.

Cockburn, Andrew and Patrick Cockburn. *Out of the Ashes: The Resurrection of Saddam Hussein*. New York, NY: Harper Perennial, 1999.

Cooper, Tom and Chris Davey. *Combat Aircraft: Iranian F-14 Tomcat Units in Combat*. Oxford: Osprey Publishing, 2004.

Cooper, Tom and Farzad Bishop. *Iran–Iraq War in the Air: 1980–1988*. Atglen, PA: Schiffer Military History, 2000.

Cordesman, Anthony H. *The Iran–Iraq War and Western Security, 1984–1987*. London: Jane's Information Group, 1987.

Iraq and the War of Sanctions: Conventional Threats and Weapons of Mass Destruction. Westport, CT: Praeger, 1999.

Cordesman, Anthony H. and Abraham R. Wagner. *The Lessons of Modern War, Volume II: The Iran–Iraq War*. Boulder, CO: Westview Press, 1990.

Coughlin, Con. *Saddam: His Rise and Fall*. New York, NY: Harper Perennial, 2005.

Cronin, Stephanie. *The Army and the Creation of the Pahlavi State in Iran, 1910–1926*. London: I. B. Tauris, 1997.

Dabashi, Hamid. *Theology of Discontent: The Ideological Foundation of the Islamic Revolution in Iran*. New Brunswick, CT: Transaction Publishing, 2005.

Dann, Uriel. "The Iraqi–Iranian War." In *Middle East Contemporary Survey, Iraq, 1976–1999, Volume VIII: 1983–84*, edited by Haim Shaked and Daniel Dishon. Boulder, CO: Westview Press, 1985.

"The Iraqi–Iranian War." In *Middle East Contemporary Survey, Iraq, 1976–1999, Volume IX: 1984–85*, edited by Itamar Rabinovich and Haim Shaked. Boulder, CO: Westview Press, 1987.

Dann, Uriel and Ofra Bengio. "Iraq." In *Middle East Contemporary Survey, Iraq, 1976–1999, Volume I: 1976–77*, edited by Colin Legum. New York, NY: Holmes & Meier Publishers, 1978.

Davis, Eric. *Memories of State: Politics, History, and Collective Identity in Modern Iraq*. Berkeley, CA: University of California Press, 2005.

de Chair, Somerset Struben. *The Golden Carpet*. New York, NY: Harcourt, Brace and Company, 1945.

Dershowitz, Alan M. *Preemption: A Knife That Cuts Both Ways*. New York, NY: W. W. Norton & Company, 2006.

Dodge, Toby. *Inventing Iraq: The Failure of Nation Building and a History Denied*. New York, NY: Columbia University Press, 2003.

"International Obligation, Domestic Pressure, and Colonial Nationalism: The Birth of the Iraqi State under the Mandate System." In *The British and French Mandates in Comparative Perspectives*, edited by Nadine Meouchy and Peter Sluglett. Leiden: Brill Publishing, 2004.

Elliot, Matthew. *"Independent Iraq" The Monarchy and British Influence, 1941–1958*. London: I. B. Tauris, 1996.

Farhi, Rarideh. "The Antinomies of Iran's War Generation." In *Iran, Iraq, and the Legacies of War*, edited by Lawrence G. Potter and Gary G. Sick. New York, NY: Palgrave Macmillan, 2004.

Farouk-Sluglett, Marion and Peter Sluglett. *Iraq since 1958: From Revolution to Dictatorship*. New York, NY: I. B. Tauris, 2001.

Fisk, Robert. *The Great War for Civilization: The Conquest of the Middle East*. New York, NY: Alfred A. Knopf, 2005.

Fuller, Graham E. and Rend Rahim Francke. *The Arab Shi'a: The Forgotten Muslims*. New York, NY: Palgrave, 2001.

Francona, Frank. *Ally to Adversary: An Eyewitness Account of Iraq's Fall from Grace*. Annapolis, MD: Naval Institute Press, 1999.

Friedman, Thomas L. *From Beirut to Jerusalem*. New York, NY: Farrar Staus Girous, 1989.

Fromkin, David. *A Peace to End All Peace: The Fall of the Ottoman Empire and the Creation of the Modern Middle East*. New York, NY: Henry Holt and Company, 1989.

Furtig, Henner. *Iran's Rivalry with Saudi Arabia between the Gulf Wars*. Reading, NY: Ithaca Press, 2006.

Gaddis, John Lewis. *The Landscape of History: How Historians Map the Past*. New York, NY: Oxford University Press, 2004.

Ganji, Babak. *Politics of Confrontation: The Foreign Policy of the USA and Revolutionary Iran*. London: Tauris Academic Studies, 2006.

Gera, Gideon. "The Iraqi–Iranian War." In *Middle East Contemporary Survey, Iraq, 1976–1999, Volume XI: 1987*, edited Itamar Rabinovich and Haim Shaked. Boulder, CO: Westview Press, 1988.

Gershovich, Moshe. "The Red Sea Mining Affair." In *Middle East Contemporary Survey, Iraq, 1976–1999, Volume VIII: 1983-84*, edited by Haim Shaked and Daniel Dishon. Boulder, CO: Westview Press, 1985.

Gibson, Bryan R. *Covert Relationship: American Foreign Policy, Intelligence, and the Iran–Iraq War, 1980–1988*. Santa Barbara, CA: Praeger, 2010.

Gieling, Saskia. *Religion and War in Revolutionary Iran*. London: I. B. Tauris, 1999.

Giles, Gregory F. "The Islamic Republic of Iran and Nuclear, Biological, and Chemical Weapons." In *Planning the Unthinkable: How New Powers Will Use Nuclear, Biological, and Chemical Weapons*, edited by Peter R. Lavoy, Scott D. Sagan, and James J. Wirtz. Ithaca, NY: Cornell University Press, 2000.

Goldstein, Lyle. *Preventive Attack and Weapons of Mass Destruction: A Comparative Historical Analysis*. Stanford University Press, 2005.

Gooch, John. "Building Buffers and Filling Vacuums: Great Britain and the Middle East, 1914–1922." In *The Making of Peace: Rulers, States, and the Aftermath of War*, edited by Williamson Murray and James Lacey. New York, NY: Cambridge University Press, 2009.

Goodarzi, Jubin M. *Syria and Iran: Diplomatic Alliance and Power Politics in the Middle East*. London: Tauris Academic Studies, 2006.

Green, Jerrold D. "Arab Politics and the Iran-Contra Affair." In *The Middle East from the Iran–Contra Affair to the Intifada*, edited by Robert O. Freedman. Syracuse University Press, 1991.

Haldane, Lieutenant General Sir Aylmer L. *The Insurrection in Mesopotamia, 1920*. London: W. Blackwood and Sons, 1922.

al-Hamdani, Lieutenant General Ra'ad Majid. *Memoir: From the Golan to the Collapse of Baghdad: Six Wars in Thirty Years*. Baghdad: Unpublished, 2003.

Hashim, Ahmed S. "Civil–Military Relations in the Islamic Republic of Iran." In *Iran, Iraq, and the Arab Gulf States*, edited by Joseph A. Kechichian. New York, NY: Palgrave, 2001.

Hastings, Max and Simon Jenkins. *The Battle for the Falklands*. New York, NY: W. W. Norton & Company, 1983.

Helms, Christine Moss. *Iraq: Eastern Flank of the Arab World*. Washington, DC: Brookings Institution Press, 1991.

Herodotus. *The Histories*. Translated by G. C. Macaulay (1890), revised by Donald Lateiner. New York, NY: Barnes and Noble Classics, 2004.

Hiltermann, Joost R. *A Poisonous Affair: America, Iraq, and the Gassing of Halabja*. New York, NY: Cambridge University Press, 2007.

Hiro, Dilip. *Iran Under the Ayatollahs*. London: Routledge, 1987.

   The Longest War: The Iran–Iraq Military Conflict. London: Grafton, 1989.

   The Iranian Labyrinth: Journeys through Theocratic Iran and Its Furies. New York, NY: Nation Books, 2005.

Hoyt, Timothy D. *Military Industry and Regional Defense Policy – India, Iraq, and Israel*. New York, NY: Routledge, 2007.

Hume, Cameron R. *The United Nations, Iran, and Iraq: How Peacemaking Changes*. Bloomington, IN: Indiana University Press, 1994.

Ismael, Tareq Y. and Rex Brynen. "Western Europe and the Middle East." In *International Relations of the Contemporary Middle East: A Study in World Politics*, edited by Tareq Y. Ismael. Syracuse University Press, 1986.

Karsh, Efraim. *The Iran–Iraq War, 1980–1988*. New York, NY: Osprey Publishing, 2009.

Karsh, Efraim and Inari Rautsi. *Saddam Hussein: A Political Biography*. New York, NY: Grove Press, 1991.

Kashani-Sabet, Firoozeh. *Frontier Fictions: Shaping the Iranian Nation, 1804–1946*. London: I. B. Tauris, 1999.

Kechichian, Joseph A. "The Gulf Cooperation Council and the Gulf War." In *The Persian Gulf War: Lessons for Strategy, Law, and Diplomacy*, edited by Christopher C. Joyner. New York, NY: Greenwood Press, 1990.

Khadduri, Majid. *Arab Contemporaries: The Role of Personalities in Politics*. Baltimore, MD: The Johns Hopkins University Press, 1973.

Khomeini, Ruhollah. *Principes De L'ayatollah Khomeiny: Poltiques, Philosophiques, Sociaux & Reglieux*. Paris: Libres-Hallier, 1979.

Kienle, Eberhard. *Ba'th v. Ba'th: The Conflict between Syria and Iraq, 1968–1989*. New York, NY: I. B. Taurus & Company, 1990.

Knox, MacGregor. *Mussolini Unleashed, Facist Italy's Last War*. Cambridge University Press, 1983.

Kramer, Martin. "The Routine of Muslim Solidarity." In *Middle East Contemporary Survey: Iraq 1976–1999, Volume IX: 1984–85*, edited by Itamar Rabinovich and Haim Shaked. Boulder, CO: Westview Press, 1987.

   Arab Awakening and Islamic Revival: The Politics of Ideas in the Middle East. New Brunswick, CT: Transaction Publishers, 2008.

Kurzman, Charles. *The Unthinkable Revolution in Iran.* Boston, MA: Harvard University Press, 2004.

Levinson, Jeffrey L. and Randy L. Edwards. *Missiles Inbound: The Attack on the Stark in the Persian Gulf.* Annapolis, MD: Naval Institute Press, 1997.

Long, Jerry M. *Saddam's War of Words: Politics, Religion, and the Iraqi Invasion of Kuwait.* Austen, TX: University of Texas Press, 2004.

Lyman, Robert. *Iraq 1941: The Battles for Basra, Habbaniya, Fallujah, and Baghdad.* Oxford: Osprey Publishing, 2006.

Mackey, Sandra. *The Reckoning, Iraq, and the Legacy of Saddam Hussein.* New York, NY: W. W. Norton & Company, 2002.

Majd, Hooman. *The Ayatollah Begs to Differ: The Paradox of Modern Iran.* New York, NY: Doubleday Publishing, 2008.

Makiya, Kanan. *Republic of Fear: The Politics of Modern Iraq.* Berkeley, CA: University of California Press, 1989.

The Monument: Art, Vulgarity, and Responsibility in Iraq. Berkeley, CA: University of California Press, 1991.

Cruelty and Silence: War, Tyranny, Uprising, and the Arab World. New York, NY: W. W. Norton & Co, 1994.

Malone, David M. *The International Struggle over Iraq: Politics in the UN Security Council, 1980–2005.* Oxford University Press, 2006.

al-Marashi, Ibrahim and Sammy Salama. *Iraq's Armed Forces: An Analytic History.* New York, NY: Routledge, 2008.

Marr, Phebe. "Iraqi Foreign Policy." In *Diplomacy in the Middle East: The International Relations of Regional and Outside Powers (Library of International Relations Series),* edited by L. Carl Brown. London: I. B. Tauris, 2004.

The Modern History of Iraq. Boulder, CO: Westview Press, 2004.

Marschall, Christin. *Iran's Persian Gulf Policy: From Khomeini to Khatami.* New York, NY: Routledge Curzon, 2003.

Matar, Fuad. "The Young President: An Interview with Saddam Hussein in 1980." In *The Saddam Hussein Reader: Selections from Leading Writers on Iraq,* edited by Turi Munthe. New York, NY: Thunder's Mouth Press, 2002.

McCarthy, Timothy V. and Jonathon B. Tucker. "Saddam's Toxic Arsenal: Chemical and Biological Weapons in the Gulf Wars." In *Planning the Unthinkable: How New Powers Will Use Nuclear, Biological, and Chemical Weapons,* edited by Peter R. Lavoy, Scott D. Sagan, and James J. Wirtz. Ithaca, NY: Cornell University Press, 2000.

McDowall, David. *A Modern History of the Kurds.* London: I. B. Tauris, 2004.

McLachlan, Keith. "Analysis of the Risk of War: Iran–Iraq Discord, 1979–1980." In *The Iran–Iraq War: The Politics of Aggression,* edited by Farhang Rajaee. Gainesville, FL: University Press of Florida, 1993.

Meho, Lokman I. and Michel G. Nehme. "The Legacy of U.S. Support to Kurds: Two Major Episodes." In *The Kurdish Question in U.S. Foreign Policy,* edited by Lokman I. Meho. Westport, CT: Praeger Publishers, 2004.

Melman, Yossi and Meir Javedanfar. *The Nuclear Sphinx of Tehran: Mahmoud Ahmadinejad and the State of Iran.* New York, NY: Carroll & Graff Publishers, 2007.

Menashri, David. "Iran (Jumhuriyye Islamiyye Iran)." In *Middle East Contemporary Survey, Iraq, 1976–1999, Volume XI: 1987*, edited by Ami Ayalon and Haim Shaked. Boulder, CO: Westview Press, 1988.

Mesbahi, Mohiaddin. "The USSR and the Iran–Iraq War: From Brezhnev to Gorbachev." In *The Iran–Iraq War: The Politics of Aggression*, edited by Farhang Rajee. Gainesville, FL: University of Florida Press, 1993.

Milani, Mohsen M. *The Making of Iran's Islamic Revolution: From Monarchy to Islamic Republic*. Boulder, CO: Westview Press, 1988.

"Iran's Persian Gulf Policy in the Post-Saddam Era." In *Contemporary Iran: Economy, Society, Politics*, edited by Ali Gheissari. Oxford University Press, 2009.

Millett, Allan R. and Williamson Murray, eds. *Military Effectiveness, Volumes 1–3*. Cambridge University Press, 2010.

Montefiore, Simon Sebag. *Stalin: The Court of the Red Tsar*. New York, NY: Alfred A. Knopf, 2004.

Moore, John, ed. *Jane's Fighting Ships: 1980–81*. London: Jane's Publishing Company, 1980.

Mufti, Malik. *Sovereign Creations: Pan-Arabism and Political Order in Syria and Iraq*. Ithaca, NY: Cornell University Press, 1996.

Murray, Williamson. *The Change in the European Balance of Power, 1938–39: The Path to Ruin*. Princeton University Press, 1984.

Nasr, Vali. *The Shi'a Revival: How Conflicts within Islam will Shape the Future*. New York, NY: W. W. Norton & Company, 2006.

Navias, Martin S. and E. R. Hooton. *Tanker Wars: The Assault on Merchant Shipping During the Iran–Iraq Conflict, 1980–1988*. London: I. B. Tauris Publishers, 1996.

Nicolle, David and Tom Cooper. *Arab Mig-19 and Mig-21 Units in Combat*. Osprey Combat Aircraft. Oxford: Osprey Publishing Limited, 2004.

Nonneman, Gerd. "The Gulf States and the Iran–Iraq War: Pattern Shifts and Continuities." In *Iran, Iraq, and the Legacies of War*, edited by Lawrence G. Potter and Gary G. Sick. New York, NY: Palgrave MacMillan, 2004.

Nordeen, Lon O. *Air Warfare in the Missile Age*. 2nd edn. Washington, DC: Smithsonian Institute Press, 2002.

O'Ballance, Edgar. *The Gulf War: Nineteen Eighty to Nineteen Eighty-Seven*. London: Brassey's Defense Publishers, 1988.

Obeidi, Mahdi and Kurt Pitzer. *The Bomb in My Garden: The Secret of Saddam's Nuclear Mastermind*. Hoboken, NJ: John Wiley & Sons, Inc, 2004.

Oren, Michael B. *Six Days of War: June 1967 and the Making of the Modern Middle East*. New York, NY: Oxford University Press, 2002.

Philip, Philip G. "The Islamic Revolution in Iran: Its Impact on Foreign Policy." In *Renegade States: The Evolution of Revolutionary Foreign Policy*, edited by Stephen Chan and Andrew J. Williams. Manchester University Press, 1994.

Pipes, Daniel. *The Hidden Hand: Middle East Fear of Conspiracy*. New York, NY: St. Martin's Griffin, 1996.

Pollack, Kenneth M. *Arabs at War: Military Effectiveness, 1948–1991*. Lincoln, NE: University of Nebraska Press, 2002.

The Persian Puzzle: The Conflict between Iran and America. New York, NY: Random House 2005.

Post, Jerrold M., ed. *The Psychological Assessment of Political Leaders: With Profiles of Saddam Hussein and Bill Clinton*. Ann Arbor, MI: University of Michigan Press, 2003.

Rabinovich, Abraham. *The Yom Kippur War: The Epic Encounter That Transformed the Middle East*. New York, NY: Schocken Books, 2004.

Roux, Georges. *Ancient Iraq*. New York, NY: Penguin Books, 1992.

Rubin, Barry. "The United States and Iraq: From Appeasement to War." In *Iraq's Road to War*, edited by Amatzia Baram and Barry Rubin. New York, NY: St Martin's Press, 1993.

Schenker, David. *Dancing with Saddam: The Strategic Tango of Jordan–Iraq Relations*. Lanham, MD: Lexington Books, 2003.

Schofield, Richard. "Position, Function, and Symbol: The Shatt al-Arab Dispute in Perspective." In *Iran, Iraq, and the Legacies of War*, edited by Lawrence G. Potter and Gary G. Sick. London: Palgrave MacMillan, 2004.

Schultz, George P. *Turmoil and Triumph: My Years as Secretary of State*. New York, NY: Charles Schribner's Sons, 1993.

Seale, Patrick. *Asad: The Struggle for the Middle East*. Berkeley, CA: University of California Press, 1988.

Shaked, Haim. "The Nuclearization of the Middle East: The Israeli Raid of Osirak." In *Middle East Contemporary Survey, Iraq, 1976–1999, Volume V: 1980–81*, edited by Colin Legum. New York, NY: Holmes & Meir Publishers, Inc., 1982.

Shawcross, William. *Allies: Why the West Had to Remove Saddam*. New York, NY: Public Affairs, 2004.

Shemirani, S. Taheri. "The War of the Cities." In *The Iran–Iraq War: The Politics of Aggression*, edited by Farhang Rajaee. Gainesville, FL: University of Florida Press, 1993.

Sick, Gary G. *All Fall Down: America's Fateful Encounter with Iran*. London: I. B. Tauris, 1985.

Sifry, Micah L. and Christopher Cerf, eds., *The Iraq War Reader: History, Documents, Opinions*. New York, NY: Simon & Schuster, 2003.

Silverfarb, Daniel and Majid Khadduri. *Britain's Informal Empire in the Middle East: A Case Study of Iraq 1929–1941*. Oxford University Press, 1986.

Simon, Reeva Spector. *Iraq Between the Two World Wars: The Creation and Implementation of a National Ideology*. New York, NY: Columbia University Press, 1986.

Slim, the Viscount Slim, Field Marshal William Joseph. *Unofficial History*. New York, NY: David McKay, 1962.

Sluglett, Peter. *Britain in Iraq: Contriving King and Country*. New York, NY: Columbia University Press, 2007.

Smolansky, Oles M. *The USSR and Iraq: The Soviet Quest for Influence*. Durham, NC: Duke University Press, 1991.

Steavenson, Wendell. *The Weight of a Mustard Seed: The Intimate Story of an Iraqi General and His Family During Thirty Years of Tyranny*. New York, NY: Harper Collins, 2009.

Styan, David. *France and Iraq: Oil, Arms, and French Policy-Making in the Middle East*. New York, NY: I. B. Tauris & Co., 2006.

Tarbush, Mohammad A. *The Role of the Military in Politics: A Case Study of Iraq to 1941*. London: Keegan Paul International, 1982.

Tehrani, Ibrahim Anvari. "Iraqi Attitudes and Interpretation of the 1975 Agreement." In *The Iran–Iraq War: The Politics of Aggression*, edited by Farhang Rajaee. Gainesville, FL: University of Florida Press, 1993.

Thesiger, Wilfred. *The Marsh Arabs*. New York, NY: Penguin Classics, 2007.

Thucydides. *The History of the Peloponnesian War*. Translated by Rex Warner. London: Penguin Books, 1954.

The Landmark Thucydides: A Comprehensive Guide to the Peloponnesian War, edited by Robert B. Strassler. New York, NY: Simon & Schuster, 1996.

Tower, John, Edmund Muskie, and Brent Scowcroft. *The Tower Commission Report: Full Text of the President's Special Review Board*. New York, NY: Bantam Books, 1987.

Treverton, Gregory. "Covert Action: Forward to the Past?" In *Covert Action: Behind the Veils of Secret Foreign Policy*, edited by Loch K. Johnson. Santa Barbara, CA: Praeger Publishers, 2006.

Tripp, Charles. *A History of Iraq*. Cambridge University Press, 2000.

Tucker, Jonathan. *War of Nerves: Chemical Warfare from World War I to al-Qaeda*. New York, NY: Pantheon Books, 2006.

Tyler, Patrick E. *A World of Trouble: The White House and the Middle East – From the Cold War to the War on Terror*. New York, NY: Farrar, Straus and Giroux, 2009.

Upton (United States Army), Major General Emory. *The Armies of Europe & Asia: Embracing Official Reports on the Armies of Japan, China, India, Persia, Italy, Russia, Austria, Germany, France, and England*. London: Simpkin, Marshall & Co, 1878.

Varzi, Roxanne. *Warring Souls: Youth, Media, and Martyrdom in Post-Revolution Iran*. Durham, NC: Duke University Press, 2006.

von Clausewitz, Carl. *On War*. Translated by Michael Howard and Peter Paret. Princeton University Press, 1976.

Wagner, J. S. "Iraq." In *Fighting Armies: Antagonists in the Middle East: A Combat Assessment*, edited by Richard A. Gabriel. Santa Barbara, CA: Greenwood Press, 1983.

Ward, Steven R. *Immortal: A Military History of Iran and Its Armed Forces*. Washington, DC: Georgetown University Press, 2009.

Wise, Harold Lee. *Inside the Danger Zone: The US Military in the Persian Gulf, 1987–1988*. Annapolis, MD: US Naval Institute Press, 2007.

Woods, Kevin M. *The Mother of All Battles: Saddam Hussein's Strategic Plan for the Persian Gulf War*. Annapolis, MD: Naval Institute Press, 2008.

Woods, Kevin M., David D. Palkki, and Mark E. Stout. *The Saddam Tapes: The Inner Workings of a Tyrant's Regime, 1978–2001*. New York, NY: Cambridge University Press, 2011.

Woods, Kevin M., Michael Pease, Mark E. Stout, Williamson Murray, and James G. Lacey. *The Iraqi Perspectives Report: Saddam's Senior Leadership on Operation Iraqi Freedom*. Annapolis, MD: Naval Institute Press, 2006.

Wright, Robin. *In the Name of God: The Khomeini Decade*. New York, NY: Simon & Schuster, 1989.

Yavari, Neguin. "National, Ethnic, and Sectarian Issues in the War." In *The Iran–Iraq War: The Politics of Aggression*, edited by Farhang Rajaee. Gainesville, FL: University of Florida Press, 1997.

Zabecki, David T. *The German 1918 Offensives: A Case Study in the Operational Level of War.* New York, NY: Taylor & Francis, 2006.

Zabih, Sepehr. *The Iranian Military in Revolution and War.* New York, NY: Routledge, 1988.

ARTICLES

"Commentary on New Lethal Weapon, 12 Apr (FBIS-MEA-83-071)." *Foreign Broadcast Information Service Daily Reports*, 1983.

"Documents and Source Material: Arab Documents on Palestine and the Arab–Israeli Conflict." *Journal of Palestinian Studies* 8, no. 2 (Winter 1979).

"Full Text: Saddam Hussein's Speech (Part 2)." *The Guardian*, 17 January 2003.

"Genocide in Iraq: The Anfal Campaign against the Kurds." *A Middle East Watch Report.* New York, NY: Human Rights Watch, 1993. www.hrw.org/reports/1993/iraqanfal/.

"Gulf War: Iraq's Confidence Trick." *Economist* 294, no. 7378 (1985).

"Iran: General Views Unit's Battle Record; Interview with General Karimi, Commander of the 77th Victorious Samen al-A'emeh Battalion During Sacred Defense Week (FTS-20000201000513)." *Open Source Center*, 1999.

"Iran: IRGC Commander Attributes Iran's Success in Iran–Iraq War to Young People (IAP-20040922000113)." *Open Source Center*, 2004.

"Iraq Ascribes a Key Defeat in '86 to Misinformation from the US." *New York Times*, 19 January 1987.

"Let's Keep Squeezing Them Harder." *Economist* 384, no. 8547 (2007).

"Resalat Interview with Former IRGC Commander: MG Mohsen Reza'i (FTS-19971023000598)." *Open Source Center*, 1997.

"RFE/RL Iran Report." *Radio Free Europe* 9, No. 38 (17 October 2006).

"Shahbazi Details Military's Activities in ETTELA'AT Interview; MG Ali Shahbazi, Head of the Joint Chiefs of Staff of the Military of the Islamic Republic of Iran (FTS-19980708000479)." *Open Source Center*, 1998.

"The Middle East and North Africa." *IISS: The Military Balance* 80, no. 1 (1980).

"The Middle East and North Africa." *IISS: The Military Balance* 81, no. 1 (1981).

"The Middle East and North Africa." *IISS: The Military Balance* 84, no. 1 (1984).

"The Middle East and North Africa." *IISS: The Military Balance* 88, no. 1 (1988).

Adib-Moghaddam, Arshin. "Inventions of the Iran–Iraq War." *Critique: Critical Middle Eastern Studies* 16, no. 1 (Spring 2007).

Ali, Javed. "Chemical Weapons and the Iran–Iraq War: A Case Study in Noncompliance." *The Nonproliferation Review* 8, no. 1 (Spring 2001).

Atkeson (USA retired), Major General Edward B. "Iran's Arsenal: Tool of Ambition." *Army*, March 1991.

Atkine, Norvell B. De. "Why Arabs Lose Wars." *Middle East Quarterly* VI, no. 4 (December 1999).

Aziz, T. M. "The Role of Muhammad Baqir al-Sadr in Shii Activism in Iraq from 1958–1980." *International Journal of Middle East Studies* 25, no. 2 (May 1993).

Baram, Amatzia. "From Militant Secularism to Islamism: The Iraqi Ba'ath Regime, 1968–2003." Occasional paper. Washington, DC: Woodrow Wilson International Center for Scholars, 2011.

al-Bazzaz, Saad. "Saad al-Bazzaz: An Insider's View of Iraq." *The Middle East Quarterly* II, no. 4 (December 1995).

Brands, Hal. "Inside the Iraqi State Records: Saddam Hussein, 'Irangate', and the United States." *The Journal of Strategic Studies* 34, no. 1 (February 2011).

Brelis, Dean and Murray J. Gart. "An Interview with Saddam Hussein." *Time Magazine*, 19 July 1982.

Chubin, Shahram. "The Last Phase of the Iran–Iraq War: From Stalemate to Ceasefire." *Third World Quarterly* 11, no. 2 (1989).

Cigar, Norman. "Iraq's Strategic Mindset and the Gulf War: Blueprint for Defeat." *Journal of Strategic Studies* 15, no. 1 (March 1992).

Cioffi-Revilla, Claudio. "Origins and Evolutions of War Politics." *International Studies Quarterly* 40, no. 1 (March 1996).

Cobban, Helena. "Feisty Saddam Sure Iraq Will Win Gulf War." *Christian Science Monitor*, 13 November 1980.

Cronin, Stephanie. "An Experimentation in Military Modernization: Constitutionalism, Political Reform, and the Iranian Gendarmerie, 1910–21." *Middle Eastern Studies* 32, no. 3 (1996).

Dawisha, Karen. "Soviet Decision-Making in the Middle East: The 1973 October War and the 1980 Gulf War." *International Affairs* 57, no. 1 (Winter 1980/81).

Deeb, Marius. "Shi'a Movements in Lebanon: Their Formation, Ideology, Social Basis, and Links with Iran and Syria." *Third World Quarterly* 10, no. 2 (1988).

Devlin, John F. "The Ba'ath Party: Rise and Metamorphosis." *The American Historical Review* 96, no. 5 (1991).

Dingeman, James and Richard Jupa. "Iranian Elite: The Islamic Revolutionary Guards Corps." *Marine Corps Gazette* 72, no. 3 (March 1988).

Dobbs, Michael. "US Had Key Role in Iraq Buildup Trade in Chemical Arms; Allowed Despite Their Use on Iranians, Kurds." *Washington Post*, 29 December 2003.

Drozdiak, William, William Stuart, and Spencer Davidson. "War in the Persian Gulf." *Time Magazine*, 6 October 1980.

Entessar, Dader. "The Kurds in Post-Revolutionary Iran and Iraq." *Third World Quarterly* 6, no. 4 (October 1984).

Eshraghi, F. "Anglo-Soviet Occupation of Iran in August 1941." *Middle Eastern Studies* 20, no. 1 (January 1984).

"Aftermath of Anglo-Soviet Occupation of Iran in August 1941." *Middle Eastern Studies* 20, no. 3 (July 1984).

Fainberg, Anthony. "Osirak and International Security." *Bulletin of the Atomic Scientists* 37, no. 8 (1981).

Farzaneh, Mateo Mohammad. "Shi'i Ideology, Iranian Secular Nationalism, and the Iran–Iraq War (1980–1988)." *Studies in Ethnicity and Nationalism* 7, no. 1 (18 March 2008).

Friedrich, Otto and James Wilde. "The Gulf: He Gives Us a Ray of Hope." *Time Magazine*, 27 August 1990.

Gasiorowski, Mark J. "The Nuzhih Plot and Iranian Politics." *International Journal of Middle East Studies* 34, no. 4 (2002).

Gray, Matthew. "Revisiting Saddam Hussein's Political Language: The Sources and Roles of Conspiracy Theories." *Arab Studies Quarterly* 32, no. 1 (2010), 28–46.

Halliday, Fred. "Year Three of the Iranian Revolution." *MERIP Reports*, no. 104 (1982), 3–5.

Hashemi-Rafsanjani, Hojjat ol-Eslam val-Moslemin. "Hashemi-Rafsanjani 26 November Sermon (FBIS-SAS-82-230)." *Foreign Broadcast Information Service Daily Reports*, 1982.

Heller, Mark. "Politics and the Military in Iraq and Jordan, 1920–1958." *Armed Forces and Society* 4, no. 1 (November 1977).

Hillenbrand, Barry, William E. Smith, and Raji Samghabadi. "The Gulf: Clouds of Desperation." *Time*, 19 March 1984.

Hunter, Shireen T. "After the Ayatollah." *Foreign Policy*, no. 66 (1987), 77–97.

Hussein, Saddam. "Saddam Husayn Address to National Assembly 4 Nov (FBIS-MEA-80-216)." *Foreign Broadcast Information Service Daily Reports*, 1980.

"Saddam Husayn: Troops to Withdraw from Iran (FBIS-MEA-82-120)." *Foreign Broadcast Information Service Daily Reports*, 1980.

"Text of President Husayn's 10 Nov Press Conference (FBIS-MEA-80-220)." *Foreign Broadcast Information Service Daily Reports*, 1980.

"Text of President Speech to National Assembly, 17 Sep (FBIS-MEA-80-183)." *Foreign Broadcast Information Service Daily Reports*, 1980.

"Saddam Hussein Addresses Arab Youth Seminar, 29 Nov (FBIS-NES-90-231)." *Foreign Broadcast Information Service Daily Reports*, 1990.

Ismael, J. S. and T. Y. Ismael. "Social Change in Islamic Society: The Political Thought of Ayatollah Khomeini." *Social Problems* 27, no. 5 (June 1980).

Johnson, Marguerite, Wilton Wynn, and William Stuart. "Persian Gulf: Choosing up Sides." *Time Magazine*, 20 October 1980.

Karsh, Efraim. "The Strategic Backdrop." *The Adelphi Papers* 27, no. 220 (1987).

Katzman, Kenneth. "The Pasdaran: Institutionalization of Revolutionary Armed Force." *Iranian Studies* 26, no. 3/4 (1993).

Kelidar, Abbas. "The Shii Imami Community and Politics in the Arab East." *Middle Eastern Studies* 19, no. 1 (January 1983).

Khomeini, Ayatollah. "We Shall Confront the World with Our Ideology (20 March 1980)." *MERIP Reports*, no. 88 (1980).

McNaugher, Thomas L. "Ballistic Missiles and Chemical Weapons: The Legacy of the Iran–Iraq War" *International Security* 15, no. 2 (1990).

Megalli, Nabila. "Who's Shooting What? Gulf Tanker Targets Laden with Confusion." *The Associated Press*, 1988.

Milani, Mohsen M. "Harvest of Shame: Tudeh and the Barzargan Government." *Middle Eastern Studies* 29, no. 2 (April 1993).

Mofid, Kamran. "Economic Reconstruction of Iraq: Financing the Peace." *Third World Quarterly* 12, no. 1 (1990).

Mohr, Charles. "New Iranian Drive Seen as Diversion." *New York Times*, 13 February 1986.

Parasiliti, Andrew and Sinan Antoon. "Friends in Need, Foes to Heed: The Iraqi Military in Politics." *Middle East Policy* 7, no. 4 (October 2000).

Power, Paul F. "The Baghdad Raid: Retrospect and Prospect." *Third World Quarterly* 8, no. 3 (1986).

Qotbzadeh, Foreign Minister Sadeq. "Text of Foreign Minister Qotbzadeh's Message to Gromyko, 14 Aug (FBIS-SAS-80-160)." *Foreign Broadcast Information Service Daily Reports*, 1980.

Ramazani, R. K. "Iran's Revolution: Patterns, Problems, and Prospects." *International Affairs* 56, no. 3 (Summer 1980).

Reed, Jack. "Iranian Missile Attack on Baghdad School Kills 32." *United Press International*, 1987.

Renfrew, Nita M. "Who Started the War?" *Foreign Policy*, 1987.

Robinson Jr., Clarence A. "Iraq, Iran Acquiring Chinese-Built Fighters." *Aviation Week & Space Technology* (11 April 1983).

Rose, Gregory F. "The Post-Revolutionary Purge of Iran's Armed Forces: A Revisionist Assessment." *Iranian Studies* 17, no. 2/3 (1984).

Rubinstein, Alvin Z. "The Soviet Union and Iran Under Khomeini." *International Affairs* 57, no. 4 (1981).

Shanahan, Rodger. "Shi'a Political Development in Iraq: The Case of the Islamic Da'wa Party." *Third World Quarterly* 25, no. 5 (2004).

Sick, Gary G. "Iran's Quest for Superpower Status." *Foreign Affairs* 65, no. 4 (Spring 1987).

    "Confronting Contradictions: The Revolution in Its Teens." *Iranian Studies* 26, no. 3/4 (1993).

Sirriyeh, Hussein. "Development of the Iraqi–Iranian Dispute, 1847–1975." *Journal of Contemporary History* 20, no. 3 (July 1985).

Spechler, Dina Rome. "The USSR and Third World Conflicts: Domestic Debate and Soviet Policy in the Middle East, 1967–1973." *World Politics* 38, no. 3 (1986).

Stafford, R. S. "Iraq and the Problem of the Assyrians." *International Affairs* 13, no. 2 (March–April 1934).

Swearingen, Will D. "Geopolitical Origins of the Iran–Iraq War." *Geographical Review* 78 (October 1988).

Takeyh, Ray. "The Iran–Iraq War: A Reassessment." *The Middle East Journal* 64, no. 3 (Summer 2010).

Taremi, Kamran. "Beyond the Axis of Evil: Ballistic Missiles in Iran's Military Thinking." *Security Dialogue* 36, no. 1 (March 2005).

Telhami, Shibley. "Arab Public Opinion and the Gulf War." *Political Science Quarterly* 108, no. 3 (Autumn 1993).

Tyler, Patrick E. "Officers Say US Aided Iraq in War Despite Use of Gas." *New York Times*, 18 August 2002.

Tyrrell, Roland. "Iran Again Rejects Iraqi Peace Terms." *United Press International*, 19 November 1980.

Ward, Steven. "Iran's Challenging Victory Narrative." *Historically Speaking* 10, no. 3 (June 2009).

Weiner, Tim. "Iraq Uses Techniques in Spying against Its Former Tutor, the US." *Philadelphia Inquirer*, 5 February 1991.

Wright, Claudia. "Religion and Strategy in the Iran–Iraq War." *Third World Quarterly* 7, no. 4 (October, 1985).

Zabih, Sepehr. "Aspects of Terrorism in Iran." *Annals of the American Academy of Political and Social Science* 463 (1982).

Zaloga, Steven. "Ballistic Missiles in the Third World: Scud and Beyond." *Jane's International Defense Review* 21, no. 11 (November 1988).

Zonis, Marvin. "The Rule of the Clerics in the Islamic Republic of Iran." *Annals of the American Academy of Political and Social Science* 482 (November 1985).

REPORTS

Brzoska, Michael and Thomas Ohlson. "Arms Trade II: The Iran–Iraq War and the Arms Trade." *Fact Sheets and Policy Briefs*. Stockholm International Peace Research Institute, 1984.

CWIHP Critical Oral History Conference: The Origins, Conduct, and Impact of the Iran–Iraq War, 1980–1988: Document Reader, edited by Malcolm Byrne and Christian Ostermann. Washington, DC: Cold War International History Project, Woodrow Wilson International Center for Scholars and the National Security Archives, 2004.

CWIHP Critical Oral History Conference: The Carter Administration and the "Arc of Crisis": 1977–1981: Document Reader, edited by Malcolm Byrne. Washington, DC: Cold War International History Project, Woodrow Wilson International Center for Scholars and the National Security Archives, 2005.

Fukuyama, Francis. "The Soviet Union and Iraq since 1968." *A RAND Note [N-1524-AF]*. Santa Monica, CA: RAND Corporation, 1980.

Katzman, Kenneth. *US Department of State Report: The People's Mojahedin Organization of Iran*. Washington, DC: Congressional Research Service, 1992.

Lambeth, Benjamin S. *Desert Storm and Its Meaning: The View from Moscow*. Santa Monica, CA: RAND Corporation, 1992.

Murray, Williamson. *Military Adaption in War*. Alexandria, VA: Institute for Defense Analyses, 2009.

Nejad, Parviz Mosalla. *The Hub of Resistance Literature and History: Khorramshahr*. Bostan, Iran: International Affairs Committee of Foundation for Preservation of Monuments and Dissemination of Value of the Holy Defense, 2006.

Pelletiere, Dr. Stephen C. and Lieutenant Colonel Douglas V. Johnson II (USA). *Lessons Learned: The Iran–Iraq War*. Carlisle Barracks, PA: US Army War College, Strategic Studies Institute, 1991.

Roberts, Mark. *Khomeini's Incorporation of the Iranian Military*. McNair Paper 48. Washington, DC: National Defense University Press, 1996.

Schahgaldian, Nikola B. and Gina Barkhordarian. *The Iranian Military Under the Islamic Republic*. Santa Monica, CA: RAND Corporation, 1987.

Schmidt, Rachel. "Global Arms Exports to Iraq, 1960–1990." *A RAND Note*. Santa Monica, CA: RAND Corporation, 1991.

SIPRI. *Fact Sheet: Chemical Warfare in the Iran–Iraq War*. Stockholm International Peace Research Institute, 1984.

United Nations. *Human Rights Report: UN Assistance Mission for Iraq*. 2009.

Wehrey, Frederic, Jorrold D. Green, Brian Nichiporuk, Alireza Nader, Lydia Hansell, Rasool Nafisi, and S. R. Bohandy. *The Rise of the Pasdaran: Assessing the Domestic Roles of Iran's Islamic Revolutionary Guards Corps*. Santa Monica, CA: RAND Corporation, 2009.

Woods, Kevin M., Williamson Murray, and Thomas Holaday. *Saddam's War: An Iraqi Military Perspective of the Iran–Iraq War.* McNair Paper 70. Washington, DC: National Defense University Press, 2009.

Woods, Kevin M., Williamson Murray, Elizabeth A. Nathan, Laila Sabara, and Ana M. Venegas. *Project 1946: Phase II.* Alexandria, VA: Institute for Defense Analyses, 2010.

Zanders, Jean Pascal. *Iranian Use of Chemical Weapons: A Critical Analysis of Past Allegations.* Center for Nonproliferation Studies, 2001, cns.miis.edu/archive/cns/programs/dc/briefs/030701.htm.

GOVERNMENT DOCUMENTS

FD-302 of Ali Hasan al-Majid al-Tikriti on 31 January 2004 in Baghdad, IQ. No. 315E-HQ-1448534-59. Washington, DC: US Federal Bureau of Investigation, 2004.

"Memorandum from RADM Grant Shart (USN) to Commander in Chief CENTCOM, RE: Formal Investigation into the Circumstances Surrounding the Attack on the USS Stark (FFG 31) on 17 May 1987."

NSDD 139: *Measures to Improve US Posture and Readiness to Developments in the Iran–Iraq War (Declassified).* No. 139. Washington, DC: The White House, 1984.

"Subject: Task Force v Lessons Learned: The Iran–Iraq War, Appendix B–Chemicals," US Office of the Secretary of Defense.

Treaties and International Agreements Registered or Filed and Recorded with the Secretariat of the United Nations. New York, NY: United Nations, 1976.

UNSCR 514. United Nations Security Council, 2383rd Meeting, 12 July 1982.

Director of Central Intelligence. *Special National Intelligence Estimate: Soviet Interests, Policies, and Prospects with Respect to the Iran–Iraq War.* Langley, VA: Central Intelligence Agency, 1980.

Interagency Intelligence Assessment: Implications of Israeli Attack on Iraq. Langley, VA: Central Intelligence Agency, 1981.

Farr, Warner D. "The Third Temple's Holy of Holies: Israel's Nuclear Weapons." In *The Counterproliferation Papers.* Maxwell Air Force Base: USAF Counterproliferation Center, 1999.

Hoffpauir, Major Michael E. (USA) *Tactical Evolution in the Iraqi Army: The Abadan Island and Fish Lake Campaigns of the Iran–Iraq War.* Army Command and General Staff College, 1991.

Jones, Ronald D. *Israeli Air Superiority in the 1967 Arab–Israeli War: An Analysis of Operational Art.* Newport, RI: Naval War College, 1996.

Murray, Williamson. "Part 1: Operations Report." In *Operations and Effects and Effectiveness. Gulf War Air Power Survey.* Washington, DC: Government Printing Office, 1993.

Playfair, Major General Ian Stanley. *The Germans Come to the Help of Their Ally, 1941.* London: Her Majesty's Stationery Office, 1956.

Scott, The Right Honorable Sir Richard, The Vice-Chancellor. *Report of the Inquiry into the Export of Defense Equipment and Dual-Use Goods to Iraq and Related Prosecutions (HC 115).* London: The House of Commons, Quadripartite Committee, 1996.

US Congress, House Select Committee to Investigate Covert Arms Transactions with Iran; US Congress, Senate Select Committee on Secret Military Assistance to Iran and the Nicaraguan Opposition. *Report of the Congressional Committee Investigating the Iran–Contra Affair: With Supplemental, Minority, and Additional Views*. Washington, DC: Government Printing Office, 1987.

US Department of Defense. "Investigative Report: Formal Investigation into the Circumstances Surrounding the Downing of Iran Air Flight 655 on 3 July 1988." 1988.

Watts, Barry D. "Part 2: Effectiveness Report." In *Operations and Effects and Effectiveness*. Gulf War Air Power Survey. Washington, DC: Government Printing Office, 1993.

Ziemke, Earl F. and Magna E. Bauer. *Moscow to Stalingrad: Decision in the East*. Washington, DC: Government Printing Office, 1987.

WEBSITES

"English Translation of the al-Dujail Judgement (Parts 1–6)." School of Law, Case Western Reserve University, www.law.case.edu/saddamtrial/dujail/opinion.asp.

"Resolution No. 6/3-E(Is): The Iraqi–Iranian Conflict." Organization of the Islamic Conference, www.oic-oci.org/english/conf/is/3/3rd-is-sum(political).htm#06.

"SIPRI International Arms Transfers Database, 1950–Present." Stockholm International Peace Research Institute, www.sipri.org/research/armaments/transfers/databases/armstransfers.

"The Mecca Declaration of the Third Islamic Summit Conference." Organization of the Islamic Conference, www.oic-oci.org/english/conf/is/3/3rd-is-sum.htm.

Aziz, Tariq. "On Arab–Iranian Relations: To Avoid Confusing the Issues Keeping the Facts Secret and Letting the Conspiracy Pass Unnoticed." Ministry of Culture and Information, www.al-moharer.net/moh232/aziz80-232.htm.

Ministry of Foreign Affairs, The State of Israel. "Statements by the Government of Israel on the Bombing of the Iraqi Nuclear Facility near Baghdad: 8 June 1981." www.mfa.gov.il/MFA/Foreign%20Relations/Israels%20Foreign%20Relations%20since%201947/1981-1982/26%20Statement%20by%20the%20Government%20of%20Israel%20on%20the%20Bo.

Sazegara, Mohsen. "What Was Once a Revolutionary Guard is Now Just a Mafia." www.sazegara.net/english/archives/2007/03/what_was_once_a_revolutionary.html.

Index